The New Testament

NEW CENTURY VERSION

With Devotional Guide and
Study Notes based on

THE SECRET KINGDOM

Pat Robertson

WORD PUBLISHING

Dallas·London·Vancouver·Melbourne

A WORD OF WELCOME

Welcome to the Secret Kingdom edition of the *New Century Version, New Testament.* I'm really excited about bringing this special edition to you because it has been specifically designed to help you, as a Christian, gain a vital sense of purpose and direction for your life . . . no matter what stage of your faith journey you're now in. Through powerful, personal study of God's Word and the principles it contains, you will renew your strength and "mount up on wings of eagles."

Several years ago I began to notice the consistency and frequency with which the Scriptures referred to the principles that Jesus set out during His earthly ministry. I had been applying many of them in my own life and in the programs we were developing at the Christian Broadcasting Network (CBN). But I began to see that there was a pattern, often overlooked, which demanded closer study.

For some time my constant prayer had been for greater wisdom and knowledge, and in time I came to a much clearer understanding of these principles. I began to see with new eyes things in the Word of God I had read dozens of times. Over the weeks, months and years, I received what I can only describe as miraculous insights, and I saw that Jesus had spoken quite precisely about how God's kingdom works.

As a result of my study, I wrote *The Secret Kingdom.* In it I noted how Jesus began His earthly ministry with an announcement of the arrival of the kingdom. And He ended his ministry by "speaking of the things pertaining to the kingdom of God." In fact, Jesus described His teachings about the kingdom as His ultimate purpose. He said, "I must preach the kingdom of God to the other cities also, for I was sent for this purpose."

From the first words of Matthew to the final words of the Revelation in the New Testament, the message of the mighty kingdom of God is trumpeted by the words of Christ. He described the kingdom as existing both then, in Bible times, and now, in current times. So, anyone who thinks that Christians are simply "hanging around" on the earth waiting for heaven has missed the point of Christ's teachings. His kingdom is not to arrive at some far-distant future time; it is here now. As Christians, it is within us, and we are within it.

Why is the kingdom secret? The principles of God's kingdom were never really secret. They were, and still are, offered freely to anyone who is willing to enter into the kingdom by faith in Jesus Christ. In fact, God wants every living soul to know and fully understand His great foundation principles because it is His desire "that no man perish."

So what's the problem? We see great stress and strain in people's lives today. Stressed and depressed souls are searching for peace and contentment through psychologists, chemical dependence, relationship hopping and other stop-gap methods. But they never find that peace because they are looking for it in all the wrong places.

Peace comes from oneness with God. The walk of faith is, by design, a journey toward greater understanding and greater unity with Him. Learning God's basic principles and laws for His kingdom will draw us closer to that unity and resulting contentment.

At last, here is a tool to help you gain that peace and oneness with God. The New Testament, *New Century Version*, with its clearly readable, everyday language, will shed light on the Scriptures as you study them. This edition contains the complete text of the New Testament from the *New Century Version*, along with ten challenging and uplifting principles of the kingdom in this front section, which have been taken from my book *The Secret Kingdom*. Together, these principles and the insightful text of the NCV will reveal God's underlying guidelines for you to live a successful and peaceful life.

Like me, you will benefit much by coming to recognize and incorporate these foundation principles of the kingdom into your life. Once the foundation is securely in place, then your spiritual growth can be rapid and solid. If you are a seeker or a new Christian, you will be able to begin your faith journey on a solid base which will support you throughout your spiritual life. As a mature Christian, you will appreciate the insights you discover by "combing" the Scriptures from a different perspective. No matter where you are in your walk with God, you will come away from this study with a better understanding of God's Word and a heart that's been refreshed.

Truly, God's kingdom is here now. Jesus said that it's among us. And since its principles undergird and penetrate the visible, material world, the laws of the kingdom will operate in our lives today.

Won't you join me now, using this special edition of the *New Century Version New Testament,* in an exploration of *The Secret Kingdom* and its eternal principles for your life? It's a journey you'll never forget.

KEYS TO THE SECRET KINGDOM

Here are the ten keys to the kingdom of God with which you can unlock a life that shows the treasure of Jesus to those around you. The symbol to the left of each law will be used later to help you identify highlighted passages in the New Testament, *New Century Version*, that *The Secret Kingdom* uses to explain and explore these laws.

 The Law of Reciprocity is God's law of "give and take." It is based on the biblical principles, "Give, and it will be given to you" and "Love your neighbor as yourself."

 The Law of Use says that we must use what the Lord has given us, putting it to work and building on it. Jesus said, "To everyone who has shall more be given."

 The Law of Perseverance is the law of struggling and keeping on. It's the "Don't give up" law. Jesus taught this principle by saying, "Ask, and God will give to you. Search, and you will find. Knock, and the door will open for you."

 The Law of Responsibility teaches us to rise to the level of responsibility we have been given. Handling responsibility well comes with being prepared for it, as taught in Jesus' parables on being prepared and alert.

 The Law of Greatness says we become great by being humble. According to Jesus, if we want to be great, we must become like little children and servants.

 The Law of Unity states that great creativity occurs when there is oneness. God's unfathomable power is released where there is harmony . . . within the individual, a family, business, or society.

 The Law of Fidelity is based on faithfulness. If we are faithful in the small things, then we will be given greater responsibilities and talents in the kingdom.

The Law of Change says that God's plan never changes, but the methods of carrying out His plan are always changing. And the greatest change of all must be in the hearts of His people.

 The Law of Miracles shows that God is willing to interrupt His natural order of day-to-day things to accomplish His ultimate purpose.

 The Law of Dominion teaches us that God wants people to rule the earth the way we were created to rule—with humility, discipline, and partnership, but not with arrogance.

HOW TO GET THE MOST FROM THIS BOOK

Applying What We Know

Once we know the principles of the kingdom, how can we apply them to the world we live in today and to our own lives? How can we take possession of these principles and apply them to the hopes and dreams of contemporary life and to the problems we face in a world that's flashing through time toward a new millennium?

That's the real beauty of this special *Secret Kingdom* edition of the *NCV New Testament*. It has been designed specifically to help you learn and apply these kingdom principles. By helping you locate and understand the teachings of God on these principles, we will help you know how they apply to your life.

Features to Help You

Here are some of the features of this edition that will help you in your study:

- **Everyday language** that clearly brings God's will for you into your daily life and times. You won't hit vocabulary roadblocks to your learning.

- **Over 300 highlighted scriptures** that will draw your attention to God's foundation teachings about His kingdom. By concentrating on these highlighted passages, you will come away with a strong basis for your spiritual growth and a clear understanding of the kingdom.

- **A personal, daily devotional section,** which develops each of the ten kingdom principles more fully over a five-day period. Each day's exploration of that kingdom law contains focused questions, Scripture references, and suggestions for further study. By turning to the suggested readings and completing the exercises in each day's agenda, you will find ample material for meditation and discussion. The daily sections are specifically designed to aid in learning and applying the principles.

- **A dictionary** in the back of the book to define more difficult words you may find in the text. These words are marked with a small superscript "d" in the text to let you know when the dictionary contains helpful information on that word.

- **The words of Jesus in red** will help you identify exactly when the Savior is speaking and what He has to say to you personally.

- **Artwork** for each of the ten kingdom principles to give you a graphic depiction of the law of God being considered.

- **Symbols,** developed from the artwork, appear in the margins to help you locate specific New Testament passages that deal with the kingdom principles you want to study. Those symbols are shown in the previous section entitled "Keys to the Secret Kingdom" next to the principles for which they stand.

- **Footnotes** at the bottom of some New Testament pages will give you additional information about customs, history, language and events for a fuller appreciation of the text in those places. These footnotes are identified with a small superscript "n" (for "note") in the NCV text.

Study Alternatives

There are many different ways you can use this material for life-changing, personal enrichment and spiritual growth. Here are a few alternative approaches you might consider, until you find one that suits your learning style best.

1. Read *The Secret Kingdom* by Pat Robertson, and use this *New Century Version New Testament* to study the Scriptures and passages he mentions. This is probably the most effective and complete way to study these concepts and conclusions.

2. **Use the devotional guide,** which follows this section, and do an

organized study of the kingdom principles on a daily devotional schedule. This approach will give you fifty days of study and meditation on God's foundation laws. By "owning" these concepts for almost two months, they will become part of you and have great impact on your life.

3. **Do a thematic study on your own.** By using the marginal symbols, turn through the New Testament and read all the passages that are noted for one of the kingdom principles. Then use your concordance to see what other passages you can discover about that law of God. Take notes as you go so that you can review your study later. Continue this approach until you have studied each of the ten laws of the kingdom.

4. **Have a small-group study.** Invite a few friends to join you in your exploration of the kingdom laws. Use *The Secret Kingdom* and this *NCV New Testament*'s devotional section to guide the group through the study. Invite open discussion of the principles and how they apply to your lives.

5. **Host a Secret Kingdom retreat** for a group of people based on *The Secret Kingdom*. Use the book and the devotional material in this book for a concentrated weekend of study.

6. **Teach a 13-week course** on the kingdom laws, using *The Secret Kingdom* and this New Testament, in your normal church setting for adults or older teens.

For Future Reference

The principles in *The Secret Kingdom* have been tested and proved for generations—in fact, since God created the world. They work; it's that simple. These principles, if you apply them every day, will serve you well all your life. They will bring you closer to oneness with God and into peace and contentment.

The *New Century Version New Testament* is designed to become your constant companion for spiritual growth. Because it speaks your everyday language, it allows God's principles to enter directly into your heart. You will learn to trust it as a good friend and guide throughout life.

You are a child of the King. The blessings contained in the following pages have been designed just for you. All you need to do is reach out and take them through sincere study of God's precious principles for his kingdom.

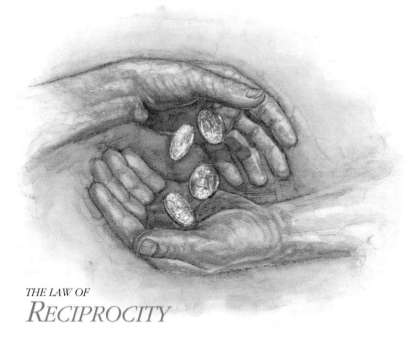

THE LAW OF
RECIPROCITY

Key Scripture: Luke 6:31-38

Reciprocity means give and take. It's the law of cause and effect, and we see it all around us. When you say, "You scratch my back and I'll scratch yours," that's reciprocity. So is the old expression, "You get what you pay for!"

Jesus gave this principle much greater importance, though. He said that God judges your heart by the way you give. When you truly love someone, you want to lavish your treasures upon him. Whatever your gifts–time, money, talent, affection–they express your love, but you hold back when your heart is cold.

There are two important lessons in the Law of Reciprocity. The first is, "Give, and it will be given to you." Jesus taught that you are blessed when you show your love by giving. The second lesson is from the Sermon on the Mount: "Love your enemies, do good to them, and lend to them without hoping to get anything back" (see Luke 6:35-38). When you give from a loving heart, God sees your gifts and rewards you accordingly. But when you give in pride, a little worldly flattery is the best you can expect in return.

This principle of the kingdom affects your relationships with your loved ones, neighbors, friends, and even strangers. It also affects your relationship with God. The Law of Reciprocity shows that you're blessed when you use what you have to bless others.

Scriptures: Matthew 6:3-4; Matthew 6:33

The Law of Reciprocity teaches that God judges your heart, and He values your giving by what He sees in your heart. God also rewards you by increasing the gifts you give. If you are generous with time and money, you will be rewarded with more time and money. Whatever you give should be given as if you are giving to God, and God will reward you in return.

At the same time, Jesus taught that you are not to be proud or boastful in giving, but to do it in secret. The Father can see what is done in secret, and the reward comes from Him (Matthew 6:3-4). And the Apostle Paul encourages you not to grow weary in doing good, for surely your reward will come in time (Galatians 6:7-10).

If you seek first and always the kingdom, doing all you have been taught, you will receive all the things you need (Matthew 6:33).

Reciprocity and Me:
1. Have you ever known someone who gives generously but wants everyone to know it? What is the value of this type of giving?
2. Would it be better not to give at all? Why?
3. How does the Law of Reciprocity affect the way you give?

Scripture: Matthew 7:1

A basic law of physics says, "For every action there is an equal and opposite reaction." The principle of thrust used in rocket engines is an example of this natural law at work. When the thrust shoots back, the rocket shoots forward. The Law of Reciprocity shows this same concept in human relations. Jesus said, "Don't judge other people, or you will be judged" (Matthew 7:1).

Jesus taught that God is the judge of human behavior. He will settle all accounts; so you are not to judge others. If you take God's judgment into your own hands, then you will be judged in return. The cause-and-effect relationship described by the Law of Reciprocity says that whatever you do to others, you receive back in kind. This principle can be applied in many ways.

Reciprocity and Me:
1. Have you ever been misjudged by another person?
2. How did it feel to be judged wrongly?
3. What can you learn from the Good Samaritan about judging others? (See Luke 10:25-37.)

Scripture: 2 Corinthians 9:6

One of the most surprising principles in the Bible says that you must give in order to receive. Paul wrote, "The person who plants a little will have a small harvest, but the person who plants a lot will have a big harvest" (2 Corinthians 9:6; compare Galatians 6:7). Farmers certainly understand the practical side of this principle. The more seed you plant, the more wheat or corn can be harvested eventually. Farmers test this aspect of the Law of Reciprocity every harvest season. But sometimes it's harder to appreciate this teaching in city life.

In 2 Corinthians 9:6-11 you can see that God provides seed for the sower and bread for food. Paul adds that if you are generous, and if you give with a cheerful heart, God will supply all your needs.

Reciprocity and Me:

1. In 2 Corinthians 9:7 Paul says that God loves the person who gives happily. Would you describe yourself as a "happy giver"? Why?
2. What type of "seeds" do you have to plant for God?
3. List three specific ways that you can begin immediately planting more seeds for a greater harvest.

Scripture: 1 Timothy 6:17

Jesus taught repeatedly about money, probably because He knew how easy it is for people to focus on riches as the way to attain happiness. But the Lord made it clear that peace and happiness do not come through this world's goods but through the treasures you store up in heaven. In Jesus' days this conflict between earthly and heavenly values was so visible that it provoked Jesus' famous comment that it's easier for a camel to go through the eye of a needle than for a rich person to enter the kingdom of God (Matthew 19:24).

The Scriptures show often that arrogance and pride lead to failure in the kingdom of God. In his advice to Timothy, the Apostle Paul says that those who are rich in this present age are not to be proud, not to trust in their riches but to turn to God. He is the source of their treasure. And He is the source of your treasure.

Reciprocity and Me:

1. How do you show by your example that you really believe this principle?
2. As you look through your checkbook register, where would you say you are storing up treasures?

Scriptures: Malachi 3:10, Revelation 22:12

"Bring to the storehouse a full tenth of what you earn so there will be food in my house. Test me in this," says the Lord All-Powerful. "I will open the windows of heaven for you and pour out all the blessings you need" (Malachi 3:10).

Underlying the teachings of Jesus was a basic sense of proportion. He said not to worry about things which do not matter but to think about the things which have eternal importance. Why treasure things easily destroyed and ignore things which endure forever?

In a world which is increasingly materialistic and controlled by possessions, people often lose sight of proportion. You may focus on your own hopes, fears, needs, and expectations and ignore the eternal perspective. In the kingdom of heaven, Jesus said, what you give away will have more value than what you keep.

Reciprocity and Me:

1. Consider how much you give away of what you have; is God able to reciprocate with riches or only meager gifts? In what ways?
2. According to the Law of Reciprocity, how can you increase God's blessings to you?
3. Write down two specific ways you will put this principle to work in your life this week.

Living in the Kingdom

My personal goals for putting The Law of Reciprocity to work in my life are these:

Short-term Goals:

Long-term Goals:

THE LAW OF
USE

Key Scripture: Matthew 25:14-30

What are the marks of success? How do you measure real accomplishment? When Jesus told his followers the Parable of the Talents toward the end of His ministry, He was dealing with these very questions.

On the surface, the story was about investing money wisely, but Jesus was actually speaking of obedience and commitment to do the work of the Master. This is the key to the Law of Use. By doing what you know the Master wants you to do, you gain His acceptance and approval. By using your gifts wisely, you fulfill God's purpose for your life.

Everyone likes to be complimented for a job well done. From childhood on, people seek recognition, to gain approval for good performance. What you most often discover is that you earn praise when you use your talents and skills effectively. Win or lose, you gain respect for doing your best.

If this principle of the Law of Use is true in daily living, it is certainly true in Christian living. The Law of Use teaches that to be successful you must use and develop your skills. You must be about the Master's business, pursuing whatever work He has given you to do until He returns.

When you are diligent in these things, the results multiply. This is described in *The Secret Kingdom* as the exponential curve, which magnifies whatever we do–both good and evil. Truly, this is one of the most powerful laws of God's kingdom.

Scripture: Matthew 25:14-30

At first sight, the idea of rewarding those who have, and holding back from those who do not have, sounds unfair. Shouldn't it be the other way around? Certainly, in modern society, governments tax the rich more heavily in order to give to the poor.

In the parable of the talents, Jesus was not addressing the idea of compassion but of fruitfulness. On several occasions Jesus taught that you should give to those who do not have, and you should "give to the poor." Here, however, He is saying that those who are fearful and unproductive will not be rewarded in the kingdom.

Because he does not trust the Master, the fearful doubter does not obey His wishes. His unfruitfulness is a sign of distrust and uncertainty. That's why the unfaithful servants were punished.

Using My Gifts:

1. Which of the three servants in the parable are you most like on a daily basis? Why?
2. If Jesus asked for an accounting of the way you have used your gifts for Him so far, what would you say?

Scripture: Mark 4:24-25

Jesus told the people gathered around Him that they were to be busy in the business of the kingdom. He had laid out principles of blessing, and He had told them to be faithful workers of the kingdom to receive those blessings.

In this passage Jesus extends the application of this teaching. He says that God will give good things to the children of the kingdom in the same way that they give to others. In other words, whatever you do for someone else you can expect in return. If you give time, you'll get time; if you give love, you'll get love; if you give money, you'll get money.

Isn't this logic upside down? Why would He give back to you what you already have? Once again, Jesus is talking about rewarding sincere efforts. Whatever you do in a spirit of love and compassion will be rewarded with love and compassion.

Using My Gifts:

1. Describe a time in your life when you gave some of your time, and you received time in return.
2. On a scale of 1 (lowest) to 5 (highest), how would you rate yourself in the way you use your gift of love?

Scriptures: John 12:35-36, John 15:5

Jesus was not a prophet to the rich and famous; He was not the darling of the privileged few. He lived and taught among ordinary, everyday people. So, He always used images that the average person could easily understand.

Today it's hard to imagine a world without electric lights—a time when nights were truly dark, lit only by small oil lamps and smoky torches. But the reality of those dark times made this teaching very graphic for His followers. Jesus is the Light of the world; He said to use this Light while you still can.

Jesus also said He is the true vine. As people who lived off the land and labored in the fields, His listeners knew the value of the true vine—the original stock from which all others are grafted. They understood they were to love the Lord with all their hearts and to help spread the news of the Messiah.

Using My Gifts:

1. Knowing that Jesus is the only true Light for our world that's lost in darkness, how are you using the Light to help others? Be specific.
2. Have you been "grafted into" the true vine? If so, how did it happen?

Scripture: Matthew 13:31-32

Small beginnings are tough. It's not easy to begin with nothing, labor patiently for years with only modest reward, and continue building in the hope of some future success. But that's exactly what Jesus wanted His followers to do. They were simple people in a simpler time, but they were given the task to plant the seeds that would someday flourish into the kingdom of God on earth.

The black mustard plant of the Middle East begins as a tiny seed no larger than a grain of sand, but it matures into a massive plant. This was the picture Jesus used to assure his followers that their hard work would not be in vain. If they *used their talents* and were faithful to their calling, the seeds they planted for the kingdom would blossom beyond their wildest imagination. And they did. But God still has seed-planting work for you to do.

Using My Gifts:

1. Seed planting can be done in a great variety of ways. What special gift did God give you to help scatter the seed (music, visitation, art, encouragement, etc.)?
2. How have you focused your gift to glorify God?

Scripture: 2 Timothy 2:14-15

The Apostle Paul was called to follow Jesus Christ in a stunning vision on the road to Damascus. He was transformed from the Pharisee who most hated and persecuted Christians to the most evangelistic follower of Jesus who has ever lived. Paul traveled from one end of the Mediterranean to the other, spoke to hostile crowds, and was tireless in his zeal. He used every ounce of his energy to spread the Good News of Jesus Christ.

So, when he told his young follower, Timothy, to be a diligent worker in the kingdom who did not need to be ashamed, he gave him an excellent example to follow—his own life. There's an old verse that says, "Just one life; 'twill soon be past. Only what's done for Christ will last." This was the truth Paul hoped to teach.

Using My Gifts:

1. Would you describe yourself as a "diligent worker in the kingdom"? Why?
2. In what specific ways can you better incorporate the Law of Use into your life this week?

Living in the Kingdom

My personal goals for putting The Law of Use to work in my life are these:

Short-term Goals:

Long-term Goals:

THE LAW OF

PERSEVERANCE

Key Scripture: Matthew 7:7-11

Everyone has heard the old saying that "success is 99 percent perspiration and 1 percent inspiration." It's quite true that a lot of good ideas never amount to anything because there is no effort behind them. The same principle is true in the kingdom; that's why Jesus told His followers to be persistent, to keep on trying, even in prayer.

In Matthew 7:7 and Luke 11:9-13 the Lord's instructions are to keep on asking, searching, and knocking, followed by the promise that your requests will be granted by the Lord. Jesus observes that no one would give bad gifts to his own children. So, he says, if we who are bad give good gifts, how much more will our heavenly Father answer those who ask Him.

Jesus told two other parables to support this teaching. The first was the story of the unfair judge, who finally agreed to do the right thing only because the persistent widow wouldn't leave him alone. The second was the story of the man who succeeded in borrowing a few loaves of bread from his neighbor because he just kept pounding on the door.

Time after time Jesus taught that success in the kingdom comes by persistence and effort. This central truth is contained in the Law of Perseverance. Whether it's a person who keeps on seeking until he finally finds the Lord, or a desperate mother praying for a wayward child, good things come when you seek first the kingdom of God and then keep on working and doing the right things.

Scripture: Luke 18:1-8

We don't really know why the widow came to the judge. We only know she had a complaint which needed a verdict, and she was persistent. We also know from this parable that even an unfair judge, without respect for God or man, was persuaded to do the right thing when the petitioner was persistent enough.

With this teaching Jesus said that perseverance and endurance were important principles of the kingdom. And if an unfair man can be persuaded to do good, how much more can your righteous and perfect heavenly Father be persuaded to hear you and grant your requests?

The principle applies to prayer, but it also applies in other areas of the Christian life. If you want blessings, if you want to experience the fullness of God's presence, then you must also persist in the godly things you do.

Being Persistent

1. Since the judge was the only one who could solve the woman's problem, did she have a *right* to keep on asking for a decision? Or was she just being an unnecessary pest?
2. Matthew 6:8 in the NCV says, "... your Father knows the things you need before you ask him." How does this fit with the Law of Persistence?

Scripture: Hebrews 10:23, 35-36

Even the most optimistic person can lose hope when constantly bombarded by trials and troubles. If you do only good things and constantly get bad things in return, you begin to wonder about the meaning of it all. This was certainly true in the early church, and the writer of Hebrews knew that those believers would be troubled by doubts, by persecution, and even death. So, he encouraged them to endure, to resist, and to hold on for the long run.

What Christ offers, and what this writer was quick to promise, was that endurance has a sure reward. Those who hold on through the difficulties and who persevere, despite the hardships, will receive the reward of eternity–what the Apostle John called the "crown of life."

Being Persistent

1. Have you ever lost your hope when facing overwhelming problems? Describe that time in your life.
2. What helps you to hold on to Christ when the going gets tough? Is it always easy to do?

Scripture: Luke 11:5-13

No promise of the Bible is greater than this: God will hear your prayers and answer them. The sovereign God of the universe listens when you seek Him diligently, and He will give you what you ask, if you are persistent.

The parable of the friend who comes at midnight for bread is another example that shows the righteousness of God contrasted with the weakness of man. If a man will rise at midnight to the knock of a persistent neighbor, how much more will God respond to our sincere and tireless prayers?

In His command to keep on asking, searching, and knocking, Jesus knew that people would sometimes ask for things not truly needed. It takes persistence to separate wishes from necessities. But in every case God is there, and He hears your prayers.

Being Persistent:

1. Would you say that your list of "necessities" gets longer or shorter as you become more persistent in prayer? Explain.
2. Do you really believe that God hears every prayer you pray? If so, why is persistence in prayer important?

 Scriptures: Romans 5:3-4; 2 Timothy 1:12

Compared to the emptiness of life without God, even turmoil and tribulation can be tolerated if they bring us nearer to Him. The early church was attacked from all sides. The believers had to learn not only to endure their hardships but to rejoice in them, since these trials produced the very qualities that made them more like Christ.

Paul said that he had joy in his troubles, knowing that his suffering would lead to hope. In the process, he would learn patience, endurance, perseverance, and develop a character that would be more pleasing to God.

To Timothy he said he was not ashamed to suffer insults, because he knew that Jesus Christ was as good as His word. He believed Jesus would keep His promise to come again and honor those who have endured to the end. He will honor you, too, if you endure.

Being Persistent:

1. Why is it so difficult to rejoice during hard times, even when we remember that we're building character?
2. Looking back at your own life, can you see a time when you should have been smiling instead of crying, now knowing what the ultimate result has been? Describe that time.

Scripture: Galatians 6:7-10

In *Your God Is Too Small,* J. B. Phillips said people have an unrealistic view of God. Do you recognize Him as a God of love, who not only created the universe but can also live within your heart? Or, do you manufacture a God who fits your own limited definitions? Perhaps, you prefer a "God-in-the-box"—a celestial Jack-in-the-box, who pops up when you turn the crank and disappears when you shut the lid. That is not the God of heaven.

But Phillips said you can discover the purpose of life in two simple principles: "Love the Lord your God with all your heart, soul, and mind" and "love your neighbor as yourself." That's persistence.

In a fallen world, permeated and overrun by sin, persistent love is difficult to find and even harder to give. Trials and testing are more common; troubles are more persistent. Endurance is tough.

Being persistent:

1. What traits would you say the person exhibits who has persistent love in his life? Do you know someone like that? What impact has that person had on you?

Living in the Kingdom

My personal goals for putting The Law of Perseverance to work in my life are these:

Short-term Goals:

Long-term Goals:

THE LAW OF
RESPONSIBILITY

Key Scripture: Luke 12:42-48

You have heard the old military expression, "Rank has its privileges." But there's another part to that saying: "Rank also has its responsibilities." Being responsible means being accountable. Sometimes it seems that leaders are a law unto themselves. Actually, those who hold great responsibility always answer to others. So, whether it's in government, business, the church, or the family, being responsible means being accountable. The heart of this teaching is Jesus' command to be faithful in whatever we've been called to do. The parable of the talents and the faithful servants teaches us to be accountable to the giver. "From everyone who has been given much," Jesus said, "much will be demanded." In the lives of Christians, the giver is God.

Among the tragedies of the past decade is the large number of scandals involving men in high-profile leadership positions. These scandals have rocked all sectors of public life—politics, business, and even religion. People who were trusted to manage large operations proved untrustworthy. They allowed greed and personal interest to sway their judgment, and they lost everything.

The Apostle Paul made it clear to Timothy that anyone who wants to be a leader must continually demonstrate strong character and moral behavior. Their values are reflected in every aspect of their lives. If you wish to receive the blessings of the kingdom, then, clearly you must take this principle to heart and live it. If you want responsibility, you must accept accountability.

Scripture: 1 Timothy 3:1-7, 8-11

The requirements for leadership laid out by the Apostles for the church are specific and demanding. Elders must not give people a reason to criticize them; they should have clear authority and leadership in the community and in their homes. They must have pleasant dispositions and be good witnesses of their faith. Deacons are to be loving, sober, and not selfish or greedy. All in all, those chosen to represent the interests of the believers must meet some very high standards.

Paul made it clear that every believer is under the same obligation to live above criticism and to be an example to the world of what it means to be a follower of Christ. Peter said believers are a chosen people, royal priests, chosen to tell about the wonderful acts of God (Peter 2:9). That's you, if you're a Christian.

Accepting My Responsibility:

1. What responsibilities have you accepted to help the work of God's kingdom?
2. In what specific area of your life do you feel you need improvement to live "above criticism"?

Scripture: James 3:13

Like Peter and John, James rose in authority and responsibility in the church after the ascension of Jesus. Having studied at the feet of the Master, James felt a burden to teach what he had discovered and to make followers who in turn could go out to the ends of the earth and teach others.

The entire book of James in the New Testament is one of the sternest challenges to live a disciplined and responsible life in Christ. The Apostle calls upon you to put your faith in action in your new life. You are to speak a new way, think new thoughts, and show by your responsible behavior that you have been changed from the inside out. You are not forced to do these things; instead, you are led to do them by the Holy Spirit. And in love you are to show meekness and wisdom.

Accepting My Responsibility:

1. When you became a Christian, how did your life change?
2. Do you feel a personal burden of responsibility to teach others about Jesus and His saving grace? Why?
3. To whom are you accountable in regard to carrying out this responsibility?

Scriptures: Mark 4:11; Matthew 16:19

Just think of the emotions of a teenager with a new car. After years of dreaming of the day, suddenly Dad holds out the keys and says, "Here; it's yours." But before the teenager drives away, there's a lot to learn and think about. A car involves new responsibilities, too.

One day Jesus called his disciples together and handed them the keys of the kingdom. What must they have felt at that moment? From the beginning it was clear that following Jesus would bring major responsibilities and certain hardships. There would be doubters and scoffers on the outside, and division and strife on the inside. There would be great victory one day and great defeat the next.

To make sure His followers understood the responsibility they were being given, Jesus told them stories and parables, and he shared many insights privately. Then, suddenly, He was gone, and it was their turn to drive.

Accepting My Responsibility:
1. Imagine that Jesus handed the keys of His kingdom to you. Describe the emotions you would feel.
2. As He walks away, Jesus says, "Here; it's up to you now." The keys are in your hand. What's the first thing you would do? Why?
3. Since it is, indeed, up to just you, will the kingdom survive?

Scripture: 1 Corinthians 9:22-27

After a torturous twenty-six-mile marathon, the runners stumble across the finish line. The winner is thrilled! Some behind him are disappointed; others are just happy to survive the demanding course. But imagine the grief of the winner when he discovers he fouled another runner along the way and has been disqualified. In one horrifying moment he plummets from first to last. Everything he has worked for is lost.

Paul compares his role of leadership with a runner who competes both against the course and himself. During the race, he must meet each person where he lives, be humble among the humble and strong among the strong. He must speak the language of those he wishes to reach and understand their individual hopes and concerns. And through it all, he must guard his own heart, never risking the outcome of the race.

Accepting My Responsibility:
1. Would you say that you have accepted your responsibility to "meet each person where he lives"? If so, how?
2. How can you "speak the language" of people you hope to reach for Christ?

Scripture: Matthew 28:18-20

In all of Scripture there is no greater commandment than this. In these verses, known as the Great Commission, Jesus sent His followers into the world to carry the Good News to every person and nation. Giving them power and dominion, He sent them first into the villages of Judea and Samaria to teach with miraculous signs and wonders. Then He gave them the keys of the kingdom.

This was not a hasty act. It was not something Jesus did lightly or without good reasons. He knew these men would be tested and that each of them would, in fact, suffer and die for the faith. But He told them He had been given all power and authority by God the Father, and He sent them forth with His blessings.

Ultimately, this is the most important application of the Law of Responsibility. If you are a follower of Jesus, you are already commissioned to make new followers for Christ, wherever you go in the world. This is the true test of accountability.

Accepting My Responsibility:

1. Don't you enjoy sharing good news with your friends and family? The *New Century Version* describes the story of Jesus as the "Good News." Make a list of three friends who need to know this Good News.
2. Will you accept your personal responsibility to share the Good News with these people, knowing you are accountable to God?

Living in the Kingdom

My personal goals for putting The Law of Responsibility to work in my life are these:

Short-term Goals:

Long-term Goals:

THE LAW OF
GREATNESS

Key Scripture: Matthew 18:1-4

What does it mean to be great? In every sport there are heroes people call great. They have nicknames which boast of their legendary qualities, like "Bear" Bryant. There are famous leaders in business and government, presidents, historical figures, even movie stars and celebrities commonly called great. So what *is* greatness?

The gospels record a humorous but instructive episode when a group of Jesus' followers were arguing over who was greatest in the kingdom. Each one probably boasted of his accomplishments, his closeness to the Master, or his leadership abilities. Finally, they went to Jesus to let Him settle the matter. Surprise!

Once again, the Lord turned the tables on them. Greatness was not power, He said, but service. Jesus was the greatest man alive, and He washed His followers' feet; He served the Passover meal; He humbled Himself even to death. To be great means to be humble, and in that humility to serve others.

A "philanthropist" is one who gives generously to others. The word means "one who loves mankind." An example of greatness through giving in our own time would be Mother Teresa of Calcutta. She lives with poverty and death, yet she attains greatness by giving herself away every day. A generation earlier most people would have said that Albert Schweitzer had this kind of greatness, too.

In humble service, through compassion, and by loving others even as we love ourselves, Jesus said, we discover the Law of Greatness.

Scripture: Luke 22:24-27

Think of the attitudes and emotions that must have run through the followers' minds that day. Seated quietly on the hillside, one of them mentioned that Jesus always picked him for the important jobs, and surely he was going to be a great leader in the kingdom. Another, insulted and angry, claimed he would be greatest; after all, he was there first, and he was always faithful to the Master.

As their argument grew, they charged down the hill to where Jesus was sitting and demanded to know whom He liked best. "Who will be the greatest in your kingdom, Master?" they demanded. Such a debate must have saddened Jesus, for it was contrary to everything He had been teaching them. In word and in action, Jesus taught that love conquers all. Humble service pays a greater dividend than worldly power. So once again, He began to teach them that important lesson.

Becoming Great:

1. The NCV shows Jesus' message clearly: "the leader should be like the servant." So, what attitudes do you think you should have to be a leader in His church?
2. How do these attitudes compare/contrast with the typical attitudes of people we often call "great"?

Scripture: Matthew 23:11-12

Jesus said the great teachings of Scripture can be summed up in the commandment to love God and your fellow man. So, to seek great rank and privilege would seem to be contrary to the things that Jesus was teaching. He made it clear that anyone who makes himself great will be made humble. Whoever makes himself humble will be made great.

Clearly, Jesus intended for there to be leaders in the church. Some would have great authority while others would be humble followers. Obviously, Jesus did not mean that authority is unimportant or evil. In fact, He claimed all authority in heaven and earth, and He gave some of those rights to His godly followers.

The important lesson is that God gives greatness to humble people, and God humbles those who are proud. If you want to be a leader for God, then you are to let Christ work through you in His own way. Whether your deeds then are great or small, you become an instrument of the Most High God.

Becoming Great:

1. Using Jesus' standard of greatness, who is the greatest person you know? How has that person affected your life?
2. Would your best friend say that you are great? Would Jesus?

Scripture: John 13:4-17

Peter, the impetuous and headstrong apostle, was always slightly out of step. He was either out front leading the charge, or holding back, protesting. But he did recognize the deity of Jesus Christ, and he bowed to Him as his leader and his Lord.

Imagine Peter's surprise one hot, dusty afternoon when Jesus knelt before him and reached out to wash his feet. "No," he yelped, "you will not wash my feet!" Peter could not imagine the Master doing such a lowly thing. But Jesus said that unless Peter allowed Him to wash his feet, Peter would have no place in the kingdom.

At that point, impetuous Peter demanded that Jesus not stop with his feet. "Then wash not only my feet, but wash my hands and my head, too!" The point Jesus had to make was that the greater must serve the lesser. In this lesson, He was teaching the Law of Greatness.

Becoming Great:
1. What actions in your life show that you recognize the deity of Jesus Christ?
2. Does your *whole* lifestyle bow to Jesus as your leader and your Lord?

 Scriptures: 1 John 5:3-5; Luke 7:28

John the Baptist must have been a conspicuous figure in the Judean wilderness. Dressed in animal skins, eating locusts and wild honey, and crying out against the sins of Israel, John would have made an awesome sight. People came from miles away to see him.

As the last of the Old Testament prophets and the man chosen by God to identify Jesus Christ as the Messiah, John also had a singular role in the kingdom of God. Jesus said, "I tell you that John is the greatest person ever born." No mere mortal had ever been blessed with such an important job, and John fulfilled it perfectly. He proclaimed Jesus as Messiah and baptized Him in the Jordan River.

But Jesus had the greatest mission: to create a New Agreement between God and humanity and to reveal the kingdom of God on earth. As great as John was, Jesus said that even the least person in the kingdom was greater than John.

Becoming Great:
1. How does it make you feel to know that, as a Christian, you are greater in the eyes of God than John the Baptist?
2. How do citizenship in God's kingdom and greatness go together? What is their common element?

Scriptures: Proverbs 22:4; James 4:6-7

Solomon, the wise king of Israel and descendant of David, was proclaimed the wisest man who ever lived. He may also have been the richest. His vast treasures, his mighty works, and his writings were astounding. But what did Solomon value most? In Proverbs 22 he said that true greatness comes not from wealth or authority, but from humility and obedience to God.

Several hundred years after Solomon's time, the Apostle James made a similar statement, calling on believers to humble themselves before God in order to become great. God does not honor the proud, he said. He humbles them. But by humbling yourself before the King of Kings, you gain power even over Satan, the prince of this world.

From beginning to end, the Law of Greatness turns the world's idea of power and authority upside down. Even amid the kings and rulers of earth, those who fall humbly before God have the greatest power of all.

Becoming Great:
1. How would you summarize the Law of Greatness?
2. To be truly great in the eyes of God, what changes would you need to make in your life?

Living in the Kingdom

My personal goals for putting The Law of Greatness to work in my life are these:

Short-term Goals:

Long-term Goals:

THE LAW OF
UNITY

Key Scriptures: Matthew 18:19-20; 1 Corinthians 12:4-7

One of the most pleasant experiences you can have is to attend a performance by a great symphony orchestra. Over the years many talented composers have contributed masterpieces to the universal repertoire. When their works are combined with the talents of an accomplished orchestra and conductor, you experience something extraordinary.

Still, as remarkable as the sound of an orchestra can be, it is made up of individuals. The majesty of the sound they make is due to their playing together in harmony and in unity.

The idea that wonderful things can be accomplished through unity was an important issue for the early church. There were many reasons to be divided; there were many sects and controversies with which to deal. Earlier, Jesus had said that any city or family that is divided against itself will not continue (Matthew 12:25), and Paul knew that a divided church could not endure. Jesus told His followers that unity would only come to the church when the different talents and gifts of the believers were combined for the good of all.

Have you ever looked at a newspaper photo up close? What you discover is that a photo is made up of thousands of tiny dots. From normal reading distance, though, those dots make a unified and natural photograph. Throughout the arts and sciences there are examples of the wonders achieved when small details are combined for the good of the whole. In essence, these are all aspects of the Law of Unity, which is one of the most dynamic laws of the kingdom.

Scripture: John 17:11, 24-26

The prayer that is commonly called "The Lord's Prayer" was actually a model which Jesus used to teach His followers. First, He taught them the basic elements of a prayer and, second, the ease of coming before the throne of God.

The personal prayer recorded in John 17, in which Christ prayed for His followers, actually deserves the title "Lord's Prayer." This is the most moving example in the Scriptures of Christ's own prayers, and its theme is unity.

Unity overcomes the greatest obstacles; division destroys even best laid plans. When Jesus prayed for unity, He used the greatest example we know— the Trinity. The *New Century Version* shows His aim clearly: Give them unity, He prayed, "so that they will be one, just as you and I are one."

Striving for Unity:

1. In your opinion, what is the greatest obstacle to unity in the church? Why?
2. Do you consider yourself a promoter of unity? If so, how? If not, why not?

Scripture: Ephesians 4:1-6, 13

Paul's plea for unity to the Christians at Ephesus is one of the most compelling appeals in the Bible. He said, "There is one body and one Spirit, and God called you to have one hope. There is one Lord, one faith, and one baptism." With such a unity of calling and commitment, there should be no stopping the church. It was from this pagan city of Ephesus, in fact, that the Good News radiated throughout the world.

There were so many obstacles to overcome in that early journey of evangelism that no division could be allowed. In Ephesus and other capitals to which Paul traveled, the apostle took pains to prune and train the early leaders, to help them unite upon the truth of the Scriptures. Even though Christians still struggle with this challenge, the model of unity was clear from the beginning.

Striving for Unity:

1. Division in a church usually begins with disunity between two individuals. If all the individuals were unified, would the church be unified?
2. Is there someone in your church with whom you are not in unity? What first step can *you* take to mend that division?

Scriptures: 1 Corinthians 3:5-11; 12:4-7

When you set out to build a structure, you need a good plan. Without a blueprint to follow, the workmen will wander off in strange directions, and the building will surely collapse.

Ironically, one of the first divisions in the church arose over of the different personalities of Paul, Barnabas, Apollos, and other early leaders. But Paul was quick to correct those who tried to create division, saying that the apostles were co-workers not competitors. Each one was doing one piece of the project.

He also said they were like farmers planting, tilling, and watering the soil. Whether planting seed or laying a foundation, it was not the workers that mattered but the thing they were creating. While each had a different role, they were unified in purpose. The focus of their labor was always the church, and Jesus Christ was the source of strength and unity.

Striving for Unity:

1. Do you see evidence of competition, and thus disunity, in your church? Describe what you see.
2. What can you do personally to help refocus "competitive" Christians' goals on Jesus Christ and off of themselves?

Scripture: Galatians 3:26-28

Most people will tell you there is no formal class system in our society. While there are higher and lower social positions based on wealth, or celebrity status, or responsibilities, the old idea of a class system has basically disappeared.

In the time of Christ, however, this was not the case. The social order ranged from emperors, regents, kings, and priests to laborers, servants, and slaves. No one dared to cross those boundaries.

So, when Paul taught that there was to be unity in the faith, he was teaching a revolutionary doctrine. He said there were no masters or slaves in the kingdom of God, no distinction between Jew and Gentile, or men and women. Jesus taught that all who claimed His promises were equally welcome in the kingdom. This teaching–the Law of Unity–has done more to change our world than any other.

Striving for Unity:

1. Are some people in your church treated differently than others due to the way they dress, the cars they drive, or their social skills? How can you help change that situation?
2. Would outcasts, people of all races, poor and abused people feel truly welcome in your church? How does this relate to unity?

Scriptures: Genesis 1:27; Acts 4:32-37
What is the nature of God? Can we know anything about God? Or is He a mystery too deep for anyone to understand?

The model of unity in the church is the unity of the Trinity. From the first chapter of Genesis you can see that God made people in His own image: "So God created human beings in his image. In the image of God he created them. He created them male and female." So, if you wish to learn about God, you can find hints by examining human nature.

One such characteristic is the need for companionship and belonging. By nature we long for closeness, for a mate, for friends, for teammates, and for partners. Unlike God, however, people have a sinful, selfish nature; so, there is always risk of division. But when unified by the Spirit of God, believers can accomplish great things. Acts 4:32-37 shows what we may yet become when we are truly united in the kingdom of heaven.

Striving for Unity:

1. How does the Law of Unity apply to your family and you?
2. What effect will your personal dedication to unity have on your relationships with friends, business associates, and your stress level?

Living in the Kingdom

My personal goals for putting The Law of Unity to work in my life are these:

Short-term Goals:

Long-term Goals:

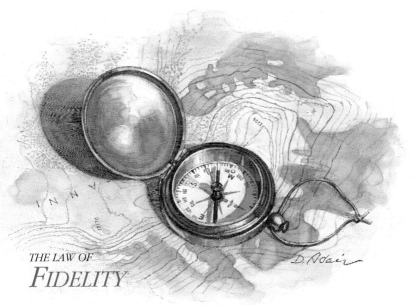

THE LAW OF
FIDELITY

Key Scripture: Matthew 24:45-47

One of the great virtues, which is desirable and highly esteemed by God is fidelity–faithfulness. It's the spiritual compass that keeps us headed due north–to God.

From beginning to end, the Scriptures reveal that God has great regard for faithfulness. In the book of Genesis, God identifies Himself as the One who is faithful. In Revelation, Jesus is identified as "the faithful and true witness" (Revelation 3:14). Through the psalmist, God says, "I will look for trustworthy people;" and further, "the Lord protects those who truly believe" (Psalms 101:6; 31:23).

Obviously, the Law of Fidelity is a central teaching of the Bible. On a practical level you may ask yourself, "Is it always something grand? Is fidelity only visible on great occasions? Is it beyond the reach of the average man or woman? Jesus showed that He was faithful unto death. Is that what fidelity demands?"

Not necessarily. In Revelation we find that God does promise a crown of life to everyone who is faithful unto death. But the parables of Jesus show that faithfulness is a matter of how we live each day. To the faithful follower, Jesus said, "You are a good and loyal servant. Because you were loyal with small things, I will let you care for much greater things" (Matthew 25:21). He also gave a promise of blessing, saying, "Come and share my joy with me."

Ultimately, the Law of Fidelity influences all our relationships–school, career, marriage, friendships. And how we respond makes all the difference.

Scriptures: Matthew 7:21-24

One of the most provocative teachings of Jesus is recorded in Matthew 7:21-24 when the Lord said that not everyone who says He is their Lord will enter the kingdom of heaven. Many will come to Him and claim to be followers who, in fact, were never part of the kingdom. As the *New Century Version* plainly shows it, Jesus will say to them, "Get away from me, you who do evil. I never knew you."

Such comments make us wonder who will be admitted. Christ gives the answer in verse 24: "Everyone who hears my words and obeys them . . . ." Jesus told the followers that such a person would be like the wise man who built his house on solid rock. In the metaphor, Christ is the rock, and whoever obeys His commandments is a true and faithful follower. This truth is the central tenet of the Law of Fidelity.

I Will Be Faithful:
1. Why will some people not enter the kingdom of God, even though they say Jesus is their Lord?
2. Does Jesus recognize you as one of His faithful followers? Why?

Scripture: Luke 16:10-13

When the applicant puts together his resumé and goes in for an interview, he puts his best foot forward. He knows that first impressions are important; so, he's well groomed and polite. He arrives on time and tries to be as pleasant as possible.

If he is successful, the prospective employer may introduce the candidate to other employees, and perhaps he will receive an offer to come to work. However, normally there is one more step: reference checking. One by one, the manager contacts previous employers to see if the applicant has been reliable. What will happen when he discovers that the young man has been indiscreet and careless in his duties?

It's bad enough to be fired from your job for careless behavior, but how much worse is it to be rejected from the kingdom of God? The Law of Fidelity shows us that God searches your heart to discover if you have been trustworthy.

I Will Be Faithful:
1. If you had to apply for a job in fidelity, would your references stand the scrutiny?
2. Name two ways you can strengthen your faithfulness, beginning this week.

Scripture: Philippians 1:27-28

Do you sometimes find it hard to live the Christian life in the everyday world? Would people laugh if they found out you were "one of them" (a Christian)? Would witnessing make your life more difficult or more dangerous?

The young churches in Asia Minor were threatened and persecuted from all sides. But Paul, who had been stoned, beaten, and jailed repeatedly for preaching the Good News of Jesus Christ, offered them his own example of faithfulness. He encouraged them to be strong and courageous in proclaiming the Word. He wrote to say that he was confident that He who had begun a good work in their hearts would be faithful to complete it. He urged them, in turn, to be faithful in all things until Christ returns.

I Will Be Faithful:
1. Tell of a tempting time recently when your fidelity to God was challenged. What did you do?
2. Do you find it easier to be faithful among your business associates or your Christian friends? Why?

 Scriptures: Matthew 10:32-39; Revelation 2:10b

A key ingredient of the Law of Fidelity is Christ's example of faithfulness. As He traveled and taught in Galilee and Judea, and in the Temple at Jerusalem, Jesus loved the very people who would one day betray and crucify Him. Knowing all along what they would do someday, He loved them faithfully and offered them the gift of salvation.

He knew that accepting Him as Messiah would be a divisive issue. Many who believed in Him would be separated from their own loved ones; they would be cursed and scorned; eventually many would be killed. But Jesus said that anyone who picked compromise and safety over Him would lose his heavenly reward, while those who remained true through thick and thin would ultimately receive a crown of life.

I Will Be Faithful:
1. Is it worth it? Could you be faithful if you knew for a fact that some day you would be killed for believing in Jesus Christ?
2. Can you see yourself being sincerely kind to a terrorist who is holding a gun to your head? In effect, that's what Jesus did.

Scripture: 1 John 1:5-10

"I will look for trustworthy people so I can live with them in the land. Only those who live innocent lives will be my servants" (Psalm 101:6).

The secrets of the kingdom of God are as available as your Bible. There is nothing truly difficult in His Word, unless your heart is hardened and you simply refuse to believe what is printed there. Usually those who have the most trouble with God's Word are those who doubt its value and seldom use it.

Many times these are also the people who say a loving God would never exclude people from heaven for something so natural as sin. But the Law of Fidelity may be the best argument against this belief. God seeks to reward those who are *faithful*. Those who live by their own rules make God a liar, and they have no part in the kingdom.

I Will Be Faithful:

1. How faithful are you to the Word of God? Do you study it often?
2. Can you truly be faithful to God if you are not truly faithful to His Word?

Living in the Kingdom

My personal goals for putting The Law of Fidelity to work in my life are these:

Short-term Goals:

Long-term Goals:

THE LAW OF
CHANGE

Key Scripture: Matthew 9:16-17

The writer of Ecclesiastes says that everything on earth has its own special season. Sunrise and sunset, night and day, summer and winter, and the cycles of life and death all teach us that change is inevitable. The book of Genesis shows that God had a purpose in creating the world; Revelation shows that He has another one in ending it. From beginning to end, the Bible teaches that God uses change to prepare our hearts for the kingdom of heaven, just as he uses change to convert a caterpillar to a butterfly.

One of the key passages teaching the Law of Change is Matthew 9:16-17, where Jesus taught that our old habits of thought could not contain the new truth He came to deliver. Jesus came to bring a new way of life, but if growth and change were to come, the followers needed to be like strong containers. To teach this lesson, He used the familiar images of putting a new patch on an old garment and of putting new wine in old wineskins. He was, of course, actually referring to the renewing of our hearts and minds.

When John the Baptist preached to the crowds on the banks of the Jordan River, he told them they must be changed from within so they could receive the Good News of salvation. Then Jesus preached the same message. He had come to introduce a New Agreement between God and humanity, and He knew that the old traditions of the Jewish faith would not be able to hold it.

In matters of faith, as in everyday life, we must understand that growth demands change, and Christ demands that we grow in Him.

Scripture: Roman 12:1-2

When Paul wrote his powerful letter to the Romans, he knew they understood the idea of sacrifice. For centuries the people of Europe had offered sacrifices to their pagan gods. Like the Phoenicians, who burned their own infant children alive at the shrine of Molech, the Romans also practiced human sacrifices.

But when Paul called for the new converts to present themselves to God as living sacrifices, he offered a dramatic new twist to the old religious ideas. For God did not want to destroy life; He wanted to bring about changes which would renew them inside and out. God did not want people to die but to live for Him. Jesus gave the perfect sacrifice of death at Calvary. His followers were asked to give Him the sacrifice of their daily lives.

In this passage Paul makes the Law of Change clear: do not be changed to the world's way of thinking, but to God's. Then you will know what is good and pleasing to the Father in heaven.

Changing My Heart and Life

1. What role do you think television has played in changing your mind to "the world's way of thinking"? Explain.
2. List three specific things you can do this week to change your thinking back to "God's way of thinking."

Scripture: Acts 2:36-38

When it was time for Jesus to leave His followers and return to the Father in heaven, He told them they were to go into all the world to preach and teach the Good News about Him. He also told them they could only have the power to do those things if they were filled with the Holy Spirit.

The coming of the Holy Spirit, recorded in Acts 2, is one of the most remarkable events recorded in the Bible. It was when the Holy Spirit of God came to the followers of Jesus. The non-believers mocked them when they saw and heard the Christians speaking in other languages. But Peter stood up to preach to the people, and he called on them to repent, or as the *New Century Version* translates it in contemporary words, to change their hearts and lives, and then to be baptized. More than 3,000 people believed the Good News and were baptized that day alone.

Jesus is still changing people's hearts, and He still sends the Holy Spirit to be their guide and comforter. He will change your heart, too, if you'll let Him.

Changing My Heart and Life

1. Is changing your heart and life an ongoing, everyday process or a one-time-for-all-time event? Explain.
2. How obvious is it to others that the Holy Spirit lives in you? Why?

Scripture: 2 Corinthians 7:9-10

In this passage, the Apostle Paul recognizes that God uses many methods to bring people to Himself. One of the most common is for people to feel sorry for the way they have behaved. They think of the things they have said and done to hurt not only God but other people, and they decide to change.

Paul says that the world is full of sadness—sadness because of loss, jealousy, anger, and sin. That kind of sadness brings death because it does not cause people to change their hearts and lives. But the sadness which leads to a change of heart and lifestyle is really a good thing, since it brings people to a new life in Jesus Christ.

This is the Law of Change in its most dynamic form, helping to change the direction of people's lives—from hell to heaven. And God created that Law of Change from the very beginning.

Changing My Heart and Life

1. What things about your relationships with your family and friends make you sad? Would changing your heart help to correct those relationship problems?
2. Pray that God will help you to change your mind and heart. Then write or call the person and let him or her know about your change of heart.

Scriptures: Luke 5:36-38; 2 Corinthians 5:17

The men who followed Jesus were hand-picked. One by one, and two by two, He selected them at the beginning of His ministry to travel with Him and to learn from Him so they would be able to take the message of the kingdom to the world. He took men who had been fishermen, tax collectors, bookkeepers, and merchants and made them teachers. He led them, step by step, through the enormous changes in their lives so that they could later lead others through the changes in their lives.

When Jesus taught them the Law of Change, He used the image of wineskins and patches to help them understand the need for a change of heart. Paul further clarified this point by saying that when you become a new creation in Christ, old things pass away, and all things become new. Change is what your faith is all about.

Changing My Heart and Life

1. As a Christian, you have also been hand-picked by God to spread His kingdom. To be effective, what changes must you make?
2. Taking an honest look at yourself, would you say that you are more like "new wine" or an "old wineskin"? Why?

Scripture: Ephesians 2:5-8

Many people consider the story of Jesus' meeting with the Jewish leader Nicodemus to be one of the most important passages in all of the Bible. In this story the Lord made the statement which has become the central truth of Christianity: Jesus Christ is our only hope for eternal life.

Jesus said to Nicodemus, "God loved the world so much that he gave his one and only Son that whoever believes in him may not be lost, but have eternal life." Because of sin, however, men and women were already condemned by God. Jesus said, "Those who do not believe have already been judged guilty . . ." (John 3:16-18). Jesus is the only way for people to escape God's wrath.

In his letter to the church at Ephesus, Paul applied this important teaching by saying that Jesus came to rescue men and women who were spiritually dead, and through the gift of God's grace you can have an inheritance in the kingdom of heaven. By letting the Law of Change work in your life, you actually receive the greatest treasure of all.

Changing My Heart and Life

1. Why does truly changing your heart automatically change your life, too?
2. Have you truly changed your heart, and therefore your life, so that you can enter the kingdom of God and continue to be molded by Him?

Living in the Kingdom

My personal goals for putting The Law of Change to work in my life are these:

Short-term Goals:

Long-term Goals:

THE LAW OF
MIRACLES

Key Scriptures: 1 Corinthians 12:8-11

The power of the miraculous may be the most misunderstood and least applied principle of our faith. The entire history of the Bible resounds with miracles. From Genesis to Revelation God reveals Himself through the miraculous; yet, today Christians fail to use this divine gift as God intended.

In Exodus, God worked countless miracles by the hand of Moses; the sun stopped in its place at Joshua's command; Elijah held back the rains for three years and called down fire from heaven. God said through Jeremiah, "Pray to me, and I will answer you. I will tell important secrets you have never heard before" (Jeremiah 33:3).

Jesus demonstrated His authority by mighty acts. He said, "God can do all things" (Mark 10:27b), and He proved that truth countless times. He told His followers that if they had faith and never doubted they would do even mightier acts, and they did.

In the book of Acts you can see how Peter, Philip, Paul, Barnabas, and others performed great miracles. In his letters to the Corinthians Paul taught that spiritual gifts, including signs and wonders, are given for the building up of the body of Christ. With so much evidence, why is there so little experience of the miraculous in Christian lives? One reason is that the flow of God's power is interrupted by sin, by doubt, and by bitterness and anger. Sin restrains the power of the Holy Spirit. Only when you come to understand and apply its truths can you hope to discover the astonishing power of the Law of Miracles.

Scripture: John 11:31-45

From the early days of His ministry, Jesus performed miracles among the people. The prophets Isaiah, Jeremiah, and Daniel had predicted that the power of God's anointed one would be revealed by signs and wonders, and Jesus used this means of declaring Himself as Messiah.

Obviously His greatest miracle was redeeming the world by rising from the grave. He gave a sample of this by raising Lazarus from the dead. Not even His closest followers believed He could do such a thing. Changing water to wine was a mighty act, but raising the dead was completely incredible.

When Jesus groaned in His spirit, it was because He was grieved by the doubt and ignorance of His followers. In John 15:11 you can see that Jesus knew well in advance that Lazarus would die. But He had power over the grave, and this was an opportunity to prove it.

The Meaning of Miracles:

1. What does it mean to your life that Jesus rose from death?
2. At first, Jesus' friends didn't believe in miracles. Do your friends believe in miracles? Why or why not?

Scripture: 1 Corinthians 12:8-11

One of the mysteries of the secret kingdom is this: the physical world is unreal, and the spiritual world is real. What you see with your eyes is only temporary, but what you cannot see endures forever. How can you grasp such strange ideas?

Among the expressions of this unseen reality is the presence of spiritual powers among us. Demons tempt and taunt you, drawing you toward evil and self-destructive acts. The Holy Spirit and ministering angels sent to you by the Father surround you and give you power.

Likewise, all Christians possess spiritual gifts designed as tools for building the kingdom of God. Though each of our gifts is different, they are all for the benefit of the kingdom. In this, God shares the very essence of His power with us.

The Meaning of Miracles:

1. How does the statement, "the physical world is unreal, and the spiritual world is real" change the way you live?
2. Do you really believe that demons and angels are among us here on earth? Why?

Scripture: Luke 24:49-53

In the history of the world, the life of Jesus is a dividing line between the old and the new. Before Christ, people lived under the sentence of death. After the crucifixion people gained new hope and new power to face the future. It's appropriate that even the calendar reflects this fact, separating the Old Agreement from the New and the age of death from the *promise of life.* After the crucifixion, Jesus walked among His followers for forty days. At one point He was seen by 500 people; but His mission during that time was to complete His teachings and prepare the church for a new role in the world.

On His last day among them, Jesus walked with the followers to the village of Bethany where He told them He was giving them His Father's promise of "life." They were to wait for the power of the Holy Spirit; and then, He miraculously ascended to heaven before their eyes.

The Meaning of Miracles:

1. What does the miracle of Jesus' ascension mean to your life today?
2. Notice how the *New Century Version* describes the response of Jesus' followers to His ascension in verse 53. How much time do you actually spend praising God?

Scripture: Acts 19:11-17

This is one of the most exciting stories in the New Testament. It reveals the nature of God's miracle-working power. It also reveals the fact, as the *New Century Version* expresses it, that ". . . God's Spirit, who is in you, is greater than the devil, who is in the world" (1 John 4:4).

God granted the power of the miraculous to testify to His presence in the church. Paul was chosen personally by Christ to take the Good News to the Gentiles. He received such power that even the garments and handkerchiefs he carried could cause miracles.

This account in Acts 19 is both comic and tragic. Evil spirits, which feared Jesus and Paul, would not respond to unbelievers who were not filled with the Spirit of God. This is still the condition of the unsaved. Without Christ, they have no power to restrain the work of Satan in the world.

The Meaning of Miracles:

1. What emotions do you feel when you read 1 John 4:4, which says that "… God's Spirit, who is in you, is greater than the devil, who is in the world"? Explain.
2. Do you consider it a miracle that God's Spirit can be in you? Why?

Scriptures: Acts 1:7-8

To most of us, power is something that comes with high office. The president has power; the head of a Fortune 500 company has power. It's harder to see the power of the Spirit within us in the same light, but that's just what Jesus expected us to do.

Very early in the Acts of the Apostles, Jesus tells us how that indwelling power would be manifested. He says, "When the Holy Spirit comes to you, you will receive power. You will be my witnesses . . . in every part of the world."

You will not go out as a defeated and helpless follower of some unknown religion, but as a servant of Jesus Christ. You are to have authority, to speak His words of power, to call upon the Jesus of miracles who said, "Those who believe will do even greater things than these." The Law of Miracles reveals the mighty power of God.

The Meaning of Miracles:

1. What is ironic about a servant (each Christian) having the power to rule the world? How is it possible?
2. How have the miracles of God touched and changed your life?

Living in the Kingdom

My personal goals for putting The Law of Miracles to work in my life are these:

Short-term Goals:

Long-term Goals:

THE LAW OF
DOMINION

Key Scriptures: Genesis 1:26-30; Philippians 4:13

Someday Jesus Christ will return in triumph over Satan. That marvelous promise is the hope of all who believe in Him as Savior and who want to experience the secrets of the kingdom of God in their lives. However, since the fall of mankind in the Garden of Eden, people have lived in a corrupted environment. In addition to the schemes of Satan, you may fall victim to your lower nature, which causes you to miss out on the abundance God offered through the Law of Dominion.

When God told Adam to be fruitful and multiply and fill the earth, He gave people authority over all other living things. If you remain faithful to His commandments, you will experience abundance and blessing. But when you turn to your own selfish interests, you allow the environment to rule over you. You may even become addicted to the things of the earth and give up your rightful authority.

From beginning to end, the Bible teaches the principle of stewardship. As a farmer looks after his fields and flocks, you are to look after the things with which you have been entrusted. Jesus told Christians to stand firm and to occupy the earth until He returns. How often we allow folly and compromise to rob us of our blessings and destroy any prospect of peace on earth.

When you apply the Law of Dominion, you learn to resist evil so that Satan and his demons must flee from you. You learn to be a responsible caretaker of the kingdom and not to let yourself become the unwitting slave of the elements over which you have been appointed to rule.

Scripture: Hebrews 2:5-9

The kingdom is full of paradoxes. Jesus, the Word, was in the beginning with God (see John 1). He was in God as one-third of the Trinity, and therefore He was God. He had the power to make the heavens and the earth, and unless He had made them they would not have been made.

This same Jesus, who made the worlds, chose to be born in a dingy stable in Bethlehem. Through His humble birth and life of service, He brought the world from darkness into light. He became lower than the angels to perform a feat no angel could ever do.

Now, while He is in heaven preparing a place for us, we are His administrators upon the earth. We rule in His place, exercising dominion over all things. This is a great honor, but it's also a duty we cannot perform without the Holy Spirit within us.

Exercising Dominion:
1. Does it make you nervous to know that Jesus has left you in charge of caring for His world? Why?
2. Make a list of five things you can do personally to take care of His world in your role.

Scripture: Luke 9:1-2

A tiny, fragile boy stood at the edge of the village until the vans carrying food and supplies finally arrived. He could hardly walk on his shriveled legs; his stomach was bloated from malnutrition, and his eye sockets bulged. But before he would accept a bite to eat, he ran back to tell the others that help had arrived.

By nature, we all want to tell others when we have good news. We want to save lives–it's human nature–and that's why the Great Commission (Matthew 28:19-20) gives us such a wonderful chance to run and tell the world the Good News. Unlike the boy, however, we do not run in weakness but in strength; for Christ has empowered us and given us dominion over every power and every spirit. How can anyone delay when so many need to know that help has come?

Exercising Dominion:
1. Does it make you feel humble or proud to know you have been given dominion over every other kind of creature God made? Explain.
2. Jesus sent the apostles out to "tell about God's kingdom." Does He expect any less of you to whom He has given such great power and dominion?

Scripture: Titus 2:11-15

In Titus 2 and 3, Paul teaches the proper relationship of the believer to the secular world. You are not to resist authority but to submit to responsible leadership knowing that you have the Spirit of God within you.

While you live in the hope of Christ's return, you are never to stop sharing the Good News of salvation. You are also to challenge other believers to live up to their calling as followers of Jesus, to remain faithful and above criticism.

Most important, in the passage above, you are taught to do all these things in a spirit of love and sincerity, giving no one cause to doubt your motives or show disrespect for the job you are doing. When you exert the force you have been given and exhort others with the words of His command, you also fulfill the Law of Dominion.

Exercising Dominion:

1. How does knowing that God's Spirit is within you allow you to submit to authority?
2. In what three specific ways can you challenge your fellow Christians to live up to their calling as followers of Jesus?

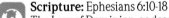

Scripture: Ephesians 6:10-18

The Law of Dominion, as described in Pat Robertson's book *The Secret Kingdom*, does not at all imply that Christianity has already won the war. Even though our side shall be victorious, and even though we serve the Conqueror, we are still engaged in armed conflict with the hostile forces of Satan.

For anyone encountering the reality of spiritual warfare, Paul's description of the "full armor of God" in Ephesians 6 is a perfect description of the way you must defend yourself against the weapons of Satan. Through the authority of the Spirit, you can speak against evil and restrain the power of demons, but you must hold on to the shield of your faith and parry the enemy's advances with the sword of the Spirit. And someday, when the battle is over, you will wear the victor's crown.

Exercising Dominion:

1. Ephesians 6:13 in the *New Century Version* says, "...put on God's full armor." How do you "put it on"?
2. Explain why your "shield of faith" protects you from the burning arrows of the Evil One.

Scripture: 1 Peter 4:10-11

Perhaps the most exceptional paradox of Christianity is that service leads to greatness, and humility gains authority. Christ honors those who honor Him, and those who serve will be served. But the world around you may often be hostile to these values.

The Apostle Peter challenged believers to go into the world and exercise gifts of speech, service, and strength. He also told them they were to give credit for all things to Jesus Christ who alone has ultimate dominion. He knew that only Christ's authority would be sufficient in times of stress.

You are to be *in* the world but not *of* it. You are to prevail over the world through the authority of the Spirit but not to succumb to its seductions. You are to maintain a standard which will put you at odds with your culture.

In this world you need the authority that comes with dominion, and you need the Holy Spirit within you. Then, if you stand firm in the power of His might, *you shall overcome!*

Exercising Dominion:

1. Give an example of someone you know whose life shows that service leads to greatness.
2. How can knowing that Christ has ultimate authority and dominion reduce the stress in your life?

Living in the Kingdom

My personal goals for putting The Law of Dominion to work in my life are these:

Short-term Goals:

Long-term Goals:

THE SECRET KINGDOM

NEW CENTURY VERSION

Contents

Contents

PREFACE

God intended for everyone to be able to understand his Word. Earliest Scriptures were in Hebrew, ideally suited for a barely literate society because of its economy of words, acrostic literary form and poetic parallelism. The New Testament was first written in the simple Greek of everyday life, not in the Latin of Roman courts or the classical Greek of the academies. Even Jesus, the Master Teacher, taught spiritual principles by comparing them to such familiar terms as pearls, seeds, rocks, trees and sheep. Likewise, the *New Century Version* translates the Scriptures in familiar, everyday words of our times.

The *New Century Version* is a translation of God's Word from the original Hebrew and Greek languages. A previous edition of the complete *New Century Version*, the *International Children's Bible*, was published in 1986.

A Trustworthy Translation

Two basic premises guided the translation process of the *New Century Version*. The first concern was that the translation be faithful to the manuscripts in the original languages. A team composed of the World Bible Translation Center and fifty additional, highly qualified and experienced Bible scholars and translators was assembled. The team included people with translation experience on such accepted versions as the *New International Version*, the *New American Standard Bible* and the *New King James Version*. The most recent scholarship and the best available Hebrew and Greek texts were used, principally the third edition of the United Bible Societies' Greek text and the latest edition of the Biblia Hebraica, along with the Septuagint.

A Clear Translation

The second concern was to make the language clear enough for anyone to read the Bible and understand it for himself. In maintaining clear language, several guidelines were followed. Vocabulary choice has been based upon *The Living Word Vocabulary* by Dr. Edgar Dale and Dr. Joseph O'Rourke (Worldbook-Childcraft International, 1981), which is the standard used by the editors of *The World Book Encyclopedia* to determine appropriate vocabulary. For difficult words which have no simpler synonyms, footnotes and dictionary references are provided. Footnotes appear at the bottom of the page and are indicated in the text by an [n] (for "note"). The dictionary/topical concordance is located at the back of the Bible with references indicated in the text by a [d].

The *New Century Version* aids understanding by putting concepts into natural terms. Modern measurements and geographical locations have been used as much as possible. For instance, terms such as "shekels," "cubits," "omer" and "hin" have been converted to modern equivalents of weights and measures. Where geographical references are identical, the modern name has been used, such as the "Mediterranean Sea" instead of "Great Sea" or "Western Sea." Also, to minimize confusion, the most familiar name for a place is used consistently, instead of using variant names for the same place. "Lake Galilee" is used throughout rather than its variant forms, "Sea of Kinnereth," "Lake Gennesaret" and "Sea of Tiberias."

Ancient customs are often unfamiliar to modern readers. Customs such as shaving a man's beard to shame him or walking between the halves of a dead animal to seal an agreement are meaningless to most people. So these are clarified either in the text or in a footnote.

Since *meanings* of words change with time, care has been taken to avoid potential misunderstandings. Frequently in the Old Testament God tells his people to "devote" something to him, as when he tells the Israelites to devote Jericho and everything in it to him. While we might understand this to mean he is telling them to keep it safe and holy, the exact opposite is true. He is telling them to destroy it totally as an offering to him. The *New Century Version* communicates the idea clearly by translating "devoted," in these situations, as "destroyed as an offering to the Lord."

Rhetorical questions have been stated according to their implied answer. The psalmist's question, "What god is so great as our God?" has been stated more directly as, "No god is as great as our God."

Figures of speech have been translated according to their meanings. For instance, the expression, "the Virgin Daughter of Zion," which is frequently used in the Old Testament, is simply translated "the people of Jerusalem."

Idiomatic expressions of the biblical languages are translated to communicate the same meaning to today's reader that would have been understood by the original audience. For example, the Hebrew idiom "he rested with his fathers" is translated by its meaning—"he died."

Obscure terms have been clarified. In the Old Testament God frequently condemns the people for their "high places" and "Asherah poles." The *New Century Version* translates these according to their meanings, which would have been understood by the Hebrews. "High places" is translated "places where gods were worshiped" and "Asherah poles" is translated "Asherah idols."

Gender language has also been translated with a concern for clarity. To avoid the misconception that "man" and "mankind" and "he" are exclusively masculine when they are being used in a generic sense, this translation has chosen to use less ambiguous language, such as "people" and "humans" and "human beings," and has prayerfully attempted throughout to choose gender language that would accurately convey the intent of the original writers. Specifically and exclusively masculine and feminine references in the text have been retained.

Following in the tradition of other English versions, the *New Century Version* indicates the divine name YHWH, the Tetragrammaton, by putting Lord, and sometimes God, in capital letters. This is to distinguish it from Adonai, another Hebrew word that is translated Lord.

Every attempt has been made to maintain proper English style, while clarifying concepts and communication. The beauty of the Hebrew parallelism in poetry and the word plays have been retained, and the images of the ancient languages have been captured in equivalent English images wherever possible.

Study Aids

Other features to enhance understanding of the text include full-color maps of Bible lands; subject headings throughout to identify speakers and topics; book subheadings to give a synopsis of each book's theme; a dictionary/topical concordance of biblical words and concepts; and footnotes identifying Old Testament quotations in the New Testament.

Our Prayer

It is with great humility and prayerfulness that this Bible is presented. We acknowledge the infallibility of God's Word and yet our own human frailty. We pray that God has worked through us as his vessels so that we all might better learn his truth for ourselves and that it might richly grow in our lives. It is to his glory that this Bible is given.

THE PUBLISHER

NEW TESTAMENT

MATTHEW

Matthew Tells the Jewish People About Jesus

The Family History of Jesus

1 This is the family history of Jesus Christ. He came from the family of David, and David came from the family of Abraham.

[2] Abraham was the father[n] of Isaac.
Isaac was the father of Jacob.
Jacob was the father of Judah and his brothers.
[3] Judah was the father of Perez and Zerah. (Their mother was Tamar.)
Perez was the father of Hezron.
Hezron was the father of Ram.
[4] Ram was the father of Amminadab.
Amminadab was the father of Nahshon.
Nahshon was the father of Salmon.
[5] Salmon was the father of Boaz. (Boaz's mother was Rahab.)
Boaz was the father of Obed. (Obed's mother was Ruth.)
Obed was the father of Jesse.
[6] Jesse was the father of King David.
David was the father of Solomon. (Solomon's mother had been Uriah's wife.)
[7] Solomon was the father of Rehoboam.
Rehoboam was the father of Abijah.
Abijah was the father of Asa.
[8] Asa was the father of Jehoshaphat.
Jehoshaphat was the father of Jehoram.
Jehoram was the ancestor of Uzziah.
[9] Uzziah was the father of Jotham.
Jotham was the father of Ahaz.
Ahaz was the father of Hezekiah.
[10] Hezekiah was the father of Manasseh.
Manasseh was the father of Amon.
Amon was the father of Josiah.
[11] Josiah was the grandfather of Jehoiachin and his brothers. (This was at the time that the people were taken to Babylon.)

[12] After they were taken to Babylon:
Jehoiachin was the father of Shealtiel.
Shealtiel was the grandfather of Zerubbabel.
[13] Zerubbabel was the father of Abiud.
Abiud was the father of Eliakim.
Eliakim was the father of Azor.
[14] Azor was the father of Zadok.
Zadok was the father of Akim.
Akim was the father of Eliud.
[15] Eliud was the father of Eleazar.
Eleazar was the father of Matthan.
Matthan was the father of Jacob.
[16] Jacob was the father of Joseph.
Joseph was the husband of Mary,
and Mary was the mother of Jesus.
Jesus is called the Christ.[d]

[17] So there were fourteen generations from Abraham to David. And there were fourteen generations from David until the people were taken to Babylon. And there were fourteen generations from the time when the people were taken to Babylon until Christ was born.

The Birth of Jesus Christ

[18] This is how the birth of Jesus Christ came about. His mother Mary was engaged[n] to marry Joseph, but before they married, she learned she was pregnant by the power of the Holy Spirit.[d] [19] Because Mary's husband, Joseph, was a good man, he did not want to disgrace her in public, so he planned to divorce her secretly.

[20] While Joseph thought about these things, an angel of the Lord came to him in a dream. The angel said, "Joseph, descendant[d] of David, don't be afraid to take Mary as your wife, because the baby in her is from the Holy Spirit. [21] She will give birth to a son, and you will name him Jesus,[n] because he will save his people from their sins."

---

father "Father" in Jewish lists of ancestors can sometimes mean grandfather or more distant relative.
engaged For the Jewish people an engagement was a lasting agreement, which could only be broken by a divorce. If a bride was unfaithful, it was considered adultery, and she could be put to death.
Jesus The name Jesus means "salvation."

22All this happened to bring about what the Lord had said through the prophet:*d* 23"The virgin*d* will be pregnant. She will have a son, and they will name him Immanuel," *n* which means "God is with us."

24When Joseph woke up, he did what the Lord's angel had told him to do. Joseph took Mary as his wife, 25but he did not have sexual relations with her until she gave birth to the son. And Joseph named him Jesus.

Wise Men Come to Visit Jesus

2 Jesus was born in the town of Bethlehem in Judea during the time when Herod was king. When Jesus was born, some wise men from the east came to Jerusalem. 2They asked, "Where is the baby who was born to be the king of the Jews? We saw his star in the east and have come to worship him."

3When King Herod heard this, he was troubled, as well as all the people in Jerusalem. 4Herod called a meeting of all the leading priests and teachers of the law and asked them where the Christ*d* would be born. 5They answered, "In the town of Bethlehem in Judea. The prophet*d* wrote about this in the Scriptures:*d*

6'But you, Bethlehem, in the land of Judah,
　are important among the tribes*d* of Judah.
A ruler will come from you
　who will be like a shepherd for my people Israel.' "　　　*Micah 5:2*

7Then Herod had a secret meeting with the wise men and learned from them the exact time they first saw the star. 8He sent the wise men to Bethlehem, saying, "Look carefully for the child. When you find him, come tell me so I can worship him too."

9After the wise men heard the king, they left. The star that they had seen in the east went before them until it stopped above the place where the child was. 10When the wise men saw the star, they were filled with joy. 11They came to the house where the child was and saw him with his mother, Mary, and they bowed down and worshiped him. They opened their gifts and gave him treasures of gold, frankincense,*d* and myrrh.*d* 12But God warned the wise men in a dream not to go back to Herod, so they returned to their own country by a different way.

Jesus' Parents Take Him to Egypt

13After they left, an angel of the Lord came to Joseph in a dream and said, "Get up! Take the child and his mother and escape to Egypt, because Herod is starting to look for the child so he can kill him. Stay in Egypt until I tell you to return."

14So Joseph got up and left for Egypt during the night with the child and his mother. 15And Joseph stayed in Egypt until Herod died. This happened to bring about what the Lord had said through the prophet:*d* "I called my son out of Egypt." *n*

Herod Kills the Baby Boys

16When Herod saw that the wise men had tricked him, he was furious. So he gave an order to kill all the baby boys in Bethlehem and in the surrounding area who were two years old or younger. This was in keeping with the time he learned from the wise men. 17So what God had said through the prophet*d* Jeremiah came true:
18"A voice was heard in Ramah
　of painful crying and deep sadness:
Rachel crying for her children.
　She refused to be comforted,
　because her children are dead."

Jeremiah 31:15

Joseph and Mary Return

19After Herod died, an angel of the Lord spoke to Joseph in a dream while he was in Egypt. 20The angel said, "Get up! Take the child and his mother and go to the land of Israel, because the people who were trying to kill the child are now dead."

21So Joseph took the child and his mother and went to Israel. 22But he heard that Archelaus was now king in Judea since his father Herod had died. So Joseph was afraid to go there. After being warned in a dream, he went to the area of Galilee, 23to a town called

---

"The virgin ... Immanuel" Quotation from Isaiah 7:14.
"I called ... Egypt." Quotation from Hosea 11:1.

Nazareth, and lived there. And so what God had said through the prophets[d] came true: "He will be called a Nazarene."[n]

The Work of John the Baptist

3 About that time John the Baptist[d] began preaching in the desert area of Judea. [2]John said, "Change your hearts and lives because the kingdom of heaven is near." [3]John the Baptist is the one Isaiah the prophet[d] was talking about when he said:

"This is a voice of one
   who calls out in the desert:
'Prepare the way for the Lord.
   Make the road straight for him.' "

Isaiah 40:3

[4]John's clothes were made from camel's hair, and he wore a leather belt around his waist. For food, he ate locusts[d] and wild honey. [5]Many people came from Jerusalem and Judea and all the area around the Jordan River to hear John. [6]They confessed their sins, and he baptized them in the Jordan River.

[7]Many of the Pharisees[d] and Sadducees[d] came to the place where John was baptizing people. When John saw them, he said, "You are all snakes! Who warned you to run away from God's coming punishment? [8]Do the things that show you really have changed your hearts and lives. [9]And don't think you can say to yourselves, 'Abraham is our father.' I tell you that God could make children for Abraham from these rocks. [10]The ax is now ready to cut down the trees, and every tree that does not produce good fruit will be cut down and thrown into the fire.[n]

[11]"I baptize you with water to show that your hearts and lives have changed. But there is one coming after me who is greater than I am, whose sandals I am not good enough to carry. He will baptize you with the Holy Spirit[d] and fire. [12]He will come ready to clean the grain, separating the good grain from the chaff.[d] He will put the good part of the grain into his barn, but he will burn the

chaff with a fire that cannot be put out."[n]

Jesus Is Baptized by John

[13]At that time Jesus came from Galilee to the Jordan River and wanted John to baptize him. [14]But John tried to stop him, saying, "Why do you come to me to be baptized? I need to be baptized by you!"

[15]Jesus answered, "Let it be this way for now. We should do all things that are God's will." So John agreed to baptize Jesus.

[16]As soon as Jesus was baptized, he came up out of the water. Then heaven opened, and he saw God's Spirit[d] coming down on him like a dove. [17]And a voice from heaven said, "This is my Son, whom I love, and I am very pleased with him."

The Temptation of Jesus

4 Then the Spirit[d] led Jesus into the desert to be tempted by the devil. [2]Jesus ate nothing for forty days and nights. After this, he was very hungry. [3]The devil came to Jesus to tempt him, saying, "If you are the Son of God, tell these rocks to become bread."

[4]Jesus answered, "It is written in the Scriptures,[d] 'A person does not live by eating only bread, but by everything God says.' "[n]

[5]Then the devil led Jesus to the holy city of Jerusalem and put him on a high place of the Temple.[d] [6]The devil said, "If you are the Son of God, jump down, because it is written in the Scriptures:

'He has put his angels in charge of you.
   They will catch you in their hands
so that you will not hit your foot on a
   rock.' "

Psalm 91:11-12

[7]Jesus answered him, "It also says in the Scriptures, 'Do not test the Lord your God.' "[n]

[8]Then the devil led Jesus to the top of a very high mountain and showed him all the kingdoms of the world and all their splendor. [9]The devil said, "If you will bow down and worship me, I will give you all these things."

[10]Jesus said to the devil, "Go away from

Nazarene   A person from the city of Nazareth, a name probably meaning "branch" (see Isaiah 11:1).
The ax . . . fire.   This means that God is ready to punish his people who do not obey him.
He will . . . out.   This means that Jesus will come to separate good people from bad people, saving the good and punishing the bad.
'A person . . . says.'   Quotation from Deuteronomy 8:3.
'Do . . . God.'   Quotation from Deuteronomy 6:16.

me, Satan! It is written in the Scriptures, 'You must worship the Lord your God and serve only him.' "[n]

[11]So the devil left Jesus, and angels came and took care of him.

Jesus Begins Work in Galilee

[12]When Jesus heard that John had been put in prison, he went back to Galilee. [13]He left Nazareth and went to live in Capernaum, a town near Lake Galilee, in the area near Zebulun and Naphtali. [14]Jesus did this to bring about what the prophet[d] Isaiah had said:

[15]"Land of Zebulun and land of Naphtali
    along the sea,
beyond the Jordan River.
    This is Galilee where the non-Jewish
        people live.
[16]These people who live in darkness
    will see a great light.
They live in a place covered with the
        shadows of death,
    but a light will shine on them."

                                    Isaiah 9:1-2

Jesus Chooses Some Followers

[17]From that time Jesus began to preach, saying, "Change your hearts and lives, because the kingdom of heaven is near."

[18]As Jesus was walking by Lake Galilee, he saw two brothers, Simon (called Peter) and his brother Andrew. They were throwing a net into the lake because they were fishermen. [19]Jesus said, "Come follow me, and I will make you fish for people." [20]So Simon and Andrew immediately left their nets and followed him.

[21]As Jesus continued walking by Lake Galilee, he saw two other brothers, James and John, the sons of Zebedee. They were in a boat with their father Zebedee, mending their nets. Jesus told them to come with him. [22]Immediately they left the boat and their father, and they followed Jesus.

Jesus Teaches and Heals People

[23]Jesus went everywhere in Galilee, teach-

ing in the synagogues,[d] preaching the Good News[d] about the kingdom of heaven, and healing all the people's diseases and sicknesses. [24]The news about Jesus spread all over Syria, and people brought all the sick to him. They were suffering from different kinds of diseases. Some were in great pain, some had demons,[d] some were epileptics,[n] and some were paralyzed. Jesus healed all of them. [25]Many people from Galilee, the Ten Towns,[n] Jerusalem, Judea, and the land across the Jordan River followed him.

Jesus Teaches the People

5 When Jesus saw the crowds, he went up on a hill and sat down. His followers came to him, [2]and he began to teach them, saying:
[3]"Those people who know they have
        great spiritual needs are happy,
    because the kingdom of heaven
        belongs to them.
[4]Those who are sad now are happy,
    because God will comfort them.
[5]Those who are humble are happy,
    because the earth will belong to them.
[6]Those who want to do right more than
        anything else are happy,
    because God will fully satisfy them.
[7]Those who show mercy to others are
        happy,
    because God will show mercy to them.
[8]Those who are pure in their thinking are
        happy,
    because they will be with God.
[9]Those who work to bring peace are
        happy,
    because God will call them his
        children.
[10]Those who are treated badly for doing
        good are happy,
    because the kingdom of heaven
        belongs to them.

[11]"People will insult you and hurt you. They will lie and say all kinds of evil things about you because you follow me. But when they do, you will be happy. [12]Rejoice and be glad, because you have a great reward wait-

---

'You . . . him.' Quotation from Deuteronomy 6:13.
epileptics People with a disease that causes them sometimes to lose control of their bodies and maybe faint, shake strongly, or not be able to move.
Ten Towns In Greek, called "Decapolis." It was an area east of Lake Galilee that once had ten main towns.

ing for you in heaven. People did the same evil things to the prophets*d* who lived before you.

You Are like Salt and Light

13"You are the salt of the earth. But if the salt loses its salty taste, it cannot be made salty again. It is good for nothing, except to be thrown out and walked on. 14"You are the light that gives light to the world. A city that is built on a hill cannot be hidden. 15And people don't hide a light under a bowl. They put it on a lampstand so the light shines for all the people in the house. 16In the same way, you should be a light for other people. Live so that they will see the good things you do and will praise your Father in heaven.

The Importance of the Law

17"Don't think that I have come to destroy the law of Moses or the teaching of the prophets.*d* I have not come to destroy them but to bring about what they said. 18I tell you the truth, nothing will disappear from the law until heaven and earth are gone. Not even the smallest letter or the smallest part of a letter will be lost until everything has happened. 19Whoever refuses to obey any command and teaches other people not to obey that command will be the least important in the kingdom of heaven. But whoever obeys the commands and teaches other people to obey them will be great in the kingdom of heaven. 20I tell you that if you are no more obedient than the teachers of the law and the Pharisees,*d* you will never enter the kingdom of heaven.

Jesus Teaches About Anger

21"You have heard that it was said to our people long ago, 'You must not murder anyone.'*n* Anyone who murders another will be judged.' 22But I tell you, if you are angry with a brother or sister,*n* you will be judged. If you say bad things to a brother or sister, you

will be judged by the council. And if you call someone a fool, you will be in danger of the fire of hell.

23"So when you offer your gift to God at the altar, and you remember that your brother or sister has something against you, 24leave your gift there at the altar. Go and make peace with that person, and then come and offer your gift.

25"If your enemy is taking you to court, become friends quickly, before you go to court. Otherwise, your enemy might turn you over to the judge, and the judge might give you to a guard to put you in jail. 26I tell you the truth, you will not leave there until you have paid everything you owe.

Jesus Teaches About Sexual Sin

27"You have heard that it was said, 'You must not be guilty of adultery.'*n* 28But I tell you that if anyone looks at a woman and wants to sin sexually with her, in his mind he has already done that sin with the woman. 29If your right eye causes you to sin, take it out and throw it away. It is better to lose one part of your body than to have your whole body thrown into hell. 30If your right hand causes you to sin, cut it off and throw it away. It is better to lose one part of your body than for your whole body to go into hell.

Jesus Teaches About Divorce

31"It was also said, 'Anyone who divorces his wife must give her a written divorce paper.'*n* 32But I tell you that anyone who divorces his wife forces her to be guilty of adultery.*d* The only reason for a man to divorce his wife is if she has sexual relations with another man. And anyone who marries that divorced woman is guilty of adultery.

Make Promises Carefully

33"You have heard that it was said to our

You ... anyone. Quotation from Exodus 20:13; Deuteronomy 5:17.
brother ... sister Although the Greek text reads "brother" here and throughout this book, Jesus' words were meant for the entire church, including men and women.
'You ... adultery.' Quotation from Exodus 20:14; Deuteronomy 5:18.
'Anyone ... divorce paper.' Quotation from Deuteronomy 24:1.

people long ago, 'Don't break your promises, but keep the promises you make to the Lord.'[n] 34But I tell you, never swear an oath. Don't swear an oath using the name of heaven, because heaven is God's throne. 35Don't swear an oath using the name of the earth, because the earth belongs to God. Don't swear an oath using the name of Jerusalem, because that is the city of the great King. 36Don't even swear by your own head, because you cannot make one hair on your head become white or black. 37Say only yes if you mean yes, and no if you mean no. If you say more than yes or no, it is from the Evil One.

Don't Fight Back

38"You have heard that it was said, 'An eye for an eye, and a tooth for a tooth.'[n] 39But I tell you, don't stand up against an evil person. If someone slaps you on the right cheek, turn to him the other cheek also. 40If someone wants to sue you in court and take your shirt, let him have your coat also. 41If someone forces you to go with him one mile, go with him two miles. 42If a person asks you for something, give it to him. Don't refuse to give to someone who wants to borrow from you.

Love All People

43"You have heard that it was said, 'Love your neighbor[n] and hate your enemies.' 44But I say to you, love your enemies. Pray for those who hurt you. 45If you do this, you will be true children of your Father in heaven. He causes the sun to rise on good people and on evil people, and he sends rain to those who do right and to those who do wrong. 46If you love only the people who love you, you will get no reward. Even the tax collectors do that. 47And if you are nice only to your friends, you are no better than other people. Even those who don't know God are nice to their friends. 48So you must be perfect, just as your Father in heaven is perfect.

Jesus Teaches About Giving

6 "Be careful! When you do good things, don't do them in front of people to be seen by them. If you do that, you will have no reward from your Father in heaven.

2"When you give to the poor, don't be like the hypocrites.[d] They blow trumpets in the synagogues[d] and on the streets so that people will see them and honor them. I tell you the truth, those hypocrites already have their full reward. 3So when you give to the poor, don't let anyone know what you are doing. 4Your giving should be done in secret. Your Father can see what is done in secret, and he will reward you.

Jesus Teaches About Prayer

5"When you pray, don't be like the hypocrites.[d] They love to stand in the synagogues[d] and on the street corners and pray so people will see them. I tell you the truth, they already have their full reward. 6When you pray, you should go into your room and close the door and pray to your Father who cannot be seen. Your Father can see what is done in secret, and he will reward you.

7"And when you pray, don't be like those people who don't know God. They continue saying things that mean nothing, thinking that God will hear them because of their many words. 8Don't be like them, because your Father knows the things you need before you ask him. 9So when you pray, you should pray like this:
'Our Father in heaven,
    may your name always be kept holy.
10May your kingdom come
    and what you want be done,
        here on earth as it is in heaven.
11Give us the food we need for each day.
12Forgive us for our sins,
        just as we have forgiven those who
            sinned against us.
13And do not cause us to be tempted,
    but save us from the Evil One.'
14Yes, if you forgive others for their sins, your Father in heaven will also forgive you for your sins. 15But if you don't forgive others,

---

'Don't . . . Lord.'   This refers to Leviticus 19:12; Numbers 30:2; Deuteronomy 23:21.
'An eye . . . tooth.'   Quotation from Exodus 21:24; Leviticus 24:20; Deuteronomy 19:21.
Love your neighbor   Quotation from Leviticus 19:18.

your Father in heaven will not forgive your sins.

Jesus Teaches About Worship

16"When you give up eating,[n] don't put on a sad face like the hypocrites.[d] They make their faces look sad to show people they are giving up eating. I tell you the truth, those hypocrites already have their full reward. 17So when you give up eating, comb your hair and wash your face. 18Then people will not know that you are giving up eating, but your Father, whom you cannot see, will see you. Your Father sees what is done in secret, and he will reward you.

God Is More Important than Money

19"Don't store treasures for yourselves here on earth where moths and rust will destroy them and thieves can break in and steal them. 20But store your treasures in heaven where they cannot be destroyed by moths or rust and where thieves cannot break in and steal them. 21Your heart will be where your treasure is.

22"The eye is a light for the body. If your eyes are good, your whole body will be full of light. 23But if your eyes are evil, your whole body will be full of darkness. And if the only light you have is really darkness, then you have the worst darkness.

24"No one can serve two masters. The person will hate one master and love the other, or will follow one master and refuse to follow the other. You cannot serve both God and worldly riches.

Don't Worry

25"So I tell you, don't worry about the food or drink you need to live, or about the clothes you need for your body. Life is more than food, and the body is more than clothes. 26Look at the birds in the air. They don't plant or harvest or store food in barns, but your heavenly Father feeds them. And you know that you are worth much more than the birds. 27You cannot add any time to your life by worrying about it.

28"And why do you worry about clothes? Look at how the lilies in the field grow. They don't work or make clothes for themselves. 29But I tell you that even Solomon with his riches was not dressed as beautifully as one of these flowers. 30God clothes the grass in the field, which is alive today but tomorrow is thrown into the fire. So you can be even more sure that God will clothe you. Don't have so little faith! 31Don't worry and say, 'What will we eat?' or 'What will we drink?' or 'What will we wear?' 32The people who don't know God keep trying to get these things, and your Father in heaven knows you need them. 33The thing you should want most is God's kingdom and doing what God wants. Then all these other things you need will be given to you. 34So don't worry about tomorrow, because tomorrow will have its own worries. Each day has enough trouble of its own.

Be Careful About Judging Others

7 "Don't judge other people, or you will be judged. 2You will be judged in the same way that you judge others, and the amount you give to others will be given to you.

3"Why do you notice the little piece of dust in your friend's eye, but you don't notice the big piece of wood in your own eye? 4How can you say to your friend, 'Let me take that little piece of dust out of your eye'? Look at yourself! You still have that big piece of wood in your own eye. 5You hypocrite![d] First, take the wood out of your own eye. Then you will see clearly to take the dust out of your friend's eye.

6"Don't give holy things to dogs, and don't throw your pearls before pigs. Pigs will only trample on them, and dogs will turn to attack you.

Ask God for What You Need

7"Ask, and God will give to you. Search, and you will find. Knock, and the door will open for you. 8Yes, everyone who asks will receive. Everyone who searches will find. And everyone who knocks will have the door opened.

---

give up eating   This is called "fasting." The people would give up eating for a special time of prayer and worship to God. It was also done to show sadness and disappointment.

9 "If your children ask for bread, which of you would give them a stone? 10 Or if your children ask for a fish, would you give them a snake? 11 Even though you are bad, you know how to give good gifts to your children. How much more your heavenly Father will give good things to those who ask him!

The Most Important Rule

12 "Do to others what you want them to do to you. This is the meaning of the law of Moses and the teaching of the prophets.*d*

The Way to Heaven Is Hard

13 "Enter through the narrow gate. The gate is wide and the road is wide that leads to hell, and many people enter through that gate. 14 But the gate is small and the road is narrow that leads to true life. Only a few people find that road.

People Know You by Your Actions

15 "Be careful of false prophets.*d* They come to you looking gentle like sheep, but they are really dangerous like wolves. 16 You will know these people by what they do. Grapes don't come from thornbushes, and figs don't come from thorny weeds. 17 In the same way, every good tree produces good fruit, but a bad tree produces bad fruit. 18 A good tree cannot produce bad fruit, and a bad tree cannot produce good fruit. 19 Every tree that does not produce good fruit is cut down and thrown into the fire. 20 In the same way, you will know these false prophets by what they do.

21 "Not all those who say that I am their Lord will enter the kingdom of heaven. The only people who will enter the kingdom of heaven are those who do what my Father in heaven wants. 22 On the last day many people will say to me, 'Lord, Lord, we spoke for you, and through you we forced out demons*d* and did many miracles.' *d* 23 Then I will tell them clearly, 'Get away from me, you who do evil. I never knew you.'

Two Kinds of People

24 "Everyone who hears my words and

obeys them is like a wise man who built his house on rock. 25 It rained hard, the floods came, and the winds blew and hit that house. But it did not fall, because it was built on rock. 26 Everyone who hears my words and does not obey them is like a foolish man who built his house on sand. 27 It rained hard, the floods came, and the winds blew and hit that house, and it fell with a big crash."

28 When Jesus finished saying these things, the people were amazed at his teaching, 29 because he did not teach like their teachers of the law. He taught like a person who had authority.

Jesus Heals a Sick Man

8 When Jesus came down from the hill, great crowds followed him. 2 Then a man with a skin disease came to Jesus. The man bowed down before him and said, "Lord, you can heal me if you will."

3 Jesus reached out his hand and touched the man and said, "I will. Be healed!" And immediately the man was healed from his disease. 4 Then Jesus said to him, "Don't tell anyone about this. But go and show yourself to the priest*n* and offer the gift Moses commanded*n* for people who are made well. This will show the people what I have done."

Jesus Heals a Soldier's Servant

5 When Jesus entered the city of Capernaum, an army officer came to him, begging for help. 6 The officer said, "Lord, my servant is at home in bed. He can't move his body and is in much pain."

7 Jesus said to the officer, "I will go and heal him."

8 The officer answered, "Lord, I am not worthy for you to come into my house. You only need to command it, and my servant will be healed. 9 I, too, am a man under the authority of others, and I have soldiers under my command. I tell one soldier, 'Go,' and he goes. I tell another soldier, 'Come,' and he comes. I say to my servant, 'Do this,' and my servant does it."

10 When Jesus heard this, he was amazed. He said to those who were following him, "I

---

show . . . priest The law of Moses said a priest must say when a Jewish person with a skin disease was well.
Moses commanded Read about this in Leviticus 14:1-32.

tell you the truth, this is the greatest faith I have found, even in Israel. [11] Many people will come from the east and from the west and will sit and eat with Abraham, Isaac, and Jacob in the kingdom of heaven. [12] But those people who should be in the kingdom will be thrown outside into the darkness, where people will cry and grind their teeth with pain."

[13] Then Jesus said to the officer, "Go home. Your servant will be healed just as you believed he would." And his servant was healed that same hour.

Jesus Heals Many People

[14] When Jesus went to Peter's house, he saw that Peter's mother-in-law was sick in bed with a fever. [15] Jesus touched her hand, and the fever left her. Then she stood up and began to serve Jesus.

[16] That evening people brought to Jesus many who had demons.[d] Jesus spoke and the demons left them, and he healed all the sick. [17] He did these things to bring about what Isaiah the prophet[d] had said:

"He took our suffering on him
    and carried our diseases."   *Isaiah 53:4*

People Want to Follow Jesus

[18] When Jesus saw the crowd around him, he told his followers to go to the other side of the lake. [19] Then a teacher of the law came to Jesus and said, "Teacher, I will follow you any place you go."

[20] Jesus said to him, "The foxes have holes to live in, and the birds have nests, but the Son of Man[d] has no place to rest his head."

[21] Another man, one of Jesus' followers, said to him, "Lord, first let me go and bury my father."

[22] But Jesus told him, "Follow me, and let the people who are dead bury their own dead."

Jesus Calms a Storm

[23] Jesus got into a boat, and his followers went with him. [24] A great storm arose on the lake so that waves covered the boat, but Jesus was sleeping. [25] His followers went to him and woke him, saying, "Lord, save us! We will drown!"

[26] Jesus answered, "Why are you afraid? You don't have enough faith." Then Jesus got up and gave a command to the wind and the waves, and it became completely calm.

[27] The men were amazed and said, "What kind of man is this? Even the wind and the waves obey him!"

Jesus Heals Two Men with Demons

[28] When Jesus arrived at the other side of the lake in the area of the Gadarene[n] people, two men who had demons[d] in them met him. These men lived in the burial caves and were so dangerous that people could not use the road by those caves. [29] They shouted, "What do you want with us, Son of God? Did you come here to torture us before the right time?"

[30] Near that place there was a large herd of pigs feeding. [31] The demons begged Jesus, "If you make us leave these men, please send us into that herd of pigs."

[32] Jesus said to them, "Go!" So the demons left the men and went into the pigs. Then the whole herd rushed down the hill into the lake and were drowned. [33] The herdsmen ran away and went into town, where they told about all of this and what had happened to the men who had demons. [34] Then the whole town went out to see Jesus. When they saw him, they begged him to leave their area.

Jesus Heals a Paralyzed Man

9 Jesus got into a boat and went back across the lake to his own town. [2] Some people brought to Jesus a man who was paralyzed and lying on a mat. When Jesus saw the faith of these people, he said to the paralyzed man, "Be encouraged, young man. Your sins are forgiven."

[3] Some of the teachers of the law said to themselves, "This man speaks as if he were God. That is blasphemy!"[n]

[4] Knowing their thoughts, Jesus said, "Why are you thinking evil thoughts? [5] Which is

Gadarene From Gadara, an area southeast of Lake Galilee.
blasphemy Saying things against God or not showing respect for God.

easier: to say, 'Your sins are forgiven,' or to tell him, 'Stand up and walk'? 6But I will prove to you that the Son of Man*d* has authority on earth to forgive sins." Then Jesus said to the paralyzed man, "Stand up, take your mat, and go home." 7And the man stood up and went home. 8When the people saw this, they were amazed and praised God for giving power like this to human beings.

Jesus Chooses Matthew

9When Jesus was leaving, he saw a man named Matthew sitting in the tax collector's booth. Jesus said to him, "Follow me," and he stood up and followed Jesus.

10As Jesus was having dinner at Matthew's house, many tax collectors and "sinners" came and ate with Jesus and his followers. 11When the Pharisees*d* saw this, they asked Jesus' followers, "Why does your teacher eat with tax collectors and sinners?"

12When Jesus heard them, he said, "It is not the healthy people who need a doctor, but the sick. 13Go and learn what this means: 'I want kindness more than I want animal sacrifices.'*n* I did not come to invite good people but to invite sinners."

Jesus' Followers Are Criticized

14Then the followers of John*n* came to Jesus and said, "Why do we and the Pharisees*d* often give up eating for a certain time,*n* but your followers don't?"

15Jesus answered, "The friends of the bridegroom are not sad while he is with them. But the time will come when the bridegroom will be taken from them, and then they will give up eating.

16"No one sews a patch of unshrunk cloth over a hole in an old coat. If he does, the patch will shrink and pull away from the coat, making the hole worse. 17Also, people never pour new wine into old leather bags. Otherwise, the bags will break, the wine will spill, and the wine bags will be ruined. But people always pour new wine into new wine bags. Then both will continue to be good."

Jesus Gives Life to a Dead Girl and Heals a Sick Woman

18While Jesus was saying these things, a leader of the synagogue*d* came to him. He bowed down before Jesus and said, "My daughter has just died. But if you come and lay your hand on her, she will live again." 19So Jesus and his followers stood up and went with the leader.

20Then a woman who had been bleeding for twelve years came behind Jesus and touched the edge of his coat. 21She was thinking, "If I can just touch his clothes, I will be healed."

22Jesus turned and saw the woman and said, "Be encouraged, dear woman. You are made well because you believed." And the woman was healed from that moment on.

23Jesus continued along with the leader and went into his house. There he saw the funeral musicians and many people crying. 24Jesus said, "Go away. The girl is not dead, only asleep." But the people laughed at him. 25After the crowd had been thrown out of the house, Jesus went into the girl's room and took hold of her hand, and she stood up. 26The news about this spread all around the area.

Jesus Heals More People

27When Jesus was leaving there, two blind men followed him. They cried out, "Have mercy on us, Son of David!"*d*

28After Jesus went inside, the blind men went with him. He asked the men, "Do you believe that I can make you see again?"

They answered, "Yes, Lord."

29Then Jesus touched their eyes and said, "Because you believe I can make you see again, it will happen." 30Then the men were able to see. But Jesus warned them strongly, saying, "Don't tell anyone about this." 31But the blind men left and spread the news about Jesus all around that area.

32When the two men were leaving, some people brought another man to Jesus. This man could not talk because he had a demon*d*

'I want ... sacrifices.' Quotation from Hosea 6:6.
John John the Baptist, who preached to people about Christ's coming (Matthew 3, Luke 3).
give up ... time This is called "fasting." The people would give up eating for a special time of prayer and worship to God. It was also done to show sadness and disappointment.

in him. [33]After Jesus forced the demon to leave the man, he was able to speak. The crowd was amazed and said, "We have never seen anything like this in Israel."

[34]But the Pharisees[d] said, "The prince of demons is the one that gives him power to force demons out."

[35]Jesus traveled through all the towns and villages, teaching in their synagogues,[d] preaching the Good News[d] about the kingdom, and healing all kinds of diseases and sicknesses. [36]When he saw the crowds, he felt sorry for them because they were hurting and helpless, like sheep without a shepherd. [37]Jesus said to his followers, "There are many people to harvest but only a few workers to help harvest them. [38]Pray to the Lord, who owns the harvest, that he will send more workers to gather his harvest."[n]

Jesus Sends Out His Apostles

10 Jesus called his twelve followers together and gave them authority to drive out evil spirits and to heal every kind of disease and sickness. [2]These are the names of the twelve apostles:[d] Simon (also called Peter) and his brother Andrew; James son of Zebedee, and his brother John; [3]Philip and Bartholomew; Thomas and Matthew, the tax collector; James son of Alphaeus, and Thaddaeus; [4]Simon the Zealot[d] and Judas Iscariot, who turned against Jesus.

[5]Jesus sent out these twelve men with the following order: "Don't go to the non-Jewish people or to any town where the Samaritans[d] live. [6]But go to the people of Israel, who are like lost sheep. [7]When you go, preach this: 'The kingdom of heaven is near.' [8]Heal the sick, raise the dead to life again, heal those who have skin diseases, and force demons[d] out of people. I give you these powers freely, so help other people freely. [9]Don't carry any money with you — gold or silver or copper. [10]Don't carry a bag or extra clothes or sandals or a walking stick. Workers should be given what they need.

[11]"When you enter a city or town, find some worthy person there and stay in that home until you leave. [12]When you enter that home, say, 'Peace be with you.' [13]If the people there welcome you, let your peace stay there. But if they don't welcome you, take back the peace you wished for them. [14]And if a home or town refuses to welcome you or listen to you, leave that place and shake its dust off your feet.[n] [15]I tell you the truth, on the Judgment Day it will be better for the towns of Sodom and Gomorrah[n] than for the people of that town.

Jesus Warns His Apostles

[16]"Listen, I am sending you out like sheep among wolves. So be as smart as snakes and as innocent as doves. [17]Be careful of people, because they will arrest you and take you to court and whip you in their synagogues.[d] [18]Because of me you will be taken to stand before governors and kings, and you will tell them and the non-Jewish people about me. [19]When you are arrested, don't worry about what to say or how to say it. At that time you will be given the things to say. [20]It will not really be you speaking but the Spirit of your Father speaking through you.

[21]"Brothers will give their own brothers to be killed, and fathers will give their own children to be killed. Children will fight against their own parents and have them put to death. [22]All people will hate you because you follow me, but those people who keep their faith until the end will be saved. [23]When you are treated badly in one city, run to another city. I tell you the truth, you will not finish going through all the cities of Israel before the Son of Man[d] comes.

[24]"A student is not better than his teacher, and a servant is not better than his master. [25]A student should be satisfied to become like his teacher; a servant should be satisfied to become like his master. If the head of the family is called Beelzebul,[d] then the other members of the family will be called worse names!

Fear God, Not People

[26]"So don't be afraid of those people, be-

"There are ... harvest."   As a farmer sends workers to harvest the grain, Jesus sends his followers to bring people to God.
shake ... feet.   A warning. It showed that they had rejected these people.
Sodom and Gomorrah   Two cities that God destroyed because the people were so evil.

cause everything that is hidden will be shown. Everything that is secret will be made known. 27I tell you these things in the dark, but I want you to tell them in the light. What you hear whispered in your ear you should shout from the housetops. 28Don't be afraid of people, who can kill the body but cannot kill the soul. The only one you should fear is the one who can destroy the soul and the body in hell. 29Two sparrows cost only a penny, but not even one of them can die without your Father's knowing it. 30God even knows how many hairs are on your head. 31So don't be afraid. You are worth much more than many sparrows.

Tell People About Your Faith

32"All those who stand before others and say they believe in me, I will say before my Father in heaven that they belong to me. 33But all who stand before others and say they do not believe in me, I will say before my Father in heaven that they do not belong to me.

34"Don't think that I came to bring peace to the earth. I did not come to bring peace, but a sword. 35I have come so that

'a son will be against his father,
    a daughter will be against her mother,
a daughter-in-law will be against her
        mother-in-law.
36 A person's enemies will be members of
        his own family.'   *Micah 7:6*

37"Those who love their father or mother more than they love me are not worthy to be my followers. Those who love their son or daughter more than they love me are not worthy to be my followers. 38Whoever is not willing to carry the cross and follow me is not worthy of me. 39Those who try to hold on to their lives will give up true life. Those who give up their lives for me will hold on to true life. 40Whoever accepts you also accepts me, and whoever accepts me also accepts the One who sent me. 41Whoever meets a prophet*d* and accepts him will receive the reward of a prophet. And whoever accepts a good person because that person is good will receive the reward of a good person. 42Those who give one of these little ones

a cup of cold water because they are my followers will truly get their reward."

Jesus and John the Baptist

11 After Jesus finished telling these things to his twelve followers, he left there and went to the towns in Galilee to teach and preach.

2John the Baptist*d* was in prison, but he heard about what Christ was doing. So John sent some of his followers to Jesus. 3They asked him, "Are you the One who is to come, or should we wait for someone else?"

4Jesus answered them, "Go tell John what you hear and see: 5The blind can see, the crippled can walk, and people with skin diseases are healed. The deaf can hear, the dead are raised to life, and the Good News*d* is preached to the poor. 6Those who do not stumble in their faith because of me are blessed."

7As John's followers were leaving, Jesus began talking to the people about John. Jesus said, "What did you go out into the desert to see? A reed*n* blown by the wind? 8What did you go out to see? A man dressed in fine clothes? No, those who wear fine clothes live in kings' palaces. 9So why did you go out? To see a prophet?*d* Yes, and I tell you, John is more than a prophet. 10This was written about him:

'I will send my messenger ahead of you,
    who will prepare the way for you.'
                                Malachi 3:1

11I tell you the truth, John the Baptist is greater than any other person ever born, but even the least important person in the kingdom of heaven is greater than John. 12Since the time John the Baptist came until now, the kingdom of heaven has been going forward in strength, and people have been trying to take it by force. 13All the prophets and the law of Moses told about what would happen until the time John came. 14And if you will believe what they said, you will believe that John is Elijah, whom they said would come. 15You people who can hear me, listen!

16"What can I say about the people of this time? What are they like? They are like chil-

---

reed It means that John was not ordinary or weak like grass blown by the wind.

dren sitting in the marketplace, who call out to each other,

17"We played music for you, but you did not dance;

we sang a sad song, but you did not cry.'

18John came and did not eat or drink like other people. So people say, 'He has a demon.'d 19The Son of Mand came, eating and drinking, and people say, 'Look at him! He eats too much and drinks too much wine, and he is a friend of tax collectors and sinners.' But wisdom is proved to be right by what it does."

Jesus Warns Unbelievers

20Then Jesus criticized the cities where he did most of his miracles,d because the people did not change their lives and stop sinning. 21He said, "How terrible for you, Korazin! How terrible for you, Bethsaida! If the same miracles I did in you had happened in Tyre and Sidon,n those people would have changed their lives a long time ago. They would have worn rough cloth and put ashes on themselves to show they had changed. 22But I tell you, on the Judgment Day it will be better for Tyre and Sidon than for you. 23And you, Capernaum,n will you be lifted up to heaven? No, you will be thrown down to the depths. If the miracles I did in you had happened in Sodom,n its people would have stopped sinning, and it would still be a city today. 24But I tell you, on the Judgment Day it will be better for Sodom than for you."

Jesus Offers Rest to People

25At that time Jesus said, "I praise you, Father, Lord of heaven and earth, because you have hidden these things from the people who are wise and smart. But you have shown them to those who are like little children. 26Yes, Father, this is what you really wanted.

27"My Father has given me all things. No one knows the Son, except the Father. And no one knows the Father, except the Son and those whom the Son chooses to tell.

28"Come to me, all of you who are tired and have heavy loads, and I will give you rest. 29Accept my teachings and learn from me, because I am gentle and humble in spirit, and you will find rest for your lives. 30The teaching that I ask you to accept is easy; the load I give you to carry is light."

Jesus Is Lord of the Sabbath

12 At that time Jesus was walking through some fields of grain on a Sabbathd day. His followers were hungry, so they began to pick the grain and eat it. 2When the Phariseesd saw this, they said to Jesus, "Look! Your followers are doing what is unlawful to do on the Sabbath day."

3Jesus answered, "Have you not read what David did when he and the people with him were hungry? 4He went into God's house, and he and those with him ate the holy bread, which was lawful only for priests to eat. 5And have you not read in the law of Moses that on every Sabbath day the priests in the Templed break this law about the Sabbath day? But the priests are not wrong for doing that. 6I tell you that there is something here that is greater than the Temple. 7The Scriptured says, 'I want kindness more than I want animal sacrifices.'n You don't really know what those words mean. If you understood them, you would not judge those who have done nothing wrong.

8"So the Son of Mand is Lord of the Sabbath day."

Jesus Heals a Man's Hand

9Jesus left there and went into their synagogue,d 10where there was a man with a crippled hand. They were looking for a reason to accuse Jesus, so they asked him, "Is it right to heal on the Sabbathd day?"n

11Jesus answered, "If any of you has a sheep, and it falls into a ditch on the Sabbath day, you will help it out of the ditch. 12Surely a human being is more important than a

---

Tyre and Sidon Towns where wicked people lived.
Korazin ... Bethsaida ... Capernaum Towns by Lake Galilee where Jesus preached to the people.
Sodom A city that God destroyed because the people were so evil.
'I ... sacrifices.' Quotation from Hosea 6:6.
"Is it right ... day?" It was against Jewish law to work on the Sabbath day.

sheep. So it is lawful to do good things on the Sabbath day."

13Then Jesus said to the man with the crippled hand, "Hold out your hand." The man held out his hand, and it became well again, like the other hand. 14But the Pharisees*d* left and made plans to kill Jesus.

Jesus Is God's Chosen Servant

15Jesus knew what the Pharisees*d* were doing, so he left that place. Many people followed him, and he healed all who were sick. 16But Jesus warned the people not to tell who he was. 17He did these things to bring about what Isaiah the prophet*d* had said:

18"Here is my servant whom I have
          chosen.
   I love him, and I am pleased with him.
   I will put my Spirit*d* upon him,
      and he will tell of my justice to all
          people.
19He will not argue or cry out;
   no one will hear his voice in the
      streets.
20He will not break a crushed blade of
      grass
   or put out even a weak flame
   until he makes justice win the victory.
21 In him will the non-Jewish people find
      hope."   *Isaiah 42:1-4*

Jesus' Power Is from God

22Then some people brought to Jesus a man who was blind and could not talk, because he had a demon.*d* Jesus healed the man so that he could talk and see. 23All the people were amazed and said, "Perhaps this man is the Son of David!"*d*

24When the Pharisees*d* heard this, they said, "Jesus uses the power of Beelzebul,*d* the ruler of demons, to force demons out of people."

25Jesus knew what the Pharisees were thinking, so he said to them, "Every kingdom that is divided against itself will be destroyed. And any city or family that is divided against itself will not continue. 26And if Satan forces out himself, then Satan is divided against himself, and his kingdom will not continue. 27You say that I use the power of Beelzebul to force out demons. If that is true, then what power do your people use to force out demons? So they will be your judges. 28But if I use the power of God's Spirit*d* to force out demons, then the kingdom of God has come to you.

29"If anyone wants to enter a strong person's house and steal his things, he must first tie up the strong person. Then he can steal the things from the house.

30"Whoever is not with me is against me. Whoever does not work with me is working against me. 31So I tell you, people can be forgiven for every sin and everything they say against God. But whoever speaks against the Holy Spirit will not be forgiven. 32Anyone who speaks against the Son of Man*d* can be forgiven, but anyone who speaks against the Holy Spirit will not be forgiven, now or in the future.

People Know You by Your Words

33"If you want good fruit, you must make the tree good. If your tree is not good, it will have bad fruit. A tree is known by the kind of fruit it produces. 34You snakes! You are evil people, so how can you say anything good? The mouth speaks the things that are in the heart. 35Good people have good things in their hearts, and so they say good things. But evil people have evil in their hearts, so they say evil things. 36And I tell you that on the Judgment Day people will be responsible for every careless thing they have said. 37The words you have said will be used to judge you. Some of your words will prove you right, but some of your words will prove you guilty."

The People Ask for a Miracle

38Then some of the Pharisees*d* and teachers of the law answered Jesus, saying, "Teacher, we want to see you work a miracle*d* as a sign."

39Jesus answered, "Evil and sinful people are the ones who want to see a miracle for a sign. But no sign will be given to them, except the sign of the prophet*d* Jonah. 40Jonah was in the stomach of the big fish for three days and three nights. In the same way, the Son of Man*d* will be in the grave three days and three nights. 41On the Judgment

Day the people from Nineveh[n] will stand up with you people who live now, and they will show that you are guilty. When Jonah preached to them, they were sorry and changed their lives. And I tell you that someone greater than Jonah is here. [42]On the Judgment Day, the Queen of the South[n] will stand up with you people who live today. She will show that you are guilty, because she came from far away to listen to Solomon's wise teaching. And I tell you that someone greater than Solomon is here.

People Today Are Full of Evil

[43]"When an evil spirit comes out of a person, it travels through dry places, looking for a place to rest, but it doesn't find it. [44]So the spirit says, 'I will go back to the house I left.' When the spirit comes back, it finds the house still empty, swept clean, and made neat. [45]Then the evil spirit goes out and brings seven other spirits even more evil than it is, and they go in and live there. So the person has even more trouble than before. It is the same way with the evil people who live today."

Jesus' True Family

[46]While Jesus was talking to the people, his mother and brothers stood outside, trying to find a way to talk to him. [47]Someone told Jesus, "Your mother and brothers are standing outside, and they want to talk to you."

[48]He answered, "Who is my mother? Who are my brothers?" [49]Then he pointed to his followers and said, "Here are my mother and my brothers. [50]My true brother and sister and mother are those who do what my Father in heaven wants."

A Story About Planting Seed

13 That same day Jesus went out of the house and sat by the lake. [2]Large crowds gathered around him, so he got into a boat and sat down, while the people stood on the shore. [3]Then Jesus used stories to teach them many things. He said: "A farmer went out to plant his seed. [4]While he was planting, some seed fell by the road, and the birds came and ate it all up. [5]Some seed fell on rocky ground, where there wasn't much dirt. That seed grew very fast, because the ground was not deep. [6]But when the sun rose, the plants dried up, because they did not have deep roots. [7]Some other seed fell among thorny weeds, which grew and choked the good plants. [8]Some other seed fell on good ground where it grew and produced a crop. Some plants made a hundred times more, some made sixty times more, and some made thirty times more. [9]You people who can hear me, listen."

Why Jesus Used Stories to Teach

[10]The followers came to Jesus and asked, "Why do you use stories to teach the people?"

[11]Jesus answered, "You have been chosen to know the secrets about the kingdom of heaven, but others cannot know these secrets. [12]Those who have understanding will be given more, and they will have all they need. But those who do not have understanding, even what they have will be taken away from them. [13]This is why I use stories to teach the people: They see, but they don't really see. They hear, but they don't really hear or understand. [14]So they show that the things Isaiah said about them are true:

'You will listen and listen, but you will
    not understand.
You will look and look, but you will
    not learn.
[15]For the minds of these people have
    become stubborn.
They do not hear with their ears,
    and they have closed their eyes.
Otherwise they might really understand
    what they see with their eyes
    and hear with their ears.
They might really understand in their
    minds
    and come back to me and be healed.'
                Isaiah 6:9-10

[16]But you are blessed, because you see with your eyes and hear with your ears. [17]I tell you

---

Nineveh The city where Jonah preached to warn the people. Read Jonah 3.
Queen of the South The Queen of Sheba. She traveled a thousand miles to learn God's wisdom from Solomon. Read 1 Kings 10:1-13.

the truth, many prophets[d] and good people wanted to see the things that you now see, but they did not see them. And they wanted to hear the things that you now hear, but they did not hear them.

Jesus Explains the Seed Story

18 "So listen to the meaning of that story about the farmer. 19 What is the seed that fell by the road? That seed is like the person who hears the message about the kingdom but does not understand it. The Evil One comes and takes away what was planted in that person's heart. 20 And what is the seed that fell on rocky ground? That seed is like the person who hears the teaching and quickly accepts it with joy. 21 But he does not let the teaching go deep into his life, so he keeps it only a short time. When trouble or persecution comes because of the teaching he accepted, he quickly gives up. 22 And what is the seed that fell among the thorny weeds? That seed is like the person who hears the teaching but lets worries about this life and the temptation of wealth stop that teaching from growing. So the teaching does not produce fruit[n] in that person's life. 23 But what is the seed that fell on the good ground? That seed is like the person who hears the teaching and understands it. That person grows and produces fruit, sometimes a hundred times more, sometimes sixty times more, and sometimes thirty times more."

A Story About Wheat and Weeds

24 Then Jesus told them another story: "The kingdom of heaven is like a man who planted good seed in his field. 25 That night, when everyone was asleep, his enemy came and planted weeds among the wheat and then left. 26 Later, the wheat sprouted and the heads of grain grew, but the weeds also grew. 27 Then the man's servants came to him and said, 'You planted good seed in your field. Where did the weeds come from?' 28 The man answered, 'An enemy planted weeds.' The servants asked, 'Do you want us to pull up the weeds?' 29 The man answered, 'No, because when you pull up the weeds, you might also pull up the wheat. 30 Let the weeds and the wheat grow together until the harvest time. At harvest time I will tell the workers, "First gather the weeds and tie them together to be burned. Then gather the wheat and bring it to my barn." ' "

Stories of Mustard Seed and Yeast

31 Then Jesus told another story: "The kingdom of heaven is like a mustard seed that a man planted in his field. 32 That seed is the smallest of all seeds, but when it grows, it is one of the largest garden plants. It becomes big enough for the wild birds to come and build nests in its branches."

33 Then Jesus told another story: "The kingdom of heaven is like yeast that a woman took and hid in a large tub of flour until it made all the dough rise."

34 Jesus used stories to tell all these things to the people; he always used stories to teach them. 35 This is as the prophet[d] said:

"I will speak using stories;
I will tell things that have been secret
    since the world was made."

Psalm 78:2

Jesus Explains About the Weeds

36 Then Jesus left the crowd and went into the house. His followers came to him and said, "Explain to us the meaning of the story about the weeds in the field."

37 Jesus answered, "The man who planted the good seed in the field is the Son of Man.[d] 38 The field is the world, and the good seed are all of God's children who belong to the kingdom. The weeds are those people who belong to the Evil One. 39 And the enemy who planted the bad seed is the devil. The harvest time is the end of the world, and the workers who gather are God's angels.

40 "Just as the weeds are pulled up and burned in the fire, so it will be at the end of the world. 41 The Son of Man will send out his angels, and they will gather out of his kingdom all who cause sin and all who do evil. 42 The angels will throw them into the blazing furnace, where the people will cry and grind their teeth with pain. 43 Then the good people will shine like the sun in the

---

produce fruit   To produce fruit means to have in your life the good things God wants.

kingdom of their Father. You people who can hear me, listen.

Stories of a Treasure and a Pearl

44"The kingdom of heaven is like a treasure hidden in a field. One day a man found the treasure, and then he hid it in the field again. He was so happy that he went and sold everything he owned to buy that field.

45"Also, the kingdom of heaven is like a man looking for fine pearls. 46When he found a very valuable pearl, he went and sold everything he had and bought it.

A Story of a Fishing Net

47"Also, the kingdom of heaven is like a net that was put into the lake and caught many different kinds of fish. 48When it was full, the fishermen pulled the net to the shore. They sat down and put all the good fish in baskets and threw away the bad fish. 49It will be this way at the end of the world. The angels will come and separate the evil people from the good people. 50The angels will throw the evil people into the blazing furnace, where people will cry and grind their teeth with pain."

51Jesus asked his followers, "Do you understand all these things?"

They answered, "Yes, we understand."

52Then Jesus said to them, "So every teacher of the law who has been taught about the kingdom of heaven is like the owner of a house. He brings out both new things and old things he has saved."

Jesus Goes to His Hometown

53When Jesus finished teaching with these stories, he left there. 54He went to his hometown and taught the people in the synagogue,*d* and they were amazed. They said, "Where did this man get this wisdom and this power to do miracles?*d* 55He is just the son of a carpenter. His mother is Mary, and his brothers are James, Joseph, Simon, and Judas. 56And all his sisters are here with us. Where then does this man get all these things?" 57So the people were upset with Jesus.

But Jesus said to them, "A prophet*d* is honored everywhere except in his hometown and in his own home."

58So he did not do many miracles there because they had no faith.

How John the Baptist Was Killed

14 At that time Herod, the ruler of Galilee, heard the reports about Jesus. 2So he said to his servants, "Jesus is John the Baptist,*d* who has risen from the dead. That is why he can work these miracles."*d*

3Sometime before this, Herod had arrested John, tied him up, and put him into prison. Herod did this because of Herodias, who had been the wife of Philip, Herod's brother. 4John had been telling Herod, "It is not lawful for you to be married to Herodias." 5Herod wanted to kill John, but he was afraid of the people, because they believed John was a prophet.*d*

6On Herod's birthday, the daughter of Herodias danced for Herod and his guests, and she pleased him. 7So he promised with an oath to give her anything she wanted. 8Herodias told her daughter what to ask for, so she said to Herod, "Give me the head of John the Baptist here on a platter." 9Although King Herod was very sad, he had made a promise, and his dinner guests had heard him. So Herod ordered that what she asked for be done. 10He sent soldiers to the prison to cut off John's head. 11And they brought it on a platter and gave it to the girl, and she took it to her mother. 12John's followers came and got his body and buried it. Then they went and told Jesus.

More than Five Thousand Fed

13When Jesus heard what had happened to John, he left in a boat and went to a lonely place by himself. But the crowds heard about it and followed him on foot from the towns. 14When he arrived, he saw a great crowd waiting. He felt sorry for them and healed those who were sick.

15When it was evening, his followers came to him and said, "No one lives in this place, and it is already late. Send the people away so they can go to the towns and buy food for themselves."

16But Jesus answered, "They don't need to go away. You give them something to eat."

17They said to him, "But we have only five loaves of bread and two fish."

[18]Jesus said, "Bring the bread and the fish to me." [19]Then he told the people to sit down on the grass. He took the five loaves and the two fish and, looking to heaven, he thanked God for the food. Jesus divided the bread and gave it to his followers, who gave it to the people. [20]All the people ate and were satisfied. Then the followers filled twelve baskets with the leftover pieces of food. [21]There were about five thousand men there who ate, not counting women and children.

Jesus Walks on the Water

[22]Immediately Jesus told his followers to get into the boat and go ahead of him across the lake. He stayed there to send the people home. [23]After he had sent them away, he went by himself up into the hills to pray. It was late, and Jesus was there alone. [24]By this time, the boat was already far away from land. It was being hit by waves, because the wind was blowing against it.

[25]Between three and six o'clock in the morning, Jesus came to them, walking on the water. [26]When his followers saw him walking on the water, they were afraid. They said, "It's a ghost!" and cried out in fear.

[27]But Jesus quickly spoke to them, "Have courage! It is I. Do not be afraid."

[28]Peter said, "Lord, if it is really you, then command me to come to you on the water."

[29]Jesus said, "Come."

And Peter left the boat and walked on the water to Jesus. [30]But when Peter saw the wind and the waves, he became afraid and began to sink. He shouted, "Lord, save me!"

[31]Immediately Jesus reached out his hand and caught Peter. Jesus said, "Your faith is small. Why did you doubt?"

[32]After they got into the boat, the wind became calm. [33]Then those who were in the boat worshiped Jesus and said, "Truly you are the Son of God!"

[34]When they had crossed the lake, they came to shore at Gennesaret. [35]When the people there recognized Jesus, they told people all around there that Jesus had come, and they brought all their sick to him. [36]They begged Jesus to let them touch just the edge of his coat, and all who touched it were healed.

Obey God's Law

15 Then some Pharisees[d] and teachers of the law came to Jesus from Jerusalem. They asked him, [2]"Why don't your followers obey the unwritten laws which have been handed down to us? They don't wash their hands before they eat."

[3]Jesus answered, "And why do you refuse to obey God's command so that you can follow your own teachings? [4]God said, 'Honor your father and your mother,'[n] and 'Anyone who says cruel things to his father or mother must be put to death.'[n] [5]But you say a person can tell his father or mother, 'I have something I could use to help you, but I have given it to God already.' [6]You teach that person not to honor his father or his mother. You rejected what God said for the sake of your own rules. [7]You are hypocrites! Isaiah was right when he said about you:

[8]'These people show honor to me with
    words,
  but their hearts are far from me.
[9]Their worship of me is worthless.
  The things they teach are nothing but
    human rules.' "   *Isaiah 29:13*

[10]After Jesus called the crowd to him, he said, "Listen and understand what I am saying. [11]It is not what people put into their mouths that makes them unclean.[d] It is what comes out of their mouths that makes them unclean."

[12]Then his followers came to him and asked, "Do you know that the Pharisees are angry because of what you said?"

[13]Jesus answered, "Every plant that my Father in heaven has not planted himself will be pulled up by the roots. [14]Stay away from the Pharisees; they are blind leaders. And if a blind person leads a blind person, both will fall into a ditch."

[15]Peter said, "Explain the example to us."

[16]Jesus said, "Do you still not understand? [17]Surely you know that all the food that enters the mouth goes into the stomach and then goes out of the body. [18]But what people

---

'Honor ... mother.'   Quotation from Exodus 20:12; Deuteronomy 5:16.
'Anyone ... death.'   Quotation from Exodus 21:17.

say with their mouths comes from the way they think; these are the things that make people unclean. [19]Out of the mind come evil thoughts, murder, adultery,*d* sexual sins, stealing, lying, and speaking evil of others. [20]These things make people unclean; eating with unwashed hands does not make them unclean."

Jesus Helps a Non-Jewish Woman

[21]Jesus left that place and went to the area of Tyre and Sidon. [22]A Canaanite woman from that area came to Jesus and cried out, "Lord, Son of David,*d* have mercy on me! My daughter has a demon,*d* and she is suffering very much."

[23]But Jesus did not answer the woman. So his followers came to Jesus and begged him, "Tell the woman to go away. She is following us and shouting."

[24]Jesus answered, "God sent me only to the lost sheep, the people of Israel."

[25]Then the woman came to Jesus again and bowed before him and said, "Lord, help me!"

[26]Jesus answered, "It is not right to take the children's bread and give it to the dogs."

[27]The woman said, "Yes, Lord, but even the dogs eat the crumbs that fall from their masters' table."

[28]Then Jesus answered, "Woman, you have great faith! I will do what you asked." And at that moment the woman's daughter was healed.

Jesus Heals Many People

[29]After leaving there, Jesus went along the shore of Lake Galilee. He went up on a hill and sat there.

[30]Great crowds came to Jesus, bringing with them the lame, the blind, the crippled, those who could not speak, and many others. They put them at Jesus' feet, and he healed them. [31]The crowd was amazed when they saw that people who could not speak before were now able to speak. The crippled were made strong. The lame could walk, and the blind could see. And they praised the God of Israel for this.

More than Four Thousand Fed

[32]Jesus called his followers to him and said, "I feel sorry for these people, because they have already been with me three days, and they have nothing to eat. I don't want to send them away hungry. They might faint while going home."

[33]His followers asked him, "How can we get enough bread to feed all these people? We are far away from any town."

[34]Jesus asked, "How many loaves of bread do you have?"

They answered, "Seven, and a few small fish."

[35]Jesus told the people to sit on the ground. [36]He took the seven loaves of bread and the fish and gave thanks to God. Then he divided the food and gave it to his followers, and they gave it to the people. [37]All the people ate and were satisfied. Then his followers filled seven baskets with the leftover pieces of food. [38]There were about four thousand men there who ate, besides women and children. [39]After sending the people home, Jesus got into the boat and went to the area of Magadan.

The Leaders Ask for a Miracle

16 The Pharisees*d* and Sadducees*d* came to Jesus, wanting to trick him. So they asked him to show them a miracle*d* from God.

[2]Jesus answered, "At sunset you say we will have good weather, because the sky is red. [3]And in the morning you say that it will be a rainy day, because the sky is dark and red. You see these signs in the sky and know what they mean. In the same way, you see the things that I am doing now, but you don't know their meaning. [4]Evil and sinful people ask for a miracle as a sign, but they will not be given any sign, except the sign of Jonah."[n] Then Jesus left them and went away.

Guard Against Wrong Teachings

[5]Jesus' followers went across the lake, but they had forgotten to bring bread. [6]Jesus said

sign of Jonah   Jonah's three days in the fish are like Jesus' three days in the tomb. The story about Jonah is in the book of Jonah.

to them, "Be careful! Beware of the yeast of the Pharisees*d* and the Sadducees."*d*

⁷His followers discussed the meaning of this, saying, "He said this because we forgot to bring bread."

⁸Knowing what they were talking about, Jesus asked them, "Why are you talking about not having bread? Your faith is small. ⁹Do you still not understand? Remember the five loaves of bread that fed the five thousand? And remember that you filled many baskets with the leftovers? ¹⁰Or the seven loaves of bread that fed the four thousand and the many baskets you filled then also? ¹¹I was not talking to you about bread. Why don't you understand that? I am telling you to beware of the yeast of the Pharisees and the Sadducees." ¹²Then the followers understood that Jesus was not telling them to beware of the yeast used in bread but to beware of the teaching of the Pharisees and the Sadducees.

Peter Says Jesus Is the Christ

¹³When Jesus came to the area of Caesarea Philippi, he asked his followers, "Who do people say the Son of Man*d* is?"

¹⁴They answered, "Some say you are John the Baptist.*d* Others say you are Elijah, and still others say you are Jeremiah or one of the prophets."*d*

¹⁵Then Jesus asked them, "And who do you say I am?"

¹⁶Simon Peter answered, "You are the Christ,*d* the Son of the living God."

¹⁷Jesus answered, "You are blessed, Simon son of Jonah, because no person taught you that. My Father in heaven showed you who I am. ¹⁸So I tell you, you are Peter.*n* On this rock I will build my church, and the power of death will not be able to defeat it. ¹⁹I will give you the keys of the kingdom of heaven; the things you don't allow on earth will be the things that God does not allow, and the things you allow on earth will be the things that God allows." ²⁰Then Jesus warned his followers not to tell anyone he was the Christ.

Jesus Says that He Must Die

²¹From that time on Jesus began telling his followers that he must go to Jerusalem, where the older Jewish leaders, the leading priests, and the teachers of the law would make him suffer many things. He told them he must be killed and then be raised from the dead on the third day.

²²Peter took Jesus aside and told him not to talk like that. He said, "God save you from those things, Lord! Those things will never happen to you!"

²³Then Jesus said to Peter, "Go away from me, Satan!*n* You are not helping me! You don't care about the things of God, but only about the things people think are important."

²⁴Then Jesus said to his followers, "If people want to follow me, they must give up the things they want. They must be willing even to give up their lives to follow me. ²⁵Those who want to save their lives will give up true life, and those who give up their lives for me will have true life. ²⁶It is worth nothing for them to have the whole world if they lose their souls. They could never pay enough to buy back their souls. ²⁷The Son of Man*d* will come again with his Father's glory and with his angels. At that time, he will reward them for what they have done. ²⁸I tell you the truth, some people standing here will see the Son of Man coming with his kingdom before they die."

Jesus Talks with Moses and Elijah

17 Six days later, Jesus took Peter, James, and John, the brother of James, up on a high mountain by themselves. ²While they watched, Jesus' appearance was changed; his face became bright like the sun, and his clothes became white as light. ³Then Moses and Elijah*n* appeared to them, talking with Jesus.

⁴Peter said to Jesus, "Lord, it is good that we are here. If you want, I will put up three tents here — one for you, one for Moses, and one for Elijah."

⁵While Peter was talking, a bright cloud

Peter   The Greek name "Peter," like the Aramaic name "Cephas," means "rock."
Satan   Name for the devil, meaning "the enemy." Jesus means that Peter was talking like Satan.
Moses and Elijah   Two of the most important Jewish leaders in the past. Moses had given them the law, and Elijah was an important prophet.

covered them. A voice came from the cloud and said, "This is my Son, whom I love, and I am very pleased with him. Listen to him!"

6When his followers heard the voice, they were so frightened they fell to the ground. 7But Jesus went to them and touched them and said, "Stand up. Don't be afraid." 8When they looked up, they saw Jesus was now alone.

9As they were coming down the mountain, Jesus commanded them not to tell anyone about what they had seen until the Son of Man*d* had risen from the dead.

10Then his followers asked him, "Why do the teachers of the law say that Elijah must come first?"

11Jesus answered, "They are right to say that Elijah is coming and that he will make everything the way it should be. 12But I tell you that Elijah has already come, and they did not recognize him. They did to him whatever they wanted to do. It will be the same with the Son of Man; those same people will make the Son of Man suffer." 13Then the followers understood that Jesus was talking about John the Baptist.*d*

Jesus Heals a Sick Boy

14When Jesus and his followers came back to the crowd, a man came to Jesus and bowed before him. 15The man said, "Lord, have mercy on my son. He has epilepsy*n* and is suffering very much, because he often falls into the fire or into the water. 16I brought him to your followers, but they could not cure him."

17Jesus answered, "You people have no faith, and your lives are all wrong. How long must I put up with you? How long must I continue to be patient with you? Bring the boy here." 18Jesus commanded the demon*d* inside the boy. Then the demon came out, and the boy was healed from that time on.

19The followers came to Jesus when he was alone and asked, "Why couldn't we force the demon out?"

20Jesus answered, "Because your faith is too small. I tell you the truth, if your faith is

as big as a mustard seed, you can say to this mountain, 'Move from here to there,' and it will move. All things will be possible for you." 21 *n*

Jesus Talks About His Death

22While Jesus' followers were gathering in Galilee, he said to them, "The Son of Man*d* will be handed over to people, 23and they will kill him. But on the third day he will be raised from the dead." And the followers were filled with sadness.

Jesus Talks About Paying Taxes

24When Jesus and his followers came to Capernaum, the men who collected the Temple*d* tax came to Peter. They asked, "Does your teacher pay the Temple tax?"

25Peter answered, "Yes, Jesus pays the tax."

Peter went into the house, but before he could speak, Jesus said to him, "What do you think? The kings of the earth collect different kinds of taxes. But who pays the taxes — the king's children or others?"

26Peter answered, "Other people pay the taxes."

Jesus said to Peter, "Then the children of the king don't have to pay taxes. 27But we don't want to upset these tax collectors. So go to the lake and fish. After you catch the first fish, open its mouth and you will find a coin. Take that coin and give it to the tax collectors for you and me."

Who Is the Greatest?

18 At that time the followers came to Jesus and asked, "Who is greatest in the kingdom of heaven?"

2Jesus called a little child to him and stood the child before his followers. 3Then he said, "I tell you the truth, you must change and become like little children. Otherwise, you will never enter the kingdom of heaven. 4The greatest person in the kingdom of heaven is the one who makes himself humble like this child.

5"Whoever accepts a child in my name ac-

---

epilepsy A disease that causes a person sometimes to lose control of his body and maybe faint, shake strongly, or not be able to move.
Verse 21 Some Greek copies add verse 21: "That kind of spirit comes out only if you use prayer and give up eating."

cepts me. [6]If one of these little children believes in me, and someone causes that child to sin, it would be better for that person to have a large stone tied around the neck and be drowned in the sea. [7]How terrible for the people of the world because of the things that cause them to sin. Such things will happen, but how terrible for the one who causes them to happen! [8]If your hand or your foot causes you to sin, cut it off and throw it away. It is better for you to lose part of your body and live forever than to have two hands and two feet and be thrown into the fire that burns forever. [9]If your eye causes you to sin, take it out and throw it away. It is better for you to have only one eye and live forever than to have two eyes and be thrown into the fire of hell.

A Lost Sheep

[10]"Be careful. Don't think these little children are worth nothing. I tell you that they have angels in heaven who are always with my Father in heaven. [11] n

[12]"If a man has a hundred sheep but one of the sheep gets lost, he will leave the other ninety-nine on the hill and go to look for the lost sheep. [13]I tell you the truth, he is happier about that one sheep than about the ninety-nine that were never lost. [14]In the same way, your Father in heaven does not want any of these little children to be lost.

When a Person Sins Against You

[15]"If your fellow believer sins against you, go and tell him in private what he did wrong. If he listens to you, you have helped that person to be your brother or sister again. [16]But if he refuses to listen, go to him again and take one or two other people with you. 'Every case may be proved by two or three witnesses.' n [17]If he refuses to listen to them, tell the church. If he refuses to listen to the church, then treat him like a person who does not believe in God or like a tax collector.

[18]"I tell you the truth, the things you don't allow on earth will be the things God does not allow. And the things you allow on earth will be the things that God allows.

[19]"Also, I tell you that if two of you on earth agree about something and pray for it, it will be done for you by my Father in heaven. [20]This is true because if two or three people come together in my name, I am there with them."

An Unforgiving Servant

[21]Then Peter came to Jesus and asked, "Lord, when my fellow believer sins against me, how many times must I forgive him? Should I forgive him as many as seven times?"

[22]Jesus answered, "I tell you, you must forgive him more than seven times. You must forgive him even if he does wrong to you seventy-seven times.

[23]"The kingdom of heaven is like a king who decided to collect the money his servants owed him. [24]When the king began to collect his money, a servant who owed him several million dollars was brought to him. [25]But the servant did not have enough money to pay his master, the king. So the master ordered that everything the servant owned should be sold, even the servant's wife and children. Then the money would be used to pay the king what the servant owed.

[26]"But the servant fell on his knees and begged, 'Be patient with me, and I will pay you everything I owe.' [27]The master felt sorry for his servant and told him he did not have to pay it back. Then he let the servant go free.

[28]"Later, that same servant found another servant who owed him a few dollars. The servant grabbed him around the neck and said, 'Pay me the money you owe me!'

[29]"The other servant fell on his knees and begged him, 'Be patient with me, and I will pay you everything I owe.'

[30]"But the first servant refused to be patient. He threw the other servant into prison until he could pay everything he owed. [31]When the other servants saw what had

---

Verse 11 Some Greek copies add verse 11: "The Son of Man came to save lost people."
'Every ... witnesses.' Quotation from Deuteronomy 19:15.

happened, they were very sorry. So they went and told their master all that had happened.

[32]"Then the master called his servant in and said, 'You evil servant! Because you begged me to forget what you owed, I told you that you did not have to pay anything. [33]You should have showed mercy to that other servant, just as I showed mercy to you.' [34]The master was very angry and put the servant in prison to be punished until he could pay everything he owed.

[35]"This king did what my heavenly Father will do to you if you do not forgive your brother or sister from your heart."

Jesus Teaches About Divorce

19 After Jesus said all these things, he left Galilee and went into the area of Judea on the other side of the Jordan River. [2]Large crowds followed him, and he healed them there.

[3]Some Pharisees[d] came to Jesus and tried to trick him. They asked, "Is it right for a man to divorce his wife for any reason he chooses?"

[4]Jesus answered, "Surely you have read in the Scriptures:[d] When God made the world, 'he made them male and female.'[n] [5]And God said, 'So a man will leave his father and mother and be united with his wife, and the two will become one body.'[n] [6]So there are not two, but one. God has joined the two together, so no one should separate them."

[7]The Pharisees asked, "Why then did Moses give a command for a man to divorce his wife by giving her divorce papers?"

[8]Jesus answered, "Moses allowed you to divorce your wives because you refused to accept God's teaching, but divorce was not allowed in the beginning. [9]I tell you that anyone who divorces his wife and marries another woman is guilty of adultery.[d] The only reason for a man to divorce his wife is if his wife has sexual relations with another man."

[10]The followers said to him, "If that is the only reason a man can divorce his wife, it is better not to marry."

[11]Jesus answered, "Not everyone can accept this teaching, but God has made some able to accept it. [12]There are different reasons why some men cannot marry. Some men were born without the ability to become fathers. Others were made that way later in life by other people. And some men have given up marriage because of the kingdom of heaven. But the person who can marry should accept this teaching about marriage."[n]

Jesus Welcomes Children

[13]Then the people brought their little children to Jesus so he could put his hands on them[n] and pray for them. His followers told them to stop, [14]but Jesus said, "Let the little children come to me. Don't stop them, because the kingdom of heaven belongs to people who are like these children." [15]After Jesus put his hands on the children, he left there.

A Rich Young Man's Question

[16]A man came to Jesus and asked, "Teacher, what good thing must I do to have life forever?"

[17]Jesus answered, "Why do you ask me about what is good? Only God is good. But if you want to have life forever, obey the commands."

[18]The man asked, "Which commands?"

Jesus answered, " 'You must not murder anyone; you must not be guilty of adultery;[d] you must not steal; you must not tell lies about your neighbor; [19]honor your father and mother;[n] and love your neighbor as you love yourself.' "[n]

[20]The young man said, "I have obeyed all these things. What else do I need to do?"

[21]Jesus answered, "If you want to be perfect, then go and sell your possessions and give the money to the poor. If you do this,

---

'he made ... female.' Quotation from Genesis 1:27 or 5:2.
'So ... body.' Quotation from Genesis 2:24.
But ... marriage. This may also mean, "The person who can accept this teaching about not marrying should accept it."
put his hands on them Showing that Jesus gave special blessings to these children.
'You ... mother.' Quotation from Exodus 20:12-16; Deuteronomy 5:16-20.
'love ... yourself.' Quotation from Leviticus 19:18.

you will have treasure in heaven. Then come and follow me."

²²But when the young man heard this, he left sorrowfully, because he was rich.

²³Then Jesus said to his followers, "I tell you the truth, it will be hard for a rich person to enter the kingdom of heaven. ²⁴Yes, I tell you that it is easier for a camel to go through the eye of a needle than for a rich person to enter the kingdom of God."

²⁵When Jesus' followers heard this, they were very surprised and asked, "Then who can be saved?"

²⁶Jesus looked at them and said, "This is something people cannot do, but God can do all things."

²⁷Peter said to Jesus, "Look, we have left everything and followed you. So what will we have?"

²⁸Jesus said to them, "I tell you the truth, when the age to come has arrived, the Son of Man^d will sit on his great throne. All of you who followed me will also sit on twelve thrones, judging the twelve tribes^d of Israel. ²⁹And all those who have left houses, brothers, sisters, father, mother, children, or farms to follow me will get much more than they left, and they will have life forever. ³⁰Many who have the highest place now will have the lowest place in the future. And many who have the lowest place now will have the highest place in the future.

A Story About Workers

20 "The kingdom of heaven is like a person who owned some land. One morning, he went out very early to hire some people to work in his vineyard. ²The man agreed to pay the workers one coin^n for working that day. Then he sent them into the vineyard to work. ³About nine o'clock the man went to the marketplace and saw some other people standing there, doing nothing. ⁴So he said to them, 'If you go and work in my vineyard, I will pay you what your work is worth.' ⁵So they went to work in the vineyard. The man went out again about twelve o'clock and three o'clock and did the same thing. ⁶About five o'clock the man went to the marketplace again and saw others stand-

ing there. He asked them, 'Why did you stand here all day doing nothing?' ⁷They answered, 'No one gave us a job.' The man said to them, 'Then you can go and work in my vineyard.'

⁸"At the end of the day, the owner of the vineyard said to the boss of all the workers, 'Call the workers and pay them. Start with the last people I hired and end with those I hired first.'

⁹"When the workers who were hired at five o'clock came to get their pay, each received one coin. ¹⁰When the workers who were hired first came to get their pay, they thought they would be paid more than the others. But each one of them also received one coin. ¹¹When they got their coin, they complained to the man who owned the land. ¹²They said, 'Those people were hired last and worked only one hour. But you paid them the same as you paid us who worked hard all day in the hot sun.' ¹³But the man who owned the vineyard said to one of those workers, 'Friend, I am being fair to you. You agreed to work for one coin. ¹⁴So take your pay and go. I want to give the man who was hired last the same pay that I gave you. ¹⁵I can do what I want with my own money. Are you jealous because I am good to those people?'

¹⁶"So those who have the last place now will have the first place in the future, and those who have the first place now will have the last place in the future."

Jesus Talks About His Own Death

¹⁷While Jesus was going to Jerusalem, he took his twelve followers aside privately and said to them, ¹⁸"Look, we are going to Jerusalem. The Son of Man^d will be turned over to the leading priests and the teachers of the law, and they will say that he must die. ¹⁹They will give the Son of Man to the non-Jewish people to laugh at him and beat him with whips and crucify him. But on the third day, he will be raised to life again."

A Mother Asks Jesus a Favor

²⁰Then the wife of Zebedee came to Jesus

---

coin A Roman denarius. One coin was the average pay for one day's work.

with her sons. She bowed before him and asked him to do something for her.

21Jesus asked, "What do you want?"

She said, "Promise that one of my sons will sit at your right side and the other will sit at your left side in your kingdom."

22But Jesus said, "You don't understand what you are asking. Can you drink the cup that I am about to drink?" n

The sons answered, "Yes, we can."

23Jesus said to them, "You will drink from my cup. But I cannot choose who will sit at my right or my left; those places belong to those for whom my Father has prepared them."

24When the other ten followers heard this, they were angry with the two brothers.

25Jesus called all the followers together and said, "You know that the rulers of the non-Jewish people love to show their power over the people. And their important leaders love to use all their authority. 26But it should not be that way among you. Whoever wants to become great among you must serve the rest of you like a servant. 27Whoever wants to become first among you must serve the rest of you like a slave. 28In the same way, the Son of Man d did not come to be served. He came to serve others and to give his life as a ransom for many people."

Jesus Heals Two Blind Men

29When Jesus and his followers were leaving Jericho, a great many people followed him. 30Two blind men sitting by the road heard that Jesus was going by, so they shouted, "Lord, Son of David, d have mercy on us!"

31The people warned the blind men to be quiet, but they shouted even more, "Lord, Son of David, have mercy on us!"

32Jesus stopped and said to the blind men, "What do you want me to do for you?"

33They answered, "Lord, we want to see."

34Jesus felt sorry for the blind men and touched their eyes, and at once they could see. Then they followed Jesus.

Jesus Enters Jerusalem as a King

21 As Jesus and his followers were coming closer to Jerusalem, they stopped at Bethphage at the hill called the Mount of Olives. d From there Jesus sent two of his followers 2and said to them, "Go to the town you can see there. When you enter it, you will quickly find a donkey tied there with its colt. Untie them and bring them to me. 3If anyone asks you why you are taking the donkeys, say that the Master needs them, and he will send them at once."

4This was to bring about what the prophet d had said:

5"Tell the people of Jerusalem,
  'Your king is coming to you.
He is gentle and riding on a donkey,
  on the colt of a donkey.' "

Isaiah 62:11; Zechariah 9:9

6The followers went and did what Jesus told them to do. 7They brought the donkey and the colt to Jesus and laid their coats on them, and Jesus sat on them. 8Many people spread their coats on the road. Others cut branches from the trees and spread them on the road. 9The people were walking ahead of Jesus and behind him, shouting,

"Praise n to the Son of David! d
God bless the One who comes in the
    name of the Lord!   *Psalm 118:26*
Praise to God in heaven!"

10When Jesus entered Jerusalem, all the city was filled with excitement. The people asked, "Who is this man?"

11The crowd said, "This man is Jesus, the prophet from the town of Nazareth in Galilee."

Jesus Goes to the Temple

12Jesus went into the Temple d and threw out all the people who were buying and selling there. He turned over the tables of those who were exchanging different kinds of money, and he upset the benches of those who were selling doves. 13Jesus said to all the people there, "It is written in the Scriptures, d 'My Temple will be called a house for

---

drink . . . drink Jesus used the idea of drinking from a cup to ask if they could accept the same terrible things that would happen to him.
Praise Literally, "Hosanna," a Hebrew word used at first in praying to God for help. At this time it was probably a shout of joy used in praising God or his Messiah.

prayer.'[n] But you are changing it into a 'hideout for robbers.' "[n]

[14]The blind and crippled people came to Jesus in the Temple, and he healed them. [15]The leading priests and the teachers of the law saw that Jesus was doing wonderful things and that the children were praising him in the Temple, saying, "Praise[n] to the Son of David."[d] All these things made the priests and the teachers of the law very angry.

[16]They asked Jesus, "Do you hear the things these children are saying?"

Jesus answered, "Yes. Haven't you read in the Scriptures, 'You have taught children and babies to sing praises'?"[n]

[17]Then Jesus left and went out of the city to Bethany, where he spent the night.

The Power of Faith

[18]Early the next morning, as Jesus was going back to the city, he became hungry. [19]Seeing a fig tree beside the road, Jesus went to it, but there were no figs on the tree, only leaves. So Jesus said to the tree, "You will never again have fruit." The tree immediately dried up.

[20]When his followers saw this, they were amazed. They asked, "How did the fig tree dry up so quickly?"

[21]Jesus answered, "I tell you the truth, if you have faith and do not doubt, you will be able to do what I did to this tree and even more. You will be able to say to this mountain, 'Go, fall into the sea.' And if you have faith, it will happen. [22]If you believe, you will get anything you ask for in prayer."

Leaders Doubt Jesus' Authority

[23]Jesus went to the Temple,[d] and while he was teaching there, the leading priests and the older leaders of the people came to him. They said, "What authority do you have to do these things? Who gave you this authority?"

[24]Jesus answered, "I also will ask you a question. If you answer me, then I will tell

you what authority I have to do these things. [25]Tell me: When John baptized people, did that come from God or just from other people?"

They argued about Jesus' question, saying, "If we answer, 'John's baptism was from God,' Jesus will say, 'Then why didn't you believe him?' [26]But if we say, 'It was from people,' we are afraid of what the crowd will do because they all believe that John was a prophet."[d]

[27]So they answered Jesus, "We don't know."

Jesus said to them, "Then I won't tell you what authority I have to do these things.

A Story About Two Sons

[28]"Tell me what you think about this: A man had two sons. He went to the first son and said, 'Son, go and work today in my vineyard.' [29]The son answered, 'I will not go.' But later the son changed his mind and went. [30]Then the father went to the other son and said, 'Son, go and work today in my vineyard.' The son answered, 'Yes, sir, I will go and work,' but he did not go. [31]Which of the two sons obeyed his father?"

The priests and leaders answered, "The first son."

Jesus said to them, "I tell you the truth, the tax collectors and the prostitutes[d] will enter the kingdom of God before you do. [32]John came to show you the right way to live. You did not believe him, but the tax collectors and prostitutes believed him. Even after seeing this, you still refused to change your ways and believe him.

A Story About God's Son

[33]"Listen to this story: There was a man who owned a vineyard. He put a wall around it and dug a hole for a winepress[d] and built a tower. Then he leased the land to some farmers and left for a trip. [34]When it was time for the grapes to be picked, he sent his servants to the farmers to get his share of the grapes. [35]But the farmers grabbed the ser-

---

'My Temple ... prayer.' Quotation from Isaiah 56:7.
'hideout for robbers.' Quotation from Jeremiah 7:11.
Praise Literally, "Hosanna," a Hebrew word used at first in praying to God for help. At this time it was probably a shout of joy used in praising God or his Messiah.
'You ... praises' Quotation from the Septuagint (Greek) version of Psalm 8:2.

vants, beat one, killed another, and then killed a third servant with stones. 36So the man sent some other servants to the farmers, even more than he sent the first time. But the farmers did the same thing to the servants that they had done before. 37So the man decided to send his son to the farmers. He said, 'They will respect my son.' 38But when the farmers saw the son, they said to each other, 'This son will inherit the vineyard. If we kill him, it will be ours!' 39Then the farmers grabbed the son, threw him out of the vineyard, and killed him. 40So what will the owner of the vineyard do to these farmers when he comes?"

41The priests and leaders said, "He will surely kill those evil men. Then he will lease the vineyard to some other farmers who will give him his share of the crop at harvest time."

42Jesus said to them, "Surely you have read this in the Scriptures:*d*

'The stone that the builders rejected
   became the cornerstone.*d*

The Lord did this,

   and it is wonderful to us.' *Psalm 118:22-23*

43"So I tell you that the kingdom of God will be taken away from you and given to people who do the things God wants in his kingdom. 44The person who falls on this stone will be broken, and on whomever that stone falls, that person will be crushed." *n*

45When the leading priests and the Pharisees*d* heard these stories, they knew Jesus was talking about them. 46They wanted to arrest him, but they were afraid of the people, because the people believed that Jesus was a prophet.*d*

A Story About a Wedding Feast

22 Jesus again used stories to teach the people. He said, 2"The kingdom of heaven is like a king who prepared a wedding feast for his son. 3The king invited some people to the feast. When the feast was ready, the king sent his servants to tell the people, but they refused to come.

4"Then the king sent other servants, saying, 'Tell those who have been invited that

my feast is ready. I have killed my best bulls and calves for the dinner, and everything is ready. Come to the wedding feast.'

5"But the people refused to listen to the servants and left to do other things. One went to work in his field, and another went to his business. 6Some of the other people grabbed the servants, beat them, and killed them. 7The king was furious and sent his army to kill the murderers and burn their city.

8"After that, the king said to his servants, 'The wedding feast is ready. I invited those people, but they were not worthy to come. 9So go to the street corners and invite everyone you find to come to my feast.' 10So the servants went into the streets and gathered all the people they could find, both good and bad. And the wedding hall was filled with guests.

11"When the king came in to see the guests, he saw a man who was not dressed for a wedding. 12The king said, 'Friend, how were you allowed to come in here? You are not dressed for a wedding.' But the man said nothing. 13So the king told some servants, 'Tie this man's hands and feet. Throw him out into the darkness, where people will cry and grind their teeth with pain.'

14"Yes, many people are invited, but only a few are chosen."

Is It Right to Pay Taxes or Not?

15Then the Pharisees*d* left that place and made plans to trap Jesus in saying something wrong. 16They sent some of their own followers and some people from the group called Herodians. *n* They said, "Teacher, we know that you are an honest man and that you teach the truth about God's way. You are not afraid of what other people think about you, because you pay no attention to who they are. 17So tell us what you think. Is it right to pay taxes to Caesar*d* or not?"

18But knowing that these leaders were trying to trick him, Jesus said, "You hypocrites!*d* Why are you trying to trap me? 19Show me a coin used for paying the tax." So the men

Verse 44 Some copies do not have verse 44.
Herodians A political group that followed Herod and his family.

showed him a coin.[n] 20Then Jesus asked, "Whose image and name are on the coin?"

21The men answered, "Caesar's."

Then Jesus said to them, "Give to Caesar the things that are Caesar's, and give to God the things that are God's."

22When the men heard what Jesus said, they were amazed and left him and went away.

Some Sadducees Try to Trick Jesus

23That same day some Sadducees[d] came to Jesus and asked him a question. (Sadducees believed that people would not rise from the dead.) 24They said, "Teacher, Moses said if a married man dies without having children, his brother must marry the widow and have children for him. 25Once there were seven brothers among us. The first one married and died. Since he had no children, his brother married the widow. 26Then the second brother also died. The same thing happened to the third brother and all the other brothers. 27Finally, the woman died. 28Since all seven men had married her, when people rise from the dead, whose wife will she be?"

29Jesus answered, "You don't understand, because you don't know what the Scriptures[d] say, and you don't know about the power of God. 30When people rise from the dead, they will not marry, nor will they be given to someone to marry. They will be like the angels in heaven. 31Surely you have read what God said to you about rising from the dead. 32God said, 'I am the God of Abraham, the God of Isaac, and the God of Jacob.'[n] God is the God of the living, not the dead."

33When the people heard this, they were amazed at Jesus' teaching.

The Most Important Command

34When the Pharisees[d] learned that the Sadducees[d] could not argue with Jesus' answers to them, the Pharisees met together. 35One Pharisee, who was an expert on the law of Moses, asked Jesus this question to test him: 36"Teacher, which command in the law is the most important?"

37Jesus answered, " 'Love the Lord your God with all your heart, all your soul, and all your mind.'[n] 38This is the first and most important command. 39And the second command is like the first: 'Love your neighbor as you love yourself.'[n] 40All the law and the writings of the prophets[d] depend on these two commands."

Jesus Questions the Pharisees

41While the Pharisees[d] were together, Jesus asked them, 42"What do you think about the Christ?[d] Whose son is he?"

They answered, "The Christ is the Son of David."[d]

43Then Jesus said to them, "Then why did David call him 'Lord'? David, speaking by the power of the Holy Spirit,[d] said,

44'The Lord said to my Lord:

Sit by me at my right side,

until I put your enemies under your
control.'   Psalm 110:1

45David calls the Christ 'Lord,' so how can the Christ be his son?"

46None of the Pharisees could answer Jesus' question, and after that day no one was brave enough to ask him any more questions.

Jesus Accuses Some Leaders

23 Then Jesus said to the crowds and to his followers, 2"The teachers of the law and the Pharisees[d] have the authority to tell you what the law of Moses says. 3So you should obey and follow whatever they tell you, but their lives are not good examples for you to follow. They tell you to do things, but they themselves don't do them. 4They make strict rules and try to force people to obey them, but they are unwilling to help those who struggle under the weight of their rules.

5"They do good things so that other people will see them. They make the boxes[n] of Scriptures[d] that they wear bigger, and they

---

coin A Roman denarius. One coin was the average pay for one day's work.
'I am ... Jacob.' Quotation from Exodus 3:6.
'Love ... mind.' Quotation from Deuteronomy 6:5.
'Love ... yourself.' Quotation from Leviticus 19:18.
boxes Small leather boxes containing four important Scriptures. Some Jews tied these to the forehead and left arm, probably to
show they were very religious.

make their special prayer clothes very long. [6]Those Pharisees and teachers of the law love to have the most important seats at feasts and in the synagogues.[d] [7]They love people to greet them with respect in the marketplaces, and they love to have people call them 'Teacher.'

[8]"But you must not be called 'Teacher,' because you have only one Teacher, and you are all brothers and sisters together. [9]And don't call any person on earth 'Father,' because you have one Father, who is in heaven. [10]And you should not be called 'Master,' because you have only one Master, the Christ.[d] [11]Whoever is your servant is the greatest among you. [12]Whoever makes himself great will be made humble. Whoever makes himself humble will be made great.

[13]"How terrible for you, teachers of the law and Pharisees! You are hypocrites![d] You close the door for people to enter the kingdom of heaven. You yourselves don't enter, and you stop others who are trying to enter. [14][n]

[15]"How terrible for you, teachers of the law and Pharisees! You are hypocrites! You travel across land and sea to find one person who will change to your ways. When you find that person, you make him more fit for hell than you are.

[16]"How terrible for you! You guide the people, but you are blind. You say, 'If people swear by the Temple[d] when they make a promise, that means nothing. But if they swear by the gold that is in the Temple, they must keep that promise.' [17]You are blind fools! Which is greater: the gold or the Temple that makes that gold holy? [18]And you say, 'If people swear by the altar when they make a promise, that means nothing. But if they swear by the gift on the altar, they must keep that promise.' [19]You are blind! Which is greater: the gift or the altar that makes the gift holy? [20]The person who swears by the altar is really using the altar and also everything on the altar. [21]And the person who swears by the Temple is really using the Temple and also everything in the Temple. [22]The person who swears by heaven is also using God's throne and the One who sits on that throne.

[23]"How terrible for you, teachers of the law and Pharisees! You are hypocrites! You give to God one-tenth of everything you earn — even your mint, dill, and cumin.[n] But you don't obey the really important teachings of the law — justice, mercy, and being loyal. These are the things you should do, as well as those other things. [24]You guide the people, but you are blind! You are like a person who picks a fly out of a drink and then swallows a camel![n]

[25]"How terrible for you, teachers of the law and Pharisees! You are hypocrites! You wash the outside of your cups and dishes, but inside they are full of things you got by cheating others and by pleasing only yourselves. [26]Pharisees, you are blind! First make the inside of the cup clean, and then the outside of the cup can be truly clean.

[27]"How terrible for you, teachers of the law and Pharisees! You are hypocrites! You are like tombs that are painted white. Outside, those tombs look fine, but inside, they are full of the bones of dead people and all kinds of unclean things. [28]It is the same with you. People look at you and think you are good, but on the inside you are full of hypocrisy and evil.

[29]"How terrible for you, teachers of the law and Pharisees! You are hypocrites! You build tombs for the prophets,[d] and you show honor to the graves of those who lived good lives. [30]You say, 'If we had lived during the time of our ancestors, we would not have helped them kill the prophets.' [31]But you give proof that you are children of those who murdered the prophets. [32]And you will complete the sin that your ancestors started.

[33]"You are snakes! A family of poisonous snakes! How are you going to escape God's judgment? [34]So I tell you this: I am sending

---

Verse 14 Some Greek copies add verse 14: "How terrible for you, teachers of the law and Pharisees. You are hypocrites. You take away widows' houses, and you say long prayers so that people will notice you. So you will have a worse punishment."
mint, dill, and cumin Small plants grown in gardens and used for spices. Only very religious people would be careful enough to give a tenth of these plants.
You ... camel! Meaning, "You worry about the smallest mistakes but commit the biggest sin."

to you prophets and wise men and teachers. Some of them you will kill and crucify. Some of them you will beat in your synagogues and chase from town to town. 35So you will be guilty for the death of all the good people who have been killed on earth — from the murder of that good man Abel to the murder of Zechariah[n] son of Berakiah, whom you murdered between the Temple and the altar. 36I tell you the truth, all of these things will happen to you people who are living now.

Jesus Feels Sorry for Jerusalem

37"Jerusalem, Jerusalem! You kill the prophets[d] and stone to death those who are sent to you. Many times I wanted to gather your people as a hen gathers her chicks under her wings, but you did not let me. 38Now your house will be left completely empty. 39I tell you, you will not see me again until that time when you will say, 'God bless the One who comes in the name of the Lord.' "[n]

The Temple Will Be Destroyed

24 As Jesus left the Temple[d] and was walking away, his followers came up to show him the Temple's buildings. 2Jesus asked, "Do you see all these buildings? I tell you the truth, not one stone will be left on another. Every stone will be thrown down to the ground."

3Later, as Jesus was sitting on the Mount of Olives,[d] his followers came to be alone with him. They said, "Tell us, when will these things happen? And what will be the sign that it is time for you to come again and for this age to end?"

4Jesus answered, "Be careful that no one fools you. 5Many will come in my name, saying, 'I am the Christ,'[d] and they will fool many people. 6You will hear about wars and stories of wars that are coming, but don't be afraid. These things must happen before the end comes. 7Nations will fight against other nations; kingdoms will fight against other kingdoms. There will be times when there is no food for people to eat, and there will be earthquakes in different places. 8These things are like the first pains when something new is about to be born.

9"Then people will arrest you, hand you over to be hurt, and kill you. They will hate you because you believe in me. 10At that time, many will lose their faith, and they will turn against each other and hate each other. 11Many false prophets[d] will come and cause many people to believe lies. 12There will be more and more evil in the world, so most people will stop showing their love for each other. 13But those people who keep their faith until the end will be saved. 14The Good News[d] about God's kingdom will be preached in all the world, to every nation. Then the end will come.

15"Daniel the prophet spoke about 'the destroying terror.'[n] You will see this standing in the holy place." (You who read this should understand what it means.) 16"At that time, the people in Judea should run away to the mountains. 17If people are on the roofs[n] of their houses, they must not go down to get anything out of their houses. 18If people are in the fields, they must not go back to get their coats. 19At that time, how terrible it will be for women who are pregnant or have nursing babies! 20Pray that it will not be winter or a Sabbath[d] day when these things happen and you have to run away, 21because at that time there will be much trouble. There will be more trouble than there has ever been since the beginning of the world until now, and nothing as bad will ever happen again. 22God has decided to make that terrible time short. Otherwise, no one would go on living. But God will make that time short to help the people he has chosen. 23At that time, someone might say to you, 'Look, there is the Christ!' Or another person might say, 'There he is!' But don't believe them. 24False Christs and false prophets will come and perform great wonders and miracles.[d] They will try to fool even the people God has chosen, if that is possible. 25Now I have warned you about this before it happens.

Abel ... Zechariah   In the order of the books of the Hebrew Old Testament, the first and last men to be murdered.
'God ... Lord.'   Quotation from Psalm 118:26.
'the destroying terror'   Mentioned in Daniel 9:27; 12:11 (see also Daniel 11:31).
roof   In Bible times houses were built with flat roofs. The roof was used for drying things such as flax and fruit. And it was used as an extra room, as a place for worship, and as a place to sleep in the summer.

26"If people tell you, 'The Christ is in the desert,' don't go there. If they say, 'The Christ is in the inner room,' don't believe it. 27When the Son of Man*d* comes, he will be seen by everyone, like lightning flashing from the east to the west. 28Wherever the dead body is, there the vultures will gather.

29"Soon after the trouble of those days,

'the sun will grow dark,

and the moon will not give its light.

The stars will fall from the sky.

And the powers of the heavens will be shaken.'   *Isaiah 13:10; 34:4*

30"At that time, the sign of the Son of Man will appear in the sky. Then all the peoples of the world will cry. They will see the Son of Man coming on clouds in the sky with great power and glory. 31He will use a loud trumpet to send his angels all around the earth, and they will gather his chosen people from every part of the world.

32"Learn a lesson from the fig tree: When its branches become green and soft and new leaves appear, you know summer is near. 33In the same way, when you see all these things happening, you will know that the time is near, ready to come. 34I tell you the truth, all these things will happen while the people of this time are still living. 35Earth and sky will be destroyed, but the words I have said will never be destroyed.

When Will Jesus Come Again?

36"No one knows when that day or time will be, not the angels in heaven, not even the Son. Only the Father knows. 37When the Son of Man*d* comes, it will be like what happened during Noah's time. 38In those days before the flood, people were eating and drinking, marrying and giving their children to be married, until the day Noah entered the boat. 39They knew nothing about what was happening until the flood came and destroyed them. It will be the same when the Son of Man comes. 40Two men will be in the field. One will be taken, and the other will be left. 41Two women will be grinding grain with a mill.*n* One will be taken, and the other will be left.

42"So always be ready, because you don't

know the day your Lord will come. 43Remember this: If the owner of the house knew what time of night a thief was coming, the owner would watch and not let the thief break in. 44So you also must be ready, because the Son of Man will come at a time you don't expect him.

45"Who is the wise and loyal servant that the master trusts to give the other servants their food at the right time? 46When the master comes and finds the servant doing his work, the servant will be blessed. 47I tell you the truth, the master will choose that servant to take care of everything he owns. 48But suppose that evil servant thinks to himself, 'My master will not come back soon,' 49and he begins to beat the other servants and eat and get drunk with others like him? 50The master will come when that servant is not ready and is not expecting him. 51Then the master will cut him in pieces and send him away to be with the hypocrites,*d* where people will cry and grind their teeth with pain.

A Story About Ten Bridesmaids

25 "At that time the kingdom of heaven will be like ten bridesmaids who took their lamps and went to wait for the bridegroom. 2Five of them were foolish and five were wise. 3The five foolish bridesmaids took their lamps, but they did not take more oil for the lamps to burn. 4The wise bridesmaids took their lamps and more oil in jars. 5Because the bridegroom was late, they became sleepy and went to sleep.

6"At midnight someone cried out, 'The bridegroom is coming! Come and meet him!' 7Then all the bridesmaids woke up and got their lamps ready. 8But the foolish ones said to the wise, 'Give us some of your oil, because our lamps are going out.' 9The wise bridesmaids answered, 'No, the oil we have might not be enough for all of us. Go to the people who sell oil and buy some for yourselves.'

10"So while the five foolish bridesmaids went to buy oil, the bridegroom came. The bridesmaids who were ready went in with the bridegroom to the wedding feast. Then the door was closed and locked.

mill Two large, round, flat rocks used for grinding grain to make flour.

11"Later the others came back and said, 'Sir, sir, open the door to let us in.' 12But the bridegroom answered, 'I tell you the truth, I don't want to know you.'

13"So always be ready, because you don't know the day or the hour the Son of Man*d* will come.

A Story About Three Servants

14"The kingdom of heaven is like a man who was going to another place for a visit. Before he left, he called for his servants and told them to take care of his things while he was gone. 15He gave one servant five bags of gold, another servant two bags of gold, and a third servant one bag of gold, to each one as much as he could handle. Then he left. 16The servant who got five bags went quickly to invest the money and earned five more bags. 17In the same way, the servant who had two bags invested them and earned two more. 18But the servant who got one bag went out and dug a hole in the ground and hid the master's money.

19"After a long time the master came home and asked the servants what they did with his money. 20The servant who was given five bags of gold brought five more bags to the master and said, 'Master, you trusted me to care for five bags of gold, so I used your five bags to earn five more.' 21The master answered, 'You did well. You are a good and loyal servant. Because you were loyal with small things, I will let you care for much greater things. Come and share my joy with me.'

22"Then the servant who had been given two bags of gold came to the master and said, 'Master, you gave me two bags of gold to care for, so I used your two bags to earn two more.' 23The master answered, 'You did well. You are a good and loyal servant. Because you were loyal with small things, I will let you care for much greater things. Come and share my joy with me.'

24"Then the servant who had been given one bag of gold came to the master and said, 'Master, I knew that you were a hard man. You harvest things you did not plant. You gather crops where you did not sow any seed. 25So I was afraid and went and hid your money in the ground. Here is your bag of

gold.' 26The master answered, 'You are a wicked and lazy servant! You say you knew that I harvest things I did not plant and that I gather crops where I did not sow any seed. 27So you should have put my gold in the bank. Then, when I came home, I would have received my gold back with interest.'

28"So the master told his other servants, 'Take the bag of gold from that servant and give it to the servant who has ten bags of gold. 29Those who have much will get more, and they will have much more than they need. But those who do not have much will have everything taken away from them.' 30Then the master said, 'Throw that useless servant outside, into the darkness where people will cry and grind their teeth with pain.'

The King Will Judge All People

31"The Son of Man*d* will come again in his great glory, with all his angels. He will be King and sit on his great throne. 32All the nations of the world will be gathered before him, and he will separate them into two groups as a shepherd separates the sheep from the goats. 33The Son of Man will put the sheep on his right and the goats on his left.

34"Then the King will say to the people on his right, 'Come, my Father has given you his blessing. Receive the kingdom God has prepared for you since the world was made. 35I was hungry, and you gave me food. I was thirsty, and you gave me something to drink. I was alone and away from home, and you invited me into your house. 36I was without clothes, and you gave me something to wear. I was sick, and you cared for me. I was in prison, and you visited me.'

37"Then the good people will answer, 'Lord, when did we see you hungry and give you food, or thirsty and give you something to drink? 38When did we see you alone and away from home and invite you into our house? When did we see you without clothes and give you something to wear? 39When did we see you sick or in prison and care for you?'

40"Then the King will answer, 'I tell you the truth, anything you did for even the least of my people here, you also did for me.'

41"Then the King will say to those on his left, 'Go away from me. You will be punished. Go into the fire that burns forever that was prepared for the devil and his angels. 42I was hungry, and you gave me nothing to eat. I was thirsty, and you gave me nothing to drink. 43I was alone and away from home, and you did not invite me into your house. I was without clothes, and you gave me nothing to wear. I was sick and in prison, and you did not care for me.'

44"Then those people will answer, 'Lord, when did we see you hungry or thirsty or alone and away from home or without clothes or sick or in prison? When did we see these things and not help you?'

45"Then the King will answer, 'I tell you the truth, anything you refused to do for even the least of my people here, you refused to do for me.'

46"These people will go off to be punished forever, but the good people will go to live forever."

The Plan to Kill Jesus

26 After Jesus finished saying all these things, he told his followers, 2"You know that the day after tomorrow is the day of the Passover⁴ Feast. On that day the Son of Man⁴ will be given to his enemies to be crucified."

3Then the leading priests and the older Jewish leaders had a meeting at the palace of the high priest, named Caiaphas. 4At the meeting, they planned to set a trap to arrest Jesus and kill him. 5But they said, "We must not do it during the feast, because the people might cause a riot."

Perfume for Jesus' Burial

6Jesus was in Bethany at the house of Simon, who had a skin disease. 7While Jesus was there, a woman approached him with an alabaster⁴ jar filled with expensive perfume. She poured this perfume on Jesus' head while he was eating.

8His followers were upset when they saw the woman do this. They asked, "Why waste that perfume? 9It could have been sold for a great deal of money and the money given to the poor."

10Knowing what had happened, Jesus said, "Why are you troubling this woman? She did an excellent thing for me. 11You will always have the poor with you, but you will not always have me. 12This woman poured perfume on my body to prepare me for burial. 13I tell you the truth, wherever the Good News⁴ is preached in all the world, what this woman has done will be told, and people will remember her."

Judas Becomes an Enemy of Jesus

14Then one of the twelve apostles, Judas Iscariot, went to talk to the leading priests. 15He said, "What will you pay me for giving Jesus to you?" And they gave him thirty silver coins. 16After that, Judas watched for the best time to turn Jesus in.

Jesus Eats the Passover Meal

17On the first day of the Feast⁴ of Unleavened Bread, the followers came to Jesus. They said, "Where do you want us to prepare for you to eat the Passover⁴ meal?"

18Jesus answered, "Go into the city to a certain man and tell him, 'The Teacher says: The chosen time is near. I will have the Passover with my followers at your house.' " 19The followers did what Jesus told them to do, and they prepared the Passover meal.

20In the evening Jesus was sitting at the table with his twelve followers. 21As they were eating, Jesus said, "I tell you the truth, one of you will turn against me."

22This made the followers very sad. Each one began to say to Jesus, "Surely, Lord, I am not the one who will turn against you, am I?"

23Jesus answered, "The man who has dipped his hand with me into the bowl is the one who will turn against me. 24The Son of Man⁴ will die, just as the Scriptures⁴ say. But how terrible it will be for the person who hands the Son of Man over to be killed. It would be better for him if he had never been born."

25Then Judas, who would give Jesus to his enemies, said to Jesus, "Teacher, surely I am not the one, am I?"

Jesus answered, "Yes, it is you."

The Lord's Supper

26While they were eating, Jesus took some bread and thanked God for it and broke it. Then he gave it to his followers and said, "Take this bread and eat it; this is my body."

27Then Jesus took a cup and thanked God for it and gave it to the followers. He said, "Every one of you drink this. 28This is my blood which is the new agreement that God makes with his people. This blood is poured out for many to forgive their sins. 29I tell you this: I will not drink of this fruit of the vine[n] again until that day when I drink it new with you in my Father's kingdom."

30After singing a hymn, they went out to the Mount of Olives.[d]

Jesus' Followers Will Leave Him

31Jesus told his followers, "Tonight you will all stumble in your faith on account of me, because it is written in the Scriptures:[d]

'I will kill the shepherd,

and the sheep will scatter.'   *Zechariah 13:7*

32But after I rise from the dead, I will go ahead of you into Galilee."

33Peter said, "Everyone else may stumble in their faith because of you, but I will not."

34Jesus said, "I tell you the truth, tonight before the rooster crows you will say three times that you don't know me."

35But Peter said, "I will never say that I don't know you! I will even die with you!" And all the other followers said the same thing.

Jesus Prays Alone

36Then Jesus went with his followers to a place called Gethsemane. He said to them, "Sit here while I go over there and pray." 37He took Peter and the two sons of Zebedee with him, and he began to be very sad and troubled. 38He said to them, "My heart is full of sorrow, to the point of death. Stay here and watch with me."

39After walking a little farther away from them, Jesus fell to the ground and prayed, "My Father, if it is possible, do not give me this cup[n] of suffering. But do what you want, not what I want." 40Then Jesus went back to his followers and found them asleep. He said to Peter, "You men could not stay awake with me for one hour? 41Stay awake and pray for strength against temptation. The

spirit wants to do what is right, but the body is weak."

42Then Jesus went away a second time and prayed, "My Father, if it is not possible for this painful thing to be taken from me, and if I must do it, I pray that what you want will be done."

43Then he went back to his followers, and again he found them asleep, because their eyes were heavy. 44So Jesus left them and went away and prayed a third time, saying the same thing.

45Then Jesus went back to his followers and said, "Are you still sleeping and resting? The time has come for the Son of Man[d] to be handed over to sinful people. 46Get up, we must go. Look, here comes the man who has turned against me."

Jesus Is Arrested

47While Jesus was still speaking, Judas, one of the twelve apostles,[d] came up. With him were many people carrying swords and clubs who had been sent from the leading priests and the older Jewish leaders of the people. 48Judas had planned to give them a signal, saying, "The man I kiss is Jesus. Arrest him." 49At once Judas went to Jesus and said, "Greetings, Teacher!" and kissed him.

50Jesus answered, "Friend, do what you came to do."

Then the people came and grabbed Jesus and arrested him. 51When that happened, one of Jesus' followers reached for his sword and pulled it out. He struck the servant of the high priest and cut off his ear.

52Jesus said to the man, "Put your sword back in its place. All who use swords will be killed with swords. 53Surely you know I could ask my Father, and he would give me more than twelve armies of angels. 54But it must happen this way to bring about what the Scriptures[d] say."

55Then Jesus said to the crowd, "You came to get me with swords and clubs as if I were a criminal. Every day I sat in the Temple[d] teaching, and you did not arrest me there. 56But all these things have happened so that

---

fruit of the vine Product of the grapevine; this may also be translated "wine."

cup Jesus is talking about the terrible things that will happen to him. Accepting these things will be very hard, like drinking a cup of something bitter.

it will come about as the prophets*d* wrote."
Then all of Jesus' followers left him and ran away.

Jesus Before the Leaders

⁵⁷Those people who arrested Jesus led him to the house of Caiaphas, the high priest, where the teachers of the law and the older Jewish leaders were gathered. ⁵⁸Peter followed far behind to the courtyard of the high priest's house, and he sat down with the guards to see what would happen to Jesus.

⁵⁹The leading priests and the whole Jewish council tried to find something false against Jesus so they could kill him. ⁶⁰Many people came and told lies about him, but the council could find no real reason to kill him. Then two people came and said, ⁶¹"This man said, 'I can destroy the Temple*d* of God and build it again in three days.'"

⁶²Then the high priest stood up and said to Jesus, "Aren't you going to answer? Don't you have something to say about their charges against you?" ⁶³But Jesus said nothing.

Again the high priest said to Jesus, "I command you by the power of the living God: Tell us if you are the Christ,*d* the Son of God."

⁶⁴Jesus answered, "Those are your words. But I tell you, in the future you will see the Son of Man*d* sitting at the right hand of God, the Powerful One, and coming on clouds in the sky."

⁶⁵When the high priest heard this, he tore his clothes and said, "This man has said things that are against God! We don't need any more witnesses; you all heard him say these things against God. ⁶⁶What do you think?"

The people answered, "He should die."

⁶⁷Then the people there spat in Jesus' face and beat him with their fists. Others slapped him. ⁶⁸They said, "Prove to us that you are a prophet,*d* you Christ! Tell us who hit you!"

Peter Says He Doesn't Know Jesus

⁶⁹At that time, as Peter was sitting in the courtyard, a servant girl came to him and said, "You also were with Jesus of Galilee."

⁷⁰But Peter said to all the people there that he was never with Jesus. He said, "I don't know what you are talking about."

⁷¹When he left the courtyard and was at the gate, another girl saw him. She said to the people there, "This man was with Jesus of Nazareth."

⁷²Again, Peter said he was never with him, saying, "I swear I don't know this man Jesus!"

⁷³A short time later, some people standing there went to Peter and said, "Surely you are one of those who followed Jesus. The way you talk shows it."

⁷⁴Then Peter began to place a curse on himself and swear, "I don't know the man." At once, a rooster crowed. ⁷⁵And Peter remembered what Jesus had told him: "Before the rooster crows, you will say three times that you don't know me." Then Peter went outside and cried painfully.

Jesus Is Taken to Pilate

27 Early the next morning, all the leading priests and older leaders of the people decided that Jesus should die. ²They tied him, led him away, and turned him over to Pilate, the governor.

Judas Kills Himself

³Judas, the one who had given Jesus to his enemies, saw that they had decided to kill Jesus. Then he was very sorry for what he had done. So he took the thirty silver coins back to the priests and the leaders, ⁴saying, "I sinned; I handed over to you an innocent man."

The leaders answered, "What is that to us? That's your problem, not ours."

⁵So Judas threw the money into the Temple.*d* Then he went off and hanged himself.

⁶The leading priests picked up the silver coins in the Temple and said, "Our law does not allow us to keep this money with the Temple money, because it has paid for a man's death." ⁷So they decided to use the coins to buy Potter's Field as a place to bury strangers who died in Jerusalem. ⁸That is why that field is still called the Field of Blood. ⁹So what Jeremiah the prophet*d* had said came true: "They took thirty silver coins. That is how little the Israelites thought he was worth. ¹⁰They used those thirty silver

coins to buy the potter's field, as the Lord commanded me." [n]

Pilate Questions Jesus

[11]Jesus stood before Pilate the governor, and Pilate asked him, "Are you the king of the Jews?"

Jesus answered, "Those are your words."

[12]When the leading priests and the older leaders accused Jesus, he said nothing.

[13]So Pilate said to Jesus, "Don't you hear them accusing you of all these things?"

[14]But Jesus said nothing in answer to Pilate, and Pilate was very surprised at this.

Pilate Tries to Free Jesus

[15]Every year at the time of Passover[d] the governor would free one prisoner whom the people chose. [16]At that time there was a man in prison, named Barabbas, who was known to be very bad. [17]When the people gathered at Pilate's house, Pilate said, "Whom do you want me to set free: Barabbas or Jesus who is called the Christ?"[d] [18]Pilate knew that the people turned Jesus in to him because they were jealous.

[19]While Pilate was sitting there on the judge's seat, his wife sent this message to him: "Don't do anything to that man, because he is innocent. Today I had a dream about him, and it troubled me very much."

[20]But the leading priests and older leaders convinced the crowd to ask for Barabbas to be freed and for Jesus to be killed.

[21]Pilate said, "I have Barabbas and Jesus. Which do you want me to set free for you?"

The people answered, "Barabbas."

[22]Pilate asked, "So what should I do with Jesus, the one called the Christ?"

They all answered, "Crucify him!"

[23]Pilate asked, "Why? What wrong has he done?"

But they shouted louder, "Crucify him!"

[24]When Pilate saw that he could do nothing about this and that a riot was starting, he took some water and washed his hands[n] in front of the crowd. Then he said, "I am not guilty of this man's death. You are the ones who are causing it!"

[25]All the people answered, "We and our children will be responsible for his death."

[26]Then he set Barabbas free. But Jesus was beaten with whips and handed over to the soldiers to be crucified.

[27]The governor's soldiers took Jesus into the governor's palace, and they all gathered around him. [28]They took off his clothes and put a red robe on him. [29]Using thorny branches, they made a crown, put it on his head, and put a stick in his right hand. Then the soldiers bowed before Jesus and made fun of him, saying, "Hail, King of the Jews!" [30]They spat on Jesus. Then they took his stick and began to beat him on the head. [31]After they finished, the soldiers took off the robe and put his own clothes on him again. Then they led him away to be crucified.

Jesus Is Crucified

[32]As the soldiers were going out of the city with Jesus, they forced a man from Cyrene, named Simon, to carry the cross for Jesus. [33]They all came to the place called Golgotha, which means the Place of the Skull. [34]The soldiers gave Jesus wine mixed with gall[n] to drink. He tasted the wine but refused to drink it. [35]When the soldiers had crucified him, they threw lots[d] to decide who would get his clothes. [36]The soldiers sat there and continued watching him. [37]They put a sign above Jesus' head with a charge against him. It said: THIS IS JESUS, THE KING OF THE JEWS. [38]Two robbers were crucified beside Jesus, one on the right and the other on the left. [39]People walked by and insulted Jesus and shook their heads, [40]saying, "You said you could destroy the Temple[d] and build it again in three days. So save yourself! Come down from that cross if you are really the Son of God!"

[41]The leading priests, the teachers of the law, and the older Jewish leaders were also making fun of Jesus. [42]They said, "He saved others, but he can't save himself! He says he is the king of Israel! If he is the king, let him

---

"They ... commanded me."   See Zechariah 11:12-13 and Jeremiah 32:6-9.
washed his hands   He did this as a sign to show that he wanted no part in what the people did.
gall   Probably a drink of wine mixed with drugs to help a person feel less pain.

come down now from the cross. Then we will believe in him. [43]He trusts in God, so let God save him now, if God really wants him. He himself said, 'I am the Son of God.' " [44]And in the same way, the robbers who were being crucified beside Jesus also insulted him.

Jesus Dies

[45]At noon the whole country became dark, and the darkness lasted for three hours. [46]About three o'clock Jesus cried out in a loud voice, "Eli, Eli, lama sabachthani?" This means, "My God, my God, why have you rejected me?"

[47]Some of the people standing there who heard this said, "He is calling Elijah." [48]Quickly one of them ran and got a sponge and filled it with vinegar and tied it to a stick and gave it to Jesus to drink. [49]But the others said, "Don't bother him. We want to see if Elijah will come to save him."

[50]But Jesus cried out again in a loud voice and died.

[51]Then the curtain in the Temple[n] was torn into two pieces, from the top to the bottom. Also, the earth shook and rocks broke apart. [52]The graves opened, and many of God's people who had died were raised from the dead. [53]They came out of the graves after Jesus was raised from the dead and went into the holy city, where they appeared to many people.

[54]When the army officer and the soldiers guarding Jesus saw this earthquake and everything else that happened, they were very frightened and said, "He really was the Son of God!"

[55]Many women who had followed Jesus from Galilee to help him were standing at a distance from the cross, watching. [56]Mary Magdalene, and Mary the mother of James and Joseph, and the mother of James and John were there.

Jesus Is Buried

[57]That evening a rich man named Joseph, a follower of Jesus from the town of Arimathea, came to Jerusalem. [58]Joseph went to Pilate and asked to have Jesus' body. So Pilate gave orders for the soldiers to give it to Joseph. [59]Then Joseph took the body and wrapped it in a clean linen cloth. [60]He put Jesus' body in a new tomb that he had cut out of a wall of rock, and he rolled a very large stone to block the entrance of the tomb. Then Joseph went away. [61]Mary Magdalene and the other woman named Mary were sitting near the tomb.

The Tomb of Jesus Is Guarded

[62]The next day, the day after Preparation[d] Day, the leading priests and the Pharisees[d] went to Pilate. [63]They said, "Sir, we remember that while that liar was still alive he said, 'After three days I will rise from the dead.' [64]So give the order for the tomb to be guarded closely till the third day. Otherwise, his followers might come and steal the body and tell people that he has risen from the dead. That lie would be even worse than the first one."

[65]Pilate said, "Take some soldiers and go guard the tomb the best way you know." [66]So they all went to the tomb and made it safe from thieves by sealing the stone in the entrance and putting soldiers there to guard it.

Jesus Rises from the Dead

28 The day after the Sabbath[d] day was the first day of the week. At dawn on the first day, Mary Magdalene and another woman named Mary went to look at the tomb.

[2]At that time there was a strong earthquake. An angel of the Lord came down from heaven, went to the tomb, and rolled the stone away from the entrance. Then he sat on the stone. [3]He was shining as bright as lightning, and his clothes were white as snow. [4]The soldiers guarding the tomb shook with fear because of the angel, and they became like dead men.

[5]The angel said to the women, "Don't be afraid. I know that you are looking for Jesus, who has been crucified. [6]He is not here. He has risen from the dead as he said he would.

---

curtain in the Temple A curtain divided the Most Holy Place from the other part of the Temple. That was the special building in Jerusalem where God commanded the Jewish people to worship him.

Come and see the place where his body was. [7]And go quickly and tell his followers, 'Jesus has risen from the dead. He is going into Galilee ahead of you, and you will see him there.' " Then the angel said, "Now I have told you."

[8]The women left the tomb quickly. They were afraid, but they were also very happy. They ran to tell Jesus' followers what had happened. [9]Suddenly, Jesus met them and said, "Greetings." The women came up to him, took hold of his feet, and worshiped him. [10]Then Jesus said to them, "Don't be afraid. Go and tell my followers to go on to Galilee, and they will see me there."

The Soldiers Report to the Leaders

[11]While the women went to tell Jesus' followers, some of the soldiers who had been guarding the tomb went into the city to tell the leading priests everything that had happened. [12]Then the priests met with the older Jewish leaders and made a plan. They paid the soldiers a large amount of money [13]and said to them, "Tell the people that Jesus' followers came during the night and stole the body while you were asleep. [14]If the governor hears about this, we will satisfy him and save you from trouble." [15]So the soldiers kept the money and did as they were told. And that story is still spread among the Jewish people even today.

Jesus Talks to His Followers

[16]The eleven followers went to Galilee to the mountain where Jesus had told them to go. [17]On the mountain they saw Jesus and worshiped him, but some of them did not believe it was really Jesus. [18]Then Jesus came to them and said, "All power in heaven and on earth is given to me. [19]So go and make followers of all people in the world. Baptize them in the name of the Father and the Son and the Holy Spirit.[d] [20]Teach them to obey everything that I have taught you, and I will be with you always, even until the end of this age."

MARK

Mark Tells About the Power of Jesus

John Prepares for Jesus

1 This is the beginning of the Good News[d] about Jesus Christ, the Son of God,[n] 2as the prophet[d] Isaiah wrote:

"I will send my messenger ahead of you,
    who will prepare your way."   *Malachi 3:1*
3"This is a voice of one
    who calls out in the desert:
'Prepare the way for the Lord.
    Make the road straight for him.' "

Isaiah 40:3

4John was baptizing people in the desert and preaching a baptism of changed hearts and lives for the forgiveness of sins. 5All the people from Judea and Jerusalem were going out to him. They confessed their sins and were baptized by him in the Jordan River. 6John wore clothes made from camel's hair, had a leather belt around his waist, and ate locusts[d] and wild honey. 7This is what John preached to the people: "There is one coming after me who is greater than I; I am not good enough even to kneel down and untie his sandals. 8I baptize you with water, but he will baptize you with the Holy Spirit."[d]

Jesus Is Baptized

9At that time Jesus came from the town of Nazareth in Galilee and was baptized by John in the Jordan River. 10Immediately, as Jesus was coming up out of the water, he saw heaven open. The Holy Spirit[d] came down on him like a dove, 11and a voice came from heaven: "You are my Son, whom I love, I am very pleased with you."

12Then the Spirit sent Jesus into the desert. 13He was in the desert forty days and was tempted by Satan. He was with the wild animals, and the angels came and took care of him.

Jesus Chooses Some Followers

14After John was put in prison, Jesus went into Galilee, preaching the Good News[d] from God. 15He said, "The right time has come. The kingdom of God is near. Change your hearts and lives and believe the Good News!"

16When Jesus was walking by Lake Galilee, he saw Simon[n] and his brother Andrew throwing a net into the lake because they were fishermen. 17Jesus said to them, "Come follow me, and I will make you fish for people." 18So Simon and Andrew immediately left their nets and followed him.

19Going a little farther, Jesus saw two more brothers, James and John, the sons of Zebedee. They were in a boat, mending their nets. 20Jesus immediately called them, and they left their father in the boat with the hired workers and followed Jesus.

Jesus Forces Out an Evil Spirit

21Jesus and his followers went to Capernaum. On the Sabbath[d] day He went to the synagogue[d] and began to teach. 22The people were amazed at his teaching, because he taught like a person who had authority, not like their teachers of the law. 23Just then, a man was there in the synagogue who had an evil spirit in him. He shouted, 24"Jesus of Nazareth! What do you want with us? Did you come to destroy us? I know who you are — God's Holy One!"

25Jesus commanded the evil spirit, "Be quiet! Come out of the man!" 26The evil spirit shook the man violently, gave a loud cry, and then came out of him.

27The people were so amazed they asked each other, "What is happening here? This man is teaching something new, and with authority. He even gives commands to evil spirits, and they obey him." 28And the news

---

the Son of God Some Greek copies omit these words.
Simon . Simon's other name was Peter.

about Jesus spread quickly everywhere in the area of Galilee.

Jesus Heals Many People

29As soon as Jesus and his followers left the synagogue,[d] they went with James and John to the home of Simon[n] and Andrew. 30Simon's mother-in-law was sick in bed with a fever, and the people told Jesus about her. 31So Jesus went to her bed, took her hand, and helped her up. The fever left her, and she began serving them.

32That evening, after the sun went down, the people brought to Jesus all who were sick and had demons[d] in them. 33The whole town gathered at the door. 34Jesus healed many who had different kinds of sicknesses, and he forced many demons to leave people. But he would not allow the demons to speak, because they knew who he was.

35Early the next morning, while it was still dark, Jesus woke and left the house. He went to a lonely place, where he prayed. 36Simon and his friends went to look for Jesus. 37When they found him, they said, "Everyone is looking for you!"

38Jesus answered, "We should go to other towns around here so I can preach there too. That is the reason I came." 39So he went everywhere in Galilee, preaching in the synagogues and forcing out demons.

Jesus Heals a Sick Man

40A man with a skin disease came to Jesus. He fell to his knees and begged Jesus, "You can heal me if you will."

41Jesus felt sorry for the man, so he reached out his hand and touched him and said, "I will. Be healed!" 42Immediately the disease left the man, and he was healed.

43Jesus told the man to go away at once, but he warned him strongly, 44"Don't tell anyone about this. But go and show yourself to the priest. And offer the gift Moses commanded for people who are made well.[n] This will show the people what I have done." 45The man left there, but he began to tell everyone that Jesus had healed him, and so he spread the news about Jesus. As a result,

Jesus could not enter a town if people saw him. He stayed in places where nobody lived, but people came to him from everywhere.

Jesus Heals a Paralyzed Man

2 A few days later, when Jesus came back to Capernaum, the news spread that he was at home. 2Many people gathered together so that there was no room in the house, not even outside the door. And Jesus was teaching them God's message. 3Four people came, carrying a paralyzed man. 4Since they could not get to Jesus because of the crowd, they dug a hole in the roof right above where he was speaking. When they got through, they lowered the mat with the paralyzed man on it. 5When Jesus saw the faith of these people, he said to the paralyzed man, "Young man, your sins are forgiven."

6Some of the teachers of the law were sitting there, thinking to themselves, 7"Why does this man say things like that? He is speaking as if he were God. Only God can forgive sins."

8Jesus knew immediately what these teachers of the law were thinking. So he said to them, "Why are you thinking these things? 9Which is easier: to tell this paralyzed man, 'Your sins are forgiven,' or to tell him, 'Stand up. Take your mat and walk'? 10But I will prove to you that the Son of Man[d] has authority on earth to forgive sins." So Jesus said to the paralyzed man, 11"I tell you, stand up, take your mat, and go home." 12Immediately the paralyzed man stood up, took his mat, and walked out while everyone was watching him.

The people were amazed and praised God. They said, "We have never seen anything like this!"

13Jesus went to the lake again. The whole crowd followed him there, and he taught them. 14While he was walking along, he saw a man named Levi son of Alphaeus, sitting in the tax collector's booth. Jesus said to him, "Follow me," and he stood up and followed Jesus.

15Later, as Jesus was having dinner at Levi's house, many tax collectors and "sin-

Simon　Simon's other name was Peter.
Moses ... well　Read about this in Leviticus 14:1-32.

ners" were eating there with Jesus and his followers. Many people like this followed Jesus. [16]When the teachers of the law who were Pharisees[d] saw Jesus eating with the tax collectors and "sinners," they asked his followers, "Why does he eat with tax collectors and sinners?"

[17]Jesus heard this and said to them, "It is not the healthy people who need a doctor, but the sick. I did not come to invite good people but to invite sinners."

Jesus' Followers Are Criticized

[18]Now the followers of John[n] and the Pharisees[d] often gave up eating for a certain time.[n] Some people came to Jesus and said, "Why do John's followers and the followers of the Pharisees often give up eating, but your followers don't?"

[19]Jesus answered, "The friends of the bridegroom do not give up eating while the bridegroom is still with them. As long as the bridegroom is with them, they cannot give up eating. [20]But the time will come when the bridegroom will be taken from them, and then they will give up eating.

[21]"No one sews a patch of unshrunk cloth over a hole in an old coat. Otherwise, the patch will shrink and pull away — the new patch will pull away from the old coat. Then the hole will be worse. [22]Also, no one ever pours new wine into old leather bags. Otherwise, the new wine will break the bags, and the wine will be ruined along with the bags. But new wine should be put into new leather bags."

Jesus Is Lord of the Sabbath

[23]One Sabbath[d] day, as Jesus was walking through some fields of grain, his followers began to pick some grain to eat. [24]The Pharisees[d] said to Jesus, "Why are your followers doing what is not lawful on the Sabbath day?"

[25]Jesus answered, "Have you never read what David did when he and those with him were hungry and needed food? [26]During the time of Abiathar the high priest, David went into God's house and ate the holy bread, which is lawful only for priests to eat. And David also gave some of the bread to those who were with him."

[27]Then Jesus said to the Pharisees, "The Sabbath day was made to help people; they were not made to be ruled by the Sabbath day. [28]So then, the Son of Man[d] is Lord even of the Sabbath day."

Jesus Heals a Man's Hand

3 Another time when Jesus went into a synagogue,[d] a man with a crippled hand was there. [2]Some people watched Jesus closely to see if he would heal the man on the Sabbath[d] day so they could accuse him.

[3]Jesus said to the man with the crippled hand, "Stand up here in the middle of everyone."

[4]Then Jesus asked the people, "Which is lawful on the Sabbath day: to do good or to do evil, to save a life or to kill?" But they said nothing to answer him.

[5]Jesus was angry as he looked at the people, and he felt very sad because they were stubborn. Then he said to the man, "Hold out your hand." The man held out his hand and it was healed. [6]Then the Pharisees[d] left and began making plans with the Herodians[n] about a way to kill Jesus.

Many People Follow Jesus

[7]Jesus left with his followers for the lake, and a large crowd from Galilee followed him. [8]Also many people came from Judea, from Jerusalem, from Idumea, from the lands across the Jordan River, and from the area of Tyre and Sidon. When they heard what Jesus was doing, many people came to him. [9]When Jesus saw the crowds, he told his followers to get a boat ready for him to keep people from crowding against him. [10]He had healed many people, so all the sick were pushing toward him to touch him. [11]When evil spirits saw Jesus, they fell down before him and shouted, "You are the Son of God!" [12]But Jesus strongly warned them not to tell who he was.

John John the Baptist, who preached to the Jewish people about Christ's coming (Mark 1:4-8).
gave ... time This is called "fasting." The people would give up eating for a special time of prayer and worship to God. It was also done to show sadness and disappointment.
Herodians A political group that followed Herod and his family.

Jesus Chooses His Twelve Apostles

13Then Jesus went up on a mountain and called to him the men he wanted, and they came to him. 14Jesus chose twelve men and called them apostles.*d* He wanted them to be with him, and he wanted to send them out to preach 15and to have the authority to force demons*d* out of people. 16These are the twelve men he chose: Simon (Jesus named him Peter), 17James and John, the sons of Zebedee (Jesus named them Boanerges, which means "Sons of Thunder"), 18Andrew, Philip, Bartholomew, Matthew, Thomas, James the son of Alphaeus, Thaddaeus, Simon the Zealot,*d* 19and Judas Iscariot, who later turned against Jesus.

Some People Say Jesus Has a Devil

20Then Jesus went home, but again a crowd gathered. There were so many people that Jesus and his followers could not eat. 21When his family heard this, they went to get him because they thought he was out of his mind. 22But the teachers of the law from Jerusalem were saying, "Beelzebul*d* is living inside him! He uses power from the ruler of demons*d* to force demons out of people."

23So Jesus called the people together and taught them with stories. He said, "Satan will not force himself out of people. 24A kingdom that is divided cannot continue, 25and a family that is divided cannot continue. 26And if Satan is against himself and fights against his own people, he cannot continue; that is the end of Satan. 27No one can enter a strong person's house and steal his things unless he first ties up the strong person. Then he can steal things from the house. 28I tell you the truth, all sins that people do and all the things people say against God can be forgiven. 29But anyone who speaks against the Holy Spirit*d* will never be forgiven; he is guilty of a sin that continues forever."

30Jesus said this because the teachers of the law said that he had an evil spirit inside him.

Jesus' True Family

31Then Jesus' mother and brothers arrived. Standing outside, they sent someone in to tell him to come out. 32Many people were sitting around Jesus, and they said to him, "Your mother and brothers are waiting for you outside."

33Jesus asked, "Who are my mother and my brothers?" 34Then he looked at those sitting around him and said, "Here are my mother and my brothers! 35My true brother and sister and mother are those who do what God wants."

A Story About Planting Seed

4 Again Jesus began teaching by the lake. A great crowd gathered around him, so he sat down in a boat near the shore. All the people stayed on the shore close to the water. 2Jesus taught them many things, using stories. He said, 3"Listen! A farmer went out to plant his seed. 4While he was planting, some seed fell by the road, and the birds came and ate it up. 5Some seed fell on rocky ground where there wasn't much dirt. That seed grew very fast, because the ground was not deep. 6But when the sun rose, the plants dried up because they did not have deep roots. 7Some other seed fell among thorny weeds, which grew and choked the good plants. So those plants did not produce a crop. 8Some other seed fell on good ground and began to grow. It got taller and produced a crop. Some plants made thirty times more, some made sixty times more, and some made a hundred times more."

9Then Jesus said, "You people who can hear me, listen!"

Jesus Tells Why He Used Stories

10Later, when Jesus was alone, the twelve apostles*d* and others around him asked him about the stories.

11Jesus said, "You can know the secret about the kingdom of God. But to other people I tell everything by using stories 12so that:

'They will look and look, but they will
   not learn.
They will listen and listen, but they
   will not understand.
If they did learn and understand,
   they would come back to me and be
      forgiven.' "   *Isaiah 6:9-10*

Jesus Explains the Seed Story

13Then Jesus said to his followers, "Don't

you understand this story? If you don't, how will you understand any story? [14]The farmer is like a person who plants God's message in people. [15]Sometimes the teaching falls on the road. This is like the people who hear the teaching of God, but Satan quickly comes and takes away the teaching that was planted in them. [16]Others are like the seed planted on rocky ground. They hear the teaching and quickly accept it with joy. [17]But since they don't allow the teaching to go deep into their lives, they keep it only a short time. When trouble or persecution comes because of the teaching they accepted, they quickly give up. [18]Others are like the seed planted among the thorny weeds. They hear the teaching, [19]but the worries of this life, the temptation of wealth, and many other evil desires keep the teaching from growing and producing fruit[n] in their lives. [20]Others are like the seed planted in the good ground. They hear the teaching and accept it. Then they grow and produce fruit — sometimes thirty times more, sometimes sixty times more, and sometimes a hundred times more."

Use What You Have

[21]Then Jesus said to them, "Do you hide a lamp under a bowl or under a bed? No! You put the lamp on a lampstand. [22]Everything that is hidden will be made clear and every secret thing will be made known. [23]You people who can hear me, listen!

[24]"Think carefully about what you hear. The way you give to others is the way God will give to you, but God will give you even more. [25]Those who have understanding will be given more. But those who do not have understanding, even what they have will be taken away from them."

Jesus Uses a Story About Seed

[26]Then Jesus said, "The kingdom of God is like someone who plants seed in the ground. [27]Night and day, whether the person is asleep or awake, the seed still grows, but the person does not know how it grows. [28]By itself the earth produces grain. First the plant grows, then the head, and then all the grain in the head. [29]When the grain is ready, the farmer cuts it, because this is the harvest time."

A Story About Mustard Seed

[30]Then Jesus said, "How can I show you what the kingdom of God is like? What story can I use to explain it? [31]The kingdom of God is like a mustard seed, the smallest seed you plant in the ground. [32]But when planted, this seed grows and becomes the largest of all garden plants. It produces large branches, and the wild birds can make nests in its shade."

[33]Jesus used many stories like these to teach the crowd God's message — as much as they could understand. [34]He always used stories to teach them. But when he and his followers were alone, Jesus explained everything to them.

Jesus Calms a Storm

[35]That evening, Jesus said to his followers, "Let's go across the lake." [36]Leaving the crowd behind, they took him in the boat just as he was. There were also other boats with them. [37]A very strong wind came up on the lake. The waves came over the sides and into the boat so that it was already full of water. [38]Jesus was at the back of the boat, sleeping with his head on a cushion. His followers woke him and said, "Teacher, don't you care that we are drowning!"

[39]Jesus stood up and commanded the wind and said to the waves, "Quiet! Be still!" Then the wind stopped, and it became completely calm.

[40]Jesus said to his followers, "Why are you afraid? Do you still have no faith?"

[41]The followers were very afraid and asked each other, "Who is this? Even the wind and the waves obey him!"

A Man with Demons Inside Him

5 Jesus and his followers went to the other side of the lake to the area of the Gerasene people. [2]When Jesus got out of the boat, instantly a man with an evil spirit came to him from the burial caves. [3]This man lived in the caves, and no one could tie him up, not even with a chain. [4]Many times people had used chains to tie the man's hands and feet,

---

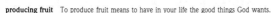

producing fruit   To produce fruit means to have in your life the good things God wants.

but he always broke them off. No one was strong enough to control him. [5]Day and night he would wander around the burial caves and on the hills, screaming and cutting himself with stones. [6]While Jesus was still far away, the man saw him, ran to him, and fell down before him.

[7]The man shouted in a loud voice, "What do you want with me, Jesus, Son of the Most High God? I command you in God's name not to torture me!" [8]He said this because Jesus was saying to him, "You evil spirit, come out of the man."

[9]Then Jesus asked him, "What is your name?"

He answered, "My name is Legion,[n] because we are many spirits." [10]He begged Jesus again and again not to send them out of that area.

[11]A large herd of pigs was feeding on a hill near there. [12]The demons[d] begged Jesus, "Send us into the pigs; let us go into them." [13]So Jesus allowed them to do this. The evil spirits left the man and went into the pigs. Then the herd of pigs — about two thousand of them — rushed down the hill into the lake and were drowned.

[14]The herdsmen ran away and went to the town and to the countryside, telling everyone about this. So people went out to see what had happened. [15]They came to Jesus and saw the man who used to have the many evil spirits, sitting, clothed, and in his right mind. And they were frightened. [16]The people who saw this told the others what had happened to the man who had the demons living in him, and they told about the pigs. [17]Then the people began to beg Jesus to leave their area.

[18]As Jesus was getting back into the boat, the man who was freed from the demons begged to go with him.

[19]But Jesus would not let him. He said, "Go home to your family and tell them how much the Lord has done for you and how he has had mercy on you." [20]So the man left and began to tell the people in the Ten Towns[n] about what Jesus had done for him. And everyone was amazed.

Jesus Gives Life to a Dead Girl and Heals a Sick Woman

[21]When Jesus went in the boat back to the other side of the lake, a large crowd gathered around him there. [22]A leader of the synagogue,[d] named Jairus, came there, saw Jesus, and fell at his feet. [23]He begged Jesus, saying again and again, "My daughter is dying. Please come and put your hands on her so she will be healed and will live." [24]So Jesus went with him.

A large crowd followed Jesus and pushed very close around him. [25]Among them was a woman who had been bleeding for twelve years. [26]She had suffered very much from many doctors and had spent all the money she had, but instead of improving, she was getting worse. [27]When the woman heard about Jesus, she came up behind him in the crowd and touched his coat. [28]She thought, "If I can just touch his clothes, I will be healed." [29]Instantly her bleeding stopped, and she felt in her body that she was healed from her disease.

[30]At once Jesus felt power go out from him. So he turned around in the crowd and asked, "Who touched my clothes?"

[31]His followers said, "Look at how many people are pushing against you! And you ask, 'Who touched me?' "

[32]But Jesus continued looking around to see who had touched him. [33]The woman, knowing that she was healed, came and fell at Jesus' feet. Shaking with fear, she told him the whole truth. [34]Jesus said to her, "Dear woman, you are made well because you believed. Go in peace; be healed of your disease."

[35]While Jesus was still speaking, some people came from the house of the synagogue leader. They said, "Your daughter is dead. There is no need to bother the teacher anymore."

[36]But Jesus paid no attention to what they said. He told the synagogue leader, "Don't be afraid; just believe."

[37]Jesus let only Peter, James, and John the brother of James go with him. [38]When they came to the house of the synagogue leader,

---

Legion Means very many. A legion was about five thousand men in the Roman army.
Ten Towns In Greek, called "Decapolis." It was an area east of Lake Galilee that once had ten main towns.

Jesus found many people there making lots of noise and crying loudly. [39]Jesus entered the house and said to them, "Why are you crying and making so much noise? The child is not dead, only asleep." [40]But they laughed at him. So, after throwing them out of the house, Jesus took the child's father and mother and his three followers into the room where the child was. [41]Taking hold of the girl's hand, he said to her, "Talitha, koum!" (This means, "Young girl, I tell you to stand up!") [42]At once the girl stood right up and began walking. (She was twelve years old.) Everyone was completely amazed. [43]Jesus gave them strict orders not to tell people about this. Then he told them to give the girl something to eat.

Jesus Goes to His Hometown

6 Jesus left there and went to his hometown, and his followers went with him. [2]On the Sabbath[d] day he taught in the synagogue.[d] Many people heard him and were amazed, saying, "Where did this man get these teachings? What is this wisdom that has been given to him? And where did he get the power to do miracles?[d] [3]He is just the carpenter, the son of Mary and the brother of James, Joseph, Judas, and Simon. And his sisters are here with us." So the people were upset with Jesus.

[4]Jesus said to them, "A prophet[d] is honored everywhere except in his hometown and with his own people and in his own home." [5]So Jesus was not able to work any miracles there except to heal a few sick people by putting his hands on them. [6]He was amazed at how many people had no faith.

Then Jesus went to other villages in that area and taught. [7]He called his twelve followers together and got ready to send them out two by two and gave them authority over evil spirits. [8]This is what Jesus commanded them: "Take nothing for your trip except a walking stick. Take no bread, no bag, and no money in your pockets. [9]Wear sandals, but take only the clothes you are wearing. [10]When you enter a house, stay there until you leave that town. [11]If the people in a cer-

tain place refuse to welcome you or listen to you, leave that place. Shake its dust off your feet[n] as a warning to them."

[12]So the followers went out and preached that people should change their hearts and lives. [13]They forced many demons[d] out and put olive oil on many sick people and healed them.

How John the Baptist Was Killed

[14]King Herod heard about Jesus, because he was now well known. Some people said, "He is John the Baptist,[d] who has risen from the dead. That is why he can work these miracles."[d]

[15]Others said, "He is Elijah."[n]

Other people said, "Jesus is a prophet,[d] like the prophets who lived long ago."

[16]When Herod heard this, he said, "I killed John by cutting off his head. Now he has risen from the dead!"

[17]Herod himself had ordered his soldiers to arrest John and put him in prison in order to please his wife, Herodias. She had been the wife of Philip, Herod's brother, but then Herod had married her. [18]John had been telling Herod, "It is not lawful for you to be married to your brother's wife." [19]So Herodias hated John and wanted to kill him. But she couldn't, [20]because Herod was afraid of John and protected him. He knew John was a good and holy man. Also, though John's preaching always bothered him, he enjoyed listening to John.

[21]Then the perfect time came for Herodias to cause John's death. On Herod's birthday, he gave a dinner party for the most important government leaders, the commanders of his army, and the most important people in Galilee. [22]When the daughter of Herodias came in and danced, she pleased Herod and the people eating with him.

So King Herod said to the girl, "Ask me for anything you want, and I will give it to you." [23]He promised her, "Anything you ask for I will give to you — up to half of my kingdom."

[24]The girl went to her mother and asked, "What should I ask for?"

Shake ... feet A warning. It showed that they were rejecting these people.
Elijah A man who spoke for God and who lived hundreds of years before Christ. See 1 Kings 17.

Her mother answered, "Ask for the head of John the Baptist."*d*

25At once the girl went back to the king and said to him, "I want the head of John the Baptist right now on a platter."

26Although the king was very sad, he had made a promise, and his dinner guests had heard it. So he did not want to refuse what she asked. 27Immediately the king sent a soldier to bring John's head. The soldier went and cut off John's head in the prison 28and brought it back on a platter. He gave it to the girl, and the girl gave it to her mother. 29When John's followers heard this, they came and got John's body and put it in a tomb.

More than Five Thousand Fed

30The apostles*d* gathered around Jesus and told him about all the things they had done and taught. 31Crowds of people were coming and going so that Jesus and his followers did not even have time to eat. He said to them, "Come away by yourselves, and we will go to a lonely place to get some rest."

32So they went in a boat by themselves to a lonely place. 33But many people saw them leave and recognized them. So from all the towns they ran to the place where Jesus was going, and they got there before him. 34When he arrived, he saw a great crowd waiting. He felt sorry for them, because they were like sheep without a shepherd. So he began to teach them many things.

35When it was late in the day, his followers came to him and said, "No one lives in this place, and it is already very late. 36Send the people away so they can go to the countryside and towns around here to buy themselves something to eat."

37But Jesus answered, "You give them something to eat."

They said to him, "We would all have to work a month to earn enough money to buy that much bread!"

38Jesus asked them, "How many loaves of bread do you have? Go and see."

When they found out, they said, "Five loaves and two fish."

39Then Jesus told his followers to have the people sit in groups on the green grass. 40So they sat in groups of fifty or a hundred.

41Jesus took the five loaves and two fish and, looking up to heaven, he thanked God for the food. He divided the bread and gave it to his followers for them to give to the people. Then he divided the two fish among them all. 42All the people ate and were satisfied. 43The followers filled twelve baskets with the leftover pieces of bread and fish. 44There were five thousand men who ate.

Jesus Walks on the Water

45Immediately Jesus told his followers to get into the boat and go ahead of him to Bethsaida across the lake. He stayed there to send the people home. 46After sending them away, he went into the hills to pray.

47That night, the boat was in the middle of the lake, and Jesus was alone on the land. 48He saw his followers struggling hard to row the boat, because the wind was blowing against them. Between three and six o'clock in the morning, Jesus came to them, walking on the water, and he wanted to walk past the boat. 49But when they saw him walking on the water, they thought he was a ghost and cried out. 50They all saw him and were afraid. But quickly Jesus spoke to them and said, "Have courage! It is I. Do not be afraid." 51Then he got into the boat with them, and the wind became calm. The followers were greatly amazed. 52They did not understand about the miracle of the five loaves, because their minds were closed.

53When they had crossed the lake, they came to shore at Gennesaret and tied the boat there. 54When they got out of the boat, people immediately recognized Jesus. 55They ran everywhere in that area and began to bring sick people on mats wherever they heard he was. 56And everywhere he went—into towns, cities, or countryside—the people brought the sick to the marketplaces. They begged him to let them touch just the edge of his coat, and all who touched it were healed.

Obey God's Law

7 When some Pharisees*d* and some teachers of the law came from Jerusalem, they gathered around Jesus. 2They saw that some of Jesus' followers ate food with hands that were not clean,*d* that is, they hadn't washed them. [3](The Pharisees and all the Jews never eat before washing their hands in a special way according to their unwritten laws. [4]And when they buy something in the market, they never eat it until they wash themselves in a special way. They also follow many other unwritten laws, such as the washing of cups, pitchers, and pots.)

[5]The Pharisees and the teachers of the law said to Jesus, "Why don't your followers obey the unwritten laws which have been handed down to us? Why do your followers eat their food with hands that are not clean?"

[6]Jesus answered, "Isaiah was right when he spoke about you hypocrites.[d] He wrote,

'These people show honor to me with words,

but their hearts are far from me.

[7]Their worship of me is worthless.

The things they teach are nothing but human rules.'　　　　　*Isaiah 29:13*

[8]You have stopped following the commands of God, and you follow only human teachings."

[9]Then Jesus said to them, "You cleverly ignore the commands of God so you can follow your own teachings. [10]Moses said, 'Honor your father and your mother,'[n] and 'Anyone who says cruel things to his father or mother must be put to death.'[n] [11]But you say a person can tell his father or mother, 'I have something I could use to help you, but it is Corban — a gift to God.' [12]You no longer let that person use that money for his father or his mother. [13]By your own rules, which you teach people, you are rejecting what God said. And you do many things like that."

[14]After Jesus called the crowd to him again, he said, "Every person should listen to me and understand what I am saying. [15]There is nothing people put into their bodies that makes them unclean. People are made unclean by the things that come out of them." [16][n]

[17]When Jesus left the people and went into the house, his followers asked him about this story. [18]Jesus said, "Do you still not understand? Surely you know that nothing that

enters someone from the outside can make that person unclean. [19]It does not go into the mind, but into the stomach. Then it goes out of the body." (When Jesus said this, he meant that no longer was any food unclean for people to eat.)

[20]And Jesus said, "The things that come out of people are the things that make them unclean. [21]All these evil things begin inside people, in the mind: evil thoughts, sexual sins, stealing, murder, adultery,[d] [22]greed, evil actions, lying, doing sinful things, jealousy, speaking evil of others, pride, and foolish living. [23]All these evil things come from inside and make people unclean."

Jesus Helps a Non-Jewish Woman

[24]Jesus left that place and went to the area around Tyre. When he went into a house, he did not want anyone to know he was there, but he could not stay hidden. [25]A woman whose daughter had an evil spirit in her heard that he was there. So she quickly came to Jesus and fell at his feet. [26]She was Greek, born in Phoenicia, in Syria. She begged Jesus to force the demon[d] out of her daughter.

[27]Jesus told the woman, "It is not right to take the children's bread and give it to the dogs. First let the children eat all they want."

[28]But she answered, "Yes, Lord, but even the dogs under the table can eat the children's crumbs."

[29]Then Jesus said, "Because of your answer, you may go. The demon has left your daughter."

[30]The woman went home and found her daughter lying in bed; the demon was gone.

Jesus Heals a Deaf Man

[31]Then Jesus left the area around Tyre and went through Sidon to Lake Galilee, to the area of the Ten Towns.[n] [32]While he was there, some people brought a man to him who was deaf and could not talk plainly. The people begged Jesus to put his hand on the man to heal him.

[33]Jesus led the man away from the crowd, by himself. He put his fingers in the man's

---

'Honor . . . mother'　Quotation from Exodus 20:12; Deuteronomy 5:16.
'Anyone . . . death.'　Quotation from Exodus 21:17.
Verse 16　Some Greek copies add verse 16: "You people who can hear me, listen!"
Ten Towns　In Greek, called "Decapolis." It was an area east of Lake Galilee that once had ten main towns.

ears and then spit and touched the man's tongue. [34]Looking up to heaven, he sighed and said to the man, "Ephphatha!" (This means, "Be opened.") [35]Instantly the man was able to hear and to use his tongue so that he spoke clearly.

[36]Jesus commanded the people not to tell anyone about what happened. But the more he commanded them, the more they told about it. [37]They were completely amazed and said, "Jesus does everything well. He makes the deaf hear! And those who can't talk he makes able to speak."

More than Four Thousand Fed

8 Another time there was a great crowd with Jesus that had nothing to eat. So Jesus called his followers and said, [2]"I feel sorry for these people, because they have already been with me for three days, and they have nothing to eat. [3]If I send them home hungry, they will faint on the way. Some of them live a long way from here."

[4]Jesus' followers answered, "How can we get enough bread to feed all these people? We are far away from any town."

[5]Jesus asked, "How many loaves of bread do you have?"

They answered, "Seven."

[6]Jesus told the people to sit on the ground. Then he took the seven loaves, gave thanks to God, and divided the bread. He gave the pieces to his followers to give to the people, and they did so. [7]The followers also had a few small fish. After Jesus gave thanks for the fish, he told his followers to give them to the people also. [8]All the people ate and were satisfied. Then his followers filled seven baskets with the leftover pieces of food. [9]There were about four thousand people who ate. After they had eaten, Jesus sent them home. [10]Then right away he got into a boat with his followers and went to the area of Dalmanutha.

The Leaders Ask for a Miracle

[11]The Pharisees[d] came to Jesus and began to ask him questions. Hoping to trap him, they asked Jesus for a miracle[d] from God. [12]Jesus sighed deeply and said, "Why do you people ask for a miracle as a sign? I tell you the truth, no sign will be given to you."

[13]Then Jesus left the Pharisees and went in the boat to the other side of the lake.

Guard Against Wrong Teachings

[14]His followers had only one loaf of bread with them in the boat; they had forgotten to bring more. [15]Jesus warned them, "Be careful! Beware of the yeast of the Pharisees[d] and the yeast of Herod."

[16]His followers discussed the meaning of this, saying, "He said this because we have no bread."

[17]Knowing what they were talking about, Jesus asked them, "Why are you talking about not having bread? Do you still not see or understand? Are your minds closed? [18]You have eyes, but you don't really see. You have ears, but you don't really listen. Remember when [19]I divided five loaves of bread for the five thousand? How many baskets did you fill with leftover pieces of food?"

They answered, "Twelve."

[20]"And when I divided seven loaves of bread for the four thousand, how many baskets did you fill with leftover pieces of food?"

They answered, "Seven."

[21]Then Jesus said to them, "Don't you understand yet?"

Jesus Heals a Blind Man

[22]Jesus and his followers came to Bethsaida. There some people brought a blind man to Jesus and begged him to touch the man. [23]So Jesus took the blind man's hand and led him out of the village. Then he spit on the man's eyes and put his hands on the man and asked, "Can you see now?"

[24]The man looked up and said, "Yes, I see people, but they look like trees walking around."

[25]Again Jesus put his hands on the man's eyes. Then the man opened his eyes wide and they were healed, and he was able to see everything clearly. [26]Jesus told him to go home, saying, "Don't go into the town."

Peter Says Jesus Is the Christ

[27]Jesus and his followers went to the towns around Caesarea Philippi. While they were traveling, Jesus asked them, "Who do people say I am?"

[28]They answered, "Some say you are John

the Baptist.*d* Others say you are Elijah,*n* and others say you are one of the prophets."*d*

29Then Jesus asked, "But who do you say I am?"

Peter answered, "You are the Christ."*d*

30Jesus warned his followers not to tell anyone who he was.

31Then Jesus began to teach them that the Son of Man*d* must suffer many things and that he would be rejected by the older Jewish leaders, the leading priests, and the teachers of the law. He told them that the Son of Man must be killed and then rise from the dead after three days. 32Jesus told them plainly what would happen. Then Peter took Jesus aside and began to tell him not to talk like that. 33But Jesus turned and looked at his followers. Then he told Peter not to talk that way. He said, "Go away from me, Satan!*n* You don't care about the things of God, but only about things people think are important."

34Then Jesus called the crowd to him, along with his followers. He said, "If people want to follow me, they must give up the things they want. They must be willing even to give up their lives to follow me. 35Those who want to save their lives will give up true life. But those who give up their lives for me and for the Good News*d* will have true life. 36It is worth nothing for them to have the whole world if they lose their souls. 37They could never pay enough to buy back their souls. 38The people who live now are living in a sinful and evil time. If people are ashamed of me and my teaching, the Son of Man*d* will be ashamed of them when he comes with his Father's glory and with the holy angels."

9 Then Jesus said to the people, "I tell you the truth, some people standing here will see the kingdom of God come with power before they die."

Jesus Talks with Moses and Elijah

2Six days later, Jesus took Peter, James, and John up on a high mountain by themselves. While they watched, Jesus' appearance was changed. 3His clothes became shining white, whiter than any person could make them. 4Then Elijah and Moses*n* appeared to them, talking with Jesus.

5Peter said to Jesus, "Teacher, it is good that we are here. Let us make three tents — one for you, one for Moses, and one for Elijah." 6Peter did not know what to say, because he and the others were so frightened.

7Then a cloud came and covered them, and a voice came from the cloud, saying, "This is my Son, whom I love. Listen to him!"

8Suddenly Peter, James, and John looked around, but they saw only Jesus there alone with them.

9As they were coming down the mountain, Jesus commanded them not to tell anyone about what they had seen until the Son of Man*d* had risen from the dead.

10So the followers obeyed Jesus, but they discussed what he meant about rising from the dead.

11Then they asked Jesus, "Why do the teachers of the law say that Elijah must come first?"

12Jesus answered, "They are right to say that Elijah must come first and make everything the way it should be. But why does the Scripture*d* say that the Son of Man will suffer much and that people will treat him as if he were nothing? 13I tell you that Elijah has already come. And people did to him whatever they wanted to do, just as the Scriptures said it would happen."

Jesus Heals a Sick Boy

14When Jesus, Peter, James, and John came back to the other followers, they saw a great crowd around them and the teachers of the law arguing with them. 15But as soon as the crowd saw Jesus, the people were surprised and ran to welcome him.

16Jesus asked, "What are you arguing about?"

17A man answered, "Teacher, I brought my son to you. He has an evil spirit in him that stops him from talking. 18When the spirit

---

Elijah　A man who spoke for God and who lived hundreds of years before Christ. See 1 Kings 17.
Satan　Name for the devil meaning "the enemy." Jesus means that Peter was talking like Satan.
Elijah and Moses　Two of the most important Jewish leaders in the past. Moses had given them the law, and Elijah was an important prophet.

attacks him, it throws him on the ground. Then my son foams at the mouth, grinds his teeth, and becomes very stiff. I asked your followers to force the evil spirit out, but they couldn't."

19Jesus answered, "You people have no faith. How long must I stay with you? How long must I put up with you? Bring the boy to me."

20So the followers brought him to Jesus. As soon as the evil spirit saw Jesus, it made the boy lose control of himself, and he fell down and rolled on the ground, foaming at the mouth.

21Jesus asked the boy's father, "How long has this been happening?"

The father answered, "Since he was very young. 22The spirit often throws him into a fire or into water to kill him. If you can do anything for him, please have pity on us and help us."

23Jesus said to the father, "You said, 'If you can!' All things are possible for the one who believes."

24Immediately the father cried out, "I do believe! Help me to believe more!"

25When Jesus saw that a crowd was quickly gathering, he ordered the evil spirit, saying, "You spirit that makes people unable to hear or speak, I command you to come out of this boy and never enter him again!"

26The evil spirit screamed and caused the boy to fall on the ground again. Then the spirit came out. The boy looked as if he were dead, and many people said, "He is dead!" 27But Jesus took hold of the boy's hand and helped him to stand up.

28When Jesus went into the house, his followers began asking him privately, "Why couldn't we force that evil spirit out?"

29Jesus answered, "That kind of spirit can only be forced out by prayer."

Jesus Talks About His Death

30Then Jesus and his followers left that place and went through Galilee. He didn't want anyone to know where he was, 31because he was teaching his followers. He said to them, "The Son of Man*d* will be handed over to people, and they will kill him. After three days, he will rise from the dead." 32But the followers did not understand what Jesus meant, and they were afraid to ask him.

Who Is the Greatest?

33Jesus and his followers went to Capernaum. When they went into a house there, he asked them, "What were you arguing about on the road?" 34But the followers did not answer, because their argument on the road was about which one of them was the greatest.

35Jesus sat down and called the twelve apostles*d* to him. He said, "Whoever wants to be the most important must be last of all and servant of all."

36Then Jesus took a small child and had him stand among them. Taking the child in his arms, he said, 37"Whoever accepts a child like this in my name accepts me. And whoever accepts me accepts the One who sent me."

Anyone Not Against Us Is for Us

38Then John said, "Teacher, we saw someone using your name to force demons*d* out of a person. We told him to stop, because he does not belong to our group."

39But Jesus said, "Don't stop him, because anyone who uses my name to do powerful things will not easily say evil things about me. 40Whoever is not against us is with us. 41I tell you the truth, whoever gives you a drink*d* of water because you belong to the Christ*d* will truly get his reward.

42"If one of these little children believes in me, and someone causes that child to sin, it would be better for that person to have a large stone tied around his neck and be drowned in the sea. 43If your hand causes you to sin, cut it off. It is better for you to lose part of your body and live forever than to have two hands and go to hell, where the fire never goes out. 44 *n* 45If your foot causes you to sin, cut it off. It is better for you to lose part of your body and live forever than to have two feet and be thrown into hell. 46 *n* 47If your eye causes you to sin, take it out. It is

Verse 44 Some Greek copies of Mark add verse 44, which is the same as verse 48.
Verse 46 Some Greek copies of Mark add verse 46, which is the same as verse 48.

better for you to enter the kingdom of God with only one eye than to have two eyes and be thrown into hell. [48]In hell the worm does not die; the fire is never put out. [49]Every person will be salted with fire.

[50]"Salt is good, but if the salt loses its salty taste, you cannot make it salty again. So, be full of salt, and have peace with each other."

Jesus Teaches About Divorce

10 Then Jesus left that place and went into the area of Judea and across the Jordan River. Again, crowds came to him, and he taught them as he usually did.

[2]Some Pharisees[d] came to Jesus and tried to trick him. They asked, "Is it right for a man to divorce his wife?"

[3]Jesus answered, "What did Moses command you to do?"

[4]They said, "Moses allowed a man to write out divorce papers and send her away."[n]

[5]Jesus said, "Moses wrote that command for you because you were stubborn. [6]But when God made the world, 'he made them male and female.'[n] [7]'So a man will leave his father and mother and be united with his wife, [8]and the two will become one body.'[n] So there are not two, but one. [9]God has joined the two together, so no one should separate them."

[10]Later, in the house, his followers asked Jesus again about the question of divorce. [11]He answered, "Anyone who divorces his wife and marries another woman is guilty of adultery[d] against her. [12]And the woman who divorces her husband and marries another man is also guilty of adultery."

Jesus Accepts Children

[13]Some people brought their little children to Jesus so he could touch them, but his followers told them to stop. [14]When Jesus saw this, he was upset and said to them, "Let the little children come to me. Don't stop them, because the kingdom of God belongs to people who are like these children. [15]I tell you the truth, you must accept the kingdom of God as if you were a little child, or you will never enter it." [16]Then Jesus took the children in his arms, put his hands on them, and blessed them.

A Rich Young Man's Question

[17]As Jesus started to leave, a man ran to him and fell on his knees before Jesus. The man asked, "Good teacher, what must I do to have life forever?"

[18]Jesus answered, "Why do you call me good? Only God is good. [19]You know the commands: 'You must not murder anyone. You must not be guilty of adultery.[d] You must not steal. You must not tell lies about your neighbor. You must not cheat. Honor your father and mother.' "[n]

[20]The man said, "Teacher, I have obeyed all these things since I was a boy."

[21]Jesus, looking at the man, loved him and said, "There is one more thing you need to do. Go and sell everything you have, and give the money to the poor, and you will have treasure in heaven. Then come and follow me."

[22]He was very sad to hear Jesus say this, and he left sorrowfully, because he was rich.

[23]Then Jesus looked at his followers and said, "How hard it will be for the rich to enter the kingdom of God!"

[24]The followers were amazed at what Jesus said. But he said again, "My children, it is very hard to enter the kingdom of God! [25]It is easier for a camel to go through the eye of a needle than for a rich person to enter the kingdom of God."

[26]The followers were even more surprised and said to each other, "Then who can be saved?"

[27]Jesus looked at them and said, "This is something people cannot do, but God can. God can do all things."

[28]Peter said to Jesus, "Look, we have left everything and followed you."

[29]Jesus said, "I tell you the truth, all those who have left houses, brothers, sisters, mother, father, children, or farms for me and for the Good News[d] [30]will get more than

---

"Moses . . . away."   Quotation from Deuteronomy 24:1.
'he made . . . female.'   Quotation from Genesis 1:27.
'So . . . body.'   Quotation from Genesis 2:24.
'You . . . mother.'   Quotation from Exodus 20:12-16; Deuteronomy 5:16-20.

they left. Here in this world they will have a hundred times more homes, brothers, sisters, mothers, children, and fields. And with those things, they will also suffer for their belief. But in the age that is coming they will have life forever. [31]Many who have the highest place now will have the lowest place in the future. And many who have the lowest place now will have the highest place in the future."

Jesus Talks About His Death

[32]As Jesus and the people with him were on the road to Jerusalem, he was leading the way. His followers were amazed, but others in the crowd who followed were afraid. Again Jesus took the twelve apostles[d] aside and began to tell them what was about to happen in Jerusalem. [33]He said, "Look, we are going to Jerusalem. The Son of Man[d] will be turned over to the leading priests and the teachers of the law. They will say that he must die, and they will turn him over to the non-Jewish people, [34]who will laugh at him and spit on him. They will beat him with whips and crucify him. But on the third day, he will rise to life again."

Two Followers Ask Jesus a Favor

[35]Then James and John, sons of Zebedee, came to Jesus and said, "Teacher, we want to ask you to do something for us."

[36]Jesus asked, "What do you want me to do for you?"

[37]They answered, "Let one of us sit at your right side and one of us sit at your left side in your glory in your kingdom."

[38]Jesus said, "You don't understand what you are asking. Can you drink the cup that I must drink? And can you be baptized with the same kind of baptism that I must go through?"[n]

[39]They answered, "Yes, we can."

Jesus said to them, "You will drink the same cup that I will drink, and you will be baptized with the same baptism that I must go through. [40]But I cannot choose who will sit at my right or my left; those places belong to those for whom they have been prepared."

[41]When the other ten followers heard this, they began to be angry with James and John.

[42]Jesus called them together and said, "The non-Jewish people have rulers. You know that those rulers love to show their power over the people, and their important leaders love to use all their authority. [43]But it should not be that way among you. Whoever wants to become great among you must serve the rest of you like a servant. [44]Whoever wants to become the first among you must serve all of you like a slave. [45]In the same way, the Son of Man[d] did not come to be served. He came to serve others and to give his life as a ransom for many people."

Jesus Heals a Blind Man

[46]Then they came to the town of Jericho. As Jesus was leaving there with his followers and a great many people, a blind beggar named Bartimaeus son of Timaeus was sitting by the road. [47]When he heard that Jesus from Nazareth was walking by, he began to shout, "Jesus, Son of David,[d] have mercy on me!"

[48]Many people warned the blind man to be quiet, but he shouted even more, "Son of David, have mercy on me!"

[49]Jesus stopped and said, "Tell the man to come here."

So they called the blind man, saying, "Cheer up! Get to your feet. Jesus is calling you." [50]The blind man jumped up, left his coat there, and went to Jesus.

[51]Jesus asked him, "What do you want me to do for you?"

The blind man answered, "Teacher, I want to see."

[52]Jesus said, "Go, you are healed because you believed." At once the man could see, and he followed Jesus on the road.

Jesus Enters Jerusalem as a King

11 As Jesus and his followers were coming closer to Jerusalem, they came to the towns of Bethphage and Bethany near the Mount of Olives.[d] From there Jesus sent two of his followers [2]and said to them, "Go to the town you can see there. When you enter it, you will quickly find a colt tied, which no one has ever ridden. Untie it and

---

Can you ... through? Jesus was asking if they could suffer the same terrible things that would happen to him.

bring it here to me. ³If anyone asks you why you are doing this, tell him its Master needs the colt, and he will send it at once. "

⁴The followers went into the town, found a colt tied in the street near the door of a house, and untied it. ⁵Some people were standing there and asked, "What are you doing? Why are you untying that colt?" ⁶The followers answered the way Jesus told them to answer, and the people let them take the colt.

⁷They brought the colt to Jesus and put their coats on it, and Jesus sat on it. ⁸Many people spread their coats on the road. Others cut branches in the fields and spread them on the road. ⁹The people were walking ahead of Jesus and behind him, shouting,

"Praise[n] God!

God bless the One who comes in the
name of the Lord!   *Psalm 118:26*

¹⁰God bless the kingdom of our father
David!

That kingdom is coming!

Praise to God in heaven!"

¹¹Jesus entered Jerusalem and went into the Temple.[d] After he had looked at everything, since it was already late, he went out to Bethany with the twelve apostles.[d]

¹²The next day as Jesus was leaving Bethany, he became hungry. ¹³Seeing a fig tree in leaf from far away, he went to see if it had any figs on it. But he found no figs, only leaves, because it was not the right season for figs. ¹⁴So Jesus said to the tree, "May no one ever eat fruit from you again." And Jesus' followers heard him say this.

Jesus Goes to the Temple

¹⁵When Jesus returned to Jerusalem, he went into the Temple[d] and began to throw out those who were buying and selling there. He turned over the tables of those who were exchanging different kinds of money, and he upset the benches of those who were selling doves. ¹⁶Jesus refused to allow anyone to carry goods through the Temple courts.

¹⁷Then he taught the people, saying, "It is written in the Scriptures,[d] 'My Temple will be called a house for prayer for people from all nations.'[n] But you are changing God's house into a 'hideout for robbers.' "[n]

¹⁸The leading priests and the teachers of the law heard all this and began trying to find a way to kill Jesus. They were afraid of him, because all the people were amazed at his teaching. ¹⁹That evening, Jesus and his followers left the city.

The Power of Faith

²⁰The next morning as Jesus was passing by with his followers, they saw the fig tree dry and dead, even to the roots. ²¹Peter remembered the tree and said to Jesus, "Teacher, look! The fig tree you cursed is dry and dead!"

²²Jesus answered, "Have faith in God. ²³I tell you the truth, you can say to this mountain, 'Go, fall into the sea.' And if you have no doubts in your mind and believe that what you say will happen, God will do it for you. ²⁴So I tell you to believe that you have received the things you ask for in prayer, and God will give them to you. ²⁵When you are praying, if you are angry with someone, forgive him so that your Father in heaven will also forgive your sins." ²⁶[n]

Leaders Doubt Jesus' Authority

²⁷Jesus and his followers went again to Jerusalem. As Jesus was walking in the Temple,[d] the leading priests, the teachers of the law, and the older leaders came to him. ²⁸They said to him, "What authority do you have to do these things? Who gave you this authority?"

²⁹Jesus answered, "I will ask you one question. If you answer me, I will tell you what authority I have to do these things. ³⁰Tell me: When John baptized people, was that authority from God or just from other people?"

³¹They argued about Jesus' question, say-

Praise Literally, "Hosanna," a Hebrew word used at first in praying to God for help, but at this time it was probably a shout of joy used in praising God or his Messiah.
'My Temple ... nations.' Quotation from Isaiah 56:7.
'hideout for robbers.' Quotation from Jeremiah 7:11.
Verse 26 Some early Greek copies add verse 26: "But if you don't forgive other people, then your Father in heaven will not forgive your sins."

ing, "If we answer, 'John's baptism was from God,' Jesus will say, 'Then why didn't you believe him?' [32]But if we say, 'It was from other people,' the crowd will be against us." (These leaders were afraid of the people, because all the people believed that John was a prophet.[d])

[33]So they answered Jesus, "We don't know."

Jesus said to them, "Then I won't tell you what authority I have to do these things."

A Story About God's Son

12 Jesus began to use stories to teach the people. He said, "A man planted a vineyard. He put a wall around it and dug a hole for a winepress[d] and built a tower. Then he leased the land to some farmers and left for a trip. [2]When it was time for the grapes to be picked, he sent a servant to the farmers to get his share of the grapes. [3]But the farmers grabbed the servant and beat him and sent him away empty-handed. [4]Then the man sent another servant. They hit him on the head and showed no respect for him. [5]So the man sent another servant, whom they killed. The man sent many other servants; the farmers beat some of them and killed others.

[6]"The man had one person left to send, his son whom he loved. He sent him last of all, saying, 'They will respect my son.'

[7]"But the farmers said to each other, 'This son will inherit the vineyard. If we kill him, it will be ours.' [8]So they took the son, killed him, and threw him out of the vineyard.

[9]"So what will the owner of the vineyard do? He will come and kill those farmers and will give the vineyard to other farmers. [10]Surely you have read this Scripture:[d]

'The stone that the builders rejected
    became the cornerstone.[d]
[11]The Lord did this,
    and it is wonderful to us.' "

                      Psalm 118:22-23

[12]The Jewish leaders knew that the story was about him. So they wanted to find a way to arrest Jesus, but they were afraid of the people. So the leaders left him and went away.

Is It Right to Pay Taxes or Not?

[13]Later, the Jewish leaders sent some Pharisees[d] and Herodians[n] to Jesus to trap him in saying something wrong. [14]They came to him and said, "Teacher, we know that you are an honest man. You are not afraid of what other people think about you, because you pay no attention to who they are. And you teach the truth about God's way. Tell us: Is it right to pay taxes to Caesar[d] or not? [15]Should we pay them, or not?"

But knowing what these men were really trying to do, Jesus said to them, "Why are you trying to trap me? Bring me a coin to look at." [16]They gave Jesus a coin, and he asked, "Whose image and name are on the coin?"

They answered, "Caesar's."

[17]Then Jesus said to them, "Give to Caesar the things that are Caesar's, and give to God the things that are God's." The men were amazed at what Jesus said.

Some Sadducees Try to Trick Jesus

[18]Then some Sadducees[d] came to Jesus and asked him a question. (Sadducees believed that people would not rise from the dead.) [19]They said, "Teacher, Moses wrote that if a man's brother dies, leaving a wife but no children, then that man must marry the widow and have children for his brother. [20]Once there were seven brothers. The first brother married and died, leaving no children. [21]So the second brother married the widow, but he also died and had no children. The same thing happened with the third brother. [22]All seven brothers married her and died, and none of the brothers had any children. Finally the woman died too. [23]Since all seven brothers had married her, when people rise from the dead, whose wife will she be?"

[24]Jesus answered, "Why don't you understand? Don't you know what the Scriptures[d] say, and don't you know about the power of God? [25]When people rise from the dead, they will not marry, nor will they be given to someone to marry. They will be like the angels in heaven. [26]Surely you have read what God said about people rising from the dead.

Herodians A political group that followed Herod and his family.

In the book in which Moses wrote about the burning bush, *n* it says that God told Moses, 'I am the God of Abraham, the God of Isaac, and the God of Jacob.' *n* 27God is the God of the living, not the dead. You Sadducees are wrong!"

The Most Important Command

28One of the teachers of the law came and heard Jesus arguing with the Sadducees.*d* Seeing that Jesus gave good answers to their questions, he asked Jesus, "Which of the commands is most important?"

29Jesus answered, "The most important command is this: 'Listen, people of Israel! The Lord our God is the only Lord. 30Love the Lord your God with all your heart, all your soul, all your mind, and all your strength.' *n* 31The second command is this: 'Love your neighbor as you love yourself.' *n* There are no commands more important than these."

32The man answered, "That was a good answer, Teacher. You were right when you said God is the only Lord and there is no other God besides him. 33One must love God with all his heart, all his mind, and all his strength. And one must love his neighbor as he loves himself. These commands are more important than all the animals and sacrifices we offer to God."

34When Jesus saw that the man answered him wisely, Jesus said to him, "You are close to the kingdom of God." And after that, no one was brave enough to ask Jesus any more questions.

35As Jesus was teaching in the Temple,*d* he asked, "Why do the teachers of the law say that the Christ*d* is the son of David? 36David himself, speaking by the Holy Spirit,*d* said:

'The Lord said to my Lord:

Sit by me at my right side,

until I put your enemies under your

control.'   *Psalm 110:1*

37David himself calls the Christ 'Lord,' so how can the Christ be his son?" The large crowd listened to Jesus with pleasure.

38Jesus continued teaching and said, "Beware of the teachers of the law. They like to walk around wearing fancy clothes, and they love for people to greet them with respect in the marketplaces. 39They love to have the most important seats in the synagogues*d* and at feasts. 40But they cheat widows and steal their houses and then try to make themselves look good by saying long prayers. They will receive a greater punishment."

True Giving

41Jesus sat near the Temple*d* money box and watched the people put in their money. Many rich people gave large sums of money. 42Then a poor widow came and put in two small copper coins, which were only worth a few cents.

43Calling his followers to him, Jesus said, "I tell you the truth, this poor widow gave more than all those rich people. 44They gave only what they did not need. This woman is very poor, but she gave all she had; she gave all she had to live on."

The Temple Will Be Destroyed

13 As Jesus was leaving the Temple,*d* one of his followers said to him, "Look, Teacher! How beautiful the buildings are! How big the stones are!"

2Jesus said, "Do you see all these great buildings? Not one stone will be left on another. Every stone will be thrown down to the ground."

3Later, as Jesus was sitting on the Mount of Olives,*d* opposite the Temple, he was alone with Peter, James, John, and Andrew. They asked Jesus, 4"Tell us, when will these things happen? And what will be the sign that they are going to happen?"

5Jesus began to answer them, "Be careful that no one fools you. 6Many people will come in my name, saying, 'I am the One,' and they will fool many people. 7When you hear about wars and stories of wars that are coming, don't be afraid. These things must happen before the end comes. 8Nations will fight against other nations, and kingdoms

---

burning bush   Read Exodus 3:1-12 in the Old Testament.
'I am ... Jacob.'   Quotation from Exodus 3:6.
'Listen ... strength.'   Quotation from Deuteronomy 6:4-5.
'Love ... yourself.'   Quotation from Leviticus 19:18.

against other kingdoms. There will be earthquakes in different places, and there will be times when there is no food for people to eat. These things are like the first pains when something new is about to be born.

[9] "You must be careful. People will arrest you and take you to court and beat you in their synagogues.[d] You will be forced to stand before kings and governors, to tell them about me. This will happen to you because you follow me. [10]But before these things happen, the Good News[d] must be told to all people. [11]When you are arrested and judged, don't worry ahead of time about what you should say. Say whatever is given you to say at that time, because it will not really be you speaking; it will be the Holy Spirit.[d]

[12] "Brothers will give their own brothers to be killed, and fathers will give their own children to be killed. Children will fight against their own parents and cause them to be put to death. [13]All people will hate you because you follow me, but those people who keep their faith until the end will be saved.

[14] "You will see 'the destroying terror'[n] standing where it should not be." (You who read this should understand what it means.) "At that time, the people in Judea should run away to the mountains. [15]If people are on the roofs[n] of their houses, they must not go down or go inside to get anything out of their houses. [16]If people are in the fields, they must not go back to get their coats. [17]At that time, how terrible it will be for women who are pregnant or have nursing babies! [18]Pray that these things will not happen in winter, [19]because those days will be full of trouble. There will be more trouble than there has ever been since the beginning, when God made the world, until now, and nothing as bad will ever happen again. [20]God has decided to make that terrible time short. Otherwise, no one would go on living. But God will make that time short to help the people he has chosen. [21]At that time, someone might say to you, 'Look, there is the Christ!'[d]

Or another person might say, 'There he is!' But don't believe them. [22]False Christs and false prophets[d] will come and perform great wonders and miracles.[d] They will try to fool even the people God has chosen, if that is possible. [23]So be careful. I have warned you about all this before it happens.

[24] "During the days after this trouble comes,

'the sun will grow dark,
  and the moon will not give its light.
[25]The stars will fall from the sky.
  And the powers of the heavens will be
    shaken.'   *Isaiah 13:10; 34:4*

[26] "Then people will see the Son of Man[d] coming in clouds with great power and glory. [27]Then he will send his angels all around the earth to gather his chosen people from every part of the earth and from every part of heaven.

[28] "Learn a lesson from the fig tree: When its branches become green and soft and new leaves appear, you know summer is near. [29]In the same way, when you see these things happening, you will know that the time is near, ready to come. [30]I tell you the truth, all these things will happen while the people of this time are still living. [31]Earth and sky will be destroyed, but the words I have said will never be destroyed.

[32] "No one knows when that day or time will be, not the angels in heaven, not even the Son. Only the Father knows. [33]Be careful! Always be ready, because you don't know when that time will be. [34]It is like a man who goes on a trip. He leaves his house and lets his servants take care of it, giving each one a special job to do. The man tells the servant guarding the door always to be watchful. [35]So always be ready, because you don't know when the owner of the house will come back. It might be in the evening, or at midnight, or in the morning while it is still dark, or when the sun rises. [36]Always be ready. Otherwise he might come back suddenly and find you sleeping. [37]I tell you this, and I say this to everyone: 'Be ready!'"

'the destroying terror'   Mentioned in Daniel 9:27; 12:11 (cf. Daniel 11:31).
roofs   In Bible times houses were built with flat roofs. The roof was used for drying things such as flax and fruit. And it was used as an extra room, as a place for worship, and as a place to sleep in the summer.

The Plan to Kill Jesus

14 It was now only two days before the Passover[d] and the Feast[d] of Unleavened Bread. The leading priests and teachers of the law were trying to find a trick to arrest Jesus and kill him. [2]But they said, "We must not do it during the feast, because the people might cause a riot."

A Woman with Perfume for Jesus

[3]Jesus was in Bethany at the house of Simon, who had a skin disease. While Jesus was eating there, a woman approached him with an alabaster[d] jar filled with very expensive perfume, made of pure nard.[d] She opened the jar and poured the perfume on Jesus' head.

[4]Some who were there became upset and said to each other, "Why waste that perfume? [5]It was worth a full year's work. It could have been sold and the money given to the poor." And they got very angry with the woman.

[6]Jesus said, "Leave her alone. Why are you troubling her? She did an excellent thing for me. [7]You will always have the poor with you, and you can help them anytime you want. But you will not always have me. [8]This woman did the only thing she could do for me; she poured perfume on my body to prepare me for burial. [9]I tell you the truth, wherever the Good News[d] is preached in all the world, what this woman has done will be told, and people will remember her."

Judas Becomes an Enemy of Jesus

[10]One of the twelve apostles, Judas Iscariot, went to talk to the leading priests to offer to hand Jesus over to them. [11]These priests were pleased about this and promised to pay Judas money. So he watched for the best time to turn Jesus in.

Jesus Eats the Passover Meal

[12]It was now the first day of the Feast[d] of Unleavened Bread when the Passover[d] lamb was sacrificed. Jesus' followers said to him, "Where do you want us to go and prepare for you to eat the Passover meal?"

[13]Jesus sent two of his followers and said to them, "Go into the city and a man carrying a jar of water will meet you. Follow him. [14]When he goes into a house, tell the owner of the house, 'The Teacher says: Where is my guest room in which I can eat the Passover meal with my followers?' [15]The owner will show you a large room upstairs that is furnished and ready. Prepare the food for us there."

[16]So the followers left and went into the city. Everything happened as Jesus had said, so they prepared the Passover meal.

[17]In the evening, Jesus went to that house with the twelve. [18]While they were all eating, Jesus said, "I tell you the truth, one of you will turn against me — one of you eating with me now."

[19]The followers were very sad to hear this. Each one began to say to Jesus, "I am not the one, am I?"

[20]Jesus answered, "It is one of the twelve — the one who dips his bread into the bowl with me. [21]The Son of Man[d] will die, just as the Scriptures[d] say. But how terrible it will be for the person who hands the Son of Man over to be killed. It would be better for him if he had never been born."

The Lord's Supper

[22]While they were eating, Jesus took some bread and thanked God for it and broke it. Then he gave it to his followers and said, "Take it; this is my body."

[23]Then Jesus took a cup and thanked God for it and gave it to the followers, and they all drank from the cup.

[24]Then Jesus said, "This is my blood which is the new agreement that God makes with his people. This blood is poured out for many. [25]I tell you the truth, I will not drink of this fruit of the vine[n] again until that day when I drink it new in the kingdom of God."

[26]After singing a hymn, they went out to the Mount of Olives.[d]

Jesus' Followers Will Leave Him

[27]Then Jesus told the followers, "You will all stumble in your faith, because it is written in the Scriptures:[d]

fruit of the vine   Product of the grapevine; this may also be translated "wine."

'I will kill the shepherd,
and the sheep will scatter.'   *Zechariah 13:7*
28But after I rise from the dead, I will go ahead of you into Galilee."

29Peter said, "Everyone else may stumble in their faith, but I will not."

30Jesus answered, "I tell you the truth, to-night before the rooster crows twice you will say three times you don't know me."

31But Peter insisted, "I will never say that I don't know you! I will even die with you!" And all the other followers said the same thing.

Jesus Prays Alone

32Jesus and his followers went to a place called Gethsemane. He said to them, "Sit here while I pray." 33Jesus took Peter, James, and John with him, and he began to be very sad and troubled. 34He said to them, "My heart is full of sorrow, to the point of death. Stay here and watch."

35After walking a little farther away from them, Jesus fell to the ground and prayed that, if possible, he would not have this time of suffering. 36He prayed, "Abba,*n* Father! You can do all things. Take away this cup*n* of suffering. But do what you want, not what I want."

37Then Jesus went back to his followers and found them asleep. He said to Peter, "Simon, are you sleeping? Couldn't you stay awake with me for one hour? 38Stay awake and pray for strength against temptation. The spirit wants to do what is right, but the body is weak."

39Again Jesus went away and prayed the same thing. 40Then he went back to his followers, and again he found them asleep, because their eyes were very heavy. And they did not know what to say to him.

41After Jesus prayed a third time, he went back to his followers and said to them, "Are you still sleeping and resting? That's enough. The time has come for the Son of Man*d* to be handed over to sinful people. 42Get up, we must go. Look, here comes the man who has turned against me."

Jesus Is Arrested

43At once, while Jesus was still speaking, Judas, one of the twelve apostles,*d* came up. With him were many people carrying swords and clubs who had been sent from the leading priests, the teachers of the law, and the older Jewish leaders.

44Judas had planned a signal for them, saying, "The man I kiss is Jesus. Arrest him and guard him while you lead him away." 45So Judas went straight to Jesus and said, "Teacher!" and kissed him. 46Then the people grabbed Jesus and arrested him. 47One of his followers standing nearby pulled out his sword and struck the servant of the high priest and cut off his ear.

48Then Jesus said, "You came to get me with swords and clubs as if I were a criminal. 49Every day I was with you teaching in the Temple,*d* and you did not arrest me there. But all these things have happened to make the Scriptures*d* come true." 50Then all of Jesus' followers left him and ran away.

51A young man, wearing only a linen cloth, was following Jesus, and the people also grabbed him. 52But the cloth he was wearing came off, and he ran away naked.

Jesus Before the Leaders

53The people who arrested Jesus led him to the house of the high priest, where all the leading priests, the older Jewish leaders, and the teachers of the law were gathered. 54Peter followed far behind and entered the courtyard of the high priest's house. There he sat with the guards, warming himself by the fire.

55The leading priests and the whole Jewish council tried to find something that Jesus had done wrong so they could kill him. But the council could find no proof of anything. 56Many people came and told false things about him, but all said different things — none of them agreed.

57Then some people stood up and lied about Jesus, saying, 58"We heard this man say, 'I will destroy this Temple*d* that people made. And three days later, I will build an-

Abba   Name that a child called his father.
cup   Jesus is talking about the terrible things that will happen to him. Accepting these things will be very hard, like drinking a cup of something bitter.

other Temple not made by people.' " ⁵⁹But even the things these people said did not agree.

⁶⁰Then the high priest stood before them and asked Jesus, "Aren't you going to answer? Don't you have something to say about their charges against you?" ⁶¹But Jesus said nothing; he did not answer.

The high priest asked Jesus another question: "Are you the Christ,*d* the Son of the blessed God?"

⁶²Jesus answered, "I am. And in the future you will see the Son of Man*d* sitting at the right hand of God, the Powerful One, and coming on clouds in the sky."

⁶³When the high priest heard this, he tore his clothes and said, "We don't need any more witnesses! ⁶⁴You all heard him say these things against God. What do you think?"

They all said that Jesus was guilty and should die. ⁶⁵Some of the people there began to spit at Jesus. They blindfolded him and beat him with their fists and said, "Prove you are a prophet!"*d* Then the guards led Jesus away and beat him.

Peter Says He Doesn't Know Jesus

⁶⁶While Peter was in the courtyard, a servant girl of the high priest came there. ⁶⁷She saw Peter warming himself at the fire and looked closely at him.

Then she said, "You also were with Jesus, that man from Nazareth."

⁶⁸But Peter said that he was never with Jesus. He said, "I don't know or understand what you are talking about." Then Peter left and went toward the entrance of the courtyard. And the rooster crowed.*n*

⁶⁹The servant girl saw Peter there, and again she said to the people who were standing nearby, "This man is one of those who followed Jesus." ⁷⁰Again Peter said that it was not true.

A short time later, some people were standing near Peter saying, "Surely you are one of those who followed Jesus, because you are from Galilee, too."

⁷¹Then Peter began to place a curse on himself and swear, "I don't know this man you're talking about!"

⁷²At once, the rooster crowed the second time. Then Peter remembered what Jesus had told him: "Before the rooster crows twice, you will say three times that you don't know me." Then Peter lost control of himself and began to cry.

Pilate Questions Jesus

15 Very early in the morning, the leading priests, the older leaders, the teachers of the law, and all the Jewish council decided what to do with Jesus. They tied him, led him away, and turned him over to Pilate, the governor.

²Pilate asked Jesus, "Are you the king of the Jews?"

Jesus answered, "Those are your words."

³The leading priests accused Jesus of many things. ⁴So Pilate asked Jesus another question, "You can see that they are accusing you of many things. Aren't you going to answer?"

⁵But Jesus still said nothing, so Pilate was very surprised.

Pilate Tries to Free Jesus

⁶Every year at the time of the Passover*d* the governor would free one prisoner whom the people chose. ⁷At that time, there was a man named Barabbas in prison who was a rebel and had committed murder during a riot. ⁸The crowd came to Pilate and began to ask him to free a prisoner as he always did.

⁹So Pilate asked them, "Do you want me to free the king of the Jews?" ¹⁰Pilate knew that the leading priests had turned Jesus in to him because they were jealous. ¹¹But the leading priests had persuaded the people to ask Pilate to free Barabbas, not Jesus.

¹²Then Pilate asked the crowd again, "So what should I do with this man you call the king of the Jews?"

¹³They shouted, "Crucify him!"

¹⁴Pilate asked, "Why? What wrong has he done?"

But they shouted even louder, "Crucify him!"

¹⁵Pilate wanted to please the crowd, so he freed Barabbas for them. After having Jesus

---

And ... crowed. A few, early Greek copies leave out this phrase.

beaten with whips, he handed Jesus over to the soldiers to be crucified.

16The soldiers took Jesus into the governor's palace (called the Praetorium) and called all the other soldiers together. 17They put a purple robe on Jesus and used thorny branches to make a crown for his head. 18They began to call out to him, "Hail, King of the Jews!" 19The soldiers beat Jesus on the head many times with a stick. They spit on him and made fun of him by bowing on their knees and worshiping him. 20After they finished, the soldiers took off the purple robe and put his own clothes on him again. Then they led him out of the palace to be crucified.

Jesus Is Crucified

21A man named Simon from Cyrene, the father of Alexander and Rufus, was coming from the fields to the city. The soldiers forced Simon to carry the cross for Jesus. 22They led Jesus to the place called Golgotha, which means the Place of the Skull. 23The soldiers tried to give Jesus wine mixed with myrrh*d* to drink, but he refused. 24The soldiers crucified Jesus and divided his clothes among themselves, throwing lots*d* to decide what each soldier would get.

25It was nine o'clock in the morning when they crucified Jesus. 26There was a sign with this charge against Jesus written on it: THE KING OF THE JEWS. 27They also put two robbers on crosses beside Jesus, one on the right, and the other on the left. 28 *n* 29People walked by and insulted Jesus and shook their heads, saying, "You said you could destroy the Temple*d* and build it again in three days. 30So save yourself! Come down from that cross!"

31The leading priests and the teachers of the law were also making fun of Jesus. They said to each other, "He saved other people, but he can't save himself. 32If he is really the Christ,*d* the king of Israel, let him come down now from the cross. When we see this, we will believe in him." The robbers who were being crucified beside Jesus also insulted him.

Jesus Dies

33At noon the whole country became dark, and the darkness lasted for three hours. 34At three o'clock Jesus cried in a loud voice, "Eloi, Eloi, lama sabachthani." This means, "My God, my God, why have you rejected me?"

35When some of the people standing there heard this, they said, "Listen! He is calling Elijah."

36Someone there ran and got a sponge, filled it with vinegar, tied it to a stick, and gave it to Jesus to drink. He said, "We want to see if Elijah will come to take him down from the cross."

37Then Jesus cried in a loud voice and died.

38The curtain in the Temple*n* was torn into two pieces, from the top to the bottom. 39When the army officer who was standing in front of the cross saw what happened when Jesus died, he said, "This man really was the Son of God!"

40Some women were standing at a distance from the cross, watching; among them were Mary Magdalene, Salome, and Mary the mother of James and Joseph. (James was her youngest son.) 41These women had followed Jesus in Galilee and helped him. Many other women were also there who had come with Jesus to Jerusalem.

Jesus Is Buried

42This was Preparation*d* Day. (That means the day before the Sabbath*d* day.) That evening, 43Joseph from Arimathea was brave enough to go to Pilate and ask for Jesus' body. Joseph, an important member of the Jewish council, was one of the people who was waiting for the kingdom of God to come. 44Pilate was amazed that Jesus would have already died, so he called the army officer who had guarded Jesus and asked him if Jesus had already died. 45The officer told Pilate that he was dead, so Pilate told Joseph he could have the body. 46Joseph bought some linen cloth, took the body down from the cross, and wrapped it in the linen. He put the

---

Verse 28 Some Greek copies add verse 28: "And the Scripture came true that says, 'They put him with criminals.'"
curtain in the Temple A curtain divided the Most Holy Place from the other part of the Temple. That was the special building in Jerusalem where God commanded the Jewish people to worship him.

body in a tomb that was cut out of a wall of rock. Then he rolled a very large stone to block the entrance of the tomb. ⁴⁷And Mary Magdalene and Mary the mother of Joseph saw the place where Jesus was laid.

Jesus Rises from the Dead

16 The day after the Sabbath*ᵈ* day, Mary Magdalene, Mary the mother of James, and Salome bought some sweet-smelling spices to put on Jesus' body. ²Very early on that day, the first day of the week, soon after sunrise, the women were on their way to the tomb. ³They said to each other, "Who will roll away for us the stone that covers the entrance of the tomb?"

⁴Then the women looked and saw that the stone had already been rolled away, even though it was very large. ⁵The women entered the tomb and saw a young man wearing a white robe and sitting on the right side, and they were afraid.

⁶But the man said, "Don't be afraid. You are looking for Jesus from Nazareth, who has been crucified. He has risen from the dead; he is not here. Look, here is the place they laid him. ⁷Now go and tell his followers and Peter, 'Jesus is going into Galilee ahead of you, and you will see him there as he told you before.' "

⁸The women were confused and shaking with fear, so they left the tomb and ran away. They did not tell anyone about what happened, because they were afraid.

Verses 9-20 are not included in two of the best and oldest Greek manuscripts of Mark.

Some Followers See Jesus

[⁹After Jesus rose from the dead early on the first day of the week, he showed himself first to Mary Magdalene. One time in the past, he had forced seven demons*ᵈ* out of her. ¹⁰After Mary saw Jesus, she went and told his followers, who were very sad and were crying. ¹¹But Mary told them that Jesus was alive. She said that she had seen him, but the followers did not believe her.

¹²Later, Jesus showed himself to two of his followers while they were walking in the country, but he did not look the same as before. ¹³These followers went back to the others and told them what had happened, but again, the followers did not believe them.

Jesus Talks to the Apostles

¹⁴Later Jesus showed himself to the eleven apostles while they were eating, and he criticized them because they had no faith. They were stubborn and refused to believe those who had seen him after he had risen from the dead.

¹⁵Jesus said to his followers, "Go everywhere in the world, and tell the Good News*ᵈ* to everyone. ¹⁶Anyone who believes and is baptized will be saved, but anyone who does not believe will be punished. ¹⁷And those who believe will be able to do these things as proof: They will use my name to force out demons.*ᵈ* They will speak in new languages.*ⁿ* ¹⁸They will pick up snakes and drink poison without being hurt. They will touch the sick, and the sick will be healed."

¹⁹After the Lord Jesus said these things to his followers, he was carried up into heaven, and he sat at the right side of God. ²⁰The followers went everywhere in the world and told the Good News to people, and the Lord helped them. The Lord proved that the Good News they told was true by giving them power to work miracles.*ᵈ*]

languages   This can also be translated "tongues."

LUKE

Luke Tells the Non-Jewish People About Jesus

Luke Writes About Jesus' Life

1 Many have tried to report on the things that happened among us. [2]They have written the same things that we learned from others—the people who saw those things from the beginning and served God by telling people his message. [3]Since I myself have studied everything carefully from the beginning, most excellent[n] Theophilus, it seemed good for me to write it out for you. I arranged it in order [4]to help you know that what you have been taught is true.

Zechariah and Elizabeth

[5]During the time Herod ruled Judea, there was a priest named Zechariah who belonged to Abijah's group.[n] Zechariah's wife, Elizabeth, came from the family of Aaron. [6]Zechariah and Elizabeth truly did what God said was good. They did everything the Lord commanded and were without fault in keeping his law. [7]But they had no children, because Elizabeth could not have a baby, and both of them were very old.

[8]One day Zechariah was serving as a priest before God, because his group was on duty. [9]According to the custom of the priests, he was chosen by lot[d] to go into the Temple of the Lord and burn incense.[d] [10]There were a great many people outside praying at the time the incense was offered. [11]Then an angel of the Lord appeared to Zechariah, standing on the right side of the incense table. [12]When he saw the angel, Zechariah was startled and frightened. [13]But the angel said to him, "Zechariah, don't be afraid. God has heard your prayer. Your wife, Elizabeth, will give birth to a son, and you will name him John. [14]He will bring you joy and gladness, and many people will be happy because of his birth. [15]John will be a great man for the Lord.

He will never drink wine or beer, and even from birth, he will be filled with the Holy Spirit.[d] [16]He will help many people of Israel return to the Lord their God. [17]He will go before the Lord in spirit and power like Elijah. He will make peace between parents and their children and will bring those who are not obeying God back to the right way of thinking, to make a people ready for the coming of the Lord."

[18]Zechariah said to the angel, "How can I know that what you say is true? I am an old man, and my wife is old, too."

[19]The angel answered him, "I am Gabriel. I stand before God, who sent me to talk to you and to tell you this good news. [20]Now, listen! You will not be able to speak until the day these things happen, because you did not believe what I told you. But they will really happen."

[21]Outside, the people were still waiting for Zechariah and were surprised that he was staying so long in the Temple. [22]When Zechariah came outside, he could not speak to them, and they knew he had seen a vision in the Temple. He could only make signs to them and remained unable to speak. [23]When his time of service at the Temple was finished, he went home.

[24]Later, Zechariah's wife, Elizabeth, became pregnant and did not go out of her house for five months. Elizabeth said, [25]"Look what the Lord has done for me! My people were ashamed[n] of me, but now the Lord has taken away that shame."

An Angel Appears to Mary

[26]During Elizabeth's sixth month of pregnancy, God sent the angel Gabriel to Nazareth, a town in Galilee, [27]to a virgin.[d] She was engaged to marry a man named Joseph

---

excellent This word was used to show respect to an important person like a king or ruler.
Abijah's group The Jewish priests were divided into twenty-four groups. See 1 Chronicles 24.
ashamed The Jewish people thought it was a disgrace for women not to have children.

from the family of David. Her name was Mary. ²⁸The angel came to her and said, "Greetings! The Lord has blessed you and is with you."

²⁹But Mary was very startled by what the angel said and wondered what this greeting might mean.

³⁰The angel said to her, "Don't be afraid, Mary; God has shown you his grace. ³¹Listen! You will become pregnant and give birth to a son, and you will name him Jesus. ³²He will be great and will be called the Son of the Most High. The Lord God will give him the throne of King David, his ancestor. ³³He will rule over the people of Jacob forever, and his kingdom will never end."

³⁴Mary said to the angel, "How will this happen since I am a virgin?"

³⁵The angel said to Mary, "The Holy Spirit*d* will come upon you, and the power of the Most High will cover you. For this reason the baby will be holy and will be called the Son of God. ³⁶Now Elizabeth, your relative, is also pregnant with a son though she is very old. Everyone thought she could not have a baby, but she has been pregnant for six months. ³⁷God can do anything!"

³⁸Mary said, "I am the servant of the Lord. Let this happen to me as you say!" Then the angel went away.

Mary Visits Elizabeth

³⁹Mary got up and went quickly to a town in the hills of Judea. ⁴⁰She came to Zechariah's house and greeted Elizabeth. ⁴¹When Elizabeth heard Mary's greeting, the unborn baby inside her jumped, and Elizabeth was filled with the Holy Spirit.*d* ⁴²She cried out in a loud voice, "God has blessed you more than any other woman, and he has blessed the baby to which you will give birth. ⁴³Why has this good thing happened to me, that the mother of my Lord comes to me? ⁴⁴When I heard your voice, the baby inside me jumped with joy. ⁴⁵You are blessed because you believed that what the Lord said to you would really happen."

Mary Praises God

⁴⁶Then Mary said,
"My soul praises the Lord;
⁴⁷ my heart rejoices in God my Savior,

⁴⁸because he has shown his concern for
    his humble servant girl.
From now on, all people will say that I
    am blessed,
⁴⁹ because the Powerful One has done
    great things for me.
His name is holy.
⁵⁰God will show his mercy forever and
    ever
to those who worship and serve him.
⁵¹He has done mighty deeds by his power.
He has scattered the people who are
    proud
and think great things about
    themselves.
⁵²He has brought down rulers from their
    thrones
and raised up the humble.
⁵³He has filled the hungry with good
    things
and sent the rich away with nothing.
⁵⁴He has helped his servant, the people of
    Israel,
remembering to show them mercy
⁵⁵as he promised to our ancestors,
    to Abraham and to his children
    forever."

⁵⁶Mary stayed with Elizabeth for about three months and then returned home.

The Birth of John

⁵⁷When it was time for Elizabeth to give birth, she had a boy. ⁵⁸Her neighbors and relatives heard how good the Lord was to her, and they rejoiced with her.

⁵⁹When the baby was eight days old, they came to circumcise*d* him. They wanted to name him Zechariah because this was his father's name, ⁶⁰but his mother said, "No! He will be named John."

⁶¹The people said to Elizabeth, "But no one in your family has this name." ⁶²Then they made signs to his father to find out what he would like to name him.

⁶³Zechariah asked for a writing tablet and wrote, "His name is John," and everyone was surprised. ⁶⁴Immediately Zechariah could talk again, and he began praising God. ⁶⁵All their neighbors became alarmed, and in all the mountains of Judea people continued talking about all these things. ⁶⁶The people who heard about them wondered, saying,

"What will this child be?" because the Lord was with him.

Zechariah Praises God

67Then Zechariah, John's father, was filled with the Holy Spirit and prophesied:*d*
68"Let us praise the Lord, the God of
   Israel,
   because he has come to help his
      people and has given them
      freedom.
69He has given us a powerful Savior
   from the family of God's servant David.
70He said that he would do this
   through his holy prophets*d* who lived
      long ago:
71He promised he would save us from our
      enemies
   and from the power of all those who
      hate us.
72He said he would give mercy to our
      fathers
   and that he would remember his holy
      promise.
73God promised Abraham, our father,
74   that he would save us from the power
      of our enemies
   so we could serve him without fear,
75being holy and good before God as long
      as we live.

76"Now you, child, will be called a
      prophet of the Most High God.
   ' You will go before the Lord to prepare
      his way.
77You will make his people know that they
      will be saved
   by having their sins forgiven.
78With the loving mercy of our God,
   a new day from heaven will dawn
      upon us.
79It will shine on those who live in
      darkness,
   in the shadow of death.
   It will guide us into the path of peace."

80And so the child grew up and became strong in spirit. John lived in the desert until the time when he came out to preach to Israel.

The Birth of Jesus

2 At that time, Augustus Caesar*d* sent an order that all people in the countries under Roman rule must list their names in a register. 2This was the first registration; *n* it was taken while Quirinius was governor of Syria. 3And all went to their own towns to be registered.

4So Joseph left Nazareth, a town in Galilee, and went to the town of Bethlehem in Judea, known as the town of David. Joseph went there because he was from the family of David. 5Joseph registered with Mary, to whom he was engaged*n* and who was now pregnant. 6While they were in Bethlehem, the time came for Mary to have the baby, 7and she gave birth to her first son. Because there were no rooms left in the inn, she wrapped the baby with pieces of cloth and laid him in a box where animals are fed.

Shepherds Hear About Jesus

8That night, some shepherds were in the fields nearby watching their sheep. 9Then an angel of the Lord stood before them. The glory of the Lord was shining around them, and they became very frightened. 10The angel said to them, "Do not be afraid. I am bringing you good news that will be a great joy to all the people. 11Today your Savior was born in the town of David. He is Christ,*d* the Lord. 12This is how you will know him: You will find a baby wrapped in pieces of cloth and lying in a feeding box."

13Then a very large group of angels from heaven joined the first angel, praising God and saying:
14"Give glory to God in heaven,
   and on earth let there be peace among
      the people who please God."

15When the angels left them and went back to heaven, the shepherds said to each other, "Let's go to Bethlehem. Let's see this thing that has happened which the Lord has told us about."

16So the shepherds went quickly and found Mary and Joseph and the baby, who was lying in a feeding box. 17When they had seen him, they told what the angels had said

---

registration Census. A counting of all the people and the things they own.
engaged For the Jewish people, an engagement was a lasting agreement. It could only be broken by divorce.

about this child. [18]Everyone was amazed at what the shepherds said to them. [19]But Mary treasured these things and continued to think about them. [20]Then the shepherds went back to their sheep, praising God and thanking him for everything they had seen and heard. It had been just as the angel had told them.

[21]When the baby was eight days old, he was circumcised[d] and was named Jesus, the name given by the angel before the baby began to grow inside Mary.

Jesus Is Presented in the Temple

[22]When the time came for Mary and Joseph to do what the law of Moses taught about being made pure,[n] they took Jesus to Jerusalem to present him to the Lord. [23](It is written in the law of the Lord: "Every firstborn[d] male shall be given to the Lord.")[n] [24]Mary and Joseph also went to offer a sacrifice, as the law of the Lord says: "You must sacrifice two doves or two young pigeons."[n]

Simeon Sees Jesus

[25]In Jerusalem lived a man named Simeon who was a good man and godly. He was waiting for the time when God would take away Israel's sorrow, and the Holy Spirit[d] was in him. [26]Simeon had been told by the Holy Spirit that he would not die before he saw the Christ[d] promised by the Lord. [27]The Spirit led Simeon to the Temple.[d] When Mary and Joseph brought the baby Jesus to the Temple to do what the law said they must do, [28]Simeon took the baby in his arms and thanked God:

[29]"Now, Lord, you can let me, your
        servant,
    die in peace as you said.
[30]With my own eyes I have seen your
        salvation,
[31] which you prepared before all people.
[32]It is a light for the non-Jewish people to
        see
    and an honor for your people, the
        Israelites."

[33]Jesus' father and mother were amazed at what Simeon had said about him. [34]Then Simeon blessed them and said to Mary, "God has chosen this child to cause the fall and rise of many in Israel. He will be a sign from God that many people will not accept [35]so that the thoughts of many will be made known. And the things that will happen will make your heart sad, too."

Anna Sees Jesus

[36]There was a prophetess,[d] Anna, from the family of Phanuel in the tribe[d] of Asher. Anna was very old. She had once been married for seven years. [37]Then her husband died, and she was a widow for eighty-four years. Anna never left the Temple but worshiped God, going without food and praying day and night. [38]Standing there at that time, she thanked God and spoke about Jesus to all who were waiting for God to free Jerusalem.

Joseph and Mary Return Home

[39]When Joseph and Mary had done everything the law of the Lord commanded, they went home to Nazareth, their own town in Galilee. [40]The little child grew and became strong. He was filled with wisdom, and God's goodness was upon him.

Jesus As a Boy

[41]Every year Jesus' parents went to Jerusalem for the Passover[d] Feast. [42]When he was twelve years old, they went to the feast as they always did. [43]After the feast days were over, they started home. The boy Jesus stayed behind in Jerusalem, but his parents did not know it. [44]Thinking that Jesus was with them in the group, they traveled for a whole day. Then they began to look for him among their family and friends. [45]When they did not find him, they went back to Jerusalem to look for him there. [46]After three days they found Jesus sitting in the Temple[d] with the teachers, listening to them and asking them questions. [47]All who heard him were amazed at his understanding and answers. [48]When Jesus' parents saw him, they were astonished. His mother said to him, "Son,

---

pure The law of Moses said that forty days after a Jewish woman gave birth to a son, she must be cleansed by a ceremony at the Temple. Read Leviticus 12:2-8.
"Every ... Lord" Quotation from Exodus 13:2.
"You ... pigeons." Quotation from Leviticus 12:8.

why did you do this to us? Your father and I were very worried about you and have been looking for you."

49Jesus said to them, "Why were you looking for me? Didn't you know that I must be in my Father's house?" 50But they did not understand the meaning of what he said.

51Jesus went with them to Nazareth and was obedient to them. But his mother kept in her mind all that had happened. 52Jesus became wiser and grew physically. People liked him, and he pleased God.

The Preaching of John

3 It was the fifteenth year of the rule of Tiberius Caesar.d These men were under Caesar: Pontius Pilate, the ruler of Judea; Herod, the ruler of Galilee; Philip, Herod's brother, the ruler of Iturea and Trachonitis; and Lysanias, the ruler of Abilene. 2Annas and Caiaphas were the high priests. At this time, the word of God came to John son of Zechariah in the desert. 3He went all over the area around the Jordan River preaching a baptism of changed hearts and lives for the forgiveness of sins. 4As it is written in the book of Isaiah the prophet:d

"This is a voice of one
    who calls out in the desert:
'Prepare the way for the Lord.
    Make the road straight for him.
5Every valley should be filled in,
    and every mountain and hill should be
        made flat.
Roads with turns should be made
        straight,
    and rough roads should be made
        smooth.
6And all people will know about the
        salvation of God!' "   Isaiah 40:3-5

7To the crowds of people who came to be baptized by John, he said, "You are all snakes! Who warned you to run away from God's coming punishment? 8Do the things that show you really have changed your hearts and lives. Don't begin to say to yourselves, 'Abraham is our father.' I tell you that God could make children for Abraham from

these rocks. 9The ax is now ready to cut down the trees, and every tree that does not produce good fruit will be cut down and thrown into the fire." n

10The people asked John, "Then what should we do?"

11John answered, "If you have two shirts, share with the person who does not have one. If you have food, share that also."

12Even tax collectors came to John to be baptized. They said to him, "Teacher, what should we do?"

13John said to them, "Don't take more taxes from people than you have been ordered to take."

14The soldiers asked John, "What about us? What should we do?"

John said to them, "Don't force people to give you money, and don't lie about them. Be satisfied with the pay you get."

15Since the people were hoping for the Christd to come, they wondered if John might be the one.

16John answered everyone, "I baptize you with water, but there is one coming who is greater than I am. I am not good enough to untie his sandals. He will baptize you with the Holy Spiritd and fire. 17He will come ready to clean the grain, separating the good grain from the chaff.d He will put the good part of the grain into his barn, but he will burn the chaff with a fire that cannot be put out." n 18And John continued to preach the Good News,d saying many other things to encourage the people.

19But John spoke against Herod, the governor, because of his sin with Herodias, the wife of Herod's brother, and because of the many other evil things Herod did. 20So Herod did something even worse: He put John in prison.

Jesus Is Baptized by John

21When all the people were being baptized by John, Jesus also was baptized. While Jesus was praying, heaven opened 22and the Holy Spiritd came down on him in the form of a dove. Then a voice came from heaven, say-

---

The ax . . . fire. This means that God is ready to punish his people who do not obey him.
He will . . . out. This means that Jesus will come to separate good people from bad people, saving the good and punishing the bad.

ing, "You are my Son, whom I love, and I am very pleased with you."

The Family History of Jesus

[23]When Jesus began his ministry, he was about thirty years old. People thought that Jesus was Joseph's son.

Joseph was the son[n] of Heli.
[24]Heli was the son of Matthat.
Matthat was the son of Levi.
Levi was the son of Melki.
Melki was the son of Jannai.
Jannai was the son of Joseph.
[25]Joseph was the son of Mattathias.
Mattathias was the son of Amos.
Amos was the son of Nahum.
Nahum was the son of Esli.
Esli was the son of Naggai.
[26]Naggai was the son of Maath.
Maath was the son of Mattathias.
Mattathias was the son of Semein.
Semein was the son of Josech.
Josech was the son of Joda.
[27]Joda was the son of Joanan.
Joanan was the son of Rhesa.
Rhesa was the son of Zerubbabel.
Zerubbabel was the grandson of Shealtiel.
Shealtiel was the son of Neri.
[28]Neri was the son of Melchi.
Melchi was the son of Addi.
Addi was the son of Cosam.
Cosam was the son of Elmadam.
Elmadam was the son of Er.
[29]Er was the son of Joshua.
Joshua was the son of Eliezer.
Eliezer was the son of Jorim.
Jorim was the son of Matthat.
Matthat was the son of Levi.
[30]Levi was the son of Simeon.
Simeon was the son of Judah.
Judah was the son of Joseph.
Joseph was the son of Jonam.
Jonam was the son of Eliakim.
[31]Eliakim was the son of Melea.
Melea was the son of Menna.
Menna was the son of Mattatha.
Mattatha was the son of Nathan.
Nathan was the son of David.
[32]David was the son of Jesse.

Jesse was the son of Obed.
Obed was the son of Boaz.
Boaz was the son of Salmon.
Salmon was the son of Nahshon.
[33]Nahshon was the son of Amminadab.
Amminadab was the son of Admin.
Admin was the son of Arni.
Arni was the son of Hezron.
Hezron was the son of Perez.
Perez was the son of Judah.
[34]Judah was the son of Jacob.
Jacob was the son of Isaac.
Isaac was the son of Abraham.
Abraham was the son of Terah.
Terah was the son of Nahor.
[35]Nahor was the son of Serug.
Serug was the son of Reu.
Reu was the son of Peleg.
Peleg was the son of Eber.
Eber was the son of Shelah.
[36]Shelah was the son of Cainan.
Cainan was the son of Arphaxad.
Arphaxad was the son of Shem.
Shem was the son of Noah.
Noah was the son of Lamech.
[37]Lamech was the son of Methuselah.
Methuselah was the son of Enoch.
Enoch was the son of Jared.
Jared was the son of Mahalalel.
Mahalalel was the son of Kenan.
[38]Kenan was the son of Enosh.
Enosh was the son of Seth.
Seth was the son of Adam.
Adam was the son of God.

Jesus Is Tempted by the Devil

4 Jesus, filled with the Holy Spirit,[d] returned from the Jordan River. The Spirit led Jesus into the desert [2]where the devil tempted Jesus for forty days. Jesus ate nothing during that time, and when those days were ended, he was very hungry.

[3]The devil said to Jesus, "If you are the Son of God, tell this rock to become bread."

[4]Jesus answered, "It is written in the Scriptures:[d] 'A person does not live by eating only bread.' "[n]

[5]Then the devil took Jesus and showed him all the kingdoms of the world in an in-

son "Son" in Jewish lists of ancestors can sometimes mean grandson or more distant relative.
'A person ... bread.' Quotation from Deuteronomy 8:3.

stant. [6]The devil said to Jesus, "I will give you all these kingdoms and all their power and glory. It has all been given to me, and I can give it to anyone I wish. [7]If you worship me, then it will all be yours."

[8]Jesus answered, "It is written in the Scriptures: 'You must worship the Lord your God and serve only him.' " [n]

[9]Then the devil led Jesus to Jerusalem and put him on a high place of the Temple.[d] He said to Jesus, "If you are the Son of God, jump down. [10]It is written in the Scriptures: 'He has put his angels in charge of you to watch over you.' *Psalm 91:11*
[11] It is also written:

'They will catch you in their hands so that you will not hit your foot on a rock.' " *Psalm 91:12*
[12]Jesus answered, "But it also says in the Scriptures: 'Do not test the Lord your God.' " [n]

[13]After the devil had tempted Jesus in every way, he left him to wait until a better time.

Jesus Teaches the People

[14]Jesus returned to Galilee in the power of the Holy Spirit,[d] and stories about him spread all through the area. [15]He began to teach in their synagogues,[d] and everyone praised him.

[16]Jesus traveled to Nazareth, where he had grown up. On the Sabbath[d] day he went to the synagogue, as he always did, and stood up to read. [17]The book of Isaiah the prophet[d] was given to him. He opened the book and found the place where this is written:
[18]"The Lord has put his Spirit in me,
because he appointed me to tell the Good News[d] to the poor.
He has sent me to tell the captives they are free
and to tell the blind that they can see again. *Isaiah 61:1*
God sent me to free those who have been treated unfairly *Isaiah 58:6*
[19] and to announce the time when the Lord will show his kindness."
Isaiah 61:2

[20]Jesus closed the book, gave it back to the assistant, and sat down. Everyone in the synagogue was watching Jesus closely. [21]He began to say to them, "While you heard these words just now, they were coming true!"

[22]All the people spoke well of Jesus and were amazed at the words of grace he spoke. They asked, "Isn't this Joseph's son?"

[23]Jesus said to them, "I know that you will tell me the old saying: 'Doctor, heal yourself.' You want to say, 'We heard about the things you did in Capernaum. Do those things here in your own town!' " [24]Then Jesus said, "I tell you the truth, a prophet is not accepted in his hometown. [25]But I tell you the truth, there were many widows in Israel during the time of Elijah. It did not rain in Israel for three and one-half years, and there was no food anywhere in the whole country. [26]But Elijah was sent to none of those widows, only to a widow in Zarephath, a town in Sidon. [27]And there were many with skin diseases living in Israel during the time of the prophet Elisha. But none of them were healed, only Naaman, who was from the country of Syria."

[28]When all the people in the synagogue heard these things, they became very angry. [29]They got up, forced Jesus out of town, and took him to the edge of the cliff on which the town was built. They planned to throw him off the edge, [30]but Jesus walked through the crowd and went on his way.

Jesus Forces Out an Evil Spirit

[31]Jesus went to Capernaum, a city in Galilee, and on the Sabbath[d] day, he taught the people. [32]They were amazed at his teaching, because he spoke with authority. [33]In the synagogue[d] a man who had within him an evil spirit shouted in a loud voice, [34]"Jesus of Nazareth! What do you want with us? Did you come to destroy us? I know who you are—God's Holy One!"

[35]Jesus commanded the evil spirit, "Be quiet! Come out of the man!" The evil spirit threw the man down to the ground before all the people and then left the man without hurting him.

'You ... him.'   Quotation from Deuteronomy 6:13.
'Do ... God.'   Quotation from Deuteronomy 6:16.

36The people were amazed and said to each other, "What does this mean? With authority and power he commands evil spirits, and they come out." 37And so the news about Jesus spread to every place in the whole area.

Jesus Heals Many People

38Jesus left the synagogue[d] and went to the home of Simon.[n] Simon's mother-in-law was sick with a high fever, and they asked Jesus to help her. 39He came to her side and commanded the fever to leave. It left her, and immediately she got up and began serving them.

40When the sun went down, the people brought those who were sick to Jesus. Putting his hands on each sick person, he healed every one of them. 41Demons[d] came out of many people, shouting, "You are the Son of God." But Jesus commanded the demons and would not allow them to speak, because they knew Jesus was the Christ.[d]

42At daybreak, Jesus went to a lonely place, but the people looked for him. When they found him, they tried to keep him from leaving. 43But Jesus said to them, "I must preach about God's kingdom to other towns, too. This is why I was sent."

44Then he kept on preaching in the synagogues[d] of Judea.

Jesus' First Followers

5 One day while Jesus was standing beside Lake Galilee, many people were pressing all around him to hear the word of God. 2Jesus saw two boats at the shore of the lake. The fishermen had left them and were washing their nets. 3Jesus got into one of the boats, the one that belonged to Simon,[n] and asked him to push off a little from the land. Then Jesus sat down and continued to teach the people from the boat.

4When Jesus had finished speaking, he said to Simon, "Take the boat into deep water, and put your nets in the water to catch some fish."

5Simon answered, "Master, we worked hard all night trying to catch fish, and we caught nothing. But you say to put the nets in the water, so I will." 6When the fishermen did as Jesus told them, they caught so many fish that the nets began to break. 7They called to their partners in the other boat to come and help them. They came and filled both boats so full that they were almost sinking.

8When Simon Peter saw what had happened, he bowed down before Jesus and said, "Go away from me, Lord. I am a sinful man!" 9He and the other fishermen were amazed at the many fish they caught, as were 10James and John, the sons of Zebedee, Simon's partners.

Jesus said to Simon, "Don't be afraid. From now on you will fish for people." 11When the men brought their boats to the shore, they left everything and followed Jesus.

Jesus Heals a Sick Man

12When Jesus was in one of the towns, there was a man covered with a skin disease. When he saw Jesus, he bowed before him and begged him, "Lord, you can heal me if you will."

13Jesus reached out his hand and touched the man and said, "I will. Be healed!" Immediately the disease disappeared. 14Then Jesus said, "Don't tell anyone about this, but go and show yourself to the priest[n] and offer a gift for your healing, as Moses commanded.[n] This will show the people what I have done."

15But the news about Jesus spread even more. Many people came to hear Jesus and to be healed of their sicknesses, 16but Jesus often slipped away to be alone so he could pray.

Jesus Heals a Paralyzed Man

17One day as Jesus was teaching the people, the Pharisees[d] and teachers of the law from every town in Galilee and Judea and from Jerusalem were there. The Lord was giving Jesus the power to heal people. 18Just

---

Simon   Simon's other name was Peter.
show . . . priest   The law of Moses said a priest must say when a Jewish person with a skin disease was well.
Moses commanded   Read about this in Leviticus 14:1-32.

then, some men were carrying on a mat a man who was paralyzed. They tried to bring him in and put him down before Jesus. [19]But because there were so many people there, they could not find a way in. So they went up on the roof and lowered the man on his mat through the ceiling into the middle of the crowd right before Jesus. [20]Seeing their faith, Jesus said, "Friend, your sins are forgiven."

[21]The Jewish teachers of the law and the Pharisees thought to themselves, "Who is this man who is speaking as if he were God? Only God can forgive sins."

[22]But Jesus knew what they were thinking and said, "Why are you thinking these things? [23]Which is easier: to say, 'Your sins are forgiven,' or to say, 'Stand up and walk'? [24]But I will prove to you that the Son of Man[d] has authority on earth to forgive sins." So Jesus said to the paralyzed man, "I tell you, stand up, take your mat, and go home."

[25]At once the man stood up before them, picked up his mat, and went home, praising God. [26]All the people were fully amazed and began to praise God. They were filled with much respect and said, "Today we have seen amazing things!"

Levi Follows Jesus

[27]After this, Jesus went out and saw a tax collector named Levi sitting in the tax collector's booth. Jesus said to him, "Follow me!" [28]So Levi got up, left everything, and followed him.

[29]Then Levi gave a big dinner for Jesus at his house. Many tax collectors and other people were eating there, too. [30]But the Pharisees[d] and the men who taught the law for the Pharisees began to complain to Jesus' followers, "Why do you eat and drink with tax collectors and sinners?"

[31]Jesus answered them, "It is not the healthy people who need a doctor, but the sick. [32]I have not come to invite good people but sinners to change their hearts and lives."

Jesus Answers a Question

[33]They said to Jesus, "John's followers often give up eating[n] for a certain time and pray, just as the Pharisees[d] do. But your followers eat and drink all the time."

[34]Jesus said to them, "You cannot make the friends of the bridegroom give up eating while he is still with them. [35]But the time will come when the bridegroom will be taken away from them, and then they will give up eating."

[36]Jesus told them this story: "No one takes cloth off a new coat to cover a hole in an old coat. Otherwise, he ruins the new coat, and the cloth from the new coat will not be the same as the old cloth. [37]Also, no one ever pours new wine into old leather bags. Otherwise, the new wine will break the bags, the wine will spill out, and the leather bags will be ruined. [38]New wine must be put into new leather bags. [39]No one after drinking old wine wants new wine, because he says, 'The old wine is better.' "

Jesus Is Lord over the Sabbath

6 One Sabbath[d] day Jesus was walking through some fields of grain. His followers picked the heads of grain, rubbed them in their hands, and ate them. [2]Some Pharisees[d] said, "Why do you do what is not lawful on the Sabbath day?"

[3]Jesus answered, "Have you not read what David did when he and those with him were hungry? [4]He went into God's house and took and ate the holy bread, which is lawful only for priests to eat. And he gave some to the people who were with him." [5]Then Jesus said to the Pharisees, "The Son of Man[d] is Lord of the Sabbath day."

Jesus Heals a Man's Hand

[6]On another Sabbath[d] day Jesus went into the synagogue[d] and was teaching, and a man with a crippled right hand was there. [7]The teachers of the law and the Pharisees[d] were watching closely to see if Jesus would heal on the Sabbath day so they could accuse him. [8]But he knew what they were thinking, and he said to the man with the crippled hand, "Stand up here in the middle of everyone." The man got up and stood there. [9]Then Jesus

---

give up eating This is called "fasting." The people would give up eating for a special time of prayer and worship to God. It was also done to show sadness and disappointment.

said to them, "I ask you, which is lawful on the Sabbath day: to do good or to do evil, to save a life or to destroy it?" 10Jesus looked around at all of them and said to the man, "Hold out your hand." The man held out his hand, and it was healed.

11But the Pharisees and the teachers of the law were very angry and discussed with each other what they could do to Jesus.

Jesus Chooses His Apostles

12At that time Jesus went off to a mountain to pray, and he spent the night praying to God. 13The next morning, Jesus called his followers to him and chose twelve of them, whom he named apostles:*d* 14Simon (Jesus named him Peter), his brother Andrew, James, John, Philip, Bartholomew, 15Matthew, Thomas, James son of Alphaeus, Simon (called the Zealot*d*), 16Judas son of James, and Judas Iscariot, who later turned Jesus over to his enemies.

Jesus Teaches and Heals

17Jesus and the apostles*d* came down from the mountain, and he stood on level ground. A large group of his followers was there, as well as many people from all around Judea, Jerusalem, and the seacoast cities of Tyre and Sidon. 18They all came to hear Jesus teach and to be healed of their sicknesses, and he healed those who were troubled by evil spirits. 19All the people were trying to touch Jesus, because power was coming from him and healing them all.

20Jesus looked at his followers and said,
"You people who are poor are happy,
    because the kingdom of God belongs
        to you.
21You people who are now hungry are
        happy,
    because you will be satisfied.
You people who are now crying are
        happy,
    because you will laugh with joy.
22"People will hate you, shut you out, insult you, and say you are evil because you follow the Son of Man.*d* But when they do, you will be happy. 23Be full of joy at that time, because you have a great reward waiting for you in heaven. Their ancestors did the same things to the prophets.*d*

24"But how terrible it will be for you who .
        are rich,
    because you have had your easy life.
25How terrible it will be for you who are
        full now,
    because you will be hungry.
    How terrible it will be for you who are
        laughing now,
    because you will be sad and cry.
26"How terrible when everyone says only good things about you, because their ancestors said the same things about the false prophets.

Love Your Enemies

27"But I say to you who are listening, love your enemies. Do good to those who hate you, 28bless those who curse you, pray for those who are cruel to you. 29If anyone slaps you on one cheek, offer him the other cheek, too. If someone takes your coat, do not stop him from taking your shirt. 30Give to everyone who asks you, and when someone takes something that is yours, don't ask for it back. 31Do to others what you would want them to do to you. 32If you love only the people who love you, what praise should you get? Even sinners love the people who love them. 33If you do good only to those who do good to you, what praise should you get? Even sinners do that! 34If you lend things to people, always hoping to get something back, what praise should you get? Even sinners lend to other sinners so that they can get back the same amount! 35But love your enemies, do good to them, and lend to them without hoping to get anything back. Then you will have a great reward, and you will be children of the Most High God, because he is kind even to people who are ungrateful and full of sin. 36Show mercy, just as your Father shows mercy.

Look at Yourselves

37"Don't judge other people, and you will not be judged. Don't accuse others of being guilty, and you will not be accused of being guilty. Forgive, and you will be forgiven. 38Give, and you will receive. You will be given much. Pressed down, shaken together, and running over, it will spill into your lap.

.The way you give to others is the way God will give to you."

39Jesus told them this story: "Can a blind person lead another blind person? No! Both of them will fall into a ditch. 40A student is not better than the teacher, but the student who has been fully trained will be like the teacher.

41"Why do you notice the little piece of dust in your friend's eye, but you don't notice the big piece of wood in your own eye? 42How can you say to your friend, 'Friend, let me take that little piece of dust out of your eye' when you cannot see that big piece of wood in your own eye! You hypocrite!d First, take the wood out of your own eye. Then you will see clearly to take the dust out of your friend's eye.

Two Kinds of Fruit

43"A good tree does not produce bad fruit, nor does a bad tree produce good fruit. 44Each tree is known by its own fruit. People don't gather figs from thornbushes, and they don't get grapes from bushes. 45Good people bring good things out of the good they stored in their hearts. But evil people bring evil things out of the evil they stored in their hearts. People speak the things that are in their hearts.

Two Kinds of People

46"Why do you call me, 'Lord, Lord,' but do not do what I say? 47I will show you what everyone is like who comes to me and hears my words and obeys. 48That person is like a man building a house who dug deep and laid the foundation on rock. When the floods came, the water tried to wash the house away, but it could not shake it, because the house was built well. 49But the one who hears my words and does not obey is like a man who built his house on the ground without a foundation. When the floods came, the house quickly fell and was completely destroyed."

Jesus Heals a Soldier's Servant

7 When Jesus finished saying all these things to the people, he went to Capernaum. 2There was an army officer who had a servant who was very important to him.

The servant was so sick he was nearly dead. 3When the officer heard about Jesus, he sent some older Jewish leaders to him to ask Jesus to come and heal his servant. 4The men went to Jesus and begged him, saying, "This officer is worthy of your help. 5He loves our people, and he built us a synagogue."d

6So Jesus went with the men. He was getting near the officer's house when the officer sent friends to say, "Lord, don't trouble yourself, because I am not worthy to have you come into my house. 7That is why I did not come to you myself. But you only need to command it, and my servant will be healed. 8I, too, am a man under the authority of others, and I have soldiers under my command. I tell one soldier, 'Go,' and he goes. I tell another soldier, 'Come,' and he comes. I say to my servant, 'Do this,' and my servant does it."

9When Jesus heard this, he was amazed. Turning to the crowd that was following him, he said, "I tell you, this is the greatest faith I have found anywhere, even in Israel."

10Those who had been sent to Jesus went back to the house where they found the servant in good health.

Jesus Brings a Man Back to Life

11Soon afterwards Jesus went to a town called Nain, and his followers and a large crowd traveled with him. 12When he came near the town gate, he saw a funeral. A mother, who was a widow, had lost her only son. A large crowd from the town was with the mother while her son was being carried out. 13When the Lord saw her, he felt very sorry for her and said, "Don't cry." 14He went up and touched the coffin, and the people who were carrying it stopped. Jesus said, "Young man, I tell you, get up!" 15And the son sat up and began to talk. Then Jesus gave him back to his mother.

16All the people were amazed and began praising God, saying, "A great prophetd has come to us! God has come to help his people."

17This news about Jesus spread through all Judea and into all the places around there.

John Asks a Question

18John's followers told him about all these

things. He called for two of his followers [19]and sent them to the Lord to ask, "Are you the One who is to come, or should we wait for someone else?"

[20]When the men came to Jesus, they said, "John the Baptist[d] sent us to you with this question: 'Are you the One who is to come, or should we wait for someone else?' "

[21]At that time, Jesus healed many people of their sicknesses, diseases, and evil spirits, and he gave sight to many blind people. [22]Then Jesus answered John's followers, "Go tell John what you saw and heard here. The blind can see, the crippled can walk, and people with skin diseases are healed. The deaf can hear, the dead are raised to life, and the Good News[d] is preached to the poor. [23]Those who do not stumble in their faith because of me are blessed!"

[24]When John's followers left, Jesus began talking to the people about John: "What did you go out into the desert to see? A reed[n] blown by the wind? [25]What did you go out to see? A man dressed in fine clothes? No, people who have fine clothes and much wealth live in kings' palaces. [26]But what did you go out to see? A prophet?[d] Yes, and I tell you, John is more than a prophet. [27]This was written about him:

'I will send my messenger ahead of you,
    who will prepare the way for you.'

Malachi 3:1

[28]I tell you, John is greater than any other person ever born, but even the least important person in the kingdom of God is greater than John."

[29](When the people, including the tax collectors, heard this, they all agreed that God's teaching was good, because they had been baptized by John. [30]But the Pharisees[d] and experts on the law refused to accept God's plan for themselves; they did not let John baptize them.)

[31]Then Jesus said, "What shall I say about the people of this time? What are they like? [32]They are like children sitting in the marketplace, calling to one another and saying,

'We played music for you, but you did
    not dance;

we sang a sad song, but you did not
    cry.'

[33]John the Baptist came and did not eat bread or drink wine, and you say, 'He has a demon[d] in him.' [34]The Son of Man[d] came eating and drinking, and you say, 'Look at him! He eats too much and drinks too much wine, and he is a friend of tax collectors and sinners!' [35]But wisdom is proved to be right by what it does."

A Woman Washes Jesus' Feet

[36]One of the Pharisees[d] asked Jesus to eat with him, so Jesus went into the Pharisee's house and sat at the table. [37]A sinful woman in the town learned that Jesus was eating at the Pharisee's house. So she brought an alabaster[d] jar of perfume [38]and stood behind Jesus at his feet, crying. She began to wash his feet with her tears, and she dried them with her hair, kissing them many times and rubbing them with the perfume. [39]When the Pharisee who asked Jesus to come to his house saw this, he thought to himself, "If Jesus were a prophet,[d] he would know that the woman touching him is a sinner!"

[40]Jesus said to the Pharisee, "Simon, I have something to say to you."

Simon said, "Teacher, tell me."

[41]Jesus said, "Two people owed money to the same banker. One owed five hundred coins[n] and the other owed fifty. [42]They had no money to pay what they owed, but the banker told both of them they did not have to pay him. Which person will love the banker more?"

[43]Simon, the Pharisee, answered, "I think it would be the one who owed him the most money."

Jesus said to Simon, "You are right." [44]Then Jesus turned toward the woman and said to Simon, "Do you see this woman? When I came into your house, you gave me no water for my feet, but she washed my feet with her tears and dried them with her hair. [45]You gave me no kiss of greeting, but she has been kissing my feet since I came in. [46]You did not put oil on my head, but she poured perfume on my feet. [47]I tell you that

---

reed It means that John was not ordinary or weak like grass blown by the wind.
coins Roman denarii. One coin was the average pay for one day's work.

her many sins are forgiven, so she showed great love. But the person who is forgiven only a little will love only a little."

48Then Jesus said to her, "Your sins are forgiven."

49The people sitting at the table began to say among themselves, "Who is this who even forgives sins?"

50Jesus said to the woman, "Because you believed, you are saved from your sins. Go in peace."

The Group with Jesus

8 After this, while Jesus was traveling through some cities and small towns, he preached and told the Good News*d* about God's kingdom. The twelve apostles*d* were with him, 2and also some women who had been healed of sicknesses and evil spirits: Mary, called Magdalene, from whom seven demons*d* had gone out; 3Joanna, the wife of Chuza (the manager of Herod's house); Susanna; and many others. These women used their own money to help Jesus and his apostles.

A Story About Planting Seed

4When a great crowd was gathered, and people were coming to Jesus from every town, he told them this story:

5"A farmer went out to plant his seed. While he was planting, some seed fell by the road. People walked on the seed, and the birds ate it up. 6Some seed fell on rock, and when it began to grow, it died because it had no water. 7Some seed fell among thorny weeds, but the weeds grew up with it and choked the good plants. 8And some seed fell on good ground and grew and made a hundred times more."

As Jesus finished the story, he called out, "You people who can hear me, listen!"

9Jesus' followers asked him what this story meant.

10Jesus said, "You have been chosen to know the secrets about the kingdom of God. But I use stories to speak to other people so that:

'They will look, but they may not see.
  They will listen, but they may not
    understand.'   *Isaiah 6:9*

11"This is what the story means: The seed is God's message. 12The seed that fell beside the road is like the people who hear God's teaching, but the devil comes and takes it away from them so they cannot believe it and be saved. 13The seed that fell on rock is like those who hear God's teaching and accept it gladly, but they don't allow the teaching to go deep into their lives. They believe for a while, but when trouble comes, they give up. 14The seed that fell among the thorny weeds is like those who hear God's teaching, but they let the worries, riches, and pleasures of this life keep them from growing and producing good fruit. 15And the seed that fell on the good ground is like those who hear God's teaching with good, honest hearts and obey it and patiently produce good fruit.

Use What You Have

16"No one after lighting a lamp covers it with a bowl or hides it under a bed. Instead, the person puts it on a lampstand so those who come in will see the light. 17Everything that is hidden will become clear, and every secret thing will be made known. 18So be careful how you listen. Those who have understanding will be given more. But those who do not have understanding, even what they think they have will be taken away from them."

Jesus' True Family

19Jesus' mother and brothers came to see him, but there was such a crowd they could not get to him. 20Someone said to Jesus, "Your mother and your brothers are standing outside, wanting to see you."

21Jesus answered them, "My mother and my brothers are those who listen to God's teaching and obey it!"

Jesus Calms a Storm

22One day Jesus and his followers got into a boat, and he said to them, "Let's go across the lake." And so they started across. 23While they were sailing, Jesus fell asleep. A very strong wind blew up on the lake, causing the boat to fill with water, and they were in danger.

24The followers went to Jesus and woke him, saying, "Master! Master! We will drown!"

Jesus got up and gave a command to the wind and the waves. They stopped, and it became calm. 25Jesus said to his followers, "Where is your faith?"

The followers were afraid and amazed and said to each other, "Who is this that commands even the wind and the water, and they obey him?"

A Man with Demons Inside Him

26Jesus and his followers sailed across the lake from Galilee to the area of the Gerasene people. 27When Jesus got out on the land, a man from the town who had demons*d* inside him came to Jesus. For a long time he had worn no clothes and had lived in the burial caves, not in a house. 28When he saw Jesus, he cried out and fell down before him. He said with a loud voice, "What do you want with me, Jesus, Son of the Most High God? I beg you, don't torture me!" 29He said this because Jesus was commanding the evil spirit to come out of the man. Many times it had taken hold of him. Though he had been kept under guard and chained hand and foot, he had broken his chains and had been forced by the demon out into a lonely place.

30Jesus asked him, "What is your name?"

He answered, "Legion," *n* because many demons were in him. 31The demons begged Jesus not to send them into eternal darkness. *n* 32A large herd of pigs was feeding on a hill, and the demons begged Jesus to allow them to go into the pigs. So Jesus allowed them to do this. 33When the demons came out of the man, they went into the pigs, and the herd ran down the hill into the lake and was drowned.

34When the herdsmen saw what had happened, they ran away and told about this in the town and the countryside. 35And people went to see what had happened. When they came to Jesus, they found the man sitting at Jesus' feet, clothed and in his right mind, because the demons were gone. But the people were frightened. 36The people who saw this happen told the others how Jesus had made the man well. 37All the people of the Gerasene country asked Jesus to leave, because

they were all very afraid. So Jesus got into the boat and went back to Galilee.

38The man whom Jesus had healed begged to go with him, but Jesus sent him away, saying, 39"Go back home and tell people how much God has done for you." So the man went all over town telling how much Jesus had done for him.

Jesus Gives Life to a Dead Girl and Heals a Sick Woman

40When Jesus got back to Galilee, a crowd welcomed him, because everyone was waiting for him. 41A man named Jairus, a leader of the synagogue,*d* came to Jesus and fell at his feet, begging him to come to his house. 42Jairus' only daughter, about twelve years old, was dying.

While Jesus was on his way to Jairus' house, the people were crowding all around him. 43A woman was in the crowd who had been bleeding for twelve years, but no one was able to heal her. 44She came up behind Jesus and touched the edge of his coat, and instantly her bleeding stopped. 45Then Jesus said, "Who touched me?"

When all the people said they had not touched him, Peter said, "Master, the people are all around you and are pushing against you."

46But Jesus said, "Someone did touch me, because I felt power go out from me." 47When the woman saw she could not hide, she came forward, shaking, and fell down before Jesus. While all the people listened, she told why she had touched him and how she had been instantly healed. 48Jesus said to her, "Dear woman, you are made well because you believed. Go in peace."

49While Jesus was still speaking, someone came from the house of the synagogue leader and said to him, "Your daughter is dead. Don't bother the teacher anymore."

50When Jesus heard this, he said to Jairus, "Don't be afraid. Just believe, and your daughter will be well."

51When Jesus went to the house, he let only Peter, John, James, and the girl's father and mother go inside with him. 52All the peo-

---

"Legion"   Means very many. A legion was about five thousand men in the Roman army.
eternal darkness   Literally, "the abyss," something like a pit or a hole that has no end.

ple were crying and feeling sad because the girl was dead, but Jesus said, "Stop crying. She is not dead, only asleep."

53The people laughed at Jesus because they knew the girl was dead. 54But Jesus took hold of her hand and called to her, "My child, stand up!" 55Her spirit came back into her, and she stood up at once. Then Jesus ordered that she be given something to eat. 56The girl's parents were amazed, but Jesus told them not to tell anyone what had happened.

Jesus Sends Out the Apostles

9 Jesus called the twelve apostles*d* together and gave them power and authority over all demons*d* and the ability to heal sicknesses. 2He sent the apostles out to tell about God's kingdom and to heal the sick. 3He said to them, "Take nothing for your trip, neither a walking stick, bag, bread, money, or extra clothes. 4When you enter a house, stay there until it is time to leave. 5If people do not welcome you, shake the dust off of your feet*n* as you leave the town, as a warning to them."

6So the apostles went out and traveled through all the towns, preaching the Good News*d* and healing people everywhere.

Herod Is Confused About Jesus

7Herod, the governor, heard about all the things that were happening and was confused, because some people said, "John the Baptist*d* has risen from the dead." 8Others said, "Elijah has come to us." And still others said, "One of the prophets*d* who lived long ago has risen from the dead." 9Herod said, "I cut off John's head, so who is this man I hear such things about?" And Herod kept trying to see Jesus.

More than Five Thousand Fed

10When the apostles*d* returned, they told Jesus everything they had done. Then Jesus took them with him to a town called Bethsaida where they could be alone together. 11But the people learned where Jesus went and followed him. He welcomed them and

talked with them about God's kingdom and healed those who needed to be healed.

12Late in the afternoon, the twelve apostles came to Jesus and said, "Send the people away. They need to go to the towns and countryside around here and find places to sleep and something to eat, because no one lives in this place."

13But Jesus said to them, "You give them something to eat."

They said, "We have only five loaves of bread and two fish, unless we go buy food for all these people." 14(There were about five thousand men there.)

Jesus said to his followers, "Tell the people to sit in groups of about fifty people."

15So the followers did this, and all the people sat down. 16Then Jesus took the five loaves of bread and two fish, and looking up to heaven, he thanked God for the food. Then he divided the food and gave it to the followers to give to the people. 17They all ate and were satisfied, and what was left over was gathered up, filling twelve baskets.

Jesus Is the Christ

18One time when Jesus was praying alone, his followers were with him, and he asked them, "Who do the people say I am?"

19They answered, "Some say you are John the Baptist.*d* Others say you are Elijah.*n* And others say you are one of the prophets*d* from long ago who has come back to life."

20Then Jesus asked, "But who do you say I am?"

Peter answered, "You are the Christ*d* from God."

21Jesus warned them not to tell anyone, saying, 22"The Son of Man*d* must suffer many things. He will be rejected by the older Jewish leaders, the leading priests, and the teachers of the law. He will be killed and after three days will be raised from the dead."

23Jesus said to all of them, "If people want to follow me, they must give up the things they want. They must be willing to give up their lives daily to follow me. 24Those who want to save their lives will give up true life. But those who give up their lives for me will

---

shake ... feet A warning. It showed that they had rejected these people.
Elijah A man who spoke for God and who lived hundreds of years before Christ. See 1 Kings 17.

have true life. 25It is worth nothing for them to have the whole world if they themselves are destroyed or lost. 26If people are ashamed of me and my teaching, then the Son of Man*d* will be ashamed of them when he comes in his glory and with the glory of the Father and the holy angels. 27I tell you the truth, some people standing here will see the kingdom of God before they die."

Jesus Talks with Moses and Elijah

28About eight days after Jesus said these things, he took Peter, John, and James and went up on a mountain to pray. 29While Jesus was praying, the appearance of his face changed, and his clothes became shining white. 30Then two men, Moses and Elijah,*n* were talking with Jesus. 31They appeared in heavenly glory, talking about his departure which he would soon bring about in Jerusalem. 32Peter and the others were very sleepy, but when they awoke fully, they saw the glory of Jesus and the two men standing with him. 33When Moses and Elijah were about to leave, Peter said to Jesus, "Master, it is good that we are here. Let us make three tents— one for you, one for Moses, and one for Elijah." (Peter did not know what he was talking about.)

34While he was saying these things, a cloud came and covered them, and they became afraid as the cloud covered them. 35A voice came from the cloud, saying, "This is my Son, whom I have chosen. Listen to him!"

36When the voice finished speaking, only Jesus was there. Peter, John, and James said nothing and told no one at that time what they had seen.

Jesus Heals a Sick Boy

37The next day, when they came down from the mountain, a large crowd met Jesus. 38A man in the crowd shouted to him, "Teacher, please come and look at my son, because he is my only child. 39An evil spirit seizes my son, and suddenly he screams. It causes him to lose control of himself and foam at the mouth. The evil spirit keeps on hurting him and almost never leaves him. 40I begged your followers to force the evil spirit out, but they could not do it."

41Jesus answered, "You people have no faith, and your lives are all wrong. How long must I stay with you and put up with you? Bring your son here."

42While the boy was coming, the demon*d* threw him on the ground and made him lose control of himself. But Jesus gave a strong command to the evil spirit and healed the boy and gave him back to his father. 43All the people were amazed at the great power of God.

Jesus Talks About His Death

While everyone was wondering about all that Jesus did, he said to his followers, 44"Don't forget what I tell you now: The Son of Man*d* will be handed over to people." 45But the followers did not understand what this meant; the meaning was hidden from them so they could not understand. But they were afraid to ask Jesus about it.

Who Is the Greatest?

46Jesus' followers began to have an argument about which one of them was the greatest. 47Jesus knew what they were thinking, so he took a little child and stood the child beside him. 48Then Jesus said, "Whoever accepts this little child in my name accepts me. And whoever accepts me accepts the One who sent me, because whoever is least among you all is really the greatest."

Anyone Not Against Us Is for Us

49John answered, "Master, we saw someone using your name to force demons*d* out of people. We told him to stop, because he does not belong to our group."

50But Jesus said to him, "Don't stop him, because whoever is not against you is for you."

A Town Rejects Jesus

51When the time was coming near for Jesus to depart, he was determined to go to Jerusalem. 52He sent some men ahead of

---

Moses and Elijah Two of the most important Jewish leaders in the past. Moses had given them the law, and Elijah was an important prophet.

him, who went into a town in Samaria to make everything ready for him. ⁵³But the people there would not welcome him, because he was set on going to Jerusalem. ⁵⁴When James and John, followers of Jesus, saw this, they said, "Lord, do you want us to call fire down from heaven and destroy those people?"ⁿ

⁵⁵But Jesus turned and scolded them. ⁵⁶Thenⁿ they went to another town.

Following Jesus

⁵⁷As they were going along the road, someone said to Jesus, "I will follow you any place you go."

⁵⁸Jesus said to them, "The foxes have holes to live in, and the birds have nests, but the Son of Manᵈ has no place to rest his head."

⁵⁹Jesus said to another man, "Follow me!"

But he said, "Lord, first let me go and bury my father."

⁶⁰But Jesus said to him, "Let the people who are dead bury their own dead. You must go and tell about the kingdom of God."

⁶¹Another man said, "I will follow you, Lord, but first let me go and say good-bye to my family."

⁶²Jesus said, "Anyone who begins to plow a field but keeps looking back is of no use in the kingdom of God."

Jesus Sends Out the Seventy-Two

10 After this, the Lord chose seventy-twoⁿ others and sent them out in pairs ahead of him into every town and place where he planned to go. ²He said to them, "There are a great many people to harvest, but there are only a few workers. So pray to God, who owns the harvest, that he will send more workers to help gather his harvest. ³Go now, but listen! I am sending you out like sheep among wolves. ⁴Don't carry a purse, a bag, or sandals, and don't waste time talking with people on the road. ⁵Before you

go into a house, say, 'Peace be with this house.' ⁶If peaceful people live there, your blessing of peace will stay with them, but if not, then your blessing will come back to you. ⁷Stay in the peaceful house, eating and drinking what the people there give you. A worker should be given his pay. Don't move from house to house. ⁸If you go into a town and the people welcome you, eat what they give you. ⁹Heal the sick who live there, and tell them, 'The kingdom of God is near you.' ¹⁰But if you go into a town, and the people don't welcome you, then go into the streets and say, ¹¹'Even the dirt from your town that sticks to our feet we wipe off against you.ⁿ But remember that the kingdom of God is near.' ¹²I tell you, on the Judgment Day it will be better for the people of Sodomⁿ than for the people of that town.

Jesus Warns Unbelievers

¹³"How terrible for you, Korazin! How terrible for you, Bethsaida! If the miraclesᵈ I did in you had happened in Tyre and Sidon,ⁿ those people would have changed their lives long ago. They would have worn rough cloth and put ashes on themselves to show they had changed. ¹⁴But on the Judgment Day it will be better for Tyre and Sidon than for you. ¹⁵And you, Capernaum,ⁿ will you be lifted up to heaven? No! You will be thrown down to the depths!

¹⁶"Whoever listens to you listens to me, and whoever refuses to accept you refuses to accept me. And whoever refuses to accept me refuses to accept the One who sent me."

Satan Falls

¹⁷When the seventy-twoⁿ came back, they were very happy and said, "Lord, even the demonsᵈ obeyed us when we used your name!"

¹⁸Jesus said, "I saw Satan fall like lightning from heaven. ¹⁹Listen, I have given you power to walk on snakes and scorpions,

Verse 54 Here, some Greek copies add: ". . . as Elijah did."
Verse 55-56 Some copies read: "But Jesus turned and scolded them. And Jesus said, 'You don't know what kind of spirit you belong to. ⁵⁶The Son of Man did not come to destroy the souls of people but to save them.' Then"
seventy-two Many Greek copies read seventy.
dirt . . . you A warning. It showed that they had rejected these people.
Sodom City that God destroyed because the people were so evil.
Tyre and Sidon Towns where wicked people lived.
Korazin, Bethsaida, Capernaum Towns by Lake Galilee where Jesus preached to the people.

power that is greater than the enemy has. So nothing will hurt you. [20]But you should not be happy because the spirits obey you but because your names are written in heaven."

Jesus Prays to the Father

[21]Then Jesus rejoiced in the Holy Spirit[d] and said, "I praise you, Father, Lord of heaven and earth, because you have hidden these things from the people who are wise and smart. But you have shown them to those who are like little children. Yes, Father, this is what you really wanted.

[22]"My Father has given me all things. No one knows who the Son is, except the Father. And no one knows who the Father is, except the Son and those whom the Son chooses to tell."

[23]Then Jesus turned to his followers and said privately, "You are blessed to see what you now see. [24]I tell you, many prophets[d] and kings wanted to see what you now see, but they did not, and they wanted to hear what you now hear, but they did not."

The Good Samaritan

[25]Then an expert on the law stood up to test Jesus, saying, "Teacher, what must I do to get life forever?"

[26]Jesus said, "What is written in the law? What do you read there?"

[27]The man answered, "Love the Lord your God with all your heart, all your soul, all your strength, and all your mind."[n] Also, "Love your neighbor as you love yourself."[n]

[28]Jesus said to him, "Your answer is right. Do this and you will live."

[29]But the man, wanting to show the importance of his question, said to Jesus, "And who is my neighbor?"

[30]Jesus answered, "As a man was going down from Jerusalem to Jericho, some robbers attacked him. They tore off his clothes, beat him, and left him lying there, almost dead. [31]It happened that a Jewish priest was going down that road. When he saw the man, he walked by on the other side. [32]Next, a Levite[n] came there, and after he went over and looked at the man, he walked by on the other side of the road. [33]Then a Samaritan[n] traveling down the road came to where the hurt man was. When he saw the man, he felt very sorry for him. [34]The Samaritan went to him, poured olive oil and wine[n] on his wounds, and bandaged them. Then he put the hurt man on his own donkey and took him to an inn where he cared for him. [35]The next day, the Samaritan brought out two coins,[n] gave them to the innkeeper, and said, 'Take care of this man. If you spend more money on him, I will pay it back to you when I come again.' "

[36]Then Jesus said, "Which one of these three men do you think was a neighbor to the man who was attacked by the robbers?"

[37]The expert on the law answered, "The one who showed him mercy."

Jesus said to him, "Then go and do what he did."

Mary and Martha

[38]While Jesus and his followers were traveling, Jesus went into a town. A woman named Martha let Jesus stay at her house. [39]Martha had a sister named Mary, who was sitting at Jesus' feet and listening to him teach. [40]But Martha was busy with all the work to be done. She went in and said, "Lord, don't you care that my sister has left me alone to do all the work? Tell her to help me."

[41]But the Lord answered her, "Martha, Martha, you are worried and upset about many things. [42]Only one thing is important. Mary has chosen the better thing, and it will never be taken away from her."

Jesus Teaches About Prayer

11 One time Jesus was praying in a certain place. When he finished, one of

---

"Love ... mind." Quotation from Deuteronomy 6:5.
"Love ... yourself." Quotation from Leviticus 19:18.
Levite Levites were members of the tribe of Levi who helped the Jewish priests with their work in the Temple. Read 1 Chronicles 23:24-32.
Samaritan Samaritans were people from Samaria. These people were part Jewish, but the Jews did not accept them as true Jews. Samaritans and Jews disliked each other.
olive oil and wine Oil and wine were used like medicine to soften and clean wounds.
coins Roman denarii. One coin was the average pay for one day's work.

his followers said to him, "Lord, teach us to pray as John taught his followers."

²Jesus said to them, "When you pray, say:

'Father, may your name always be kept holy.

May your kingdom come.

³Give us the food we need for each day.

⁴Forgive us for our sins,

because we forgive everyone who has done wrong to us.

And do not cause us to be tempted.' "

Continue to Ask

⁵Then Jesus said to them, "Suppose one of you went to your friend's house at midnight and said to him, 'Friend, loan me three loaves of bread. ⁶A friend of mine has come into town to visit me, but I have nothing for him to eat.' ⁷Your friend inside the house answers, 'Don't bother me! The door is already locked, and my children and I are in bed. I cannot get up and give you anything.' ⁸I tell you, if friendship is not enough to make him get up to give you the bread, your boldness will make him get up and give you whatever you need. ⁹So I tell you, ask, and God will give to you. Search, and you will find. Knock, and the door will open for you. ¹⁰Yes, everyone who asks will receive. The one who searches will find. And everyone who knocks will have the door opened. ¹¹If your children ask for a fish, which of you would give them a snake instead? ¹²Or, if your children ask for an egg, would you give them a scorpion? ¹³Even though you are bad, you know how to give good things to your children. How much more your heavenly Father will give the Holy Spirit*d* to those who ask him!"

Jesus' Power Is from God

¹⁴One time Jesus was sending out a demon*d* that could not talk. When the demon came out, the man who had been unable to speak, then spoke. The people were amazed. ¹⁵But some of them said, "Jesus uses the power of Beelzebul,*d* the ruler of demons, to force demons out of people."

¹⁶Other people, wanting to test Jesus, asked him to give them a sign from heaven. ¹⁷But knowing their thoughts, he said to them, "Every kingdom that is divided against itself will be destroyed. And a family that is divided against itself will not continue. ¹⁸So if Satan is divided against himself, his kingdom will not continue. You say that I use the power of Beelzebul to force out demons. ¹⁹But if I use the power of Beelzebul to force out demons, what power do your people use to force demons out? So they will be your judges. ²⁰But if I use the power of God to force out demons, then the kingdom of God has come to you.

²¹"When a strong person with many weapons guards his own house, his possessions are safe. ²²But when someone stronger comes and defeats him, the stronger one will take away the weapons the first man trusted and will give away the possessions.

²³"Anyone who is not with me is against me, and anyone who does not work with me is working against me.

The Empty Person

²⁴"When an evil spirit comes out of a person, it travels through dry places, looking for a place to rest. But when it finds no place, it says, 'I will go back to the house I left.' ²⁵And when it comes back, it finds that house swept clean and made neat. ²⁶Then the evil spirit goes out and brings seven other spirits more evil than it is, and they go in and live there. So the person has even more trouble than before."

People Who Are Truly Happy

²⁷As Jesus was saying these things, a woman in the crowd called out to Jesus, "Happy is the mother who gave birth to you and nursed you."

²⁸But Jesus said, "No, happy are those who hear the teaching of God and obey it."

The People Want a Miracle

²⁹As the crowd grew larger, Jesus said, "The people who live today are evil. They want to see a miracle*d* for a sign, but no sign will be given them, except the sign of Jonah. *n* ³⁰As Jonah was a sign for those people who lived in Nineveh, the Son of Man*d* will be a sign for the people of this time. ³¹On the

---

sign of Jonah   Jonah's three days in the fish are like Jesus' three days in the tomb. See Matthew 12:40.

Judgment Day the Queen of the South[n] will stand up with the people who live now. She will show they are guilty, because she came from far away to listen to Solomon's wise teaching. And I tell you that someone greater than Solomon is here. [32]On the Judgment Day the people of Nineveh will stand up with the people who live now, and they will show that you are guilty. When Jonah preached to them, they were sorry and changed their lives. And I tell you that someone greater than Jonah is here.

Be a Light for the World

[33]"No one lights a lamp and puts it in a secret place or under a bowl, but on a lamp-stand so the people who come in can see. [34]Your eye is a light for the body. When your eyes are good, your whole body will be full of light. But when your eyes are evil, your whole body will be full of darkness. [35]So be careful not to let the light in you become darkness. [36]If your whole body is full of light, and none of it is dark, then you will shine bright, as when a lamp shines on you."

Jesus Accuses the Pharisees

[37]After Jesus had finished speaking, a Pharisee[d] asked Jesus to eat with him. So Jesus went in and sat at the table. [38]But the Pharisee was surprised when he saw that Jesus did not wash his hands[n] before the meal. [39]The Lord said to him, "You Pharisees clean the outside of the cup and the dish, but inside you are full of greed and evil. [40]You foolish people! The same one who made what is outside also made what is inside. [41]So give what is in your dishes to the poor, and then you will be fully clean. [42]How terrible for you Pharisees! You give God one-tenth of even your mint, your rue, and every other plant in your garden. But you fail to be fair to others and to love God. These are the things you should do while continuing to do those other things. [43]How terrible for you Pharisees, because you love to have the most important seats in the synagogues,[d] and you love to be greeted with respect in the marketplaces.

[44]How terrible for you, because you are like hidden graves, which people walk on without knowing."

Jesus Talks to Experts on the Law

[45]One of the experts on the law said to Jesus, "Teacher, when you say these things, you are insulting us, too."

[46]Jesus answered, "How terrible for you, you experts on the law! You make strict rules that are very hard for people to obey, but you yourselves don't even try to follow those rules. [47]How terrible for you, because you build tombs for the prophets[d] whom your ancestors killed! [48]And now you show that you approve of what your ancestors did. They killed the prophets, and you build tombs for them! [49]This is why in his wisdom God said, 'I will send prophets and apostles[d] to them. They will kill some, and they will treat others cruelly.' [50]So you who live now will be punished for the deaths of all the prophets who were killed since the beginning of the world— [51]from the killing of Abel to the killing of Zechariah,[n] who died between the altar and the Temple.[d] Yes, I tell you that you who are alive now will be punished for them all.

[52]"How terrible for you, you experts on the law. You have taken away the key to learning about God. You yourselves would not learn, and you stopped others from learning, too."

[53]When Jesus left, the teachers of the law and the Pharisees[d] began to give him trouble, asking him questions about many things, [54]trying to catch him saying something wrong.

Don't Be Like the Pharisees

12 So many thousands of people had gathered that they were stepping on each other. Jesus spoke first to his followers, saying, "Beware of the yeast of the Pharisees,[d] because they are hypocrites.[d] [2]Everything that is hidden will be shown, and everything that is secret will be made known. [3]What you have said in the dark will be

---

Queen of the South   The Queen of Sheba. She traveled a thousand miles to learn God's wisdom from Solomon. Read 1 Kings 10:1-3.
wash his hands   This was a Jewish religious custom that the Pharisees thought was very important.
Abel . . . Zechariah   In the Hebrew Old Testament, the first and last men to be murdered.

heard in the light, and what you have whispered in an inner room will be shouted from the housetops.

4"I tell you, my friends, don't be afraid of people who can kill the body but after that can do nothing more to hurt you. 5I will show you the one to fear. Fear the one who has the power to kill you and also to throw you into hell. Yes, this is the one you should fear.

6"Five sparrows are sold for only two pennies, and God does not forget any of them. 7But God even knows how many hairs you have on your head. Don't be afraid. You are worth much more than many sparrows.

Don't Be Ashamed of Jesus

8"I tell you, all those who stand before others and say they believe in me, I, the Son of Man,*d* will say before the angels of God that they belong to me. 9But all who stand before others and say they do not believe in me, I will say before the angels of God that they do not belong to me.

10"Anyone who speaks against the Son of Man*d* can be forgiven, but anyone who speaks against the Holy Spirit*d* will not be forgiven.

11"When you are brought into the synagogues*d* before the leaders and other powerful people, don't worry about how to defend yourself or what to say. 12At that time the Holy Spirit will teach you what you must say."

Jesus Warns Against Selfishness

13Someone in the crowd said to Jesus, "Teacher, tell my brother to divide with me the property our father left us."

14But Jesus said to him, "Who said I should judge or decide between you?" 15Then Jesus said to them, "Be careful and guard against all kinds of greed. Life is not measured by how much one owns."

16Then Jesus told this story: "There was a rich man who had some land, which grew a good crop. 17He thought to himself, 'What will I do? I have no place to keep all my crops.' 18Then he said, 'This is what I will do: I will tear down my barns and build bigger ones, and there I will store all my grain and other goods. 19Then I can say to myself, "I

have enough good things stored to last for many years. Rest, eat, drink, and enjoy life!"

20"But God said to him, 'Foolish man! Tonight your life will be taken from you. So who will get those things you have prepared for yourself?'

21"This is how it will be for those who store up things for themselves and are not rich toward God."

Don't Worry

22Jesus said to his followers, "So I tell you, don't worry about the food you need to live, or about the clothes you need for your body. 23Life is more than food, and the body is more than clothes. 24Look at the birds. They don't plant or harvest, they don't have storerooms or barns, but God feeds them. And you are worth much more than birds. 25You cannot add any time to your life by worrying about it. 26If you cannot do even the little things, then why worry about the big things? 27Consider how the lilies grow; they don't work or make clothes for themselves. But I tell you that even Solomon with his riches was not dressed as beautifully as one of these flowers. 28God clothes the grass in the field, which is alive today but tomorrow is thrown into the fire. So how much more will God clothe you? Don't have so little faith! 29Don't always think about what you will eat or what you will drink, and don't keep worrying. 30All the people in the world are trying to get these things, and your Father knows you need them. 31But seek God's kingdom, and all the other things you need will be given to you.

Don't Trust in Money

32"Don't fear, little flock, because your Father wants to give you the kingdom. 33Sell your possessions and give to the poor. Get for yourselves purses that will not wear out, the treasure in heaven that never runs out, where thieves can't steal and moths can't destroy. 34Your heart will be where your treasure is.

Always Be Ready

35"Be dressed, ready for service, and have your lamps shining. 36Be like servants who are waiting for their master to come home from a wedding party. When he comes and knocks, the servants immediately open the door for him. **37**They will be blessed when their master comes home, because he sees that they were watching for him. I tell you the truth, the master will dress himself to serve and tell the servants to sit at the table, and he will serve them. **38**Those servants will be happy when he comes in and finds them still waiting, even if it is midnight or later.

39"Remember this: If the owner of the house knew what time a thief was coming, he would not allow the thief to enter his house. **40**So you also must be ready, because the Son of Man*d* will come at a time when you don't expect him!"

Who Is the Trusted Servant?

41Peter said, "Lord, did you tell this story to us or to all people?"

42The Lord said, "Who is the wise and trusted servant that the master trusts to give the other servants their food at the right time? **43**When the master comes and finds the servant doing his work, the servant will be blessed. **44**I tell you the truth, the master will choose that servant to take care of everything he owns. **45**But suppose the servant thinks to himself, 'My master will not come back soon,' and he begins to beat the other servants, men and women, and to eat and drink and get drunk. **46**The master will come when that servant is not ready and is not expecting him. Then the master will cut him in pieces and send him away to be with the others who don't obey.

47"The servant who knows what his master wants but is not ready, or who does not do what the master wants, will be beaten with many blows! **48**But the servant who does not know what his master wants and does things that should be punished will be beaten with few blows. From everyone who has been given much, much will be demanded. And from the one trusted with much, much more will be expected.

Jesus Causes Division

49"I came to set fire to the world, and I wish it were already burning! **50**I have a baptism*n* to suffer through, and I feel very troubled until it is over. **51**Do you think I came to give peace to the earth? No, I tell you, I came to divide it. **52**From now on, a family with five people will be divided, three against two, and two against three. **53**They will be divided: father against son and son against father, mother against daughter and daughter against mother, mother-in-law against daughter-in-law and daughter-in-law against mother-in-law."

Understanding the Times

54Then Jesus said to the people, "When you see clouds coming up in the west, you say, 'It's going to rain,' and it happens. **55**When you feel the wind begin to blow from the south, you say, 'It will be a hot day,' and it happens. **56**Hypocrites!*d* You know how to understand the appearance of the earth and sky. Why don't you understand what is happening now?

Settle Your Problems

57"Why can't you decide for yourselves what is right? **58**If your enemy is taking you to court, try hard to settle it on the way. If you don't, your enemy might take you to the judge, and the judge might turn you over to the officer, and the officer might throw you into jail. **59**I tell you, you will not get out of there until you have paid everything you owe."

Change Your Hearts

13 At that time some people were there who told Jesus that Pilate*n* had killed some people from Galilee while they were worshiping. He mixed their blood with the blood of the animals they were sacrificing to God. **2**Jesus answered, "Do you think this happened to them because they were more sinful than all others from Galilee? **3**No, I tell you. But unless you change your hearts and lives, you will be destroyed as they were! **4**What about those eighteen people who died when the tower of Siloam fell on them? Do you think they were more sinful than all the

I . . . baptism　Jesus was talking about the suffering he would soon go through.
Pilate　Pontius Pilate was the Roman governor of Judea from A.D. 26 to A.D. 36.

others who live in Jerusalem? [5]No, I tell you. But unless you change your hearts and lives, you will all be destroyed too!"

The Useless Tree

[6]Jesus told this story: "A man had a fig tree planted in his vineyard. He came looking for some fruit on the tree, but he found none. [7]So the man said to his gardener, 'I have been looking for fruit on this tree for three years, but I never find any. Cut it down. Why should it waste the ground?' [8]But the servant answered, 'Master, let the tree have one more year to produce fruit. Let me dig up the dirt around it and put on some fertilizer. [9]If the tree produces fruit next year, good. But if not, you can cut it down.' "

Jesus Heals on the Sabbath

[10]Jesus was teaching in one of the synagogues[d] on the Sabbath[d] day. [11]A woman was there who, for eighteen years, had an evil spirit in her that made her crippled. Her back was always bent; she could not stand up straight. [12]When Jesus saw her, he called her over and said, "Woman, you are free from your sickness." [13]Jesus put his hands on her, and immediately she was able to stand up straight and began praising God.

[14]The synagogue leader was angry because Jesus healed on the Sabbath day. He said to the people, "There are six days when one has to work. So come to be healed on one of those days, and not on the Sabbath day."

[15]The Lord answered, "You hypocrites![d] Doesn't each of you untie your work animals and lead them to drink water every day — even on the Sabbath day? [16]This woman that I healed, a daughter of Abraham, has been held by Satan for eighteen years. Surely it is not wrong for her to be freed from her sickness on a Sabbath day!" [17]When Jesus said this, all of those who were criticizing him were ashamed, but the entire crowd rejoiced at all the wonderful things Jesus was doing.

Stories of Mustard Seed and Yeast

[18]Then Jesus said, "What is God's kingdom like? What can I compare it with? [19]It is like a mustard seed that a man plants in his garden. The seed grows and becomes a tree, and the wild birds build nests in its branches."

[20]Jesus said again, "What can I compare God's kingdom with? [21]It is like yeast that a woman took and hid in a large tub of flour until it made all the dough rise."

The Narrow Door

[22]Jesus was teaching in every town and village as he traveled toward Jerusalem. [23]Someone said to Jesus, "Lord, will only a few people be saved?"

Jesus said, [24]"Try hard to enter through the narrow door, because many people will try to enter there, but they will not be able. [25]When the owner of the house gets up and closes the door, you can stand outside and knock on the door and say, 'Sir, open the door for us.' But he will answer, 'I don't know you or where you come from.' [26]Then you will say, 'We ate and drank with you, and you taught in the streets of our town.' [27]But he will say to you, 'I don't know you or where you come from. Go away from me, all you who do evil!' [28]You will cry and grind your teeth with pain when you see Abraham, Isaac, Jacob, and all the prophets[d] in God's kingdom, but you yourselves thrown outside. [29]People will come from the east, west, north, and south and will sit down at the table in the kingdom of God. [30]There are those who have the lowest place in life now who will have the highest place in the future. And there are those who have the highest place now who will have the lowest place in the future."

Jesus Will Die in Jerusalem

[31]At that time some Pharisees[d] came to Jesus and said, "Go away from here! Herod wants to kill you!"

[32]Jesus said to them, "Go tell that fox Herod, 'Today and tomorrow I am forcing demons[d] out and healing people. Then, on the third day, I will reach my goal.' [33]Yet I must be on my way today and tomorrow and the next day. Surely it cannot be right for a prophet[d] to be killed anywhere except in Jerusalem.

[34]"Jerusalem, Jerusalem! You kill the prophets and stone to death those who are sent to you. Many times I wanted to gather

your people as a hen gathers her chicks under her wings, but you would not let me. [35]Now your house is left completely empty. I tell you, you will not see me until that time when you will say, 'God bless the One who comes in the name of the Lord.' " [n]

Healing on the Sabbath

14 On a Sabbath[d] day, when Jesus went to eat at the home of a leading Pharisee,[d] the people were watching Jesus very closely. [2]And in front of him was a man with dropsy.[n] [3]Jesus said to the Pharisees and experts on the law, "Is it right or wrong to heal on the Sabbath day?" [4]But they would not answer his question. So Jesus took the man, healed him, and sent him away. [5]Jesus said to the Pharisees and teachers of the law, "If your child or ox falls into a well on the Sabbath day, will you not pull him out quickly?" [6]And they could not answer him.

Don't Make Yourself Important

[7]When Jesus noticed that some of the guests were choosing the best places to sit, he told this story: [8]"When someone invites you to a wedding feast, don't take the most important seat, because someone more important than you may have been invited. [9]The host, who invited both of you, will come to you and say, 'Give this person your seat.' Then you will be embarrassed and will have to move to the last place. [10]So when you are invited, go sit in a seat that is not important. When the host comes to you, he may say, 'Friend, move up here to a more important place.' Then all the other guests will respect you. [11]All who make themselves great will be made humble, but those who make themselves humble will be made great."

You Will Be Rewarded

[12]Then Jesus said to the man who had invited him, "When you give a lunch or a dinner, don't invite only your friends, your family, your other relatives, and your rich neighbors. At another time they will invite you to eat with them, and you will be repaid.

[13]Instead, when you give a feast, invite the poor, the crippled, the lame, and the blind. [14]Then you will be blessed, because they have nothing and cannot pay you back. But you will be repaid when the good people rise from the dead."

A Story About a Big Banquet

[15]One of those at the table with Jesus heard these things and said to him, "Happy are the people who will share in the meal in God's kingdom."

[16]Jesus said to him, "A man gave a big banquet and invited many people. [17]When it was time to eat, the man sent his servant to tell the guests, 'Come. Everything is ready.'

[18]"But all the guests made excuses. The first one said, 'I have just bought a field, and I must go look at it. Please excuse me.' [19]Another said, 'I have just bought five pairs of oxen; I must go and try them. Please excuse me.' [20]A third person said, 'I just got married; I can't come.' [21]So the servant returned and told his master what had happened. Then the master became angry and said, 'Go at once into the streets and alleys of the town, and bring in the poor, the crippled, the blind, and the lame.' [22]Later the servant said to him, 'Master, I did what you commanded, but we still have room.' [23]The master said to the servant, 'Go out to the roads and country lanes, and urge the people there to come so my house will be full. [24]I tell you, none of those whom I invited first will eat with me.' "

The Cost of Being Jesus' Follower

[25]Large crowds were traveling with Jesus, and he turned and said to them, [26]"If anyone comes to me but loves his father, mother, wife, children, brothers, or sisters — or even life — more than me, he cannot be my follower. [27]Whoever is not willing to carry the cross and follow me cannot be my follower. [28]If you want to build a tower, you first sit down and decide how much it will cost, to see if you have enough money to finish the job. [29]If you don't, you might lay the foundation, but you would not be able to finish. Then all who would see it would make fun

'God . . . Lord.' Quotation from Psalm 118:26.
dropsy A sickness that causes the body to swell larger and larger.

of you, [30]saying, 'This person began to build but was not able to finish.'

[31]"If a king is going to fight another king, first he will sit down and plan. He will decide if he and his ten thousand soldiers can defeat the other king who has twenty thousand soldiers. [32]If he can't, then while the other king is still far away, he will send some people to speak to him and ask for peace. [33]In the same way, you must give up everything you have to be my follower.

Don't Lose Your Influence

[34]"Salt is good, but if it loses its salty taste, you cannot make it salty again. [35]It is no good for the soil or for manure; it is thrown away.

"You people who can hear me, listen."

A Lost Sheep, a Lost Coin

15 The tax collectors and sinners all came to listen to Jesus. [2]But the Pharisees[d] and the teachers of the law began to complain: "Look, this man welcomes sinners and even eats with them."

[3]Then Jesus told them this story: [4]"Suppose one of you has a hundred sheep but loses one of them. Then he will leave the other ninety-nine sheep in the open field and go out and look for the lost sheep until he finds it. [5]And when he finds it, he happily puts it on his shoulders [6]and goes home. He calls to his friends and neighbors and says, 'Be happy with me because I found my lost sheep.' [7]In the same way, I tell you there is more joy in heaven over one sinner who changes his heart and life, than over ninety-nine good people who don't need to change.

[8]"Suppose a woman has ten silver coins,[n] but loses one. She will light a lamp, sweep the house, and look carefully for the coin until she finds it. [9]And when she finds it, she will call her friends and neighbors and say, 'Be happy with me because I have found the coin that I lost.' [10]In the same way, there is joy in the presence of the angels of God when one sinner changes his heart and life."

The Son Who Left Home

[11]Then Jesus said, "A man had two sons.

[12]The younger son said to his father, 'Give me my share of the property.' So the father divided the property between his two sons. [13]Then the younger son gathered up all that was his and traveled far away to another country. There he wasted his money in foolish living. [14]After he had spent everything, a time came when there was no food anywhere in the country, and the son was poor and hungry. [15]So he got a job with one of the citizens there who sent the son into the fields to feed pigs. [16]The son was so hungry that he wanted to eat the pods the pigs were eating, but no one gave him anything. [17]When he realized what he was doing, he thought, 'All of my father's servants have plenty of food. But I am here, almost dying with hunger. [18]I will leave and return to my father and say to him, "Father, I have sinned against God and have done wrong to you. [19]I am no longer worthy to be called your son, but let me be like one of your servants." ' [20]So the son left and went to his father.

"While the son was still a long way off, his father saw him and felt sorry for his son. So the father ran to him and hugged and kissed him. [21]The son said, 'Father, I have sinned against God and have done wrong to you. I am no longer worthy to be called your son.' [22]But the father said to his servants, 'Hurry! Bring the best clothes and put them on him. Also, put a ring on his finger and sandals on his feet. [23]And get our fat calf and kill it so we can have a feast and celebrate. [24]My son was dead, but now he is alive again! He was lost, but now he is found!' So they began to celebrate.

[25]"The older son was in the field, and as he came closer to the house, he heard the sound of music and dancing. [26]So he called to one of the servants and asked what all this meant. [27]The servant said, 'Your brother has come back, and your father killed the fat calf, because your brother came home safely.' [28]The older son was angry and would not go in to the feast. So his father went out and begged him to come in. [29]But the older son said to his father, 'I have served you like a slave for many years and have always obeyed your commands. But you never gave me

silver coins Roman denarii. One coin was the average pay for one day's work.

even a young goat to have at a feast with my friends. 30But your other son, who wasted all your money on prostitutes,*d* comes home, and you kill the fat calf for him!' 31The father said to him, 'Son, you are always with me, and all that I have is yours. 32We had to celebrate and be happy because your brother was dead, but now he is alive. He was lost, but now he is found.' "

True Wealth

16 Jesus also said to his followers, "Once there was a rich man who had a manager to take care of his business. This manager was accused of cheating him. 2So he called the manager in and said to him, 'What is this I hear about you? Give me a report of what you have done with my money, because you can't be my manager any longer.' 3The manager thought to himself, 'What will I do since my master is taking my job away from me? I am not strong enough to dig ditches, and I am ashamed to beg. 4I know what I'll do so that when I lose my job people will welcome me into their homes.'

5"So the manager called in everyone who owed the master any money. He asked the first one, 'How much do you owe?' 6He answered, 'Eight hundred gallons of olive oil.' The manager said to him, 'Take your bill, sit down quickly, and write four hundred gallons.' 7Then the manager asked another one, 'How much do you owe?' He answered, 'One thousand bushels of wheat.' Then the manager said to him, 'Take your bill and write eight hundred bushels.' 8So, the master praised the dishonest manager for being smart. Yes, worldly people are smarter with their own kind than spiritual people are.

9"I tell you, make friends for yourselves using worldly riches so that when those riches are gone, you will be welcomed in those homes that continue forever. 10Whoever can be trusted with a little can also be trusted with a lot, and whoever is dishonest with a little is dishonest with a lot. 11If you cannot be trusted with worldly riches, then who will trust you with true riches? 12And if you cannot be trusted with things that belong to someone else, who will give you things of your own?

13"No servant can serve two masters. The servant will hate one master and love the other, or will follow one master and refuse to follow the other. You cannot serve both God and worldly riches."

God's Law Cannot Be Changed

14The Pharisees,*d* who loved money, were listening to all these things and made fun of Jesus. 15He said to them, "You make yourselves look good in front of people, but God knows what is really in your hearts. What is important to people is hateful in God's sight.

16"The law of Moses and the writings of the prophets*d* were preached until John*n* came. Since then the Good News*d* about the kingdom of God is being told, and everyone tries to enter it by force. 17It would be easier for heaven and earth to pass away than for the smallest part of a letter in the law to be changed.

Divorce and Remarriage

18"If a man divorces his wife and marries another woman, he is guilty of adultery,*d* and the man who marries a divorced woman is also guilty of adultery."

The Rich Man and Lazarus

19Jesus said, "There was a rich man who always dressed in the finest clothes and lived in luxury every day. 20And a very poor man named Lazarus, whose body was covered with sores, was laid at the rich man's gate. 21He wanted to eat only the small pieces of food that fell from the rich man's table. And the dogs would come and lick his sores. 22Later, Lazarus died, and the angels carried him to the arms of Abraham.*d* The rich man died, too, and was buried. 23In the place of the dead, he was in much pain. The rich man saw Abraham far away with Lazarus at his side. 24He called, 'Father Abraham, have mercy on me! Send Lazarus to dip his finger in water and cool my tongue, because I am suffering in this fire!' 25But Abraham said, 'Child, remember when you were alive you had the good things in life, but bad things

---

John   John the Baptist, who preached to people about Christ's coming (Matthew 3, Luke 3).

happened to Lazarus. Now he is comforted here, and you are suffering. 26Besides, there is a big pit between you and us, so no one can cross over to you, and no one can leave there and come here.' 27The rich man said, 'Father, then please send Lazarus to my father's house. 28I have five brothers, and Lazarus could warn them so that they will not come to this place of pain.' 29But Abraham said, 'They have the law of Moses and the writings of the prophets;*d* let them learn from them.' 30The rich man said, 'No, father Abraham! If someone goes to them from the dead, they would believe and change their hearts and lives.' 31But Abraham said to him, 'If they will not listen to Moses and the prophets, they will not listen to someone who comes back from the dead.' "

Sin and Forgiveness

17 Jesus said to his followers, "Things that cause people to sin will happen, but how terrible for the person who causes them to happen! 2It would be better for you to be thrown into the sea with a large stone around your neck than to cause one of these little ones to sin. 3So be careful!

"If another follower sins, warn him, and if he is sorry and stops sinning, forgive him. 4If he sins against you seven times in one day and says that he is sorry each time, forgive him."

How Big Is Your Faith?

5The apostles*d* said to the Lord, "Give us more faith!"

6The Lord said, "If your faith were the size of a mustard seed, you could say to this mulberry tree, 'Dig yourself up and plant yourself in the sea,' and it would obey you.

Be Good Servants

7"Suppose one of you has a servant who has been plowing the ground or caring for the sheep. When the servant comes in from working in the field, would you say, 'Come in and sit down to eat'? 8No, you would say to him, 'Prepare something for me to eat. Then get yourself ready and serve me. After

I finish eating and drinking, you can eat.' 9The servant does not get any special thanks for doing what his master commanded. 10It is the same with you. When you have done everything you are told to do, you should say, 'We are unworthy servants; we have only done the work we should do.' "

Be Thankful

11While Jesus was on his way to Jerusalem, he was going through the area between Samaria and Galilee. 12As he came into a small town, ten men who had a skin disease met him there. They did not come close to Jesus 13but called to him, "Jesus! Master! Have mercy on us!"

14When Jesus saw the men, he said, "Go and show yourselves to the priests."*n*

As the ten men were going, they were healed. 15When one of them saw that he was healed, he went back to Jesus, praising God in a loud voice. 16Then he bowed down at Jesus' feet and thanked him. (And this man was a Samaritan.*d*) 17Jesus said, "Weren't ten men healed? Where are the other nine? 18Is this Samaritan the only one who came back to thank God?" 19Then Jesus said to him, "Stand up and go on your way. You were healed because you believed."

God's Kingdom Is Within You

20Some of the Pharisees*d* asked Jesus, "When will the kingdom of God come?"

Jesus answered, "God's kingdom is coming, but not in a way that you will be able to see with your eyes. 21People will not say, 'Look, here it is!' or, 'There it is!' because God's kingdom is within*n* you."

22Then Jesus said to his followers, "The time will come when you will want very much to see one of the days of the Son of Man.*d* But you will not see it. 23People will say to you, 'Look, there he is!' or, 'Look, here he is!' Stay where you are; don't go away and search.

When Jesus Comes Again

24"When the Son of Man*d* comes again, he will shine like lightning, which flashes across

---

show . . . priests The law of Moses said a priest must say when a Jewish person with a skin disease became well.
within Or "among."

the sky and lights it up from one side to the other. 25But first he must suffer many things and be rejected by the people of this time. 26When the Son of Man comes again, it will be as it was when Noah lived. 27People were eating, drinking, marrying, and giving their children to be married until the day Noah entered the boat. Then the flood came and killed them all. 28It will be the same as during the time of Lot. People were eating, drinking, buying, selling, planting, and building. 29But the day Lot left Sodom,n fire and sulfur rained down from the sky and killed them all. 30This is how it will be when the Son of Man comes again.

31"On that day, a person who is on the roof and whose belongings are in the house should not go inside to get them. A person who is in the field should not go back home. 32Remember Lot's wife. n 33Those who try to keep their lives will lose them. But those who give up their lives will save them. 34I tell you, on that night two people will be sleeping in one bed; one will be taken and the other will be left. 35There will be two women grinding grain together; one will be taken, and the other will be left." 36 n

37The followers asked Jesus, "Where will this be, Lord?"

Jesus answered, "Where there is a dead body, there the vultures will gather."

God Will Answer His People

18 Then Jesus used this story to teach his followers that they should always pray and never lose hope. 2"In a certain town there was a judge who did not respect God or care about people. 3In that same town there was a widow who kept coming to this judge, saying, 'Give me my rights against my enemy.' 4For a while the judge refused to help her. But afterwards, he thought to himself, 'Even though I don't respect God or care about people, 5I will see that she gets her rights. Otherwise she will continue to bother me until I am worn out.'"

6The Lord said, "Listen to what the unfair judge said. 7God will always give what is right to his people who cry to him night and day, and he will not be slow to answer them. 8I tell you, God will help his people quickly. But when the Son of Mand comes again, will he find those on earth who believe in him?"

Being Right with God

9Jesus told this story to some people who thought they were very good and looked down on everyone else: 10"A Phariseed and a tax collector both went to the Templed to pray. 11The Pharisee stood alone and prayed, 'God, I thank you that I am not like other people who steal, cheat, or take part in adultery,d or even like this tax collector. 12I give up eatingn twice a week, and I give one-tenth of everything I get!'

13"The tax collector, standing at a distance, would not even look up to heaven. But he beat on his chest because he was so sad. He said, 'God, have mercy on me, a sinner.' 14I tell you, when this man went home, he was right with God, but the Pharisee was not. All who make themselves great will be made humble, but all who make themselves humble will be made great."

Who Will Enter God's Kingdom?

15Some people brought even their babies to Jesus so he could touch them. When the followers saw this, they told them to stop. 16But Jesus called for the children, saying, "Let the little children come to me. Don't stop them, because the kingdom of God belongs to people who are like these children. 17I tell you the truth, you must accept the kingdom of God as if you were a child, or you will never enter it."

A Rich Man's Question

18A certain leader asked Jesus, "Good Teacher, what must I do to have life forever?"

19Jesus said to him, "Why do you call me good? Only God is good. 20You know the commands: 'You must not be guilty of adul-

Sodom   City that God destroyed because the people were so evil.
Lot's wife   A story about what happened to Lot's wife is found in Genesis 19:15-17, 26.
Verse 36   A few Greek copies add verse 36: "Two people will be in the field. One will be taken, and the other will be left."
give up eating   This is called "fasting." The people would give up eating for a special time of prayer and worship to God. It was also done to show sadness and disappointment.

tery.*d* You must not murder anyone. You must not steal. You must not tell lies about your neighbor. Honor your father and mother.' "*n*

21But the leader said, "I have obeyed all these commands since I was a boy."

22When Jesus heard this, he said to him, "There is still one more thing you need to do. Sell everything you have and give it to the poor, and you will have treasure in heaven. Then come and follow me." 23But when the man heard this, he became very sad, because he was very rich.

24Jesus looked at him and said, "It is very hard for rich people to enter the kingdom of God. 25It is easier for a camel to go through the eye of a needle than for a rich person to enter the kingdom of God."

Who Can Be Saved?

26When the people heard this, they asked, "Then who can be saved?"

27Jesus answered, "God can do things that are not possible for people to do."

28Peter said, "Look, we have left everything and followed you."

29Jesus said, "I tell you the truth, all those who have left houses, wives, brothers, parents, or children for the kingdom of God 30will get much more in this life. And in the age that is coming, they will have life forever."

Jesus Will Rise from the Dead

31Then Jesus took the twelve apostles*d* aside and said to them, "We are going to Jerusalem. Everything the prophets*d* wrote about the Son of Man*d* will happen. 32He will be turned over to those who are not Jews. They will laugh at him, insult him, spit on him, 33beat him with whips, and kill him. But on the third day, he will rise to life again." 34The apostles did not understand this; the meaning was hidden from them, and they did not realize what was said.

Jesus Heals a Blind Man

35As Jesus came near the city of Jericho, a blind man was sitting beside the road, begging. 36When he heard the people coming

down the road, he asked, "What is happening?"

37They told him, "Jesus, from Nazareth, is going by."

38The blind man cried out, "Jesus, Son of David,*d* have mercy on me!"

39The people leading the group warned the blind man to be quiet. But the blind man shouted even more, "Son of David, have mercy on me!"

40Jesus stopped and ordered the blind man to be brought to him. When he came near, Jesus asked him, 41"What do you want me to do for you?"

He said, "Lord, I want to see."

42Jesus said to him, "Then see. You are healed because you believed."

43At once the man was able to see, and he followed Jesus, thanking God. All the people who saw this praised God.

Zacchaeus Meets Jesus

19 Jesus was going through the city of Jericho. 2A man was there named Zacchaeus, who was a very important tax collector, and he was wealthy. 3He wanted to see who Jesus was, but he was not able because he was too short to see above the crowd. 4He ran ahead to a place where Jesus would come, and he climbed a sycamore tree so he could see him. 5When Jesus came to that place, he looked up and said to him, "Zacchaeus, hurry and come down! I must stay at your house today."

6Zacchaeus came down quickly and welcomed him gladly. 7All the people saw this and began to complain, "Jesus is staying with a sinner!"

8But Zacchaeus stood and said to the Lord, "I will give half of my possessions to the poor. And if I have cheated anyone, I will pay back four times more."

9Jesus said to him, "Salvation has come to this house today, because this man also belongs to the family of Abraham. 10The Son of Man*d* came to find lost people and save them."

A Story About Three Servants

11As the people were listening to this,

'You ... mother.' Quotation from Exodus 20:12-16; Deuteronomy 5:16-20.

Jesus told them a story because he was near Jerusalem and they thought God's kingdom would appear immediately. 12He said: "A very important man went to a country far away to be made a king and then to return home. 13So he called ten of his servants and gave a coin*n* to each servant. He said, 'Do business with this money until I get back.' 14But the people in the kingdom hated the man. So they sent a group to follow him and say, 'We don't want this man to be our king.'

15"But the man became king. When he returned home, he said, 'Call those servants who have my money so I can know how much they earned with it.'

16"The first servant came and said, 'Sir, I earned ten coins with the one you gave me.' 17The king said to the servant, 'Excellent! You are a good servant. Since I can trust you with small things, I will let you rule over ten of my cities.'

18"The second servant said, 'Sir, I earned five coins with your one.' 19The king said to this servant, 'You can rule over five cities.'

20"Then another servant came in and said to the king, 'Sir, here is your coin which I wrapped in a piece of cloth and hid. 21I was afraid of you, because you are a hard man. You even take money that you didn't earn and gather food that you didn't plant.' 22Then the king said to the servant, 'I will condemn you by your own words, you evil servant. You knew that I am a hard man, taking money that I didn't earn and gathering food that I didn't plant. 23Why then didn't you put my money in the bank? Then when I came back, my money would have earned some interest.'

24"The king said to the men who were standing by, 'Take the coin away from this servant and give it to the servant who earned ten coins.' 25They said, 'But sir, that servant already has ten coins.' 26The king said, 'Those who have will be given more, but those who do not have anything will have everything taken away from them. 27Now where are my enemies who didn't want me to be king? Bring them here and kill them before me.' "

Jesus Enters Jerusalem as a King

28After Jesus said this, he went on toward Jerusalem. 29As Jesus came near Bethphage and Bethany, towns near the hill called the Mount of Olives,*d* he sent out two of his followers. 30He said, "Go to the town you can see there. When you enter it, you will find a colt tied there, which no one has ever ridden. Untie it and bring it here to me. 31If anyone asks you why you are untying it, say that the Master needs it."

32The two followers went into town and found the colt just as Jesus had told them. 33As they were untying it, its owners came out and asked the followers, "Why are you untying our colt?"

34The followers answered, "The Master needs it." 35So they brought it to Jesus, threw their coats on the colt's back, and put Jesus on it. 36As Jesus rode toward Jerusalem, others spread their coats on the road before him.

37As he was coming close to Jerusalem, on the way down the Mount of Olives, the whole crowd of followers began joyfully shouting praise to God for all the miracles*d* they had seen. 38They said,

"God bless the king who comes in the
        name of the Lord!   *Psalm 118:26*
There is peace in heaven and glory to
        God!"

39Some of the Pharisees*d* in the crowd said to Jesus, "Teacher, tell your followers not to say these things."

40But Jesus answered, "I tell you, if my followers didn't say these things, then the stones would cry out."

Jesus Cries for Jerusalem

41As Jesus came near Jerusalem, he saw the city and cried for it, 42saying, "I wish you knew today what would bring you peace. But now it is hidden from you. 43The time is coming when your enemies will build a wall around you and will hold you in on all sides. 44They will destroy you and all your people, and not one stone will be left on another. All this will happen because you did not recognize the time when God came to save you."

---

coin A Greek "mina." One mina was enough money to pay a person for working three months.

Jesus Goes to the Temple

[45]Jesus went into the Temple[d] and began to throw out the people who were selling things there. [46]He said, "It is written in the Scriptures,[d] 'My Temple will be a house for prayer.'[n] But you have changed it into a 'hideout for robbers'!"[n]

[47]Jesus taught in the Temple every day. The leading priests, the experts on the law, and some of the leaders of the people wanted to kill Jesus. [48]But they did not know how they could do it, because all the people were listening closely to him.

Jewish Leaders Question Jesus

20 One day Jesus was in the Temple,[d] teaching the people and telling them the Good News.[d] The leading priests, teachers of the law, and older Jewish leaders came up to talk with him, [2]saying, "Tell us what authority you have to do these things? Who gave you this authority?"

[3]Jesus answered, "I will also ask you a question. Tell me: [4]When John baptized people, was that authority from God or just from other people?"

[5]They argued about this, saying, "If we answer, 'John's baptism was from God,' Jesus will say, 'Then why did you not believe him?' [6]But if we say, 'It was from other people,' all the people will stone us to death, because they believe John was a prophet."[d] [7]So they answered that they didn't know where it came from.

[8]Jesus said to them, "Then I won't tell you what authority I have to do these things."

A Story About God's Son

[9]Then Jesus told the people this story: "A man planted a vineyard and leased it to some farmers. Then he went away for a long time. [10]When it was time for the grapes to be picked, he sent a servant to the farmers to get some of the grapes. But they beat the servant and sent him away empty-handed. [11]Then he sent another servant. They beat this servant also, and showed no respect for him, and sent him away empty-handed. [12]So the man

sent a third servant. The farmers wounded him and threw him out. [13]The owner of the vineyard said, 'What will I do now? I will send my son whom I love. Maybe they will respect him.' [14]But when the farmers saw the son, they said to each other, 'This son will inherit the vineyard. If we kill him, it will be ours.' [15]So the farmers threw the son out of the vineyard and killed him.

"What will the owner of this vineyard do to them? [16]He will come and kill those farmers and will give the vineyard to other farmers."

When the people heard this story, they said, "Let this never happen!"

[17]But Jesus looked at them and said, "Then what does this verse mean:

'The stone that the builders rejected
   became the cornerstone'?[d]   Psalm 118:22

[18]Everyone who falls on that stone will be broken, and the person on whom it falls, that person will be crushed!"

[19]The teachers of the law and the leading priests wanted to arrest Jesus at once, because they knew the story was about them. But they were afraid of what the people would do.

Is It Right to Pay Taxes or Not?

[20]So they watched Jesus and sent some spies who acted as if they were sincere. They wanted to trap Jesus in saying something wrong so they could hand him over to the authority and power of the governor. [21]So the spies asked Jesus, "Teacher, we know that what you say and teach is true. You pay no attention to who people are, and you always teach the truth about God's way. [22]Tell us, is it right for us to pay taxes to Caesar[d] or not?"

[23]But Jesus, knowing they were trying to trick him, said, [24]"Show me a coin. Whose image and name are on it?"

They said, "Caesar's."

[25]Jesus said to them, "Then give to Caesar the things that are Caesar's, and give to God the things that are God's."

[26]So they were not able to trap Jesus in anything he said in the presence of the peo-

---

'My Temple ... prayer.' Quotation from Isaiah 56:7.
'hideout for robbers' Quotation from Jeremiah 7:11.

ple. And being amazed at his answer, they became silent.

Some Sadducees Try to Trick Jesus

27Some Sadducees,*d* who believed people would not rise from the dead, came to Jesus. 28They asked, "Teacher, Moses wrote that if a man's brother dies and leaves a wife but no children, then that man must marry the widow and have children for his brother. 29Once there were seven brothers. The first brother married and died, but had no children. 30Then the second brother married the widow, and he died. 31And the third brother married the widow, and he died. The same thing happened with all seven brothers; they died and had no children. 32Finally, the woman died also. 33Since all seven brothers had married her, whose wife will she be when people rise from the dead?"

34Jesus said to them, "On earth, people marry and are given to someone to marry. 35But those who will be worthy to be raised from the dead and live again will not marry, nor will they be given to someone to marry. 36In that life they are like angels and cannot die. They are children of God, because they have been raised from the dead. 37Even Moses clearly showed that the dead are raised to life. When he wrote about the burning bush,*n* he said that the Lord is 'the God of Abraham, the God of Isaac, and the God of Jacob.'*n* 38God is the God of the living, not the dead, because all people are alive to him."

39Some of the teachers of the law said, "Teacher, your answer was good." 40No one was brave enough to ask him another question.

Is the Christ the Son of David?

41Then Jesus said, "Why do people say that the Christ*d* is the Son of David?*d* 42In the book of Psalms, David himself says:

'The Lord said to my Lord:
    Sit by me at my right side,
43   until I put your enemies under your
        control.'*n*   *Psalm 110:1*

44David calls the Christ 'Lord,' so how can the Christ be his son?"

Jesus Accuses Some Leaders

45While all the people were listening, Jesus said to his followers, 46"Beware of the teachers of the law. They like to walk around wearing fancy clothes, and they love for people to greet them with respect in the marketplaces. They love to have the most important seats in the synagogues*d* and at feasts. 47But they cheat widows and steal their houses and then try to make themselves look good by saying long prayers. They will receive a greater punishment."

True Giving

21 As Jesus looked up, he saw some rich people putting their gifts into the Temple*d* money box.*n* 2Then he saw a poor widow putting two small copper coins into the box. 3He said, "I tell you the truth, this poor widow gave more than all those rich people. 4They gave only what they did not need. This woman is very poor, but she gave all she had to live on."

The Temple Will Be Destroyed

5Some people were talking about the Temple*d* and how it was decorated with beautiful stones and gifts offered to God.

But Jesus said, 6"As for these things you are looking at, the time will come when not one stone will be left on another. Every stone will be thrown down."

7They asked Jesus, "Teacher, when will these things happen? What will be the sign that they are about to take place?"

8Jesus said, "Be careful so you are not fooled. Many people will come in my name, saying, 'I am the One' and, 'The time has come!' But don't follow them. 9When you hear about wars and riots, don't be afraid, because these things must happen first, but the end will come later."

10Then he said to them, "Nations will fight against other nations, and kingdoms against other kingdoms. 11In various places there

---

burning bush   Read Exodus 3:1-12 in the Old Testament.
'the God of . . . Jacob'   These words are taken from Exodus 3:6.
until . . . control   Literally, "until I make your enemies a footstool for your feet."
money box   A special box in the Jewish place of worship where people put their gifts to God.

will be great earthquakes, sicknesses, and a lack of food. Fearful events and great signs will come from heaven.

12 "But before all these things happen, people will arrest you and treat you cruelly. They will judge you in their synagogues*d* and put you in jail and force you to stand before kings and governors, because you follow me. 13 But this will give you an opportunity to tell about me. 14 Make up your minds not to worry ahead of time about what you will say. 15 I will give you the wisdom to say things that none of your enemies will be able to stand against or prove wrong. 16 Even your parents, brothers, relatives, and friends will turn against you, and they will kill some of you. 17 All people will hate you because you follow me. 18 But none of these things can really harm you. 19 By continuing to have faith you will save your lives.

Jerusalem Will Be Destroyed

20 "When you see armies all around Jerusalem, you will know it will soon be destroyed. 21 At that time, the people in Judea should run away to the mountains. The people in Jerusalem must get out, and those who are near the city should not go in. 22 These are the days of punishment to bring about all that is written in the Scriptures.*d* 23 How terrible it will be for women who are pregnant or have nursing babies! Great trouble will come upon this land, and God will be angry with these people. 24 They will be killed by the sword and taken as prisoners to all nations. Jerusalem will be crushed by non-Jewish people until their time is over.

Don't Fear

25 "There will be signs in the sun, moon, and stars. On earth, nations will be afraid and confused because of the roar and fury of the sea. 26 People will be so afraid they will faint, wondering what is happening to the world, because the powers of the heavens will be shaken. 27 Then people will see the Son of Man*d* coming in a cloud with power and great glory. 28 When these things begin to happen, look up and hold your heads high, because the time when God will free you is near!"

Jesus' Words Will Live Forever

29 Then Jesus told this story: "Look at the fig tree and all the other trees. 30 When their leaves appear, you know that summer is near. 31 In the same way, when you see these things happening, you will know that God's kingdom is near.

32 "I tell you the truth, all these things will happen while the people of this time are still living. 33 Earth and sky will be destroyed, but the words I have spoken will never be destroyed.

Be Ready All the Time

34 "Be careful not to spend your time feasting, drinking, or worrying about worldly things. If you do, that day might come on you suddenly, 35 like a trap on all people on earth. 36 So be ready all the time. Pray that you will be strong enough to escape all these things that will happen and that you will be able to stand before the Son of Man."*d*

37 During the day, Jesus taught the people in the Temple,*d* and at night he went out of the city and stayed on the Mount of Olives.*d* 38 Every morning all the people got up early to go to the Temple to listen to him.

Judas Becomes an Enemy of Jesus

22 It was almost time for the Feast*d* of Unleavened Bread, called the Passover*d* Feast. 2 The leading priests and teachers of the law were trying to find a way to kill Jesus, because they were afraid of the people.

3 Satan entered Judas Iscariot, one of Jesus' twelve apostles.*d* 4 Judas went to the leading priests and some of the soldiers who guarded the Temple*d* and talked to them about a way to hand Jesus over to them. 5 They were pleased and agreed to give Judas money. 6 He agreed and watched for the best time to hand Jesus over to them when he was away from the crowd.

Jesus Eats the Passover Meal

7 The Day of Unleavened*d* Bread came when the Passover*d* lambs had to be sacrificed. 8 Jesus said to Peter and John, "Go and prepare the Passover meal for us to eat."

9 They asked, "Where do you want us to prepare it?" 10 Jesus said to them, "After you

go into the city, a man carrying a jar of water will meet you. Follow him into the house that he enters, 11and tell the owner of the house, 'The Teacher says: Where is the guest room in which I may eat the Passover meal with my followers?' 12Then he will show you a large, furnished room upstairs. Prepare the Passover meal there."

13So Peter and John left and found everything as Jesus had said. And they prepared the Passover meal.

The Lord's Supper

14When the time came, Jesus and the apostles*d* were sitting at the table. 15He said to them, "I wanted very much to eat this Passover*d* meal with you before I suffer. 16I will not eat another Passover meal until it is given its true meaning in the kingdom of God."

17Then Jesus took a cup, gave thanks, and said, "Take this cup and share it among yourselves. 18I will not drink again from the fruit of the vine*n* until God's kingdom comes."

19Then Jesus took some bread, gave thanks, broke it, and gave it to the apostles, saying, "This is my body, which I am giving for you. Do this to remember me." 20In the same way, after supper, Jesus took the cup and said, "This cup is the new agreement that God makes with his people. This new agreement begins with my blood which is poured out for you.

Who Will Turn Against Jesus?

21"But one of you will turn against me, and his hand is with mine on the table. 22What God has planned for the Son of Man*d* will happen, but how terrible it will be for that one who turns against the Son of Man."

23Then the apostles*d* asked each other which one of them would do that.

Be Like a Servant

24The apostles*d* also began to argue about which one of them was the most important. 25But Jesus said to them, "The kings of the non-Jewish people rule over them, and those who have authority over others like to be called 'friends of the people.' 26But you must not be like that. Instead, the greatest among you should be like the youngest, and the leader should be like the servant. 27Who is more important: the one sitting at the table or the one serving? You think the one at the table is more important, but I am like a servant among you.

28"You have stayed with me through my struggles. 29Just as my Father has given me a kingdom, I also give you a kingdom 30so you may eat and drink at my table in my kingdom. And you will sit on thrones, judging the twelve tribes*d* of Israel.

Don't Lose Your Faith!

31"Simon, Simon, Satan has asked to test all of you as a farmer sifts his wheat. 32I have prayed that you will not lose your faith! Help your brothers be stronger when you come back to me."

33But Peter said to Jesus, "Lord, I am ready to go with you to prison and even to die with you!"

34But Jesus said, "Peter, before the rooster crows this day, you will say three times that you don't know me."

Be Ready for Trouble

35Then Jesus said to the apostles,*d* "When I sent you out without a purse, a bag, or sandals, did you need anything?"

They said, "No."

36He said to them, "But now if you have a purse or a bag, carry that with you. If you don't have a sword, sell your coat and buy one. 37The Scripture*d* says, 'He was treated like a criminal,'*n* and I tell you this scripture must have its full meaning. It was written about me, and it is happening now."

38His followers said, "Look, Lord, here are two swords."

He said to them, "That is enough."

Jesus Prays Alone

39Jesus left the city and went to the Mount of Olives,*d* as he often did, and his followers went with him. 40When he reached the

---

fruit of the vine Product of the grapevine; this may also be translated "wine."
'He ... criminal' Quotation from Isaiah 53:12.

place, he said to them, "Pray for strength against temptation."

41Then Jesus went about a stone's throw away from them. He kneeled down and prayed, 42"Father, if you are willing, take away this cup*n* of suffering. But do what you want, not what I want." 43Then an angel from heaven appeared to him to strengthen him. 44Being full of pain, Jesus prayed even harder. His sweat was like drops of blood falling to the ground. 45When he finished praying, he went to his followers and found them asleep because of their sadness. 46Jesus said to them, "Why are you sleeping? Get up and pray for strength against temptation."

Jesus Is Arrested

47While Jesus was speaking, a crowd came up, and Judas, one of the twelve apostles,*d* was leading them. He came close to Jesus so he could kiss him.

48But Jesus said to him, "Judas, are you using the kiss to give the Son of Man*d* to his enemies?"

49When those who were standing around him saw what was happening, they said, "Lord, should we strike them with our swords?" 50And one of them struck the servant of the high priest and cut off his right ear.

51Jesus said, "Stop! No more of this." Then he touched the servant's ear and healed him.

52Those who came to arrest Jesus were the leading priests, the soldiers who guarded the Temple,*d* and the older Jewish leaders. Jesus said to them, "You came out here with swords and clubs as though I were a criminal. 53I was with you every day in the Temple, and you didn't arrest me there. But this is your time—the time when darkness rules."

Peter Says He Doesn't Know Jesus

54They arrested Jesus, and led him away, and brought him into the house of the high priest. Peter followed far behind them. 55After the soldiers started a fire in the middle of the courtyard and sat together, Peter sat with them. 56A servant girl saw Peter sitting there

in the firelight, and looking closely at him, she said, "This man was also with him."

57But Peter said this was not true; he said, "Woman, I don't know him."

58A short time later, another person saw Peter and said, "You are also one of them."

But Peter said, "Man, I am not!"

59About an hour later, another man insisted, "Certainly this man was with him, because he is from Galilee, too."

60But Peter said, "Man, I don't know what you are talking about!"

At once, while Peter was still speaking, a rooster crowed. 61Then the Lord turned and looked straight at Peter. And Peter remembered what the Lord had said: "Before the rooster crows this day, you will say three times that you don't know me." 62Then Peter went outside and cried painfully.

The People Make Fun of Jesus

63The men who were guarding Jesus began making fun of him and beating him. 64They blindfolded him and said, "Prove that you are a prophet,*d* and tell us who hit you." 65They said many cruel things to Jesus.

Jesus Before the Leaders

66When day came, the council of the older leaders of the people, both the leading priests and the teachers of the law, came together and led Jesus to their highest court. 67They said, "If you are the Christ,*d* tell us."

Jesus said to them, "If I tell you, you will not believe me. 68And if I ask you, you will not answer. 69But from now on, the Son of Man*d* will sit at the right hand of the powerful God."

70They all said, "Then are you the Son of God?"

Jesus said to them, "You say that I am."

71They said, "Why do we need witnesses now? We ourselves heard him say this."

Pilate Questions Jesus

23 Then the whole group stood up and led Jesus to Pilate.*n* 2They began to accuse Jesus, saying, "We caught this man

---

cup Jesus is talking about the painful things that will happen to him. Accepting these things will be hard, like drinking a cup of something bitter.
Pilate Pontius Pilate was the Roman governor of Judea from A.D. 26 to A.D. 36.

telling things that mislead our people. He says that we should not pay taxes to Caesar,*d* and he calls himself the Christ,*d* a king."

³Pilate asked Jesus, "Are you the king of the Jews?"

Jesus answered, "Those are your words."

⁴Pilate said to the leading priests and the people, "I find nothing against this man."

⁵They were insisting, saying, "But Jesus makes trouble with the people, teaching all around Judea. He began in Galilee, and now he is here."

Pilate Sends Jesus to Herod

⁶Pilate heard this and asked if Jesus was from Galilee. ⁷Since Jesus was under Herod's authority, Pilate sent Jesus to Herod, who was in Jerusalem at that time. ⁸When Herod saw Jesus, he was very glad, because he had heard about Jesus and had wanted to meet him for a long time. He was hoping to see Jesus work a miracle.*d* ⁹Herod asked Jesus many questions, but Jesus said nothing. ¹⁰The leading priests and teachers of the law were standing there, strongly accusing Jesus. ¹¹After Herod and his soldiers had made fun of Jesus, they dressed him in a kingly robe and sent him back to Pilate. ¹²In the past, Pilate and Herod had always been enemies, but on that day they became friends.

Jesus Must Die

¹³Pilate called the people together with the leading priests and the Jewish leaders. ¹⁴He said to them, "You brought this man to me, saying he makes trouble among the people. But I have questioned him before you all, and I have not found him guilty of what you say. ¹⁵Also, Herod found nothing wrong with him; he sent him back to us. Look, he has done nothing for which he should die. ¹⁶So, after I punish him, I will let him go free." ¹⁷ *n*

¹⁸But the people shouted together, "Take this man away! Let Barabbas go free!" ¹⁹(Barabbas was a man who was in prison for his part in a riot in the city and for murder.)

²⁰Pilate wanted to let Jesus go free and told this to the crowd. ²¹But they shouted again, "Crucify him! Crucify him!"

²²A third time Pilate said to them, "Why? What wrong has he done? I can find no reason to kill him. So I will have him punished and set him free."

²³But they continued to shout, demanding that Jesus be crucified. Their yelling became so loud that ²⁴Pilate decided to give them what they wanted. ²⁵He set free the man who was in jail for rioting and murder, and he handed Jesus over to them to do with him as they wished.

Jesus Is Crucified

²⁶As they led Jesus away, Simon, a man from Cyrene, was coming in from the fields. They forced him to carry Jesus' cross and to walk behind him.

²⁷A large crowd of people was following Jesus, including some women who were sad and crying for him. ²⁸But Jesus turned and said to them, "Women of Jerusalem, don't cry for me. Cry for yourselves and for your children. ²⁹The time is coming when people will say, 'Happy are the women who cannot have children and who have no babies to nurse.' ³⁰Then people will say to the mountains, 'Fall on us!' And they will say to the hills, 'Cover us!' ³¹If they act like this now when life is good, what will happen when bad times come?" *n*

³²There were also two criminals led out with Jesus to be put to death. ³³When they came to a place called the Skull, the soldiers crucified Jesus and the criminals — one on his right and the other on his left. ³⁴Jesus said, "Father, forgive them, because they don't know what they are doing." *n*

The soldiers threw lots*d* to decide who would get his clothes. ³⁵The people stood there watching. And the leaders made fun of Jesus, saying, "He saved others. Let him save himself if he is God's Chosen One, the Christ."*d*

³⁶The soldiers also made fun of him, coming to Jesus and offering him some vinegar. ³⁷They said, "If you are the king of the Jews,

---

Verse 17 A few Greek copies add verse 17: "Every year at the Passover Feast, Pilate had to release one prisoner to the people."
If . . . come? Literally, "If they do these things in the green tree, what will happen in the dry?"
Verse 34 Some early Greek copies do not have this part of the verse.

save yourself!" [38]At the top of the cross these words were written: THIS IS THE KING OF THE JEWS.

[39]One of the criminals on a cross began to shout insults at Jesus: "Aren't you the Christ? Then save yourself and us."

[40]But the other criminal stopped him and said, "You should fear God! You are getting the same punishment he is. [41]We are punished justly, getting what we deserve for what we did. But this man has done nothing wrong." [42]Then he said, "Jesus, remember me when you come into your kingdom."

[43]Jesus said to him, "I tell you the truth, today you will be with me in paradise." [n]

Jesus Dies

[44]It was about noon, and the whole land became dark until three o'clock in the afternoon, [45]because the sun did not shine. The curtain in the Temple[n] was torn in two. [46]Jesus cried out in a loud voice, "Father, I give you my life." After Jesus said this, he died.

[47]When the army officer there saw what happened, he praised God, saying, "Surely this was a good man!"

[48]When all the people who had gathered there to watch saw what happened, they returned home, beating their chests because they were so sad. [49]But those who were close friends of Jesus, including the women who had followed him from Galilee, stood at a distance and watched.

Joseph Takes Jesus' Body

[50]There was a good and religious man named Joseph who was a member of the Jewish council. [51]But he had not agreed to the other leaders' plans and actions against Jesus. He was from the Jewish town of Arimathea and was waiting for the kingdom of God to come. [52]Joseph went to Pilate to ask for the body of Jesus. [53]He took the body down from the cross, wrapped it in cloth, and put it in a tomb that was cut out of a wall of rock. This tomb had never been used before. [54]This was late on Preparation[d] Day,

and when the sun went down, the Sabbath[d] day would begin.

[55]The women who had come from Galilee with Jesus followed Joseph and saw the tomb and how Jesus' body was laid. [56]Then the women left to prepare spices and perfumes.

On the Sabbath day they rested, as the law of Moses commanded.

Jesus Rises from the Dead

24 Very early on the first day of the week, at dawn, the women came to the tomb, bringing the spices they had prepared. [2]They found the stone rolled away from the entrance of the tomb, [3]but when they went in, they did not find the body of the Lord Jesus. [4]While they were wondering about this, two men in shining clothes suddenly stood beside them. [5]The women were very afraid and bowed their heads to the ground. The men said to them, "Why are you looking for a living person in this place for the dead? [6]He is not here; he has risen from the dead. Do you remember what he told you in Galilee? [7]He said the Son of Man[d] must be handed over to sinful people, be crucified, and rise from the dead on the third day." [8]Then the women remembered what Jesus had said.

[9]The women left the tomb and told all these things to the eleven apostles[d] and the other followers. [10]It was Mary Magdalene, Joanna, Mary the mother of James, and some other women who told the apostles everything that had happened at the tomb. [11]But they did not believe the women, because it sounded like nonsense. [12]But Peter got up and ran to the tomb. Bending down and looking in, he saw only the cloth that Jesus' body had been wrapped in. Peter went away to his home, wondering about what had happened.

Jesus on the Road to Emmaus

[13]That same day two of Jesus' followers were going to a town named Emmaus, about seven miles from Jerusalem. [14]They were talking about everything that had happened.

---

paradise A place where people who are obedient to God go when they die.
curtain in the Temple A curtain divided the Most Holy Place from the other part of the Temple, the special building in Jerusalem where God commanded the Jewish people to worship him.

15While they were talking and discussing, Jesus himself came near and began walking with them, 16but they were kept from recognizing him. 17Then he said, "What are these things you are talking about while you walk?"

The two followers stopped, looking very sad. 18The one named Cleopas answered, "Are you the only visitor in Jerusalem who does not know what just happened there?"

19Jesus said to them, "What are you talking about?"

They said, "About Jesus of Nazareth. He was a prophet*d* who said and did many powerful things before God and all the people. 20Our leaders and the leading priests handed him over to be sentenced to death, and they crucified him. 21But we were hoping that he would free Israel. Besides this, it is now the third day since this happened. 22And today some women among us amazed us. Early this morning they went to the tomb, 23but they did not find his body there. They came and told us that they had seen a vision of angels who said that Jesus was alive! 24So some of our group went to the tomb, too. They found it just as the women said, but they did not see Jesus."

25Then Jesus said to them, "You are foolish and slow to believe everything the prophets said. 26They said that the Christ*d* must suffer these things before he enters his glory." 27Then starting with what Moses and all the prophets had said about him, Jesus began to explain everything that had been written about himself in the Scriptures.*d*

28They came near the town of Emmaus, and Jesus acted as if he were going farther. 29But they begged him, "Stay with us, because it is late; it is almost night." So he went in to stay with them.

30When Jesus was at the table with them, he took some bread, gave thanks, divided it, and gave it to them. 31And then, they were allowed to recognize Jesus. But when they saw who he was, he disappeared. 32They said to each other, "It felt like a fire burning in us when Jesus talked to us on the road and explained the Scriptures to us."

33So the two followers got up at once and went back to Jerusalem. There they found the eleven apostles*d* and others gathered. 34They were saying, "The Lord really has risen from the dead! He showed himself to Simon."

35Then the two followers told what had happened on the road and how they recognized Jesus when he divided the bread.

Jesus Appears to His Followers

36While the two followers were telling this, Jesus himself stood right in the middle of them and said, "Peace be with you."

37They were fearful and terrified and thought they were seeing a ghost. 38But Jesus said, "Why are you troubled? Why do you doubt what you see? 39Look at my hands and my feet. It is I myself! Touch me and see, because a ghost does not have a living body as you see I have."

40After Jesus said this, he showed them his hands and feet. 41While they still could not believe it because they were amazed and happy, Jesus said to them, "Do you have any food here?" 42They gave him a piece of broiled fish. 43While the followers watched, Jesus took the fish and ate it.

44He said to them, "Remember when I was with you before? I said that everything written about me must happen—everything in the law of Moses, the books of the prophets,*d* and the Psalms."

45Then Jesus opened their minds so they could understand the Scriptures.*d* 46He said to them, "It is written that the Christ*d* would suffer and rise from the dead on the third day 47and that a change of hearts and lives and forgiveness of sins would be preached in his name to all nations, starting at Jerusalem. 48You are witnesses of these things. 49I will send you what my Father has promised, but you must stay in Jerusalem until you have received that power from heaven."

Jesus Goes Back to Heaven

50Jesus led his followers as far as Bethany, and he raised his hands and blessed them. 51While he was blessing them, he was separated from them and carried into heaven. 52They worshiped him and returned to Jerusalem very happy. 53They stayed in the Temple*d* all the time, praising God.

JOHN

John Tells About Jesus, the Son of God

Christ Comes to the World

1 In the beginning there was the Word.[n] The Word was with God, and the Word was God. [2]He was with God in the beginning. [3]All things were made by him, and nothing was made without him. [4]In him there was life, and that life was the light of all people. [5]The Light shines in the darkness, and the darkness has not overpowered it.

[6]There was a man named John[n] who was sent by God. [7]He came to tell people the truth about the Light so that through him all people could hear about the Light and believe. [8]John was not the Light, but he came to tell people the truth about the Light. [9]The true Light that gives light to all was coming into the world!

[10]The Word was in the world, and the world was made by him, but the world did not know him. [11]He came to the world that was his own, but his own people did not accept him. [12]But to all who did accept him and believe in him he gave the right to become children of God. [13]They did not become his children in any human way — by any human parents or human desire. They were born of God.

[14]The Word became a human and lived among us. We saw his glory — the glory that belongs to the only Son of the Father — and he was full of grace and truth. [15]John tells the truth about him and cries out, saying, "This is the One I told you about: 'The One who comes after me is greater than I am, because he was living before me.' "

[16]Because he was full of grace and truth, from him we all received one gift after an-other. [17]The law was given through Moses, but grace and truth came through Jesus Christ. [18]No one has ever seen God. But God the only Son is very close to the Father,[n] and he has shown us what God is like.

John Tells People About Jesus

[19]Here is the truth John[n] told when the Jews in Jerusalem sent priests and Levites to ask him, "Who are you?"

[20]John spoke freely and did not refuse to answer. He said, "I am not the Christ."[d]

[21]So they asked him, "Then who are you? Are you Elijah?"[n]

He answered, "No, I am not."

"Are you the Prophet?"[n] they asked.

He answered, "No."

[22]Then they said, "Who are you? Give us an answer to tell those who sent us. What do you say about yourself?"

[23]John told them in the words of the prophet Isaiah:

"I am the voice of one
 calling out in the desert:
'Make the road straight for the Lord.' "

Isaiah 40:3

[24]Some Pharisees[d] who had been sent asked John: [25]"If you are not the Christ or Elijah or the Prophet, why do you baptize people?"

[26]John answered, "I baptize with water, but there is one here with you that you don't know about. [27]He is the One who comes af-ter me. I am not good enough to untie the strings of his sandals."

[28]This all happened at Bethany on the other side of the Jordan River, where John was baptizing people.

Word The Greek word is "logos," meaning any kind of communication; it could be translated "message." Here, it means Christ, because Christ was the way God told people about himself.
John John the Baptist, who preached to people about Christ's coming (Matthew 3, Luke 3).
But . . . Father This could be translated, "But the only God is very close to the Father." Also, some Greek copies say, "But the only Son is very close to the Father."
Elijah A man who spoke for God. He lived hundreds of years before Christ and was expected to return before Christ (Malachi 4:5-6).
Prophet They probably meant the prophet that God told Moses he would send (Deuteronomy 18:15-19).

[29]The next day John saw Jesus coming toward him. John said, "Look, the Lamb of God,[n] who takes away the sin of the world! [30]This is the One I was talking about when I said, 'A man will come after me, but he is greater than I am, because he was living before me.' [31]Even I did not know who he was, although I came baptizing with water so that the people of Israel would know who he is."

[32-33]Then John said, "I saw the Spirit come down from heaven in the form of a dove and rest on him. Until then I did not know who the Christ was. But the God who sent me to baptize with water told me, 'You will see the Spirit[d] come down and rest on a man; he is the One who will baptize with the Holy Spirit.' [34]I have seen this happen, and I tell you the truth: This man is the Son of God."

The First Followers of Jesus

[35]The next day John[n] was there again with two of his followers. [36]When he saw Jesus walking by, he said, "Look, the Lamb of God!"[n]

[37]The two followers heard John say this, so they followed Jesus. [38]When Jesus turned and saw them following him, he asked, "What are you looking for?"

They said, "Rabbi, where are you staying?" ("Rabbi" means "Teacher.")

[39]He answered, "Come and see." So the two men went with Jesus and saw where he was staying and stayed there with him that day. It was about four o'clock in the afternoon.

[40]One of the two men who followed Jesus after they heard John speak about him was Andrew, Simon Peter's brother. [41]The first thing Andrew did was to find his brother Simon and say to him, "We have found the Messiah." ("Messiah" means "Christ."[d])

[42]Then Andrew took Simon to Jesus. Jesus looked at him and said, "You are Simon son of John. You will be called Cephas." ("Cephas" means "Peter."[n])

[43]The next day Jesus decided to go to Galilee. He found Philip and said to him, "Follow me." [44]Philip was from the town of Bethsaida, where Andrew and Peter lived. [45]Philip found Nathanael and told him, "We have found the man that Moses wrote about in the law, and the prophets[d] also wrote about him. He is Jesus, the son of Joseph, from Nazareth."

[46]But Nathanael said to Philip, "Can anything good come from Nazareth?"

Philip answered, "Come and see."

[47]As Jesus saw Nathanael coming toward him, he said, "Here is truly an Israelite. There is nothing false in him."

[48]Nathanael asked, "How do you know me?"

Jesus answered, "I saw you when you were under the fig tree, before Philip told you about me."

[49]Then Nathanael said to Jesus, "Teacher, you are the Son of God; you are the King of Israel."

[50]Jesus said to Nathanael, "Do you believe simply because I told you I saw you under the fig tree? You will see greater things than that." [51]And Jesus said to them, "I tell you the truth, you will all see heaven open and 'angels of God going up and coming down'[n] on the Son of Man."[d]

The Wedding at Cana

2 Two days later there was a wedding in the town of Cana in Galilee. Jesus' mother was there, [2]and Jesus and his followers were also invited to the wedding. [3]When all the wine was gone, Jesus' mother said to him, "They have no more wine."

[4]Jesus answered, "Dear woman, why come to me? My time has not yet come."

[5]His mother said to the servants, "Do whatever he tells you to do."

[6]In that place there were six stone water jars that the Jews used in their washing ceremony.[n] Each jar held about twenty or thirty gallons.

[7]Jesus said to the servants, "Fill the jars

Lamb of God   Name for Jesus. Jesus is like the lambs that were offered for a sacrifice to God.
John   John the Baptist, who preached to people about Christ's coming (Matthew 3, Luke 3).
Peter   The Greek name "Peter," like the Aramaic name "Cephas," means "rock."
'angels ... down'   These words are from Genesis 28:12.
washing ceremony   The Jewish people washed themselves in special ways before eating, before worshiping in the Temple, and at other special times.

with water." So they filled the jars to the top.

[8]Then he said to them, "Now take some out and give it to the master of the feast."

So they took the water to the master. [9]When he tasted it, the water had become wine. He did not know where the wine came from, but the servants who had brought the water knew. The master of the wedding called the bridegroom [10]and said to him, "People always serve the best wine first. Later, after the guests have been drinking awhile, they serve the cheaper wine. But you have saved the best wine till now."

[11]So in Cana of Galilee Jesus did his first miracle.[d] There he showed his glory, and his followers believed in him.

Jesus in the Temple

[12]After this, Jesus went to the town of Capernaum with his mother, brothers, and followers. They stayed there for just a few days. [13]When it was almost time for the Jewish Passover[d] Feast, Jesus went to Jerusalem. [14]In the Temple[d] he found people selling cattle, sheep, and doves. He saw others sitting at tables, exchanging different kinds of money. [15]Jesus made a whip out of cords and forced all of them, both the sheep and cattle, to leave the Temple. He turned over the tables and scattered the money of those who were exchanging it. [16]Then he said to those who were selling pigeons, "Take these things out of here! Don't make my Father's house a place for buying and selling!"

[17]When this happened, the followers remembered what was written in the Scriptures:[d] "My strong love for your Temple completely controls me."[n]

[18]The Jews said to Jesus, "Show us a miracle[d] to prove you have the right to do these things."

[19]Jesus answered them, "Destroy this temple, and I will build it again in three days."

[20]The Jews answered, "It took forty-six years to build this Temple! Do you really believe you can build it again in three days?"

[21](But the temple Jesus meant was his own body. [22]After Jesus was raised from the dead, his followers remembered that Jesus had said this. Then they believed the Scripture[d] and the words Jesus had said.)

[23]When Jesus was in Jerusalem for the Passover Feast, many people believed in him because they saw the miracles he did. [24]But Jesus did not trust himself to them because he knew them all. [25]He did not need anyone to tell him about people, because he knew what was in people's minds.

Nicodemus Comes to Jesus

3 There was a man named Nicodemus who was one of the Pharisees[d] and an important Jewish leader. [2]One night Nicodemus came to Jesus and said, "Teacher, we know you are a teacher sent from God, because no one can do the miracles[d] you do unless God is with him."

[3]Jesus answered, "I tell you the truth, unless one is born again, he cannot be in God's kingdom."

[4]Nicodemus said, "But if a person is already old, how can he be born again? He cannot enter his mother's body again. So how can a person be born a second time?"

[5]But Jesus answered, "I tell you the truth, unless one is born from water and the Spirit,[d] he cannot enter God's kingdom. [6]Human life comes from human parents, but spiritual life comes from the Spirit. [7]Don't be surprised when I tell you, 'You must all be born again.' [8]The wind blows where it wants to and you hear the sound of it, but you don't know where the wind comes from or where it is going. It is the same with every person who is born from the Spirit."

[9]Nicodemus asked, "How can this happen?"

[10]Jesus said, "You are an important teacher in Israel, and you don't understand these things? [11]I tell you the truth, we talk about what we know, and we tell about what we have seen, but you don't accept what we tell you. [12]I have told you about things here on earth, and you do not believe me. So you will not believe me if I tell you about things of heaven. [13]The only one who has ever gone up to heaven is the One who came down from heaven — the Son of Man.[d]

[14]"Just as Moses lifted up the snake in the

"My . . . me." Quotation from Psalm 69:9.

desert,*n* the Son of Man must also be lifted up. [15]So that everyone who believes can have eternal life in him.

[16]"God loved the world so much that he gave his one and only Son so that whoever believes in him may not be lost, but have eternal life. [17]God did not send his Son into the world to judge the world guilty, but to save the world through him. [18]People who believe in God's Son are not judged guilty. Those who do not believe have already been judged guilty, because they have not believed in God's one and only Son. [19]They are judged by this fact: The Light has come into the world, but they did not want light. They wanted darkness, because they were doing evil things. [20]All who do evil hate the light and will not come to the light, because it will show all the evil things they do. [21]But those who follow the true way come to the light, and it shows that the things they do were done through God."

Jesus and John the Baptist

[22]After this, Jesus and his followers went into the area of Judea, where he stayed with his followers and baptized people. [23]John was also baptizing in Aenon, near Salim, because there was plenty of water there. People were going there to be baptized. [24](This was before John was put into prison.)

[25]Some of John's followers had an argument with a Jew about religious washing.*n* [26]So they came to John and said, "Teacher, remember the man who was with you on the other side of the Jordan River, the one you spoke about so much? He is baptizing, and everyone is going to him."

[27]John answered, "A man can get only what God gives him. [28]You yourselves heard me say, 'I am not the Christ,*d* but I am the one sent to prepare the way for him.' [29]The bride belongs only to the bridegroom. But the friend who helps the bridegroom stands by and listens to him. He is thrilled that he gets to hear the bridegroom's voice. In the same way, I am really happy. [30]He must be-

come greater, and I must become less important.

The One Who Comes from Heaven

[31]"The One who comes from above is greater than all. The one who is from the earth belongs to the earth and talks about things on the earth. But the One who comes from heaven is greater than all. [32]He tells what he has seen and heard, but no one accepts what he says. [33]Whoever accepts what he says has proven that God is true. [34]The One whom God sent speaks the words of God, because God gives him the Spirit*d* fully. [35]The Father loves the Son and has given him power over everything. [36]Those who believe in the Son have eternal life, but those who do not obey the Son will never have life. God's anger stays on them."

Jesus and a Samaritan Woman

4 The Pharisees*d* heard that Jesus was making and baptizing more followers than John, [2]although Jesus himself did not baptize people, but his followers did. [3]Jesus knew that the Pharisees had heard about him, so he left Judea and went back to Galilee. [4]But on the way he had to go through the country of Samaria.

[5]In Samaria Jesus came to the town called Sychar, which is near the field Jacob gave to his son Joseph. [6]Jacob's well was there. Jesus was tired from his long trip, so he sat down beside the well. It was about twelve o'clock noon. [7]When a Samaritan*d* woman came to the well to get some water, Jesus said to her, "Please give me a drink." [8](This happened while Jesus' followers were in town buying some food.)

[9]The woman said, "I am surprised that you ask me for a drink, since you are a Jewish man and I am a Samaritan woman." (Jewish people are not friends with Samaritans.*n*)

[10]Jesus said, "If you only knew the free gift of God and who it is that is asking you for water, you would have asked him, and he would have given you living water."

Moses ... desert When the Israelites were dying from snake bites, God told Moses to put a brass snake on a pole. The people who looked at the snake were healed (Numbers 21:4-9).
religious washing The Jewish people washed themselves in special ways before eating, before worshiping in the Temple, and at other special times.
Jewish people ... Samaritans This can also be translated "Jewish people don't use things that Samaritans have used."

[11]The woman said, "Sir, where will you get this living water? The well is very deep, and you have nothing to get water with. [12]Are you greater than Jacob, our father, who gave us this well and drank from it himself along with his sons and flocks?"

[13]Jesus answered, "Everyone who drinks this water will be thirsty again, [14]but whoever drinks the water I give will never be thirsty. The water I give will become a spring of water gushing up inside that person, giving eternal life."

[15]The woman said to him, "Sir, give me this water so I will never be thirsty again and will not have to come back here to get more water."

[16]Jesus told her, "Go get your husband and come back here."

[17]The woman answered, "I have no husband."

Jesus said to her, "You are right to say you have no husband. [18]Really you have had five husbands, and the man you live with now is not your husband. You told the truth."

[19]The woman said, "Sir, I can see that you are a prophet.[d] [20]Our ancestors worshiped on this mountain, but you Jews say that Jerusalem is the place where people must worship."

[21]Jesus said, "Believe me, woman. The time is coming when neither in Jerusalem nor on this mountain will you actually worship the Father. [22]You Samaritans worship something you don't understand. We understand what we worship, because salvation comes from the Jews. [23]The time is coming when the true worshipers will worship the Father in spirit and truth, and that time is here already. You see, the Father too is actively seeking such people to worship him. [24]God is spirit, and those who worship him must worship in spirit and truth."

[25]The woman said, "I know that the Messiah is coming." (Messiah is the One called Christ.[d]) "When the Messiah comes, he will explain everything to us."

[26]Then Jesus said, "I am he — I, the one talking to you."

[27]Just then his followers came back from town and were surprised to see him talking with a woman. But none of them asked, "What do you want?" or "Why are you talking with her?"

[28]Then the woman left her water jar and went back to town. She said to the people, [29]"Come and see a man who told me everything I ever did. Do you think he might be the Christ?" [30]So the people left the town and went to see Jesus.

[31]Meanwhile, his followers were begging him, "Teacher, eat something."

[32]But Jesus answered, "I have food to eat that you know nothing about."

[33]So the followers asked themselves, "Did somebody already bring him food?"

[34]Jesus said, "My food is to do what the One who sent me wants me to do and to finish his work. [35]You have a saying, 'Four more months till harvest.' But I tell you, open your eyes and look at the fields ready for harvest now. [36]Already, the one who harvests is being paid and is gathering crops for eternal life. So the one who plants and the one who harvests celebrate at the same time. [37]Here the saying is true, 'One person plants, and another harvests.' [38]I sent you to harvest a crop that you did not work on. Others did the work, and you get to finish up their work."[n]

[39]Many of the Samaritans in that town believed in Jesus because of what the woman said: "He told me everything I ever did." [40]When the Samaritans came to Jesus, they begged him to stay with them, so he stayed there two more days. [41]And many more believed because of the things he said.

[42]They said to the woman, "First we believed in Jesus because of your speech, but now we believe because we heard him ourselves. We know that this man really is the Savior of the world."

Jesus Heals an Officer's Son

[43]Two days later, Jesus left and went to Galilee. [44](Jesus had said before that a prophet[d] is not respected in his own country.) [45]When Jesus arrived in Galilee, the people there welcomed him. They had seen all the things he did at the Passover[d] Feast in Jerusalem, because they had been there, too.

But I ... their work. As a farmer sends workers to harvest grain, Jesus sends his followers out to bring people to God.

46Jesus went again to visit Cana in Galilee where he had changed the water into wine. One of the king's important officers lived in the city of Capernaum, and his son was sick. 47When he heard that Jesus had come from Judea to Galilee, he went to Jesus and begged him to come to Capernaum and heal his son, because his son was almost dead. 48Jesus said to him, "You people must see signs and miracles[d] before you will believe in me."

49The officer said, "Sir, come before my child dies."

50Jesus answered, "Go. Your son will live."

The man believed what Jesus told him and went home. 51On the way the man's servants came and met him and told him, "Your son is alive."

52The man asked, "What time did my son begin to get well?"

They answered, "Yesterday at one o'clock the fever left him."

53The father knew that one o'clock was the exact time that Jesus had said, "Your son will live." So the man and all the people who lived in his house believed in Jesus.

54That was the second miracle Jesus did after coming from Judea to Galilee.

Jesus Heals a Man at a Pool

5 Later Jesus went to Jerusalem for a special Jewish feast. 2In Jerusalem there is a pool with five covered porches, which is called Bethzatha[n] in the Jewish language.[n] This pool is near the Sheep Gate. 3Many sick people were lying on the porches beside the pool. Some were blind, some were crippled, and some were paralyzed.[n] 5A man was lying there who had been sick for thirty-eight years. 6When Jesus saw the man and knew that he had been sick for such a long time, Jesus asked him, "Do you want to be well?"

7The sick man answered, "Sir, there is no one to help me get into the pool when the water starts moving. While I am coming to the water, someone else always gets in before me."

8Then Jesus said, "Stand up. Pick up your mat and walk." 9And immediately the man was well; he picked up his mat and began to walk.

The day this happened was a Sabbath[d] day. 10So the Jews said to the man who had been healed, "Today is the Sabbath. It is against our law for you to carry your mat on the Sabbath day."

11But he answered, "The man who made me well told me, 'Pick up your mat and walk.'"

12Then they asked him, "Who is the man who told you to pick up your mat and walk?"

13But the man who had been healed did not know who it was, because there were many people in that place, and Jesus had left.

14Later, Jesus found the man at the Temple[d] and said to him, "See, you are well now. Stop sinning so that something worse does not happen to you."

15Then the man left and told the Jews that Jesus was the one who had made him well.

16Because Jesus was doing this on the Sabbath day, the Jews began to persecute him. 17But Jesus said to them, "My Father never stops working, and so I keep working, too."

18This made the Jews try still harder to kill him. They said, "First Jesus was breaking the law about the Sabbath day. Now he says that God is his own Father, making himself equal with God!"

Jesus Has God's Authority

19But Jesus said, "I tell you the truth, the Son can do nothing alone. The Son does only what he sees the Father doing, because the Son does whatever the Father does. 20The Father loves the Son and shows the Son all the things he himself does. But the Father will show the Son even greater things than this so that you can all be amazed. 21Just as the Father raises the dead and gives them life, so also the Son gives life to those he wants to. 22In fact, the Father judges no one, but he has given the Son power to do all the judging 23so that all people will honor the Son as much as

---

Bethzatha Also called Bethsaida or Bethesda, a pool of water north of the Temple in Jerusalem.
Jewish language Hebrew or Aramaic, the languages of the Jewish people in the first century.
Verse 3 Some Greek copies add "and they waited for the water to move." A few later copies add verse 4: "Sometimes an angel of the Lord came down to the pool and stirred up the water. After the angel did this, the first person to go into the pool was healed from any sickness he had."

they honor the Father. Anyone who does not honor the Son does not honor the Father who sent him.

24"I tell you the truth, whoever hears what I say and believes in the One who sent me has eternal life. That person will not be judged guilty but has already left death and entered life. 25I tell you the truth, the time is coming and is already here when the dead will hear the voice of the Son of God, and those who hear will have life. 26Life comes from the Father himself, and he has allowed the Son to have life in himself as well. 27And the Father has given the Son the power to judge, because he is the Son of Man.*d* 28Don't be surprised at this: A time is coming when all who are dead and in their graves will hear his voice. 29Then they will come out of their graves. Those who did good will rise and have life forever, but those who did evil will rise to be judged guilty.

Jesus Is God's Son

30"I can do nothing alone. I judge only the way I am told, so my judgment is fair. I don't try to please myself, but I try to please the One who sent me.

31"If only I tell people about myself, what I say is not true. 32But there is another who tells about me, and I know that the things he says about me are true.

33"You have sent people to John, and he has told you the truth. 34It is not that I accept such human telling; I tell you this so you can be saved. 35John was like a burning and shining lamp, and you were happy to enjoy his light for a while.

36"But I have a proof about myself that is greater than that of John. The things I do, which are the things my Father gave me to do, prove that the Father sent me. 37And the Father himself who sent me has given proof about me. You have never heard his voice or seen what he looks like. 38His teaching does not live in you, because you don't believe in the One the Father sent. 39You carefully study the Scriptures*d* because you think they give you eternal life. They do in fact tell about me, 40but you refuse to come to me to have that life.

41"I don't need praise from people. 42But I know you—I know that you don't have

God's love in you. 43I have come from my Father and speak for him, but you don't accept me. But when another person comes, speaking only for himself, you will accept him. 44You try to get praise from each other, but you do not try to get the praise that comes from the only God. So how can you believe? 45Don't think that I will stand before the Father and say you are wrong. The one who says you are wrong is Moses, the one you hoped would save you. 46If you really believed Moses, you would believe me, because Moses wrote about me. 47But if you don't believe what Moses wrote, how can you believe what I say?"

More than Five Thousand Fed

6 After this, Jesus went across Lake Galilee (or, Lake Tiberias). 2Many people followed him because they saw the miracles*d* he did to heal the sick. 3Jesus went up on a hill and sat down there with his followers. 4It was almost the time for the Jewish Passover*d* Feast.

5When Jesus looked up and saw a large crowd coming toward him, he said to Philip, "Where can we buy enough bread for all these people to eat?" 6(Jesus asked Philip this question to test him, because Jesus already knew what he planned to do.)

7Philip answered, "We would all have to work a month to buy enough bread for each person to have only a little piece."

8Another one of his followers, Andrew, Simon Peter's brother, said, 9"Here is a boy with five loaves of barley bread and two little fish, but that is not enough for so many people."

10Jesus said, "Tell the people to sit down." This was a very grassy place, and about five thousand men sat down there. 11Then Jesus took the loaves of bread, thanked God for them, and gave them to the people who were sitting there. He did the same with the fish, giving as much as the people wanted.

12When they had all had enough to eat, Jesus said to his followers, "Gather the leftover pieces of fish and bread so that nothing is wasted." 13So they gathered up the pieces and filled twelve baskets with the pieces left from the five barley loaves.

14When the people saw this miracle*d*

that Jesus did, they said, "He must truly be the Prophet[n] who is coming into the world."

15Jesus knew that the people planned to come and take him by force and make him their king, so he left and went into the hills alone.

Jesus Walks on the Water

16That evening Jesus' followers went down to Lake Galilee. 17It was dark now, and Jesus had not yet come to them. The followers got into a boat and started across the lake to Capernaum. 18By now a strong wind was blowing, and the waves on the lake were getting bigger. 19When they had rowed the boat about three or four miles, they saw Jesus walking on the water, coming toward the boat. The followers were afraid, 20but Jesus said to them, "It is I. Do not be afraid." 21Then they were glad to take him into the boat. At once the boat came to land at the place where they wanted to go.

The People Seek Jesus

22The next day the people who had stayed on the other side of the lake knew that Jesus had not gone in the boat with his followers but that they had left without him. And they knew that only one boat had been there. 23But then some boats came from Tiberias and landed near the place where the people had eaten the bread after the Lord had given thanks. 24When the people saw that Jesus and his followers were not there now, they got into boats and went to Capernaum to find Jesus.

Jesus, the Bread of Life

25When the people found Jesus on the other side of the lake, they asked him, "Teacher, when did you come here?"

26Jesus answered, "I tell you the truth, you aren't looking for me because you saw me do miracles.[d] You are looking for me because you ate the bread and were satisfied. 27Don't work for the food that spoils. Work for the food that stays good always and gives eternal

life. The Son of Man[d] will give you this food, because on him God the Father has put his power."

28The people asked Jesus, "What are the things God wants us to do?"

29Jesus answered, "The work God wants you to do is this: Believe the One he sent."

30So the people asked, "What miracle will you do? If we see a miracle, we will believe you. What will you do? 31Our fathers ate the manna[d] in the desert. This is written in the Scriptures:[d] 'He gave them bread from heaven to eat.' "[n]

32Jesus said, "I tell you the truth, it was not Moses who gave you bread from heaven; it is my Father who is giving you the true bread from heaven. 33God's bread is the One who comes down from heaven and gives life to the world."

34The people said, "Sir, give us this bread always."

35Then Jesus said, "I am the bread that gives life. Whoever comes to me will never be hungry, and whoever believes in me will never be thirsty. 36But as I told you before, you have seen me and still don't believe. 37The Father gives me my people. Every one of them will come to me, and I will always accept them. 38I came down from heaven to do what God wants me to do, not what I want to do. 39Here is what the One who sent me wants me to do: I must not lose even one whom God gave me, but I must raise them all on the last day. 40Those who see the Son and believe in him have eternal life, and I will raise them on the last day. This is what my Father wants."

41The Jews began to complain about Jesus because he said, "I am the bread that comes down from heaven." 42They said, "This is Jesus, the son of Joseph. We know his father and mother. How can he say, 'I came down from heaven'?"

43But Jesus answered, "Stop complaining to each other. 44The Father is the One who sent me. No one can come to me unless the Father draws him to me, and I will raise that person up on the last day. 45It is written in the prophets,[d] 'They will all be taught by

---

Prophet   They probably meant the prophet that God told Moses he would send (Deuteronomy 18:15-19).
'He gave ... eat.'   Quotation from Psalm 78:24.

God.'[n] Everyone who listens to the Father and learns from him comes to me. [46]No one has seen the Father except the One who is from God; only he has seen the Father. [47]I tell you the truth, whoever believes has eternal life. [48]I am the bread that gives life. [49]Your ancestors ate the manna in the desert, but still they died. [50]Here is the bread that comes down from heaven. Anyone who eats this bread will never die. [51]I am the living bread that came down from heaven. Anyone who eats this bread will live forever. This bread is my flesh, which I will give up so that the world may have life."

[52]Then the Jews began to argue among themselves, saying, "How can this man give us his flesh to eat?"

[53]Jesus said, "I tell you the truth, you must eat the flesh of the Son of Man and drink his blood. Otherwise, you won't have real life in you. [54]Those who eat my flesh and drink my blood have eternal life, and I will raise them up on the last day. [55]My flesh is true food, and my blood is true drink. [56]Those who eat my flesh and drink my blood live in me, and I live in them. [57]The living Father sent me, and I live because of the Father. So whoever eats me will live because of me. [58]I am not like the bread your ancestors ate. They ate that bread and still died. I am the bread that came down from heaven, and whoever eats this bread will live forever." [59]Jesus said all these things while he was teaching in the synagogue[d] in Capernaum.

The Words of Eternal Life

[60]When the followers of Jesus heard this, many of them said, "This teaching is hard. Who can accept it?"

[61]Knowing that his followers were complaining about this, Jesus said, "Does this teaching bother you? [62]Then will it also bother you to see the Son of Man[d] going back to the place where he came from? [63]It is the Spirit that gives life. The flesh doesn't give life. The words I told you are spirit, and they give life. [64]But some of you don't believe." (Jesus knew from the beginning who did not believe and who would turn against him.)

[65]Jesus said, "That is the reason I said, 'If the Father does not bring a person to me, that one cannot come.' "

[66]After Jesus said this, many of his followers left him and stopped following him.

[67]Jesus asked the twelve followers, "Do you want to leave, too?"

[68]Simon Peter answered him, "Lord, where would we go? You have the words that give eternal life. [69]We believe and know that you are the Holy One from God."

[70]Then Jesus answered, "I chose all twelve of you, but one of you is a devil."

[71]Jesus was talking about Judas, the son of Simon Iscariot. Judas was one of the twelve, but later he was going to turn against Jesus.

Jesus' Brothers Don't Believe

7 After this, Jesus traveled around Galilee. He did not want to travel in Judea, because the Jews there wanted to kill him. [2]It was time for the Jewish Feast[d] of Shelters. [3]So Jesus' brothers said to him, "You should leave here and go to Judea so your followers there can see the miracles[d] you do. [4]Anyone who wants to be well known does not hide what he does. If you are doing these things, show yourself to the world." [5](Even Jesus' brothers did not believe in him.)

[6]Jesus said to his brothers, "The right time for me has not yet come, but any time is right for you. [7]The world cannot hate you, but it hates me, because I tell it the evil things it does. [8]So you go to the feast. I will not go yet to this feast, because the right time for me has not yet come." [9]After saying this, Jesus stayed in Galilee.

[10]But after Jesus' brothers had gone to the feast, Jesus went also. But he did not let people see him. [11]At the feast the Jews were looking for him and saying, "Where is that man?"

[12]Within the large crowd there, many people were whispering to each other about Jesus. Some said, "He is a good man."

Others said, "No, he fools the people." [13]But no one was brave enough to talk about Jesus openly, because they were afraid of the Jews.

'They . . . God.' Quotation from Isaiah 54:13.

Jesus Teaches at the Feast

14When the feast was about half over, Jesus went to the Temple*d* and began to teach. 15The Jews were amazed and said, "This man has never studied in school. How did he learn so much?"

16Jesus answered, "The things I teach are not my own, but they come from him who sent me. 17If people choose to do what God wants, they will know that my teaching comes from God and not from me. 18Those who teach their own ideas are trying to get honor for themselves. But those who try to bring honor to the one who sent him speak the truth, and there is nothing false in them. 19Moses gave you the law, *n* but none of you obeys that law. Why are you trying to kill me?"

20The people answered, "A demon*d* has come into you. We are not trying to kill you."

21Jesus said to them, "I did one miracle, *d* and you are all amazed. 22Moses gave you the law about circumcision. *d* (But really Moses did not give you circumcision; it came from our ancestors.) And yet you circumcise a baby on a Sabbath*d* day. 23If a baby can be circumcised on a Sabbath day to obey the law of Moses, why are you angry at me for healing a person's whole body on the Sabbath day? 24Stop judging by the way things look, but judge by what is really right."

Is Jesus the Christ?

25Then some of the people who lived in Jerusalem said, "This is the man they are trying to kill. 26But he is teaching where everyone can see and hear him, and no one is trying to stop him. Maybe the leaders have decided he really is the Christ. *d* 27But we know where this man is from. And when the real Christ comes, no one will know where he comes from."

28Jesus, teaching in the Temple, *d* cried out, "Yes, you know me, and you know where I am from. But I have not come by my own authority. I was sent by the One who is true, whom you don't know. 29But I know him, because I am from him, and he sent me."

30When Jesus said this, the people tried to take him. But no one was able to touch him, because it was not yet the right time. 31But many of the people believed in Jesus. They said, "When the Christ comes, will he do more miracles*d* than this man has done?"

The Leaders Try to Arrest Jesus

32The Pharisees*d* heard the crowd whispering these things about Jesus. So the leading priests and the Pharisees sent some Temple*d* guards to arrest him. 33Jesus said, "I will be with you a little while longer. Then I will go back to the One who sent me. 34You will look for me, but you will not find me. And you cannot come where I am."

35The Jews said to each other, "Where will this man go so we cannot find him? Will he go to the Greek cities where our people live and teach the Greek people there? 36What did he mean when he said, 'You will look for me, but you will not find me,' and 'You cannot come where I am'?"

Jesus Talks About the Spirit

37On the last and most important day of the feast Jesus stood up and said in a loud voice, "Let anyone who is thirsty come to me and drink. 38If anyone believes in me, rivers of living water will flow out from that person's heart, as the Scripture*d* says." 39Jesus was talking about the Holy Spirit. *d* The Spirit had not yet been given, because Jesus had not yet been raised to glory. But later, those who believed in Jesus would receive the Spirit.

The People Argue About Jesus

40When the people heard Jesus' words, some of them said, "This man really is the Prophet." *n*

41Others said, "He is the Christ."*d*

Still others said, "The Christ will not come from Galilee. 42The Scripture*d* says that the Christ will come from David's family and from Bethlehem, the town where David lived." 43So the people did not agree with each other about Jesus. 44Some of them

---

law Moses gave God's people the law that God gave him on Mount Sinai (Exodus 34:29-32).
Prophet They probably meant the prophet God told Moses he would send (Deuteronomy 18:15-19).

wanted to arrest him, but no one was able to touch him.

Some Leaders Won't Believe

45The Temple*d* guards went back to the leading priests and the Pharisees,*d* who asked, "Why didn't you bring Jesus?"

46The guards answered, "The words he says are greater than the words of any other person who has ever spoken!"

47The Pharisees answered, "So Jesus has fooled you also! 48Have any of the leaders or the Pharisees believed in him? No! 49But these people, who know nothing about the law, are under God's curse."

50Nicodemus, who had gone to see Jesus before, was in that group.*n* He said, 51"Our law does not judge a man without hearing him and knowing what he has done."

52They answered, "Are you from Galilee, too? Study the Scriptures,*d* and you will learn that no prophet*d* comes from Galilee."

Some early Greek manuscripts do not contain 7:53 — 8:11.

[53And everyone left and went home.

The Woman Caught in Adultery

8 Jesus went to the Mount of Olives.*d* 2But early in the morning he went back to the Temple,*d* and all the people came to him, and he sat and taught them. 3The teachers of the law and the Pharisees*d* brought a woman who had been caught in adultery.*d* They forced her to stand before the people. 4They said to Jesus, "Teacher, this woman was caught having sexual relations with a man who is not her husband. 5The law of Moses commands that we stone to death every woman who does this. What do you say we should do?" 6They were asking this to trick Jesus so that they could have some charge against him.

But Jesus bent over and started writing on the ground with his finger. 7When they continued to ask Jesus their question, he raised up and said, "Anyone here who has never sinned can throw the first stone at her."

8Then Jesus bent over again and wrote on the ground.

9Those who heard Jesus began to leave one by one, first the older men and then the others. Jesus was left there alone with the woman standing before him. 10Jesus raised up again and asked her, "Woman, where are they? Has no one judged you guilty?"

11She answered, "No one, sir."

Then Jesus said, "I also don't judge you guilty. You may go now, but don't sin anymore."]

Jesus Is the Light of the World

12Later, Jesus talked to the people again, saying, "I am the light of the world. The person who follows me will never live in darkness but will have the light that gives life."

13The Pharisees*d* said to Jesus, "When you talk about yourself, you are the only one to say these things are true. We cannot accept what you say."

14Jesus answered, "Yes, I am saying these things about myself, but they are true. I know where I came from and where I am going. But you don't know where I came from or where I am going. 15You judge by human standards. I am not judging anyone. 16But when I do judge, my judging is true, because I am not alone. The Father who sent me is with me. 17Your own law says that when two witnesses say the same thing, you must accept what they say. 18I am one of the witnesses who speaks about myself, and the Father who sent me is the other witness."

19They asked, "Where is your father?"

Jesus answered, "You don't know me or my Father. If you knew me, you would know my Father, too." 20Jesus said these things while he was teaching in the Temple,*d* near where the money is kept. But no one arrested him, because the right time for him had not yet come.

The People Misunderstand Jesus

21Again, Jesus said to the people, "I will leave you, and you will look for me, but you

Nicodemus ... group   The story about Nicodemus going and talking to Jesus is in John 3:1-21.

will die in your sins. You cannot come where I am going."

²²So the Jews asked, "Will Jesus kill himself? Is that why he said, 'You cannot come where I am going'?"

²³Jesus said, "You people are from here below, but I am from above. You belong to this world, but I don't belong to this world. ²⁴So I told you that you would die in your sins. Yes, you will die in your sins if you don't believe that I am he."

²⁵They asked, "Then who are you?"

Jesus answered, "I am what I have told you from the beginning. ²⁶I have many things to say and decide about you. But I tell people only the things I have heard from the One who sent me, and he speaks the truth."

²⁷The people did not understand that he was talking to them about the Father. ²⁸So Jesus said to them, "When you lift up the Son of Man,ᵈ you will know that I am he. You will know that these things I do are not by my own authority but that I say only what the Father has taught me. ²⁹The One who sent me is with me. I always do what is pleasing to him, so he has not left me alone." ³⁰While Jesus was saying these things, many people believed in him.

Freedom from Sin

³¹So Jesus said to the Jews who believed in him, "If you continue to obey my teaching, you are truly my followers. ³²Then you will know the truth, and the truth will make you free."

³³They answered, "We are Abraham's children, and we have never been anyone's slaves. So why do you say we will be free?"

³⁴Jesus answered, "I tell you the truth, everyone who lives in sin is a slave to sin. ³⁵A slave does not stay with a family forever, but a son belongs to the family forever. ³⁶So if the Son makes you free, you will be truly free. ³⁷I know you are Abraham's children, but you want to kill me because you don't accept my teaching. ³⁸I am telling you what my Father has shown me, but you do what your father has told you."

³⁹They answered, "Our father is Abraham."

Jesus said, "If you were really Abraham's children, you would do the things Abraham did. ⁴⁰I am a man who has told you the truth which I heard from God, but you are trying to kill me. Abraham did nothing like that. ⁴¹So you are doing the things your own father did."

But they said, "We are not like children who never knew who their father was. God is our Father; he is the only Father we have."

⁴²Jesus said to them, "If God were really your Father, you would love me, because I came from God and now I am here. I did not come by my own authority; God sent me. ⁴³You don't understand what I say, because you cannot accept my teaching. ⁴⁴You belong to your father the devil, and you want to do what he wants. He was a murderer from the beginning and was against the truth, because there is no truth in him. When he tells a lie, he shows what he is really like, because he is a liar and the father of lies. ⁴⁵But because I speak the truth, you don't believe me. ⁴⁶Can any of you prove that I am guilty of sin? If I am telling the truth, why don't you believe me? ⁴⁷The person who belongs to God accepts what God says. But you don't accept what God says, because you don't belong to God."

Jesus Is Greater than Abraham

⁴⁸The Jews answered, "We say you are a Samaritanᵈ and have a demonᵈ in you. Are we not right?"

⁴⁹Jesus answered, "I have no demon in me. I give honor to my Father, but you dishonor me. ⁵⁰I am not trying to get honor for myself. There is One who wants this honor for me, and he is the judge. ⁵¹I tell you the truth, whoever obeys my teaching will never die."

⁵²The Jews said to Jesus, "Now we know that you have a demon in you! Even Abraham and the prophetsᵈ died. But you say, 'Whoever obeys my teaching will never die.' ⁵³Do you think you are greater than our father Abraham, who died? And the prophets died, too. Who do you think you are?"

⁵⁴Jesus answered, "If I give honor to myself, that honor is worth nothing. The One who gives me honor is my Father, and you say he is your God. ⁵⁵You don't really know him, but I know him. If I said I did not know him, I would be a liar like you. But I

do know him, and I obey what he says.
⁵⁶Your father Abraham was very happy that
he would see my day. He saw that day and
was glad."

⁵⁷The Jews said to him, "You have never
seen Abraham! You are not even fifty years
old."

⁵⁸Jesus answered, "I tell you the truth, before Abraham was even born, I am!" ⁵⁹When
Jesus said this, the people picked up stones to
throw at him. But Jesus hid himself, and then
he left the Temple.ᵈ

Jesus Heals a Man Born Blind

9 As Jesus was walking along, he saw a
man who had been born blind. ²His followers asked him, "Teacher, whose sin
caused this man to be born blind — his own
sin or his parents' sin?"

³Jesus answered, "It is not this man's sin
or his parents' sin that made him be blind.
This man was born blind so that God's power
could be shown in him. ⁴While it is daytime,
we must continue doing the work of the One
who sent me. Night is coming, when no one
can work. ⁵While I am in the world, I am the
light of the world."

⁶After Jesus said this, he spit on the ground
and made some mud with it and put the mud
on the man's eyes. ⁷Then he told the man,
"Go and wash in the Pool of Siloam." (Siloam
means Sent.) So the man went, washed, and
came back seeing.

⁸The neighbors and some people who had
earlier seen this man begging said, "Isn't this
the same man who used to sit and beg?"

⁹Some said, "He is the one," but others
said, "No, he only looks like him."

The man himself said, "I am the man."

¹⁰They asked, "How did you get your
sight?"

¹¹He answered, "The man named Jesus
made some mud and put it on my eyes. Then
he told me to go to Siloam and wash. So I
went and washed, and then I could see."

¹²They asked him, "Where is this man?"

"I don't know," he answered.

Pharisees Question the Healing

¹³Then the people took to the Phariseesᵈ
the man who had been blind. ¹⁴The day Jesus
had made mud and healed his eyes was a

Sabbathᵈ day. ¹⁵So now the Pharisees asked
the man, "How did you get your sight?"

He answered, "He put mud on my eyes, I
washed, and now I see."

¹⁶So some of the Pharisees were saying,
"This man does not keep the Sabbath day, so
he is not from God."

But others said, "A man who is a sinner
can't do miraclesᵈ like these." So they could
not agree with each other.

¹⁷They asked the man again, "What do
you say about him since it was your eyes he
opened?"

The man answered, "He is a prophet."ᵈ

¹⁸The Jews did not believe that he had
been blind and could now see again. So they
sent for the man's parents ¹⁹and asked them,
"Is this your son who you say was born
blind? Then how does he now see?"

²⁰His parents answered, "We know that
this is our son and that he was born blind.
²¹But we don't know how he can now see.
We don't know who opened his eyes. Ask
him. He is old enough to speak for himself."
²²His parents said this because they were
afraid of the Jews, who had already decided
that anyone who said Jesus was the Christᵈ
would be put out of the synagogue.ᵈ ²³That
is why his parents said, "He is old enough.
Ask him."

²⁴So for the second time, they called the
man who had been blind. They said, "You
should give God the glory by telling the
truth. We know that this man is a sinner."

²⁵He answered, "I don't know if he is a
sinner. One thing I do know: I was blind,
and now I see."

²⁶They asked, "What did he do to you?
How did he make you see again?"

²⁷He answered, "I already told you, and
you didn't listen. Why do you want to hear
it again? Do you want to become his followers, too?"

²⁸Then they insulted him and said, "You
are his follower, but we are followers of Moses. ²⁹We know that God spoke to Moses,
but we don't even know where this man
comes from."

³⁰The man answered, "This is a very
strange thing. You don't know where he
comes from, and yet he opened my eyes.
³¹We all know that God does not listen to

sinners, but he listens to anyone who worships and obeys him. [32]Nobody has ever heard of anyone giving sight to a man born blind. [33]If this man were not from God, he could do nothing."

[34]They answered, "You were born full of sin! Are you trying to teach us?" And they threw him out.

Spiritual Blindness

[35]When Jesus heard that they had thrown him out, Jesus found him and said, "Do you believe in the Son of Man?"[d]

[36]He asked, "Who is the Son of Man, sir, so that I can believe in him?"

[37]Jesus said to him, "You have seen him. The Son of Man is the one talking with you."

[38]He said, "Lord, I believe!" Then the man worshiped Jesus.

[39]Jesus said, "I came into this world so that the world could be judged. I came so that the blind[n] would see and so that those who see will become blind."

[40]Some of the Pharisees[d] who were nearby heard Jesus say this and asked, "Are you saying we are blind, too?"

[41]Jesus said, "If you were blind, you would not be guilty of sin. But since you keep saying you see, your guilt remains."

The Shepherd and His Sheep

10 Jesus said, "I tell you the truth, the person who does not enter the sheepfold by the door, but climbs in some other way, is a thief and a robber. [2]The one who enters by the door is the shepherd of the sheep. [3]The one who guards the door opens it for him. And the sheep listen to the voice of the shepherd. He calls his own sheep by name and leads them out. [4]When he brings all his sheep out, he goes ahead of them, and they follow him because they know his voice. [5]But they will never follow a stranger. They will run away from him because they don't know his voice." [6]Jesus told the people this story, but they did not understand what it meant.

Jesus Is the Good Shepherd

[7]So Jesus said again, "I tell you the truth,

I am the door for the sheep. [8]All the people who came before me were thieves and robbers. The sheep did not listen to them. [9]I am the door, and the person who enters through me will be saved and will be able to come in and go out and find pasture. [10]A thief comes to steal and kill and destroy, but I came to give life — life in all its fullness.

[11]"I am the good shepherd. The good shepherd gives his life for the sheep. [12]The worker who is paid to keep the sheep is different from the shepherd who owns them. When the worker sees a wolf coming, he runs away and leaves the sheep alone. Then the wolf attacks the sheep and scatters them. [13]The man runs away because he is only a paid worker and does not really care about the sheep.

[14-15]"I am the good shepherd. I know my sheep, as the Father knows me. And my sheep know me, as I know the Father. I give my life for the sheep. [16]I have other sheep that are not in this flock, and I must bring them also. They will listen to my voice, and there will be one flock and one shepherd. [17]The Father loves me because I give my life so that I can take it back again. [18]No one takes it away from me; I give my own life freely. I have the right to give my life, and I have the right to take it back. This is what my Father commanded me to do."

[19]Again the Jews did not agree with each other because of these words of Jesus. [20]Many of them said, "A demon[d] has come into him and made him crazy. Why listen to him?"

[21]But others said, "A man who is crazy with a demon does not say things like this. Can a demon open the eyes of the blind?"

Jesus Is Rejected

[22]The time came for the Feast[d] of Dedication at Jerusalem. It was winter, [23]and Jesus was walking in the Temple[d] in Solomon's Porch.[d] [24]The Jews gathered around him and said, "How long will you make us wonder about you? If you are the Christ,[d] tell us plainly."

[25]Jesus answered, "I told you already, but you did not believe. The miracles[d] I do in my

---

blind Jesus is talking about people who are spiritually blind, not physically blind.

Father's name show who I am. 26But you don't believe, because you are not my sheep. 27My sheep listen to my voice; I know them, and they follow me. 28I give them eternal life, and they will never die, and no one can steal them out of my hand. 29My Father gave my sheep to me. He is greater than all, and no person can steal my sheep out of my Father's hand. 30The Father and I are one."

31Again the Jews picked up stones to kill Jesus. 32But he said to them, "I have done many good works from the Father. Which of these good works are you killing me for?"

33The Jews answered, "We are not killing you because of any good work you did, but because you speak against God. You are only a human, but you say you are the same as God!"

34Jesus answered, "It is written in your law that God said, 'I said, you are gods.'n 35This Scriptured called those people gods who received God's message, and Scripture is always true. 36So why do you say that I speak against God because I said, 'I am God's Son'? I am the one God chose and sent into the world. 37If I don't do what my Father does, then don't believe me. 38But if I do what my Father does, even though you don't believe in me, believe what I do. Then you will know and understand that the Father is in me and I am in the Father."

39They tried to take Jesus again, but he escaped from them.

40Then he went back across the Jordan River to the place where John had first baptized. Jesus stayed there, 41and many people came to him and said, "John never did a miracle, but everything John said about this man is true." 42And in that place many believed in Jesus.

The Death of Lazarus

11 A man named Lazarus was sick. He lived in the town of Bethany, where Mary and her sister Martha lived. 2Mary was the woman who later put perfume on the Lord and wiped his feet with her hair. Mary's brother was Lazarus, the man who was now sick. 3So Mary and Martha sent someone to tell Jesus, "Lord, the one you love is sick."

4When Jesus heard this, he said, "This sickness will not end in death. It is for the glory of God, to bring glory to the Son of God." 5Jesus loved Martha and her sister and Lazarus. 6But when he heard that Lazarus was sick, he stayed where he was for two more days. 7Then Jesus said to his followers, "Let's go back to Judea."

8The followers said, "But Teacher, the Jews there tried to stone you to death only a short time ago. Now you want to go back there?"

9Jesus answered, "Are there not twelve hours in the day? If anyone walks in the daylight, he will not stumble, because he can see by this world's light. 10But if anyone walks at night, he stumbles because there is no light to help him see."

11After Jesus said this, he added, "Our friend Lazarus has fallen asleep, but I am going there to wake him."

12The followers said, "But Lord, if he is only asleep, he will be all right."

13Jesus meant that Lazarus was dead, but his followers thought he meant Lazarus really sleeping. 14So then Jesus said plainly, "Lazarus is dead. 15And I am glad for your sakes I was not there so that you may believe. But let's go to him now."

16Then Thomas (the one called Didymus) said to the other followers, "Let us also go so that we can die with him."

Jesus in Bethany

17When Jesus arrived, he learned that Lazarus had already been dead and in the tomb for four days. 18Bethany was about two miles from Jerusalem. 19Many of the Jews had come there to comfort Martha and Mary about their brother.

20When Martha heard that Jesus was coming, she went out to meet him, but Mary stayed home. 21Martha said to Jesus, "Lord, if you had been here, my brother would not have died. 22But I know that even now God will give you anything you ask."

23Jesus said, "Your brother will rise and live again."

24Martha answered, "I know that he will

'I ... gods.' Quotation from Psalm 82:6.

rise and live again in the resurrection[n] on the last day."

25Jesus said to her, "I am the resurrection and the life. Those who believe in me will have life even if they die. 26And everyone who lives and believes in me will never die. Martha, do you believe this?"

27Martha answered, "Yes, Lord. I believe that you are the Christ,[d] the Son of God, the One coming to the world."

Jesus Cries

28After Martha said this, she went back and talked to her sister Mary alone. Martha said, "The Teacher is here and he is asking for you." 29When Mary heard this, she got up quickly and went to Jesus. 30Jesus had not yet come into the town but was still at the place where Martha had met him. 31The Jews were with Mary in the house, comforting her. When they saw her stand and leave quickly, they followed her, thinking she was going to the tomb to cry there. 32But Mary went to the place where Jesus was. When she saw him, she fell at his feet and said, "Lord, if you had been here, my brother would not have died."

33When Jesus saw Mary crying and the Jews who came with her also crying, he was upset and was deeply troubled. 34He asked, "Where did you bury him?"

"Come and see, Lord," they said.

35Jesus cried.

36So the Jews said, "See how much he loved him."

37But some of them said, "If Jesus opened the eyes of the blind man, why couldn't he keep Lazarus from dying?"

Jesus Raises Lazarus

38Again feeling very upset, Jesus came to the tomb. It was a cave with a large stone covering the entrance. 39Jesus said, "Move the stone away."

Martha, the sister of the dead man, said, "But, Lord, it has been four days since he died. There will be a bad smell."

40Then Jesus said to her, "Didn't I tell you that if you believed you would see the glory of God?"

41So they moved the stone away from the entrance. Then Jesus looked up and said, "Father, I thank you that you heard me. 42I know that you always hear me, but I said these things because of the people here around me. I want them to believe that you sent me." 43After Jesus said this, he cried out in a loud voice, "Lazarus, come out!" 44The dead man came out, his hands and feet wrapped with pieces of cloth, and a cloth around his face.

Jesus said to them, "Take the cloth off of him and let him go."

The Plan to Kill Jesus

45Many of the Jews, who had come to visit Mary and saw what Jesus did, believed in him. 46But some of them went to the Pharisees[d] and told them what Jesus had done. 47Then the leading priests and Pharisees called a meeting of the Jewish council. They asked, "What should we do? This man is doing many miracles.[d] 48If we let him continue doing these things, everyone will believe in him. Then the Romans will come and take away our Temple[d] and our nation."

49One of the men there was Caiaphas, the high priest that year. He said, "You people know nothing! 50You don't realize that it is better for one man to die for the people than for the whole nation to be destroyed."

51Caiaphas did not think of this himself. As high priest that year, he was really prophesying[d] that Jesus would die for the Jewish nation 52and for God's scattered children to bring them all together and make them one.

53That day they started planning to kill Jesus. 54So Jesus no longer traveled openly among the Jews. He left there and went to a place near the desert, to a town called Ephraim and stayed there with his followers.

55It was almost time for the Jewish Passover[d] Feast. Many from the country went up to Jerusalem before the Passover to do the special things to make themselves pure. 56The people looked for Jesus and stood in the Temple asking each other, "Is he coming to the Feast? What do you think?" 57But the leading priests and the Pharisees had given orders that if anyone knew where Jesus was,

---

resurrection Being raised from the dead to live again.

he must tell them. Then they could arrest him.

Jesus with Friends in Bethany

12 Six days before the Passover[d] Feast, Jesus went to Bethany, where Lazarus lived. (Lazarus is the man Jesus raised from the dead.) [2]There they had a dinner for Jesus. Martha served the food, and Lazarus was one of the people eating with Jesus. [3]Mary brought in a pint of very expensive perfume made from pure nard.[d] She poured the perfume on Jesus' feet, and then she wiped his feet with her hair. And the sweet smell from the perfume filled the whole house.

[4]Judas Iscariot, one of Jesus' followers who would later turn against him, was there. Judas said, [5]"This perfume was worth three hundred coins.[n] Why wasn't it sold and the money given to the poor?" [6]But Judas did not really care about the poor; he said this because he was a thief. He was the one who kept the money box, and he often stole from it.

[7]Jesus answered, "Leave her alone. It was right for her to save this perfume for today, the day for me to be prepared for burial. [8]You will always have the poor with you, but you will not always have me."

The Plot Against Lazarus

[9]A large crowd of Jews heard that Jesus was in Bethany. So they went there to see not only Jesus but Lazarus, whom Jesus raised from the dead. [10]So the leading priests made plans to kill Lazarus, too. [11]Because of Lazarus many of the Jews were leaving them and believing in Jesus.

Jesus Enters Jerusalem

[12]The next day a great crowd who had come to Jerusalem for the Passover[d] Feast heard that Jesus was coming there. [13]So they took branches of palm trees and went out to meet Jesus, shouting,
"Praise[n] God!

God bless the One who comes in the
    name of the Lord!
God bless the King of Israel!" *Psalm 118:25-26*
[14]Jesus found a colt and sat on it. This was as the Scripture[d] says,
[15]"Don't be afraid, people of Jerusalem!
Your king is coming,
    sitting on the colt of a donkey."
                                          Zechariah 9:9
[16]The followers of Jesus did not understand this at first. But after Jesus was raised to glory, they remembered that this had been written about him and that they had done these things to him.

People Tell About Jesus

[17]There had been many people with Jesus when he raised Lazarus from the dead and told him to come out of the tomb. Now they were telling others about what Jesus did. [18]Many people went out to meet Jesus, because they had heard about this miracle.[d] [19]So the Pharisees[d] said to each other, "You can see that nothing is going right for us. Look! The whole world is following him."

Jesus Talks About His Death

[20]There were some Greek people, too, who came to Jerusalem to worship at the Passover[d] Feast. [21]They went to Philip, who was from Bethsaida in Galilee, and said, "Sir, we would like to see Jesus." [22]Philip told Andrew, and then Andrew and Philip told Jesus.

[23]Jesus said to them, "The time has come for the Son of Man[d] to receive his glory. [24]I tell you the truth, a grain of wheat must fall to the ground and die to make many seeds. But if it never dies, it remains only a single seed. [25]Those who love their lives will lose them, but those who hate their lives in this world will keep true life forever. [26]Whoever serves me must follow me. Then my servant will be with me everywhere I am. My Father will honor anyone who serves me.

[27]"Now I am very troubled. Should I say, 'Father, save me from this time'? No, I came to this time so I could suffer. [28]Father, bring glory to your name!"

coins One coin, a denarius, was the average pay for one day's work.
Praise Literally, "Hosanna," a Hebrew word used at first in praying to God for help, but at this time it was probably a shout of joy used in praising God or his Messiah.

Then a voice came from heaven, "I have brought glory to it, and I will do it again."

²⁹The crowd standing there, who heard the voice, said it was thunder.

But others said, "An angel has spoken to him."

³⁰Jesus said, "That voice was for your sake, not mine. ³¹Now is the time for the world to be judged; now the ruler of this world will be thrown down. ³²If I am lifted up from the earth, I will draw all people toward me." ³³Jesus said this to show how he would die.

³⁴The crowd said, "We have heard from the law that the Christ*ᵈ* will live forever. So why do you say, 'The Son of Man must be lifted up'? Who is this 'Son of Man'?"

³⁵Then Jesus said, "The light will be with you for a little longer, so walk while you have the light. Then the darkness will not catch you. If you walk in the darkness, you will not know where you are going. ³⁶Believe in the light while you still have it so that you will become children of light." When Jesus had said this, he left and hid himself from them.

Some People Won't Believe in Jesus

³⁷Though Jesus had done many miracles*ᵈ* in front of the people, they still did not believe in him. ³⁸This was to bring about what Isaiah the prophet*ᵈ* had said:

"Lord, who believed what we told them?
Who saw the Lord's power in this?"

Isaiah 53:1

³⁹This is why the people could not believe: Isaiah also had said,

⁴⁰"He has blinded their eyes,
and he has closed their minds.
Otherwise they would see with their eyes
and understand in their minds
and come back to me and be healed."

Isaiah 6:10

⁴¹Isaiah said this because he saw Jesus' glory and spoke about him.

⁴²But many believed in Jesus, even many of the leaders. But because of the Pharisees,*ᵈ* they did not say they believed in him for fear they would be put out of the synagogue.*ᵈ* ⁴³They loved praise from people more than praise from God.

⁴⁴Then Jesus cried out, "Whoever believes in me is really believing in the One who sent me. ⁴⁵Whoever sees me sees the One who sent me. ⁴⁶I have come as light into the world so that whoever believes in me would not stay in darkness.

⁴⁷"Anyone who hears my words and does not obey them, I do not judge, because I did not come to judge the world, but to save the world. ⁴⁸There is a judge for those who refuse to believe in me and do not accept my words. The word I have taught will be their judge on the last day. ⁴⁹The things I taught were not from myself. The Father who sent me told me what to say and what to teach. ⁵⁰And I know that eternal life comes from what the Father commands. So whatever I say is what the Father told me to say."

Jesus Washes His Followers' Feet

13 It was almost time for the Jewish Passover*ᵈ* Feast. Jesus knew that it was time for him to leave this world and go back to the Father. He had always loved those who were his own in the world, and he loved them all the way to the end.

²Jesus and his followers were at the evening meal. The devil had already persuaded Judas Iscariot, the son of Simon, to turn against Jesus. ³Jesus knew that the Father had given him power over everything and that he had come from God and was going back to God. ⁴So during the meal Jesus stood up and took off his outer clothing. Taking a towel, he wrapped it around his waist. ⁵Then he poured water into a bowl and began to wash the followers' feet, drying them with the towel that was wrapped around him.

⁶Jesus came to Simon Peter, who said to him, "Lord, are you going to wash my feet?"

⁷Jesus answered, "You don't understand now what I am doing, but you will understand later."

⁸Peter said, "No, you will never wash my feet."

Jesus answered, "If I don't wash your feet, you are not one of my people."

⁹Simon Peter answered, "Lord, then wash not only my feet, but wash my hands and my head, too!"

¹⁰Jesus said, "After a person has had a bath, his whole body is clean. He needs only to wash his feet. And you men are clean,*ᵈ* but not all of you." ¹¹Jesus knew who would turn

against him, and that is why he said, "Not all of you are clean."

12When he had finished washing their feet, he put on his clothes and sat down again. He asked, "Do you understand what I have just done for you? 13You call me 'Teacher' and 'Lord,' and you are right, because that is what I am. 14If I, your Lord and Teacher, have washed your feet, you also should wash each other's feet. 15I did this as an example so that you should do as I have done for you. 16I tell you the truth, a servant is not greater than his master. A messenger is not greater than the one who sent him. 17If you know these things, you will be happy if you do them.

18"I am not talking about all of you. I know those I have chosen. But this is to bring about what the Scripture*d* said: 'The man who ate at my table has turned against me.'*n* 19I am telling you this now before it happens so that when it happens, you will believe that I am he. 20I tell you the truth, whoever accepts anyone I send also accepts me. And whoever accepts me also accepts the One who sent me."

Jesus Talks About His Death

21After Jesus said this, he was very troubled. He said openly, "I tell you the truth, one of you will turn against me."

22The followers all looked at each other, because they did not know whom Jesus was talking about. 23One of the followers sitting*n* next to Jesus was the follower Jesus loved. 24Simon Peter motioned to him to ask Jesus whom he was talking about.

25That follower leaned closer to Jesus and asked, "Lord, who is it?"

26Jesus answered, "I will dip this bread into the dish. The man I give it to is the man who will turn against me." So Jesus took a piece of bread, dipped it, and gave it to Judas Iscariot, the son of Simon. 27As soon as Judas took the bread, Satan entered him. Jesus said to him, "The thing that you will do—do it quickly." 28No one at the table understood why Jesus said this to Judas. 29Since he was the one who kept the money box, some of the followers thought Jesus was telling him to buy what was needed for the feast or to give something to the poor.

30Judas took the bread Jesus gave him and immediately went out. It was night.

31When Judas was gone, Jesus said, "Now the Son of Man*d* receives his glory, and God receives glory through him. 32If God receives glory through him, then God will give glory to the Son through himself. And God will give him glory quickly."

33Jesus said, "My children, I will be with you only a little longer. You will look for me, and what I told the Jews, I tell you now: Where I am going you cannot come.

34"I give you a new command: Love each other. You must love each other as I have loved you. 35All people will know that you are my followers if you love each other."

Peter Will Say He Doesn't Know Jesus

36Simon Peter asked Jesus, "Lord, where are you going?"

Jesus answered, "Where I am going you cannot follow now, but you will follow later."

37Peter asked, "Lord, why can't I follow you now? I am ready to die for you!"

38Jesus answered, "Are you ready to die for me? I tell you the truth, before the rooster crows, you will say three times that you don't know me."

Jesus Comforts His Followers

14 Jesus said, "Don't let your hearts be troubled. Trust in God, and trust in me. 2There are many rooms in my Father's house; I would not tell you this if it were not true. I am going there to prepare a place for you. 3After I go and prepare a place for you, I will come back and take you to be with me so that you may be where I am. 4You know the way to the place where I am going."

5Thomas said to Jesus, "Lord, we don't know where you are going. So how can we know the way?"

6Jesus answered, "I am the way, and the truth, and the life. The only way to the Father is through me. 7If you really knew me,

---

'The man ... me.' Quotation from Psalm 41:9.
sitting Literally, "lying." The people of that time ate lying down and leaning on one arm.

you would know my Father, too. But now you do know him, and you have seen him."

8Philip said to him, "Lord, show us the Father. That is all we need."

9Jesus answered, "I have been with you a long time now. Do you still not know me, Philip? Whoever has seen me has seen the Father. So why do you say, 'Show us the Father'? 10Don't you believe that I am in the Father and the Father is in me? The words I say to you don't come from me, but the Father lives in me and does his own work. 11Believe me when I say that I am in the Father and the Father is in me. Or believe because of the miracles*d* I have done. 12I tell you the truth, whoever believes in me will do the same things that I do. Those who believe will do even greater things than these, because I am going to the Father. 13And if you ask for anything in my name, I will do it for you so that the Father's glory will be shown through the Son. 14If you ask me for anything in my name, I will do it.

The Promise of the Holy Spirit

15"If you love me, you will obey my commands. 16I will ask the Father, and he will give you another Helper*n* to be with you forever— 17the Spirit*d* of truth. The world cannot accept him, because it does not see him or know him. But you know him, because he lives with you and he will be in you.

18"I will not leave you all alone like orphans; I will come back to you. 19In a little while the world will not see me anymore, but you will see me. Because I live, you will live, too. 20On that day you will know that I am in my Father, and that you are in me and I am in you. 21Those who know my commands and obey them are the ones who love me, and my Father will love those who love me. I will love them and will show myself to them."

22Then Judas (not Judas Iscariot) said, "But, Lord, why do you plan to show yourself to us and not to the rest of the world?"

23Jesus answered, "If people love me, they will obey my teaching. My Father will love them, and we will come to them and make our home with them. 24Those who do not

love me do not obey my teaching. This teaching that you hear is not really mine; it is from my Father, who sent me.

25"I have told you all these things while I am with you. 26But the Helper will teach you everything and will cause you to remember all that I told you. This Helper is the Holy Spirit whom the Father will send in my name.

27"I leave you peace; my peace I give you. I do not give it to you as the world does. So don't let your hearts be troubled or afraid. 28You heard me say to you, 'I am going, but I am coming back to you.' If you loved me, you should be happy that I am going back to the Father, because he is greater than I am. 29I have told you this now, before it happens, so that when it happens, you will believe. 30I will not talk with you much longer, because the ruler of this world is coming. He has no power over me, 31but the world must know that I love the Father, so I do exactly what the Father told me to do.

"Come now, let us go.

Jesus Is Like a Vine

15 "I am the true vine; my Father is the gardener. 2He cuts off every branch of mine that does not produce fruit. And he trims and cleans every branch that produces fruit so that it will produce even more fruit. 3You are already clean*d* because of the words I have spoken to you. 4Remain in me, and I will remain in you. A branch cannot produce fruit alone but must remain in the vine. In the same way, you cannot produce fruit alone but must remain in me.

5"I am the vine, and you are the branches. If any remain in me and I remain in them, they produce much fruit. But without me they can do nothing. 6If any do not remain in me, they are like a branch that is thrown away and then dies. People pick up dead branches, throw them into the fire, and burn them. 7If you remain in me and follow my teachings, you can ask anything you want, and it will be given to you. 8You should produce much fruit and show that you are my followers, which brings glory to my Father. 9I loved you as the Father loved me. Now re-

---

Helper   "Counselor" or "Comforter." Jesus is talking about the Holy Spirit.

main in my love. 10I have obeyed my Father's commands, and I remain in his love. In the same way, if you obey my commands, you will remain in my love. 11I have told you these things so that you can have the same joy I have and so that your joy will be the fullest possible joy.

12"This is my command: Love each other as I have loved you. 13The greatest love a person can show is to die for his friends. 14You are my friends if you do what I command you. 15I no longer call you servants, because a servant does not know what his master is doing. But I call you friends, because I have made known to you everything I heard from my Father. 16You did not choose me; I chose you. And I gave you this work: to go and produce fruit, fruit that will last. Then the Father will give you anything you ask for in my name. 17This is my command: Love each other.

Jesus Warns His Followers

18"If the world hates you, remember that it hated me first. 19If you belonged to the world, it would love you as it loves its own. But I have chosen you out of the world, so you don't belong to it. That is why the world hates you. 20Remember what I told you: A servant is not greater than his master. If people did wrong to me, they will do wrong to you, too. And if they obeyed my teaching, they will obey yours, too. 21They will do all this to you on account of me, because they do not know the One who sent me. 22If I had not come and spoken to them, they would not be guilty of sin, but now they have no excuse for their sin. 23Whoever hates me also hates my Father. 24I did works among them that no one else has ever done. If I had not done these works, they would not be guilty of sin. But now they have seen what I have done, and yet they have hated both me and my Father. 25But this happened so that what is written in their law would be true: 'They hated me for no reason.'n

26"I will send you the Helpern from the Father; he is the Spirit of truth who comes from the Father. When he comes, he will tell

about me, 27and you also must tell people about me, because you have been with me from the beginning.

16 "I have told you these things to keep you from giving up. 2People will put you out of their synagogues.d Yes, the time is coming when those who kill you will think they are offering service to God. 3They will do this because they have not known the Father and they have not known me. 4I have told you these things now so that when the time comes you will remember that I warned you.

The Work of the Holy Spirit

"I did not tell you these things at the beginning, because I was with you then. 5Now I am going back to the One who sent me. But none of you asks me, 'Where are you going?' 6Your hearts are filled with sadness because I have told you these things. 7But I tell you the truth, it is better for you that I go away. When I go away, I will send the Helpern to you. If I do not go away, the Helper will not come. 8When the Helper comes, he will prove to the people of the world the truth about sin, about being right with God, and about judgment. 9He will prove to them that sin is not believing in me. 10He will prove to them that being right with God comes from my going to the Father and not being seen anymore. 11And the Helper will prove to them that judgment happened when the ruler of this world was judged.

12"I have many more things to say to you, but they are too much for you now. 13But when the Spiritd of truth comes, he will lead you into all truth. He will not speak his own words, but he will speak only what he hears, and he will tell you what is to come. 14The Spirit of truth will bring glory to me, because he will take what I have to say and tell it to you. 15All that the Father has is mine. That is why I said that the Spirit will take what I have to say and tell it to you.

Sadness Will Become Happiness

16"After a little while you will not see me,

'They ... reason.' These words could be from Psalm 35:19 or Psalm 69:4.
Helper "Counselor" or "Comforter." Jesus is talking about the Holy Spirit.

and then after a little while you will see me again."

¹⁷Some of the followers said to each other, "What does Jesus mean when he says, 'After a little while you will not see me, and then after a little while you will see me again'? And what does he mean when he says, 'Because I am going to the Father'?" ¹⁸They also asked, "What does he mean by 'a little while'? We don't understand what he is saying."

¹⁹Jesus saw that the followers wanted to ask him about this, so he said to them, "Are you asking each other what I meant when I said, 'After a little while you will not see me, and then after a little while you will see me again'? ²⁰I tell you the truth, you will cry and be sad, but the world will be happy. You will be sad, but your sadness will become joy. ²¹When a woman gives birth to a baby, she has pain, because her time has come. But when her baby is born, she forgets the pain, because she is so happy that a child has been born into the world. ²²It is the same with you. Now you are sad, but I will see you again and you will be happy, and no one will take away your joy. ²³In that day you will not ask me for anything. I tell you the truth, my Father will give you anything you ask for in my name. ²⁴Until now you have not asked for anything in my name. Ask and you will receive, so that your joy will be the fullest possible joy.

Victory over the World

²⁵"I have told you these things, using stories that hide the meaning. But the time will come when I will not use stories like that to tell you things; I will speak to you in plain words about the Father. ²⁶In that day you will ask the Father for things in my name. I mean, I will not need to ask the Father for you. ²⁷The Father himself loves you. He loves you because you loved me and believed that I came from God. ²⁸I came from the Father into the world. Now I am leaving the world and going back to the Father."

²⁹Then the followers of Jesus said, "You are speaking clearly to us now and are not using stories that are hard to understand. ³⁰We can see now that you know all things. You can answer a person's question even be-fore it is asked. This makes us believe you came from God."

³¹Jesus answered, "So now you believe? ³²Listen to me; a time is coming when you will be scattered, each to his own home. That time is now here. You will leave me alone, but I am never really alone, because the Father is with me.

³³"I told you these things so that you can have peace in me. In this world you will have trouble, but be brave! I have defeated the world."

Jesus Prays for His Followers

17 After Jesus said these things, he looked toward heaven and prayed, "Father, the time has come. Give glory to your Son so that the Son can give glory to you. ²You gave the Son power over all people so that the Son could give eternal life to all those you gave him. ³And this is eternal life: that people know you, the only true God, and that they know Jesus Christ, the One you sent. ⁴Having finished the work you gave me to do, I brought you glory on earth. ⁵And now, Father, give me glory with you; give me the glory I had with you before the world was made.

⁶"I showed what you are like to those you gave me from the world. They belonged to you, and you gave them to me, and they have obeyed your teaching. ⁷Now they know that everything you gave me comes from you. ⁸I gave them the teachings you gave me, and they accepted them. They knew that I truly came from you, and they believed that you sent me. ⁹I am praying for them. I am not praying for people in the world but for those you gave me, because they are yours. ¹⁰All I have is yours, and all you have is mine. And my glory is shown through them. ¹¹I am coming to you; I will not stay in the world any longer. But they are still in the world. Holy Father, keep them safe by the power of your name, the name you gave me, so that they will be one, just as you and I are one. ¹²While I was with them, I kept them safe by the power of your name, the name you gave me. I protected them, and only one of them, the one worthy of destruction, was lost so that the Scripture*d* would come true.

¹³"I am coming to you now. But I pray

these things while I am still in the world so that these followers can have all of my joy in them. [14]I have given them your teaching. And the world has hated them, because they don't belong to the world, just as I don't belong to the world. [15]I am not asking you to take them out of the world but to keep them safe from the Evil One. [16]They don't belong to the world, just as I don't belong to the world. [17]Make them ready for your service through your truth; your teaching is truth. [18]I have sent them into the world, just as you sent me into the world. [19]For their sake, I am making myself ready to serve so that they can be ready for their service of the truth.

[20]"I pray for these followers, but I am also praying for all those who will believe in me because of their teaching. [21]Father, I pray that they can be one. As you are in me and I am in you, I pray that they can also be one in us. Then the world will believe that you sent me. [22]I have given these people the glory that you gave me so that they can be one, just as you and I are one. [23]I will be in them and you will be in me so that they will be completely one. Then the world will know that you sent me and that you loved them just as much as you loved me.

[24]"Father, I want these people that you gave me to be with me where I am. I want them to see my glory, which you gave me because you loved me before the world was made. [25]Father, you are the One who is good. The world does not know you, but I know you, and these people know you sent me. [26]I showed them what you are like, and I will show them again. Then they will have the same love that you have for me, and I will live in them."

Jesus Is Arrested

18 When Jesus finished praying, he went with his followers across the Kidron Valley. On the other side there was a garden, and Jesus and his followers went into it.

[2]Judas knew where this place was, because Jesus met there often with his followers. Judas was the one who turned against Jesus. [3]So Judas came there with a group of soldiers and some guards from the leading priests and the Pharisees.[d] They were carrying torches, lanterns, and weapons.

[4]Knowing everything that would happen to him, Jesus went out and asked, "Who is it you are looking for?"

[5]They answered, "Jesus from Nazareth."

"I am he," Jesus said. (Judas, the one who turned against Jesus, was standing there with them.) [6]When Jesus said, "I am he," they moved back and fell to the ground.

[7]Jesus asked them again, "Who is it you are looking for?"

They said, "Jesus of Nazareth."

[8]"I told you that I am he," Jesus said. "So if you are looking for me, let the others go." [9]This happened so that the words Jesus said before would come true: "I have not lost any of the ones you gave me."

[10]Simon Peter, who had a sword, pulled it out and struck the servant of the high priest, cutting off his right ear. (The servant's name was Malchus.) [11]Jesus said to Peter, "Put your sword back. Shouldn't I drink the cup[n] the Father gave me?"

Jesus Is Brought Before Annas

[12]Then the soldiers with their commander and the Jewish guards arrested Jesus. They tied him [13]and led him first to Annas, the father-in-law of Caiaphas, the high priest that year. [14]Caiaphas was the one who told the Jews that it would be better if one man died for all the people.

Peter Says He Doesn't Know Jesus

[15]Simon Peter and another one of Jesus' followers went along after Jesus. This follower knew the high priest, so he went with Jesus into the high priest's courtyard. [16]But Peter waited outside near the door. The follower who knew the high priest came back outside, spoke to the girl at the door, and brought Peter inside. [17]The girl at the door said to Peter, "Aren't you also one of that man's followers?"

Peter answered, "No, I am not!"

[18]It was cold, so the servants and guards

---

cup   Jesus is talking about the painful things that will happen to him. Accepting these things will be very hard, like drinking a cup of something bitter.

had built a fire and were standing around it, warming themselves. Peter also was standing with them, warming himself.

The High Priest Questions Jesus

[19]The high priest asked Jesus questions about his followers and his teaching. [20]Jesus answered, "I have spoken openly to every-one. I have always taught in synagogues[d] and in the Temple,[d] where all the Jews come to-gether. I never said anything in secret. [21]So why do you question me? Ask the people who heard my teaching. They know what I said."

[22]When Jesus said this, one of the guards standing there hit him. The guard said, "Is that the way you answer the high priest?"

[23]Jesus answered him, "If I said something wrong, then show what it was. But if what I said is true, why do you hit me?"

[24]Then Annas sent Jesus, who was still tied, to Caiaphas the high priest.

Peter Says Again He Doesn't Know Jesus

[25]As Simon Peter was standing and warm-ing himself, they said to him, "Aren't you one of that man's followers?"

Peter said it was not true; he said, "No, I am not."

[26]One of the servants of the high priest was there. This servant was a relative of the man whose ear Peter had cut off. The servant said, "Didn't I see you with him in the gar-den?"

[27]Again Peter said it wasn't true. At once a rooster crowed.

Jesus Is Brought Before Pilate

[28]Early in the morning they led Jesus from Caiaphas's house to the Roman governor's palace. They would not go inside the palace, because they did not want to make them-selves unclean;[n] they wanted to eat the Passover[d] meal. [29]So Pilate went outside to them and asked, "What charges do you bring against this man?"

[30]They answered, "If he were not a crimi-nal, we wouldn't have brought him to you."

[31]Pilate said to them, "Take him your-selves and judge him by your own law."

"But we are not allowed to put anyone to death," the Jews answered. [32](This happened so that what Jesus said about how he would die would come true.)

[33]Then Pilate went back inside the palace and called Jesus to him and asked, "Are you the king of the Jews?"

[34]Jesus said, "Is that your own question, or did others tell you about me?"

[35]Pilate answered, "I am not Jewish. It was your own people and their leading priests who handed you over to me. What have you done wrong?"

[36]Jesus answered, "My kingdom does not belong to this world. If it belonged to this world, my servants would fight so that I would not be given over to the Jews. But my kingdom is from another place."

[37]Pilate said, "So you are a king!"

Jesus answered, "You are the one saying I am a king. This is why I was born and came into the world: to tell people the truth. And everyone who belongs to the truth listens to me."

[38]Pilate said, "What is truth?" After he said this, he went out to the Jews again and said to them, "I find nothing against this man. [39]But it is your custom that I free one pris-oner to you at Passover time. Do you want me to free the 'king of the Jews'?"

[40]They shouted back, "No, not him! Let Barabbas go free!" (Barabbas was a robber.)

19 Then Pilate ordered that Jesus be taken away and whipped. [2]The sol-diers made a crown from some thorny branches and put it on Jesus' head and put a purple robe around him. [3]Then they came to him many times and said, "Hail, King of the Jews!" and hit him in the face.

[4]Again Pilate came out and said to them, "Look, I am bringing Jesus out to you. I want you to know that I find nothing against him." [5]So Jesus came out, wearing the crown of thorns and the purple robe. Pilate said to them, "Here is the man!"

[6]When the leading priests and the guards saw Jesus, they shouted, "Crucify him! Cru-cify him!"

But Pilate answered, "Crucify him your-selves, because I find nothing against him."

---

unclean Going into a non-Jewish place would make them unfit to eat the Passover Feast, according to Jewish law.

7The Jews answered, "We have a law that says he should die, because he said he is the Son of God."

8When Pilate heard this, he was even more afraid. 9He went back inside the palace and asked Jesus, "Where do you come from?" But Jesus did not answer him. 10Pilate said, "You refuse to speak to me? Don't you know I have power to set you free and power to have you crucified?"

11Jesus answered, "The only power you have over me is the power given to you by God. The man who turned me in to you is guilty of a greater sin."

12After this, Pilate tried to let Jesus go. But the Jews cried out, "Anyone who makes himself king is against Caesar. If you let this man go, you are no friend of Caesar."

13When Pilate heard what they were saying, he brought Jesus out and sat down on the judge's seat at the place called The Stone Pavement. (In the Jewish language[n] the name is Gabbatha.) 14It was about noon on Preparation[d] Day of Passover[d] week. Pilate said to the Jews, "Here is your king!"

15They shouted, "Take him away! Take him away! Crucify him!"

Pilate asked them, "Do you want me to crucify your king?"

The leading priests answered, "The only king we have is Caesar."

16So Pilate handed Jesus over to them to be crucified.

Jesus Is Crucified

The soldiers took charge of Jesus. 17Carrying his own cross, Jesus went out to a place called The Place of the Skull, which in the Jewish language[n] is called Golgotha. 18There they crucified Jesus. They also crucified two other men, one on each side, with Jesus in the middle. 19Pilate wrote a sign and put it on the cross. It read: JESUS OF NAZARETH, THE KING OF THE JEWS. 20The sign was written in the Jewish language, in Latin, and in Greek. Many of the Jews read the sign, because the place where Jesus was crucified was near the city. 21The leading Jewish priests said to Pi-

late, "Don't write, 'The King of the Jews.' But write, 'This man said, "I am the King of the Jews." ' "

22Pilate answered, "What I have written, I have written."

23After the soldiers crucified Jesus, they took his clothes and divided them into four parts, with each soldier getting one part. They also took his long shirt, which was all one piece of cloth, woven from top to bottom. 24So the soldiers said to each other, "We should not tear this into parts. Let's throw lots[d] to see who will get it." This happened so that this Scripture would come true:[d]

"They divided my clothes among them,
   and they threw lots[d] for my clothing."

Psalm 22:18

So the soldiers did this.

25Standing near his cross were Jesus' mother, his mother's sister, Mary the wife of Clopas, and Mary Magdalene. 26When Jesus saw his mother and the follower he loved standing nearby, he said to his mother, "Dear woman, here is your son." 27Then he said to the follower, "Here is your mother." From that time on, the follower took her to live in his home.

Jesus Dies

28After this, Jesus knew that everything had been done. So that the Scripture[d] would come true, he said, "I am thirsty."[n] 29There was a jar full of vinegar there, so the soldiers soaked a sponge in it, put the sponge on a branch of a hyssop plant, and lifted it to Jesus' mouth. 30When Jesus tasted the vinegar, he said, "It is finished." Then he bowed his head and died.

31This day was Preparation[d] Day, and the next day was a special Sabbath[d] day. Since the Jews did not want the bodies to stay on the cross on the Sabbath day, they asked Pilate to order that the legs of the men be broken[n] and the bodies be taken away. 32So the soldiers came and broke the legs of the first man on the cross beside Jesus. Then they broke the legs of the man on the other cross

---

Jewish language   Hebrew or Aramaic, the languages of the Jewish people in the first century.
"I am thirsty."   Read Psalms 22:15; 69:21.
broken   The breaking of their bones would make them die sooner.

beside Jesus. [33]But when the soldiers came to Jesus and saw that he was already dead, they did not break his legs. [34]But one of the soldiers stuck his spear into Jesus' side, and at once blood and water came out. [35](The one who saw this happen is the one who told us this, and whatever he says is true. And he knows that he tells the truth, and he tells it so that you might believe.) [36]These things happened to make the Scripture come true: "Not one of his bones will be broken." [n] [37]And another Scripture says, "They will look at the one they stabbed." [n]

Jesus Is Buried

[38]Later, Joseph from Arimathea asked Pilate if he could take the body of Jesus. (Joseph was a secret follower of Jesus, because he was afraid of the Jews.) Pilate gave his permission, so Joseph came and took Jesus' body away. [39]Nicodemus, who earlier had come to Jesus at night, went with Joseph. He brought about seventy-five pounds of myrrh[d] and aloes.[d] [40]These two men took Jesus' body and wrapped it with the spices in pieces of linen cloth, which is how the Jewish people bury the dead. [41]In the place where Jesus was crucified, there was a garden. In the garden was a new tomb that had never been used before. [42]The men laid Jesus in that tomb because it was nearby, and the Jews were preparing to start their Sabbath[d] day.

Jesus' Tomb Is Empty

20 Early on the first day of the week, Mary Magdalene went to the tomb while it was still dark. When she saw that the large stone had been moved away from the tomb, [2]she ran to Simon Peter and the follower whom Jesus loved. Mary said, "They have taken the Lord out of the tomb, and we don't know where they have put him."

[3]So Peter and the other follower started for the tomb. [4]They were both running, but the other follower ran faster than Peter and reached the tomb first. [5]He bent down and looked in and saw the strips of linen cloth lying there, but he did not go in. [6]Then following him, Simon Peter arrived and went into the tomb and saw the strips of linen lying there. [7]He also saw the cloth that had been around Jesus' head, which was folded up and laid in a different place from the strips of linen. [8]Then the other follower, who had reached the tomb first, also went in. He saw and believed. [9](They did not yet understand from the Scriptures[d] that Jesus must rise from the dead.)

Jesus Appears to Mary Magdalene

[10]Then the followers went back home. [11]But Mary stood outside the tomb, crying. As she was crying, she bent down and looked inside the tomb. [12]She saw two angels dressed in white, sitting where Jesus' body had been, one at the head and one at the feet.

[13]They asked her, "Woman, why are you crying?"

She answered, "They have taken away my Lord, and I don't know where they have put him." [14]When Mary said this, she turned around and saw Jesus standing there, but she did not know it was Jesus.

[15]Jesus asked her, "Woman, why are you crying? Whom are you looking for?"

Thinking he was the gardener, she said to him, "Did you take him away, sir? Tell me where you put him, and I will get him."

[16]Jesus said to her, "Mary."

Mary turned toward Jesus and said in the Jewish language,[n] "Rabboni." (This means Teacher.)

[17]Jesus said to her, "Don't hold on to me, because I have not yet gone up to the Father. But go to my brothers and tell them, 'I am going back to my Father and your Father, to my God and your God.' "

[18]Mary Magdalene went and said to the followers, "I saw the Lord!" And she told them what Jesus had said to her.

Jesus Appears to His Followers

[19]When it was evening on the first day of the week, the followers were together. The doors were locked, because they were afraid

---

"Not one ... broken." Quotation from Psalm 34:20. The idea is from Exodus 12:46; Numbers 9:12.
"They ... stabbed." Quotation from Zechariah 12:10.
Jewish language Hebrew or Aramaic, the languages of the Jewish people in the first century.

of the Jews. Then Jesus came and stood right in the middle of them and said, "Peace be with you." 20After he said this, he showed them his hands and his side. The followers were thrilled when they saw the Lord.

21Then Jesus said again, "Peace be with you. As the Father sent me, I now send you." 22After he said this, he breathed on them and said, "Receive the Holy Spirit.*d* 23If you forgive anyone his sins, they are forgiven. If you don't forgive them, they are not forgiven."

Jesus Appears to Thomas

24Thomas (called Didymus), who was one of the twelve, was not with them when Jesus came. 25The other followers kept telling Thomas, "We saw the Lord."

But Thomas said, "I will not believe it until I see the nail marks in his hands and put my finger where the nails were and put my hand into his side."

26A week later the followers were in the house again, and Thomas was with them. The doors were locked, but Jesus came in and stood right in the middle of them. He said, "Peace be with you." 27Then he said to Thomas, "Put your finger here, and look at my hands. Put your hand here in my side. Stop being an unbeliever and believe."

28Thomas said to him, "My Lord and my God!"

29Then Jesus told him, "You believe because you see me. Those who believe without seeing me will be truly happy."

Why John Wrote This Book

30Jesus did many other miracles*d* in the presence of his followers that are not written in this book. 31But these are written so that you may believe that Jesus is the Christ,*d* the Son of God. Then, by believing, you may have life through his name.

Jesus Appears to Seven Followers

21 Later, Jesus showed himself to his followers again—this time at Lake Galilee.*n* This is how he showed himself: 2Some of the followers were together: Simon Peter, Thomas (called Didymus), Nathanael from Cana in Galilee, the two sons of Zebe-

dee, and two other followers. 3Simon Peter said, "I am going out to fish."

The others said, "We will go with you." So they went out and got into the boat. They fished that night but caught nothing.

4Early the next morning Jesus stood on the shore, but the followers did not know it was Jesus. 5Then he said to them, "Friends, did you catch any fish?"

They answered, "No."

6He said, "Throw your net on the right side of the boat, and you will find some." So they did, and they caught so many fish they could not pull the net back into the boat.

7The follower whom Jesus loved said to Peter, "It is the Lord!" When Peter heard him say this, he wrapped his coat around himself. (Peter had taken his clothes off.) Then he jumped into the water. 8The other followers went to shore in the boat, dragging the net full of fish. They were not very far from shore, only about a hundred yards. 9When the followers stepped out of the boat and onto the shore, they saw a fire of hot coals. There were fish on the fire, and there was bread.

10Then Jesus said, "Bring some of the fish you just caught."

11Simon Peter went into the boat and pulled the net to the shore. It was full of big fish, one hundred fifty-three in all, but even though there were so many, the net did not tear. 12Jesus said to them, "Come and eat." None of the followers dared ask him, "Who are you?" because they knew it was the Lord. 13Jesus came and took the bread and gave it to them, along with the fish.

14This was now the third time Jesus showed himself to his followers after he was raised from the dead.

Jesus Talks to Peter

15When they finished eating, Jesus said to Simon Peter, "Simon son of John do you love me more than these?"

He answered, "Yes, Lord, you know that I love you."

Jesus said, "Feed my lambs."

16Again Jesus said, "Simon son of John do you love me?"

Lake Galilee Literally, "Sea of Tiberias."

He answered, "Yes, Lord, you know that I love you."

Jesus said, "Take care of my sheep."

[17]A third time he said, "Simon son of John do you love me?"

Peter was hurt because Jesus asked him the third time, "Do you love me?" Peter said, "Lord, you know everything; you know that I love you!"

He said to him, "Feed my sheep. [18]I tell you the truth, when you were younger, you tied your own belt and went where you wanted. But when you are old, you will put out your hands and someone else will tie you and take you where you don't want to go." [19](Jesus said this to show how Peter would die to give glory to God.) Then Jesus said to Peter, "Follow me!"

[20]Peter turned and saw that the follower Jesus loved was walking behind them. (This was the follower who had leaned against Jesus at the supper and had said, "Lord, who will turn against you?") [21]When Peter saw him behind them, he asked Jesus, "Lord, what about him?"

[22]Jesus answered, "If I want him to live until I come back, that is not your business. You follow me."

[23]So a story spread among the followers that this one would not die. But Jesus did not say he would not die. He only said, "If I want him to live until I come back, that is not your business."

[24]That follower is the one who is telling these things and who has now written them down. We know that what he says is true.

[25]There are many other things Jesus did. If every one of them were written down, I suppose the whole world would not be big enough for all the books that would be written.

ACTS

The Good News of Jesus Spreads

Luke Writes Another Book

1 To Theophilus.
The first book I wrote was about every-thing Jesus began to do and teach ²until the day he was taken up into heaven. Before this, with the help of the Holy Spirit,*d* Jesus told the apostles he had chosen what they should do. ³After his death, he showed himself to them and proved in many ways that he was alive. The apostles saw Jesus during the forty days after he was raised from the dead, and he spoke to them about the kingdom of God. ⁴Once when he was eating with them, he told them not to leave Jerusalem. He said, "Wait here to receive the promise from the Father which I told you about. ⁵John baptized people with water, but in a few days you will be baptized with the Holy Spirit."

Jesus Is Taken Up Into Heaven

⁶When the apostles*d* were all together, they asked Jesus, "Lord, are you now going to give the kingdom back to Israel?"

⁷Jesus said to them, "The Father is the only One who has the authority to decide dates and times. These things are not for you to know. ⁸But when the Holy Spirit*d* comes to you, you will receive power. You will be my witnesses—in Jerusalem, in all of Judea, in Samaria, and in every part of the world."

⁹After he said this, as they were watching, he was lifted up, and a cloud hid him from their sight. ¹⁰As he was going, they were looking into the sky. Suddenly, two men wearing white clothes stood beside them. ¹¹They said, "Men of Galilee, why are you standing here looking into the sky? Jesus, whom you saw taken up from you into heaven, will come back in the same way you saw him go."

A New Apostle Is Chosen

¹²Then they went back to Jerusalem from the Mount of Olives.*d* (This mountain is about half a mile from Jerusalem.) ¹³When they entered the city, they went to the up-stairs room where they were staying. Peter, John, James, Andrew, Philip, Thomas, Bar-tholomew, Matthew, James son of Alphaeus, Simon (known as the Zealot*d*), and Judas son of James were there. ¹⁴They all continued praying together with some women, includ-ing Mary the mother of Jesus, and Jesus' brothers.

¹⁵During this time there was a meeting of the believers (about one hundred twenty of them.) Peter stood up and said, ¹⁶⁻¹⁷"Brothers and sisters,*n* in the Scriptures*d* the Holy Spirit*d* said through David something that must happen involving Judas. He was one of our own group and served together with us. He led those who arrested Jesus." ¹⁸(Judas bought a field with the money he got for his evil act. But he fell to his death, his body burst open, and all his intestines poured out. ¹⁹Everyone in Jerusalem learned about this so they named this place Akeldama. In their language Akeldama means "Field of Blood.") ²⁰"In the Book of Psalms," Peter said, "this is written:

'May his place be empty;
leave no one to live in it.'   *Psalm 69:25*

And it is also written:

'Let another man replace him as leader.'
                                    Psalm 109:8

²¹⁻²²"So now a man must become a wit-ness with us of Jesus' being raised from the dead. He must be one of the men who were part of our group during all the time the Lord Jesus was among us—from the time John was baptizing people until the day Jesus was taken up from us to heaven."

Brothers and sisters Although the Greek text says "Brothers" here and throughout this book, the words of the speakers were meant for the entire church, including men and women.

23They put the names of two men before the group. One was Joseph Barsabbas, who was also called Justus. The other was Matthias. 24-25The apostles prayed, "Lord, you know the thoughts of everyone. Show us which one of these two you have chosen to do this work. Show us who should be an apostle*d* in place of Judas, who turned away and went where he belongs." 26Then they used lots*d* to choose between them, and the lots showed that Matthias was the one. So he became an apostle with the other eleven.

The Coming of the Holy Spirit

2 When the day of Pentecost*d* came, they were all together in one place. 2Suddenly a noise like a strong, blowing wind came from heaven and filled the whole house where they were sitting. 3They saw something like flames of fire that were separated and stood over each person there. 4They were all filled with the Holy Spirit,*d* and they began to speak different languages*n* by the power the Holy Spirit was giving them.

5There were some religious Jews staying in Jerusalem who were from every country in the world. 6When they heard this noise, a crowd came together. They were all surprised, because each one heard them speaking in his own language. 7They were completely amazed at this. They said, "Look! Aren't all these people that we hear speaking from Galilee? 8Then how is it possible that we each hear them in our own languages? We are from different places: 9Parthia, Media, Elam, Mesopotamia, Judea, Cappadocia, Pontus, Asia, 10Phrygia, Pamphylia, Egypt, the areas of Libya near Cyrene, Rome 11(both Jews and those who had become Jews), Crete, and Arabia. But we hear them telling in our own languages about the great things God has done!" 12They were all amazed and confused, asking each other, "What does this mean?"

13But others were making fun of them, saying, "They have had too much wine."

Peter Speaks to the People

14But Peter stood up with the eleven apostles,*d* and in a loud voice he spoke to the crowd: "My fellow Jews, and all of you who are in Jerusalem, listen to me. Pay attention to what I have to say. 15These people are not drunk, as you think; it is only nine o'clock in the morning! 16But Joel the prophet*d* wrote about what is happening here today:

17"God says: In the last days
  I will pour out my Spirit*d* on all kinds
    of people.
Your sons and daughters will prophesy.*d*
Your young men will see visions,
  and your old men will dream dreams.
18At that time I will pour out my Spirit
  also on my male slaves and female
    slaves,
and they will prophesy.
19I will show miracles*d*
  in the sky and on the earth:
  blood, fire, and thick smoke.
20The sun will become dark,
  the moon red as blood,
  before the overwhelming and glorious
    day of the Lord will come.
21Then anyone who calls on the Lord
  will be saved.'   *Joel 2:28-32*

22"People of Israel, listen to these words: Jesus from Nazareth was a very special man. God clearly showed this to you by the miracles,*d* wonders, and signs he did through Jesus. You all know this, because it happened right here among you. 23Jesus was given to you, and with the help of those who don't know the law, you put him to death by nailing him to a cross. But this was God's plan which he had made long ago; he knew all this would happen. 24God raised Jesus from the dead and set him free from the pain of death, because death could not hold him. 25For David said this about him:

'I keep the Lord before me always.
  Because he is close by my side,
  I will not be hurt.
26So I am glad, and I rejoice.
  Even my body has hope,
27because you will not leave me in the
    grave.
  You will not let your Holy One rot.
28You will teach me how to live a holy
    life.

---

languages   This can also be translated "tongues."

Being with you will fill me with joy.'

Psalm 16:8-11

29"Brothers and sisters, I can tell you truly that David, our ancestor, died and was buried. His grave is still here with us today. 30He was a prophet*d* and knew God had promised him that he would make a person from David's family a king just as he was.*n* 31Knowing this before it happened, David talked about the Christ*d* rising from the dead. He said:

'He was not left in the grave.

His body did not rot.'

32So Jesus is the One whom God raised from the dead. And we are all witnesses to this. 33Jesus was lifted up to heaven and is now at God's right side. The Father has given the Holy Spirit*d* to Jesus as he promised. So Jesus has poured out that Spirit, and this is what you now see and hear. 34David was not the one who was lifted up to heaven, but he said:

'The Lord said to my Lord,

"Sit by me at my right side,

35   until I put your enemies under your control." '*n*

Psalm 110:1

36"So, all the people of Israel should know this truly: God has made Jesus—the man you nailed to the cross—both Lord and Christ."

37When the people heard this, they felt guilty and asked Peter and the other apostles, "What shall we do?"

38Peter said to them, "Change your hearts and lives and be baptized, each one of you, in the name of Jesus Christ for the forgiveness of your sins. And you will receive the gift of the Holy Spirit. 39This promise is for you, for your children, and for all who are far away. It is for everyone the Lord our God calls to himself."

40Peter warned them with many other words. He begged them, "Save yourselves from the evil of today's people!" 41Then those people who accepted what Peter said were baptized. About three thousand people were added to the number of believers that day. 42They spent their time learning the apostles' teaching, sharing, breaking bread,*n* and praying together.

The Believers Share

43The apostles*d* were doing many miracles*d* and signs, and everyone felt great respect for God. 44All the believers were together and shared everything. 45They would sell their land and the things they owned and then divide the money and give it to anyone who needed it. 46The believers met together in the Temple*d* every day. They ate together in their homes, happy to share their food with joyful hearts. 47They praised God and were liked by all the people. Every day the Lord added those who were being saved to the group of believers.

Peter Heals a Crippled Man

3 One day Peter and John went to the Temple*d* at three o'clock, the time set each day for the afternoon prayer service. 2There, at the Temple gate called Beautiful Gate, was a man who had been crippled all his life. Every day he was carried to this gate to beg for money from the people going into the Temple. 3The man saw Peter and John going into the Temple and asked them for money. 4Peter and John looked straight at him and said, "Look at us!" 5The man looked at them, thinking they were going to give him some money. 6But Peter said, "I don't have any silver or gold, but I do have something else I can give you. By the power of Jesus Christ from Nazareth, stand up and walk!" 7Then Peter took the man's right hand and lifted him up. Immediately the man's feet and ankles became strong. 8He jumped up, stood on his feet, and began to walk. He went into the Temple with them, walking and jumping and praising God. 9-10All the people recognized him as the crippled man who always sat by the Beautiful Gate begging for money. Now they saw this same man walking and praising God, and they were amazed. They wondered how this could happen.

God ... was See 2 Samuel 7:13; Psalm 132:11.

until ... control Literally, "until I make your enemies a footstool for your feet."

breaking bread This may mean a meal as in verse 46, or the Lord's Supper, the special meal Jesus told his followers to eat to remember him (Luke 22:14-20).

Peter Speaks to the People

11While the man was holding on to Peter and John, all the people were amazed and ran to them at Solomon's Porch.[d] 12When Peter saw this, he said to them, "People of Israel, why are you surprised? You are looking at us as if it were our own power or goodness that made this man walk. 13The God of Abraham, Isaac, and Jacob, the God of our ancestors, gave glory to Jesus, his servant. But you handed him over to be killed. Pilate decided to let him go free, but you told Pilate you did not want Jesus. 14You did not want the One who is holy and good but asked Pilate to give you a murderer[n] instead. 15And so you killed the One who gives life, but God raised him from the dead. We are witnesses to this. 16It was faith in Jesus that made this crippled man well. You can see this man, and you know him. He was made completely well because of trust in Jesus, and you all saw it happen!

17"Brothers and sisters, I know you did those things to Jesus because neither you nor your leaders understood what you were doing. 18God said through the prophets[d] that his Christ[d] would suffer and die. And now God has made these things come true in this way. 19So you must change your hearts and lives! Come back to God, and he will forgive your sins. Then the Lord will send the time of rest. 20And he will send Jesus, the One he chose to be the Christ. 21But Jesus must stay in heaven until the time comes when all things will be made right again. God told about this time long ago when he spoke through his holy prophets. 22Moses said, 'The Lord your God will give you a prophet like me, who is one of your own people. You must listen to everything he tells you. 23Anyone who does not listen to that prophet will die, cut off from God's people.'[n] 24Samuel, and all the other prophets who spoke for God after Samuel, told about this time now. 25You are descendants[d] of the prophets. You have received the agreement God made with your ancestors. He said to your father Abraham,

'Through your descendants[d] all the nations on the earth will be blessed.'[n] 26God has raised up his servant Jesus and sent him to you first to bless you by turning each of you away from doing evil."

Peter and John at the Council

4 While Peter and John were speaking to the people, Jewish priests, the captain of the soldiers that guarded the Temple,[d] and Sadducees[d] came up to them. 2They were upset because the two apostles[d] were teaching the people and were preaching that people will rise from the dead through the power of Jesus. 3The Jewish leaders grabbed Peter and John and put them in jail. Since it was already night, they kept them in jail until the next day. 4But many of those who had heard Peter and John preach believed the things they said. There were now about five thousand in the group of believers.

5The next day the Jewish rulers, the older Jewish leaders, and the teachers of the law met in Jerusalem. 6Annas the high priest, Caiaphas, John, and Alexander were there, as well as everyone from the high priest's family. 7They made Peter and John stand before them and then asked them, "By what power or authority did you do this?"

8Then Peter, filled with the Holy Spirit,[d] said to them, "Rulers of the people and you older leaders, 9are you questioning us about a good thing that was done to a crippled man? Are you asking us who made him well? 10We want all of you and all the Jewish people to know that this man was made well by the power of Jesus Christ from Nazareth. You crucified him, but God raised him from the dead. This man was crippled, but he is now well and able to stand here before you because of the power of Jesus. 11Jesus is

'the stone[n] that you builders rejected,
    which has become the cornerstone.'[d]

Psalm 118:22

12Jesus is the only One who can save people. His name is the only power in the world that has been given to save people. We must be saved through him."

---

murderer Barabbas, the man the crowd asked Pilate to set free instead of Jesus (Luke 23:18).
'The Lord . . . people.' Quotation from Deuteronomy 18:15, 19.
'Through . . . blessed.' Quotation from Genesis 22:18; 26:4.
stone A symbol meaning Jesus.

¹³The Jewish leaders saw that Peter and John were not afraid to speak, and they understood that these men had no special training or education. So they were amazed. Then they realized that Peter and John had been with Jesus. ¹⁴Because they saw the healed man standing there beside the two apostles, they could say nothing against them. ¹⁵After the Jewish leaders ordered them to leave the meeting, they began to talk to each other. ¹⁶They said, "What shall we do with these men? Everyone in Jerusalem knows they have done a great miracle,*d* and we cannot say it is not true. ¹⁷But to keep it from spreading among the people, we must warn them not to talk to people anymore using that name."

¹⁸So they called Peter and John in again and told them not to speak or to teach at all in the name of Jesus. ¹⁹But Peter and John answered them, "You decide what God would want. Should we obey you or God? ²⁰We cannot keep quiet. We must speak about what we have seen and heard." ²¹The Jewish leaders warned the apostles again and let them go free. They could not find a way to punish them, because all the people were praising God for what had been done. ²²The man who received the miracle of healing was more than forty years old.

The Believers Pray

²³After Peter and John left the meeting of Jewish leaders, they went to their own group and told them everything the leading priests and the older Jewish leaders had said to them. ²⁴When the believers heard this, they prayed to God together, "Lord, you are the One who made the sky, the earth, the sea, and everything in them. ²⁵By the Holy Spirit,*d* through our father David your servant, you said:

'Why are the nations so angry?
Why are the people making useless plans?
²⁶The kings of the earth prepare to fight,
and their leaders make plans together against the Lord
and his Christ.'*d*   *Psalm 2:1-2*

²⁷These things really happened with Herod, Pontius Pilate, those who are not Jews, and the Jewish people all came together against

Jesus here in Jerusalem. Jesus is your holy servant, the One you made to be the Christ. ²⁸These people made your plan happen because of your power and your will. ²⁹And now, Lord, listen to their threats. Lord, help us, your servants, to speak your word without fear. ³⁰Help us to be brave by showing us your power to heal. Give proofs and make miracles*d* happen by the power of Jesus, your holy servant."

³¹After they had prayed, the place where they were meeting was shaken. They were all filled with the Holy Spirit,*d* and they spoke God's word without fear.

The Believers Share

³²The group of believers were united in their hearts and spirit. All those in the group acted as though their private property belonged to everyone in the group. In fact, they shared everything. ³³With great power the apostles*d* were telling people that the Lord Jesus was truly raised from the dead. And God blessed all the believers very much. ³⁴No one in the group needed anything. From time to time those who owned fields or houses sold them, brought the money, ³⁵and gave it to the apostles. Then the money was given to anyone who needed it.

³⁶One of the believers was named Joseph, a Levite born in Cyprus. The apostles called him Barnabas (which means "one who encourages"). ³⁷Joseph owned a field, sold it, brought the money, and gave it to the apostles.

Ananias and Sapphira Die

5 But a man named Ananias and his wife Sapphira sold some land. ²He kept back part of the money for himself; his wife knew about this and agreed to it. But he brought the rest of the money and gave it to the apostles.*d* ³Peter said, "Ananias, why did you let Satan rule your thoughts to lie to the Holy Spirit*d* and to keep for yourself part of the money you received for the land? ⁴Before you sold the land, it belonged to you. And even after you sold it, you could have used the money any way you wanted. Why did you think of doing this? You lied to God, not to us!" ⁵⁻⁶When Ananias heard this, he fell down and died. Some young men came in,

wrapped up his body, carried it out, and buried it. And everyone who heard about this was filled with fear.

7About three hours later his wife came in, but she did not know what had happened. 8Peter said to her, "Tell me, was the money you got for your field this much?"

Sapphira answered, "Yes, that was the price."

9Peter said to her, "Why did you and your husband agree to test the Spirit of the Lord? Look! The men who buried your husband are at the door, and they will carry you out." 10At that moment Sapphira fell down by his feet and died. When the young men came in and saw that she was dead, they carried her out and buried her beside her husband. 11The whole church and all the others who heard about these things were filled with fear.

The Apostles Heal Many

12The apostles*d* did many signs and miracles*d* among the people. And they would all meet together on Solomon's Porch.*d* 13None of the others dared to join them, but all the people respected them. 14More and more men and women believed in the Lord and were added to the group of believers. 15The people placed their sick on beds and mats in the streets, hoping that when Peter passed by at least his shadow might fall on them. 16Crowds came from all the towns around Jerusalem, bringing their sick and those who were bothered by evil spirits, and all of them were healed.

Leaders Try to Stop the Apostles

17The high priest and all his friends (a group called the Sadducees*d*) became very jealous. 18They took the apostles*d* and put them in jail. 19But during the night, an angel of the Lord opened the doors of the jail and led the apostles outside. The angel said, 20"Go stand in the Temple*d* and tell the people everything about this new life." 21When the apostles heard this, they obeyed and went into the Temple early in the morning and continued teaching.

When the high priest and his friends arrived, they called a meeting of the Jewish leaders and all the important older Jewish men. They sent some men to the jail to bring the apostles to them. 22But, upon arriving, the officers could not find the apostles. So they went back and reported to the Jewish leaders. 23They said, "The jail was closed and locked, and the guards were standing at the doors. But when we opened the doors, the jail was empty!" 24Hearing this, the captain of the Temple guards and the leading priests were confused and wondered what was happening.

25Then someone came and told them, "Listen! The men you put in jail are standing in the Temple teaching the people." 26Then the captain and his men went out and brought the apostles back. But the soldiers did not use force, because they were afraid the people would stone them to death.

27The soldiers brought the apostles to the meeting and made them stand before the Jewish leaders. The high priest questioned them, 28saying, "We gave you strict orders not to continue teaching in that name. But look, you have filled Jerusalem with your teaching and are trying to make us responsible for this man's death."

29Peter and the other apostles answered, "We must obey God, not human authority! 30You killed Jesus by hanging him on a cross. But God, the God of our ancestors, raised Jesus up from the dead! 31Jesus is the One whom God raised to be on his right side, as Leader and Savior. Through him, all Jewish people could change their hearts and lives and have their sins forgiven. 32We saw all these things happen. The Holy Spirit,*d* whom God has given to all who obey him, also proves these things are true."

33When the Jewish leaders heard this, they became angry and wanted to kill them. 34But a Pharisee*d* named Gamaliel stood up in the meeting. He was a teacher of the law, and all the people respected him. He ordered the apostles to leave the meeting for a little while. 35Then he said, "People of Israel, be careful what you are planning to do to these men. 36Remember when Theudas appeared? He said he was a great man, and about four hundred men joined him. But he was killed, and all his followers were scattered; they were able to do nothing. 37Later, a man named Judas came from Galilee at the time of the registration.[n] He also led a group of followers and was killed, and all his followers were scattered. 38And so now I tell you: Stay away from these men, and leave them alone. If their plan comes from human authority, it will fail. 39But if it is from God, you will not be able to stop them. You might even be fighting against God himself!"

The Jewish leaders agreed with what Gamaliel said. 40They called the apostles in, beat them, and told them not to speak in the name of Jesus again. Then they let them go free. 41The apostles left the meeting full of joy because they were given the honor of suffering disgrace for Jesus. 42Every day in the Temple and in people's homes they continued teaching the people and telling the Good News — that Jesus is the Christ.[d]

Seven Leaders Are Chosen

6 The number of followers was growing. But during this same time, the Greek-speaking followers had an argument with the other Jewish followers. The Greek-speaking widows were not getting their share of the food that was given out every day. 2The twelve apostles[d] called the whole group of followers together and said, "It is not right for us to stop our work of teaching God's word in order to serve tables. 3So, brothers and sisters, choose seven of your own men who are good, full of the Spirit[d] and full of wisdom. We will put them in charge of this work. 4Then we can continue to pray and to teach the word of God."

5The whole group liked the idea, so they chose these seven men: Stephen (a man with great faith and full of the Holy Spirit), Philip,[n] Procorus, Nicanor, Timon, Parmenas, and Nicolas (a man from Antioch who had become a Jew). 6Then they put these men before the apostles, who prayed and laid their hands[n] on them.

7The word of God was continuing to spread. The group of followers in Jerusalem increased, and a great number of the Jewish priests believed and obeyed.

Stephen Is Accused

8Stephen was richly blessed by God who gave him the power to do great miracles[d] and signs among the people. 9But some Jewish people were against him. They belonged to the synagogue[d] of Free Men[n] (as it was called), which included Jewish people from Cyrene, Alexandria, Cilicia, and Asia. They all came and argued with Stephen.

10But the Spirit[d] was helping him to speak with wisdom, and his words were so strong that they could not argue with him. 11So they secretly urged some men to say, "We heard Stephen speak against Moses and against God."

12This upset the people, the older Jewish leaders, and the teachers of the law. They came and grabbed Stephen and brought him to a meeting of the Jewish leaders. 13They brought in some people to tell lies about Stephen, saying, "This man is always speaking against this holy place and the law of Moses. 14We heard him say that Jesus from Nazareth will destroy this place and that Jesus will change the customs Moses gave us." 15All the people in the meeting were watching Stephen closely and saw that his face looked like the face of an angel.

Stephen's Speech

7 The high priest said to Stephen, "Are these things true?"

2Stephen answered, "Brothers and fathers, listen to me. Our glorious God appeared to Abraham, our ancestor, in Mesopotamia before he lived in Haran. 3God said to Abraham, 'Leave your country and your relatives, and go to the land I will show you.'[n] 4So Abraham left the country of Chaldea and went to live in Haran. After Abraham's father died, God sent him to this place where you now live. 5God did not give Abraham any of this land, not even a foot of it. But God promised that he would give this land to him and his descendants,[d] even before Abraham had a child. 6This is what God said to him: 'Your descendants will be strangers in a land they

---

registration Census. A counting of all the people and the things they own.
Philip Not the apostle named Philip.
laid their hands The laying on of hands had many purposes, including the giving of a blessing, power, or authority.
Free Men Jewish people who had been slaves or whose fathers had been slaves, but were now free.
'Leave . . . you.' Quotation from Genesis 12:1.

don't own. The people there will make them slaves and will mistreat them for four hundred years. [7]But I will punish the nation where they are slaves. Then your descendants will leave that land and will worship me in this place.'[n] [8]God made an agreement with Abraham, the sign of which was circumcision.[d] And so when Abraham had his son Isaac, Abraham circumcised him when he was eight days old. Isaac also circumcised his son Jacob, and Jacob did the same for his sons, the twelve ancestors[n] of our people.

[9]"Jacob's sons became jealous of Joseph and sold him to be a slave in Egypt. But God was with him [10]and saved him from all his troubles. The king of Egypt liked Joseph and respected him because of the wisdom God gave him. The king made him governor of Egypt and put him in charge of all the people in his palace.

[11]"Then all the land of Egypt and Canaan became so dry that nothing would grow, and the people suffered very much. Jacob's sons, our ancestors, could not find anything to eat. [12]But when Jacob heard there was grain in Egypt, he sent his sons there. This was their first trip to Egypt. [13]When they went there a second time, Joseph told his brothers who he was, and the king learned about Joseph's family. [14]Then Joseph sent messengers to invite Jacob, his father, to come to Egypt along with all his relatives (seventy-five persons altogether). [15]So Jacob went down to Egypt, where he and his sons died. [16]Later their bodies were moved to Shechem and put in a grave there. (It was the same grave Abraham had bought for a sum of money from the sons of Hamor in Shechem.)

[17]"The promise God made to Abraham was soon to come true, and the number of people in Egypt grew large. [18]Then a new king, who did not know who Joseph was, began to rule Egypt. [19]This king tricked our people and was cruel to our ancestors, forcing them to leave their babies outside to die. [20]At this time Moses was born, and he was very beautiful. For three months Moses was cared for in his father's house. [21]When they put Moses outside, the king's daughter adopted him and raised him as if he were her own son. [22]The Egyptians taught Moses everything they knew, and he was a powerful man in what he said and did.

[23]"When Moses was about forty years old, he thought it would be good to visit his own people, the people of Israel. [24]Moses saw an Egyptian mistreating an Israelite, so he defended the Israelite and punished the Egyptian by killing him. [25]Moses thought his own people would understand that God was using him to save them, but they did not. [26]The next day when Moses saw two men of Israel fighting, he tried to make peace between them. He said, 'Men, you are brothers. Why are you hurting each other?' [27]The man who was hurting the other pushed Moses away and said, 'Who made you our ruler and judge? [28]Are you going to kill me as you killed the Egyptian yesterday?'[n] [29]When Moses heard him say this, he left Egypt and went to live in the land of Midian where he was a stranger. While Moses lived in Midian, he had two sons.

[30]"Forty years later an angel appeared to Moses in the flames of a burning bush as he was in the desert near Mount Sinai. [31]When Moses saw this, he was amazed and went near to look closer. Moses heard the Lord's voice say, [32]'I am the God of your ancestors, the God of Abraham, Isaac, and Jacob.'[n] Moses began to shake with fear and was afraid to look. [33]The Lord said to him, 'Take off your sandals, because you are standing on holy ground. [34]I have seen the troubles my people have suffered in Egypt. I have heard their cries and have come down to save them. And now, Moses, I am sending you back to Egypt.'[n]

[35]"This Moses was the same man the two men of Israel rejected, saying, 'Who made you a ruler and judge?'[n] Moses is the same man God sent to be a ruler and savior, with

---

'Your descendants . . . place.'   Quotation from Genesis 15:13-14 and Exodus 3:12.
twelve ancestors   Important ancestors of the Jewish people; the leaders of the twelve Jewish tribes.
'Who . . . yesterday?'   Quotation from Exodus 2:14.
'I am . . . Jacob.'   Quotation from Exodus 3:6.
'Take . . . Egypt.'   Quotation from Exodus 3:5-10.
'Who . . . judge?'   Quotation from Exodus 2:14.

the help of the angel that Moses saw in the burning bush. [36]So Moses led the people out of Egypt. He worked miracles[d] and signs in Egypt, at the Red Sea,[d] and then in the desert for forty years. [37]This is the same Moses that said to the people of Israel, 'God will give you a prophet[d] like me, who is one of your own people.'[n] [38]This is the Moses who was with the gathering of the Israelites in the desert. He was with the angel that spoke to him at Mount Sinai, and he was with our ancestors. He received commands from God that give life, and he gave those commands to us.

[39]"But our ancestors did not want to obey Moses. They rejected him and wanted to go back to Egypt. [40]They said to Aaron, 'Make us gods who will lead us. Moses led us out of Egypt, but we don't know what has happened to him.'[n] [41]So the people made an idol that looked like a calf. Then they brought sacrifices to it and were proud of what they had made with their own hands. [42]But God turned against them and did not try to stop them from worshiping the sun, moon, and stars. This is what is written in the book of the prophets: God says,

'People of Israel, you did not bring me
        sacrifices and offerings
    while you traveled in the desert for
        forty years.
[43]You have carried with you
    the tent to worship Molech[d]
    and the idols of the star god Rephan
        that you made to worship.
So I will send you away beyond
        Babylon.'   *Amos 5:25-27*

[44]"The Holy Tent[d] where God spoke to our ancestors was with them in the desert. God told Moses how to make this Tent, and he made it like the plan God showed him. [45]Later, Joshua led our ancestors to capture the lands of the other nations. Our people went in, and God forced the other people out. When our people went into this new land, they took with them this same Tent they had received from their ancestors. They kept it until the time of David, [46]who pleased God and asked God to let him build a house

for him, the God of Jacob. [47]But Solomon was the one who built the Temple.[d]

[48]"But the Most High does not live in houses that people build with their hands. As the prophet says:
[49]'Heaven is my throne,
    and the earth is my footstool.
So do you think you can build a house
        for me? says the Lord.
    Do I need a place to rest?
[50]Remember, my hand made all these
        things!' "   *Isaiah 66:1-2*

[51]Stephen continued speaking: "You stubborn people! You have not given your hearts to God, nor will you listen to him! You are always against what the Holy Spirit[d] is trying to tell you, just as your ancestors were. [52]Your ancestors tried to hurt every prophet who ever lived. Those prophets said long ago that the One who is good would come, but your ancestors killed them. And now you have turned against and killed the One who is good. [53]You received the law of Moses, which God gave you through his angels, but you haven't obeyed it."

Stephen Is Killed

[54]When the leaders heard this, they became furious. They were so mad they were grinding their teeth at Stephen. [55]But Stephen was full of the Holy Spirit.[d] He looked up to heaven and saw the glory of God and Jesus standing at God's right side. [56]He said, "Look! I see heaven open and the Son of Man[d] standing at God's right side."

[57]Then they shouted loudly and covered their ears and all ran at Stephen. [58]They took him out of the city and began to throw stones at him to kill him. And those who told lies against Stephen left their coats with a young man named Saul. [59]While they were throwing stones, Stephen prayed, "Lord Jesus, receive my spirit." [60]He fell on his knees and cried in a loud voice, "Lord, do not hold this sin against them." After Stephen said this, he died.

8 Saul agreed that the killing of Stephen was good.

'**God . . . people.**' Quotation from Deuteronomy 18:15.
'**Make . . . him.**' Quotation from Exodus 32:1.

Troubles for the Believers

On that day the church of Jerusalem began to be persecuted,[d] and all the believers, except the apostles,[d] were scattered throughout Judea and Samaria.

2And some religious people buried Stephen and cried loudly for him. 3Saul was also trying to destroy the church, going from house to house, dragging out men and women and putting them in jail. 4And wherever they were scattered, they told people the Good News.[d]

Philip Preaches in Samaria

5Philip[n] went to the city of Samaria and preached about the Christ.[d] 6When the people there heard Philip and saw the miracles[d] he was doing, they all listened carefully to what he said. 7Many of these people had evil spirits in them, but Philip made the evil spirits leave. The spirits made a loud noise when they came out. Philip also healed many weak and crippled people there. 8So the people in that city were very happy.

9But there was a man named Simon in that city. Before Philip came there, Simon had practiced magic and amazed all the people of Samaria. He bragged and called himself a great man. 10All the people — the least important and the most important — paid attention to Simon, saying, "This man has the power of God, called 'the Great Power'!" 11Simon had amazed them with his magic so long that the people became his followers. 12But when Philip told them the Good News[d] about the kingdom of God and the power of Jesus Christ, men and women believed Philip and were baptized. 13Simon himself believed, and after he was baptized, he stayed very close to Philip. When he saw the miracles and the powerful things Philip did, Simon was amazed.

14When the apostles[d] who were still in Jerusalem heard that the people of Samaria had accepted the word of God, they sent Peter and John to them. 15When Peter and John arrived, they prayed that the Samaritan believers might receive the Holy Spirit.[d] 16These people had been baptized in the name of the Lord Jesus, but the Holy Spirit had not yet come upon any of them. 17Then, when the two apostles began laying their hands on the people, they received the Holy Spirit.

18Simon saw that the Spirit was given to people when the apostles laid their hands on them. So he offered the apostles money, 19saying, "Give me also this power so that anyone on whom I lay my hands will receive the Holy Spirit."

20Peter said to him, "You and your money should both be destroyed, because you thought you could buy God's gift with money. 21You cannot share with us in this work since your heart is not right before God. 22Change your heart! Turn away from this evil thing you have done, and pray to the Lord. Maybe he will forgive you for thinking this. 23I see that you are full of bitter jealousy and ruled by sin."

24Simon answered, "Both of you pray for me to the Lord so the things you have said will not happen to me."

25After Peter and John told the people what they had seen Jesus do and after they had spoken the message of the Lord, they went back to Jerusalem. On the way, they went through many Samaritan towns and preached the Good News to the people.

Philip Teaches an Ethiopian

26An angel of the Lord said to Philip,[n] "Get ready and go south to the road that leads down to Gaza from Jerusalem — the desert road." 27So Philip got ready and went. On the road he saw a man from Ethiopia, a eunuch.[d] He was an important officer in the service of Candace, the queen of the Ethiopians; he was responsible for taking care of all her money. He had gone to Jerusalem to worship. 28Now, as he was on his way home, he was sitting in his chariot reading from the Book of Isaiah, the prophet.[d] 29The Spirit[d] said to Philip, "Go to that chariot and stay near it."

30So when Philip ran toward the chariot, he heard the man reading from Isaiah the prophet. Philip asked, "Do you understand what you are reading?"

31He answered, "How can I understand

Philip Not the apostle named Philip.

unless someone explains it to me?" Then he invited Philip to climb in and sit with him. [32]The portion of Scripture[d] he was reading was this:

"He was like a sheep being led to be killed.

He was quiet, as a lamb is quiet while its wool is being cut;

he never opened his mouth.

[33] He was shamed and was treated unfairly.

He died without children to continue his family.

His life on earth has ended."   *Isaiah 53:7-8*

[34]The officer said to Philip, "Please tell me, who is the prophet talking about — himself or someone else?" [35]Philip began to speak, and starting with this same Scripture, he told the man the Good News[d] about Jesus.

[36]While they were traveling down the road, they came to some water. The officer said, "Look, here is water. What is stopping me from being baptized?" [37] [n] [38]Then the officer commanded the chariot to stop. Both Philip and the officer went down into the water, and Philip baptized him. [39]When they came up out of the water, the Spirit of the Lord took Philip away; the officer never saw him again. And the officer continued on his way home, full of joy. [40]But Philip appeared in a city called Azotus and preached the Good News in all the towns on the way from Azotus to Caesarea.

Saul Is Converted

9 In Jerusalem Saul was still threatening the followers of the Lord by saying he would kill them. So he went to the high priest [2]and asked him to write letters to the synagogues[d] in the city of Damascus. Then if Saul found any followers of Christ's Way, men or women, he would arrest them and bring them back to Jerusalem.

[3]So Saul headed toward Damascus. As he came near the city, a bright light from heaven suddenly flashed around him. [4]Saul fell to the ground and heard a voice saying to him, "Saul, Saul! Why are you persecuting me?"

[5]Saul said, "Who are you, Lord?"

The voice answered, "I am Jesus, whom you are persecuting. [6]Get up now and go into the city. Someone there will tell you what you must do."

[7]The people traveling with Saul stood there but said nothing. They heard the voice, but they saw no one. [8]Saul got up from the ground and opened his eyes, but he could not see. So those with Saul took his hand and led him into Damascus. [9]For three days Saul could not see and did not eat or drink.

[10]There was a follower of Jesus in Damascus named Ananias. The Lord spoke to Ananias in a vision, "Ananias!"

Ananias answered, "Here I am, Lord."

[11]The Lord said to him, "Get up and go to Straight Street. Find the house of Judas,[n] and ask for a man named Saul from the city of Tarsus. He is there now, praying. [12]Saul has seen a vision in which a man named Ananias comes to him and lays his hands on him. Then he is able to see again."

[13]But Ananias answered, "Lord, many people have told me about this man and the terrible things he did to your holy people in Jerusalem. [14]Now he has come here to Damascus, and the leading priests have given him the power to arrest everyone who worships you."

[15]But the Lord said to Ananias, "Go! I have chosen Saul for an important work. He must tell about me to those who are not Jews, to kings, and to the people of Israel. [16]I will show him how much he must suffer for my name."

[17]So Ananias went to the house of Judas. He laid his hands on Saul and said, "Brother Saul, the Lord Jesus sent me. He is the one you saw on the road on your way here. He sent me so that you can see again and be filled with the Holy Spirit."[d] [18]Immediately, something that looked like fish scales fell from Saul's eyes, and he was able to see again! Then Saul got up and was baptized. [19]After he ate some food, his strength returned.

Verse 37 Some late copies of Acts add verse 37: "Philip answered, 'If you believe with all your heart, you can.' The officer said, 'I believe that Jesus Christ is the Son of God.' "
Judas This is not either of the apostles named Judas.

Saul Preaches in Damascus

Saul stayed with the followers of Jesus in Damascus for a few days. 20Soon he began to preach about Jesus in the synagogues,*d* saying, "Jesus is the Son of God."

21All the people who heard him were amazed. They said, "This is the man who was in Jerusalem trying to destroy those who trust in this name! He came here to arrest the followers of Jesus and take them back to the leading priests."

22But Saul grew more powerful. His proofs that Jesus is the Christ*d* were so strong that the Jewish people in Damascus could not argue with him.

23After many days, some Jewish people made plans to kill Saul. 24They were watching the city gates day and night, but Saul learned about their plan. 25One night some followers of Saul helped him leave the city by lowering him in a basket through an opening in the city wall.

Saul Preaches in Jerusalem

26When Saul went to Jerusalem, he tried to join the group of followers, but they were all afraid of him. They did not believe he was really a follower. 27But Barnabas accepted Saul and took him to the apostles.*d* Barnabas explained to them that Saul had seen the Lord on the road and the Lord had spoken to Saul. Then he told them how boldly Saul had preached in the name of Jesus in Damascus.

28And so Saul stayed with the followers, going everywhere in Jerusalem, preaching boldly in the name of the Lord. 29He would often talk and argue with the Jewish people who spoke Greek, but they were trying to kill him. 30When the followers learned about this, they took Saul to Caesarea and from there sent him to Tarsus.

31The church everywhere in Judea, Galilee, and Samaria had a time of peace and became stronger. Respecting the Lord by the way they lived, and being encouraged by the Holy Spirit,*d* the group of believers continued to grow.

Peter Heals Aeneas

32As Peter was traveling through all the area, he visited God's people who lived in Lydda. 33There he met a man named Aeneas, who was paralyzed and had not been able to leave his bed for the past eight years. 34Peter said to him, "Aeneas, Jesus Christ heals you. Stand up and make your bed." Aeneas stood up immediately. 35All the people living in Lydda and on the Plain of Sharon saw him and turned to the Lord.

Peter Heals Tabitha

36In the city of Joppa there was a follower named Tabitha (whose Greek name was Dorcas). She was always doing good deeds and kind acts. 37While Peter was in Lydda, Tabitha became sick and died. Her body was washed and put in a room upstairs. 38Since Lydda is near Joppa and the followers in Joppa heard that Peter was in Lydda, they sent two messengers to Peter. They begged him, "Hurry, please come to us!" 39So Peter got ready and went with them. When he arrived, they took him to the upstairs room where all the widows stood around Peter, crying. They showed him the shirts and coats Tabitha had made when she was still alive. 40Peter sent everyone out of the room and kneeled and prayed. Then he turned to the body and said, "Tabitha, stand up." She opened her eyes, and when she saw Peter, she sat up. 41He gave her his hand and helped her up. Then he called the saints*d* and the widows into the room and showed them that Tabitha was alive. 42People everywhere in Joppa learned about this, and many believed in the Lord. 43Peter stayed in Joppa for many days with a man named Simon who was a tanner.

Peter Teaches Cornelius

10 At Caesarea there was a man named Cornelius, an officer in the Italian group of the Roman army. 2Cornelius was a religious man. He and all the other people who lived in his house worshiped the true God. He gave much of his money to the poor and prayed to God often. 3One afternoon about three o'clock, Cornelius clearly saw a vision. An angel of God came to him and said, "Cornelius!"

4Cornelius stared at the angel. He became afraid and said, "What do you want, Lord?"

The angel said, "God has heard your

prayers. He has seen that you give to the poor, and he remembers you. [5]Send some men now to Joppa to bring back a man named Simon who is also called Peter. [6]He is staying with a man, also named Simon, who is a tanner and has a house beside the sea." [7]When the angel who spoke to Cornelius left, Cornelius called two of his servants and a soldier, a religious man who worked for him. [8]Cornelius explained everything to them and sent them to Joppa.

[9]About noon the next day as they came near Joppa, Peter was going up to the roof[n] to pray. [10]He was hungry and wanted to eat, but while the food was being prepared, he had a vision. [11]He saw heaven opened and something coming down that looked like a big sheet being lowered to earth by its four corners. [12]In it were all kinds of animals, reptiles, and birds. [13]Then a voice said to Peter, "Get up, Peter; kill and eat."

[14]But Peter said, "No, Lord! I have never eaten food that is unholy or unclean."[d]

[15]But the voice said to him again, "God has made these things clean so don't call them 'unholy'!" [16]This happened three times, and at once the sheet was taken back to heaven.

[17]While Peter was wondering what this vision meant, the men Cornelius sent had found Simon's house and were standing at the gate. [18]They asked, "Is Simon Peter staying here?"

[19]While Peter was still thinking about the vision, the Spirit[d] said to him, "Listen, three men are looking for you. [20]Get up and go downstairs. Go with them without doubting, because I have sent them to you."

[21]So Peter went down to the men and said, "I am the one you are looking for. Why did you come here?"

[22]They said, "A holy angel spoke to Cornelius, an army officer and a good man; he worships God. All the Jewish people respect him. The angel told Cornelius to ask you to come to his house so that he can hear what you have to say." [23]So Peter asked the men to come in and spend the night.

The next day Peter got ready and went with them, and some of the followers from Joppa joined him. [24]On the following day they came to Caesarea. Cornelius was waiting for them and had called together his relatives and close friends. [25]When Peter entered, Cornelius met him, fell at his feet, and worshiped him. [26]But Peter helped him up, saying, "Stand up. I too am only a human." [27]As he talked with Cornelius, Peter went inside where he saw many people gathered. [28]He said, "You people understand that it is against our Jewish law for Jewish people to associate with or visit anyone who is not Jewish. But God has shown me that I should not call any person 'unholy' or 'unclean.' [29]That is why I did not argue when I was asked to come here. Now, please tell me why you sent for me."

[30]Cornelius said, "Four days ago, I was praying in my house at this same time—three o'clock in the afternoon. Suddenly, there was a man standing before me wearing shining clothes. [31]He said, 'Cornelius, God has heard your prayer and has seen that you give to the poor and remembers you. [32]So send some men to Joppa and ask Simon Peter to come. Peter is staying in the house of a man, also named Simon, who is a tanner and has a house beside the sea.' [33]So I sent for you immediately, and it was very good of you to come. Now we are all here before God to hear everything the Lord has commanded you to tell us."

[34]Peter began to speak: "I really understand now that to God every person is the same. [35]In every country God accepts anyone who worships him and does what is right. [36]You know the message that God has sent to the people of Israel is the Good News[d] that peace has come through Jesus Christ. Jesus is the Lord of all people! [37]You know what has happened all over Judea, beginning in Galilee after John[n] preached to the people about baptism. [38]You know about Jesus from Nazareth, that God gave him the Holy Spirit[d] and power. You know how Jesus went everywhere doing good and healing those who

---

roof In Bible times houses were built with flat roofs. The roof was used for drying things such as flax and fruit. And it was used as an extra room, as a place for worship, and as a place to sleep in the summer.
John John the Baptist, who preached to people about Christ's coming (Luke 3).

were ruled by the devil, because God was with him. 39We saw what Jesus did in Judea and in Jerusalem, but the Jews in Jerusalem killed him by hanging him on a cross. 40Yet, on the third day, God raised Jesus to life and caused him to be seen, 41not by all the people, but only by the witnesses God had already chosen. And we are those witnesses who ate and drank with him after he was raised from the dead. 42He told us to preach to the people and to tell them that he is the one whom God chose to be the judge of the living and the dead. 43All the prophets say it is true that all who believe in Jesus will be forgiven of their sins through Jesus' name."

44While Peter was still saying this, the Holy Spirit*d* came down on all those who were listening. 45The Jewish believers who came with Peter were amazed that the gift of the Holy Spirit had been given even to those who were not Jews. 46These Jewish believers heard them speaking in different languages*n* and praising God. Then Peter said, 47"Can anyone keep these people from being baptized with water? They have received the Holy Spirit just as we did!" 48So Peter ordered that they be baptized in the name of Jesus Christ. Then they asked Peter to stay with them for a few days.

Peter Returns to Jerusalem

11 The apostles*d* and the believers in Judea heard that some who were not Jewish had accepted God's teaching too. 2But when Peter came to Jerusalem, some Jewish believers argued with him. 3They said, "You went into the homes of people who are not circumcised*d* and ate with them!"

4So Peter explained the whole story to them. 5He said, "I was in the city of Joppa, and while I was praying, I had a vision. I saw something that looked like a big sheet being lowered from heaven by its four corners. It came very close to me. 6I looked inside it and saw animals, wild beasts, reptiles, and birds. 7I heard a voice say to me, 'Get up, Peter. Kill and eat.' 8But I said, 'No, Lord! I have never eaten anything that is unholy or unclean.'*d* 9But the voice from heaven spoke again,

'God has made these things clean, so don't call them unholy.' 10This happened three times. Then the whole thing was taken back to heaven. 11Right then three men who were sent to me from Caesarea came to the house where I was staying. 12The Spirit*d* told me to go with them without doubting. These six believers here also went with me, and we entered the house of Cornelius. 13He told us about the angel he saw standing in his house. The angel said to him, 'Send some men to Joppa and invite Simon Peter to come. 14By the words he will say to you, you and all your family will be saved.' 15When I began my speech, the Holy Spirit came on them just as he came on us at the beginning. 16Then I remembered the words of the Lord. He said, 'John baptized with water, but you will be baptized with the Holy Spirit.' 17Since God gave them the same gift he gave us who believed in the Lord Jesus Christ, how could I stop the work of God?"

18When the Jewish believers heard this, they stopped arguing. They praised God and said, "So God is allowing even those who are not Jewish to turn to him and live."

The Good News Comes to Antioch

19Many of the believers were scattered when they were persecuted after Stephen was killed. Some of them went as far as Phoenicia, Cyprus, and Antioch telling the message to others, but only to Jews. 20Some of these believers were people from Cyprus and Cyrene. When they came to Antioch, they spoke also to Greeks, telling them the Good News*d* about the Lord Jesus. 21The Lord was helping the believers, and a large group of people believed and turned to the Lord.

22The church in Jerusalem heard about all of this, so they sent Barnabas to Antioch. 23-24Barnabas was a good man, full of the Holy Spirit*d* and full of faith. When he reached Antioch and saw how God had blessed the people, he was glad. He encouraged all the believers in Antioch always to obey the Lord with all their hearts, and many people became followers of the Lord.

25Then Barnabas went to the city of Tarsus to look for Saul, 26and when he found Saul,

languages   This can also be translated "tongues."

he brought him to Antioch. For a whole year Saul and Barnabas met with the church and taught many people there. In Antioch the followers were called Christians for the first time.

27About that time some prophets*d* came from Jerusalem to Antioch. 28One of them, named Agabus, stood up and spoke with the help of the Holy Spirit. He said, "A very hard time is coming to the whole world. There will be no food to eat." (This happened when Claudius ruled.) 29The believers all decided to help the followers who lived in Judea, as much as each one could. 30They gathered the money and gave it to Barnabas and Saul, who brought it to the elders*d* in Judea.

Herod Agrippa Hurts the Church

12 During that same time King Herod began to mistreat some who belonged to the church. 2He ordered James, the brother of John, to be killed by the sword. 3Herod saw that the Jewish people liked this, so he decided to arrest Peter, too. (This happened during the time of the Feast*d* of Unleavened Bread.)

4After Herod arrested Peter, he put him in jail and handed him over to be guarded by sixteen soldiers. Herod planned to bring Peter before the people for trial after the Passover*d* Feast. 5So Peter was kept in jail, but the church prayed earnestly to God for him.

Peter Leaves the Jail

6The night before Herod was to bring him to trial, Peter was sleeping between two soldiers, bound with two chains. Other soldiers were guarding the door of the jail. 7Suddenly, an angel of the Lord stood there, and a light shined in the cell. The angel struck Peter on the side and woke him up. "Hurry! Get up!" the angel said. And the chains fell off Peter's hands. 8Then the angel told him, "Get dressed and put on your sandals." And Peter did. Then the angel said, "Put on your coat and follow me." 9So Peter followed him out, but he did not know if what the angel was doing was real; he thought he might be seeing a vision. 10They went past the first and second guards and came to the iron gate that separated them from the city. The gate opened by itself for them, and they went

through it. When they had walked down one street, the angel suddenly left him.

11Then Peter realized what had happened. He thought, "Now I know that the Lord really sent his angel to me. He rescued me from Herod and from all the things the Jewish people thought would happen."

12When he considered this, he went to the home of Mary, the mother of John Mark. Many people were gathered there, praying. 13Peter knocked on the outside door, and a servant girl named Rhoda came to answer it. 14When she recognized Peter's voice, she was so happy she forgot to open the door. Instead, she ran inside and told the group, "Peter is at the door!"

15They said to her, "You are crazy!" But she kept on saying it was true, so they said, "It must be Peter's angel."

16Peter continued to knock, and when they opened the door, they saw him and were amazed. 17Peter made a sign with his hand to tell them to be quiet. He explained how the Lord led him out of the jail, and he said, "Tell James and the other believers what happened." Then he left to go to another place.

18The next day the soldiers were very upset and wondered what had happened to Peter. 19Herod looked everywhere for him but could not find him. So he questioned the guards and ordered that they be killed.

The Death of Herod Agrippa

Later Herod moved from Judea and went to the city of Caesarea, where he stayed. 20Herod was very angry with the people of Tyre and Sidon, but the people of those cities all came in a group to him. After convincing Blastus, the king's personal servant, to be on their side, they asked Herod for peace, because their country got its food from his country.

21On a chosen day Herod put on his royal robes, sat on his throne, and made a speech to the people. 22They shouted, "This is the voice of a god, not a human!" 23Because Herod did not give the glory to God, an angel of the Lord immediately caused him to become sick, and he was eaten by worms and died.

²⁴God's message continued to spread and reach people.

²⁵After Barnabas and Saul finished their task in Jerusalem, they returned to Antioch, taking John Mark with them.

Barnabas and Saul Are Chosen

13 In the church at Antioch there were these prophets[d] and teachers: Barnabas, Simeon (also called Niger), Lucius (from the city of Cyrene), Manaen (who had grown up with Herod, the ruler), and Saul. ²They were all worshiping the Lord and giving up eating for a certain time.[n] During this time the Holy Spirit[d] said to them, "Set apart for me Barnabas and Saul to do a special work for which I have chosen them."

³So after they gave up eating and prayed, they laid their hands on[n] Barnabas and Saul and sent them out.

Barnabas and Saul in Cyprus

⁴Barnabas and Saul, sent out by the Holy Spirit,[d] went to the city of Seleucia. From there they sailed to the island of Cyprus. ⁵When they came to Salamis, they preached the Good News[d] of God in the Jewish synagogues.[d] John Mark was with them to help.

⁶They went across the whole island to Paphos where they met a Jewish magician named Bar-Jesus. He was a false prophet[d] ⁷who always stayed close to Sergius Paulus, the governor and a smart man. He asked Barnabas and Saul to come to him, because he wanted to hear the message of God. ⁸But Elymas, the magician, was against them. (Elymas is the name for Bar-Jesus in the Greek language.) He tried to stop the governor from believing in Jesus. ⁹But Saul, who was also called Paul, was filled with the Holy Spirit. He looked straight at Elymas ¹⁰and said, "You son of the devil! You are an enemy of everything that is right! You are full of evil tricks and lies, always trying to change the Lord's truths into lies. ¹¹Now the Lord will touch you, and you will be blind. For a time you will not be able to see anything—not even the light from the sun."

Then everything became dark for Elymas, and he walked around, trying to find someone to lead him by the hand. ¹²When the governor saw this, he believed because he was amazed at the teaching about the Lord.

Paul and Barnabas Leave Cyprus

¹³Paul and those with him sailed from Paphos and came to Perga, in Pamphylia. There John Mark left them to return to Jerusalem. ¹⁴They continued their trip from Perga and went to Antioch, a city in Pisidia. On the Sabbath[d] day they went into the synagogue[d] and sat down. ¹⁵After the law of Moses and the writings of the prophets[d] were read, the leaders of the synagogue sent a message to Paul and Barnabas: "Brothers, if you have any message that will encourage the people, please speak."

¹⁶Paul stood up, raised his hand, and said, "You Israelites and you who worship God, please listen! ¹⁷The God of the Israelites chose our ancestors. He made the people great during the time they lived in Egypt, and he brought them out of that country with great power. ¹⁸And he was patient with them for forty years in the desert. ¹⁹God destroyed seven nations in the land of Canaan and gave the land to his people. ²⁰All this happened in about four hundred fifty years.

"After this, God gave them judges until the time of Samuel the prophet. ²¹Then the people asked for a king, so God gave them Saul son of Kish. Saul was from the tribe[d] of Benjamin and was king for forty years. ²²After God took him away, God made David their king. God said about him: 'I have found in David son of Jesse the kind of man I want. He will do all I want him to do.' ²³So God has brought Jesus, one of David's descendants,[d] to Israel to be its Savior,[d] as he promised. ²⁴Before Jesus came, John[n] preached to all the people of Israel about a baptism of changed hearts and lives. ²⁵When he was finishing his work, he said, 'Who do you think I am? I am not the Christ.[d] He is coming later, and I am not worthy to untie his sandals.'

---

giving up . . . time   This is called "fasting." The people would give up eating for a special time of prayer and worship to God. It was also done to show sadness and disappointment.
laid their hands on   The laying on of hands had many purposes, including the giving of a blessing, power, or authority.
John   John the Baptist, who preached to people about Christ's coming (Luke 3).

26"Brothers, sons of the family of Abraham, and those of you who are not Jews who worship God, listen! The news about this salvation has been sent to us. 27Those who live in Jerusalem and their leaders did not realize that Jesus was the Savior. They did not understand the words that the prophets wrote, which are read every Sabbath*d* day. But they made them come true when they said Jesus was guilty. 28They could not find any real reason for Jesus to be put to death, but they asked Pilate to have him killed. 29When they had done to him all that the Scriptures*d* had said, they took him down from the cross and laid him in a tomb. 30But God raised him up from the dead! 31After this, for many days, those who had gone with Jesus from Galilee to Jerusalem saw him. They are now his witnesses to the people. 32We tell you the Good News*d* about the promise God made to our ancestors. 33God has made this promise come true for us, his children, by raising Jesus from the dead. We read about this also in Psalm 2:

'You are my Son.
   Today I have become your Father.'

Psalm 2:7

34God raised Jesus from the dead, and he will never go back to the grave and become dust. So God said:

'I will give you the holy and sure
      blessings
   that I promised to David.'   *Isaiah 55:3*

35But in another place God says:

'You will not let your Holy One rot.'

Psalm 16:10

36David did God's will during his lifetime. Then he died and was buried beside his ancestors, and his body did rot in the grave. 37But the One God raised from the dead did not rot in the grave. 38-39Brothers, understand what we are telling you: You can have forgiveness of your sins through Jesus. The law of Moses could not free you from your sins. But through Jesus everyone who believes is free from all sins. 40Be careful! Don't let what the prophets said happen to you: 41'Listen, you people who doubt!

You can wonder, and then die.
I will do something in your lifetime

that you won't believe even when you
      are told about it!' "   *Habakkuk 1:5*

42While Paul and Barnabas were leaving the synagogue, the people asked them to tell them more about these things on the next Sabbath. 43When the meeting was over, many Jews and those who had changed to the Jewish religion and who worshiped God followed Paul and Barnabas from that place. Paul and Barnabas were persuading them to continue trusting in God's grace.

44On the next Sabbath day, almost everyone in the city came to hear the word of the Lord. 45Seeing the crowd, the Jewish people became very jealous and said insulting things and argued against what Paul said. 46But Paul and Barnabas spoke very boldly, saying, "We must speak the message of God to you first. But you refuse to listen. You are judging yourselves not worthy of having eternal life! So we will now go to the people of other nations. 47This is what the Lord told us to do, saying:

'I have made you a light for the nations;
   you will show people all over the
      world the way to be saved.' "

Isaiah 49:6

48When those who were not Jewish heard Paul say this, they were happy and gave honor to the message of the Lord. And the people who were chosen to have life forever believed the message.

49So the message of the Lord was spreading through the whole country. 50But the Jewish people stirred up some of the important religious women and the leaders of the city. They started trouble against Paul and Barnabas and forced them out of their area. 51So Paul and Barnabas shook the dust off their feet*n* and went to Iconium. 52But the followers were filled with joy and the Holy Spirit.*d*

Paul and Barnabas in Iconium

14 In Iconium, Paul and Barnabas went as usual to the Jewish synagogue.*d* They spoke so well that a great many Jews and Greeks believed. 2But some of the Jews who did not believe excited the non-Jewish people and turned them against the believ-

---

shook . . . feet A warning. It showed that they had rejected these people.

ers. [3]Paul and Barnabas stayed in Iconium a long time and spoke bravely for the Lord. He showed that their message about his grace was true by giving them the power to work miracles[d] and signs. [4]But the city was divided. Some of the people agreed with the Jews, and others believed the apostles.[d]

[5]Some who were not Jews, some Jews, and some of their rulers wanted to mistreat Paul and Barnabas and to stone them to death. [6]When Paul and Barnabas learned about this, they ran away to Lystra and Derbe, cities in Lycaonia, and to the areas around those cities. [7]They announced the Good News[d] there, too.

Paul in Lystra and Derbe

[8]In Lystra there sat a man who had been born crippled; he had never walked. [9]As this man was listening to Paul speak, Paul looked straight at him and saw that he believed God could heal him. [10]So he cried out, "Stand up on your feet!" The man jumped up and began walking around. [11]When the crowds saw what Paul did, they shouted in the Lycaonian language, "The gods have become like humans and have come down to us!" [12]Then the people began to call Barnabas "Zeus"[n] and Paul "Hermes,"[n] because he was the main speaker. [13]The priest in the temple of Zeus, which was near the city, brought some bulls and flowers to the city gates. He and the people wanted to offer a sacrifice to Paul and Barnabas. [14]But when the apostles,[d] Barnabas and Paul, heard about it, they tore their clothes. They ran in among the people, shouting, [15]"Friends, why are you doing these things? We are only human beings like you. We are bringing you the Good News[d] and are telling you to turn away from these worthless things and turn to the living God. He is the One who made the sky, the earth, the sea, and everything in them. [16]In the past, God let all the nations do what they wanted. [17]Yet he proved he is real by showing kindness, by giving you rain from heaven and crops at the right times, by giving you food and filling your hearts with joy." [18]Even

with these words, they were barely able to keep the crowd from offering sacrifices to them.

[19]Then some Jewish people came from Antioch and Iconium and persuaded the people to turn against Paul. So they threw stones at him and dragged him out of town, thinking they had killed him. [20]But the followers gathered around him, and he got up and went back into the town. The next day he and Barnabas left and went to the city of Derbe.

The Return to Antioch in Syria

[21]Paul and Barnabas told the Good News[d] in Derbe, and many became followers. Paul and Barnabas returned to Lystra, Iconium, and Antioch, [22]making the followers of Jesus stronger and helping them stay in the faith. They said, "We must suffer many things to enter God's kingdom." [23]They chose elders[d] for each church, by praying and giving up eating for a certain time.[n] These elders had trusted the Lord, so Paul and Barnabas put them in the Lord's care.

[24]Then they went through Pisidia and came to Pamphylia. [25]When they had preached the message in Perga, they went down to Attalia. [26]And from there they sailed away to Antioch where the believers had put them into God's care and had sent them out to do this work. Now they had finished.

[27]When they arrived in Antioch, Paul and Barnabas gathered the church together. They told the church all about what God had done with them and how God had made it possible for those who were not Jewish to believe. [28]And they stayed there a long time with the followers.

The Meeting at Jerusalem

15 Then some people came to Antioch from Judea and began teaching the non-Jewish believers: "You cannot be saved if you are not circumcised[d] as Moses taught us." [2]Paul and Barnabas were against this teaching and argued with them about it. So the church decided to send Paul, Barnabas, and some others to Jerusalem where they

---

"Zeus"   The Greeks believed in many gods, of whom Zeus was most important.
"Hermes"   The Greeks believed he was a messenger for the other gods.
giving . . . time   This is called "fasting." The people would give up eating for a special time of prayer and worship to God. It was also done to show sadness and disappointment.

could talk more about this with the apostles*d* and elders.*d*

³The church helped them leave on the trip, and they went through the countries of Phoenicia and Samaria, telling all about how those who were not Jewish had turned to God. This made all the believers very happy. ⁴When they arrived in Jerusalem, they were welcomed by the apostles, the elders, and the church. Paul, Barnabas, and the others told about everything God had done with them. ⁵But some of the believers who belonged to the Pharisee*d* group came forward and said, "The non-Jewish believers must be circumcised. They must be told to obey the law of Moses."

⁶The apostles and the elders gathered to consider this problem. ⁷After a long debate, Peter stood up and said to them, "Brothers, you know that in the early days God chose me from among you to preach the Good News*d* to those who are not Jewish. They heard the Good News from me, and they believed. ⁸God, who knows the thoughts of everyone, accepted them. He showed this to us by giving them the Holy Spirit,*d* just as he did to us. ⁹To God, those people are not different from us. When they believed, he made their hearts pure. ¹⁰So now why are you testing God by putting a heavy load around the necks of the non-Jewish believers? It is a load that neither we nor our ancestors were able to carry. ¹¹But we believe that we and they too will be saved by the grace of the Lord Jesus."

¹²Then the whole group became quiet. They listened to Paul and Barnabas tell about all the miracles*d* and signs that God did through them among the non-Jewish people. ¹³After they finished speaking, James said, "Brothers, listen to me. ¹⁴Simon has told us how God showed his love for the non-Jewish people. For the first time he is accepting from among them a people to be his own. ¹⁵The words of the prophets*d* agree with this too:

¹⁶'After these things I will return.

The kingdom of David is like a fallen tent.

But I will rebuild its ruins,

and I will set it up.

¹⁷Then those people who are left alive may ask the Lord for help,

and the other nations that belong to me,

says the Lord,

who will make it happen.

¹⁸ And these things have been known for a long time.'   *Amos 9:11-12*

¹⁹"So I think we should not bother the non-Jewish people who are turning to God. ²⁰Instead, we should write a letter to them telling them these things: Stay away from food that has been offered to idols (which makes it unclean*d*), any kind of sexual sin, eating animals that have been strangled, and blood. ²¹They should do these things, because for a long time in every city the law of Moses has been taught. And it is still read in the synagogue*d* every Sabbath*d* day."

Letter to Non-Jewish Believers

²²The apostles,*d* the elders,*d* and the whole church decided to send some of their men with Paul and Barnabas to Antioch. They chose Judas Barsabbas and Silas, who were respected by the believers. ²³They sent the following letter with them:

From the apostles and elders, your brothers.

To all the non-Jewish believers in Antioch, Syria, and Cilicia:

Greetings!

²⁴We have heard that some of our group have come to you and said things that trouble and upset you. But we did not tell them to do this. ²⁵We have all agreed to choose some messengers and send them to you with our dear friends Barnabas and Paul— ²⁶people who have given their lives to serve our Lord Jesus Christ. ²⁷So we are sending Judas and Silas, who will tell you the same things. ²⁸It has pleased the Holy Spirit*d* that you should not have a heavy load to carry, and we agree. You need to do only these things: ²⁹Stay away from any food that has been offered to idols, eating any animals that have been strangled, and blood, and any kind of sexual sin. If you stay away from these things, you will do well.

Good-bye.

³⁰So they left Jerusalem and went to Anti-

och where they gathered the church and gave them the letter. 31When they read it, they were very happy because of the encouraging message. 32Judas and Silas, who were also prophets,*d* said many things to encourage the believers and make them stronger. 33After some time Judas and Silas were sent off in peace by the believers, and they went back to those who had sent them. 34 *n*

35But Paul and Barnabas stayed in Antioch and, along with many others, preached the Good News*d* and taught the people the message of the Lord.

Paul and Barnabas Separate

36After some time, Paul said to Barnabas, "We should go back to all those towns where we preached the message of the Lord. Let's visit the believers and see how they are doing."

37Barnabas wanted to take John Mark with them, 38but he had left them at Pamphylia; he did not continue with them in the work. So Paul did not think it was a good idea to take him. 39Paul and Barnabas had such a serious argument about this that they separated and went different ways. Barnabas took Mark and sailed to Cyprus, 40but Paul chose Silas and left. The believers in Antioch put Paul into the Lord's care, 41and he went through Syria and Cilicia, giving strength to the churches.

Timothy Goes with Paul

16 Paul came to Derbe and Lystra, where a follower named Timothy lived. Timothy's mother was Jewish and a believer, but his father was a Greek.

2The believers in Lystra and Iconium respected Timothy and said good things about him. 3Paul wanted Timothy to travel with him, but all the Jews living in that area knew that Timothy's father was Greek. So Paul circumcised*d* Timothy to please the Jews. 4Paul and those with him traveled from town to town and gave the decisions made by the apostles*d* and elders*d* in Jerusalem for the people to obey. 5So the churches became

stronger in the faith and grew larger every day.

Paul Is Called Out of Asia

6Paul and those with him went through the areas of Phrygia and Galatia since the Holy Spirit*d* did not let them preach the Good News*d* in the country of Asia. 7When they came near the country of Mysia, they tried to go into Bithynia, but the Spirit of Jesus did not let them. 8So they passed by Mysia and went to Troas. 9That night Paul saw in a vision a man from Macedonia. The man stood and begged, "Come over to Macedonia and help us." 10After Paul had seen the vision, we immediately prepared to leave for Macedonia, understanding that God had called us to tell the Good News to those people.

Lydia Becomes a Christian

11We left Troas and sailed straight to the island of Samothrace. The next day we sailed to Neapolis. *n* 12Then we went by land to Philippi, a Roman colony*n* and the leading city in that part of Macedonia. We stayed there for several days.

13On the Sabbath*d* day we went outside the city gate to the river where we thought we would find a special place for prayer. Some women had gathered there, so we sat down and talked with them. 14One of the listeners was a woman named Lydia from the city of Thyatira whose job was selling purple cloth. She worshiped God, and he opened her mind to pay attention to what Paul was saying. 15She and all the people in her house were baptized. Then she invited us to her home, saying, "If you think I am truly a believer in the Lord, then come stay in my house." And she persuaded us to stay with her.

Paul and Silas in Jail

16Once, while we were going to the place for prayer, a servant girl met us. She had a special spirit*n* in her, and she earned a lot of money for her owners by telling fortunes.

Verse 34 Some Greek copies add verse 34: ". . . but Silas decided to remain there."
Neapolis City in Macedonia. It was the first city Paul visited on the continent of Europe.
Roman colony A town begun by Romans with Roman laws, customs, and privileges.
spirit This was a spirit from the devil, which caused her to say she had special knowledge.

[17]This girl followed Paul and us, shouting, "These men are servants of the Most High God. They are telling you how you can be saved."

[18]She kept this up for many days. This bothered Paul, so he turned and said to the spirit, "By the power of Jesus Christ, I command you to come out of her!" Immediately, the spirit came out.

[19]When the owners of the servant girl saw this, they knew that now they could not use her to make money. So they grabbed Paul and Silas and dragged them before the city rulers in the marketplace. [20]They brought Paul and Silas to the Roman rulers and said, "These men are Jews and are making trouble in our city. [21]They are teaching things that are not right for us as Romans to do."

[22]The crowd joined the attack against them. The Roman officers tore the clothes of Paul and Silas and had them beaten with rods. [23]Then Paul and Silas were thrown into jail, and the jailer was ordered to guard them carefully. [24]When he heard this order, he put them far inside the jail and pinned their feet down between large blocks of wood.

[25]About midnight Paul and Silas were praying and singing songs to God as the other prisoners listened. [26]Suddenly, there was a strong earthquake that shook the foundation of the jail. Then all the doors of the jail broke open, and all the prisoners were freed from their chains. [27]The jailer woke up and saw that the jail doors were open. Thinking that the prisoners had already escaped, he got his sword and was about to kill himself.[n] [28]But Paul shouted, "Don't hurt yourself! We are all here."

[29]The jailer told someone to bring a light. Then he ran inside and, shaking with fear, fell down before Paul and Silas. [30]He brought them outside and said, "Men, what must I do to be saved?"

[31]They said to him, "Believe in the Lord Jesus and you will be saved—you and all the people in your house." [32]So Paul and Silas told the message of the Lord to the jailer and all the people in his house. [33]At that hour of the night the jailer took Paul and Silas and washed their wounds. Then he and all his people were baptized immediately. [34]After this the jailer took Paul and Silas home and gave them food. He and his family were very happy because they now believed in God.

[35]The next morning, the Roman officers sent the police to tell the jailer, "Let these men go free."

[36]The jailer said to Paul, "The officers have sent an order to let you go free. You can leave now. Go in peace."

[37]But Paul said to the police, "They beat us in public without a trial, even though we are Roman citizens.[n] And they threw us in jail. Now they want to make us go away quietly. No! Let them come themselves and bring us out."

[38]The police told the Roman officers what Paul said. When the officers heard that Paul and Silas were Roman citizens, they were afraid. [39]So they came and told Paul and Silas they were sorry and took them out of jail and asked them to leave the city. [40]So when they came out of the jail, they went to Lydia's house where they saw some of the believers and encouraged them. Then they left.

Paul and Silas in Thessalonica

17 Paul and Silas traveled through Amphipolis and Apollonia and came to Thessalonica where there was a Jewish synagogue.[d] [2]Paul went into the synagogue as he always did, and on each Sabbath[d] day for three weeks, he talked with the Jews about the Scriptures.[d] [3]He explained and proved that the Christ[d] must die and then rise from the dead. He said, "This Jesus I am telling you about is the Christ." [4]Some of the Jews were convinced and joined Paul and Silas, along with many of the Greeks who worshiped God and many of the important women.

[5]But the Jews became jealous. So they got some evil men from the marketplace, formed a mob, and started a riot. They ran to Jason's house, looking for Paul and Silas, wanting to bring them out to the people. [6]But when they did not find them, they dragged Jason and some other believers to the leaders of the

kill himself He thought the leaders would kill him for letting the prisoners escape.
Roman citizens Roman law said that Roman citizens must not be beaten before they had a trial.

city. The people were yelling, "These people have made trouble everywhere in the world, and now they have come here too! [7]Jason is keeping them in his house. All of them do things against the laws of Caesar,[d] saying there is another king, called Jesus."

[8]When the people and the leaders of the city heard these things, they became very upset. [9]They made Jason and the others put up a sum of money. Then they let the believers go free.

Paul and Silas Go to Berea

[10]That same night the believers sent Paul and Silas to Berea where they went to the Jewish synagogue.[d] [11]These Jews were more willing to listen than the Jews in Thessalonica. The Bereans were eager to hear what Paul and Silas said and studied the Scriptures[d] every day to find out if these things were true. [12]So, many of them believed, as well as many important Greek women and men. [13]But the Jews in Thessalonica learned that Paul was preaching the word of God in Berea, too. So they came there, upsetting the people and making trouble. [14]The believers quickly sent Paul away to the coast, but Silas and Timothy stayed in Berea. [15]The people leading Paul went with him to Athens. Then they carried a message from Paul back to Silas and Timothy for them to come to him as soon as they could.

Paul Preaches in Athens

[16]While Paul was waiting for Silas and Timothy in Athens, he was troubled because he saw that the city was full of idols. [17]In the synagogue,[d] he talked with the Jews and the Greeks who worshiped God. He also talked every day with people in the marketplace.

[18]Some of the Epicurean and Stoic philosophers[n] argued with him, saying, "This man doesn't know what he is talking about. What is he trying to say?" Others said, "He seems to be telling us about some other gods," because Paul was telling them about Jesus and his rising from the dead. [19]They got Paul and took him to a meeting of the Areopagus,[n]

where they said, "Please explain to us this new idea you have been teaching. [20]The things you are saying are new to us, and we want to know what this teaching means." [21](All the people of Athens and those from other countries who lived there always used their time to talk about the newest ideas.)

[22]Then Paul stood before the meeting of the Areopagus and said, "People of Athens, I can see you are very religious in all things. [23]As I was going through your city, I saw the objects you worship. I found an altar that had these words written on it: TO A GOD WHO IS NOT KNOWN. You worship a god that you don't know, and this is the God I am telling you about! [24]The God who made the whole world and everything in it is the Lord of the land and the sky. He does not live in temples built by human hands. [25]This God is the One who gives life, breath, and everything else to people. He does not need any help from them; he has everything he needs. [26]God began by making one person, and from him came all the different people who live everywhere in the world. God decided exactly when and where they must live. [27]God wanted them to look for him and perhaps search all around for him and find him, though he is not far from any of us: [28]'We live in him. We walk in him. We are in him.' Some of your own poets have said: 'For we are his children.' [29]Since we are God's children, you must not think that God is like something that people imagine or make from gold, silver, or rock. [30]In the past, people did not understand God, and he ignored this. But now, God tells all people in the world to change their hearts and lives. [31]God has set a day that he will judge all the world with fairness, by the man he chose long ago. And God has proved this to everyone by raising that man from the dead!"

[32]When the people heard about Jesus being raised from the dead, some of them laughed. But others said, "We will hear more about this from you later." [33]So Paul went away from them. [34]But some of the people believed Paul and joined him. Among those

Epicurean and Stoic philosophers Philosophers were those who searched for truth. Epicureans believed that pleasure, especially pleasures of the mind, were the goal of life. Stoics believed that life should be without feelings of joy or grief.
Areopagus A council or group of important leaders in Athens. They were like judges.

who believed was Dionysius, a member of the Areopagus, a woman named Damaris, and some others.

Paul in Corinth

18 Later Paul left Athens and went to Corinth. [2]Here he met a Jew named Aquila who had been born in the country of Pontus. But Aquila and his wife, Priscilla, had recently moved to Corinth from Italy, because Claudius[n] commanded that all Jews must leave Rome. Paul went to visit Aquila and Priscilla. [3]Because they were tentmakers, just as he was, he stayed with them and worked with them. [4]Every Sabbath[d] day he talked with the Jews and Greeks in the synagogue,[d] trying to persuade them to believe in Jesus.

[5]Silas and Timothy came from Macedonia and joined Paul in Corinth. After this, Paul spent all his time telling people the Good News,[d] showing the Jews that Jesus is the Christ.[d] [6]But they would not accept Paul's teaching and said some evil things. So he shook off the dust from his clothes[n] and said to them, "If you are not saved, it will be your own fault! I have done all I can do! After this, I will go only to those who are not Jewish." [7]Paul left the synagogue and moved into the home of Titius Justus, next to the synagogue. This man worshiped God. [8]Crispus was the leader of that synagogue, and he and all the people living in his house believed in the Lord. Many others in Corinth also listened to Paul and believed and were baptized.

[9]During the night, the Lord told Paul in a vision: "Don't be afraid. Continue talking to people and don't be quiet. [10]I am with you, and no one will hurt you because many of my people are in this city." [11]Paul stayed there for a year and a half, teaching God's word to the people.

Paul Is Brought Before Gallio

[12]When Gallio was the governor of the country of Southern Greece, some of the Jews came together against Paul and took him to the court. [13]They said, "This man is teaching people to worship God in a way that is against our law."

[14]Paul was about to say something, but Gallio spoke to the Jews, saying, "I would listen to you Jews if you were complaining about a crime or some wrong. [15]But the things you are saying are only questions about words and names—arguments about your own law. So you must solve this problem yourselves. I don't want to be a judge of these things." [16]And Gallio made them leave the court.

[17]Then they all grabbed Sosthenes, the leader of the synagogue,[d] and beat him there before the court. But this did not bother Gallio.

Paul Returns to Antioch

[18]Paul stayed with the believers for many more days. Then he left and sailed for Syria, with Priscilla and Aquila. At Cenchrea Paul cut off his hair,[n] because he had made a promise to God. [19]Then they went to Ephesus, where Paul left Priscilla and Aquila. While Paul was there, he went into the synagogue[d] and talked with the Jews. [20]When they asked him to stay with them longer, he refused. [21]But as he left, he said, "I will come back to you again if God wants me to." And so he sailed away from Ephesus.

[22]When Paul landed at Caesarea, he went and gave greetings to the church in Jerusalem. After that, Paul went to Antioch. [23]He stayed there for a while and then left and went through the regions of Galatia and Phrygia. He traveled from town to town in these regions, giving strength to all the followers.

Apollos in Ephesus and Corinth

[24]A Jew named Apollos came to Ephesus. He was born in the city of Alexandria and was a good speaker who knew the Scriptures[d] well. [25]He had been taught about the way of the Lord and was always very excited when he spoke and taught the truth about Jesus. But the only baptism Apollos knew about was the baptism that John[n] taught.

Claudius The emperor (ruler) of Rome, A.D. 41-54.
shook ... clothes This was a warning to show that Paul was finished talking to the Jews in that city.
cut ... hair Jews did this to show that the time of a special promise to God was finished.
John John the Baptist, who preached to people about Christ's coming (Luke 3).

26Apollos began to speak very boldly in the synagogue,*d* and when Priscilla and Aquila heard him, they took him to their home and helped him better understand the way of God. 27Now Apollos wanted to go to the country of Southern Greece. So the believers helped him and wrote a letter to the followers there, asking them to accept him. These followers had believed in Jesus because of God's grace, and when Apollos arrived, he helped them very much. 28He argued very strongly with the Jews before all the people, clearly proving with the Scriptures that Jesus is the Christ.*d*

Paul in Ephesus

19 While Apollos was in Corinth, Paul was visiting some places on the way to Ephesus. There he found some followers 2and asked them, "Did you receive the Holy Spirit*d* when you believed?"

They said, "We have never even heard of a Holy Spirit."

3So he asked, "What kind of baptism did you have?"

They said, "It was the baptism that John*n* taught."

4Paul said, "John's baptism was a baptism of changed hearts and lives. He told people to believe in the one who would come after him, and that one is Jesus."

5When they heard this, they were baptized in the name of the Lord Jesus. 6Then Paul laid his hands on them,*n* and the Holy Spirit came upon them. They began speaking different languages*n* and prophesying.*d* 7There were about twelve people in this group.

8Paul went into the synagogue*d* and spoke out boldly for three months. He talked with the Jews and persuaded them to accept the things he said about the kingdom of God. 9But some of the Jews became stubborn. They refused to believe and said evil things about the Way of Jesus before all the people. So Paul left them, and taking the followers with him, he went to the school of a man named Tyrannus. There Paul talked with

people every day 10for two years. Because of his work, every Jew and Greek in the country of Asia heard the word of the Lord.

The Sons of Sceva

11God used Paul to do some very special miracles.*d* 12Some people took handkerchiefs and clothes that Paul had used and put them on the sick. When they did this, the sick were healed and evil spirits left them.

13But some Jews also were traveling around and making evil spirits go out of people. They tried to use the name of the Lord Jesus to force the evil spirits out. They would say, "By the same Jesus that Paul talks about, I order you to come out!" 14Seven sons of Sceva, a leading Jewish priest, were doing this.

15But one time an evil spirit said to them, "I know Jesus, and I know about Paul, but who are you?"

16Then the man who had the evil spirit jumped on them. Because he was so much stronger than all of them, they ran away from the house naked and hurt. 17All the people in Ephesus — Jews and Greeks — learned about this and were filled with fear and gave great honor to the Lord Jesus. 18Many of the believers began to confess openly and tell all the evil things they had done. 19Some of them who had used magic brought their magic books and burned them before everyone. Those books were worth about fifty thousand silver coins.*n*

20So in a powerful way the word of the Lord kept spreading and growing.

21After these things, Paul decided to go to Jerusalem, planning to go through the countries of Macedonia and Southern Greece and then on to Jerusalem. He said, "After I have been to Jerusalem, I must also visit Rome." 22Paul sent Timothy and Erastus, two of his helpers, ahead to Macedonia, but he himself stayed in Asia for a while.

Trouble in Ephesus

23And during that time, there was some serious trouble in Ephesus about the Way of

---

John John the Baptist, who preached to people about Christ's coming (Luke 3).
laid his hands on them The laying on of hands had many purposes, including the giving of a blessing, power, or authority.
languages This can also be translated "tongues."
fifty thousand silver coins Probably drachmas. One coin was enough to pay a worker for one day's labor.

Jesus. [24]A man named Demetrius, who worked with silver, made little silver models that looked like the temple of the goddess Artemis.[n] Those who did this work made much money. [25]Demetrius had a meeting with them and some others who did the same kind of work. He told them, "Men, you know that we make a lot of money from our business. [26]But look at what this man Paul is doing. He has convinced and turned away many people in Ephesus and in almost all of Asia! He says the gods made by human hands are not real. [27]There is a danger that our business will lose its good name, but there is also another danger: People will begin to think that the temple of the great goddess Artemis is not important. Her greatness will be destroyed, and Artemis is the goddess that everyone in Asia and the whole world worships."

[28]When the others heard this, they became very angry and shouted, "Artemis, the goddess of Ephesus, is great!" [29]The whole city became confused. The people grabbed Gaius and Aristarchus, who were from Macedonia and were traveling with Paul, and ran to the theater. [30]Paul wanted to go in and talk to the crowd, but the followers did not let him. [31]Also, some leaders of Asia who were friends of Paul sent him a message, begging him not to go into the theater. [32]Some people were shouting one thing, and some were shouting another. The meeting was completely confused; most of them did not know why they had come together. [33]The Jews put a man named Alexander in front of the people, and some of them told him what to do. Alexander waved his hand so he could explain things to the people. [34]But when they saw that Alexander was a Jew, they all shouted the same thing for two hours: "Great is Artemis of Ephesus!"

[35]Then the city clerk made the crowd be quiet. He said, "People of Ephesus, everyone knows that Ephesus is the city that keeps the temple of the great goddess Artemis and her holy stone[n] that fell from heaven. [36]Since no one can say this is not true, you should be quiet. Stop and think before you do anything. [37]You brought these men here, but they have not said anything evil against our goddess or stolen anything from her temple. [38]If Demetrius and those who work with him have a charge against anyone they should go to the courts and judges where they can argue with each other. [39]If there is something else you want to talk about, it can be decided at the regular town meeting of the people. [40]I say this because some people might see this trouble today and say that we are rioting. We could not explain this, because there is no real reason for this meeting." [41]After the city clerk said these things, he told the people to go home.

Paul In Macedonia and Greece

20 When the trouble stopped, Paul sent for the followers to come to him. After he encouraged them and then told them good-bye, he left and went to the country of Macedonia. [2]He said many things to strengthen the followers in the different places on his way through Macedonia. Then he went to Greece, [3]where he stayed for three months. He was ready to sail for Syria, but some Jews were planning something against him. So Paul decided to go back through Macedonia to Syria. [4]The men who went with him were Sopater son of Pyrrhus, from the city of Berea; Aristarchus and Secundus, from the city of Thessalonica; Gaius, from Derbe; Timothy; and Tychicus and Trophimus, two men from the country of Asia. [5]These men went on ahead and waited for us at Troas. [6]We sailed from Philippi after the Feast[d] of Unleavened Bread. Five days later we met them in Troas, where we stayed for seven days.

Paul's Last Visit to Troas

[7]On the first day of the week,[n] we all met together to break bread,[n] and Paul spoke to

---

Artemis A Greek goddess that the people of Asia Minor worshiped.
holy stone Probably a meteorite or stone that the people thought looked like Artemis.
first day of the week Sunday, which for the Jews began at sunset on our Saturday. But if in this part of Asia a different system of time was used, then the meeting was on our Sunday night.
break bread Probably the Lord's Supper, the special meal that Jesus told his followers to eat to remember him (Luke 22:14-20).

the group. Because he was planning to leave the next day, he kept on talking until midnight. [8]We were all together in a room upstairs, and there were many lamps in the room. [9]A young man named Eutychus was sitting in the window. As Paul continued talking, Eutychus was falling into a deep sleep. Finally, he went sound asleep and fell to the ground from the third floor. When they picked him up, he was dead. [10]Paul went down to Eutychus, knelt down, and put his arms around him. He said, "Don't worry. He is alive now." [11]Then Paul went upstairs again, broke bread, and ate. He spoke to them a long time, until it was early morning, and then he left. [12]They took the young man home alive and were greatly comforted.

The Trip from Troas to Miletus

[13]We went on ahead of Paul and sailed for the city of Assos, where he wanted to join us on the ship. Paul planned it this way because he wanted to go to Assos by land. [14]When he met us there, we took him aboard and went to Mitylene. [15]We sailed from Mitylene and the next day came to a place near Chios. The following day we sailed to Samos, and the next day we reached Miletus. [16]Paul had already decided not to stop at Ephesus, because he did not want to stay too long in the country of Asia. He was hurrying to be in Jerusalem on the day of Pentecost,[d] if that were possible.

The Elders from Ephesus

[17]Now from Miletus Paul sent to Ephesus and called for the elders[d] of the church. [18]When they came to him, he said, "You know about my life from the first day I came to Asia. You know the way I lived all the time I was with you. [19]The Jews made plans against me, which troubled me very much. But you know I always served the Lord unselfishly, and I often cried. [20]You know I preached to you and did not hold back anything that would help you. You know that I taught you in public and in your homes. [21]I warned both Jews and Greeks to change their lives and turn to God and believe in our Lord Jesus. [22]But now I must obey the Holy Spirit[d] and go to Jerusalem. I don't know what will happen to me there. [23]I know only that in every city the Holy Spirit tells me that troubles and even jail wait for me. [24]I don't care about my own life. The most important thing is that I complete my mission, the work that the Lord Jesus gave me — to tell people the Good News[d] about God's grace.

[25]"And now, I know that none of you among whom I was preaching the kingdom of God will ever see me again. [26]So today I tell you that if any of you should be lost, I am not responsible, [27]because I have told you everything God wants you to know. [28]Be careful for yourselves and for all the people the Holy Spirit has given to you to care for. You must be like shepherds to the church of God,[n] which he bought with the death of his own son. [29]I know that after I leave, some people will come like wild wolves and try to destroy the flock. [30]Also, some from your own group will rise up and twist the truth and will lead away followers after them. [31]So be careful! Always remember that for three years, day and night, I never stopped warning each of you, and I often cried over you.

[32]"Now I am putting you in the care of God and the message about his grace. It is able to give you strength, and it will give you the blessings God has for all his holy people. [33]When I was with you, I never wanted anyone's money or fine clothes. [34]You know I always worked to take care of my own needs and the needs of those who were with me. [35]I showed you in all things that you should work as I did and help the weak. I taught you to remember the words Jesus said: 'It is more blessed to give than to receive.' "

[36]When Paul had said this, he knelt down with all of them and prayed. [37-38]And they all cried because Paul had said they would never see him again. They put their arms around him and kissed him. Then they went with him to the ship.

Paul Goes to Jerusalem

21 After we all said good-bye to them, we sailed straight to the island of Cos. The next day we reached Rhodes, and

---

of God   Some Greek copies say, "of the Lord."

from there we went to Patara. [2]There we found a ship going to Phoenicia, so we went aboard and sailed away. [3]We sailed near the island of Cyprus, seeing it to the north, but we sailed on to Syria. We stopped at Tyre because the ship needed to unload its cargo there. [4]We found some followers in Tyre and stayed with them for seven days. Through the Holy Spirit[d] they warned Paul not to go to Jerusalem. [5]When we finished our visit, we left and continued our trip. All the followers, even the women and children, came outside the city with us. After we all knelt on the beach and prayed, [6]we said good-bye and got on the ship, and the followers went back home.

[7]We continued our trip from Tyre and arrived at Ptolemais, where we greeted the believers and stayed with them for a day. [8]The next day we left Ptolemais and went to the city of Caesarea. There we went into the home of Philip the preacher,[d] one of the seven helpers,[n] and stayed with him. [9]He had four unmarried daughters who had the gift of prophesying.[d] [10]After we had been there for some time, a prophet named Agabus arrived from Judea. [11]He came to us and borrowed Paul's belt and used it to tie his own hands and feet. He said, "The Holy Spirit says, 'This is how the Jews in Jerusalem will tie up the man who wears this belt. Then they will give him to those who are not Jews.' "

[12]When we all heard this, we and the people there begged Paul not to go to Jerusalem. [13]But he said, "Why are you crying and making me so sad? I am not only ready to be tied up in Jerusalem, I am ready to die for the Lord Jesus!"

[14]We could not persuade him to stay away from Jerusalem. So we stopped begging him and said, "We pray that what the Lord wants will be done."

[15]After this, we got ready and started on our way to Jerusalem. [16]Some of the followers from Caesarea went with us and took us to the home of Mnason, where we would stay. He was from Cyprus and was one of the first followers.

Paul Visits James

[17]In Jerusalem the believers were glad to see us. [18]The next day Paul went with us to visit James, and all the elders[d] were there. [19]Paul greeted them and told them everything God had done among the non-Jewish people through him. [20]When they heard this, they praised God. Then they said to Paul, "Brother, you can see that many thousands of Jews have become believers. And they think it is very important to obey the law of Moses. [21]They have heard about your teaching, that you tell the Jews who live among those who are not Jews to leave the law of Moses. They have heard that you tell them not to circumcise[d] their children and not to obey Jewish customs. [22]What should we do? They will learn that you have come. [23]So we will tell you what to do: Four of our men have made a promise to God. [24]Take these men with you and share in their cleansing ceremony.[n] Pay their expenses so they can shave their heads.[n] Then it will prove to everyone that what they have heard about you is not true and that you follow the law of Moses in your own life. [25]We have already sent a letter to the non-Jewish believers. The letter said: 'Do not eat food that has been offered to idols, or blood, or animals that have been strangled. Do not take part in sexual sin.' "

[26]The next day Paul took the four men and shared in the cleansing ceremony with them. Then he went to the Temple[d] and announced the time when the days of the cleansing ceremony would be finished. On the last day an offering would be given for each of the men.

[27]When the seven days were almost over, some Jews from Asia saw Paul at the Temple. They caused all the people to be upset and grabbed Paul. [28]They shouted, "People of Israel, help us! This is the man who goes everywhere teaching against the law of Moses,

---

helpers The seven men chosen for a special work described in Acts 6:1-6.
cleansing ceremony The special things Jews did to end the Nazirite promise.
shave their heads The Jews did this to show that their promise was finished.

against our people, and against this Temple. Now he has brought some Greeks into the Temple and has made this holy place unclean!"[d] 29(The Jews said this because they had seen Trophimus, a man from Ephesus, with Paul in Jerusalem. The Jews thought that Paul had brought him into the Temple.)

30All the people in Jerusalem became upset. Together they ran, took Paul, and dragged him out of the Temple. The Temple doors were closed immediately. 31While they were trying to kill Paul, the commander of the Roman army in Jerusalem learned that there was trouble in the whole city. 32Immediately he took some officers and soldiers and ran to the place where the crowd was gathered. When the people saw them, they stopped beating Paul. 33The commander went to Paul and arrested him. He told his soldiers to tie Paul with two chains. Then he asked who he was and what he had done wrong. 34Some in the crowd were yelling one thing, and some were yelling another. Because of all this confusion and shouting, the commander could not learn what had happened. So he ordered the soldiers to take Paul to the army building. 35When Paul came to the steps, the soldiers had to carry him because the people were ready to hurt him. 36The whole mob was following them, shouting, "Kill him!"

37As the soldiers were about to take Paul into the army building, he spoke to the commander, "May I say something to you?"

The commander said, "Do you speak Greek? 38I thought you were the Egyptian who started some trouble against the government not long ago and led four thousand killers out to the desert."

39Paul said, "No, I am a Jew from Tarsus in the country of Cilicia. I am a citizen of that important city. Please, let me speak to the people."

40The commander gave permission, so Paul stood on the steps and waved his hand to quiet the people. When there was silence, he spoke to them in the Jewish language.[n]

Paul Speaks to the People

22 Paul said, "Friends, fellow Jews, listen to my defense to you." 2When the Jews heard him speaking the Jewish language,[n] they became very quiet. Paul said, 3"I am a Jew, born in Tarsus in the country of Cilicia, but I grew up in this city. I was a student of Gamaliel,[n] who carefully taught me everything about the law of our ancestors. I was very serious about serving God, just as are all of you here today. 4I persecuted the people who followed the Way of Jesus, and some of them were even killed. I arrested men and women and put them in jail. 5The high priest and the whole council of older Jewish leaders can tell you this is true. They gave me letters to the Jewish brothers in Damascus. So I was going there to arrest these people and bring them back to Jerusalem to be punished.

6"About noon when I came near Damascus, a bright light from heaven suddenly flashed all around me. 7I fell to the ground and heard a voice saying, 'Saul, Saul, why are you persecuting me?' 8I asked, 'Who are you, Lord?' The voice said, 'I am Jesus from Nazareth whom you are persecuting.' 9Those who were with me did not hear the voice, but they saw the light. 10I said, 'What shall I do, Lord?' The Lord answered, 'Get up and go to Damascus. There you will be told about all the things I have planned for you to do.' 11I could not see, because the bright light had made me blind. So my companions led me into Damascus.

12"There a man named Ananias came to me. He was a religious man; he obeyed the law of Moses, and all the Jews who lived there respected him. 13He stood by me and said, 'Brother Saul, see again!' Immediately I was able to see him. 14He said, 'The God of our ancestors chose you long ago to know his plan, to see the Righteous One, and to hear words from him. 15You will be his witness to all people, telling them about what you have seen and heard. 16Now, why wait any longer? Get up, be baptized, and wash your sins away, trusting in him to save you.'

17"Later, when I returned to Jerusalem, I

Jewish language Hebrew or Aramaic, the languages of the Jews in the first century.
Gamaliel A very important teacher of the Pharisees, a Jewish religious group (Acts 5:34).

was praying in the Temple,[d] and I saw a vision. 18I saw the Lord saying to me, 'Hurry! Leave Jerusalem now! The people here will not accept the truth about me.' 19But I said, 'Lord, they know that in every synagogue[d] I put the believers in jail and beat them. 20They also know I was there when Stephen, your witness, was killed. I stood there agreeing and holding the coats of those who were killing him!' 21But the Lord said to me, 'Leave now. I will send you far away to the non-Jewish people.' "

22The crowd listened to Paul until he said this. Then they began shouting, "Kill him! Get him out of the world! He should not be allowed to live!" 23They shouted, threw off their coats,[n] and threw dust into the air.[n]

24Then the commander ordered the soldiers to take Paul into the army building and beat him. He wanted to make Paul tell why the people were shouting against him like this. 25But as the soldiers were tying him up, preparing to beat him, Paul said to an officer nearby, "Do you have the right to beat a Roman citizen[n] who has not been proven guilty?"

26When the officer heard this, he went to the commander and reported it. The officer said, "Do you know what you are doing? This man is a Roman citizen."

27The commander came to Paul and said, "Tell me, are you really a Roman citizen?"

He answered, "Yes."

28The commander said, "I paid a lot of money to become a Roman citizen."

But Paul said, "I was born a citizen."

29The men who were preparing to question Paul moved away from him immediately. The commander was frightened because he had already tied Paul, and Paul was a Roman citizen.

Paul Speaks to Jewish Leaders

30The next day the commander decided to learn why the Jews were accusing Paul. So he ordered the leading priests and the Jewish council to meet. The commander took Paul's chains off. Then he brought Paul out and stood him before their meeting.

23 Paul looked at the Jewish council and said, "Brothers, I have lived my life without guilt feelings before God up to this day." 2Ananias,[n] the high priest, heard this and told the men who were standing near Paul to hit him on the mouth. 3Paul said to Ananias, "God will hit you, too! You are like a wall that has been painted white. You sit there and judge me, using the law of Moses, but you are telling them to hit me, and that is against the law."

4The men standing near Paul said to him, "You cannot insult God's high priest like that!"

5Paul said, "Brothers, I did not know this man was the high priest. It is written in the Scriptures,[d] 'You must not curse a leader of your people.' "[n]

6Some of the men in the meeting were Sadducees,[d] and others were Pharisees.[d] Knowing this, Paul shouted to them, "My brothers, I am a Pharisee, and my father was a Pharisee. I am on trial here because I believe that people will rise from the dead."

7When Paul said this, there was an argument between the Pharisees and the Sadducees, and the group was divided. 8(The Sadducees do not believe in angels or spirits or that people will rise from the dead. But the Pharisees believe in them all.) 9So there was a great uproar. Some of the teachers of the law, who were Pharisees, stood up and argued, "We find nothing wrong with this man. Maybe an angel or a spirit did speak to him."

10The argument was beginning to turn into such a fight that the commander was afraid the Jews would tear Paul to pieces. So he told the soldiers to go down and take Paul away and put him in the army building.

11The next night the Lord came and stood by Paul. He said, "Be brave! You have told people in Jerusalem about me. You must do the same in Rome."

12In the morning some of the Jews made

---

threw off their coats This showed that the Jews were very angry with Paul.
threw dust into the air This showed even greater anger.
Roman citizen Roman law said that Roman citizens must not be beaten before they had a trial.
Ananias This is not the same man named Ananias in Acts 22:12.
'You ... people.' Quotation from Exodus 22:28.

a plan to kill Paul, and they took an oath not to eat or drink anything until they had killed him. [13]There were more than forty Jews who made this plan. [14]They went to the leading priests and the older Jewish leaders and said, "We have taken an oath not to eat or drink until we have killed Paul. [15]So this is what we want you to do: Send a message to the commander to bring Paul out to you as though you want to ask him more questions. We will be waiting to kill him while he is on the way here."

[16]But Paul's nephew heard about this plan and went to the army building and told Paul. [17]Then Paul called one of the officers and said, "Take this young man to the commander. He has a message for him."

[18]So the officer brought Paul's nephew to the commander and said, "The prisoner, Paul, asked me to bring this young man to you. He wants to tell you something."

[19]The commander took the young man's hand and led him to a place where they could be alone. He asked, "What do you want to tell me?"

[20]The young man said, "The Jews have decided to ask you to bring Paul down to their council meeting tomorrow. They want you to think they are going to ask him more questions. [21]But don't believe them! More than forty men are hiding and waiting to kill Paul. They have all taken an oath not to eat or drink until they have killed him. Now they are waiting for you to agree."

[22]The commander sent the young man away, ordering him, "Don't tell anyone that you have told me about their plan."

Paul Is Sent to Caesarea

[23]Then the commander called two officers and said, "I need some men to go to Caesarea. Get two hundred soldiers, seventy horsemen, and two hundred men with spears ready to leave at nine o'clock tonight. [24]Get some horses for Paul to ride so he can be taken to Governor Felix safely." [25]And he wrote a letter that said:

[26]From Claudius Lysias.

To the Most Excellent Governor Felix:

Greetings.

[27]The Jews had taken this man and planned to kill him. But I learned that he is a Roman citizen, so I went with my soldiers and saved him. [28]I wanted to know why they were accusing him, so I brought him before their council meeting. [29]I learned that the Jews said Paul did some things that were wrong by their own laws, but no charge was worthy of jail or death. [30]When I was told that some of the Jews were planning to kill Paul, I sent him to you at once. I also told those Jews to tell you what they have against him.

[31]So the soldiers did what they were told and took Paul and brought him to the city of Antipatris that night. [32]The next day the horsemen went with Paul to Caesarea, but the other soldiers went back to the army building in Jerusalem. [33]When the horsemen came to Caesarea and gave the letter to the governor, they turned Paul over to him. [34]The governor read the letter and asked Paul, "What area are you from?" When he learned that Paul was from Cilicia, [35]he said, "I will hear your case when those who are against you come here, too." Then the governor gave orders for Paul to be kept under guard in Herod's palace.

Paul Is Accused

24 Five days later Ananias, the high priest, went to the city of Caesarea with some of the older Jewish leaders and a lawyer named Tertullus. They had come to make charges against Paul before the governor. [2]Paul was called into the meeting, and Tertullus began to accuse him, saying, "Most Excellent Felix! Our people enjoy much peace because of you, and many wrong things in our country are being made right through your wise help. [3]We accept these things always and in every place, and we are thankful for them. [4]But not wanting to take any more of your time, I beg you to be kind and listen to our few words. [5]We have found this man to be a troublemaker, stirring up the Jews everywhere in the world. He is a leader of the Nazarene[d] group. [6]Also, he was trying to make the Temple[d] unclean,[d] but we stopped him.[n] [8]By asking him questions yourself, you can decide if all these things are true." [9]The other Jews agreed and said that all of this was true.

[10]When the governor made a sign for Paul to speak, Paul said, "Governor Felix, I know you have been a judge over this nation for a long time. So I am happy to defend myself before you. [11]You can learn for yourself that I went to worship in Jerusalem only twelve days ago. [12]Those who are accusing me did not find me arguing with anyone in the Temple or stirring up the people in the synagogues[d] or in the city. [13]They cannot prove the things they are saying against me now. [14]But I will tell you this: I worship the God of our ancestors as a follower of the Way of Jesus. The Jews say that the Way of Jesus is not the right way. But I believe everything that is taught in the law of Moses and that is written in the books of the Prophets.[d] [15]I have the same hope in God that they have — the hope that all people, good and bad, will surely be raised from the dead. [16]This is why I always try to do what I believe is right before God and people.

[17]"After being away from Jerusalem for several years, I went back to bring money to my people and to offer sacrifices. [18]I was doing this when they found me in the Temple. I had finished the cleansing ceremony and had not made any trouble; no people were gathering around me. [19]But there were some Jews from the country of Asia who should be here, standing before you. If I have really done anything wrong, they are the ones who should accuse me. [20]Or ask these Jews here if they found any wrong in me when I stood before the Jewish council in Jerusalem. [21]But I did shout one thing when I stood before them: 'You are judging me today because I believe that people will rise from the dead!' "

[22]Felix already understood much about the Way of Jesus. He stopped the trial and said, "When commander Lysias comes here, I will decide your case." [23]Felix told the officer to keep Paul guarded but to give him some freedom and to let his friends bring what he needed.

Paul Speaks to Felix and His Wife

[24]After some days Felix came with his wife, Drusilla, who was Jewish, and asked for Paul to be brought to him. He listened to Paul talk about believing in Christ Jesus. [25]But Felix became afraid when Paul spoke about living right, self-control, and the time when God will judge the world. He said, "Go away now. When I have more time, I will call for you." [26]At the same time Felix hoped that Paul would give him some money, so he often sent for Paul and talked with him.

[27]But after two years, Felix was replaced by Porcius Festus as governor. But Felix had left Paul in prison to please the Jews.

Paul Asks to See Caesar

25 Three days after Festus became governor, he went from Caesarea to Jerusalem. [2]There the leading priests and the important Jewish leaders made charges against Paul before Festus. [3]They asked Festus to do them a favor. They wanted him to send Paul back to Jerusalem, because they had a plan to kill him on the way. [4]But Festus answered that Paul would be kept in Caesarea and that he himself was returning there soon. [5]He said, "Some of your leaders should go with me. They can accuse the man there in Caesarea, if he has really done something wrong."

[6]Festus stayed in Jerusalem another eight or ten days and then went back to Caesarea. The next day he told the soldiers to bring Paul before him. Festus was seated on the judge's seat [7]when Paul came into the room. The Jewish people who had come from Jerusalem stood around him, making serious charges against him, which they could not prove. [8]This is what Paul said to defend himself: "I have done nothing wrong against the Jewish law, against the Temple,[d] or against Caesar."[d]

[9]But Festus wanted to please the Jews. So he asked Paul, "Do you want to go to Jerusalem for me to judge you there on these charges?"

[10]Paul said, "I am standing at Caesar's judgment seat now, where I should be

---

Verse 6 Some Greek copies add 6b-8a: "And we wanted to judge him by our own law. [7]But the officer Lysias came and used much force to take him from us. [8]And Lysias commanded those who wanted to accuse Paul to come to you."

judged. I have done nothing wrong to the Jews; you know this is true. [11]If I have done something wrong and the law says I must die, I do not ask to be saved from death. But if these charges are not true, then no one can give me to them. I want Caesar to hear my case!"

[12]Festus talked about this with his advisors. Then he said, "You have asked to see Caesar, so you will go to Caesar!"

Paul Before King Agrippa

[13]A few days later King Agrippa and Bernice came to Caesarea to visit Festus. [14]They stayed there for some time, and Festus told the king about Paul's case. Festus said, "There is a man that Felix left in prison. [15]When I went to Jerusalem, the leading priests and the older Jewish leaders there made charges against him, asking me to sentence him to death. [16]But I answered, 'When a man is accused of a crime, Romans do not hand him over until he has been allowed to face his accusers and defend himself against their charges.' [17]So when these Jews came here to Caesarea for the trial, I did not waste time. The next day I sat on the judge's seat and commanded that the man be brought in. [18]The Jews stood up and accused him, but not of any serious crime as I thought they would. [19]The things they said were about their own religion and about a man named Jesus who died. But Paul said that he is still alive. [20]Not knowing how to find out about these questions, I asked Paul, 'Do you want to go to Jerusalem and be judged there?' [21]But he asked to be kept in Caesarea. He wants a decision from the emperor.[n] So I ordered that he be held until I could send him to Caesar.[d]"

[22]Agrippa said to Festus, "I would also like to hear this man myself."

Festus said, "Tomorrow you will hear him."

[23]The next day Agrippa and Bernice appeared with great show, acting like very important people. They went into the judgment room with the army leaders and the important men of Caesarea. Then Festus ordered the soldiers to bring Paul in. [24]Festus said,

"King Agrippa and all who are gathered here with us, you see this man. All the Jewish people, here and in Jerusalem, have complained to me about him, shouting that he should not live any longer. [25]When I judged him, I found no reason to order his death. But since he asked to be judged by Caesar, I decided to send him. [26]But I have nothing definite to write the emperor about him. So I have brought him before all of you — especially you, King Agrippa. I hope you can question him and give me something to write. [27]I think it is foolish to send a prisoner to Caesar without telling what charges are against him."

Paul Defends Himself

26 Agrippa said to Paul, "You may now speak to defend yourself."

Then Paul raised his hand and began to speak. [2]He said, "King Agrippa, I am very happy to stand before you and will answer all the charges the Jewish people make against me. [3]You know so much about all the Jewish customs and the things the Jews argue about, so please listen to me patiently.

[4]"All the Jewish people know about my whole life, how I lived from the beginning in my own country and later in Jerusalem. [5]They have known me for a long time. If they want to, they can tell you that I was a good Pharisee.[d] And the Pharisees obey the laws of the Jewish religion more carefully than any other group. [6]Now I am on trial because I hope for the promise that God made to our ancestors. [7]This is the promise that the twelve tribes[d] of our people hope to receive as they serve God day and night. My king, the Jews have accused me because I hope for this same promise! [8]Why do any of you people think it is impossible for God to raise people from the dead?

[9]"I, too, thought I ought to do many things against Jesus from Nazareth. [10]And that is what I did in Jerusalem. The leading priests gave me the power to put many of God's people in jail, and when they were being killed, I agreed it was a good thing. [11]In every synagogue,[d] I often punished them and tried to make them speak against Jesus. I was so an-

---

emperor   The ruler of the Roman Empire, which was almost all the known world.

gry against them I even went to other cities to find them and punish them.

[12]"One time the leading priests gave me permission and the power to go to Damascus. [13]On the way there, at noon, I saw a light from heaven. It was brighter than the sun and flashed all around me and those who were traveling with me. [14]We all fell to the ground. Then I heard a voice speaking to me in the Jewish language,[n] saying, 'Saul, Saul, why are you persecuting me? You are only hurting yourself by fighting me.' [15]I said, 'Who are you, Lord?' The Lord said, 'I am Jesus, the one you are persecuting. [16]Stand up! I have chosen you to be my servant and my witness — you will tell people the things that you have seen and the things that I will show you. This is why I have come to you today. [17]I will keep you safe from your own people and also from those who are not Jewish. I am sending you to them [18]to open their eyes so that they may turn away from darkness to the light, away from the power of Satan and to God. Then their sins can be forgiven, and they can have a place with those people who have been made holy by believing in me.'

[19]"King Agrippa, after I had this vision from heaven, I obeyed it. [20]I began telling people that they should change their hearts and lives and turn to God and do things to show they really had changed. I told this first to those in Damascus, then in Jerusalem, and in every part of Judea, and also to those who are not Jewish. [21]This is why the Jews took me and were trying to kill me in the Temple.[d] [22]But God has helped me, and so I stand here today, telling all people, small and great, what I have seen. But I am saying only what Moses and the prophets[d] said would happen — [23]that the Christ[d] would die, and as the first to rise from the dead, he would bring light to the Jewish and non-Jewish people."

Paul Tries to Persuade Agrippa

[24]While Paul was saying these things to defend himself, Festus said loudly, "Paul, you are out of your mind! Too much study has driven you crazy!"

[25]Paul said, "Most excellent Festus, I am not crazy. My words are true and sensible. [26]King Agrippa knows about these things, and I can speak freely to him. I know he has heard about all of these things, because they did not happen off in a corner. [27]King Agrippa, do you believe what the prophets[d] wrote? I know you believe."

[28]King Agrippa said to Paul, "Do you think you can persuade me to become a Christian in such a short time?"

[29]Paul said, "Whether it is a short or a long time, I pray to God that not only you but every person listening to me today would be saved and be like me — except for these chains I have."

[30]Then King Agrippa, Governor Festus, Bernice, and all the people sitting with them stood up [31]and left the room. Talking to each other, they said, "There is no reason why this man should die or be put in jail." [32]And Agrippa said to Festus, "We could let this man go free, but he has asked Caesar[d] to hear his case."

Paul Sails for Rome

27 It was decided that we would sail for Italy. An officer named Julius, who served in the emperor's[n] army, guarded Paul and some other prisoners. [2]We got on a ship that was from the city of Adramyttium and was about to sail to different ports in the country of Asia. Aristarchus, a man from the city of Thessalonica in Macedonia, went with us. [3]The next day we came to Sidon. Julius was very good to Paul and gave him freedom to go visit his friends, who took care of his needs. [4]We left Sidon and sailed close to the island of Cyprus, because the wind was blowing against us. [5]We went across the sea by Cilicia and Pamphylia and landed at the city of Myra, in Lycia. [6]There the officer found a ship from Alexandria that was going to Italy, so he put us on it.

[7]We sailed slowly for many days. We had a hard time reaching Cnidus because the

---

Jewish language   Hebrew or Aramaic, the languages of the Jews in the first century.
emperor   The ruler of the Roman Empire, which was almost all the known world.

wind was blowing against us, and we could not go any farther. So we sailed by the south side of the island of Crete near Salmone. [8]Sailing past it was hard. Then we came to a place called Fair Havens, near the city of Lasea.

[9]We had lost much time, and it was now dangerous to sail, because it was already after the Day of Cleansing.[n] So Paul warned them, [10]"Men, I can see there will be a lot of trouble on this trip. The ship, the cargo, and even our lives may be lost." [11]But the captain and the owner of the ship did not agree with Paul, and the officer believed what the captain and owner of the ship said. [12]Since that harbor was not a good place for the ship to stay for the winter, most of the men decided that the ship should leave. They hoped we could go to Phoenix and stay there for the winter. Phoenix, a city on the island of Crete, had a harbor which faced southwest and northwest.

The Storm

[13]When a good wind began to blow from the south, the men on the ship thought, "This is the wind we wanted, and now we have it." So they pulled up the anchor, and we sailed very close to the island of Crete. [14]But then a very strong wind named the "northeaster" came from the island. [15]The ship was caught in it and could not sail against it. So we stopped trying and let the wind carry us. [16]When we went below a small island named Cauda, we were barely able to bring in the lifeboat. [17]After the men took the lifeboat in, they tied ropes around the ship to hold it together. The men were afraid that the ship would hit the sandbanks of Syrtis,[n] so they lowered the sail and let the wind carry the ship. [18]The next day the storm was blowing us so hard that the men threw out some of the cargo. [19]A day later with their own hands they threw out the ship's equipment. [20]When we could not see the sun or the stars for many days, and the storm was very bad, we lost all hope of being saved.

[21]After the men had gone without food for a long time, Paul stood up before them and said, "Men, you should have listened to me. You should not have sailed from Crete. Then you would not have all this trouble and loss. [22]But now I tell you to cheer up because none of you will die. Only the ship will be lost. [23]Last night an angel came to me from the God I belong to and worship. [24]The angel said, 'Paul, do not be afraid. You must stand before Caesar.[d] And God has promised you that he will save the lives of everyone sailing with you.' [25]So men, have courage. I trust in God that everything will happen as his angel told me. [26]But we will crash on an island."

[27]On the fourteenth night we were still being carried around in the Adriatic Sea.[n] About midnight the sailors thought we were close to land, [28]so they lowered a rope with a weight on the end of it into the water. They found that the water was one hundred twenty feet deep. They went a little farther and lowered the rope again. It was ninety feet deep. [29]The sailors were afraid that we would hit the rocks, so they threw four anchors into the water and prayed for daylight to come. [30]Some of the sailors wanted to leave the ship, and they lowered the lifeboat, pretending they were throwing more anchors from the front of the ship. [31]But Paul told the officer and the other soldiers, "If these men do not stay in the ship, your lives cannot be saved." [32]So the soldiers cut the ropes and let the lifeboat fall into the water.

[33]Just before dawn Paul began persuading all the people to eat something. He said, "For the past fourteen days you have been waiting and watching and not eating. [34]Now I beg you to eat something. You need it to stay alive. None of you will lose even one hair off your heads." [35]After he said this, Paul took some bread and thanked God for it before all of them. He broke off a piece and began eating. [36]They all felt better and started eating, too. [37]There were two hundred seventy-six people on the ship. [38]When they had eaten all they wanted, they began making the ship lighter by throwing the grain into the sea.

Day of Cleansing   An important Jewish holy day in the fall of the year. This was the time of year that bad storms arose on the sea.
Syrtis   Shallow area in the sea near the Libyan coast.
Adriatic Sea   The sea between Greece and Italy, including the central Mediterranean.

The Ship Is Destroyed

[39] When daylight came, the sailors saw land. They did not know what land it was, but they saw a bay with a beach and wanted to sail the ship to the beach if they could. [40] So they cut the ropes to the anchors and left the anchors in the sea. At the same time, they untied the ropes that were holding the rudders. Then they raised the front sail into the wind and sailed toward the beach. [41] But the ship hit a sandbank. The front of the ship stuck there and could not move, but the back of the ship began to break up from the big waves.

[42] The soldiers decided to kill the prisoners so none of them could swim away and escape. [43] But Julius, the officer, wanted to let Paul live and did not allow the soldiers to kill the prisoners. Instead he ordered everyone who could swim to jump into the water first and swim to land. [44] The rest were to follow using wooden boards or pieces of the ship. And this is how all the people made it safely to land.

Paul on the Island of Malta

28 When we were safe on land, we learned that the island was called Malta. [2] The people who lived there were very good to us. Because it was raining and very cold, they made a fire and welcomed all of us. [3] Paul gathered a pile of sticks and was putting them on the fire when a poisonous snake came out because of the heat and bit him on the hand. [4] The people living on the island saw the snake hanging from Paul's hand and said to each other, "This man must be a murderer! He did not die in the sea, but Justice[n] does not want him to live." [5] But Paul shook the snake off into the fire and was not hurt. [6] The people thought that Paul would swell up or fall down dead. They waited and watched him for a long time, but nothing bad happened to him. So they changed their minds and said, "He is a god!"

[7] There were some fields around there owned by Publius, an important man on the island. He welcomed us into his home and was very good to us for three days. [8] Publius' father was sick with a fever and dysentery.[n] Paul went to him, prayed, and put his hands on the man and healed him. [9] After this, all the other sick people on the island came to Paul, and he healed them, too. [10-11] The people on the island gave us many honors. When we were ready to leave, three months later, they gave us the things we needed.

Paul Goes to Rome

We got on a ship from Alexandria that had stayed on the island during the winter. On the front of the ship was the sign of the twin gods.[n] [12] We stopped at Syracuse for three days. [13] From there we sailed to Rhegium. The next day a wind began to blow from the south, and a day later we came to Puteoli. [14] We found some believers there who asked us to stay with them for a week. Finally, we came to Rome. [15] The believers in Rome heard that we were there and came out as far as the Market of Appius[n] and the Three Inns[n] to meet us. When Paul saw them, he was encouraged and thanked God.

Paul in Rome

[16] When we arrived at Rome, Paul was allowed to live alone, with the soldier who guarded him.

[17] Three days later Paul sent for the Jewish leaders there. When they came together, he said, "Brothers, I have done nothing against our people or the customs of our ancestors. But I was arrested in Jerusalem and given to the Romans. [18] After they asked me many questions, they could find no reason why I should be killed. They wanted to let me go free, [19] but the Jewish people there argued against that. So I had to ask to come to Rome to have my trial before Caesar.[d] But I have no charge to bring against my own people. [20] That is why I wanted to see you and talk with you. I am bound with this chain because I believe in the hope of Israel."

[21] They answered Paul, "We have received

Justice The people thought there was a god named Justice who would punish bad people.
dysentery A sickness like diarrhea.
twin gods Statues of Castor and Pollux, gods in old Greek tales.
Market of Appius A town about twenty-seven miles from Rome.
Three Inns A town about thirty miles from Rome.

no letters from Judea about you. None of our Jewish brothers who have come from there brought news or told us anything bad about you. 22But we want to hear your ideas, because we know that people everywhere are speaking against this religious group."

23Paul and the Jewish people chose a day for a meeting and on that day many more of the Jews met with Paul at the place he was staying. He spoke to them all day long. Using the law of Moses and the prophets'*d* writings, he explained the kingdom of God, and he tried to persuade them to believe these things about Jesus. 24Some believed what Paul said, but others did not. 25So they argued and began leaving after Paul said one more thing to them: "The Holy Spirit*d* spoke the truth to your ancestors through Isaiah the prophet, saying,

26'Go to this people and say:

You will listen and listen, but you will
    not understand.

You will look and look, but you will
    not learn,

27because these people have become
    stubborn.

They don't hear with their ears,
    and they have closed their eyes.

Otherwise, they might really understand
    what they see with their eyes
    and hear with their ears.

They might really understand in their
    minds

    and come back to me and be healed.'

Isaiah 6:9-10

28"I want you to know that God has also sent his salvation to those who are not Jewish, and they will listen!" 29 *n*

30Paul stayed two full years in his own rented house and welcomed all people who came to visit him. 31He boldly preached about the kingdom of God and taught about the Lord Jesus Christ, and no one tried to stop him.

Verse 29   Some late Greek copies add verse 29: "After Paul said this, the Jews left. They were arguing very much with each other."

ROMANS

God's Plan to Save Us

1 From Paul, a servant of Christ Jesus. God called me to be an apostle[d] and chose me to tell the Good News.[d]

[2]God promised this Good News long ago through his prophets,[d] as it is written in the Holy Scriptures.[d] [3-4]The Good News is about God's Son, Jesus Christ our Lord. As a man, he was born from the family of David. But through the Spirit[d] of holiness he was appointed to be God's Son with great power by rising from the dead. [5]Through Christ, God gave me the special work of an apostle, which was to lead people of all nations to believe and obey. I do this work for him. [6]And you who are in Rome are also called to belong to Jesus Christ.

[7]To all of you in Rome whom God loves and has called to be his holy people:

Grace and peace to you from God our Father and the Lord Jesus Christ.

A Prayer of Thanks

[8]First I want to say that I thank my God through Jesus Christ for all of you, because people everywhere in the world are talking about your faith. [9]God, whom I serve with my whole heart by telling the Good News[d] about his Son, knows that I always mention you [10]every time I pray. I pray that I will be allowed to come to you, and this will happen if God wants it. [11]I want very much to see you, to give you some spiritual gift to make you strong. [12]I mean that I want us to help each other with the faith we have. Your faith will help me, and my faith will help you. [13]Brothers and sisters,[n] I want you to know that I planned many times to come to you, but this has not been possible. I wanted to come so that I could help you grow spiritually as I have helped the other non-Jewish people.

[14]I have a duty to all people — Greeks and those who are not Greeks, the wise and the foolish. [15]That is why I want so much to preach the Good News to you in Rome.

[16]I am proud of the Good News, because it is the power God uses to save everyone who believes — to save the Jews first, and also to save those who are not Jews. [17]The Good News shows how God makes people right with himself — that it begins and ends with faith. As the Scripture[d] says, "But those who are right with God will live by trusting in him."[n]

All People Have Done Wrong

[18]God's anger is shown from heaven against all the evil and wrong things people do. By their own evil lives they hide the truth. [19]God shows his anger because some knowledge of him has been made clear to them. Yes, God has shown himself to them. [20]There are things about him that people cannot see — his eternal power and all the things that make him God. But since the beginning of the world those things have been easy to understand by what God has made. So people have no excuse for the bad things they do. [21]They knew God, but they did not give glory to God or thank him. Their thinking became useless. Their foolish minds were filled with darkness. [22]They said they were wise, but they became fools. [23]They traded the glory of God who lives forever for the worship of idols made to look like earthly people, birds, animals, and snakes.

[24]Because they did these things, God left them and let them go their sinful way, wanting only to do evil. As a result, they became full of sexual sin, using their bodies wrongly with each other. [25]They traded the truth of God for a lie. They worshiped and served

Brothers and sisters Although the Greek text says "Brothers" here and throughout this book, Paul's words were meant for the entire church, including men and women.
"But those . . . him." Quotation from Habakkuk 2:4.

what had been created instead of the God who created those things, who should be praised forever. Amen.

²⁶Because people did those things, God left them and let them do the shameful things they wanted to do. Women stopped having natural sex and started having sex with other women. ²⁷In the same way, men stopped having natural sex and began wanting each other. Men did shameful things with other men, and in their bodies they received the punishment for those wrongs.

²⁸People did not think it was important to have a true knowledge of God. So God left them and allowed them to have their own worthless thinking and to do things they should not do. ²⁹They are filled with every kind of sin, evil, selfishness, and hatred. They are full of jealousy, murder, fighting, lying, and thinking the worst about each other. They gossip ³⁰and say evil things about each other. They hate God. They are rude and conceited and brag about themselves. They invent ways of doing evil. They do not obey their parents. ³¹They are foolish, they do not keep their promises, and they show no kindness or mercy to others. ³²They know God's law says that those who live like this should die. But they themselves not only continue to do these evil things, they applaud others who do them.

You People Also Are Sinful

2 If you think you can judge others, you are wrong. When you judge them, you are really judging yourself guilty, because you do the same things they do. ²God judges those who do wrong things, and we know that his judging is right. ³You judge those who do wrong, but you do wrong yourselves. Do you think you will be able to escape the judgment of God? ⁴He has been very kind and patient, waiting for you to change, but you think nothing of his kindness. Perhaps you do not understand that God is kind to you so you will change your hearts and lives. ⁵But you are stubborn and refuse to change, so you are making your own punishment even greater on the day he shows his anger. On that day everyone will see God's right judgments. ⁶God will reward or punish every person for what that person has done. ⁷Some

people, by always continuing to do good, live for God's glory, for honor, and for life that has no end. God will give them life forever. ⁸But other people are selfish. They refuse to follow truth and, instead, follow evil. God will give them his punishment and anger. ⁹He will give trouble and suffering to everyone who does evil — to the Jews first and also to those who are not Jews. ¹⁰But he will give glory, honor, and peace to everyone who does good — to the Jews first and also to those who are not Jews. ¹¹For God judges all people in the same way.

¹²People who do not have the law and who are sinners will be lost, although they do not have the law. And, in the same way, those who have the law and are sinners will be judged by the law. ¹³Hearing the law does not make people right with God. It is those who obey the law who will be right with him. ¹⁴(Those who are not Jews do not have the law, but when they freely do what the law commands, they are the law for themselves. This is true even though they do not have the law. ¹⁵They show that in their hearts they know what is right and wrong, just as the law commands. And they show this by their consciences. Sometimes their thoughts tell them they did wrong, and sometimes their thoughts tell them they did right.) ¹⁶All these things will happen on the day when God, through Christ Jesus, will judge people's secret thoughts. The Good News*d* that I preach says this.

The Jews and the Law

¹⁷What about you? You call yourself a Jew. You trust in the law of Moses and brag that you are close to God. ¹⁸You know what he wants you to do and what is important, because you have learned the law. ¹⁹You think you are a guide for the blind and a light for those who are in darkness. ²⁰You think you can show foolish people what is right and teach those who know nothing. You have the law; so you think you know everything and have all truth. ²¹You teach others, so why don't you teach yourself? You tell others not to steal, but you steal. ²²You say that others must not take part in adultery,*d* but you are guilty of that sin. You hate idols, but you steal from temples. ²³You brag about having

God's law, but you bring shame to God by breaking his law, [24]just as the Scriptures[d] say: "Those who are not Jews speak against God's name because of you." [n]

[25]If you follow the law, your circumcision[d] has meaning. But if you break the law, it is as if you were never circumcised. [26]People who are not Jews are not circumcised, but if they do what the law says, it is as if they were circumcised. [27]You Jews have the written law and circumcision, but you break the law. So those who are not circumcised in their bodies, but still obey the law, will show that you are guilty. [28]They can do this because a person is not a true Jew if he is only a Jew in his physical body; true circumcision is not only on the outside of the body. [29]A person is a Jew only if he is a Jew inside; true circumcision is done in the heart by the Spirit,[d] not by the written law. Such a person gets praise from God rather than from people.

3 So, do Jews have anything that other people do not have? Is there anything special about being circumcised? [2]Yes, of course, there is in every way. The most important thing is this: God trusted the Jews with his teachings. [3]If some Jews were not faithful to him, will that stop God from doing what he promised? [4]No! God will continue to be true even when every person is false. As the Scriptures[d] say:

"So you will be shown to be right when you speak,
and you will win your case."   *Psalm 51:4*

[5]When we do wrong, that shows more clearly that God is right. So can we say that God is wrong to punish us? (I am talking as people might talk.) [6]No! If God could not punish us, he could not judge the world.

[7]A person might say, "When I lie, it really gives him glory, because my lie shows God's truth. So why am I judged a sinner?" [8]It would be the same to say, "We should do evil so that good will come." Some people find fault with us and say we teach this, but they are wrong and deserve the punishment they will receive.

All People Are Guilty

[9]So are we Jews better than others? No! We have already said that Jews and those who are not Jews are all guilty of sin. [10]As the Scriptures[d] say:

"There is no one who always does what is right,
not even one.
[11] There is no one who understands.
There is no one who looks to God for help.
[12]All have turned away.
Together, everyone has become useless.
There is no one who does anything good;
there is not even one."   *Psalm 14:1-3*
[13]"Their throats are like open graves;
they use their tongues for telling lies."   *Psalm 5:9*
"Their words are like snake poison."   *Psalm 140:3*
[14] "Their mouths are full of cursing and hate."   *Psalm 10:7*
[15]"They are always ready to kill people.
[16] Everywhere they go they cause ruin and misery.
[17]They don't know how to live in peace."   *Isaiah 59:7-8*
[18] "They have no fear of God."   *Psalm 36:1*

[19]We know that the law's commands are for those who have the law. This stops all excuses and brings the whole world under God's judgment, [20]because no one can be made right with God by following the law. The law only shows us our sin.

How God Makes People Right

[21]But God has a way to make people right with him without the law, and he has now shown us that way which the law and the prophets[d] told us about. [22]God makes people right with himself through their faith in Jesus Christ. This is true for all who believe in Christ, because all people are the same: [23]All have sinned and are not good enough for God's glory, [24]and all need to be made right with God by his grace, which is a free gift. They need to be made free from sin through Jesus Christ. [25]God gave him as a way to forgive sin through faith in the blood of Jesus' death. This showed that God always does

---

"Those . . . you." Quotation from Isaiah 52:5; Ezekiel 36:20.

what is right and fair, as in the past when he was patient and did not punish people for their sins. [26]And God gave Jesus to show today that he does what is right. God did this so he could judge rightly and so he could make right any person who has faith in Jesus.

[27]So do we have a reason to brag about ourselves? No! And why not? It is the way of faith that stops all bragging, not the way of trying to obey the law. [28]A person is made right with God through faith, not through obeying the law. [29]Is God only the God of the Jews? Is he not also the God of those who are not Jews? [30]Of course he is, because there is only one God. He will make Jews right with him by their faith, and he will also make those who are not Jews right with him through their faith. [31]So do we destroy the law by following the way of faith? No! Faith causes us to be what the law truly wants.

The Example of Abraham

4 So what can we say that Abraham,[n] the father of our people, learned about faith? [2]If Abraham was made right by the things he did, he had a reason to brag. But this is not God's view, [3]because the Scripture[d] says, "Abraham believed God, and God accepted Abraham's faith, and that faith made him right with God."[n]

[4]When people work, their pay is not given as a gift, but as something earned. [5]But people cannot do any work that will make them right with God. So they must trust in him, who makes even evil people right in his sight. Then God accepts their faith, and that makes them right with him. [6]David said the same thing. He said that people are truly blessed when God, without paying attention to good deeds, makes people right with himself.

[7]"Happy are they
   whose sins are forgiven,
   whose wrongs are pardoned.
[8]Happy is the person
   whom the Lord does not consider
      guilty."   *Psalm 32:1-2*

[9]Is this blessing only for those who are circumcised[d] or also for those who are not cir-

cumcised? We have already said that God accepted Abraham's faith and that faith made him right with God. [10]So how did this happen? Did God accept Abraham before or after he was circumcised? It was before his circumcision. [11]Abraham was circumcised to show that he was right with God through faith before he was circumcised. So Abraham is the father of all those who believe but are not circumcised; he is the father of all believers who are accepted as being right with God. [12]And Abraham is also the father of those who have been circumcised and who live following the faith that our father Abraham had before he was circumcised.

God Keeps His Promise

[13]Abraham[n] and his descendants[d] received the promise that they would get the whole world. He did not receive that promise through the law, but through being right with God by his faith. [14]If people could receive what God promised by following the law, then faith is worthless. And God's promise to Abraham is worthless, [15]because the law can only bring God's anger. But if there is no law, there is nothing to disobey.

[16]So people receive God's promise by having faith. This happens so the promise can be a free gift. Then all of Abraham's children can have that promise. It is not only for those who live under the law of Moses but for anyone who lives with faith like that of Abraham, who is the father of us all. [17]As it is written in the Scriptures:[d] "I am making you a father of many nations."[n] This is true before God, the God Abraham believed, the God who gives life to the dead and who creates something out of nothing.

[18]There was no hope that Abraham would have children. But Abraham believed God and continued hoping, and so he became the father of many nations. As God told him, "Your descendants also will be too many to count."[n] [19]Abraham was almost a hundred years old, much past the age for having children, and Sarah could not have children. Abraham thought about all this, but his faith

Abraham Most respected ancestor of the Jews. Every Jew hoped to see Abraham.
"Abraham . . . God." Quotation from Genesis 15:6.
"I . . . nations." Quotation from Genesis 17:5.
"Your . . . count." Quotation from Genesis 15:5.

in God did not become weak. [20]He never doubted that God would keep his promise, and he never stopped believing. He grew stronger in his faith and gave praise to God. [21]Abraham felt sure that God was able to do what he had promised. [22]So, "God accepted Abraham's faith, and that faith made him right with God." [n] [23]Those words ("God accepted Abraham's faith") were written not only for Abraham [24]but also for us. God will accept us also because we believe in the One who raised Jesus our Lord from the dead. [25]Jesus was given to die for our sins, and he was raised from the dead to make us right with God.

Right with God

5 Since we have been made right with God by our faith, we have peace with God. This happened through our Lord Jesus Christ, [2]who has brought us into that blessing of God's grace that we now enjoy. And we are happy because of the hope we have of sharing God's glory. [3]We also have joy with our troubles, because we know that these troubles produce patience. [4]And patience produces character, and character produces hope. [5]And this hope will never disappoint us, because God has poured out his love to fill our hearts. He gave us his love through the Holy Spirit, [d] whom God has given to us.

[6]When we were unable to help ourselves, at the moment of our need, Christ died for us, although we were living against God. [7]Very few people will die to save the life of someone else. Although perhaps for a good person someone might possibly die. [8]But God shows his great love for us in this way: Christ died for us while we were still sinners.

[9]So through Christ we will surely be saved from God's anger, because we have been made right with God by the blood of Christ's death. [10]While we were God's enemies, he made friends with us through the death of his Son. Surely, now that we are his friends, he will save us through his Son's life. [11]And not only that, but now we are also very happy in God through our Lord Jesus Christ. Through him we are now God's friends again.

Adam and Christ Compared

[12]Sin came into the world because of what one man did, and with sin came death. This is why everyone must die — because everyone sinned. [13]Sin was in the world before the law of Moses, but sin is not counted against us as breaking a command when there is no law. [14]But from the time of Adam to the time of Moses, everyone had to die, even those who had not sinned by breaking a command, as Adam had.

Adam was like the One who was coming in the future. [15]But God's free gift is not like Adam's sin. Many people died because of the sin of that one man. But the grace from God was much greater; many people received God's gift of life by the grace of the one man, Jesus Christ. [16]After Adam sinned once, he was judged guilty. But the gift of God is different. God's free gift came after many sins, and it makes people right with God. [17]One man sinned, and so death ruled all people because of that one man. But now those people who accept God's full grace and the great gift of being made right with him will surely have true life and rule through the one man, Jesus Christ.

[18]So as one sin of Adam brought the punishment of death to all people, one good act that Christ did makes all people right with God. And that brings true life for all. [19]One man disobeyed God, and many became sinners. In the same way, one man obeyed God, and many will be made right. [20]The law came to make sin worse. But when sin grew worse, God's grace increased. [21]Sin once used death to rule us, but God gave people more of his grace so that grace could rule by making people right with him. And this brings life forever through Jesus Christ our Lord.

Dead to Sin but Alive in Christ

6 So do you think we should continue sinning so that God will give us even more grace? [2]No! We died to our old sinful lives, so how can we continue living with sin? [3]Did you forget that all of us became part of Christ when we were baptized? We shared his death in our baptism. [4]When we were baptized, we were buried with Christ and shared his death. So, just as Christ was raised from the dead by the wonderful power of the Father, we also can live a new life.

5Christ died, and we have been joined with him by dying too. So we will also be joined with him by rising from the dead as he did. 6We know that our old life died with Christ on the cross so that our sinful selves would have no power over us and we would not be slaves to sin. 7Anyone who has died is made free from sin's control.

8If we died with Christ, we know we will also live with him. 9Christ was raised from the dead, and we know that he cannot die again. Death has no power over him now. 10Yes, when Christ died, he died to defeat the power of sin one time—enough for all time. He now has a new life, and his new life is with God. 11In the same way, you should see yourselves as being dead to the power of sin and alive with God through Christ Jesus.

12So, do not let sin control your life here on earth so that you do what your sinful self wants to do. 13Do not offer the parts of your body to serve sin, as things to be used in doing evil. Instead, offer yourselves to God as people who have died and now live. Offer the parts of your body to God to be used in doing good. 14Sin will not be your master, because you are not under law but under God's grace.

Be Slaves of Righteousness

15So what should we do? Should we sin because we are under grace and not under law? No! 16Surely you know that when you give yourselves like slaves to obey someone, then you are really slaves of that person. The person you obey is your master. You can follow sin, which brings spiritual death, or you can obey God, which makes you right with him. 17In the past you were slaves to sin—sin controlled you. But thank God, you fully obeyed the things that you were taught. 18You were made free from sin, and now you are slaves to goodness. 19I use this example because this is hard for you to understand. In the past you offered the parts of your body to be slaves to sin and evil; you lived only for

evil. In the same way now you must give yourselves to be slaves of goodness. Then you will live only for God.

20In the past you were slaves to sin, and goodness did not control you. 21You did evil things, and now you are ashamed of them. Those things only bring death. 22But now you are free from sin and have become slaves of God. This brings you a life that is only for God, and this gives you life forever. 23When people sin, they earn what sin pays—death. But God gives us a free gift—life forever in Christ Jesus our Lord.

An Example from Marriage

7 Brothers and sisters, all of you understand the law of Moses. So surely you know that the law rules over people only while they are alive. 2For example, a woman must stay married to her husband as long as he is alive. But if her husband dies, she is free from the law of marriage. 3But if she marries another man while her husband is still alive, the law says she is guilty of adultery.*d* But if her husband dies, she is free from the law of marriage. Then if she marries another man, she is not guilty of adultery.

4In the same way, my brothers and sisters, your old selves died, and you became free from the law through the body of Christ. This happened so that you might belong to someone else—the One who was raised from the dead—and so that we might be used in service to God. 5In the past, we were ruled by our sinful selves. The law made us want to do sinful things that controlled our bodies, so the things we did were bringing us death. 6In the past, the law held us like prisoners, but our old selves died, and we were made free from the law. So now we serve God in a new way with the Spirit,*d* and not in the old way with written rules.

Our Fight Against Sin

7You might think I am saying that sin and the law are the same thing. That is not true. But the law was the only way I could learn what sin meant. I would never have known what it means to want to take something belonging to someone else if the law had not said, "You must not want to take your neighbor's things." [n] [8]And sin found a way to use that command and cause me to want all kinds of things I should not want. But without the law, sin has no power. [9]I was alive before I knew the law. But when the law's command came to me, then sin began to live, [10]and I died. The command was meant to bring life, but for me it brought death. [11]Sin found a way to fool me by using the command to make me die.

[12]So the law is holy, and the command is holy and right and good. [13]Does this mean that something that is good brought death to me? No! Sin used something that is good to bring death to me. This happened so that I could see what sin is really like; the command was used to show that sin is very evil.

The War Within Us

[14]We know that the law is spiritual, but I am not spiritual since sin rules me as if I were its slave. [15]I do not understand the things I do. I do not do what I want to do, and I do the things I hate. [16]And if I do not want to do the hated things I do, that means I agree that the law is good. [17]But I am not really the one who is doing these hated things; it is sin living in me that does them. [18]Yes, I know that nothing good lives in me — I mean nothing good lives in the part of me that is earthly and sinful. I want to do the things that are good, but I do not do them. [19]I do not do the good things I want to do, but I do the bad things I do not want to do. [20]So if I do things I do not want to do, then I am not the one doing them. It is sin living in me that does those things.

[21]So I have learned this rule: When I want to do good, evil is there with me. [22]In my mind, I am happy with God's law. [23]But I see another law working in my body, which makes war against the law that my mind accepts. That other law working in my body is the law of sin, and it makes me its prisoner. [24]What a miserable man I am! Who will save me from this body that brings me death? [25]I thank God for saving me through Jesus Christ our Lord!

So in my mind I am a slave to God's law, but in my sinful self I am a slave to the law of sin.

Be Ruled by the Spirit

8 So now, those who are in Christ Jesus are not judged guilty. [2]Through Christ Jesus the law of the Spirit[d] that brings life made me free from the law that brings sin and death. [3]The law was without power, because the law was made weak by our sinful selves. But God did what the law could not do. He sent his own Son to earth with the same human life that others use for sin. By sending his Son to be an offering to pay for sin, God used a human life to destroy sin. [4]He did this so that we could be the kind of people the law correctly wants us to be. Now we do not live following our sinful selves, but we live following the Spirit.

[5]Those who live following their sinful selves think only about things that their sinful selves want. But those who live following the Spirit are thinking about the things the Spirit wants them to do. [6]If people's thinking is controlled by the sinful self, there is death. But if their thinking is controlled by the Spirit, there is life and peace. [7]When people's thinking is controlled by the sinful self, they are against God, because they refuse to obey God's law and really are not even able to obey God's law. [8]Those people who are ruled by their sinful selves cannot please God.

[9]But you are not ruled by your sinful selves. You are ruled by the Spirit, if that Spirit of God really lives in you. But the person who does not have the Spirit of Christ does not belong to Christ. [10]Your body will always be dead because of sin. But if Christ is in you, then the Spirit gives you life, because Christ made you right with God. [11]God raised Jesus from the dead, and if God's Spirit is living in you, he will also give life to your bodies that die. God is the One who raised Christ from the dead, and he will give life through his Spirit that lives in you.

[12]So, my brothers and sisters, we must not be ruled by our sinful selves or live the way our sinful selves want. [13]If you use your lives to do the wrong things your sinful selves

---

"You ... things." Quotation from Exodus 20:17.

want, you will die spiritually. But if you use the Spirit's help to stop doing the wrong things you do with your body, you will have true life.

[14]The true children of God are those who let God's Spirit lead them. [15]The Spirit we received does not make us slaves again to fear; it makes us children of God. With that Spirit we cry out, "Father." [n] [16]And the Spirit himself joins with our spirits to say we are God's children. [17]If we are God's children, we will receive blessings from God together with Christ. But we must suffer as Christ suffered so that we will have glory as Christ has glory.

Our Future Glory

[18]The sufferings we have now are nothing compared to the great glory that will be shown to us. [19]Everything God made is waiting with excitement for God to show his children's glory completely. [20]Everything God made was changed to become useless, not by its own wish but because God wanted it and because all along there was this hope: [21]that everything God made would be set free from ruin to have the freedom and glory that belong to God's children.

[22]We know that everything God made has been waiting until now in pain, like a woman ready to give birth. [23]Not only the world, but we also have been waiting with pain inside us. We have the Spirit[d] as the first part of God's promise. So we are waiting for God to finish making us his own children, which means our bodies will be made free. [24]We were saved, and we have this hope. If we see what we are waiting for, that is not really hope. People do not hope for something they already have. [25]But we are hoping for something we do not have yet, and we are waiting for it patiently.

[26]Also, the Spirit helps us with our weakness. We do not know how to pray as we should. But the Spirit himself speaks to God for us, even begs God for us with deep feelings that words cannot explain. [27]God can see what is in people's hearts. And he knows what is in the mind of the Spirit, because the Spirit speaks to God for his people in the way God wants.

[28]We know that in everything God works for the good of those who love him. They are the people he called, because that was his plan. [29]God knew them before he made the world, and he decided that they would be like his Son so that Jesus would be the firstborn[n] of many brothers. [30]God planned for them to be like his Son; and those he planned to be like his Son, he also called; and those he called, he also made right with him; and those he made right, he also glorified.

God's Love in Christ Jesus

[31]So what should we say about this? If God is with us, no one can defeat us. [32]He did not spare his own Son but gave him for us all. So with Jesus, God will surely give us all things. [33]Who can accuse the people God has chosen? No one, because God is the One who makes them right. [34]Who can say God's people are guilty? No one, because Christ Jesus died, but he was also raised from the dead, and now he is on God's right side, begging God for us. [35]Can anything separate us from the love Christ has for us? Can troubles or problems or sufferings or hunger or nakedness or danger or violent death? [36]As it is written in the Scriptures:[d]

"For you we are in danger of death all
    the time.
People think we are worth no more
    than sheep to be killed."   *Psalm 44:22*

[37]But in all these things we have full victory through God who showed his love for us. [38]Yes, I am sure that neither death, nor life, nor angels, nor ruling spirits, nothing now, nothing in the future, no powers, [39]nothing above us, nothing below us, nor anything else in the whole world will ever be able to separate us from the love of God that is in Christ Jesus our Lord.

God and the Jewish People

9 I am in Christ, and I am telling you the truth; I do not lie. My conscience is ruled by the Holy Spirit,[d] and it tells me I am not lying. [2]I have great sorrow and always

---

"Father"   Literally, "Abba, Father." Jewish children called their fathers "Abba."
firstborn   Here this probably means that Christ was the first in God's family to share God's glory.

feel much sadness. ³I wish I could help my Jewish brothers and sisters, my people. I would even wish that I were cursed and cut off from Christ if that would help them. ⁴They are the people of Israel, God's chosen children. They have seen the glory of God, and they have the agreements that God made between himself and his people. God gave them the law of Moses and the right way of worship and his promises. ⁵They are the descendants*d* of our great ancestors, and they are the earthly family into which Christ was born, who is God over all. Praise him forever!*n* Amen.

⁶It is not that God failed to keep his promise to them. But only some of the people of Israel are truly God's people,*n* ⁷and only some of Abraham's*n* descendants are true children of Abraham. But God said to Abraham: "The descendants I promised you will be from Isaac."*n* ⁸This means that not all of Abraham's descendants are God's true children. Abraham's true children are those who become God's children because of the promise God made to Abraham. ⁹God's promise to Abraham was this: "At the right time I will return, and Sarah will have a son."*n* ¹⁰And that is not all. Rebekah's sons had the same father, our father Isaac. ¹¹⁻¹²But before the two boys were born, God told Rebekah, "The older will serve the younger."*n* This was before the boys had done anything good or bad. God said this so that the one chosen would be chosen because of God's own plan. He was chosen because he was the one God wanted to call, not because of anything he did. ¹³As the Scripture*d* says, "I loved Jacob, but I hated Esau."*n*

¹⁴So what should we say about this? Is God unfair? In no way. ¹⁵God said to Moses, "I will show kindness to anyone to whom I want to show kindness, and I will show mercy to anyone to whom I want to show mercy."*n* ¹⁶So God will choose the one to whom he decides to show mercy; his choice does not depend on what people want or try to do. ¹⁷The Scripture says to the king of Egypt: "I made you king for this reason: to show my power in you so that my name will be talked about in all the earth."*n* ¹⁸So God shows mercy where he wants to show mercy, and he makes stubborn the people he wants to make stubborn.

¹⁹So one of you will ask me: "Then why does God blame us for our sins? Who can fight his will?" ²⁰You are only human, and human beings have no right to question God. An object should not ask the person who made it, "Why did you make me like this?" ²¹The potter can make anything he wants to make. He can use the same clay to make one thing for special use and another thing for daily use.

²²It is the same way with God. He wanted to show his anger and to let people see his power. But he patiently stayed with those people he was angry with — people who were made ready to be destroyed. ²³He waited with patience so that he could make known his rich glory to the people who receive his mercy. He has prepared these people to have his glory, ²⁴and we are those people whom God called. He called us not from the Jews only but also from those who are not Jews. ²⁵As the Scripture says in Hosea:

"I will say, 'You are my people'
    to those I had called 'not my people.'
And I will show my love
    to those people I did not love."

Hosea 2:1, 23

²⁶"They were called,
    'You are not my people,'
but later they will be called
    'children of the living God.' "   *Hosea 1:10*
²⁷And Isaiah cries out about Israel:
"The people of Israel are many,
    like the grains of sand by the sea.
But only a few of them will be saved,

---

born ... forever!   This can also mean, "born. May God, who rules over all things, be praised forever!"
God's people   Literally, "Israel," the people God chose to bring his blessings to the world.
Abraham   Most respected ancestor of the Jews. Every Jew hoped to see Abraham.
"The descendants ... Isaac."   Quotation from Genesis 21:12.
"At ... son."   Quotation from Genesis 18:10, 14.
"The older ... younger."   Quotation from Genesis 25:23.
"I ... Esau."   Quotation from Malachi 1:2-3.
"I ... mercy."   Quotation from Exodus 33:19.
"I ... earth."   Quotation from Exodus 9:16.

²⁸ because the Lord will quickly and completely punish the people on the earth." *Isaiah 10:22-23*

²⁹It is as Isaiah said:

"The Lord All-Powerful
    allowed a few of our descendants to
        live.
Otherwise we would have been
    completely destroyed
    like the cities of Sodom and
        Gomorrah." *n* *Isaiah 1:9*

³⁰So what does all this mean? Those who are not Jews were not trying to make themselves right with God, but they were made right with God because of their faith. ³¹The people of Israel tried to follow a law to make themselves right with God. But they did not succeed, ³²because they tried to make themselves right by the things they did instead of trusting in God to make them right. They stumbled over the stone that causes people to stumble. ³³As it is written in the Scripture:

"I will put in Jerusalem a stone that
    causes people to stumble,
a rock that makes them fall.
Anyone who trusts in him will never be
        disappointed." *Isaiah 8:14; 28:16*

10 Brothers and sisters, the thing I want most is for all the Jews to be saved. That is my prayer to God. ²I can say this about them: They really try to follow God, but they do not know the right way. ³Because they did not know the way that God makes people right with him, they tried to make themselves right in their own way. So they did not accept God's way of making people right. ⁴Christ ended the law so that everyone who believes in him may be right with God.

⁵Moses writes about being made right by following the law. He says, "A person who obeys these things will live because of them." *n* ⁶But this is what the Scripture says about being made right through faith: "Don't say to yourself, 'Who will go up into heaven?' " (That means, "Who will go up to heaven and bring Christ down to earth?") ⁷"And do not say, 'Who will go down into the world below?' " (That means, "Who will go down and bring Christ up from the dead?") ⁸This is what the Scripture says: "The word is near you; it is in your mouth and in your heart." *n* That is the teaching of faith that we are telling. ⁹If you use your mouth to say, "Jesus is Lord," and if you believe in your heart that God raised Jesus from the dead, you will be saved. ¹⁰We believe with our hearts, and so we are made right with God. And we use our mouths to say that we believe, and so we are saved. ¹¹As the Scripture says, "Anyone who trusts in him will never be disappointed." *n* ¹²That Scripture says "anyone" because there is no difference between those who are Jews and those who are not. The same Lord is the Lord of all and gives many blessings to all who trust in him, ¹³as the Scripture says, "Anyone who calls on the Lord will be saved." *n*

¹⁴But before people can ask the Lord for help, they must believe in him; and before they can believe in him, they must hear about him; and for them to hear about the Lord, someone must tell them; ¹⁵and before someone can go and tell them, that person must be sent. It is written, "How beautiful is the person who comes to bring good news." *n*

¹⁶But not all the Jews accepted the good news. Isaiah said, "Lord, who believed what we told them?" *n* ¹⁷So faith comes from hearing the Good News, *d* and people hear the Good News when someone tells them about Christ.

¹⁸But I ask: Didn't people hear the Good News? Yes, they heard — as the Scripture says:

"Their message went out through all the
        world;
    their words go everywhere on earth." *Psalm 19:4*

Sodom and Gomorrah   Two cities that God destroyed because the people were so evil.
"A person ... them."   Quotation from Leviticus 18:5.
Verses 6-8   Quotations from Deuteronomy 9:4; 30:12-14; Psalm 107:26.
"Anyone ... disappointed."   Quotation from Isaiah 28:16.
"Anyone ... saved."   Quotation from Joel 2:32.
"How ... news."   Quotation from Isaiah 52:7.
"Lord, ... them?"   Quotation from Isaiah 53:1.

[19]Again I ask: Didn't the people of Israel understand? Yes, they did understand. First, Moses says:

"I will use those who are not a nation to make you jealous.

I will use a nation that does not understand to make you angry."

Deuteronomy 32:21

[20]Then Isaiah is bold enough to say:

"I was found by those who were not asking me for help.

I made myself known to people who were not looking for me."   *Isaiah 65:1*

[21]But about Israel God says,

"All day long I stood ready to accept people who disobey and are stubborn."

Isaiah 65:2

God Shows Mercy to All People

11 So I ask: Did God throw out his people? No! I myself am an Israelite from the family of Abraham, from the tribe[d] of Benjamin. [2]God chose the Israelites to be his people before they were born, and he has not thrown his people out. Surely you know what the Scripture[d] says about Elijah, how he prayed to God against the people of Israel. [3]"Lord," he said, "they have killed your prophets,[d] and they have destroyed your altars. I am the only prophet left, and now they are trying to kill me, too."[n] [4]But what answer did God give Elijah? He said, "But I have left seven thousand people in Israel who have never bowed down before Baal."[n] [5]It is the same now. There are a few people that God has chosen by his grace. [6]And if he chose them by grace, it is not for the things they have done. If they could be made God's people by what they did, God's gift of grace would not really be a gift.

[7]So, this is what has happened: Although the Israelites tried to be right with God, they did not succeed, but the ones God chose did become right with him. The others were made stubborn and refused to listen to God. [8]As it is written in the Scriptures:[d]

"God gave the people a dull mind so they could not understand."

Isaiah 29:10

"He closed their eyes so they could not see

and their ears so they could not hear. This continues until today."   *Deuteronomy 29:4*

[9]And David says:

"Let their own feasts trap them and cause their ruin;

let their feasts cause them to stumble and be paid back.

[10]Let their eyes be closed so they cannot see

and their backs be forever weak from troubles."   *Psalm 69:22-23*

[11]So I ask: When the Jews fell, did that fall destroy them? No! But their mistake brought salvation to those who are not Jews, in order to make the Jews jealous. [12]The Jews' mistake brought rich blessings for the world, and the Jews' loss brought rich blessings for the non-Jewish people. So surely the world will receive much richer blessings when enough Jews become the kind of people God wants.

[13]Now I am speaking to you who are not Jews. I am an apostle[d] to those who are not Jews, and since I have that work, I will make the most of it. [14]I hope I can make my own people jealous and, in that way, help some of them to be saved. [15]When God turned away from the Jews, he became friends with other people in the world. So when God accepts the Jews, surely that will bring them life after death.

[16]If the first piece of bread is offered to God, then the whole loaf is made holy. If the roots of a tree are holy, then the tree's branches are holy too.

[17]It is as if some of the branches from an olive tree have been broken off. You non-Jewish people are like the branch of a wild olive tree that has been joined to that first tree. You now share the strength and life of the first tree, the Jews. [18]So do not brag about those branches that were broken off. If you brag, remember that you do not support the root, but the root supports you. [19]You will say, "Branches were broken off so that I could be joined to their tree." [20]That is true. But those branches were broken off because

---

"They . . . too."   Quotation from 1 Kings 19:10, 14.
"But . . . Baal."   Quotation from 1 Kings 19:18.

they did not believe, and you continue to be part of the tree only because you believe. Do not be proud, but be afraid. [21]If God did not let the natural branches of that tree stay, then he will not let you stay if you don't believe.

[22]So you see that God is kind and also very strict. He punishes those who stop following him. But God is kind to you, if you continue following in his kindness. If you do not, you will be cut off from the tree. [23]And if the Jews will believe in God again, he will accept them back. God is able to put them back where they were. [24]It is not natural for a wild branch to be part of a good tree. And you who are not Jews are like a branch cut from a wild olive tree and joined to a good olive tree. But since those Jews are like a branch that grew from the good tree, surely they can be joined to their own tree again.

[25]I want you to understand this secret, brothers and sisters, so you will understand that you do not know everything: Part of Israel has been made stubborn, but that will change when many who are not Jews have come to God. [26]And that is how all Israel will be saved. It is written in the Scriptures:

"The Savior will come from Jerusalem;
he will take away all evil from the
family of Jacob.[n]
[27]And I will make this agreement with
those people
when I take away their sins."

Isaiah 59:20-21; 27:9

[28]The Jews refuse to accept the Good News,[d] so they are God's enemies. This has happened to help you who are not Jews. But the Jews are still God's chosen people, and he loves them very much because of the promises he made to their ancestors. [29]God never changes his mind about the people he calls and the things he gives them. [30]At one time you refused to obey God. But now you have received mercy, because those people refused to obey. [31]And now the Jews refuse to obey, because God showed mercy to you. But this happened so that they also can receive mercy from him. [32]God has given all people over to their stubborn ways so that he can show mercy to all.

Praise to God

[33]Yes, God's riches are very great, and his wisdom and knowledge have no end! No one can explain the things God decides or understand his ways. [34]As the Scripture[d] says,

"Who has known the mind of the Lord,
or who has been able to give him
advice?" *Isaiah 40:13*
[35]"No one has ever given God anything
that he must pay back." *Job 41:11*
[36]Yes, God made all things, and everything continues through him and for him. To him be the glory forever! Amen.

Give Your Lives to God

12 So brothers and sisters, since God has shown us great mercy, I beg you to offer your lives as a living sacrifice to him. Your offering must be only for God and pleasing to him, which is the spiritual way for you to worship. [2]Do not change yourselves to be like the people of this world, but be changed within by a new way of thinking. Then you will be able to decide what God wants for you; you will know what is good and pleasing to him and what is perfect. [3]Because God has given me a special gift, I have something to say to everyone among you. Do not think you are better than you are. You must decide what you really are by the amount of faith God has given you. [4]Each one of us has a body with many parts, and these parts all have different uses. [5]In the same way, we are many, but in Christ we are all one body. Each one is a part of that body, and each part belongs to all the other parts. [6]We all have different gifts, each of which came because of the grace God gave us. The person who has the gift of prophecy[d] should use that gift in agreement with the faith. [7]Anyone who has the gift of serving should serve. Anyone who has the gift of teaching should teach. [8]Whoever has the gift of encouraging others should encourage. Whoever has the gift of giving to others should give freely. Anyone who has the gift of being a leader should try hard when he leads. Whoever has the gift of showing mercy to others should do so with joy.

[9]Your love must be real. Hate what is evil, and hold on to what is good. [10]Love each

Jacob Father of the twelve family groups of Israel, the people God chose to be his people.

other like brothers and sisters. Give each other more honor than you want for yourselves. [11]Do not be lazy but work hard, serving the Lord with all your heart. [12]Be joyful because you have hope. Be patient when trouble comes, and pray at all times. [13]Share with God's people who need help. Bring strangers in need into your homes.

[14]Wish good for those who harm you; wish them well and do not curse them. [15]Be happy with those who are happy, and be sad with those who are sad. [16]Live in peace with each other. Do not be proud, but make friends with those who seem unimportant. Do not think how smart you are.

[17]If someone does wrong to you, do not pay him back by doing wrong to him. Try to do what everyone thinks is right. [18]Do your best to live in peace with everyone. [19]My friends, do not try to punish others when they wrong you, but wait for God to punish them with his anger. It is written: "I will punish those who do wrong; I will repay them," [n] says the Lord. [20]But you should do this:

"If your enemy is hungry, feed him;
    if he is thirsty, give him a drink.
Doing this will be like pouring burning
    coals on his head."   *Proverbs 25:21-22*
[21]Do not let evil defeat you, but defeat evil by doing good.

Christians Should Obey the Law

13 All of you must yield to the government rulers. No one rules unless God has given him the power to rule, and no one rules now without that power from God. [2]So those who are against the government are really against what God has commanded. And they will bring punishment on themselves. [3]Those who do right do not have to fear the rulers; only those who do wrong fear them. Do you want to be unafraid of the rulers? Then do what is right, and they will praise you. [4]The ruler is God's servant to help you. But if you do wrong, then be afraid.

He has the power to punish; he is God's servant to punish those who do wrong. [5]So you must yield to the government, not only because you might be punished, but because you know it is right.

[6]This is also why you pay taxes. Rulers are working for God and give their time to their work. [7]Pay everyone, then, what you owe. If you owe any kind of tax, pay it. Show respect and honor to them all.

Loving Others

[8]Do not owe people anything, except always owe love to each other, because the person who loves others has obeyed all the law. [9]The law says, "You must not be guilty of adultery.[d] You must not murder anyone. You must not steal. You must not want to take your neighbor's things." [n] All these commands and all others are really only one rule: "Love your neighbor as you love yourself." [n] [10]Love never hurts a neighbor, so loving is obeying all the law.

[11]Do this because we live in an important time. It is now time for you to wake up from your sleep, because our salvation is nearer now than when we first believed. [12]The "night" [n] is almost finished, and the "day" [n] is almost here. So we should stop doing things that belong to darkness and take up the weapons used for fighting in the light. [13]Let us live in a right way, like people who belong to the day. We should not have wild parties or get drunk. There should be no sexual sins of any kind, no fighting or jealousy. [14]But clothe yourselves with the Lord Jesus Christ and forget about satisfying your sinful self.

Do Not Criticize Other People

14 Accept into your group someone who is weak in faith, and do not argue about opinions. [2]One person believes it is right to eat all kinds of food. [n] But another, who is weak, believes it is right to eat only vegetables. [3]The one who knows that it is

---

"I ... them"   Quotation from Deuteronomy 32:35.
"You ... things."   Quotation from Exodus 20:13-15, 17.
"Love ... yourself."   Quotation from Leviticus 19:18.
"night"   This is used as a symbol of the sinful world we live in. This world will soon end.
"day"   This is used as a symbol of the good time that is coming, when we will be with God.
all ... food   The Jewish law said there were some foods Jews should not eat. When Jews became Christians, some of them did not understand they could now eat all foods.

right to eat any kind of food must not reject the one who eats only vegetables. And the person who eats only vegetables must not think that the one who eats all foods is wrong, because God has accepted that person. [4]You cannot judge another person's servant. The master decides if the servant is doing well or not. And the Lord's servant will do well because the Lord helps him do well.

[5]Some think that one day is more important than another, and others think that every day is the same. Let all be sure in their own mind. [6]Those who think one day is more important than other days are doing that for the Lord. And those who eat all kinds of food are doing that for the Lord, and they give thanks to God. Others who refuse to eat some foods do that for the Lord, and they give thanks to God. [7]We do not live or die for ourselves. [8]If we live, we are living for the Lord, and if we die, we are dying for the Lord. So living or dying, we belong to the Lord.

[9]The reason Christ died and rose from the dead to live again was so he would be Lord over both the dead and the living. [10]So why do you judge your brothers or sisters in Christ? And why do you think you are better than they are? We will all stand before God to be judged, [11]because it is written in the Scriptures:[d]

" 'As surely as I live,' says the Lord,
  'Everyone will bow before me;
  everyone will say that I am God.' "

Isaiah 45:23

[12]So each of us will have to answer to God.

Do Not Cause Others to Sin

[13]For that reason we should stop judging each other. We must make up our minds not to do anything that will make another Christian sin. [14]I am in the Lord Jesus, and I know that there is no food that is wrong to eat. But if a person believes something is wrong, that thing is wrong for him. [15]If you hurt your brother's or sister's faith because of something you eat, you are not really following the way of love. Do not destroy someone's faith by eating food he thinks is wrong, because

Christ died for him. [16]Do not allow what you think is good to become what others say is evil. [17]In the kingdom of God, eating and drinking are not important. The important things are living right with God, peace, and joy in the Holy Spirit.[d] [18]Anyone who serves Christ by living this way is pleasing God and will be accepted by other people.

[19]So let us try to do what makes peace and helps one another. [20]Do not let the eating of food destroy the work of God. All foods are all right to eat, but it is wrong to eat food that causes someone else to sin. [21]It is better not to eat meat or drink wine or do anything that will cause your brother or sister to sin.

[22]Your beliefs about these things should be kept secret between you and God. People are happy if they can do what they think is right without feeling guilty. [23]But those who eat something without being sure it is right are wrong because they did not believe it was right. Anything that is done without believing it is right is a sin.

15 We who are strong in faith should help the weak with their weaknesses, and not please only ourselves. [2]Let each of us please our neighbors for their good, to help them be stronger in faith. [3]Even Christ did not live to please himself. It was as the Scriptures[d] said: "When people insult you, it hurts me."[n] [4]Everything that was written in the past was written to teach us. The Scriptures give us patience and encouragement so that we can have hope. [5]Patience and encouragement come from God. And I pray that God will help you all agree with each other the way Christ Jesus wants. [6]Then you will all be joined together, and you will give glory to God the Father of our Lord Jesus Christ. [7]Christ accepted you, so you should accept each other, which will bring glory to God. [8]I tell you that Christ became a servant of the Jews to show that God's promises to the Jewish ancestors are true. [9]And he also did this so that those who are not Jews could give glory to God for the mercy he gives to them. It is written in the Scriptures:

"So I will praise you among the
  non-Jewish people.

"When . . . me." Quotation from Psalm 69:9.

I will sing praises to your name."

Psalm 18:49

[10]The Scripture also says,

"Be happy, you who are not Jews,
together with his people."

Deuteronomy 32:43

[11]Again the Scripture says,

"All you who are not Jews, praise the
Lord.

All you people, sing praises to him."

Psalm 117:1

[12]And Isaiah says,

"A new king will come from the family
of Jesse.[n]

He will come to rule over the
non-Jewish people,

and they will have hope because of
him."

Isaiah 11:10

[13]I pray that the God who gives hope will
fill you with much joy and peace while you
trust in him. Then your hope will overflow
by the power of the Holy Spirit.[d]

Paul Talks About His Work

[14]My brothers and sisters, I am sure that
you are full of goodness. I know that you
have all the knowledge you need and that
you are able to teach each other. [15]But I have
written to you very openly about some things
I wanted you to remember. I did this because
God gave me this special gift: [16]to be a minister of Christ Jesus to those who are not Jews.
I served God by teaching his Good News,[d] so
that the non-Jewish people could be an offering that God would accept — an offering
made holy by the Holy Spirit.[d]

[17]So I am proud of what I have done for
God in Christ Jesus. [18]I will not talk about
anything except what Christ has done
through me in leading those who are not
Jews to obey God. They have obeyed God
because of what I have said and done, [19]be-
cause of the power of miracles[d] and the great
things they saw, and because of the power of
the Holy Spirit. I preached the Good News
from Jerusalem all the way around to Illyri-
cum, and so I have finished that part of my
work. [20]I always want to preach the Good
News in places where people have never

heard of Christ, because I do not want to
build on the work someone else has already
started. [21]But it is written in the Scriptures:[d]

"Those who were not told about him
will see,

and those who have not heard about
him will understand."   *Isaiah 52:15*

Paul's Plan to Visit Rome

[22]This is the reason I was stopped many
times from coming to you. [23]Now I have finished my work here. Since for many years I
have wanted to come to you, [24]I hope to visit
you on my way to Spain. After I enjoy being
with you for a while, I hope you can help me
on my trip. [25]Now I am going to Jerusalem to
help God's people. [26]The believers in Macedonia and Southern Greece were happy to
give their money to help the poor among
God's people at Jerusalem. [27]They were
happy to do this, and really they owe it to
them. These who are not Jews have shared
in the Jews' spiritual blessings, so they should
use their material possessions to help the
Jews. [28]After I am sure the poor in Jerusalem
get the money that has been given for them,
I will leave for Spain and stop and visit you.
[29]I know that when I come to you I will bring
Christ's full blessing.

[30]Brothers and sisters, I beg you to help me
in my work by praying to God for me. Do this
because of our Lord Jesus and the love that
the Holy Spirit[d] gives us. [31]Pray that I will be
saved from the non-believers in Judea and
that this help I bring to Jerusalem will please
God's people there. [32]Then, if God wants me
to, I will come to you with joy, and together
you and I will have a time of rest. [33]The God
who gives peace be with you all. Amen.

Greetings to the Christians

16 I recommend to you our sister
Phoebe, who is a helper[n] in the
church in Cenchrea. [2]I ask you to accept her
in the Lord in the way God's people should.
Help her with anything she needs, because
she has helped me and many other people
also.

[3]Give my greetings to Priscilla and Aquila,

Jesse Jesse was the father of David, king of Israel. Jesus was from their family.
helper Literally, "deaconess." This might mean the same as one of the special women helpers in 1 Timothy 3:11.

who work together with me in Christ Jesus [4]and who risked their own lives to save my life. I am thankful to them, and all the non-Jewish churches are thankful as well. [5]Also, greet for me the church that meets at their house.

Greetings to my dear friend Epenetus, who was the first person in the country of Asia to follow Christ. [6]Greetings to Mary, who worked very hard for you. [7]Greetings to Andronicus and Junia, my relatives, who were in prison with me. They are very important apostles. They were believers in Christ before I was. [8]Greetings to Ampliatus, my dear friend in the Lord. [9]Greetings to Urbanus, a worker together with me for Christ. And greetings to my dear friend Stachys. [10]Greetings to Apelles, who was tested and proved that he truly loves Christ. Greetings to all those who are in the family of Aristobulus. [11]Greetings to Herodion, my fellow citizen. Greetings to all those in the family of Narcissus who belong to the Lord. [12]Greetings to Tryphena and Tryphosa, women who work very hard for the Lord. Greetings to my dear friend Persis, who also has worked very hard for the Lord. [13]Greetings to Rufus, who is a special person in the Lord, and to his mother, who has been like a mother to me also. [14]Greetings to Asyncritus, Phlegon, Hermes, Patrobas, Hermas, and all the brothers who are with them. [15]Greetings to Philologus and Julia, Nereus and his sister, and Olympas, and to all God's people with them. [16]Greet each other with a holy kiss. All of Christ's churches send greetings to you.

[17]Brothers and sisters, I ask you to look out for those who cause people to be against each other and who upset other people's faith. They are against the true teaching you learned, so stay away from them. [18]Such people are not serving our Lord Christ but are only doing what pleases themselves. They use fancy talk and fine words to fool the minds of those who do not know about evil. [19]All the believers have heard that you obey, so I am very happy because of you. But I want you to be wise in what is good and innocent in what is evil.

[20]The God who brings peace will soon defeat Satan and give you power over him.

The grace of our Lord Jesus be with you.

[21]Timothy, a worker together with me, sends greetings, as well as Lucius, Jason, and Sosipater, my relatives.

[22]I am Tertius, and I am writing this letter from Paul. I send greetings to you in the Lord.

[23]Gaius is letting me and the whole church here use his home. He also sends greetings to you, as do Erastus, the city treasurer, and our brother Quartus. [24] *n*

[25]Glory to God who can make you strong in faith by the Good News[d] that I tell people and by the message about Jesus Christ. The message about Christ is the secret that was hidden for long ages past but is now made known. [26]It has been made clear through the writings of the prophets.[d] And by the command of the eternal God it is made known to all nations that they might believe and obey.

[27]To the only wise God be glory forever through Jesus Christ! Amen.

Verse 24 Some Greek copies add verse 24: "The grace of our Lord Jesus Christ be with all of you. Amen."

1 CORINTHIANS

Help for a Church with Problems

1 From Paul. God called me to be an apostle*d* of Christ Jesus because that is what God wanted. Also from Sosthenes, our brother in Christ.

²To the church of God in Corinth, to you who have been made holy in Christ Jesus. You were called to be God's holy people with all people everywhere who pray in the name of the Lord Jesus Christ — their Lord and ours:

³Grace and peace to you from God our Father and the Lord Jesus Christ.

Paul Gives Thanks to God

⁴I always thank my God for you because of the grace God has given you in Christ Jesus. ⁵I thank God because in Christ you have been made rich in every way, in all your speaking and in all your knowledge. ⁶Just as our witness about Christ has been guaranteed to you, ⁷so you have every gift from God while you wait for our Lord Jesus Christ to come again. ⁸Jesus will keep you strong until the end so that there will be no wrong in you on the day our Lord Jesus Christ comes again. ⁹God, who has called you to share everything with his Son, Jesus Christ our Lord, is faithful.

Problems in the Church

¹⁰I beg you, brothers and sisters,*n* by the name of our Lord Jesus Christ that all of you agree with each other and not be split into groups. I beg that you be completely joined together by having the same kind of thinking and the same purpose. ¹¹My brothers and sisters, some people from Chloe's family have told me quite plainly that there are quarrels among you. ¹²This is what I mean: One of you says, "I follow Paul"; another says, "I

follow Apollos"; another says, "I follow Peter"; and another says, "I follow Christ." ¹³Christ has been divided up into different groups! Did Paul die on the cross for you? No! Were you baptized in the name of Paul? No! ¹⁴I thank God I did not baptize any of you except Crispus and Gaius ¹⁵so that now no one can say you were baptized in my name. ¹⁶(I also baptized the family of Stephanas, but I do not remember that I baptized anyone else.) ¹⁷Christ did not send me to baptize people but to preach the Good News.*d* And he sent me to preach the Good News without using words of human wisdom so that the cross*n* of Christ would not lose its power.

Christ Is God's Power and Wisdom

¹⁸The teaching about the cross is foolishness to those who are being lost, but to us who are being saved it is the power of God. ¹⁹It is written in the Scriptures:*d*

"I will cause the wise men to lose their
    wisdom;
I will make the wise men unable to
    understand." *Isaiah 29:14*

²⁰Where is the wise person? Where is the educated person? Where is the skilled talker of this world? God has made the wisdom of the world foolish. ²¹In the wisdom of God the world did not know God through its own wisdom. So God chose to use the message that sounds foolish to save those who believe. ²²The Jews ask for miracles,*d* and the Greeks want wisdom. ²³But we preach a crucified Christ. This is a big problem to the Jews, and it is foolishness to those who are not Jews. ²⁴But Christ is the power of God and the wisdom of God to those people God has called — Jews and Greeks. ²⁵Even the foolishness of God is wiser than human wis-

---

brothers and sisters Although the Greek text says "brothers" here and throughout this book, Paul's words were meant for the entire church, including men and women.
cross Paul uses the cross as a picture of the gospel, the story of Christ's death and rising from the dead to pay for people's sins. The cross, or Christ's death, was God's way to save people.

dom, and the weakness of God is stronger than human strength.

26Brothers and sisters, look at what you were when God called you. Not many of you were wise in the way the world judges wisdom. Not many of you had great influence. Not many of you came from important families. 27But God chose the foolish things of the world to shame the wise, and he chose the weak things of the world to shame the strong. 28He chose what the world thinks is unimportant and what the world looks down on and thinks is nothing in order to destroy what the world thinks is important. 29God did this so that no one can brag in his presence. 30Because of God you are in Christ Jesus, who has become for us wisdom from God. In Christ we are put right with God, and have been made holy, and have been set free from sin. 31So, as the Scripture*d* says, "If someone wants to brag, he should brag only about the Lord." *n*

The Message of Christ's Death

2 Dear brothers and sisters, when I came to you, I did not come preaching God's secret with fancy words or a show of human wisdom. 2I decided that while I was with you I would forget about everything except Jesus Christ and his death on the cross. 3So when I came to you, I was weak and fearful and trembling. 4My teaching and preaching were not with words of human wisdom that persuade people but with proof of the power that the Spirit*d* gives. 5This was so that your faith would be in God's power and not in human wisdom.

God's Wisdom

6However, I speak a wisdom to those who are mature. But this wisdom is not from this world or from the rulers of this world, who are losing their power. 7I speak God's secret wisdom, which he has kept hidden. Before the world began, God planned this wisdom for our glory. 8None of the rulers of this world understood it. If they had, they would not have crucified the Lord of glory. 9But as it is written in the Scriptures:*d*

"No one has ever seen this,
    and no one has ever heard about it.
No one has ever imagined
    what God has prepared for those
    who love him."   *Isaiah 64:4*

10But God has shown us these things through the Spirit.*d*

The Spirit searches out all things, even the deep secrets of God. 11Who knows the thoughts that another person has? Only a person's spirit that lives within him knows his thoughts. It is the same with God. No one knows the thoughts of God except the Spirit of God. 12Now we did not receive the spirit of the world, but we received the Spirit that is from God so that we can know all that God has given us. 13And we speak about these things, not with words taught us by human wisdom but with words taught us by the Spirit. And so we explain spiritual truths to spiritual people. 14A person who does not have the Spirit does not accept the truths that come from the Spirit of God. That person thinks they are foolish and cannot understand them, because they can only be judged to be true by the Spirit. 15The spiritual person is able to judge all things, but no one can judge him. The Scripture says:

16"Who has known the mind of the Lord?
    Who has been able to teach him?"

                                Isaiah 40:13

But we have the mind of Christ.

Following People Is Wrong

3 Brothers and sisters, in the past I could not talk to you as I talk to spiritual people. I had to talk to you as I would to people without the Spirit — babies in Christ. 2The teaching I gave you was like milk, not solid food, because you were not able to take solid food. And even now you are not ready. 3You are still not spiritual, because there is jealousy and quarreling among you, and this shows that you are not spiritual. You are acting like people of the world. 4One of you says, "I belong to Paul," and another says, "I belong to Apollos." When you say things like this, you are acting like people of the world.

5Is Apollos important? No! Is Paul important? No! We are only servants of God who

---

"If ... Lord."   Quotation from Jeremiah 9:24.

helped you believe. Each one of us did the work God gave us to do. ⁶I planted the seed, and Apollos watered it. But God is the One who made it grow. ⁷So the one who plants is not important, and the one who waters is not important. Only God, who makes things grow, is important. ⁸The one who plants and the one who waters have the same purpose, and each will be rewarded for his own work. ⁹We are God's workers, working together; you are like God's farm, God's house.

¹⁰Using the gift God gave me, I laid the foundation of that house like an expert builder. Others are building on that foundation, but all people should be careful how they build on it. ¹¹The foundation that has already been laid is Jesus Christ, and no one can lay down any other foundation. ¹²But if people build on that foundation, using gold, silver, jewels, wood, grass, or straw, ¹³their work will be clearly seen, because the Day of Judgment[n] will make it visible. That Day will appear with fire, and the fire will test everyone's work to show what sort of work it was. ¹⁴If the building that has been put on the foundation still stands, the builder will get a reward. ¹⁵But if the building is burned up, the builder will suffer loss. The builder will be saved, but it will be as one who escaped from a fire.

¹⁶Don't you know that you are God's temple and that God's Spirit[d] lives in you? ¹⁷If anyone destroys God's temple, God will destroy that person, because God's temple is holy and you are that temple.

¹⁸Do not fool yourselves. If you think you are wise in this world, you should become a fool so that you can become truly wise, ¹⁹because the wisdom of this world is foolishness with God. It is written in the Scriptures,[d] "He catches those who are wise in their own clever traps."[n] ²⁰It is also written in the Scriptures, "The Lord knows what wise people think. He knows their thoughts are just a puff of wind."[n] ²¹So you should not brag about human leaders. All things belong to you: ²²Paul, Apollos, and Peter; the world, life, death, the present, and the future—all

these belong to you. ²³And you belong to Christ, and Christ belongs to God.

Apostles Are Servants of Christ

4 People should think of us as servants of Christ, the ones God has trusted with his secrets. ²Now in this way those who are trusted with something valuable must show they are worthy of that trust. ³As for myself, I do not care if I am judged by you or by any human court. I do not even judge myself. ⁴I know of no wrong I have done, but this does not make me right before the Lord. The Lord is the One who judges me. ⁵So do not judge before the right time; wait until the Lord comes. He will bring to light things that are now hidden in darkness, and will make known the secret purposes of people's hearts. Then God will praise each one of them.

⁶Brothers and sisters, I have used Apollos and myself as examples so you could learn through us the meaning of the saying, "Follow only what is written in the Scriptures."[d] Then you will not be more proud of one person than another. ⁷Who says you are better than others? What do you have that was not given to you? And if it was given to you, why do you brag as if you did not receive it as a gift?

⁸You think you already have everything you need. You think you are rich. You think you have become kings without us. I wish you really were kings so we could be kings together with you. ⁹But it seems to me that God has put us apostles[d] in last place, like those sentenced to die. We are like a show for the whole world to see—angels and people. ¹⁰We are fools for Christ's sake, but you are very wise in Christ. We are weak, but you are strong. You receive honor, but we are shamed. ¹¹Even to this very hour we do not have enough to eat or drink or to wear. We are often beaten, and we have no homes in which to live. ¹²We work hard with our own hands for our food. When people curse us, we bless them. When they hurt us, we put up with it. ¹³When they tell evil lies

Day of Judgment   The day Christ will come to judge all people and take his people home to live with him.
"He . . . traps."   Quotation from Job 5:13.
"The Lord . . . wind."   Quotation from Psalm 94:11.

about us, we speak nice words about them. Even today, we are treated as though we were the garbage of the world — the filth of the earth.

[14]I am not trying to make you feel ashamed. I am writing this to give you a warning as my own dear children. [15]For though you may have ten thousand teachers in Christ, you do not have many fathers. Through the Good News[d] I became your father in Christ Jesus, [16]so I beg you, please follow my example. [17]That is why I am sending to you Timothy, my son in the Lord. I love Timothy, and he is faithful. He will help you remember my way of life in Christ Jesus, just as I teach it in all the churches everywhere.

[18]Some of you have become proud, thinking that I will not come to you again. [19]But I will come to you very soon if the Lord wishes. Then I will know what the proud ones do, not what they say, [20]because the kingdom of God is present not in talk but in power. [21]Which do you want: that I come to you with punishment or with love and gentleness?

Wickedness in the Church

5 It is actually being said that there is sexual sin among you. And it is a kind that does not happen even among people who do not know God. A man there has his father's wife. [2]And you are proud! You should have been filled with sadness so that the man who did this should be put out of your group. [3]I am not there with you in person, but I am with you in spirit. And I have already judged the man who did that sin as if I were really there. [4]When you meet together in the name of our Lord Jesus, and I meet with you in spirit with the power of our Lord Jesus, [5]then hand this man over to Satan. So his sinful self[n] will be destroyed, and his spirit will be saved on the day of the Lord.

[6]Your bragging is not good. You know the saying, "Just a little yeast makes the whole batch of dough rise." [7]Take out all the old yeast so that you will be a new batch of dough without yeast, which you really are.

For Christ, our Passover[d] lamb, has been sacrificed. [8]So let us celebrate this feast, but not with the bread that has the old yeast — the yeast of sin and wickedness. Let us celebrate this feast with the bread that has no yeast — the bread of goodness and truth.

[9]I wrote you in my earlier letter not to associate with those who sin sexually. [10]But I did not mean you should not associate with those of this world who sin sexually, or with the greedy, or robbers, or those who worship idols. To get away from them you would have to leave this world. [11]I am writing to tell you that you must not associate with those who call themselves believers in Christ but who sin sexually, or are greedy, or worship idols, or abuse others with words, or get drunk, or cheat people. Do not even eat with people like that.

[12-13]It is not my business to judge those who are not part of the church. God will judge them. But you must judge the people who are part of the church. The Scripture[d] says, "You must get rid of the evil person among you."[n]

Judging Problems Among Christians

6 When you have something against another Christian, how can you bring yourself to go before judges who are not right with God? Why do you not let God's people decide who is right? [2]Surely you know that God's people will judge the world. So if you are to judge the world, are you not able to judge small cases as well? [3]You know that in the future we will judge angels, so surely we can judge the ordinary things of this life. [4]If you have ordinary cases that must be judged, are you going to appoint people as judges who mean nothing to the church? [5]I say this to shame you. Surely there is someone among you wise enough to judge a complaint between believers. [6]But now one believer goes to court against another believer — and you do this in front of unbelievers!

[7]The fact that you have lawsuits against each other shows that you are already defeated. Why not let yourselves be wronged? Why not let yourselves be cheated? [8]But you

---

sinful self Literally, "flesh." This could also mean his body.
"You ... you." Quotation from Deuteronomy 17:7; 19:19; 22:21, 24; 24:7.

yourselves do wrong and cheat, and you do this to other believers!

9-10Surely you know that the people who do wrong will not inherit God's kingdom. Do not be fooled. Those who sin sexually, worship idols, take part in adultery,*d* those who are male prostitutes,*d* or men who have sexual relations with other men, those who steal, are greedy, get drunk, lie about others, or rob — these people will not inherit God's kingdom. 11In the past, some of you were like that, but you were washed clean. You were made holy, and you were made right with God in the name of the Lord Jesus Christ and in the Spirit of our God.

Use Your Bodies for God's Glory

12"I am allowed to do all things," but all things are not good for me to do. "I am allowed to do all things," but I will not let anything make me its slave. 13"Food is for the stomach, and the stomach for food," but God will destroy them both. The body is not for sexual sin but for the Lord, and the Lord is for the body. 14By his power God has raised the Lord from the dead and will also raise us from the dead. 15Surely you know that your bodies are parts of Christ himself. So I must never take the parts of Christ and join them to a prostitute!*d* 16It is written in the Scriptures,*d* "The two will become one body."*n* So you should know that anyone who joins with a prostitute becomes one body with the prostitute. 17But the one who joins with the Lord is one spirit with the Lord.

18So run away from sexual sin. Every other sin people do is outside their bodies, but those who sin sexually sin against their own bodies. 19You should know that your body is a temple for the Holy Spirit*d* who is in you. You have received the Holy Spirit from God. So you do not belong to yourselves, 20because you were bought by God for a price. So honor God with your bodies.

About Marriage

7 Now I will discuss the things you wrote me about. It is good for a man not to have sexual relations with a woman. 2But because sexual sin is a danger, each man should have his own wife, and each woman should have her own husband. 3The husband should give his wife all that he owes her as his wife. And the wife should give her husband all that she owes him as her husband. 4The wife does not have full rights over her own body; her husband shares them. And the husband does not have full rights over his own body; his wife shares them. 5Do not refuse to give your bodies to each other, unless you both agree to stay away from sexual relations for a time so you can give your time to prayer. Then come together again so Satan cannot tempt you because of a lack of self-control. 6I say this to give you permission to stay away from sexual relations for a time. It is not a command to do so. 7I wish that everyone were like me, but each person has his own gift from God. One has one gift, another has another gift.

8Now for those who are not married and for the widows I say this: It is good for them to stay unmarried as I am. 9But if they cannot control themselves, they should marry. It is better to marry than to burn with sexual desire.

10Now I give this command for the married people. (The command is not from me; it is from the Lord.) A wife should not leave her husband. 11But if she does leave, she must not marry again, or she should make up with her husband. Also the husband should not divorce his wife.

12For all the others I say this (I am saying this, not the Lord): If a Christian man has a wife who is not a believer, and she is happy to live with him, he must not divorce her. 13And if a Christian woman has a husband who is not a believer, and he is happy to live with her, she must not divorce him. 14The husband who is not a believer is made holy through his believing wife. And the wife who is not a believer is made holy through her believing husband. If this were not true, your children would not be clean,*d* but now your children are holy.

15But if those who are not believers decide to leave, let them leave. When this happens, the Christian man or woman is free. But God called us to live in peace. 16Wife, you don't

---

"The two . . . body." Quotation from Genesis 2:24.

know; maybe you will save your husband. And husband, you don't know; maybe you will save your wife.

Live as God Called You

[17]But in any case each one of you should continue to live the way God has given you to live — the way you were when God called you. This is a rule I make in all the churches. [18]If a man was already circumcised[d] when he was called, he should not undo his circumcision. If a man was without circumcision when he was called, he should not be circumcised. [19]It is not important if a man is circumcised or not. The important thing is obeying God's commands. [20]Each one of you should stay the way you were when God called you. [21]If you were a slave when God called you, do not let that bother you. But if you can be free, then make good use of your freedom. [22]Those who were slaves when the Lord called them are free persons who belong to the Lord. In the same way, those who were free when they were called are now Christ's slaves. [23]You all were bought at a great price, so do not become slaves of people. [24]Brothers and sisters, each of you should stay as you were when you were called, and stay there with God.

Questions About Getting Married

[25]Now I write about people who are not married. I have no command from the Lord about this; I give my opinion. But I can be trusted, because the Lord has shown me mercy. [26]The present time is a time of trouble, so I think it is good for you to stay the way you are. [27]If you have a wife, do not try to become free from her. If you are not married, do not try to find a wife. [28]But if you decide to marry, you have not sinned. And if a girl who has never married decides to marry, she has not sinned. But those who marry will have trouble in this life, and I want you to be free from trouble.

[29]Brothers and sisters, this is what I mean: We do not have much time left. So starting now, those who have wives should live as if they had no wives. [30]Those who are crying should live as if they were not crying. Those who are happy should live as if they were not happy. Those who buy things should live as if they own nothing. [31]Those who use the things of the world should live as if they were not using them, because this world in its present form will soon be gone.

[32]I want you to be free from worry. A man who is not married is busy with the Lord's work, trying to please the Lord. [33]But a man who is married is busy with things of the world, trying to please his wife. [34]He must think about two things — pleasing his wife and pleasing the Lord. A woman who is not married or a girl who has never married is busy with the Lord's work. She wants to be holy in body and spirit. But a married woman is busy with things of the world, as to how she can please her husband. [35]I am saying this to help you, not to limit you. But I want you to live in the right way, to give yourselves fully to the Lord without concern for other things.

[36]If a man thinks he is not doing the right thing with the girl he is engaged to, if she is almost past the best age to marry and he feels he should marry her, he should do what he wants. They should get married. It is no sin. [37]But if a man is sure in his mind that there is no need for marriage, and has his own desires under control, and has decided not to marry the one to whom he is engaged, he is doing the right thing. [38]So the man who marries his girl does right, but the man who does not marry will do better.

[39]A woman must stay with her husband as long as he lives. But if her husband dies, she is free to marry any man she wants, but she must marry in the Lord. [40]The woman is happier if she does not marry again. This is my opinion, but I believe I also have God's Spirit.

About Food Offered to Idols

8 Now I will write about meat that is sacrificed to idols. We know that "we all have knowledge." Knowledge puffs you up with pride, but love builds up. [2]If you think you know something, you do not yet know anything as you should. [3]But if any person loves God, that person is known by God.

[4]So this is what I say about eating meat sacrificed to idols: We know that an idol is really nothing in the world, and we know there is only one God. [5]Even though there are things called gods, in heaven or on earth

(and there are many "gods" and "lords"), ⁶for us there is only one God — our Father. All things came from him, and we live for him. And there is only one Lord — Jesus Christ. All things were made through him, and we also were made through him.

⁷But not all people know this. Some people are still so used to idols that when they eat meat, they still think of it as being sacrificed to an idol. Because their conscience is weak, when they eat it, they feel guilty. ⁸But food will not bring us closer to God. Refusing to eat does not make us less pleasing to God, and eating does not make us better in God's sight.

⁹But be careful that your freedom does not cause those who are weak in faith to fall into sin. ¹⁰You have "knowledge," so you eat in an idol's temple. *n* But someone who is weak in faith might see you eating there and be encouraged to eat meat sacrificed to idols while thinking it is wrong to do so. ¹¹This weak believer for whom Christ died is ruined because of your "knowledge." ¹²When you sin against your brothers and sisters in Christ like this and cause them to do what they feel is wrong, you are also sinning against Christ. ¹³So if the food I eat causes them to fall into sin, I will never eat meat again so that I will not cause any of them to sin.

Paul Is like the Other Apostles

9 I am a free man. I am an apostle.*d* I have seen Jesus our Lord. You people are all an example of my work in the Lord. ²If others do not accept me as an apostle, surely you do, because you are proof that I am an apostle in the Lord.

³This is the answer I give people who want to judge me: ⁴Do we not have the right to eat and drink? ⁵Do we not have the right to bring a believing wife with us when we travel as do the other apostles and the Lord's brothers and Peter? ⁶Are Barnabas and I the only ones who must work to earn our living? ⁷No soldier ever serves in the army and pays his own salary. No one ever plants a vineyard without eating some of the grapes. No person takes

care of a flock without drinking some of the milk.

⁸I do not say this by human authority; God's law also says the same thing. ⁹It is written in the law of Moses: "When an ox is working in the grain, do not cover its mouth to keep it from eating." *n* When God said this, was he thinking only about oxen? No. ¹⁰He was really talking about us. Yes, that Scripture*d* was written for us, because it goes on to say: "The one who plows and the one who works in the grain should hope to get some of the grain for their work." ¹¹Since we planted spiritual seed among you, is it too much if we should harvest from you some things for this life? ¹²If others have the right to get something from you, surely we have this right, too. But we do not use it. No, we put up with everything ourselves so that we will not keep anyone from believing the Good News*d* of Christ. ¹³Surely you know that those who work at the Temple*d* get their food from the Temple, and those who serve at the altar get part of what is offered at the altar. ¹⁴In the same way, the Lord has commanded that those who tell the Good News should get their living from this work.

¹⁵But I have not used any of these rights. And I am not writing this now to get anything from you. I would rather die than to have my reason for bragging taken away. ¹⁶Telling the Good News does not give me any reason for bragging. Telling the Good News is my duty — something I must do. And how terrible it will be for me if I do not tell the Good News. ¹⁷If I preach because it is my own choice, I have a reward. But if I preach and it is not my choice to do so, I am only doing the duty that was given to me. ¹⁸So what reward do I get? This is my reward: that when I tell the Good News I can offer it freely. I do not use my full rights in my work of preaching the Good News.

¹⁹I am free and belong to no one. But I make myself a slave to all people to win as many as I can. ²⁰To the Jews I became like a Jew to win the Jews. I myself am not ruled by the law. But to those who are ruled by the

---

idol's temple   Building where a god is worshiped.
"When an ox . . . eating."   Quotation from Deuteronomy 25:4.

law I became like a person who is ruled by the law. I did this to win those who are ruled by the law. [21]To those who are without the law I became like a person who is without the law. I did this to win those people who are without the law. (But really, I am not without God's law — I am ruled by Christ's law.) [22]To those who are weak, I became weak so I could win the weak. I have become all things to all people so I could save some of them in any way possible. [23]I do all this because of the Good News and so I can share in its blessings.

[24]You know that in a race all the runners run, but only one gets the prize. So run to win! [25]All those who compete in the games use self-control so they can win a crown. That crown is an earthly thing that lasts only a short time, but our crown will never be destroyed. [26]So I do not run without a goal. I fight like a boxer who is hitting something — not just the air. [27]I treat my body hard and make it my slave so that I myself will not be disqualified after I have preached to others.

Warnings from Israel's Past

10 Brothers and sisters, I want you to know what happened to our ancestors who followed Moses. They were all under the cloud and all went through the sea. [2]They were all baptized as followers of Moses in the cloud and in the sea. [3]They all ate the same spiritual food, [4]and all drank the same spiritual drink. They drank from that spiritual rock that followed them, and that rock was Christ. [5]But God was not pleased with most of them, so they died in the desert.

[6]And these things happened as examples for us, to stop us from wanting evil things as those people did. [7]Do not worship idols, as some of them did. Just as it is written in the Scriptures: *d* "They sat down to eat and drink, and then they got up and sinned sexually." *n* [8]We must not take part in sexual sins, as some of them did. In one day twenty-three thousand of them died because of their sins. [9]We must not test Christ as some of them

did; they were killed by snakes. [10]Do not complain as some of them did; they were killed by the angel that destroys.

[11]The things that happened to those people are examples. They were written down to teach us, because we live in a time when all these things of the past have reached their goal. [12]If you think you are strong, you should be careful not to fall. [13]The only temptation that has come to you is that which everyone has. But you can trust God, who will not permit you to be tempted more than you can stand. But when you are tempted, he will also give you a way to escape so that you will be able to stand it.

[14]So, my dear friends, run away from the worship of idols. [15]I am speaking to you as to intelligent people; judge for yourselves what I say. [16]We give thanks for the cup of blessing, *n* which is a sharing in the blood of Christ. And the bread that we break is a sharing in the body of Christ. [17]Because there is one loaf of bread, we who are many are one body, because we all share that one loaf.

[18]Think about the Israelites: Do not those who eat the sacrifices share in the altar? [19]I do not mean that the food sacrificed to an idol is important. I do not mean that an idol is anything at all. [20]But I say that what is sacrificed to idols is offered to demons, *d* not to God. And I do not want you to share anything with demons. [21]You cannot drink the cup of the Lord and the cup of demons also. You cannot share in the Lord's table and the table of demons. [22]Are we trying to make the Lord jealous? We are not stronger than he is, are we?

How to Use Christian Freedom

[23]"We are allowed to do all things," but all things are not good for us to do. "We are allowed to do all things," but not all things help others grow stronger. [24]Do not look out only for yourselves. Look out for the good of others also.

[25]Eat any meat that is sold in the meat market. Do not ask questions to see if it is meat you think is wrong to eat. [26]You may

---

"They ... sexually." Quotation from Exodus 32:6.
cup of blessing The cup of the fruit of the vine that Christians thank God for and drink at the Lord's Supper.

eat it, "because the earth belongs to the Lord, and everything in it." [n]

27Those who are not believers may invite you to eat with them. If you want to go, eat anything that is put before you. Do not ask questions to see if you think it might be wrong to eat. 28But if anyone says to you, "That food was offered to idols," do not eat it. Do not eat it because of that person who told you and because eating it might be thought to be wrong. 29I don't mean you think it is wrong, but the other person might. But why, you ask, should my freedom be judged by someone else's conscience? 30If I eat the meal with thankfulness, why am I criticized because of something for which I thank God?

31The answer is, if you eat or drink, or if you do anything, do it all for the glory of God. 32Never do anything that might hurt others—Jews, Greeks, or God's church—33just as I, also, try to please everybody in every way. I am not trying to do what is good for me but what is good for most people so they can be saved.

11 Follow my example, as I follow the example of Christ.

Being Under Authority

2I praise you because you remember me in everything, and you follow closely the teachings just as I gave them to you. 3But I want you to understand this: The head of every man is Christ, the head of a woman is the man,[n] and the head of Christ is God. 4Every man who prays or prophesies[d] with his head covered brings shame to his head. 5But every woman who prays or prophesies with her head uncovered brings shame to her head. She is the same as a woman who has her head shaved. 6If a woman does not cover her head, she should have her hair cut off. But since it is shameful for a woman to cut off her hair or to shave her head, she should cover her head. 7But a man should not cover his head, because he is the likeness and glory of God. But woman is man's glory. 8Man did not come from woman, but woman came

from man. 9And man was not made for woman, but woman was made for man. 10So that is why a woman should have a symbol of authority on her head, because of the angels.

11But in the Lord women are not independent of men, and men are not independent of women. 12This is true because woman came from man, but also man is born from woman. But everything comes from God. 13Decide this for yourselves: Is it right for a woman to pray to God with her head uncovered? 14Even nature itself teaches you that wearing long hair is shameful for a man. 15But long hair is a woman's glory. Long hair is given to her as a covering. 16Some people may still want to argue about this, but I would add that neither we nor the churches of God have any other practice.

The Lord's Supper

17In the things I tell you now I do not praise you, because when you come together you do more harm than good. 18First, I hear that when you meet together as a church you are divided, and I believe some of this. 19(It is necessary to have differences among you so that it may be clear which of you really have God's approval.) 20When you come together, you are not really eating the Lord's Supper.[n] 21This is because when you eat, each person eats without waiting for the others. Some people do not get enough to eat, while others have too much to drink. 22You can eat and drink in your own homes! You seem to think God's church is not important, and you embarrass those who are poor. What should I tell you? Should I praise you? I do not praise you for doing this.

23The teaching I gave you is the same teaching I received from the Lord: On the night when the Lord Jesus was handed over to be killed, he took bread 24and gave thanks for it. Then he broke the bread and said, "This is my body; it is for you. Do this to remember me." 25In the same way, after they ate, Jesus took the cup. He said, "This cup is the new agreement that is sealed with the

"because ... it"   Quotation from Psalms 24:1; 50:12; 89:11.
the man   This could also mean "her husband."
Lord's Supper   The meal Jesus told his followers to eat to remember him (Luke 22:14-20).

blood of my death. When you drink this, do it to remember me." ²⁶Every time you eat this bread and drink this cup you are telling others about the Lord's death until he comes.

²⁷So a person who eats the bread or drinks the cup of the Lord in a way that is not worthy of it will be guilty of sinning against the body and the blood of the Lord. ²⁸Look into your own hearts before you eat the bread and drink the cup, ²⁹because all who eat the bread and drink the cup without recognizing the body eat and drink judgment against themselves. ³⁰That is why many in your group are sick and weak, and many have died. ³¹But if we judged ourselves in the right way, God would not judge us. ³²But when the Lord judges us, he punishes us so that we will not be destroyed along with the world.

³³So my brothers and sisters, when you come together to eat, wait for each other. ³⁴Anyone who is too hungry should eat at home so that in meeting together you will not bring God's judgment on yourselves. I will tell you what to do about the other things when I come.

Gifts from the Holy Spirit

12 Now, brothers and sisters, I want you to understand about spiritual gifts. ²You know the way you lived before you were believers. You let yourselves be influenced and led away to worship idols — things that could not speak. ³So I want you to understand that no one who is speaking with the help of God's Spirit says, "Jesus be cursed." And no one can say, "Jesus is Lord," without the help of the Holy Spirit.*d*

⁴There are different kinds of gifts, but they are all from the same Spirit. ⁵There are different ways to serve but the same Lord to serve. ⁶And there are different ways that God works through people but the same God. God works in all of us in everything we do. ⁷Something from the Spirit can be seen in each person, for the common good. ⁸The Spirit gives one person the ability to speak with wisdom, and the same Spirit gives another the ability to speak with knowledge. ⁹The same Spirit gives faith to one person. And, to another, that one Spirit gives gifts of

healing. ¹⁰The Spirit gives to another person the power to do miracles,*d* to another the ability to prophesy.*d* And he gives to another the ability to know the difference between good and evil spirits. The Spirit gives one person the ability to speak in different kinds of languages*n* and to another the ability to interpret those languages. ¹¹One Spirit, the same Spirit, does all these things, and the Spirit decides what to give each person.

The Body of Christ Works Together

¹²A person's body is only one thing, but it has many parts. Though there are many parts to a body, all those parts make only one body. Christ is like that also. ¹³Some of us are Jews, and some are Greeks. Some of us are slaves, and some are free. But we were all baptized into one body through one Spirit.*d* And we were all made to share in the one Spirit.

¹⁴The human body has many parts. ¹⁵The foot might say, "Because I am not a hand, I am not part of the body." But saying this would not stop the foot from being a part of the body. ¹⁶The ear might say, "Because I am not an eye, I am not part of the body." But saying this would not stop the ear from being a part of the body. ¹⁷If the whole body were an eye, it would not be able to hear. If the whole body were an ear, it would not be able to smell. ¹⁸⁻¹⁹If each part of the body were the same part, there would be no body. But truly God put all the parts, each one of them, in the body as he wanted them. ²⁰So then there are many parts, but only one body.

²¹The eye cannot say to the hand, "I don't need you!" And the head cannot say to the foot, "I don't need you!" ²²No! Those parts of the body that seem to be the weaker are really necessary. ²³And the parts of the body we think are less are the parts to which we give the most honor. We give special respect to the parts we want to hide. ²⁴The more respectable parts of our body need no special care. But God put the body together and gave more honor to the parts that need it ²⁵so our body would not be divided. God wanted the different parts to care the same for each other. ²⁶If one part of the body suffers, all the

---

languages   This can also be translated "tongues."

other parts suffer with it. Or if one part of our body is honored, all the other parts share its honor.

27Together you are the body of Christ, and each one of you is a part of that body. 28In the church God has given a place first to apostles,*d* second to prophets,*d* and third to teachers. Then God has given a place to those who do miracles,*d* those who have gifts of healing, those who can help others, those who are able to govern, and those who can speak in different languages.*n* 29Not all are apostles. Not all are prophets. Not all are teachers. Not all do miracles. 30Not all have gifts of healing. Not all speak in different languages. Not all interpret those languages. 31But you should truly want to have the greater gifts.

Love Is the Greatest Gift

And now I will show you the best way of all.

13 I may speak in different languages*n* of people or even angels. But if I do not have love, I am only a noisy bell or a crashing cymbal. 2I may have the gift of prophecy.*d* I may understand all the secret things of God and have all knowledge, and I may have faith so great I can move mountains. But even with all these things, if I do not have love, then I am nothing. 3I may give away everything I have, and I may even give my body as an offering to be burned.*n* But I gain nothing if I do not have love.

4Love is patient and kind. Love is not jealous, it does not brag, and it is not proud. 5Love is not rude, is not selfish, and does not get upset with others. Love does not count up wrongs that have been done. 6Love is not happy with evil but is happy with the truth. 7Love patiently accepts all things. It always trusts, always hopes, and always remains strong.

8Love never ends. There are gifts of prophecy,*d* but they will be ended. There are gifts of speaking in different languages, but those gifts will stop. There is the gift of knowledge, but it will come to an end. 9The reason is that our knowledge and our ability to prophesy are not perfect. 10But when perfection

comes, the things that are not perfect will end. 11When I was a child, I talked like a child, I thought like a child, I reasoned like a child. When I became a man, I stopped those childish ways. 12It is the same with us. Now we see a dim reflection, as if we were looking into a mirror, but then we shall see clearly. Now I know only a part, but then I will know fully, as God has known me. 13So these three things continue forever: faith, hope, and love. And the greatest of these is love.

Desire Spiritual Gifts

14 You should seek after love, and you should truly want to have the spiritual gifts, especially the gift of prophecy.*d* 2I will explain why. Those who have the gift of speaking in different languages*n* are not speaking to people; they are speaking to God. No one understands them; they are speaking secret things through the Spirit.*d* 3But those who prophesy are speaking to people to give them strength, encouragement, and comfort. 4The ones who speak in different languages are helping only themselves, but those who prophesy are helping the whole church. 5I wish all of you had the gift of speaking in different kinds of languages, but more, I wish you would prophesy. Those who prophesy are greater than those who can only speak in different languages — unless someone is there who can explain what is said so that the whole church can be helped.

6Brothers and sisters, will it help you if I come to you speaking in different languages? No! It will help you only if I bring you a new truth or some new knowledge, or prophecy, or teaching. 7It is the same as with lifeless things that make sounds — like a flute or a harp. If they do not make clear musical notes, you will not know what is being played. 8And in a war, if the trumpet does not give a clear sound, who will prepare for battle? 9It is the same with you. Unless you speak clearly with your tongue, no one can understand what you are saying. You will be talking into the air! 10It may be true that there are all kinds of sounds in the world,

languages   This can also be translated "tongues."
Verse 3   Other Greek copies read: "hand over my body in order that I may brag."

and none is without meaning. [11]But unless I understand the meaning of what someone says to me, I will be a foreigner to him, and he will be a foreigner to me. [12]It is the same with you. Since you want spiritual gifts very much, seek most of all to have the gifts that help the church grow stronger.

[13]The one who has the gift of speaking in a different language should pray for the gift to interpret what is spoken. [14]If I pray in a different language, my spirit is praying, but my mind does nothing. [15]So what should I do? I will pray with my spirit, but I will also pray with my mind. I will sing with my spirit, but I will also sing with my mind. [16]If you praise God with your spirit, those persons there without understanding cannot say amen[n] to your prayer of thanks, because they do not know what you are saying. [17]You may be thanking God in a good way, but the other person is not helped.

[18]I thank God that I speak in different kinds of languages more than all of you. [19]But in the church meetings I would rather speak five words I understand in order to teach others than thousands of words in a different language.

[20]Brothers and sisters, do not think like children. In evil things be like babies, but in your thinking you should be like adults. [21]It is written in the Scriptures:[d]

"With people who use strange words and foreign languages
I will speak to these people.
But even then they will not listen to me,"   *Isaiah 28:11-12*

says the Lord.

[22]So the gift of speaking in different kinds of languages is a proof for those who do not believe, not for those who do believe. And prophecy is for people who believe, not for those who do not believe. [23]Suppose the whole church meets together and everyone speaks in different languages. If some people come in who do not understand or do not believe, they will say you are crazy. [24]But suppose everyone is prophesying and some people come in who do not believe or do not understand. If everyone is prophesying, their

sin will be shown to them, and they will be judged by all that they hear. [25]The secret things in their hearts will be made known. So they will bow down and worship God saying, "Truly, God is with you."

Meetings Should Help the Church

[26]So, brothers and sisters, what should you do? When you meet together, one person has a song, and another has a teaching. Another has a new truth from God. Another speaks in a different language,[n] and another person interprets that language. The purpose of all these things should be to help the church grow strong. [27]When you meet together, if anyone speaks in a different language, it should be only two, or not more than three, who speak. They should speak one after the other, and someone else should interpret. [28]But if there is no interpreter, then those who speak in a different language should be quiet in the church meeting. They should speak only to themselves and to God.

[29]Only two or three prophets[d] should speak, and the others should judge what they say. [30]If a message from God comes to another person who is sitting, the first speaker should stop. [31]You can all prophesy one after the other. In this way all the people can be taught and encouraged. [32]The spirits of prophets are under the control of the prophets themselves. [33]God is not a God of confusion but a God of peace.

As is true in all the churches of God's people, [34]women should keep quiet in the church meetings. They are not allowed to speak, but they must yield to this rule as the law says. [35]If they want to learn something, they should ask their own husbands at home. It is shameful for a woman to speak in the church meeting. [36]Did God's teaching come from you? Or are you the only ones to whom it has come?

[37]Those who think they are prophets or spiritual persons should understand that what I am writing to you is the Lord's command. [38]Those who ignore this will be ignored by God.

[39]So my brothers and sisters, you should

---

amen   To say amen means to agree with the things that were said.
language   This can also be translated "tongue."

truly want to prophesy. But do not stop people from using the gift of speaking in different kinds of languages. [40]But let everything be done in a right and orderly way.

The Good News About Christ

15 Now, brothers and sisters, I want you to remember the Good News[d] I brought to you. You received this Good News and continue strong in it. [2]And you are being saved by it if you continue believing what I told you. If you do not, then you believed for nothing.

[3]I passed on to you what I received, of which this was most important: that Christ died for our sins, as the Scriptures[d] say; [4]that he was buried and was raised to life on the third day as the Scriptures say; [5]and that he was seen by Peter and then by the twelve apostles.[d] [6]After that, Jesus was seen by more than five hundred of the believers at the same time. Most of them are still living today, but some have died. [7]Then he was seen by James and later by all the apostles. [8]Last of all he was seen by me — as by a person not born at the normal time. [9]All the other apostles are greater than I am. I am not even good enough to be called an apostle, because I persecuted the church of God. [10]But God's grace has made me what I am, and his grace to me was not wasted. I worked harder than all the other apostles. (But it was not I really; it was God's grace that was with me.) [11]So if I preached to you or the other apostles preached to you, we all preach the same thing, and this is what you believed.

We Will Be Raised from the Dead

[12]Now since we preached that Christ was raised from the dead, why do some of you say that people will not be raised from the dead? [13]If no one is ever raised from the dead, then Christ has not been raised. [14]And if Christ has not been raised, then our preaching is worth nothing, and your faith is worth nothing. [15]And also, we are guilty of lying about God, because we testified of him that he raised Christ from the dead. But if people are not raised from the dead, then

God never raised Christ. [16]If the dead are not raised, Christ has not been raised either. [17]And if Christ has not been raised, then your faith has nothing to it; you are still guilty of your sins. [18]And those in Christ who have already died are lost. [19]If our hope in Christ is for this life only, we should be pitied more than anyone else in the world.

[20]But Christ has truly been raised from the dead — the first one and proof that those who sleep in death will also be raised. [21]Death has come because of what one man did, but the rising from death also comes because of one man. [22]In Adam all of us die. In the same way, in Christ all of us will be made alive again. [23]But everyone will be raised to life in the right order. Christ was first to be raised. When Christ comes again, those who belong to him will be raised to life, [24]and then the end will come. At that time Christ will destroy all rulers, authorities, and powers, and he will hand over the kingdom to God the Father. [25]Christ must rule until he puts all enemies under his control. [26]The last enemy to be destroyed will be death. [27]The Scripture[d] says that God put all things under his control.[n] When it says "all things" are under him, it is clear this does not include God himself. God is the One who put everything under his control. [28]After everything has been put under the Son, then he will put himself under God, who had put all things under him. Then God will be the complete ruler over everything.

[29]If the dead are never raised, what will people do who are being baptized for the dead? If the dead are not raised at all, why are people being baptized for them?

[30]And what about us? Why do we put ourselves in danger every hour? [31]I die every day. That is true, brothers and sisters, just as it is true that I brag about you in Christ Jesus our Lord. [32]If I fought wild animals in Ephesus only with human hopes, I have gained nothing. If the dead are not raised, "Let us eat and drink, because tomorrow we will die."[n]

[33]Do not be fooled: "Bad friends will ruin good habits." [34]Come back to your right way

God put ... control. From Psalm 8:6.
"Let us ... die." Quotation from Isaiah 22:13; 56:12.

of thinking and stop sinning. Some of you do not know God—I say this to shame you.

What Kind of Body Will We Have?

[35]But someone may ask, "How are the dead raised? What kind of body will they have?" [36]Foolish person! When you sow a seed, it must die in the ground before it can live and grow. [37]And when you sow it, it does not have the same "body" it will have later. What you sow is only a bare seed, maybe wheat or something else. [38]But God gives it a body that he has planned for it, and God gives each kind of seed its own body. [39]All things made of flesh are not the same: People have one kind of flesh, animals have another, birds have another, and fish have another. [40]Also there are heavenly bodies and earthly bodies. But the beauty of the heavenly bodies is one kind, and the beauty of the earthly bodies is another. [41]The sun has one kind of beauty, the moon has another beauty, and the stars have another. And each star is different in its beauty.

[42]It is the same with the dead who are raised to life. The body that is "planted" will ruin and decay, but it is raised to a life that cannot be destroyed. [43]When the body is "planted," it is without honor, but it is raised in glory. When the body is "planted," it is weak, but when it is raised, it is powerful. [44]The body that is "planted" is a physical body. When it is raised, it is a spiritual body.

There is a physical body, and there is also a spiritual body. [45]It is written in the Scriptures:[d] "The first man, Adam, became a living person."[n] But the last Adam became a spirit that gives life. [46]The spiritual did not come first, but the physical and then the spiritual. [47]The first man came from the dust of the earth. The second man came from heaven. [48]People who belong to the earth are like the first man of earth. But those people who belong to heaven are like the man of heaven. [49]Just as we were made like the man of earth, so we will also be made like the man of heaven.

[50]I tell you this, brothers and sisters: Flesh and blood cannot have a part in the kingdom of God. Something that will ruin cannot have a part in something that never ruins. [51]But look! I tell you this secret: We will not all sleep in death, but we will all be changed. [52]It will take only a second—as quickly as an eye blinks—when the last trumpet sounds. The trumpet will sound, and those who have died will be raised to live forever, and we will all be changed. [53]This body that can be destroyed must clothe itself with something that can never be destroyed. And this body that dies must clothe itself with something that can never die. [54]So this body that can be destroyed will clothe itself with that which can never be destroyed, and this body that dies will clothe itself with that which can never die. When this happens, this Scripture will be made true:

"Death is destroyed forever in victory."

Isaiah 25:8

[55]"Death, where is your victory?
    Death, where is your pain?"   *Hosea 13:14*
[56]Death's power to hurt is sin, and the power of sin is the law. [57]But we thank God! He gives us the victory through our Lord Jesus Christ.

[58]So my dear brothers and sisters, stand strong. Do not let anything change you. Always give yourselves fully to the work of the Lord, because you know that your work in the Lord is never wasted.

The Gift for Other Believers

16 Now I will write about the collection of money for God's people. Do the same thing I told the Galatian churches to do: [2]On the first day of every week, each one of you should put aside money as you have been blessed. Save it up so you will not have to collect money after I come. [3]When I arrive, I will send whomever you approve to take your gift to Jerusalem. I will send them with letters of introduction, [4]and if it seems good for me to go also, they will go along with me.

Paul's Plans

[5]I plan to go through Macedonia, so I will come to you after I go through there. [6]Perhaps I will stay with you for a time or even all winter. Then you can help me on my trip,

"The first ... person." Quotation from Genesis 2:7.

wherever I go. [7]I do not want to see you now just in passing. I hope to stay a longer time with you if the Lord allows it. [8]But I will stay at Ephesus until Pentecost,[d] [9]because a good opportunity for a great and growing work has been given to me now. And there are many people working against me.

[10]If Timothy comes to you, see to it that he has nothing to fear with you, because he is working for the Lord just as I am. [11]So none of you should treat Timothy as unimportant, but help him on his trip in peace so that he can come back to me. I am expecting him to come with the brothers.

[12]Now about our brother Apollos: I strongly encouraged him to visit you with the other brothers. He did not at all want to come now; he will come when he has the opportunity.

Paul Ends His Letter

[13]Be alert. Continue strong in the faith. Have courage, and be strong. [14]Do everything in love.

[15]You know that the family of Stephanas were the first believers in Southern Greece and that they have given themselves to the service of God's people. I ask you, brothers and sisters, [16]to follow the leading of people like these and anyone else who works and serves with them.

[17]I am happy that Stephanas, Fortunatus, and Achaicus have come. You are not here, but they have filled your place. [18]They have refreshed my spirit and yours. You should recognize the value of people like these.

[19]The churches in the country of Asia send greetings to you. Aquila and Priscilla greet you in the Lord, as does the church that meets in their house. [20]All the brothers and sisters here send greetings. Give each other a holy kiss when you meet.

[21]I, Paul, am writing this greeting with my own hand.

[22]If anyone does not love the Lord, let him be separated from God — lost forever!

Come, O Lord!

[23]The grace of the Lord Jesus be with you. [24]My love be with all of you in Christ Jesus.

2 CORINTHIANS

Paul Answers Those Who Accuse Him

1 From Paul, an apostle*d* of Christ Jesus. I am an apostle because that is what God wanted. Also from Timothy our brother in Christ.

To the church of God in Corinth, and to all of God's people everywhere in Southern Greece:

²Grace and peace to you from God our Father and the Lord Jesus Christ.

Paul Gives Thanks to God

³Praise be to the God and Father of our Lord Jesus Christ. God is the Father who is full of mercy and all comfort. ⁴He comforts us every time we have trouble, so when others have trouble, we can comfort them with the same comfort God gives us. ⁵We share in the many sufferings of Christ. In the same way, much comfort comes to us through Christ. ⁶If we have troubles, it is for your comfort and salvation, and if we have comfort, you also have comfort. This helps you to accept patiently the same sufferings we have. ⁷Our hope for you is strong, knowing that you share in our sufferings and also in the comfort we receive.

⁸Brothers and sisters,*n* we want you to know about the trouble we suffered in Asia. We had great burdens there that were beyond our own strength. We even gave up hope of living. ⁹Truly, in our own hearts we believed we would die. But this happened so we would not trust in ourselves but in God, who raises people from the dead. ¹⁰God saved us from these great dangers of death, and he will continue to save us. We have put our hope in him, and he will save us again. ¹¹And you can help us with your prayers. Then many people will give thanks for us — that God blessed us because of their many prayers.

The Change in Paul's Plans

¹²This is what we are proud of, and I can say it with a clear conscience: In everything we have done in the world, and especially with you, we have had an honest and sincere heart from God. We did this by God's grace, not by the kind of wisdom the world has. ¹³⁻¹⁴We write to you only what you can read and understand. And I hope that as you have understood some things about us, you may come to know everything about us. Then you can be proud of us, as we will be proud of you on the day our Lord Jesus Christ comes again.

¹⁵I was so sure of all this that I made plans to visit you first so you could be blessed twice. ¹⁶I planned to visit you on my way to Macedonia and again on my way back. I wanted to get help from you for my trip to Judea. ¹⁷Do you think that I made these plans without really meaning it? Or maybe you think I make plans as the world does, so that I say yes, yes and at the same time no, no.

¹⁸But if you can believe God, you can believe that what we tell you is never both yes and no. ¹⁹The Son of God, Jesus Christ, that Silas and Timothy and I preached to you, was not yes and no. In Christ it has always been yes. ²⁰The yes to all of God's promises is in Christ, and through Christ we say yes to the glory of God. ²¹Remember, God is the One who makes you and us strong in Christ. God made us his chosen people. ²²He put his mark on us to show that we are his, and he put his Spirit*d* in our hearts to be a guarantee for all he has promised.

²³I tell you this, and I ask God to be my witness that this is true: The reason I did not come back to Corinth was to keep you from being punished or hurt. ²⁴We are not trying to control your faith. You are strong in faith.

But we are workers with you for your own joy.

2 So I decided that my next visit to you would not be another one to make you sad. [2]If I make you sad, who will make me glad? Only you can make me glad — particularly the person whom I made sad. [3]I wrote you a letter for this reason: that when I came to you I would not be made sad by the people who should make me happy. I felt sure of all of you, that you would share my joy. [4]When I wrote to you before, I was very troubled and unhappy in my heart, and I wrote with many tears. I did not write to make you sad, but to let you know how much I love you.

Forgive the Sinner

[5]Someone there among you has caused sadness, not to me, but to all of you. I mean he caused sadness to all in some way. (I do not want to make it sound worse than it really is.) [6]The punishment that most of you gave him is enough for him. [7]But now you should forgive him and comfort him to keep him from having too much sadness and giving up completely. [8]So I beg you to show that you love him. [9]I wrote you to test you and to see if you obey in everything. [10]If you forgive someone, I also forgive him. And what I have forgiven — if I had anything to forgive — I forgave it for you, as if Christ were with me. [11]I did this so that Satan would not win anything from us, because we know very well what Satan's plans are.

Paul's Concern in Troas

[12]When I came to Troas to preach the Good News[d] of Christ, the Lord gave me a good opportunity there. [13]But I had no peace, because I did not find my brother Titus. So I said good-bye to them at Troas and went to Macedonia.

Victory Through Christ

[14]But thanks be to God, who always leads us in victory through Christ. God uses us to spread his knowledge everywhere like a sweet-smelling perfume. [15]Our offering to God is this: We are the sweet smell of Christ among those who are being saved and among those who are being lost. [16]To those who are lost, we are the smell of death that brings death, but to those who are being saved, we are the smell of life that brings life. So who is able to do this work? [17]We do not sell the word of God for a profit as many other people do. But in Christ we speak the truth before God, as messengers of God.

Servants of the New Agreement

3 Are we starting to brag about ourselves again? Do we need letters of introduction to you or from you, like some other people? [2]You yourselves are our letter, written on our hearts, known and read by everyone. [3]You show that you are a letter from Christ sent through us. This letter is not written with ink but with the Spirit[d] of the living God. It is not written on stone tablets[n] but on human hearts.

[4]We can say this, because through Christ we feel certain before God. [5]We are not saying that we can do this work ourselves. It is God who makes us able to do all that we do. [6]He made us able to be servants of a new agreement from himself to his people. This new agreement is not a written law, but it is of the Spirit. The written law brings death, but the Spirit gives life.

[7]The law that brought death was written in words on stone. It came with God's glory, which made Moses' face so bright that the Israelites could not continue to look at it. But that glory later disappeared. [8]So surely the new way that brings the Spirit has even more glory. [9]If the law that judged people guilty of sin had glory, surely the new way that makes people right with God has much greater glory. [10]That old law had glory, but it really loses its glory when it is compared to the much greater glory of this new way. [11]If that law which disappeared came with glory, then this new way which continues forever has much greater glory.

[12]We have this hope, so we are very bold. [13]We are not like Moses, who put a covering over his face so the Israelites would not see it. The glory was disappearing, and Moses did not want them to see it end. [14]But their

---

stone tablets   Meaning the law of Moses that was written on stone tablets (Exodus 24:12; 25:16).

minds were closed, and even today that same covering hides the meaning when they read the old agreement. That covering is taken away only through Christ. [15]Even today, when they read the law of Moses, there is a covering over their minds. [16]But when a person changes and follows the Lord, that covering is taken away. [17]The Lord is the Spirit, and where the Spirit of the Lord is, there is freedom. [18]Our faces, then, are not covered. We all show the Lord's glory, and we are being changed to be like him. This change in us brings ever greater glory, which comes from the Lord, who is the Spirit.

Preaching the Good News

4 God, with his mercy, gave us this work to do, so we don't give up. [2]But we have turned away from secret and shameful ways. We use no trickery, and we do not change the teaching of God. We teach the truth plainly, showing everyone who we are. Then they can know in their hearts what kind of people we are in God's sight. [3]If the Good News[d] that we preach is hidden, it is hidden only to those who are lost. [4]The devil who rules this world has blinded the minds of those who do not believe. They cannot see the light of the Good News — the Good News about the glory of Christ, who is exactly like God. [5]We do not preach about ourselves, but we preach that Jesus Christ is Lord and that we are your servants for Jesus. [6]God once said, "Let the light shine out of the darkness!" This is the same God who made his light shine in our hearts by letting us know the glory of God that is in the face of Christ.

Spiritual Treasure in Clay Jars

[7]We have this treasure from God, but we are like clay jars that hold the treasure. This shows that the great power is from God, not from us. [8]We have troubles all around us, but we are not defeated. We do not know what to do, but we do not give up the hope of living. [9]We are persecuted, but God does not leave us. We are hurt sometimes, but we are not destroyed. [10]We carry the death of Jesus in our own bodies so that the life of Jesus can

also be seen in our bodies. [11]We are alive, but for Jesus we are always in danger of death so that the life of Jesus can be seen in our bodies that die. [12]So death is working in us, but life is working in you.

[13]It is written in the Scriptures,[d] "I believed, so I spoke."[n] Our faith is like this, too. We believe, and so we speak. [14]God raised the Lord Jesus from the dead, and we know that God will also raise us with Jesus. God will bring us together with you, and we will stand before him. [15]All these things are for you. And so the grace of God that is being given to more and more people will bring increasing thanks to God for his glory.

Living by Faith

[16]So we do not give up. Our physical body is becoming older and weaker, but our spirit inside us is made new every day. [17]We have small troubles for a while now, but they are helping us gain an eternal glory that is much greater than the troubles. [18]We set our eyes not on what we see but on what we cannot see. What we see will last only a short time, but what we cannot see will last forever.

5 We know that our body — the tent we live in here on earth — will be destroyed. But when that happens, God will have a house for us. It will not be a house made by human hands; instead, it will be a home in heaven that will last forever. [2]But now we groan in this tent. We want God to give us our heavenly home, [3]because it will clothe us so we will not be naked. [4]While we live in this body, we have burdens, and we groan. We do not want to be naked, but we want to be clothed with our heavenly home. Then this body that dies will be fully covered with life. [5]This is what God made us for, and he has given us the Spirit[d] to be a guarantee for this new life.

[6]So we always have courage. We know that while we live in this body, we are away from the Lord. [7]We live by what we believe, not by what we can see. [8]So I say that we have courage. We really want to be away from this body and be at home with the Lord. [9]Our only goal is to please God whether we

"I . . . spoke."　Quotation from Psalm 116:10.

live here or there, [10]because we must all stand before Christ to be judged. Each of us will receive what we should get — good or bad — for the things we did in the earthly body.

Becoming Friends with God

[11]Since we know what it means to fear the Lord, we try to help people accept the truth about us. God knows what we really are, and I hope that in your hearts you know, too. [12]We are not trying to prove ourselves to you again, but we are telling you about ourselves so you will be proud of us. Then you will have an answer for those who are proud about things that can be seen rather than what is in the heart. [13]If we are out of our minds, it is for God. If we have our right minds, it is for you. [14]The love of Christ controls us, because we know that One died for all, so all have died. [15]Christ died for all so that those who live would not continue to live for themselves. He died for them and was raised from the dead so that they would live for him.

[16]From this time on we do not think of anyone as the world does. In the past we thought of Christ as the world thinks, but we no longer think of him in that way. [17]If anyone belongs to Christ, there is a new creation. The old things have gone; everything is made new! [18]All this is from God. Through Christ, God made peace between us and himself, and God gave us the work of telling everyone about the peace we can have with him. [19]God was in Christ, making peace between the world and himself. In Christ, God did not hold the world guilty of its sins. And he gave us this message of peace. [20]So we have been sent to speak for Christ. It is as if God is calling to you through us. We speak for Christ when we beg you to be at peace with God. [21]Christ had no sin, but God made him become sin so that in Christ we could become right with God.

6 We are workers together with God, so we beg you: Do not let the grace that you received from God be for nothing. [2]God says,

"At the right time I heard your prayers.

On the day of salvation I helped you."

Isaiah 49:8

I tell you that the "right time" is now, and the "day of salvation" is now.

[3]We do not want anyone to find fault with our work, so nothing we do will be a problem for anyone. [4]But in every way we show we are servants of God: in accepting many hard things, in troubles, in difficulties, and in great problems. [5]We are beaten and thrown into prison. We meet those who become upset with us and start riots. We work hard, and sometimes we get no sleep or food. [6]We show we are servants of God by our pure lives, our understanding, patience, and kindness, by the Holy Spirit,[d] by true love, [7]by speaking the truth, and by God's power. We use our right living to defend ourselves against everything. [8]Some people honor us, but others blame us. Some people say evil things about us, but others say good things. Some people say we are liars, but we speak the truth. [9]We are not known, but we are well known. We seem to be dying, but we continue to live. We are punished, but we are not killed. [10]We have much sadness, but we are always rejoicing. We are poor, but we are making many people rich in faith. We have nothing, but really we have everything.

[11]We have spoken freely to you in Corinth and have opened our hearts to you. [12]Our feelings of love for you have not stopped, but you have stopped your feelings of love for us. [13]I speak to you as if you were my children. Do to us as we have done — open your hearts to us.

Warning About Non-Christians

[14]You are not the same as those who do not believe. So do not join yourselves to them. Good and bad do not belong together. Light and darkness cannot share together. [15]How can Christ and Belial, the devil, have any agreement? What can a believer have together with a nonbeliever? [16]The temple of God cannot have any agreement with idols, and we are the temple of the living God. As God said: "I will live with them and walk with them. And I will be their God, and they will be my people." [n]

"I . . . people." Quotation from Leviticus 26:11-12; Jeremiah 32:38; Ezekiel 37:27.

17"Leave those people,
  and be separate, says the Lord.
Touch nothing that is unclean,*d*
  and I will accept you."

Isaiah 52:11; Ezekiel 20:34, 41

18"I will be your father,
  and you will be my sons and
    daughters,
says the Lord Almighty."   *2 Samuel 7:14; 7:8*

7 Dear friends, we have these promises from God, so we should make ourselves pure — free from anything that makes body or soul unclean. We should try to become holy in the way we live, because we respect God.

Paul's Joy

2Open your hearts to us. We have not done wrong to anyone, we have not ruined the faith of anyone, and we have not cheated anyone. 3I do not say this to blame you. I told you before that we love you so much we would live or die with you. 4I feel very sure of you and am very proud of you. You give me much comfort, and in all of our troubles I have great joy.

5When we came into Macedonia, we had no rest. We found trouble all around us. We had fighting on the outside and fear on the inside. 6But God, who comforts those who are troubled, comforted us when Titus came. 7We were comforted, not only by his coming but also by the comfort you gave him. Titus told us about your wish to see me and that you are very sorry for what you did. He also told me about your great care for me, and when I heard this, I was much happier.

8Even if my letter made you sad, I am not sorry I wrote it. At first I was sorry, because it made you sad, but you were sad only for a short time. 9Now I am happy, not because you were made sad, but because your sorrow made you change your lives. You became sad in the way God wanted you to, so you were not hurt by us in any way. 10The kind of sorrow God wants makes people change their hearts and lives. This leads to salvation, and you cannot be sorry for that. But the kind of sorrow the world has brings death. 11See what this sorrow — the sorrow God wanted

you to have — has done to you: It has made you very serious. It made you want to prove you were not wrong. It made you angry and afraid. It made you want to see me. It made you care. It made you want the right thing to be done. You proved you were innocent in the problem. 12I wrote that letter, not because of the one who did the wrong or because of the person who was hurt. I wrote the letter so you could see, before God, the great care you have for us. 13That is why we were comforted.

Not only were we very comforted, we were even happier to see that Titus was so happy. All of you made him feel much better. 14I bragged to Titus about you, and you showed that I was right. Everything we said to you was true, and you have proved that what we bragged about to Titus is true. 15And his love for you is stronger when he remembers that you were all ready to obey. You welcomed him with respect and fear. 16I am very happy that I can trust you fully.

Christian Giving

8 And now, brothers and sisters, we want you to know about the grace God gave the churches in Macedonia. 2They have been tested by great troubles, and they are very poor. But they gave much because of their great joy. 3I can tell you that they gave as much as they were able and even more than they could afford. No one told them to do it. 4But they begged and pleaded with us to let them share in this service for God's people. 5And they gave in a way we did not expect: They first gave themselves to the Lord and to us. This is what God wants. 6So we asked Titus to help you finish this special work of grace since he is the one who started it. 7You are rich in everything — in faith, in speaking, in knowledge, in truly wanting to help, and in the love you learned from us. In the same way, be strong also in the grace of giving.

8I am not commanding you to give. But I want to see if your love is true by comparing you with others that really want to help. 9You know the grace of our Lord Jesus Christ. You know that Christ was rich, but for you he became poor so that by his becoming poor you might become rich.

[10]This is what I think you should do: Last year you were the first to want to give, and you were the first who gave. [11]So now finish the work you started. Then your "doing" will be equal to your "wanting to do." Give from what you have. [12]If you want to give, your gift will be accepted. It will be judged by what you have, not by what you do not have. [13]We do not want you to have troubles while other people are at ease, but we want everything to be equal. [14]At this time you have plenty. What you have can help others who are in need. Then later, when they have plenty, they can help you when you are in need, and all will be equal. [15]As it is written in the Scriptures,[d] "The person who gathered more did not have too much, nor did the person who gathered less have too little."[n]

Titus and His Companions Help

[16]I thank God because he gave Titus the same love for you that I have. [17]Titus accepted what we asked him to do. He wanted very much to go to you, and this was his own idea. [18]We are sending with him the brother who is praised by all the churches because of his service in preaching the Good News.[d] [19]Also, this brother was chosen by the churches to go with us when we deliver this gift of money. We are doing this service to bring glory to the Lord and to show that we really want to help.

[20]We are being careful so that no one will criticize us for the way we are handling this large gift. [21]We are trying hard to do what the Lord accepts as right and also what people think is right.

[22]Also, we are sending with them our brother, who is always ready to help. He has proved this to us in many ways, and he wants to help even more now, because he has much faith in you.

[23]Now about Titus — he is my partner who is working with me to help you. And about the other brothers — they are sent from the churches, and they bring glory to Christ. [24]So show these men the proof of your love and the reason we are proud of you. Then all the churches can see it.

Help for Fellow Christians

9 I really do not need to write you about this help for God's people. [2]I know you want to help. I have been bragging about this to the people in Macedonia, telling them that you in Southern Greece have been ready to give since last year. And your desire to give has made most of them ready to give also. [3]But I am sending the brothers to you so that our bragging about you in this will not be empty words. I want you to be ready, as I said you would be. [4]If any of the people from Macedonia come with me and find that you are not ready, we will be ashamed that we were so sure of you. (And you will be ashamed, too!) [5]So I thought I should ask these brothers to go to you before we do. They will finish getting in order the generous gift you promised so it will be ready when we come. And it will be a generous gift — not one that you did not want to give.

[6]Remember this: The person who plants a little will have a small harvest, but the person who plants a lot will have a big harvest. [7]Each one should give as you have decided in your heart to give. You should not be sad when you give, and you should not give because you feel forced to give. God loves the person who gives happily. [8]And God can give you more blessings than you need. Then you will always have plenty of everything — enough to give to every good work. [9]It is written in the Scriptures:[d]

"He gives freely to the poor.
The things he does are right and will
    continue forever." *Psalm 112:9*

[10]God is the One who gives seed to the farmer and bread for food. He will give you all the seed you need and make it grow so there will be a great harvest from your goodness. [11]He will make you rich in every way so that you can always give freely. And your giving through us will cause many to give thanks to God. [12]This service you do not only helps the needs of God's people, it also brings many more thanks to God. [13]It is a proof of your faith. Many people will praise God because you obey the Good News[d] of Christ — the gospel you say you believe — and because

---

"The person . . . little." Quotation from Exodus 16:18.

you freely share with them and with all others. [14]And when they pray, they will wish they could be with you because of the great grace that God has given you. [15]Thanks be to God for his gift that is too wonderful for words.

Paul Defends His Ministry

10 I, Paul, am begging you with the gentleness and the kindness of Christ. Some people say that I am easy on you when I am with you and bold when I am away. [2]They think we live in a worldly way, and I plan to be very bold with them when I come. I beg you that when I come I will not need to use that same boldness with you. [3]We do live in the world, but we do not fight in the same way the world fights. [4]We fight with weapons that are different from those the world uses. Our weapons have power from God that can destroy the enemy's strong places. We destroy people's arguments [5]and every proud thing that raises itself against the knowledge of God. We capture every thought and make it give up and obey Christ. [6]We are ready to punish anyone there who does not obey, but first we want you to obey fully.

[7]You must look at the facts before you. If you feel sure that you belong to Christ, you must remember that we belong to Christ just as you do. [8]It is true that we brag freely about the authority the Lord gave us. But this authority is to build you up, not to tear you down. So I will not be ashamed. [9]I do not want you to think I am trying to scare you with my letters. [10]Some people say, "Paul's letters are powerful and sound important, but when he is with us, he is weak. And his speaking is nothing." [11]They should know this: We are not there with you now, so we say these things in letters. But when we are there with you, we will show the same authority that we show in our letters.

[12]We do not dare to compare ourselves with those who think they are very important. They use themselves to measure themselves, and they judge themselves by what they themselves are. This shows that they know nothing. [13]But we will not brag about

things outside the work that was given us to do. We will limit our bragging to the work that God gave us, and this includes our work with you. [14]We are not bragging too much, as we would be if we had not already come to you. But we have come to you with the Good News*d* of Christ. [15]We limit our bragging to the work that is ours, not what others have done. We hope that as your faith continues to grow, you will help our work to grow much larger. [16]We want to tell the Good News in the areas beyond your city. We do not want to brag about work that has already been done in another person's area. [17]But, "If someone wants to brag, he should brag only about the Lord." *n* [18]It is not those who say they are good who are accepted but those who the Lord thinks are good.

Paul and the False Apostles

11 I wish you would be patient with me even when I am a little foolish, but you are already doing that. [2]I am jealous over you with a jealousy that comes from God. I promised to give you to Christ, as your only husband. I want to give you as his pure bride. [3]But I am afraid that your minds will be led away from your true and pure following of Christ just as Eve was tricked by the snake with his evil ways. [4]You are very patient with anyone who comes to you and preaches a different Jesus from the one we preached. You are very willing to accept a spirit or gospel that is different from the Spirit*d* and Good News*d* you received from us.

[5]I do not think that those "great apostles" are any better than I am. [6]I may not be a trained speaker, but I do have knowledge. We have shown this to you clearly in every way.

[7]I preached God's Good News to you without pay. I made myself unimportant to make you important. Do you think that was wrong? [8]I accepted pay from other churches, taking their money so I could serve you. [9]If I needed something when I was with you, I did not trouble any of you. The brothers who came from Macedonia gave me all that I needed. I did not allow myself to depend on you in any way, and I will never depend on

"If . . . Lord." Quotation from Jeremiah 9:24.

you. [10]No one in Southern Greece will stop me from bragging about that. I say this with the truth of Christ in me. [11]And why do I not depend on you? Do you think it is because I do not love you? God knows that I love you.

[12]And I will continue doing what I am doing now, because I want to stop those people from having a reason to brag. They would like to say that the work they brag about is the same as ours. [13]Such men are not true apostles[d] but are workers who lie. They change themselves to look like apostles of Christ. [14]This does not surprise us. Even Satan changes himself to look like an angel of light. [n] [15]So it does not surprise us if Satan's servants also make themselves look like servants who work for what is right. But in the end they will be punished for what they do.

Paul Tells About His Sufferings

[16]I tell you again: No one should think I am a fool. But if you think so, accept me as you would accept a fool. Then I can brag a little, too. [17]When I brag because I feel sure of myself, I am not talking as the Lord would talk but as a fool. [18]Many people are bragging about their lives in the world. So I will brag too. [19]You are wise, so you will gladly be patient with fools! [20]You are even patient with those who order you around, or use you, or trick you, or think they are better than you, or hit you in the face. [21]It is shameful to me to say this, but we were too "weak" to do those things to you!

But if anyone else is brave enough to brag, then I also will be brave and brag. (I am talking as a fool.) [22]Are they Hebrews?[n] So am I. Are they Israelites? So am I. Are they from Abraham's family? So am I. [23]Are they serving Christ? I am serving him more. (I am crazy to talk like this.) I have worked much harder than they. I have been in prison more often. I have been hurt more in beatings. I have been near death many times. [24]Five times the Jews have given me their punishment of thirty-nine lashes with a whip. [25]Three different times I was beaten with

rods. One time I was almost stoned to death. Three times I was in ships that wrecked, and one of those times I spent a night and a day in the sea. [26]I have gone on many travels and have been in danger from rivers, thieves, my own people, the Jews, and those who are not Jews. I have been in danger in cities, in places where no one lives, and on the sea. And I have been in danger with false Christians. [27]I have done hard and tiring work, and many times I did not sleep. I have been hungry and thirsty, and many times I have been without food. I have been cold and without clothes. [28]Besides all this, there is on me every day the load of my concern for all the churches. [29]I feel weak every time someone is weak, and I feel upset every time someone is led into sin.

[30]If I must brag, I will brag about the things that show I am weak. [31]God knows I am not lying. He is the God and Father of the Lord Jesus Christ, and he is to be praised forever. [32]When I was in Damascus, the governor under King Aretas wanted to arrest me, so he put guards around the city. [33]But my friends lowered me in a basket through a hole in the city wall. So I escaped from the governor.

A Special Blessing in Paul's Life

12 I must continue to brag. It will do no good, but I will talk now about visions and revelations[n] from the Lord. [2]I know a man in Christ who was taken up to the third heaven fourteen years ago. I do not know whether the man was in his body or out of his body, but God knows. [3-4]And I know that this man was taken up to paradise.[n] I don't know if he was in his body or away from his body, but God knows. He heard things he is not able to explain, things that no human is allowed to tell. [5]I will brag about a man like that, but I will not brag about myself, except about my weaknesses. [6]But if I wanted to brag about myself, I would not be a fool, because I would be telling the truth. But I will not brag about myself. I do

---

angel of light   Messenger from God. The devil fools people so that they think he is from God.
Hebrews   A name for the Jews that some Jews were very proud of.
revelations   Revelation is making known a truth that was hidden.
paradise   A place where good people go when they die.

not want people to think more of me than what they see me do or hear me say.

⁷So that I would not become too proud of the wonderful things that were shown to me, a painful physical problem *n* was given to me. This problem was a messenger from Satan, sent to beat me and keep me from being too proud. ⁸I begged the Lord three times to take this problem away from me. ⁹But he said to me, "My grace is enough for you. When you are weak, my power is made perfect in you." So I am very happy to brag about my weaknesses. Then Christ's power can live in me. ¹⁰For this reason I am happy when I have weaknesses, insults, hard times, sufferings, and all kinds of troubles for Christ. Because when I am weak, then I am truly strong.

Paul's Love for the Christians

¹¹I have been talking like a fool, but you made me do it. You are the ones who should say good things about me. I am worth nothing, but those "great apostles" are not worth any more than I am! ¹²When I was with you, I patiently did the things that prove I am an apostle*d*—signs, wonders, and miracles.*d* ¹³So you received everything that the other churches have received. Only one thing was different: I was not a burden to you. Forgive me for this!

¹⁴I am now ready to visit you the third time, and I will not be a burden to you. I want nothing from you, except you. Children should not have to save up to give to their parents. Parents should save to give to their children. ¹⁵So I am happy to give everything I have for you, even myself. If I love you more, will you love me less?

¹⁶It is clear I was not a burden to you, but you think I was tricky and lied to catch you. ¹⁷Did I cheat you by using any of the messengers I sent to you? No, you know I did not. ¹⁸I asked Titus to go to you, and I sent our brother with him. Titus did not cheat you, did he? No, you know that Titus and I did the same thing and with the same spirit.

¹⁹Do you think we have been defending ourselves to you all this time? We have been speaking in Christ and before God. You are our dear friends, and everything we do is to make you stronger. ²⁰I am afraid that when I come, you will not be what I want you to be, and I will not be what you want me to be. I am afraid that among you there may be arguing, jealousy, anger, selfish fighting, evil talk, gossip, pride, and confusion. ²¹I am afraid that when I come to you again, my God will make me ashamed before you. I may be saddened by many of those who have sinned because they have not changed their hearts or turned from their sexual sins and the shameful things they have done.

Final Warnings and Greetings

13 I will come to you for the third time. "Every case must be proved by two or three witnesses." *n* ²When I was with you the second time, I gave a warning to those who had sinned. Now I am away from you, and I give a warning to all the others. When I come to you again, I will not be easy with them. ³You want proof that Christ is speaking through me. My proof is that he is not weak among you, but he is powerful. ⁴It is true that he was weak when he was killed on the cross, but he lives now by God's power. It is true that we are weak in Christ, but for you we will be alive in Christ by God's power.

⁵Look closely at yourselves. Test yourselves to see if you are living in the faith. You know that Jesus Christ is in you — unless you fail the test. ⁶But I hope you will see that we ourselves have not failed the test. ⁷We pray to God that you will not do anything wrong. It is not important to see that we have passed the test, but it is important that you do what is right, even if it seems we have failed. ⁸We cannot do anything against the truth, but only for the truth. ⁹We are happy to be weak, if you are strong, and we pray that you will become complete. ¹⁰I am writing this while I am away from you so that when I come I will not have to be harsh in my use of authority. The Lord gave me this authority to build you up, not to tear you down.

---

painful physical problem   Literally, "thorn in the flesh."
"Every . . . witnesses."   Quotation from Deuteronomy 19:15.

[11]Now, brothers and sisters, I say goodbye. Try to be complete. Do what I have asked you to do. Agree with each other, and live in peace. Then the God of love and peace will be with you.

[12]Greet each other with a holy kiss. [13]All of God's holy people send greetings to you.

[14]The grace of the Lord Jesus Christ, the love of God, and the fellowship of the Holy Spirit[d] be with you all.

GALATIANS

Christians Are Saved by Grace

1 From Paul, an apostle.[d] I was not chosen to be an apostle by human beings, nor was I sent from human beings. I was made an apostle through Jesus Christ and God the Father who raised Jesus from the dead. [2]This letter is also from all those of God's family[n] who are with me.

To the churches in Galatia:[n]

[3]Grace and peace to you from God our Father and the Lord Jesus Christ. [4]Jesus gave himself for our sins to free us from this evil world we live in, as God the Father planned. [5]The glory belongs to God forever and ever. Amen.

The Only Good News

[6]God, by his grace through Christ, called you to become his people. So I am amazed that you are turning away so quickly and believing something different than the Good News.[d] [7]Really, there is no other Good News. But some people are confusing you; they want to change the Good News of Christ. [8]We preached to you the Good News. So if we ourselves, or even an angel from heaven, should preach to you something different, we should be judged guilty! [9]I said this before, and now I say it again: You have already accepted the Good News. If anyone is preaching something different to you, he should be judged guilty!

[10]Do you think I am trying to make people accept me? No, God is the One I am trying to please. Am I trying to please people? If I still wanted to please people, I would not be a servant of Christ.

Paul's Authority Is from God

[11]Brothers and sisters,[n] I want you to know that the Good News[d] I preached to you was not made up by human beings. [12]I did not get it from humans, nor did anyone teach it to me, but Jesus Christ showed it to me.

[13]You have heard about my past life in the Jewish religion. I attacked the church of God and tried to destroy it. [14]I was becoming a leader in the Jewish religion, doing better than most other Jews of my age. I tried harder than anyone else to follow the teachings handed down by our ancestors.

[15]But God had special plans for me and set me apart for his work even before I was born. He called me through his grace [16]and showed his son to me so that I might tell the Good News about him to those who are not Jewish. When God called me, I did not get advice or help from any person. [17]I did not go to Jerusalem to see those who were apostles[d] before I was. But, without waiting, I went away to Arabia and later went back to Damascus.

[18]After three years I went to Jerusalem to meet Peter and stayed with him for fifteen days. [19]I met no other apostles, except James, the brother of the Lord. [20]God knows that these things I write are not lies. [21]Later, I went to the areas of Syria and Cilicia.

[22]In Judea the churches in Christ had never met me. [23]They had only heard it said, "This man who was attacking us is now preaching the same faith that he once tried to destroy." [24]And these believers praised God because of me.

Other Apostles Accepted Paul

2 After fourteen years I went to Jerusalem again, this time with Barnabas. I also

---

those ... family The Greek text says "brothers."
Galatia Probably the same country where Paul preached and began churches on his first missionary trip. Read the book of Acts, chapters 13 and 14.
Brothers and sisters Although the Greek text says "Brothers" here and throughout this book, Paul's words were meant for the entire church, including men and women.

took Titus with me. [2]I went because God showed me I should go. I met with the believers there, and in private I told their leaders the Good News[d] that I preach to the non-Jewish people. I did not want my past work and the work I am now doing to be wasted. [3]Titus was with me, but he was not forced to be circumcised,[d] even though he was a Greek. [4]We talked about this problem because some false believers had come into our group secretly. They came in like spies to overturn the freedom we have in Christ Jesus. They wanted to make us slaves. [5]But we did not give in to those false believers for a minute. We wanted the truth of the Good News to continue for you.

[6]Those leaders who seemed to be important did not change the Good News that I preach. (It doesn't matter to me if they were "important" or not. To God everyone is the same.) [7]But these leaders saw that I had been given the work of telling the Good News to those who are not Jewish, just as Peter had the work of telling the Jews. [8]God gave Peter the power to work as an apostle[d] for the Jewish people. But he also gave me the power to work as an apostle for those who are not Jews. [9]James, Peter, and John, who seemed to be the leaders, understood that God had given me this special grace, so they accepted Barnabas and me. They agreed that they would go to the Jewish people and that we should go to those who are not Jewish. [10]The only thing they asked us was to remember to help the poor — something I really wanted to do.

Paul Shows that Peter Was Wrong

[11]When Peter came to Antioch, I challenged him to his face, because he was wrong. [12]Peter ate with the non-Jewish people until some Jewish people sent from James came to Antioch. When they arrived, Peter stopped eating with those who weren't Jewish, and he separated himself from them. He was afraid of the Jews. [13]So Peter was a hypocrite,[d] as were the other Jewish believers who joined with him. Even Barnabas was influenced by what these Jewish believers did. [14]When I saw they were not following the truth of the Good News,[d] I spoke to Peter in

front of them all. I said, "Peter, you are a Jew, but you are not living like a Jew. You are living like those who are not Jewish. So why do you now try to force those who are not Jewish to live like Jews?"

[15]We were not born as non-Jewish "sinners," but as Jews. [16]Yet we know that a person is made right with God not by following the law, but by trusting in Jesus Christ. So we, too, have put our faith in Christ Jesus, that we might be made right with God because we trusted in Christ. It is not because we followed the law, because no one can be made right with God by following the law.

[17]We Jews came to Christ, trying to be made right with God, and it became clear that we are sinners, too. Does this mean that Christ encourages sin? No! [18]But I would really be wrong to begin teaching again those things that I gave up. [19]It was the law that put me to death, and I died to the law so that I can now live for God. [20]I was put to death on the cross with Christ, and I do not live anymore — it is Christ who lives in me. I still live in my body, but I live by faith in the Son of God who loved me and gave himself to save me. [21]By saying these things I am not going against God's grace. Just the opposite, if the law could make us right with God, then Christ's death would be useless.

Blessing Comes Through Faith

3 You people in Galatia were told very clearly about the death of Jesus Christ on the cross. But you were foolish; you let someone trick you. [2]Tell me this one thing: How did you receive the Holy Spirit?[d] Did you receive the Spirit by following the law? No, you received the Spirit because you heard the Good News[d] and believed it. [3]You began your life in Christ by the Spirit. Now are you trying to make it complete by your own power? That is foolish. [4]Were all your experiences wasted? I hope not! [5]Does God give you the Spirit and work miracles[d] among you because you follow the law? No, he does these things because you heard the Good News and believed it.

[6]The Scriptures[d] say the same thing about Abraham: "Abraham believed God, and God accepted Abraham's faith, and that faith

made him right with God." [n] [7]So you should know that the true children of Abraham are those who have faith. [8]The Scriptures, telling what would happen in the future, said that God would make the non-Jewish people right through their faith. This Good News was told to Abraham beforehand, as the Scripture says: "All nations will be blessed through you." [n] [9]So all who believe as Abraham believed are blessed just as Abraham was. [10]But those who depend on following the law to make them right are under a curse, because the Scriptures say, "Anyone will be cursed who does not always obey what is written in the Book of the Law." [n] [11]Now it is clear that no one can be made right with God by the law, because the Scriptures say, "Those who are right with God will live by trusting in him." [n] [12]The law is not based on faith. It says, "A person who obeys these things will live because of them." [n] [13]Christ took away the curse the law put on us. He changed places with us and put himself under that curse. It is written in the Scriptures, "Anyone whose body is displayed on a tree [n] is cursed." [14]Christ did this so that God's blessing promised to Abraham might come through Jesus Christ to those who are not Jews. Jesus died so that by our believing we could receive the Spirit that God promised.

The Law and the Promise

[15]Brothers and sisters, let us think in human terms: Even an agreement made between two persons is firm. After that agreement is accepted by both people, no one can stop it or add anything to it. [16]God made promises both to Abraham and to his descendant. [d] God did not say, "and to your descendants." That would mean many people. But God said, "and to your descendant." That means only one person; that person is Christ. [17]This is what I mean: God had an agreement with Abraham and promised to keep it.

The law, which came four hundred thirty years later, cannot change that agreement and so destroy God's promise to Abraham. [18]If the law could give us Abraham's blessing, then the promise would not be necessary. But that is not possible, because God freely gave his blessings to Abraham through the promise he had made.

[19]So what was the law for? It was given to show that the wrong things people do are against God's will. And it continued until the special descendant, who had been promised, came. The law was given through angels who used Moses for a mediator [n] to give the law to people. [20]But a mediator is not needed when there is only one side, and God is only one.

The Purpose of the Law of Moses

[21]Does this mean that the law is against God's promises? Never! That would be true only if the law could make us right. But God did not give a law that can bring life. [22]Instead, the Scriptures [d] showed that the whole world is bound by sin. This was so the promise would be given through faith to people who believe in Jesus Christ.

[23]Before this faith came, we were all held prisoners by the law. We had no freedom until God showed us the way of faith that was coming. [24]In other words, the law was our guardian leading us to Christ so that we could be made right with God through faith. [25]Now the way of faith has come, and we no longer live under a guardian.

[26-27]You were all baptized into Christ, and so you were all clothed with Christ. This means that you are all children of God through faith in Christ Jesus. [28]In Christ, there is no difference between Jew and Greek, slave and free person, male and female. You are all the same in Christ Jesus. [29]You belong to Christ, so you are Abraham's descendants. [d] You will inherit all of God's

"**Abraham . . . God.**" Quotation from Genesis 15:6.
"**All . . . you.**" Quotation from Genesis 12:3 and 18:18.
"**Anyone . . . Law.**" Quotation from Deuteronomy 27:26.
"**Those . . . him.**" Quotation from Habakkuk 2:4.
"**A person . . . them.**" Quotation from Leviticus 18:5.
displayed on a tree Deuteronomy 21:22-23 says that when a person was killed for doing wrong, the body was hung on a tree to show shame. Paul means that the cross of Jesus was like that.
mediator A person who helps one person talk to or give something to another person.

blessings because of the promise God made to Abraham.

4 I want to tell you this: While those who will inherit their fathers' property are still children, they are no different from slaves. It does not matter that the children own everything. [2]While they are children, they must obey those who are chosen to care for them. But when the children reach the age set by their fathers, they are free. [3]It is the same for us. We were once like children, slaves to the useless rules of this world. [4]But when the right time came, God sent his Son who was born of a woman and lived under the law. [5]God did this so he could buy freedom for those who were under the law and so we could become his children.

[6]Since you are God's children, God sent the Spirit of his Son into your hearts, and the Spirit[d] cries out, "Father."[n] [7]So now you are not a slave; you are God's child, and God will give you the blessing he promised, because you are his child.

Paul's Love for the Christians

[8]In the past you did not know God. You were slaves to gods that were not real. [9]But now you know the true God. Really, it is God who knows you. So why do you turn back to those weak and useless rules you followed before? Do you want to be slaves to those things again? [10]You still follow teachings about special days, months, seasons, and years. [11]I am afraid for you, that my work for you has been wasted.

[12]Brothers and sisters, I became like you, so I beg you to become like me. You were very good to me before. [13]You remember that it was because of an illness that I came to you the first time, preaching the Good News.[d] [14]Though my sickness was a trouble for you, you did not hate me or make me leave. But you welcomed me as an angel from God, as if I were Jesus Christ himself! [15]You were very happy then, but where is that joy now? I am ready to testify that you would have taken out your eyes and given them to me if that were possible. [16]Now am I your enemy because I tell you the truth?

[17]Those people[n] are working hard to persuade you, but this is not good for you. They want to persuade you to turn against us and follow only them. [18]It is good for people to show interest in you, but only if their purpose is good. This is always true, not just when I am with you. [19]My little children, again I feel the pain of childbirth for you until you truly become like Christ. [20]I wish I could be with you now and could change the way I am talking to you, because I do not know what to think about you.

The Example of Hagar and Sarah

[21]Some of you still want to be under the law. Tell me, do you know what the law says? [22]The Scriptures[d] say that Abraham had two sons. The mother of one son was a slave woman, and the mother of the other son was a free woman. [23]Abraham's son from the slave woman was born in the normal human way. But the son from the free woman was born because of the promise God made to Abraham.

[24]This story teaches something else: The two women are like the two agreements between God and his people. One agreement is the law that God made on Mount Sinai,[n] and the people who are under this agreement are like slaves. The mother named Hagar is like that agreement. [25]She is like Mount Sinai in Arabia and is a picture of the earthly Jewish city of Jerusalem. This city and its people, the Jews, are slaves to the law. [26]But the heavenly Jerusalem, which is above, is like the free woman. She is our mother. [27]It is written in the Scriptures:

"Be happy, Jerusalem.
   You are like a woman who never gave
      birth to children.
Start singing and shout for joy.
   You never felt the pain of giving birth,
but you will have more children
   than the woman who has a husband."

Isaiah 54:1

[28]My brothers and sisters, you are God's children because of his promise, as Isaac was

---

"Father"   Literally, "Abba, Father." Jewish children called their fathers "Abba."
Those people   They are the false teachers who were bothering the believers in Galatia (Galatians 1:7).
Mount Sinai   Mountain in Arabia where God gave his laws to Moses (Exodus 19 and 20).

then. [29]The son who was born in the normal way treated the other son badly. It is the same today. [30]But what does the Scripture say? "Throw out the slave woman and her son. The son of the slave woman should not inherit anything. The son of the free woman should receive it all."[n] [31]So, my brothers and sisters, we are not children of the slave woman, but of the free woman.

Keep Your Freedom

5 We have freedom now, because Christ made us free. So stand strong. Do not change and go back into the slavery of the law. [2]Listen, I Paul tell you that if you go back to the law by being circumcised,[d] Christ does you no good. [3]Again, I warn every man: If you allow yourselves to be circumcised, you must follow all the law. [4]If you try to be made right with God through the law, your life with Christ is over — you have left God's grace. [5]But we have the true hope that comes from being made right with God, and by the Spirit we wait eagerly for this hope. [6]When we are in Christ Jesus, it is not important if we are circumcised or not. The important thing is faith — the kind of faith that works through love.

[7]You were running a good race. Who stopped you from following the true way? [8]This change did not come from the One who chose you. [9]Be careful! "Just a little yeast makes the whole batch of dough rise." [10]But I trust in the Lord that you will not believe those different ideas. Whoever is confusing you with such ideas will be punished.

[11]My brothers and sisters, I do not teach that a man must be circumcised. If I teach circumcision, why am I still being attacked? If I still taught circumcision, my preaching about the cross would not be a problem. [12]I wish the people who are bothering you would castrate[n] themselves!

[13]My brothers and sisters, God called you to be free, but do not use your freedom as an excuse to do what pleases your sinful self.

Serve each other with love. [14]The whole law is made complete in this one command: "Love your neighbor as you love yourself."[n] [15]If you go on hurting each other and tearing each other apart, be careful, or you will completely destroy each other.

The Spirit and Human Nature

[16]So I tell you: Live by following the Spirit.[d] Then you will not do what your sinful selves want. [17]Our sinful selves want what is against the Spirit, and the Spirit wants what is against our sinful selves. The two are against each other, so you cannot do just what you please. [18]But if the Spirit is leading you, you are not under the law.

[19]The wrong things the sinful self does are clear: being sexually unfaithful, not being pure, taking part in sexual sins, [20]worshiping gods, doing witchcraft,[d] hating, making trouble, being jealous, being angry, being selfish, making people angry with each other, causing divisions among people, [21]feeling envy, being drunk, having wild and wasteful parties, and doing other things like these. I warn you now as I warned you before: Those who do these things will not inherit God's kingdom. [22]But the Spirit produces the fruit of love, joy, peace, patience, kindness, goodness, faithfulness, [23]gentleness, self-control. There is no law that says these things are wrong. [24]Those who belong to Christ Jesus have crucified their own sinful selves. They have given up their old selfish feelings and the evil things they wanted to do. [25]We get our new life from the Spirit, so we should follow the Spirit. [26]We must not be proud or make trouble with each other or be jealous of each other.

Help Each Other

6 Brothers and sisters, if someone in your group does something wrong, you who are spiritual should go to that person and gently help make him right again. But be careful, because you might be tempted to sin, too. [2]By helping each other with your trou-

---

"Throw ... all." Quotation from Genesis 21:10.
castrate To cut off part of the male sex organ. Paul uses this word because it is similar to "circumcision." Paul wanted to show that he is very upset with the false teachers.
"Love ... yourself." Quotation from Leviticus 19:18.

bles, you truly obey the law of Christ. [3]If anyone thinks he is important when he really is not, he is only fooling himself. [4]Each person should judge his own actions and not compare himself with others. Then he can be proud for what he himself has done. [5]Each person must be responsible for himself.

[6]Anyone who is learning the teaching of God should share all the good things he has with his teacher.

Life Is like Planting a Field

 [7]Do not be fooled: You cannot cheat God. People harvest only what they plant. [8]If they plant to satisfy their sinful selves, their sinful selves will bring them ruin. But if they plant to please the Spirit,[d] they will receive eternal life from the Spirit. [9]We must not become tired of doing good. We will receive our harvest of eternal life at the right time if we do not give up. [10]When we have the opportunity to help anyone, we should do it. But we should give special attention to those who are in the family of believers.

Paul Ends His Letter

[11]See what large letters I use to write this myself. [12]Some people are trying to force you to be circumcised[d] so the Jews will accept them. They are afraid they will be attacked if they follow only the cross of Christ.[n] [13]Those who are circumcised do not obey the law themselves, but they want you to be circumcised so they can brag about what they forced you to do. [14]I hope I will never brag about things like that. The cross of our Lord Jesus Christ is my only reason for bragging. Through the cross of Jesus my world was crucified, and I died to the world. [15]It is not important if a man is circumcised or uncircumcised. The important thing is being the new people God has made. [16]Peace and mercy to those who follow this rule — and to all of God's people.

[17]So do not give me any more trouble. I have scars on my body that show[n] I belong to Christ Jesus.

[18]My brothers and sisters, the grace of our Lord Jesus Christ be with your spirit. Amen.

---

cross of Christ Paul uses the cross as a picture of the gospel, the story of Christ's death and rising from the dead to pay for our sins. The cross, or Christ's death, was God's way to save us.

that show Many times Paul was beaten and whipped by people who were against him because he was teaching about Christ. The scars were from these beatings.

EPHESIANS

God Unites His People

1 From Paul, an apostle*d* of Christ Jesus. I am an apostle because that is what God wanted.

To God's holy people living in Ephesus, believers in Christ Jesus:

²Grace and peace to you from God our Father and the Lord Jesus Christ.

Spiritual Blessings in Christ

³Praise be to the God and Father of our Lord Jesus Christ. In Christ, God has given us every spiritual blessing in the heavenly world. ⁴That is, in Christ, he chose us before the world was made so that we would be his holy people — people without blame before him. ⁵Because of his love, God had already decided to make us his own children through Jesus Christ. That was what he wanted and what pleased him, ⁶and it brings praise to God because of his wonderful grace. God gave that grace to us freely, in Christ, the One he loves. ⁷In Christ we are set free by the blood of his death, and so we have forgiveness of sins. How rich is God's grace, ⁸which he has given to us so fully and freely. God, with full wisdom and understanding, ⁹let us know his secret purpose. This was what God wanted, and he planned to do it through Christ. ¹⁰His goal was to carry out his plan, when the right time came, that all things in heaven and on earth would be joined together in Christ as the head.

¹¹In Christ we were chosen to be God's people, because from the very beginning God had decided this in keeping with his plan. And he is the One who makes everything agree with what he decides and wants. ¹²We are the first people who hoped in Christ, and we were chosen so that we would bring praise to God's glory. ¹³So it is with you. When you heard the true teaching — the Good News*d* about your salvation — you believed in Christ. And in Christ, God put his special mark of ownership on you by giving you the Holy Spirit*d* that he had promised. ¹⁴That Holy Spirit is the guarantee that we will receive what God promised for his people until God gives full freedom to those who are his — to bring praise to God's glory.

Paul's Prayer

¹⁵That is why since I heard about your faith in the Lord Jesus and your love for all God's people, ¹⁶I have not stopped giving thanks to God for you. I always remember you in my prayers, ¹⁷asking the God of our Lord Jesus Christ, the glorious Father, to give you a spirit of wisdom and revelation*d* so that you will know him better. ¹⁸I pray also that you will have greater understanding in your heart so you will know the hope to which he has called us and that you will know how rich and glorious are the blessings God has promised his holy people. ¹⁹And you will know that God's power is very great for us who believe. That power is the same as the great strength ²⁰God used to raise Christ from the dead and put him at his right side in the heavenly world. ²¹God has put Christ over all rulers, authorities, powers, and kings, not only in this world but also in the next. ²²God put everything under his power and made him the head over everything for the church, ²³which is Christ's body. The church is filled with Christ, and Christ fills everything in every way.

We Now Have Life

2 In the past you were spiritually dead because of your sins and the things you did against God. ²Yes, in the past you lived the way the world lives, following the ruler of the evil powers that are above the earth. That same spirit is now working in those who refuse to obey God. ³In the past all of us lived like them, trying to please our sinful selves and doing all the things our bodies and minds wanted. We should have suffered God's anger because of the way we were. We were the same as all other people.

[4]But God's mercy is great, and he loved us very much. [5]Though we were spiritually dead because of the things we did against God, he gave us new life with Christ. You have been saved by God's grace. [6]And he raised us up with Christ and gave us a seat with him in the heavens. He did this for those in Christ Jesus [7]so that for all future time he could show the very great riches of his grace by being kind to us in Christ Jesus. [8]I mean that you have been saved by grace through believing. You did not save yourselves; it was a gift from God. [9]It was not the result of your own efforts, so you cannot brag about it. [10]God has made us what we are. In Christ Jesus, God made us to do good works, which God planned in advance for us to live our lives doing.

One in Christ

[11]You were not born Jewish. You are the people the Jews call "uncircumcised."[n] Those who call you "uncircumcised" call themselves "circumcised."[d] (Their circumcision is only something they themselves do on their bodies.) [12]Remember that in the past you were without Christ. You were not citizens of Israel, and you had no part in the agreements[n] with the promise that God made to his people. You had no hope, and you did not know God. [13]But now in Christ Jesus, you who were far away from God are brought near through the blood of Christ's death. [14]Christ himself is our peace. He made both Jewish people and those who are not Jews one people. They were separated as if there were a wall between them, but Christ broke down that wall of hate by giving his own body. [15]The Jewish law had many commands and rules, but Christ ended that law. His purpose was to make the two groups of people become one new people in him and in this way make peace. [16]It was also Christ's purpose to end the hatred between the two groups, to make them into one body, and to bring them back to God. Christ did all this

with his death on the cross. [17]Christ came and preached peace to you who were far away from God, and to those who were near to God. [18]Yes, it is through Christ we all have the right to come to the Father in one Spirit.[d]

[19]Now you who are not Jewish are not foreigners or strangers any longer, but are citizens together with God's holy people. You belong to God's family. [20]You are like a building that was built on the foundation of the apostles[d] and prophets.[d] Christ Jesus himself is the most important stone[n] in that building, [21]and that whole building is joined together in Christ. He makes it grow and become a holy temple in the Lord. [22]And in Christ you, too, are being built together with the Jews into a place where God lives through the Spirit.

Paul's Work in Telling the Good News

3 So I, Paul, am a prisoner of Christ Jesus for you who are not Jews. [2]Surely you have heard that God gave me this work through his grace to help you. [3]He let me know his secret by showing it to me. I have already written a little about this. [4]If you read what I wrote then, you can see that I truly understand the secret about the Christ.[d] [5]People who lived in other times were not told that secret. But now, through the Spirit,[d] God has shown that secret to his holy apostles[d] and prophets.[d] [6]This is that secret: that through the Good News[d] those who are not Jews will share with the Jews in God's blessing. They belong to the same body, and they share together in the promise that God made in Christ Jesus.

[7]By God's special gift of grace given to me through his power, I became a servant to tell that Good News. [8]I am the least important of all God's people, but God gave me this gift — to tell those who are not Jews the Good News about the riches of Christ, which are too great to understand fully. [9]And God gave me the work of telling all people about the plan for his secret, which has been hidden in him since the beginning of time. He is the One who created everything. [10]His purpose

---

uncircumcised   People not having the mark of circumcision as the Jews had.
agreements   The agreements that God gave to his people in the Old Testament.
most important stone   Literally, "cornerstone." The first and most important stone in a building.

was that through the church all the rulers and powers in the heavenly world will now know God's wisdom, which has so many forms. [11]This agrees with the purpose God had since the beginning of time, and he carried out his plan through Christ Jesus our Lord. [12]In Christ we can come before God with freedom and without fear. We can do this through faith in Christ. [13]So I ask you not to become discouraged because of the sufferings I am having for you. My sufferings are for your glory.

The Love of Christ

[14]So I bow in prayer before the Father [15]from whom every family in heaven and on earth gets its true name. [16]I ask the Father in his great glory to give you the power to be strong inwardly through his Spirit.[d] [17]I pray that Christ will live in your hearts by faith and that your life will be strong in love and be built on love. [18]And I pray that you and all God's holy people will have the power to understand the greatness of Christ's love — how wide and how long and how high and how deep that love is. [19]Christ's love is greater than anyone can ever know, but I pray that you will be able to know that love. Then you can be filled with the fullness of God.

[20]With God's power working in us, God can do much, much more than anything we can ask or imagine. [21]To him be glory in the church and in Christ Jesus for all time, forever and ever. Amen.

The Unity of the Body

4 I am in prison because I belong to the Lord. God chose you to be his people, so I urge you now to live the life to which God called you. [2]Always be humble, gentle, and patient, accepting each other in love. [3]You are joined together with peace through the Spirit,[d] so make every effort to continue together in this way. [4]There is one body and one Spirit, and God called you to have one hope. [5]There is one Lord, one faith, and one baptism. [6]There is one God and Father of everything. He rules everything and is everywhere and is in everything.

[7]Christ gave each one of us the special gift of grace, showing how generous he is. [8]That is why it says in the Scriptures,[d]

"When he went up to the heights,
he led a parade of captives,
and he gave gifts to people."   *Psalm 68:18*

[9]When it says, "He went up," what does it mean? It means that he first came down to the earth. [10]So Jesus came down, and he is the same One who went up above all the sky. Christ did that to fill everything with his presence. [11]And Christ gave gifts to people — he made some to be apostles,[d] some to be prophets,[d] some to go and tell the Good News,[d] and some to have the work of caring for and teaching God's people. [12]Christ gave those gifts to prepare God's holy people for the work of serving, to make the body of Christ stronger. [13]This work must continue until we are all joined together in the same faith and in the same knowledge of the Son of God. We must become like a mature person, growing until we become like Christ and have his perfection.

[14]Then we will no longer be babies. We will not be tossed about like a ship that the waves carry one way and then another. We will not be influenced by every new teaching we hear from people who are trying to fool us. They make plans and try any kind of trick to fool people into following the wrong path. [15]No! Speaking the truth with love, we will grow up in every way into Christ, who is the head. [16]The whole body depends on Christ, and all the parts of the body are joined and held together. Each part does its own work to make the whole body grow and be strong with love.

The Way You Should Live

[17]In the Lord's name, I tell you this. Do not continue living like those who do not believe. Their thoughts are worth nothing. [18]They do not understand, and they know nothing, because they refuse to listen. So they cannot have the life that God gives. [19]They have lost all feeling of shame, and they use their lives for doing evil. They continually want to do all kinds of evil. [20]But what you learned in Christ was not like this. [21]I know that you heard about him, and you are in him, so you were taught the truth that is in Jesus. [22]You were taught to leave your old self — to stop living the evil way you lived before. That old self becomes worse, because

people are fooled by the evil things they want to do. 23But you were taught to be made new in your hearts, 24to become a new person. That new person is made to be like God — made to be truly good and holy.

25So you must stop telling lies. Tell each other the truth, because we all belong to each other in the same body.[n] 26When you are angry, do not sin, and be sure to stop being angry before the end of the day. 27Do not give the devil a way to defeat you. 28Those who are stealing must stop stealing and start working. They should earn an honest living for themselves. Then they will have something to share with those who are poor.

29When you talk, do not say harmful things, but say what people need — words that will help others become stronger. Then what you say will do good to those who listen to you. 30And do not make the Holy Spirit[d] sad. The Spirit is God's proof that you belong to him. God gave you the Spirit to show that God will make you free when the final day comes. 31Do not be bitter or angry or mad. Never shout angrily or say things to hurt others. Never do anything evil. 32Be kind and loving to each other, and forgive each other just as God forgave you in Christ.

Living in the Light

5 You are God's children whom he loves, so try to be like him. 2Live a life of love just as Christ loved us and gave himself for us as a sweet-smelling offering and sacrifice to God.

3But there must be no sexual sin among you, or any kind of evil or greed. Those things are not right for God's holy people. 4Also, there must be no evil talk among you, and you must not speak foolishly or tell evil jokes. These things are not right for you. Instead, you should be giving thanks to God. 5You can be sure of this: No one will have a place in the kingdom of Christ and of God who sins sexually, or does evil things, or is greedy. Anyone who is greedy is serving a false god. 6Do not let anyone fool you by telling you things that are not true, because these things

will bring God's anger on those who do not obey him. 7So have nothing to do with them. 8In the past you were full of darkness, but now you are full of light in the Lord. So live like children who belong to the light. 9Light brings every kind of goodness, right living, and truth. 10Try to learn what pleases the Lord. 11Have nothing to do with the things done in darkness, which are not worth anything. But show that they are wrong. 12It is shameful even to talk about what those people do in secret. 13But the light makes all things easy to see, 14and everything that is made easy to see can become light. This is why it is said:

"Wake up, sleeper!
    Rise from death,
    and Christ will shine on you."

15So be very careful how you live. Do not live like those who are not wise, but live wisely. 16Use every chance you have for doing good, because these are evil times. 17So do not be foolish but learn what the Lord wants you to do. 18Do not be drunk with wine, which will ruin you, but be filled with the Spirit.[d] 19Speak to each other with psalms, hymns, and spiritual songs, singing and making music in your hearts to the Lord. 20Always give thanks to God the Father for everything, in the name of our Lord Jesus Christ.

Wives and Husbands

21Yield to obey each other because you respect Christ.

22Wives, yield to your husbands, as you do to the Lord, 23because the husband is the head of the wife, as Christ is the head of the church. And he is the Savior of the body, which is the church. 24As the church yields to Christ, so you wives should yield to your husbands in everything.

25Husbands, love your wives as Christ loved the church and gave himself for it 26to make it belong to God. Christ used the word to make the church clean by washing it with water. 27He died so that he could give the church to himself like a bride in all her beauty. He died so that the church could be

---

Tell ... body. Quotation from Zechariah 8:16.

pure and without fault, with no evil or sin or any other wrong thing in it. [28]In the same way, husbands should love their wives as they love their own bodies. The man who loves his wife loves himself. [29]No one ever hates his own body, but feeds and takes care of it. And that is what Christ does for the church, [30]because we are parts of his body. [31]The Scripture says, "So a man will leave his father and mother and be united with his wife, and the two will become one body." [n] [32]That secret is very important — I am talking about Christ and the church. [33]But each one of you must love his wife as he loves himself, and a wife must respect her husband.

Children and Parents

6 Children, obey your parents as the Lord wants, because this is the right thing to do. [2]The command says, "Honor your father and mother." [n] This is the first command that has a promise with it — [3]"Then everything will be well with you, and you will have a long life on the earth." [n]

[4]Fathers, do not make your children angry, but raise them with the training and teaching of the Lord.

Slaves and Masters

[5]Slaves, obey your masters here on earth with fear and respect and from a sincere heart, just as you obey Christ. [6]You must do this not only while they are watching you, to please them. With all your heart you must do what God wants as people who are obeying Christ. [7]Do your work with enthusiasm. Work as if you were serving the Lord, not as if you were serving only men and women. [8]Remember that the Lord will give a reward to everyone, slave or free, for doing good.

[9]Masters, in the same way, be good to your slaves. Do not threaten them. Remember that the One who is your Master and their Master is in heaven, and he treats everyone alike.

Wear the Full Armor of God

[10]Finally, be strong in the Lord and in his great power. [11]Put on the full armor of God so that you can fight against the devil's evil tricks. [12]Our fight is not against people on earth but against the rulers and authorities and the powers of this world's darkness, against the spiritual powers of evil in the heavenly world. [13]That is why you need to put on God's full armor. Then on the day of evil you will be able to stand strong. And when you have finished the whole fight, you will still be standing. [14]So stand strong, with the belt of truth tied around your waist and the protection of right living on your chest. [15]On your feet wear the Good News [d] of peace to help you stand strong. [16]And also use the shield of faith with which you can stop all the burning arrows of the Evil One. [17]Accept God's salvation as your helmet, and take the sword of the Spirit, [d] which is the word of God. [18]Pray in the Spirit at all times with all kinds of prayers, asking for everything you need. To do this you must always be ready and never give up. Always pray for all God's people.

[19]Also pray for me that when I speak, God will give me words so that I can tell the secret of the Good News without fear. [20]I have been sent to preach this Good News, and I am doing that now, here in prison. Pray that when I preach the Good News I will speak without fear, as I should.

Final Greetings

[21]I am sending to you Tychicus, our brother whom we love and a faithful servant of the Lord's work. He will tell you everything that is happening with me. Then you will know how I am and what I am doing. [22]I am sending him to you for this reason — so that you will know how we are, and he can encourage you.

[23]Peace and love with faith to you from God the Father and the Lord Jesus Christ. [24]Grace to all of you who love our Lord Jesus Christ with love that never ends.

"So . . . body."   Quotation from Genesis 2:24.
"Honor . . . mother."   Quotation from Exodus 20:12; Deuteronomy 5:16.
"Then . . . earth."   Quotation from Exodus 20:12; Deuteronomy 5:16.

PHILIPPIANS

Serve Others with Joy

1 From Paul and Timothy, servants of Christ Jesus.

To all of God's holy people in Christ Jesus who live in Philippi, including your elders*d* and deacons:*d*

²Grace and peace to you from God our Father and the Lord Jesus Christ.

Paul's Prayer

³I thank my God every time I remember you, ⁴always praying with joy for all of you. ⁵I thank God for the help you gave me while I preached the Good News*d*—help you gave from the first day you believed until now. ⁶God began doing a good work in you, and I am sure he will continue it until it is finished when Jesus Christ comes again.

⁷And I know that I am right to think like this about all of you, because I have you in my heart. All of you share in God's grace with me while I am in prison and while I am defending and proving the truth of the Good News. ⁸God knows that I want to see you very much, because I love all of you with the love of Christ Jesus.

⁹This is my prayer for you: that your love will grow more and more; that you will have knowledge and understanding with your love; ¹⁰that you will see the difference between good and bad and will choose the good; that you will be pure and without wrong for the coming of Christ; ¹¹that you will do many good things with the help of Christ to bring glory and praise to God.

Paul's Troubles Help the Work

¹²I want you brothers and sisters*n* to know that what has happened to me has helped to spread the Good News.*d* ¹³All the palace guards and everyone else knows that I am in prison because I am a believer in Christ. ¹⁴Because I am in prison, most of the believers have become more bold in Christ and are not afraid to speak the word of God.

¹⁵It is true that some preach about Christ because they are jealous and ambitious, but others preach about Christ because they want to help. ¹⁶They preach because they have love, and they know that God gave me the work of defending the Good News. ¹⁷But the others preach about Christ for selfish and wrong reasons, wanting to make trouble for me in prison.

¹⁸But it doesn't matter. The important thing is that in every way, whether for right or wrong reasons, they are preaching about Christ. So I am happy, and I will continue to be happy. ¹⁹Because you are praying for me and the Spirit of Jesus Christ is helping me, I know this trouble will bring my freedom. ²⁰I expect and hope that I will not fail Christ in anything but that I will have the courage now, as always, to show the greatness of Christ in my life here on earth, whether I live or die. ²¹To me the only important thing about living is Christ, and dying would be profit for me. ²²If I continue living in my body, I will be able to work for the Lord. I do not know what to choose—living or dying. ²³It is hard to choose between the two. I want to leave this life and be with Christ, which is much better, ²⁴but you need me here in my body. ²⁵Since I am sure of this, I know I will stay with you to help you grow and have joy in your faith. ²⁶You will be very happy in Christ Jesus when I am with you again.

²⁷Only one thing concerns me: Be sure that you live in a way that brings honor to the Good News of Christ. Then whether I come and visit you or am away from you, I will hear that you are standing strong with one

---

brothers and sisters Although the Greek text says "brothers" here and throughout this book, Paul's words were meant for the entire church, including men and women.

purpose, that you work together as one for the faith of the Good News, 28and that you are not afraid of those who are against you. All of this is proof that your enemies will be destroyed but that you will be saved by God. 29God gave you the honor not only of believing in Christ but also of suffering for him, both of which bring glory to Christ. 30When I was with you, you saw the struggles I had, and you hear about the struggles I am having now. You yourselves are having the same kind of struggles.

2 Does your life in Christ give you strength? Does his love comfort you? Do we share together in the spirit? Do you have mercy and kindness? 2If so, make me very happy by having the same thoughts, sharing the same love, and having one mind and purpose. 3When you do things, do not let selfishness or pride be your guide. Instead, be humble and give more honor to others than to yourselves. 4Do not be interested only in your own life, but be interested in the lives of others.

Be Unselfish like Christ

5In your lives you must think and act like Christ Jesus.

6Christ himself was like God in
everything.
But he did not think that being equal
with God was something to be
used for his own benefit.
7But he gave up his place with God and
made himself nothing.
He was born to be a man
and became like a servant.
8And when he was living as a man,
he humbled himself and was fully
obedient to God,
even when that caused his
death — death on a cross.
9So God raised him to the highest place.
God made his name greater than every
other name
10so that every knee will bow to the name
of Jesus —
everyone in heaven, on earth, and
under the earth.
11And everyone will confess that Jesus
Christ is Lord
and bring glory to God the Father.

Be the People God Wants You to Be

12My dear friends, you have always obeyed God when I was with you. It is even more important that you obey now while I am away from you. Keep on working to complete your salvation with fear and trembling, 13because God is working in you to help you want to do and be able to do what pleases him.

14Do everything without complaining or arguing. 15Then you will be innocent and without any wrong. You will be God's children without fault. But you are living with crooked and mean people all around you, among whom you shine like stars in the dark world. 16You offer the teaching that gives life. So when Christ comes again, I can be happy because my work was not wasted. I ran the race and won.

17Your faith makes you offer your lives as a sacrifice in serving God. If I have to offer my own blood with your sacrifice, I will be happy and full of joy with all of you. 18You also should be happy and full of joy with me.

Timothy and Epaphroditus

19I hope in the Lord Jesus to send Timothy to you soon. I will be happy to learn how you are. 20I have no one else like Timothy, who truly cares for you. 21Other people are interested only in their own lives, not in the work of Jesus Christ. 22You know the kind of person Timothy is. You know he has served with me in telling the Good News, *d* as a son serves his father. 23I plan to send him to you quickly when I know what will happen to me. 24I am sure that the Lord will help me to come to you soon.

25Epaphroditus, my brother in Christ, works and serves with me in the army of Christ. When I needed help, you sent him to me. I think now that I must send him back to you, 26because he wants very much to see all of you. He is worried because you heard that he was sick. 27Yes, he was sick, and nearly died, but God had mercy on him and me too so that I would not have more sadness. 28I want very much to send him to you so that when you see him you can be happy, and I can stop worrying about you. 29Welcome him in the Lord with much joy. Give honor to people like him, [30]because he almost died for the work of Christ. He risked his life to give me the help you could not give in your service to me.

The Importance of Christ

3 My brothers and sisters, be full of joy in the Lord. It is no trouble for me to write the same things to you again, and it will help you to be more ready. [2]Watch out for those who do evil, who are like dogs, who demand to cut[n] the body. [3]We are the ones who are truly circumcised.[d] We worship God through his Spirit,[d] and our pride is in Christ Jesus. We do not put trust in ourselves or anything we can do, [4]although I might be able to put trust in myself. If anyone thinks he has a reason to trust in himself, he should know that I have greater reason for trusting in myself. [5]I was circumcised eight days after my birth. I am from the people of Israel and the tribe[d] of Benjamin. I am a Hebrew, and my parents were Hebrews. I had a strict view of the law, which is why I became a Pharisee.[d] [6]I was so enthusiastic I tried to hurt the church. No one could find fault with the way I obeyed the law of Moses. [7]Those things were important to me, but now I think they are worth nothing because of Christ. [8]Not only those things, but I think that all things are worth nothing compared with the greatness of knowing Christ Jesus my Lord. Because of him, I have lost all those things, and now I know they are worthless trash. This allows me to have Christ [9]and to belong to him. Now I am right with God, not because I followed the law, but because I believed in Christ. God uses my faith to make me right with him. [10]I want to know Christ and the power that raised him from the dead. I want to share in his sufferings and become like him in his death. [11]Then I have hope that I myself will be raised from the dead.

Continuing Toward Our Goal

[12]I do not mean that I am already as God wants me to be. I have not yet reached that goal, but I continue trying to reach it and to make it mine. Christ wants me to do that, which is the reason he made me his. [13]Brothers and sisters, I know that I have not yet reached that goal, but there is one thing I always do. Forgetting the past and straining toward what is ahead, [14]I keep trying to reach the goal and get the prize for which God called me through Christ to the life above.

[15]All of us who are spiritually mature should think this way, too. And if there are things you do not agree with, God will make them clear to you. [16]But we should continue following the truth we already have.

[17]Brothers and sisters, all of you should try to follow my example and to copy those who live the way we showed you. [18]Many people live like enemies of the cross of Christ. I have often told you about them, and it makes me cry to tell you about them now. [19]In the end, they will be destroyed. They do whatever their bodies want, they are proud of their shameful acts, and they think only about earthly things. [20]But our homeland is in heaven, and we are waiting for our Savior, the Lord Jesus Christ, to come from heaven. [21]By his power to rule all things, he will change our simple bodies and make them like his own glorious body.

What the Christians Are to Do

4 My dear brothers and sisters, I love you and want to see you. You bring me joy and make me proud of you, so stand strong in the Lord as I have told you.

[2]I ask Euodia and Syntyche to agree in the Lord. [3]And I ask you, my faithful friend, to help these women. They served with me in telling the Good News,[d] together with Clement and others who worked with me, whose names are written in the book of life.[n]

[4]Be full of joy in the Lord always. I will say again, be full of joy.

[5]Let everyone see that you are gentle and kind. The Lord is coming soon. [6]Do not worry about anything, but pray and ask God for everything you need, always giving thanks. [7]And God's peace, which is so great we cannot understand it, will keep your hearts and minds in Christ Jesus.

---

cut The word in Greek is like the word "circumcise," but it means "to cut completely off."
book of life God's book that has the names of all God's chosen people (Revelation 3:5; 21:27).

[8]Brothers and sisters, think about the things that are good and worthy of praise. Think about the things that are true and honorable and right and pure and beautiful and respected. [9]Do what you learned and received from me, what I told you, and what you saw me do. And the God who gives peace will be with you.

Paul Thanks the Christians

[10]I am very happy in the Lord that you have shown your care for me again. You continued to care about me, but there was no way for you to show it. [11]I am not telling you this because I need anything. I have learned to be satisfied with the things I have and with everything that happens. [12]I know how to live when I am poor, and I know how to live when I have plenty. I have learned the secret of being happy at any time in everything that happens, when I have enough to eat and when I go hungry, when I have more than I need and when I do not have enough. [13]I can do all things through Christ, because he gives me strength.

[14]But it was good that you helped me when I needed it. [15]You Philippians remember when I first preached the Good News[d] there. When I left Macedonia, you were the only church that gave me help. [16]Several times you sent me things I needed when I was in Thessalonica. [17]Really, it is not that I want to receive gifts from you, but I want you to have the good that comes from giving. [18]And now I have everything, and more. I have all I need, because Epaphroditus brought your gift to me. It is like a sweet-smelling sacrifice offered to God, who accepts that sacrifice and is pleased with it. [19]My God will use his wonderful riches in Christ Jesus to give you everything you need. [20]Glory to our God and Father forever and ever! Amen.

[21]Greet each of God's people in Christ. Those who are with me send greetings to you. [22]All of God's people greet you, particularly those from the palace of Caesar.[d]

[23]The grace of the Lord Jesus Christ be with you all.

COLOSSIANS

Only Christ Can Save People

1 From Paul, an apostle[d] of Christ Jesus. I am an apostle because that is what God wanted. Also from Timothy, our brother.

[2]To the holy and faithful brothers and sisters[n] in Christ that live in Colosse:

Grace and peace to you from God our Father.

[3]In our prayers for you we always thank God, the Father of our Lord Jesus Christ, [4]because we have heard about the faith you have in Christ Jesus and the love you have for all of God's people. [5]You have this faith and love because of your hope, and what you hope for is kept safe for you in heaven. You learned about this hope when you heard the message about the truth, the Good News[d] [6]that was told to you. Everywhere in the world that Good News is bringing blessings and is growing. This has happened with you, too, since you heard the Good News and understood the truth about the grace of God. [7]You learned about God's grace from Epaphras, whom we love. He works together with us and is a faithful servant of Christ for us. [8]He also told us about the love you have from the Holy Spirit.[d]

[9]Because of this, since the day we heard about you, we have continued praying for you, asking God that you will know fully what he wants. We pray that you will also have great wisdom and understanding in spiritual things [10]so that you will live the kind of life that honors and pleases the Lord in every way. You will produce fruit in every good work and grow in the knowledge of God. [11]God will strengthen you with his own great power so that you will not give up when troubles come, but you will be patient. [12]And you will joyfully give thanks to the Father who has made you able to have a share in all that he has prepared for his people in the kingdom of light. [13]God has freed us from the power of darkness, and he brought us into the kingdom of his dear Son. [14]The Son paid for our sins, and in him we have forgiveness.

The Importance of Christ

[15]No one can see God, but Jesus Christ is exactly like him. He ranks higher than everything that has been made. [16]Through his power all things were made — things in heaven and on earth, things seen and unseen, all powers, authorities, lords, and rulers. All things were made through Christ and for Christ. [17]He was there before anything was made, and all things continue because of him. [18]He is the head of the body, which is the church. Everything comes from him. He is the first one who was raised from the dead. So in all things Jesus has first place. [19]God was pleased for all of himself to live in Christ. [20]And through Christ, God has brought all things back to himself again — things on earth and things in heaven. God made peace through the blood of Christ's death on the cross.

[21]At one time you were separated from God. You were his enemies in your minds, and the evil things you did were against God. [22]But now God has made you his friends again. He did this through Christ's death in the body so that he might bring you into God's presence as people who are holy, with no wrong, and with nothing of which God can judge you guilty. [23]This will happen if you continue strong and sure in your faith. You must not be moved away from the hope brought to you by the Good News that you heard. That same Good News has been told to everyone in the world, and I, Paul, help in preaching that Good News.

---

brothers and sisters Although the Greek text says "brothers" here and throughout this book, Paul's words were meant for the entire church, including men and women.

Paul's Work for the Church

24I am happy in my sufferings for you. There are things that Christ must still suffer through his body, the church. I am accepting, in my body, my part of these things that must be suffered. 25I became a servant of the church because God gave me a special work to do that helps you, and that work is to tell fully the message of God. 26This message is the secret that was hidden from everyone since the beginning of time, but now it is made known to God's holy people. 27God decided to let his people know this rich and glorious secret which he has for all people. This secret is Christ himself, who is in you. He is our only hope for glory. 28So we continue to preach Christ to each person, using all wisdom to warn and to teach everyone, in order to bring each one into God's presence as a mature person in Christ. 29To do this, I work and struggle, using Christ's great strength that works so powerfully in me.

2 I want you to know how hard I work for you, those in Laodicea, and others who have never seen me. 2I want them to be strengthened and joined together with love so that they may be rich in their understanding. This leads to their knowing fully God's secret, that is, Christ himself. 3In him all the treasures of wisdom and knowledge are safely kept.

4I say this so that no one can fool you by arguments that seem good, but are false. 5Though I am absent from you in my body, my heart is with you, and I am happy to see your good lives and your strong faith in Christ.

Continue to Live in Christ

6As you received Christ Jesus the Lord, so continue to live in him. 7Keep your roots deep in him and have your lives built on him. Be strong in the faith, just as you were taught, and always be thankful.

8Be sure that no one leads you away with false and empty teaching that is only human, which comes from the ruling spirits of this world, and not from Christ. 9All of God lives in Christ fully (even when Christ was on earth), 10and you have a full and true life in Christ, who is ruler over all rulers and powers.

11Also in Christ you had a different kind of circumcision,d a circumcision not done by hands. It was through Christ's circumcision, that is, his death, that you were made free from the power of your sinful self. 12When you were baptized, you were buried with Christ, and you were raised up with him through your faith in God's power that was shown when he raised Christ from the dead. 13When you were spiritually dead because of your sins and because you were not free from the power of your sinful self, God made you alive with Christ, and he forgave all our sins. 14He canceled the debt, which listed all the rules we failed to follow. He took away that record with its rules and nailed it to the cross. 15God stripped the spiritual rulers and powers of their authority. With the cross, he won the victory and showed the world that they were powerless.

Don't Follow People's Rules

16So do not let anyone make rules for you about eating and drinking or about a religious feast, a New Moond Festival, or a Sabbathd day. 17These things were like a shadow of what was to come. But what is true and real has come and is found in Christ. 18Do not let anyone disqualify you by making you humiliate yourself and worship angels. Such people enter into visions, which fill them with foolish pride because of their human way of thinking. 19They do not hold tightly to Christ, the head. It is from him that all the parts of the body are cared for and held together. So it grows in the way God wants it to grow.

20Since you died with Christ and were made free from the ruling spirits of the world, why do you act as if you still belong to this world by following rules like these: 21"Don't eat this," "Don't taste that," "Don't even touch that thing"? 22These rules refer to earthly things that are gone as soon as they are used. They are only man-made commands and teachings. 23They seem to be wise, but they are only part of a man-made religion. They make people pretend not to be proud and make them punish their bodies, but they do not really control the evil desires of the sinful self.

Your New Life in Christ

3 Since you were raised from the dead with Christ, aim at what is in heaven, where Christ is sitting at the right hand of God. [2]Think only about the things in heaven, not the things on earth. [3]Your old sinful self has died, and your new life is kept with Christ in God. [4]Christ is our life, and when he comes again, you will share in his glory.

[5]So put all evil things out of your life: sexual sinning, doing evil, letting evil thoughts control you, wanting things that are evil, and greed. This is really serving a false god. [6]These things make God angry.[n] [7]In your past, evil life you also did these things.

[8]But now also put these things out of your life: anger, bad temper, doing or saying things to hurt others, and using evil words when you talk. [9]Do not lie to each other. You have left your old sinful life and the things you did before. [10]You have begun to live the new life, in which you are being made new and are becoming like the One who made you. This new life brings you the true knowledge of God. [11]In the new life there is no difference between Greeks and Jews, those who are circumcised[d] and those who are not circumcised, or people who are foreigners, or Scythians.[n] There is no difference between slaves and free people. But Christ is in all believers, and Christ is all that is important.

[12]God has chosen you and made you his holy people. He loves you. So always do these things: Show mercy to others, be kind, humble, gentle, and patient. [13]Get along with each other, and forgive each other. If someone does wrong to you, forgive that person because the Lord forgave you. [14]Do all these things; but most important, love each other. Love is what holds you all together in perfect unity. [15]Let the peace that Christ gives control your thinking, because you were all called together in one body[n] to have peace. Always be thankful. [16]Let the teaching of Christ live in you richly. Use all

wisdom to teach and instruct each other by singing psalms, hymns, and spiritual songs with thankfulness in your hearts to God. [17]Everything you do or say should be done to obey Jesus your Lord. And in all you do, give thanks to God the Father through Jesus.

Your New Life with Other People

[18]Wives, yield to the authority of your husbands, because this is the right thing to do in the Lord.

[19]Husbands, love your wives and be gentle with them.

[20]Children, obey your parents in all things, because this pleases the Lord.

[21]Fathers, do not nag your children. If you are too hard to please, they may want to stop trying.

[22]Slaves, obey your masters in all things. Do not obey just when they are watching you, to gain their favor, but serve them honestly, because you respect the Lord. [23]In all the work you are doing, work the best you can. Work as if you were doing it for the Lord, not for people. [24]Remember that you will receive your reward from the Lord, which he promised to his people. You are serving the Lord Christ. [25]But remember that anyone who does wrong will be punished for that wrong, and the Lord treats everyone the same.

4 Masters, give what is good and fair to your slaves. Remember that you have a Master in heaven.

What the Christians Are to Do

[2]Continue praying, keeping alert, and always thanking God. [3]Also pray for us that God will give us an opportunity to tell people his message. Pray that we can preach the secret that God has made known about Christ. This is why I am in prison. [4]Pray that I can speak in a way that will make it clear, as I should.

[5]Be wise in the way you act with people who are not believers, making the most of every opportunity. [6]When you talk, you

---

These ... angry Some Greek copies add: "against the people who do not obey God."
Scythians The Scythians were known as very wild and cruel people.
body The spiritual body of Christ, meaning the church or his people.

should always be kind and pleasant so you will be able to answer everyone in the way you should.

News About the People with Paul

⁷Tychicus is my dear brother in Christ and a faithful minister and servant with me in the Lord. He will tell you all the things that are happening to me. ⁸This is why I am sending him: so you may know how we are and he may encourage you. ⁹I send him with Onesimus, a faithful and dear brother in Christ, and one of your group. They will tell you all that has happened here.

¹⁰Aristarchus, a prisoner with me, and Mark, the cousin of Barnabas, greet you. (I have already told you what to do about Mark. If he comes, welcome him.) ¹¹Jesus, who is called Justus, also greets you. These are the only Jewish believers who work with me for the kingdom of God, and they have been a comfort to me.

¹²Epaphras, a servant of Jesus Christ, from your group, also greets you. He always prays for you that you will grow to be spiritually mature and have everything God wants for you. ¹³I know he has worked hard for you and the people in Laodicea and in Hierapolis. ¹⁴Demas and our dear friend Luke, the doctor, greet you.

¹⁵Greet the brothers in Laodicea. And greet Nympha and the church that meets in her house. ¹⁶After this letter is read to you, be sure it is also read to the church in Laodicea. And you read the letter that I wrote to Laodicea. ¹⁷Tell Archippus, "Be sure to finish the work the Lord gave you."

¹⁸I, Paul, greet you and write this with my own hand. Remember me in prison. Grace be with you.

1 THESSALONIANS

Paul Encourages New Christians

1 From Paul, Silas, and Timothy.
To the church in Thessalonica, the church in God the Father and the Lord Jesus Christ:

Grace and peace to you.

The Faith of the Thessalonians

²We always thank God for all of you and mention you when we pray. ³We continually recall before God our Father the things you have done because of your faith and the work you have done because of your love. And we thank him that you continue to be strong because of your hope in our Lord Jesus Christ.

⁴Brothers and sisters, *n* God loves you, and we know he has chosen you, ⁵because the Good News*d* we brought to you came not only with words, but with power, with the Holy Spirit,*d* and with sure knowledge that it is true. Also you know how we lived when we were with you in order to help you. ⁶And you became like us and like the Lord. You suffered much, but still you accepted the teaching with the joy that comes from the Holy Spirit. ⁷So you became an example to all the believers in Macedonia and Southern Greece. ⁸And the Lord's teaching spread from you not only into Macedonia and Southern Greece, but now your faith in God has become known everywhere. So we do not need to say anything about it. ⁹People everywhere are telling about the way you accepted us when we were there with you. They tell how you stopped worshiping idols and began serving the living and true God. ¹⁰And you wait for God's Son, whom God raised from the dead, to come from heaven. He is Jesus, who saves us from God's angry judgment that is sure to come.

Paul's Work in Thessalonica

2 Brothers and sisters, you know our visit to you was not a failure. ²Before we came to you, we suffered in Philippi. People there insulted us, as you know, and many people were against us. But our God helped us to be brave and to tell you his Good News.*d* ³Our appeal does not come from lies or wrong reasons, nor were we trying to trick you. ⁴But we speak the Good News because God tested us and trusted us to do it. When we speak, we are not trying to please people, but God, who tests our hearts. ⁵You know that we never tried to influence you by saying nice things about you. We were not trying to get your money; we had no selfishness to hide from you. God knows that this is true. ⁶We were not looking for human praise, from you or anyone else, ⁷even though as apostles*d* of Christ we could have used our authority over you.

But we were very gentle with you, like a mother caring for her little children. ⁸Because we loved you, we were happy to share not only God's Good News with you, but even our own lives. You had become so dear to us! ⁹Brothers and sisters, I know you remember our hard work and difficulties. We worked night and day so we would not burden any of you while we preached God's Good News to you.

¹⁰When we were with you, we lived in a holy and honest way, without fault. You know this is true, and so does God. ¹¹You know that we treated each of you as a father treats his own children. ¹²We encouraged you, we urged you, and we insisted that you live good lives for God, who calls you to his glorious kingdom.

¹³Also, we always thank God because when you heard his message from us, you

---

Brothers and sisters Although the Greek text says "Brothers" here and throughout this book, Paul's words were meant for the entire church, including men and women.

accepted it as the word of God, not the words of humans. And it really is God's message which works in you who believe. [14]Brothers and sisters, your experiences have been like those of God's churches in Christ that are in Judea.[n] You suffered from the people of your own country, as they suffered from the Jews, [15]who killed both the Lord Jesus and the prophets[d] and forced us to leave that country. They do not please God and are against all people. [16]They try to stop us from teaching those who are not Jews so they may be saved. By doing this, they are increasing their sins to the limit. The anger of God has come to them at last.

Paul Wants to Visit Them Again

[17]Brothers and sisters, though we were separated from you for a short time, our thoughts were still with you. We wanted very much to see you and tried hard to do so. [18]We wanted to come to you. I, Paul, tried to come more than once, but Satan stopped us. [19]You are our hope, our joy, and the crown we will take pride in when our Lord Jesus Christ comes. [20]Truly you are our glory and our joy.

3 When we could not wait any longer, we decided it was best to stay in Athens alone [2]and send Timothy to you. Timothy, our brother, works with us for God and helps us tell people the Good News[d] about Christ. We sent him to strengthen and encourage you in your faith [3]so none of you would be upset by these troubles. You yourselves know that we must face these troubles. [4]Even when we were with you, we told you we all would have to suffer, and you know it has happened. [5]Because of this, when I could wait no longer, I sent Timothy to you so I could learn about your faith. I was afraid the devil had tempted you, and then our hard work would have been wasted.

[6]But Timothy now has come back to us from you and has brought us good news about your faith and love. He told us that you always remember us in a good way and that you want to see us just as much as we want to see you. [7]So, brothers and sisters, while

we have much trouble and suffering, we are encouraged about you because of your faith. [8]Our life is really full if you stand strong in the Lord. [9]We have so much joy before our God because of you. We cannot thank him enough for all the joy we feel. [10]Night and day we continue praying with all our heart that we can see you again and give you all the things you need to make your faith strong.

[11]Now may our God and Father himself and our Lord Jesus prepare the way for us to come to you. [12]May the Lord make your love grow more and multiply for each other and for all people so that you will love others as we love you. [13]May your hearts be made strong so that you will be holy and without fault before our God and Father when our Lord Jesus comes with all his holy ones.

A Life that Pleases God

4 Brothers and sisters, we taught you how to live in a way that will please God, and you are living that way. Now we ask and encourage you in the Lord Jesus to live that way even more. [2]You know what we told you to do by the authority of the Lord Jesus. [3]God wants you to be holy and to stay away from sexual sins. [4]He wants each of you to learn to control your own body[n] in a way that is holy and honorable. [5]Don't use your body for sexual sin like the people who do not know God. [6]Also, do not wrong or cheat another Christian in this way. The Lord will punish people who do those things as we have already told you and warned you. [7]God called us to be holy and does not want us to live in sin. [8]So the person who refuses to obey this teaching is disobeying God, not simply a human teaching. And God is the One who gives us his Holy Spirit.[d]

[9]We do not need to write you about having love for your Christian family, because God has already taught you to love each other. [10]And truly you do love the Christians in all of Macedonia. Brothers and sisters, now we encourage you to love them even more.

[11]Do all you can to live a peaceful life.

Judea The Jewish land where Jesus lived and taught and where the church first began.
learn ... body This might also mean "learn to live with your own wife."

Take care of your own business, and do your own work as we have already told you. [12]If you do, then people who are not believers will respect you, and you will not have to depend on others for what you need.

The Lord's Coming

[13]Brothers and sisters, we want you to know about those Christians who have died so you will not be sad, as others who have no hope. [14]We believe that Jesus died and that he rose again. So, because of him, God will raise with Jesus those who have died. [15]What we tell you now is the Lord's own message. We who are living when the Lord comes again will not go before those who have already died. [16]The Lord himself will come down from heaven with a loud command, with the voice of the archangel,[n] and with the trumpet call of God. And those who have died believing in Christ will rise first. [17]After that, we who are still alive will be gathered up with them in the clouds to meet the Lord in the air. And we will be with the Lord forever. [18]So encourage each other with these words.

Be Ready for the Lord's Coming

5 Now, brothers and sisters, we do not need to write you about times and dates. [2]You know very well that the day the Lord comes again will be a surprise, like a thief that comes in the night. [3]While people are saying, "We have peace and we are safe," they will be destroyed quickly. It is like pains that come quickly to a woman having a baby. Those people will not escape. [4]But you, brothers and sisters, are not living in darkness, and so that day will not surprise you like a thief. [5]You are all people who belong to the light and to the day. We do not belong to the night or to darkness. [6]So we should not be like other people who are sleeping, but we should be alert and have self-control. [7]Those who sleep, sleep at night. Those who get drunk, get drunk at night. [8]But we belong

to the day, so we should control ourselves. We should wear faith and love to protect us, and the hope of salvation should be our helmet. [9]God did not choose us to suffer his anger but to have salvation through our Lord Jesus Christ. [10]Jesus died for us so that we can live together with him, whether we are alive or dead when he comes. [11]So encourage each other and give each other strength, just as you are doing now.

Final Instructions and Greetings

[12]Now, brothers and sisters, we ask you to appreciate those who work hard among you, who lead you in the Lord and teach you. [13]Respect them with a very special love because of the work they do.

Live in peace with each other. [14]We ask you, brothers and sisters, to warn those who do not work. Encourage the people who are afraid. Help those who are weak. Be patient with everyone. [15]Be sure that no one pays back wrong for wrong, but always try to do what is good for each other and for all people.

[16]Always be joyful. [17]Pray continually, [18]and give thanks whatever happens. That is what God wants for you in Christ Jesus.

[19]Do not hold back the work of the Holy Spirit.[d] [20]Do not treat prophecy[d] as if it were unimportant. [21]But test everything. Keep what is good, [22]and stay away from everything that is evil.

[23]Now may God himself, the God of peace, make you pure, belonging only to him. May your whole self—spirit, soul, and body—be kept safe and without fault when our Lord Jesus Christ comes. [24]You can trust the One who calls you to do that for you.

[25]Brothers and sisters, pray for us.

[26]Give each other a holy kiss when you meet. [27]I tell you by the authority of the Lord to read this letter to all the believers.

[28]The grace of our Lord Jesus Christ be with you.

archangel The leader among God's angels or messengers.

2 THESSALONIANS

The Problems of New Christians

1 From Paul, Silas, and Timothy.
To the church in Thessalonica in God our Father and the Lord Jesus Christ:

²Grace and peace to you from God the Father and the Lord Jesus Christ.

Paul Talks About God's Judgment

³We must always thank God for you, brothers and sisters. [n] This is only right, because your faith is growing more and more, and the love that every one of you has for each other is increasing. ⁴So we brag about you to the other churches of God. We tell them about the way you continue to be strong and have faith even though you are being treated badly and are suffering many troubles.

⁵This is proof that God is right in his judgment. He wants you to be counted worthy of his kingdom for which you are suffering. ⁶God will do what is right. He will give trouble to those who trouble you. ⁷And he will give rest to you who are troubled and to us also when the Lord Jesus appears with burning fire from heaven with his powerful angels. ⁸Then he will punish those who do not know God and who do not obey the Good News [d] about our Lord Jesus Christ. ⁹Those people will be punished with a destruction that continues forever. They will be kept away from the Lord and from his great power. ¹⁰This will happen on the day when the Lord Jesus comes to receive glory because of his holy people. And all the people who have believed will be amazed at Jesus. You will be in that group, because you believed what we told you.

¹¹That is why we always pray for you, asking our God to help you live the kind of life he called you to live. We pray that with his power God will help you do the good things you want and perform the works that come from your faith. ¹²We pray all this so that the name of our Lord Jesus Christ will have glory in you, and you will have glory in him. That glory comes from the grace of our God and the Lord Jesus Christ.

Evil Things Will Happen

2 Brothers and sisters, we have something to say about the coming of our Lord Jesus Christ and the time when we will meet together with him. ²Do not become easily upset in your thinking or afraid if you hear that the day of the Lord has already come. Someone may say this in a prophecy [d] or in a message or in a letter as if it came from us. ³Do not let anyone fool you in any way. That day of the Lord will not come until the turning away [n] from God happens and the Man of Evil, who is on his way to hell, appears. ⁴He will be against and put himself above anything called God or anything that people worship. And that Man of Evil will even go into God's Temple [d] and sit there and say that he is God.

⁵I told you when I was with you that all this would happen. Do you not remember? ⁶And now you know what is stopping that Man of Evil so he will appear at the right time. ⁷The secret power of evil is already working in the world, but there is one who is stopping that power. And he will continue to stop it until he is taken out of the way. ⁸Then that Man of Evil will appear, and the Lord Jesus will kill him with the breath that comes from his mouth and will destroy him with the glory of his coming. ⁹The Man of Evil will come by the power of Satan. He will have great power, and he will do many differ-

---

brothers and sisters Although the Greek text says "brothers" here and throughout this book, Paul's words were meant for the entire church, including men and women.
turning away Or "the rebellion."

ent false miracles,^d signs, and wonders. ¹⁰He will use every kind of evil to trick those who are lost. They will die, because they refused to love the truth. (If they loved the truth, they would be saved.) ¹¹For this reason God sends them something powerful that leads them away from the truth so they will believe a lie. ¹²So all those will be judged guilty who did not believe the truth, but enjoyed doing evil.

You Are Chosen for Salvation

¹³Brothers and sisters, whom the Lord loves, God chose you from the beginning to be saved. So we must always thank God for you. You are saved by the Spirit^d that makes you holy and by your faith in the truth. ¹⁴God used the Good News^d that we preached to call you to be saved so you can share in the glory of our Lord Jesus Christ. ¹⁵So, brothers and sisters, stand strong and continue to believe the teachings we gave you in our speaking and in our letter.

¹⁶⁻¹⁷May our Lord Jesus Christ himself and God our Father encourage you and strengthen you in every good thing you do and say. God loved us, and through his grace he gave us a good hope and encouragement that continues forever.

Pray for Us

3 And now, brothers and sisters, pray for us that the Lord's teaching will continue to spread quickly and that people will give honor to that teaching, just as happened with you. ²And pray that we will be protected from stubborn and evil people, because not all people believe. ³But the Lord is faithful and will give you strength and will protect you from the Evil One. ⁴The Lord makes us feel sure that you are doing and will continue to do the things

we told you. ⁵May the Lord lead your hearts into God's love and Christ's patience.

The Duty to Work

⁶Brothers and sisters, by the authority of our Lord Jesus Christ we command you to stay away from any believer who refuses to work and does not follow the teaching we gave you. ⁷You yourselves know that you should live as we live. We were not lazy when we were with you. ⁸And when we ate another person's food, we always paid for it. We worked very hard night and day so we would not be an expense to any of you. ⁹We had the right to ask you to help us, but we worked to take care of ourselves so we would be an example for you to follow. ¹⁰When we were with you, we gave you this rule: "Anyone who refuses to work should not eat."

¹¹We hear that some people in your group refuse to work. They do nothing but busy themselves in other people's lives. ¹²We command those people and beg them in the Lord Jesus Christ to work quietly and earn their own food. ¹³But you, brothers and sisters, never become tired of doing good.

¹⁴If some people do not obey what we tell you in this letter, then take note of them. Have nothing to do with them so they will feel ashamed. ¹⁵But do not treat them as enemies. Warn them as fellow believers.

Final Words

¹⁶Now may the Lord of peace give you peace at all times and in every way. The Lord be with all of you.

¹⁷I, Paul, end this letter now in my own handwriting. All my letters have this to show they are from me. This is the way I write.

¹⁸The grace of our Lord Jesus Christ be with you all.

1 TIMOTHY

Advice to a Young Preacher

1 From Paul, an apostle*d* of Christ Jesus, by the command of God our Savior and Christ Jesus our hope.

²To Timothy, a true child to me because you believe:

Grace, mercy, and peace from God the Father and Christ Jesus our Lord.

Warning Against False Teaching

³I asked you to stay longer in Ephesus when I went into Macedonia so you could command some people there to stop teaching false things. ⁴Tell them not to spend their time on stories that are not true and on long lists of names in family histories. These things only bring arguments; they do not help God's work, which is done in faith. ⁵The purpose of this command is for people to have love, a love that comes from a pure heart and a good conscience and a true faith. ⁶Some people have missed these things and turned to useless talk. ⁷They want to be teachers of the law, but they do not understand either what they are talking about or what they are sure about.

⁸But we know that the law is good if someone uses it lawfully. ⁹We also know that the law is not made for good people but for those who are against the law and for those who refuse to follow it. It is for people who are against God and are sinful, who are not holy and have no religion, who kill their fathers and mothers, who murder, ¹⁰who take part in sexual sins, who have sexual relations with people of the same sex, who sell slaves, who tell lies, who speak falsely, and who do anything against the true teaching of God. ¹¹That teaching is part of the Good News*d* of the blessed God that he gave me to tell.

Thanks for God's Mercy

¹²I thank Christ Jesus our Lord, who gave me strength, because he trusted me and gave me this work of serving him. ¹³In the past I spoke against Christ and persecuted him and did all kinds of things to hurt him. But God showed me mercy, because I did not know what I was doing. I did not believe. ¹⁴But the grace of our Lord was fully given to me, and with that grace came the faith and love that are in Christ Jesus.

¹⁵What I say is true, and you should fully accept it: Christ Jesus came into the world to save sinners, of whom I am the worst. ¹⁶But I was given mercy so that in me, the worst of all sinners, Christ Jesus could show that he has patience without limit. His patience with me made me an example for those who would believe in him and have life forever. ¹⁷To the King that rules forever, who will never die, who cannot be seen, the only God, be honor and glory forever and ever. Amen.

¹⁸Timothy, my child, I am giving you a command that agrees with the prophecies*d* that were given about you in the past. I tell you this so you can follow them and fight the good fight. ¹⁹Continue to have faith and do what you know is right. Some people have rejected this, and their faith has been shipwrecked. ²⁰Hymenaeus and Alexander have done that, and I have given them to Satan so they will learn not to speak against God.

Some Rules for Men and Women

2 First, I tell you to pray for all people, asking God for what they need and being thankful to him. ²Pray for rulers and for all who have authority so that we can have quiet and peaceful lives full of worship and respect for God. ³This is good, and it pleases God our Savior, ⁴who wants all people to be saved and to know the truth. ⁵There is one God and one way human beings can reach God. That way is through Christ Jesus, who is himself human. ⁶He gave himself as a payment to free all people. He is proof that came at the right time. ⁷That is why I was chosen to tell the Good News*d* and to be an apostle.*d*

(I am telling the truth; I am not lying.) I was chosen to teach those who are not Jews to believe and to know the truth.

⁸So, I want the men everywhere to pray, lifting up their hands in a holy manner, without anger and arguments.

⁹Also, women should wear proper clothes that show respect and self-control, not using braided hair or gold or pearls or expensive clothes. ¹⁰Instead, they should do good deeds, which is right for women who say they worship God.

¹¹Let a woman learn by listening quietly and being ready to cooperate in everything. ¹²But I do not allow a woman to teach or to have authority over a man, but to listen quietly, ¹³because Adam was formed first and then Eve. ¹⁴And Adam was not tricked, but the woman was tricked and became a sinner. ¹⁵But she will be saved through having children if they continue in faith, love, and holiness, with self-control.

Elders in the Church

 3 What I say is true: Anyone wanting to become an elder*d* desires a good work. ²An elder must not give people a reason to criticize him, and he must have only one wife. He must be self-controlled, wise, respected by others, ready to welcome guests, and able to teach. ³He must not drink too much wine or like to fight, but rather be gentle and peaceable, not loving money. ⁴He must be a good family leader, having children who cooperate with full respect. ⁵(If someone does not know how to lead the family, how can that person take care of God's church?) ⁶But an elder must not be a new believer, or he might be too proud of himself and be judged guilty just as the devil was. ⁷An elder must also have the respect of people who are not in the church so he will not be criticized by others and caught in the devil's trap.

Deacons in the Church

⁸In the same way, deacons*d* must be respected by others, not saying things they do not mean. They must not drink too much wine or try to get rich by cheating others.

⁹With a clear conscience they must follow the secret of the faith that God made known to us. ¹⁰Test them first. Then let them serve as deacons if you find nothing wrong in them. ¹¹In the same way, women*n* must be respected by others. They must not speak evil of others. They must be self-controlled and trustworthy in everything. ¹²Deacons must have only one wife and be good leaders of their children and their own families. ¹³Those who serve well as deacons are making an honorable place for themselves, and they will be very bold in their faith in Christ Jesus.

The Secret of Our Life

¹⁴Although I hope I can come to you soon, I am writing these things to you now. ¹⁵Then, even if I am delayed, you will know how to live in the family of God. That family is the church of the living God, the support and foundation of the truth. ¹⁶Without doubt, the secret of our life of worship is great:

He was shown to us in a human body,
    proved right in spirit,*d*
and seen by angels.
    He was preached to those who are not
    Jews,
believed in by the world,
    and taken up in glory.

A Warning About False Teachers

4 Now the Holy Spirit*d* clearly says that in the later times some people will stop believing the faith. They will follow spirits that lie and teachings of demons.*d* ²Such teachings come from the false words of liars whose consciences are destroyed as if by a hot iron. ³They forbid people to marry and tell them not to eat certain foods which God created to be eaten with thanks by people who believe and know the truth. ⁴Everything God made is good, and nothing should be refused if it is accepted with thanks, ⁵because it is made holy by what God has said and by prayer.

Be a Good Servant of Christ

⁶By telling these things to the brothers and

---

women This might mean the wives of the deacons, or it might mean women who serve in the same way as deacons.

sisters,[n] you will be a good servant of Christ Jesus. You will be made strong by the words of the faith and the good teaching which you have been following. [7]But do not follow foolish stories that disagree with God's truth, but train yourself to serve God. [8]Training your body helps you in some ways, but serving God helps you in every way by bringing you blessings in this life and in the future life, too. [9]What I say is true, and you should fully accept it. [10]This is why we work and struggle: We hope in the living God who is the Savior of all people, especially of those who believe.

[11]Command and teach these things. [12]Do not let anyone treat you as if you are unimportant because you are young. Instead, be an example to the believers with your words, your actions, your love, your faith, and your pure life. [13]Until I come, continue to read the Scriptures[d] to the people, strengthen them, and teach them. [14]Use the gift you have, which was given to you through prophecy[d] when the group of elders[d] laid their hands on[n] you. [15]Continue to do those things; give your life to doing them so your progress may be seen by everyone. [16]Be careful in your life and in your teaching. If you continue to live and teach rightly, you will save both yourself and those who listen to you.

Rules for Living with Others

5 Do not speak angrily to an older man, but plead with him as if he were your father. Treat younger men like brothers, [2]older women like mothers, and younger women like sisters. Always treat them in a pure way.

[3]Take care of widows who are truly widows. [4]But if a widow has children or grandchildren, let them first learn to do their duty to their own family and to repay their parents or grandparents. That pleases God. [5]The true widow, who is all alone, puts her hope in God and continues to pray night and day for God's help. [6]But the widow who uses her life to please herself is really dead while she is alive. [7]Tell the believers to do these things so

that no one can criticize them. [8]Whoever does not care for his own relatives, especially his own family members, has turned against the faith and is worse than someone who does not believe in God.

[9]To be on the list of widows, a woman must be at least sixty years old. She must have been faithful to her husband. [10]She must be known for her good works — works such as raising her children, welcoming strangers, washing the feet of God's people, helping those in trouble, and giving her life to do all kinds of good deeds.

[11]But do not put younger widows on that list. After they give themselves to Christ, they are pulled away from him by their physical needs, and then they want to marry again. [12]They will be judged for not doing what they first promised to do. [13]Besides that, they learn to waste their time, going from house to house. And they not only waste their time but also begin to gossip and busy themselves with other people's lives, saying things they should not say. [14]So I want the younger widows to marry, have children, and manage their homes. Then no enemy will have any reason to criticize them. [15]But some have already turned away to follow Satan.

[16]If any woman who is a believer has widows in her family, she should care for them herself. The church should not have to care for them. Then it will be able to take care of those who are truly widows.

[17]The elders[d] who lead the church well should receive double honor, especially those who work hard by speaking and teaching, [18]because the Scripture[d] says: "When an ox is working in the grain, do not cover its mouth to keep it from eating,"[n] and "A worker should be given his pay."[n]

[19]Do not listen to someone who accuses an elder, without two or three witnesses. [20]Tell those who continue sinning that they are wrong. Do this in front of the whole church so that the others will have a warning.

brothers and sisters Although the Greek text says "brothers" here and throughout this book, Paul's words refer to the entire church, including men and women.
laid their hands on The laying on of hands had many purposes, including the giving of a blessing, power, or authority.
"When ... eating," Quotation from Deuteronomy 25:4.
"A worker ... pay." Quotation from Luke 10:7.

21Before God and Christ Jesus and the chosen angels, I command you to do these things without showing favor of any kind to anyone.

22Think carefully before you lay your hands on[n] anyone, and don't share in the sins of others. Keep yourself pure.

23Stop drinking only water, but drink a little wine to help your stomach and your frequent sicknesses.

24The sins of some people are easy to see even before they are judged, but the sins of others are seen only later. 25So also good deeds are easy to see, but even those that are not easily seen cannot stay hidden.

6 All who are slaves under a yoke[d] should show full respect to their masters so no one will speak against God's name and our teaching. 2The slaves whose masters are believers should not show their masters any less respect because they are believers. They should serve their masters even better, because they are helping believers they love.

You must teach and preach these things.

False Teaching and True Riches

3Anyone who has a different teaching does not agree with the true teaching of our Lord Jesus Christ and the teaching that shows the true way to serve God. 4This person is full of pride and understands nothing, but is sick with a love for arguing and fighting about words. This brings jealousy, fighting, speaking against others, evil mistrust, 5and constant quarrels from those who have evil minds and have lost the truth. They think that serving God is a way to get rich.

6Serving God does make us very rich, if we are satisfied with what we have. 7We brought nothing into the world, so we can take nothing out. 8But, if we have food and clothes, we will be satisfied with that. 9Those who want to become rich bring temptation to themselves and are caught in a trap. They want many foolish and harmful things that ruin and destroy people. 10The love of money causes all kinds of evil. Some people have left the faith, because they wanted to get more money, but they have caused themselves much sorrow.

Some Things to Remember

11But you, man of God, run away from all those things. Instead, live in the right way, serve God, have faith, love, patience, and gentleness. 12Fight the good fight of faith, grabbing hold of the life that continues forever. You were called to have that life when you confessed the good confession before many witnesses. 13In the sight of God, who gives life to everything, and of Christ Jesus, I give you a command. Christ Jesus made the good confession when he stood before Pontius Pilate. 14Do what you were commanded to do without wrong or blame until our Lord Jesus Christ comes again. 15God will make that happen at the right time. He is the blessed and only Ruler, the King of all kings and the Lord of all lords. 16He is the only One who never dies. He lives in light so bright no one can go near it. No one has ever seen God, or can see him. May honor and power belong to God forever. Amen.

17Command those who are rich with things of this world not to be proud. Tell them to hope in God, not in their uncertain riches. God richly gives us everything to enjoy. 18Tell the rich people to do good, to be rich in doing good deeds, to be generous and ready to share. 19By doing that, they will be saving a treasure for themselves as a strong foundation for the future. Then they will be able to have the life that is true life.

20Timothy, guard what God has trusted to you. Stay away from foolish, useless talk and from the arguments of what is falsely called "knowledge." 21By saying they have that "knowledge," some have missed the true faith.

Grace be with you.

---

lay your hands on   The laying on of hands had many purposes, including the giving of a blessing, power, or authority.

2 TIMOTHY

Paul Encourages Timothy

1 From Paul, an apostle[d] of Christ Jesus by the will of God. God sent me to tell about the promise of life that is in Christ Jesus.

[2]To Timothy, a dear child to me:

Grace, mercy, and peace to you from God the Father and Christ Jesus our Lord.

Encouragement for Timothy

[3]I thank God as I always mention you in my prayers, day and night. I serve him, doing what I know is right as my ancestors did. [4]Remembering that you cried for me, I want very much to see you so I can be filled with joy. [5]I remember your true faith. That faith first lived in your grandmother Lois and in your mother Eunice, and I know you now have that same faith. [6]This is why I remind you to keep using the gift God gave you when I laid my hands on[n] you. Now let it grow, as a small flame grows into a fire. [7]God did not give us a spirit that makes us afraid but a spirit of power and love and self-control.

[8]So do not be ashamed to tell people about our Lord Jesus, and do not be ashamed of me, in prison for the Lord. But suffer with me for the Good News.[d] God, who gives us the strength to do that, [9]saved us and made us his holy people. That was not because of anything we did ourselves but because of God's purpose and grace. That grace was given to us through Christ Jesus before time began, [10]but it is now shown to us by the coming of our Savior Christ Jesus. He destroyed death, and through the Good News he showed us the way to have life that cannot be destroyed. [11]I was chosen to tell that Good News and to be an apostle[d] and a teacher. [12]I am suffering now because I tell the Good News, but I am not ashamed, because I know Jesus, the One in whom I have believed. And I am sure he is able to protect what he has trusted me with until that day.[n] [13]Follow the pattern of true teachings that you heard from me in faith and love, which are in Christ Jesus. [14]Protect the truth that you were given; protect it with the help of the Holy Spirit[d] who lives in us.

[15]You know that everyone in the country of Asia has left me, even Phygelus and Hermogenes. [16]May the Lord show mercy to the family of Onesiphorus, who has often helped me and was not ashamed that I was in prison. [17]When he came to Rome, he looked eagerly for me until he found me. [18]May the Lord allow him to find mercy from the Lord on that day. You know how many ways he helped me in Ephesus.

A Loyal Soldier of Christ Jesus

2 You then, Timothy, my child, be strong in the grace we have in Christ Jesus. [2]You should teach people whom you can trust the things you and many others have heard me say. Then they will be able to teach others. [3]Share in the troubles we have like a good soldier of Christ Jesus. [4]A soldier wants to please the enlisting officer, so no one serving in the army wastes time with everyday matters. [5]Also an athlete who takes part in a contest must obey all the rules in order to win. [6]The farmer who works hard should be the first person to get some of the food that was grown. [7]Think about what I am saying, because the Lord will give you the ability to understand everything.

[8]Remember Jesus Christ, who was raised from the dead, who is from the family of David. This is the Good News[d] I preach, [9]and I am suffering because of it to the point of being bound with chains like a criminal. But God's teaching is not in chains. [10]So I patiently accept all these troubles so that those

---

laid my hands on The laying on of hands had many purposes, including the giving of a blessing, power, or authority.
day The day Christ will come to judge all people and take his people to live with him.

whom God has chosen can have the salvation that is in Christ Jesus. With that salvation comes glory that never ends.

[11] This teaching is true:

If we died with him, we will also live with him.

[12] If we accept suffering, we will also rule with him.

If we refuse to accept him, he will refuse to accept us.

[13] If we are not faithful, he will still be faithful,

because he cannot be false to himself.

A Worker Pleasing to God

[14] Continue teaching these things, warning people in God's presence not to argue about words. It does not help anyone, and it ruins those who listen. [15] Make every effort to give yourself to God as the kind of person he will accept. Be a worker who is not ashamed and who uses the true teaching in the right way. [16] Stay away from foolish, useless talk, because that will lead people further away from God. [17] Their evil teaching will spread like a sickness inside the body. Hymenaeus and Philetus are like that. [18] They have left the true teaching, saying that the rising from the dead has already taken place, and so they are destroying the faith of some people. [19] But God's strong foundation continues to stand. These words are written on the seal: "The Lord knows those who belong to him," [n] and "Everyone who wants to belong to the Lord must stop doing wrong."

[20] In a large house there are not only things made of gold and silver, but also things made of wood and clay. Some things are used for special purposes, and others are made for ordinary jobs. [21] All who make themselves clean[d] from evil will be used for special purposes. They will be made holy, useful to the Master, ready to do any good work.

[22] But run away from the evil young people like to do. Try hard to live right and to have faith, love, and peace, together with those who trust in the Lord from pure hearts. [23] Stay away from foolish and stupid arguments, because you know they grow into quarrels. [24] And a servant of the Lord must not quarrel but must be kind to everyone, a good teacher, and patient. [25] The Lord's servant must gently teach those who disagree. Then maybe God will let them change their minds so they can accept the truth. [26] And they may wake up and escape from the trap of the devil, who catches them to do what he wants.

The Last Days

3 Remember this! In the last days there will be many troubles, [2] because people will love themselves, love money, brag, and be proud. They will say evil things against others and will not obey their parents or be thankful or be the kind of people God wants. [3] They will not love others, will refuse to forgive, will gossip, and will not control themselves. They will be cruel, will hate what is good, [4] will turn against their friends, and will do foolish things without thinking. They will be conceited, will love pleasure instead of God, [5] and will act as if they serve God but will not have his power. Stay away from those people. [6] Some of them go into homes and get control of silly women who are full of sin and are led by many evil desires. [7] These women are always learning new teachings, but they are never able to understand the truth fully. [8] Just as Jannes and Jambres were against Moses, these people are against the truth. Their thinking has been ruined, and they have failed in trying to follow the faith. [9] But they will not be successful in what they do, because as with Jannes and Jambres, everyone will see that they are foolish.

Obey the Teachings

[10] But you have followed what I teach, the way I live, my goal, faith, patience, and love. You know I never give up. [11] You know how I have been hurt and have suffered, as in Antioch, Iconium, and Lystra. I have suffered, but the Lord saved me from all those troubles. [12] Everyone who wants to live as God desires, in Christ Jesus, will be hurt. [13] But people who are evil and cheat others will go from bad to worse. They will fool others, but they will also be fooling themselves.

"The Lord ... him" Quotation from Numbers 16:5.

[14]But you should continue following the teachings you learned. You know they are true, because you trust those who taught you. [15]Since you were a child you have known the Holy Scriptures[d] which are able to make you wise. And that wisdom leads to salvation through faith in Christ Jesus. [16]All Scripture is given by God and is useful for teaching, for showing people what is wrong in their lives, for correcting faults, and for teaching how to live right. [17]Using the Scriptures, the person who serves God will be capable, having all that is needed to do every good work.

4 I give you a command in the presence of God and Christ Jesus, the One who will judge the living and the dead, and by his coming and his kingdom: [2]Preach the Good News.[d] Be ready at all times, and tell people what they need to do. Tell them when they are wrong. Encourage them with great patience and careful teaching, [3]because the time will come when people will not listen to the true teaching but will find many more teachers who please them by saying the things they want to hear. [4]They will stop listening to the truth and will begin to follow false stories. [5]But you should control yourself at all times, accept troubles, do the work of telling the Good News, and complete all the duties of a servant of God.

[6]My life is being given as an offering to God, and the time has come for me to leave this life. [7]I have fought the good fight, I have finished the race, I have kept the faith. [8]Now, a crown is being held for me — a crown for being right with God. The Lord, the judge who judges rightly, will give the crown to me on that day[n] — not only to me but to all those who have waited with love for him to come again.

Personal Words

[9]Do your best to come to me as soon as you can, [10]because Demas, who loved this world, left me and went to Thessalonica. Crescens went to Galatia, and Titus went to Dalmatia. [11]Luke is the only one still with me. Get Mark and bring him with you when you come, because he can help me in my work here. [12]I sent Tychicus to Ephesus. [13]When I was in Troas, I left my coat there with Carpus. So when you come, bring it to me, along with my books, particularly the ones written on parchment.[n]

[14]Alexander the metalworker did many harmful things against me. The Lord will punish him for what he did. [15]You also should be careful that he does not hurt you, because he fought strongly against our teaching.

[16]The first time I defended myself, no one helped me; everyone left me. May they be forgiven. [17]But the Lord stayed with me and gave me strength so I could fully tell the Good News[d] to all those who are not Jews. So I was saved from the lion's mouth. [18]The Lord will save me when anyone tries to hurt me, and he will bring me safely to his heavenly kingdom. Glory forever and ever be the Lord's. Amen.

Final Greetings

[19]Greet Priscilla and Aquila and the family of Onesiphorus. [20]Erastus stayed in Corinth, and I left Trophimus sick in Miletus. [21]Try as hard as you can to come to me before winter.

Eubulus sends greetings to you. Also Pudens, Linus, Claudia, and all the brothers and sisters in Christ greet you.

[22]The Lord be with your spirit. Grace be with you.

---

day   The day Christ will come to judge all people and take his people to live with him.
parchment   A writing paper made from the skins of sheep.

TITUS

Paul Instructs Titus

1 From Paul, a servant of God and an apostle[d] of Jesus Christ. I was sent to help the faith of God's chosen people and to help them know the truth that shows people how to serve God. [2]That faith and that knowledge come from the hope for life forever, which God promised to us before time began. And God cannot lie. [3]At the right time God let the world know about that life through preaching. He trusted me with that work, and I preached by the command of God our Savior.

[4]To Titus, my true child in the faith we share:

Grace and peace from God the Father and Christ Jesus our Savior.

Titus' Work in Crete

[5]I left you in Crete so you could finish doing the things that still needed to be done and so you could appoint elders[d] in every town, as I directed you. [6]An elder must not be guilty of doing wrong, must have only one wife, and must have believing children. They must not be known as children who are wild and do not cooperate. [7]As God's manager, an elder must not be guilty of doing wrong, being selfish, or becoming angry quickly. He must not drink too much wine, like to fight, or try to get rich by cheating others. [8]An elder must be ready to welcome guests, love what is good, be wise, live right, and be holy and self-controlled. [9]By holding on to the trustworthy word just as we teach it, an elder can help people by using true teaching, and he can show those who are against the true teaching that they are wrong.

[10]There are many people who refuse to cooperate, who talk about worthless things and lead others into the wrong way—mainly those who say all who are not Jews must be circumcised.[d] [11]These people must be stopped, because they are upsetting whole families by teaching things they should not

teach, which they do to get rich by cheating people. [12]Even one of their own prophets said, "Cretans are always liars, evil animals, and lazy people who do nothing but eat." [13]The words that prophet said are true. So firmly tell those people they are wrong so they may become strong in the faith, [14]not accepting Jewish false stories and the commands of people who reject the truth. [15]To those who are pure, all things are pure, but to those who are full of sin and do not believe, nothing is pure. Both their minds and their consciences have been ruined. [16]They say they know God, but their actions show they do not accept him. They are hateful people, they refuse to obey, and they are useless for doing anything good.

Following the True Teaching

2 But you must tell everyone what to do to follow the true teaching. [2]Teach older men to be self-controlled, serious, wise, strong in faith, in love, and in patience.

[3]In the same way, teach older women to be holy in their behavior, not speaking against others or enslaved to too much wine, but teaching what is good. [4]Then they can teach the young women to love their husbands, to love their children, [5]to be wise and pure, to be good workers at home, to be kind, and to yield to their husbands. Then no one will be able to criticize the teaching God gave us.

[6]In the same way, encourage young men to be wise. [7]In every way be an example of doing good deeds. When you teach, do it with honesty and seriousness. [8]Speak the truth so that you cannot be criticized. Then those who are against you will be ashamed because there is nothing bad to say about us.

[9]Slaves should yield to their own masters at all times, trying to please them and not arguing with them. [10]They should not steal from them but should show their masters

they can be fully trusted so that in everything they do they will make the teaching of God our Savior attractive.

¹¹That is the way we should live, because God's grace that can save everyone has come. ¹²It teaches us not to live against God nor to do the evil things the world wants to do. Instead, that grace teaches us to live now in a wise and right way and in a way that shows we serve God. ¹³We should live like that while we wait for our great hope and the coming of the glory of our great God and Savior Jesus Christ. ¹⁴He gave himself for us so he might pay the price to free us from all evil and to make us pure people who belong only to him — people who are always wanting to do good deeds.

¹⁵Say these things and encourage the people and tell them what is wrong in their lives, with all authority. Do not let anyone treat you as if you were unimportant.

The Right Way to Live

3 Remind the believers to yield to the authority of rulers and government leaders, to obey them, to be ready to do good, ²to speak no evil about anyone, to live in peace, and to be gentle and polite to all people.

³In the past we also were foolish. We did not obey, we were wrong, and we were slaves to many things our bodies wanted and enjoyed. We spent our lives doing evil and being jealous. People hated us, and we hated each other. ⁴But when the kindness and love of God our Savior was shown, ⁵he saved us because of his mercy. It was not because of

good deeds we did to be right with him. He saved us through the washing that made us new people through the Holy Spirit.ᵈ ⁶God poured out richly upon us that Holy Spirit through Jesus Christ our Savior. ⁷Being made right with God by his grace, we could have the hope of receiving the life that never ends.

⁸This teaching is true, and I want you to be sure the people understand these things. Then those who believe in God will be careful to use their lives for doing good. These things are good and will help everyone.

⁹But stay away from those who have foolish arguments and talk about useless family histories and argue and quarrel about the law. Those things are worth nothing and will not help anyone. ¹⁰After a first and second warning, avoid someone who causes arguments. ¹¹You can know that such people are evil and sinful; their own sins prove them wrong.

Some Things to Remember

¹²When I send Artemas or Tychicus to you, make every effort to come to me at Nicopolis, because I have decided to stay there this winter. ¹³Do all you can to help Zenas the lawyer and Apollos on their journey so that they have everything they need. ¹⁴Our people must learn to use their lives for doing good deeds to provide what is necessary so that their lives will not be useless.

¹⁵All who are with me greet you. Greet those who love us in the faith.

Grace be with you all.

PHILEMON

A Slave Becomes a Christian

¹From Paul, a prisoner of Christ Jesus, and from Timothy, our brother.

To Philemon, our dear friend and worker with us; ²to Apphia, our sister; to Archippus, a worker with us; and to the church that meets in your home:

³Grace and peace to you from God our Father and the Lord Jesus Christ.

Philemon's Love and Faith

⁴I always thank my God when I mention you in my prayers, ⁵because I hear about the love you have for all God's holy people and the faith you have in the Lord Jesus. ⁶I pray that the faith you share may make you understand every blessing we have in Christ. ⁷I have great joy and comfort, my brother, because the love you have shown to God's people has refreshed them.

Accept Onesimus as a Brother

⁸So, in Christ, I could be bold and order you to do what is right. ⁹But because I love you, I am pleading with you instead. I, Paul, an old man now and also a prisoner for Christ Jesus, ¹⁰am pleading with you for my child Onesimus, who became my child while I was in prison. ¹¹In the past he was useless to you, but now he has become useful for both you and me.

¹²I am sending him back to you, and with him I am sending my own heart. ¹³I wanted to keep him with me so that in your place he might help me while I am in prison for the Good News.ᵈ ¹⁴But I did not want to do anything without asking you first so that any good you do for me will be because you want to do it, not because I forced you. ¹⁵Maybe Onesimus was separated from you for a short time so you could have him back forever— ¹⁶no longer as a slave, but better than a slave, as a loved brother. I love him very much, but you will love him even more, both as a person and as a believer in the Lord.

¹⁷So if you consider me your partner, welcome Onesimus as you would welcome me. ¹⁸If he has done anything wrong to you or if he owes you anything, charge that to me. ¹⁹I, Paul, am writing this with my own hand. I will pay it back, and I will say nothing about what you owe me for your own life. ²⁰So, my brother, I ask that you do this for me in the Lord: Refresh my heart in Christ. ²¹I write this letter, knowing that you will do what I ask you and even more.

²²One more thing—prepare a room for me in which to stay, because I hope God will answer your prayers and I will be able to come to you.

Final Greetings

²³Epaphras, a prisoner with me for Christ Jesus, sends greetings to you. ²⁴And also Mark, Aristarchus, Demas, and Luke, workers together with me, send greetings.

²⁵The grace of our Lord Jesus Christ be with your spirit.

HEBREWS

A Better Life Through Christ

God Spoke Through His Son

1 In the past God spoke to our ancestors through the prophets*d* many times and in many different ways. ²But now in these last days God has spoken to us through his Son. God has chosen his Son to own all things, and through him he made the world. ³The Son reflects the glory of God and shows exactly what God is like. He holds everything together with his powerful word. When the Son made people clean from their sins, he sat down at the right side of God, the Great One in heaven. ⁴The Son became much greater than the angels, and God gave him a name that is much greater than theirs.

⁵This is because God never said to any of the angels,

"You are my Son.
   Today I have become your Father."

Psalm 2:7

Nor did God say of any angel,

"I will be his Father,
   and he will be my Son." *2 Samuel 7:14*

⁶And when God brings his firstborn Son into the world, he says,

"Let all God's angels worship him." *n*

Psalm 97:7

⁷This is what God said about the angels:

"God makes his angels become like winds.
   He makes his servants become like flames of fire." *Psalm 104:4*

⁸But God said this about his Son:

"God, your throne will last forever and ever.
   You will rule your kingdom with fairness.
⁹You love right and hate evil,
   so God has chosen you from among your friends;

he has set you apart with much joy."

Psalm 45:6-7

¹⁰God also says,

"Lord, in the beginning you made the earth,
   and your hands made the skies.
¹¹They will be destroyed, but you will remain.
   They will all wear out like clothes.
¹²You will fold them like a coat.
   And, like clothes, you will change them.
But you never change,
   and your life will never end."

Psalm 102:25-27

¹³And God never said this to an angel:

"Sit by me at my right side
until I put your enemies under your
   control." *n* *Psalm 110:1*

¹⁴All the angels are spirits who serve God and are sent to help those who will receive salvation.

Our Salvation Is Great

2 So we must be more careful to follow what we were taught. Then we will not stray away from the truth. ²The teaching God spoke through angels was shown to be true, and anyone who did not follow it or obey it received the punishment that was earned. ³So surely we also will be punished if we ignore this great salvation. The Lord himself first told about this salvation, and it was proven true to us by those who heard him. ⁴God also proved it by using wonders, great signs, many kinds of miracles,*d* and by giving people gifts through the Holy Spirit,*d* just as he wanted.

Christ Became like Humans

5 God did not choose angels to be the rulers

"Let . . . him." These words are found in Deuteronomy 32:43 in the Septuagint, the Greek version of the Old Testament, and in a Hebrew copy among the Dead Sea Scrolls.
until . . . control. Literally, "until I make your enemies a footstool for your feet."

of the new world that was coming, which is what we have been talking about. [6]It is written in the Scriptures,[d]

"Why are people important to you?
Why do you take care of human
   beings?
[7]You made them a little lower than the
   angels
and crowned them with glory and
   honor.
[8] You put all things under their control."
                                           Psalm 8:4-6

When God put everything under their control, there was nothing left that they did not rule. Still, we do not yet see them ruling over everything. [9]But we see Jesus, who for a short time was made lower than the angels. And now he is wearing a crown of glory and honor because he suffered and died. And by God's grace, he died for everyone.

[10]God is the One who made all things, and all things are for his glory. He wanted to have many children share his glory, so he made the One who leads people to salvation perfect through suffering.

[11]Jesus, who makes people holy, and those who are made holy are from the same family. So he is not ashamed to call them his brothers and sisters. [n] [12]He says,

"Then, I will tell my fellow Israelites
   about you;
I will praise you in the public
   meeting."   *Psalm 22:22*
[13]He also says,
"I will trust in God."   *Isaiah 8:17*
And he also says,
"I am here, and with me are the
   children God has given me."
                                Isaiah 8:18

[14]Since these children are people with physical bodies, Jesus himself became like them. He did this so that, by dying, he could destroy the one who has the power of death —the devil— [15]and free those who were like slaves all their lives because of their fear of death. [16]Clearly, it is not angels that Jesus helps, but the people who are from Abra-

ham. [n] [17]For this reason Jesus had to be made like his brothers in every way so he could be their merciful and faithful high priest in service to God. Then Jesus could bring forgiveness for their sins. [18]And now he can help those who are tempted, because he himself suffered and was tempted.

Jesus Is Greater than Moses

3 So all of you holy brothers and sisters, who were called by God, think about Jesus, who was sent to us and is the high priest of our faith. [2]Jesus was faithful to God as Moses was in God's family. [3]Jesus has more honor than Moses, just as the builder of a house has more honor than the house itself. [4]Every house is built by someone, but the builder of everything is God himself. [5]Moses was faithful in God's family as a servant, and he told what God would say in the future. [6]But Christ is faithful as a Son over God's house. And we are God's house if we keep on being very sure about our great hope.

We Must Continue to Follow God

[7]So it is as the Holy Spirit[d] says:
"Today listen to what he says.
[8]Do not be stubborn as in the past
   when you turned against God,
when you tested God in the desert.
[9]There your ancestors tried me and tested
   me
   and saw the things I did for forty
      years.
[10]I was angry with them.
   I said, 'They are not loyal to me
   and have not understood my ways.'
[11]I was angry and made a promise,
   'They will never enter my rest.' "[n]
                                   Psalm 95:7-11

[12]So brothers and sisters, be careful that none of you has an evil, unbelieving heart that will turn you away from the living God. [13]But encourage each other every day while it is "today." [n] Help each other so none of you will become hardened because sin has

---

brothers and sisters   Although the Greek text says "brothers" here and throughout this book, the writer's words were meant for the entire church, including men and women.
Abraham   Most respected ancestor of the Jews. Every Jew hoped to see Abraham.
rest   A place of rest God promised to give his people.
"today"   This word is taken from verse 7. It means that it is important to do these things now.

tricked you. [14]We all share in Christ if we keep till the end the sure faith we had in the beginning. [15]This is what the Scripture[d] says:

"Today listen to what he says.

Do not be stubborn as in the past
when you turned against God."

Psalm 95:7-8

[16]Who heard God's voice and was against him? It was all those people Moses led out of Egypt. [17]And with whom was God angry for forty years? He was angry with those who sinned, who died in the desert. [18]And to whom was God talking when he promised that they would never enter his rest? He was talking to those who did not obey him. [19]So we see they were not allowed to enter and have God's rest, because they did not believe.

4 Now, since God has left us the promise that we may enter his rest, let us be very careful so none of you will fail to enter. [2]The Good News[d] was preached to us just as it was to them. But the teaching they heard did not help them, because they heard it but did not accept it with faith. [3]We who have believed are able to enter and have God's rest. As God has said,

"I was angry and made a promise,
'They will never enter my rest.' "

Psalm 95:11

But God's work was finished from the time he made the world. [4]In the Scriptures[d] he talked about the seventh day of the week: "And on the seventh day God rested from all his works."[n] [5]And again in the Scripture God said, "They will never enter my rest."

[6]It is still true that some people will enter God's rest, but those who first heard the way to be saved did not enter, because they did not obey. [7]So God planned another day, called "today." He spoke about that day through David a long time later in the same Scripture used before:

"Today listen to what he says.

Do not be stubborn." *Psalm 95:7-8*

[8]We know that Joshua[n] did not lead the people into that rest, because God spoke later

about another day. [9]This shows that the rest[n] for God's people is still coming. [10]Anyone who enters God's rest will rest from his work as God did. [11]Let us try as hard as we can to enter God's rest so that no one will fail by following the example of those who refused to obey.

[12]God's word is alive and working and is sharper than a double-edged sword. It cuts all the way into us, where the soul and the spirit are joined, to the center of our joints and bones. And it judges the thoughts and feelings in our hearts. [13]Nothing in all the world can be hidden from God. Everything is clear and lies open before him, and to him we must explain the way we have lived.

Jesus Is Our High Priest

[14]Since we have a great high priest, Jesus the Son of God, who has gone into heaven, let us hold on to the faith we have. [15]For our high priest is able to understand our weaknesses. When he lived on earth, he was tempted in every way that we are, but he did not sin. [16]Let us, then, feel very sure that we can come before God's throne where there is grace. There we can receive mercy and grace to help us when we need it.

5 Every high priest is chosen from among other people. He is given the work of going before God for them to offer gifts and sacrifices for sins. [2]Since he himself is weak, he is able to be gentle with those who do not understand and who are doing wrong things. [3]Because he is weak, the high priest must offer sacrifices for his own sins and also for the sins of the people.

[4]To be a high priest is an honor, but no one chooses himself for this work. He must be called by God as Aaron[n] was. [5]So also Christ did not choose himself to have the honor of being a high priest, but God chose him. God said to him,

"You are my Son.

Today I have become your Father."

Psalm 2:7

[6]And in another Scripture[d] God says,

"And . . . works." Quotation from Genesis 2:2.
Joshua After Moses died, Joshua became leader of the Jewish people and led them into the land that God promised to give them.
rest Literally, "sabbath rest," meaning a sharing in the rest that God began after he created the world.
Aaron Aaron was Moses' brother and the first Jewish high priest.

"You are a priest forever,
    a priest like Melchizedek." [n]   *Psalm 110:4*
[7]While Jesus lived on earth, he prayed to God and asked God for help. He prayed with loud cries and tears to the One who could save him from death, and his prayer was heard because he trusted God. [8]Even though Jesus was the Son of God, he learned obedience by what he suffered. [9]And because his obedience was perfect, he was able to give eternal salvation to all who obey him. [10]In this way God made Jesus a high priest, a priest like Melchizedek.

Warning Against Falling Away

[11]We have much to say about this, but it is hard to explain because you are so slow to understand. [12]By now you should be teachers, but you need someone to teach you again the first lessons of God's message. You still need the teaching that is like milk. You are not ready for solid food. [13]Anyone who lives on milk is still a baby and knows nothing about right teaching. [14]But solid food is for those who are grown up. They have practiced in order to know the difference between good and evil.

[6] So let us go on to grown-up teaching. Let us not go back over the beginning lessons we learned about Christ. We should not again start teaching about faith in God and about turning away from those acts that lead to death. [2]We should not return to the teaching about baptisms, [n] about laying on of hands, [n] about the raising of the dead and eternal judgment. [3]And we will go on to grown-up teaching if God allows.

[4]Some people cannot be brought back again to a changed life. They were once in God's light, and enjoyed heaven's gift, and shared in the Holy Spirit. [d] [5]They found out how good God's word is, and they received the powers of his new world. [6]But they fell away from Christ. It is impossible to bring them back to a changed life again, because they are nailing the Son of God to a cross again and are shaming him in front of others. [7]Some people are like land that gets plenty

of rain. The land produces a good crop for those who work it, and it receives God's blessings. [8]Other people are like land that grows thorns and weeds and is worthless. It is in danger of being cursed by God and will be destroyed by fire.

[9]Dear friends, we are saying this to you, but we really expect better things from you that will lead to your salvation. [10]God is fair; he will not forget the work you did and the love you showed for him by helping his people. And he will remember that you are still helping them. [11]We want each of you to go on with the same hard work all your lives so you will surely get what you hope for. [12]We do not want you to become lazy. Be like those who through faith and patience will receive what God has promised.

[13]God made a promise to Abraham. And as there is no one greater than God, he used himself when he swore to Abraham, [14]saying, "I will surely bless you and give you many descendants." [n] [15]Abraham waited patiently for this to happen, and he received what God promised.

[16]People always use the name of someone greater than themselves when they swear. The oath proves that what they say is true, and this ends all arguing. [17]God wanted to prove that his promise was true to those who would get what he promised. And he wanted them to understand clearly that his purposes never change, so he made an oath. [18]These two things cannot change: God cannot lie when he makes a promise, and he cannot lie when he makes an oath. These things encourage us who came to God for safety. They give us strength to hold on to the hope we have been given. [19]We have this hope as an anchor for the soul, sure and strong. It enters behind the curtain in the Most Holy Place in heaven, [20]where Jesus has gone ahead of us and for us. He has become the high priest forever, a priest like Melchizedek. [n]

The Priest Melchizedek

[7] Melchizedek [n] was the king of Salem and a priest for God Most High. He met

---

Melchizedek   A priest and king who lived in the time of Abraham. (Read Genesis 14:17-24.)
baptisms   The word here may refer to Christian baptism, or it may refer to the Jewish ceremonial washings.
laying on of hands   The laying on of hands had many purposes, including the giving of a blessing, power, or authority.
"I . . . descendants."   Quotation from Genesis 22:17.

Abraham when Abraham was coming back after defeating the kings. When they met, Melchizedek blessed Abraham, [2]and Abraham gave him a tenth of everything he had brought back from the battle. First, Melchizedek's name means "king of goodness," and he is king of Salem, which means "king of peace." [3]No one knows who Melchizedek's father or mother was,[n] where he came from, when he was born, or when he died. Melchizedek is like the Son of God; he continues being a priest forever.

[4]You can see how great Melchizedek was. Abraham, the great father, gave him a tenth of everything that he won in battle. [5]Now the law says that those in the tribe[d] of Levi who become priests must collect a tenth from the people — their own people — even though the priests and the people are from the family of Abraham. [6]Melchizedek was not from the tribe of Levi, but he collected a tenth from Abraham. And he blessed Abraham, the man who had God's promises. [7]Now everyone knows that the more important person blesses the less important person. [8]Priests receive a tenth, even though they are only men who live and then die. But Melchizedek, who received a tenth from Abraham, continues living, as the Scripture[d] says. [9]We might even say that Levi, who receives a tenth, also paid it when Abraham paid Melchizedek a tenth. [10]Levi was not yet born, but he was in the body of his ancestor when Melchizedek met Abraham.

[11]The people were given the law[n] based on a system of priests from the tribe of Levi, but they could not be made perfect through that system. So there was a need for another priest to come, a priest like Melchizedek, not Aaron. [12]And when a different kind of priest comes, the law must be changed, too. [13]We are saying these things about Christ, who belonged to a different tribe. No one from that tribe ever served as a priest at the altar. [14]It is clear that our Lord came from the tribe of Judah, and Moses said nothing about priests belonging to that tribe.

Jesus Is like Melchizedek

[15]And this becomes even more clear when we see that another priest comes who is like Melchizedek.[n] [16]He was not made a priest by human rules and laws but through the power of his life, which continues forever. [17]It is said about him,

"You are a priest forever,
    a priest like Melchizedek."   Psalm 110:4

[18]The old rule is now set aside, because it was weak and useless. [19]The law of Moses could not make anything perfect. But now a better hope has been given to us, and with this hope we can come near to God. [20]It is important that God did this with an oath. Others became priests without an oath, [21]but Christ became a priest with God's oath. God said:

"The Lord has made a promise
    and will not change his mind.
'You are a priest forever.' "   Psalm 110:4

[22]This means that Jesus is the guarantee of a better agreement[n] from God to his people.

[23]When one of the other priests died, he could not continue being a priest. So there were many priests. [24]But because Jesus lives forever, he will never stop serving as priest. [25]So he is able always to save those who come to God through him because he always lives, asking God to help them.

[26]Jesus is the kind of high priest we need. He is holy, sinless, pure, not influenced by sinners, and he is raised above the heavens. [27]He is not like the other priests who had to offer sacrifices every day, first for their own sins, and then for the sins of the people. Christ offered his sacrifice only once and for all time when he offered himself. [28]The law chooses high priests who are people with weaknesses, but the word of God's oath came later than the law. It made God's Son to be the high priest, and that Son has been made perfect forever.

Jesus Is Our High Priest

8 Here is the point of what we are saying: We have a high priest who sits on the

---

No . . . was   Literally, "Melchizedek was without father, without mother, without genealogy."
The . . . law   This refers to the people of Israel who were given the law of Moses.
Melchizedek   A priest and king who lived in the time of Abraham. (Read Genesis 14:17-24.)
agreement   God gives a contract or agreement to his people. For the Jews, this agreement was the law of Moses. But now God has given a better agreement to his people through Christ.

right side of God's throne in heaven. [2]Our high priest serves in the Most Holy Place, the true place of worship that was made by God, not by humans.

[3]Every high priest has the work of offering gifts and sacrifices to God. So our high priest must also offer something to God. [4]If our high priest were now living on earth, he would not be a priest, because there are already priests here who follow the law by offering gifts to God. [5]The work they do as priests is only a copy and a shadow of what is in heaven. This is why God warned Moses when he was ready to build the Holy Tent:[d] "Be very careful to make everything by the plan I showed you on the mountain." [n] [6]But the priestly work that has been given to Jesus is much greater than the work that was given to the other priests. In the same way, the new agreement that Jesus brought from God to his people is much greater than the old one. And the new agreement is based on promises of better things.

[7]If there had been nothing wrong with the first agreement,[n] there would have been no need for a second agreement. [8]But God found something wrong with his people. He says:

"Look, the time is coming, says the Lord,
    when I will make a new agreement
  with the people of Israel
    and the people of Judah.
[9]It will not be like the agreement
    I made with their ancestors
  when I took them by the hand
    to bring them out of Egypt.
  But they broke that agreement,
    and I turned away from them, says the Lord.
[10]This is the agreement I will make
    with the people of Israel at that time,
    says the Lord.
  I will put my teachings in their minds
    and write them on their hearts.
  I will be their God,
    and they will be my people.
[11]People will no longer have to teach their
    neighbors and relatives
  to know the Lord,

because all people will know me,
    from the least to the most important.
[12]I will forgive them for the wicked things
        they did,
    and I will not remember their sins
        anymore."   *Jeremiah 31:31-34*

[13]God called this a new agreement, so he has made the first agreement old. And anything that is old and worn out is ready to disappear.

The Old Agreement

9 The first agreement[n] had rules for worship and a man-made place for worship. [2]The Holy Tent[d] was set up for this. The first area in the Tent was called the Holy Place. In it were the lamp and the table with the bread that was made holy for God. [3]Behind the second curtain was a room called the Most Holy Place. [4]In it was a golden altar for burning incense[d] and the Ark[d] covered with gold that held the old agreement. Inside this Ark was a golden jar of manna,[d] Aaron's rod that once grew leaves, and the stone tablets of the old agreement. [5]Above the Ark were the creatures that showed God's glory, whose wings reached over the lid. But we cannot tell everything about these things now.

[6]When everything in the Tent was made ready in this way, the priests went into the first room every day to worship. [7]But only the high priest could go into the second room, and he did that only once a year. He could never enter the inner room without taking blood with him, which he offered to God for himself and for sins the people did without knowing they did them. [8]The Holy Spirit[d] uses this to show that the way into the Most Holy Place was not open while the system of the old Holy Tent was still being used. [9]This is an example for the present time. It shows that the gifts and sacrifices offered cannot make the conscience of the worshiper perfect. [10]These gifts and sacrifices were only about food and drink and special washings. They were rules for the body, to be followed until the time of God's new way.

"Be ... mountain." Quotation from Exodus 25:40.
first agreement The contract God gave the Jewish people when he gave them the law of Moses.

The New Agreement

[11]But when Christ came as the high priest of the good things we now have, he entered the greater and more perfect tent. It is not made by humans and does not belong to this world. [12]Christ entered the Most Holy Place only once — and for all time. He did not take with him the blood of goats and calves. His sacrifice was his own blood, and by it he set us free from sin forever. [13]The blood of goats and bulls and the ashes of a cow are sprinkled on the people who are unclean,[d] and this makes their bodies clean again. [14]How much more is done by the blood of Christ. He offered himself through the eternal Spirit[n] as a perfect sacrifice to God. His blood will make our consciences pure from useless acts so we may serve the living God.

[15]For this reason Christ brings a new agreement from God to his people. Those who are called by God can now receive the blessings he has promised, blessings that will last forever. They can have those things because Christ died so that the people who lived under the first agreement could be set free from sin.

[16]When there is a will,[n] it must be proven that the one who wrote that will is dead. [17]A will means nothing while the person is alive; it can be used only after the person dies. [18]This is why even the first agreement could not begin without blood to show death. [19]First, Moses told all the people every command in the law. Next he took the blood of calves and mixed it with water. Then he used red wool and a branch of the hyssop plant to sprinkle it on the book of the law and on all the people. [20]He said, "This is the blood that begins the Agreement that God commanded you to obey."[n] [21]In the same way, Moses sprinkled the blood on the Holy Tent[d] and over all the things used in worship. [22]The law says that almost everything must be made clean by blood, and sins cannot be forgiven without blood to show death.

Christ's Death Takes Away Sins

[23]So the copies of the real things in heaven had to be made clean[d] by animal sacrifices. But the real things in heaven need much better sacrifices. [24]Christ did not go into the Most Holy Place made by humans, which is only a copy of the real one. He went into heaven itself and is there now before God to help us. [25]The high priest enters the Most Holy Place once every year with blood that is not his own. But Christ did not offer himself many times. [26]Then he would have had to suffer many times since the world was made. But Christ came only once and for all time at just the right time to take away all sin by sacrificing himself. [27]Just as everyone must die once and be judged, [28]so Christ was offered as a sacrifice one time to take away the sins of many people. And he will come a second time, not to offer himself for sin, but to bring salvation to those who are waiting for him.

10 The law is only an unclear picture of the good things coming in the future; it is not the real thing. The people under the law offer the same sacrifices every year, but these sacrifices can never make perfect those who come near to worship God. [2]If the law could make them perfect, the sacrifices would have already stopped. The worshipers would be made clean, and they would no longer have a sense of sin. [3]But these sacrifices remind them of their sins every year, [4]because it is impossible for the blood of bulls and goats to take away sins.

[5]So when Christ came into the world, he said:

"You do not want sacrifices and
　　offerings,
but you have prepared a body for me.
[6]You do not ask for burnt offerings
　and offerings to take away sins.
[7]Then I said, 'Look, I have come.
　It is written about me in the book.
　God, I have come to do what you
　　want.' "　　　　　　　*Psalm 40:6-8*

[8]In this Scripture[d] he first said, "You do not

Spirit　This refers to the Holy Spirit, to Christ's own spirit, or to the spiritual and eternal nature of his sacrifice.

will　A legal document that shows how a person's money and property are to be distributed at the time of death. This is the same word in Greek as "agreement" in verse 15.

"This . . . obey."　Quotation from Exodus 24:8.

want sacrifices and offerings. You do not ask for burnt offerings and offerings to take away sins." (These are all sacrifices that the law commands.) [9]Then he said, "Look, I have come to do what you want." God ends the first system of sacrifices so he can set up the new system. [10]And because of this, we are made holy through the sacrifice Christ made in his body once and for all time.

[11]Every day the priests stand and do their religious service, often offering the same sacrifices. Those sacrifices can never take away sins. [12]But after Christ offered one sacrifice for sins, forever, he sat down at the right side of God. [13]And now Christ waits there for his enemies to be put under his power. [14]With one sacrifice he made perfect forever those who are being made holy.

[15]The Holy Spirit[d] also tells us about this. First he says:

[16]"This is the agreement[n] I will make
with them at that time, says the Lord.
I will put my teachings in their hearts
and write them on their minds."

Jeremiah 31:33

[17]Then he says:

"Their sins and the evil things they do—
I will not remember anymore."

Jeremiah 31:34

[18]Now when these have been forgiven, there is no more need for a sacrifice for sins.

Continue to Trust God

[19]So, brothers and sisters, we are completely free to enter the Most Holy Place without fear because of the blood of Jesus' death. [20]We can enter through a new and living way that Jesus opened for us. It leads through the curtain—Christ's body. [21]And since we have a great priest over God's house, [22]let us come near to God with a sincere heart and a sure faith, because we have been made free from a guilty conscience, and our bodies have been washed with pure water. [23]Let us hold firmly to the hope that we have confessed, because we can trust God to do what he promised.

[24]Let us think about each other and help each other to show love and do good deeds. [25]You should not stay away from the church meetings, as some are doing, but you should meet together and encourage each other. Do this even more as you see the day[n] coming.

[26]If we decide to go on sinning after we have learned the truth, there is no longer any sacrifice for sins. [27]There is nothing but fear in waiting for the judgment and the terrible fire that will destroy all those who live against God. [28]Anyone who refused to obey the law of Moses was found guilty from the proof given by two or three witnesses. He was put to death without mercy. [29]So what do you think should be done to those who do not respect the Son of God, who look at the blood of the agreement that made them holy as no different from others' blood, who insult the Spirit[d] of God's grace? Surely they should have a much worse punishment. [30]We know that God said, "I will punish those who do wrong; I will repay them."[n] And he also said, "The Lord will judge his people."[n] [31]It is a terrible thing to fall into the hands of the living God.

[32]Remember those days in the past when you first learned the truth. You had a hard struggle with many sufferings, but you continued strong. [33]Sometimes you were hurt and attacked before crowds of people, and sometimes you shared with those who were being treated that way. [34]You helped the prisoners. You even had joy when all that you owned was taken from you, because you knew you had something better and more lasting.

[35]So do not lose the courage you had in the past, which has a great reward. [36]You must hold on, so you can do what God wants and receive what he has promised. [37]For in a very short time,

"The One who is coming will come
and will not be delayed.
[38]The person who is right with me
will live by trusting in me.
But if he turns back with fear,

---

agreement God gives a contract or agreement to his people. For the Jews, this agreement was the law of Moses. But now God has given a better agreement to his people through Christ.
day The day Christ will come to judge all people and take his people to live with him.
"I . . . them." Quotation from Deuteronomy 32:35.
"The Lord . . . people." Quotation from Deuteronomy 32:36; Psalm 135:14.

I will not be pleased with him."

Habakkuk 2:3-4

[39]But we are not those who turn back and are lost. We are people who have faith and are saved.

What Is Faith?

11 Faith means being sure of the things we hope for and knowing that something is real even if we do not see it. [2]Faith is the reason we remember great people who lived in the past.

[3]It is by faith we understand that the whole world was made by God's command so what we see was made by something that cannot be seen.

[4]It was by faith that Abel offered God a better sacrifice than Cain did. God said he was pleased with the gifts Abel offered and called Abel a good man because of his faith. Abel died, but through his faith he is still speaking.

[5]It was by faith that Enoch was taken to heaven so he would not die. He could not be found, because God had taken him away. Before he was taken, the Scripture[d] says that he was a man who truly pleased God. [6]Without faith no one can please God. Anyone who comes to God must believe that he is real and that he rewards those who truly want to find him.

[7]It was by faith that Noah heard God's warnings about things he could not yet see. He obeyed God and built a large boat to save his family. By his faith, Noah showed that the world was wrong, and he became one of those who are made right with God through faith.

[8]It was by faith Abraham obeyed God's call to go to another place God promised to give him. He left his own country, not knowing where he was to go. [9]It was by faith that he lived like a foreigner in the country God promised to give him. He lived in tents with Isaac and Jacob, who had received that same promise from God. [10]Abraham was waiting for the city[n] that has real foundations — the city planned and built by God.

[11]He was too old to have children, and Sarah could not have children. It was by faith that Abraham was made able to become a father, because he trusted God to do what he had promised. [12]This man was so old he was almost dead, but from him came as many descendants as there are stars in the sky. Like the sand on the seashore, they could not be counted.

[13]All these great people died in faith. They did not get the things that God promised his people, but they saw them coming far in the future and were glad. They said they were like visitors and strangers on earth. [14]When people say such things, they show they are looking for a country that will be their own. [15]If they had been thinking about the country they had left, they could have gone back. [16]But they were waiting for a better country — a heavenly country. So God is not ashamed to be called their God, because he has prepared a city for them.

[17]It was by faith that Abraham, when God tested him, offered his son Isaac as a sacrifice. God made the promises to Abraham, but Abraham was ready to offer his own son as a sacrifice. [18]God had said, "The descendants I promised you will be from Isaac."[n] [19]Abraham believed that God could raise the dead, and really, it was as if Abraham got Isaac back from death.

[20]It was by faith that Isaac blessed the future of Jacob and Esau. [21]It was by faith that Jacob, as he was dying, blessed each one of Joseph's sons. Then he worshiped as he leaned on the top of his walking stick.

[22]It was by faith that Joseph, while he was dying, spoke about the Israelites leaving Egypt and gave instructions about what to do with his body.

[23]It was by faith that Moses' parents hid him for three months after he was born. They saw that Moses was a beautiful baby, and they were not afraid to disobey the king's order.

[24]It was by faith that Moses, when he grew up, refused to be called the son of the king of Egypt's daughter. [25]He chose to suffer with God's people instead of enjoying sin for a short time. [26]He thought it was better to

city The spiritual "city" where God's people live with him. Also called "the heavenly Jerusalem." (See Hebrews 12:22.)
"The descendants ... Isaac." Quotation from Genesis 21:12.

suffer for the Christ[d] than to have all the treasures of Egypt, because he was looking for God's reward. [27]It was by faith that Moses left Egypt and was not afraid of the king's anger. Moses continued strong as if he could see the God that no one can see. [28]It was by faith that Moses prepared the Passover[d] and spread the blood on the doors so the one who brings death would not kill the firstborn[d] sons of Israel.

[29]It was by faith that the people crossed the Red Sea as if it were dry land. But when the Egyptians tried it, they were drowned.

[30]It was by faith that the walls of Jericho fell after the people had marched around them for seven days.

[31]It was by faith that Rahab, the prostitute,[d] welcomed the spies and was not killed with those who refused to obey God.

[32]Do I need to give more examples? I do not have time to tell you about Gideon, Barak, Samson, Jephthah, David, Samuel, and the prophets.[d] [33]Through their faith they defeated kingdoms. They did what was right, received God's promises, and shut the mouths of lions. [34]They stopped great fires and were saved from being killed with swords. They were weak, and yet were made strong. They were powerful in battle and defeated other armies. [35]Women received their dead relatives raised back to life. Others were tortured and refused to accept their freedom so they could be raised from the dead to a better life. [36]Some were laughed at and beaten. Others were put in chains and thrown into prison. [37]They were stoned to death, they were cut in half, and they were killed with swords. Some wore the skins of sheep and goats. They were poor, abused, and treated badly. [38]The world was not good enough for them! They wandered in deserts and mountains, living in caves and holes in the earth.

[39]All these people are known for their faith, but none of them received what God had promised. [40]God planned to give us something better so that they would be made perfect, but only together with us.

Follow Jesus' Example

12 We have around us many people whose lives tell us what faith means.

So let us run the race that is before us and never give up. We should remove from our lives anything that would get in the way and the sin that so easily holds us back. [2]Let us look only to Jesus, the One who began our faith and who makes it perfect. He suffered death on the cross. But he accepted the shame as if it were nothing because of the joy that God put before him. And now he is sitting at the right side of God's throne. [3]Think about Jesus' example. He held on while wicked people were doing evil things to him. So do not get tired and stop trying.

God Is like a Father

[4]You are struggling against sin, but your struggles have not yet caused you to be killed. [5]You have forgotten the encouraging words that call you his children:

"My child, don't think the Lord's
    discipline is worth nothing,
    and don't stop trying when he corrects
        you.
[6]The Lord disciplines those he loves,
    and he punishes everyone he accepts
        as his child."   *Proverbs 3:11-12*

[7]So hold on through your sufferings, because they are like a father's discipline. God is treating you as children. All children are disciplined by their fathers. [8]If you are never disciplined (and every child must be disciplined), you are not true children. [9]We have all had fathers here on earth who disciplined us, and we respected them. So it is even more important that we accept discipline from the Father of our spirits so we will have life. [10]Our fathers on earth disciplined us for a short time in the way they thought was best. But God disciplines us to help us, so we can become holy as he is. [11]We do not enjoy being disciplined. It is painful, but later, after we have learned from it, we have peace, because we start living in the right way.

Be Careful How You Live

[12]You have become weak, so make yourselves strong again. [13]Live in the right way so that you will be saved and your weakness will not cause you to be lost.

[14]Try to live in peace with all people, and try to live free from sin. Anyone whose life is not holy will never see the Lord. [15]Be careful

that no one fails to receive God's grace and begins to cause trouble among you. A person like that can ruin many of you. [16]Be careful that no one takes part in sexual sin or is like Esau and never thinks about God. As the oldest son, Esau would have received everything from his father, but he sold all that for a single meal. [17]You remember that after Esau did this, he wanted to get his father's blessing, but his father refused. Esau could find no way to change what he had done, even though he wanted the blessing so much that he cried.

[18]You have not come to a mountain that can be touched and that is burning with fire. You have not come to darkness, sadness, and storms. [19]You have not come to the noise of a trumpet or to the sound of a voice like the one the people of Israel heard and begged not to hear another word. [20]They did not want to hear the command: "If anything, even an animal, touches the mountain, it must be put to death with stones." [n] [21]What they saw was so terrible that Moses said, "I am shaking with fear." [n]

[22]But you have come to Mount Zion, [n] to the city of the living God, the heavenly Jerusalem. You have come to thousands of angels gathered together with joy. [23]You have come to the meeting of God's firstborn [n] children whose names are written in heaven. You have come to God, the judge of all people, and to the spirits of good people who have been made perfect. [24]You have come to Jesus, the One who brought the new agreement from God to his people, and you have come to the sprinkled blood [n] that has a better message than the blood of Abel. [n]

[25]So be careful and do not refuse to listen when God speaks. Others refused to listen to him when he warned them on earth, and they did not escape. So it will be worse for us if we refuse to listen to God who warns us from heaven. [26]When he spoke before, his voice shook the earth, but now he has prom-

ised, "Once again I will shake not only the earth but also the heavens." [n] [27]The words "once again" clearly show us that everything that was made — things that can be shaken — will be destroyed. Only the things that cannot be shaken will remain.

[28]So let us be thankful, because we have a kingdom that cannot be shaken. We should worship God in a way that pleases him with respect and fear, [29]because our God is like a fire that burns things up.

13 Keep on loving each other as brothers and sisters. [2]Remember to welcome strangers, because some who have done this have welcomed angels without knowing it. [3]Remember those who are in prison as if you were in prison with them. Remember those who are suffering as if you were suffering with them.

[4]Marriage should be honored by everyone, and husband and wife should keep their marriage pure. God will judge as guilty those who take part in sexual sins. [5]Keep your lives free from the love of money, and be satisfied with what you have. God has said,

"I will never leave you;
I will never forget you." *Deuteronomy 31:6*
[6]So we can be sure when we say,
"I will not be afraid, because the Lord is my helper.
People can't do anything to me."
Psalm 118:6

[7]Remember your leaders who taught God's message to you. Remember how they lived and died, and copy their faith. [8]Jesus Christ is the same yesterday, today, and forever.

[9]Do not let all kinds of strange teachings lead you into the wrong way. Your hearts should be strengthened by God's grace, not by obeying rules about foods, which do not help those who obey them.

[10]We have a sacrifice, but the priests who serve in the Holy Tent [d] cannot eat from it. [11]The high priest carries the blood of animals

---

"If . . . stones." Quotation from Exodus 19:12-13.
"I . . . fear." Quotation from Deuteronomy 9:19.
Mount Zion Another name for Jerusalem, here meaning the spiritual city of God's people.
firstborn The first son born in a Jewish family was given the most important place in the family and received special blessings. All of God's children are like that.
sprinkled blood The blood of Jesus' death.
Abel The son of Adam and Eve, who was killed by his brother Cain (Genesis 4:8).
"Once . . . heavens." Quotation from Haggai 2:6, 21.

into the Most Holy Place where he offers this blood for sins. But the bodies of the animals are burned outside the camp. [12]So Jesus also suffered outside the city to make his people holy with his own blood. [13]So let us go to Jesus outside the camp, holding on as he did when we are abused.

[14]Here on earth we do not have a city that lasts forever, but we are looking for the city that we will have in the future. [15]So through Jesus let us always offer to God our sacrifice of praise, coming from lips that speak his name. [16]Do not forget to do good to others, and share with them, because such sacrifices please God.

[17]Obey your leaders and act under their authority. They are watching over you, because they are responsible for your souls. Obey them so that they will do this work with joy, not sadness. It will not help you to make their work hard.

[18]Pray for us. We are sure that we have a clear conscience, because we always want to do the right thing. [19]I especially beg you to pray so that God will send me back to you soon.

[20-21]I pray that the God of peace will give you every good thing you need so you can do what he wants. God raised from the dead our Lord Jesus, the Great Shepherd of the sheep, because of the blood of his death. His blood began the eternal agreement that God made with his people. I pray that God will do in us what pleases him, through Jesus Christ, and to him be glory forever and ever. Amen.

[22]My brothers and sisters, I beg you to listen patiently to this message I have written to encourage you, because it is not very long. [23]I want you to know that our brother Timothy has been let out of prison. If he arrives soon, we will both come to see you.

[24]Greet all your leaders and all of God's people. Those from Italy send greetings to you.

[25]Grace be with you all.

JAMES

How to Live as a Christian

1 From James, a servant of God and of the Lord Jesus Christ.

To all of God's people who are scattered everywhere in the world:

Greetings.

Faith and Wisdom

²My brothers and sisters,[n] when you have many kinds of troubles, you should be full of joy, ³because you know that these troubles test your faith, and this will give you patience. ⁴Let your patience show itself perfectly in what you do. Then you will be perfect and complete and will have everything you need. ⁵But if any of you needs wisdom, you should ask God for it. He is generous and enjoys giving to all people, so he will give you wisdom. ⁶But when you ask God, you must believe and not doubt. Anyone who doubts is like a wave in the sea, blown up and down by the wind. ⁷⁻⁸Such doubters are thinking two different things at the same time, and they cannot decide about anything they do. They should not think they will receive anything from the Lord.

True Riches

⁹Believers who are poor should be proud, because God has made them spiritually rich. ¹⁰Those who are rich should be proud, because God has shown them that they are spiritually poor. The rich will die like a wild flower in the grass. ¹¹The sun rises with burning heat and dries up the plants. The flower falls off, and its beauty is gone. In the same way the rich will die while they are still taking care of business.

Temptation Is Not from God

¹²When people are tempted and still continue strong, they should be happy. After they have proved their faith, God will reward them with life forever. God promised this to all those who love him. ¹³When people are tempted, they should not say, "God is tempting me." Evil cannot tempt God, and God himself does not tempt anyone. ¹⁴But people are tempted when their own evil desire leads them away and traps them. ¹⁵This desire leads to sin, and then the sin grows and brings death.

¹⁶My dear brothers and sisters, do not be fooled about this. ¹⁷Every good action and every perfect gift is from God. These good gifts come down from the Creator of the sun, moon, and stars, who does not change like their shifting shadows. ¹⁸God decided to give us life through the word of truth so we might be the most important of all the things he made.

Listening and Obeying

¹⁹My dear brothers and sisters, always be willing to listen and slow to speak. Do not become angry easily, ²⁰because anger will not help you live the right kind of life God wants. ²¹So put out of your life every evil thing and every kind of wrong. Then in gentleness accept God's teaching that is planted in your hearts, which can save you.

²²Do what God's teaching says; when you only listen and do nothing, you are fooling yourselves. ²³Those who hear God's teaching and do nothing are like people who look at themselves in a mirror. ²⁴They see their faces and then go away and quickly forget what they looked like. ²⁵But the truly happy people are those who carefully study God's perfect law that makes people free, and they continue to study it. They do not forget what they heard, but they obey what God's teaching says. Those who do this will be made happy.

---

brothers and sisters Although the Greek text says "brothers" here and throughout this book, James' words were meant for the entire church, including men and women.

The True Way to Worship God

26People who think they are religious but say things they should not say are just fooling themselves. Their "religion" is worth nothing. 27Religion that God accepts as pure and without fault is this: caring for orphans or widows who need help, and keeping yourself free from the world's evil influence.

Love All People

2 My dear brothers and sisters, as believers in our glorious Lord Jesus Christ, never think some people are more important than others. 2Suppose someone comes into your church meeting wearing nice clothes and a gold ring. At the same time a poor person comes in wearing old, dirty clothes. 3You show special attention to the one wearing nice clothes and say, "Please, sit here in this good seat." But you say to the poor person, "Stand over there," or, "Sit on the floor by my feet." 4What are you doing? You are making some people more important than others, and with evil thoughts you are deciding that one person is better.

5Listen, my dear brothers and sisters! God chose the poor in the world to be rich with faith and to receive the kingdom God promised to those who love him. 6But you show no respect to the poor. The rich are always trying to control your lives. They are the ones who take you to court. 7And they are the ones who speak against Jesus, who owns you.

8This royal law is found in the Scriptures: *d* "Love your neighbor as you love yourself." *n* If you obey this law, you are doing right. 9But if you treat one person as being more important than another, you are sinning. You are guilty of breaking God's law. 10A person who follows all of God's law but fails to obey even one command is guilty of breaking all the commands in that law. 11The same God who said, "You must not be guilty of adultery," *d, n* also said, "You must not murder anyone." *n* So if you do not take part in adultery but you murder someone, you are guilty of breaking

all of God's law. 12In everything you say and do, remember that you will be judged by the law that makes people free. 13So you must show mercy to others, or God will not show mercy to you when he judges you. But the person who shows mercy can stand without fear at the judgment.

Faith and Good Works

14My brothers and sisters, if people say they have faith, but do nothing, their faith is worth nothing. Can faith like that save them? 15A brother or sister in Christ might need clothes or food. 16If you say to that person, "God be with you! I hope you stay warm and get plenty to eat," but you do not give what that person needs, your words are worth nothing. 17In the same way, faith that is alone — that does nothing — is dead.

18Someone might say, "You have faith, but I have deeds." Show me your faith without doing anything, and I will show you my faith by what I do. 19You believe there is one God. Good! But the demons *d* believe that, too, and they tremble with fear.

20You foolish person! Must you be shown that faith that does nothing is worth nothing? 21Abraham, our ancestor, was made right with God by what he did when he offered his son Isaac on the altar. 22So you see that Abraham's faith and the things he did worked together. His faith was made perfect by what he did. 23This shows the full meaning of the Scripture *d* that says: "Abraham believed God, and God accepted Abraham's faith, and that faith made him right with God." *n* And Abraham was called God's friend. *n* 24So you see that people are made right with God by what they do, not by faith only.

25Another example is Rahab, a prostitute, *d* who was made right with God by something she did. She welcomed the spies into her home and helped them escape by a different road.

26Just as a person's body that does not have a spirit is dead, so faith that does nothing is dead!

"Love . . . yourself." Quotation from Leviticus 19:18.
"You . . . adultery." Quotation from Exodus 20:14 and Deuteronomy 5:18.
"You . . . anyone." Quotation from Exodus 20:13 and Deuteronomy 5:17.
"Abraham . . . God." Quotation from Genesis 15:6.
God's friend These words about Abraham are found in 2 Chronicles 20:7 and Isaiah 41:8.

Controlling the Things We Say

3 My brothers and sisters, not many of you should become teachers, because you know that we who teach will be judged more strictly. [2]We all make many mistakes. If people never said anything wrong, they would be perfect and able to control their entire selves, too. [3]When we put bits into the mouths of horses to make them obey us, we can control their whole bodies. [4]Also a ship is very big, and it is pushed by strong winds. But a very small rudder controls that big ship, making it go wherever the pilot wants. [5]It is the same with the tongue. It is a small part of the body, but it brags about great things.

A big forest fire can be started with only a little flame. [6]And the tongue is like a fire. It is a whole world of evil among the parts of our bodies. The tongue spreads its evil through the whole body. The tongue is set on fire by hell, and it starts a fire that influences all of life. [7]People can tame every kind of wild animal, bird, reptile, and fish, and they have tamed them, [8]but no one can tame the tongue. It is wild and evil and full of deadly poison. [9]We use our tongues to praise our Lord and Father, but then we curse people, whom God made like himself. [10]Praises and curses come from the same mouth! My brothers and sisters, this should not happen. [11]Do good and bad water flow from the same spring? [12]My brothers and sisters, can a fig tree make olives, or can a grapevine make figs? No! And a well full of salty water cannot give good water.

True Wisdom

[13]Are there those among you who are truly wise and understanding? Then they should show it by living right and doing good things with a gentleness that comes from wisdom. [14]But if you are selfish and have bitter jealousy in your hearts, do not brag. Your bragging is a lie that hides the truth. [15]That kind of "wisdom" does not come from God but from the world. It is not spiritual; it is from the devil. [16]Where jealousy and selfishness are, there will be confusion and every kind of evil. [17]But the wisdom that comes from God is first of all pure, then peaceful, gentle, and easy to please. This wisdom is always ready to help those who are troubled and to do good for others. It is always fair and honest. [18]People who work for peace in a peaceful way plant a good crop of right-living.

Give Yourselves to God

4 Do you know where your fights and arguments come from? They come from the selfish desires that war within you. [2]You want things, but you do not have them. So you are ready to kill and are jealous of other people, but you still cannot get what you want. So you argue and fight. You do not get what you want, because you do not ask God. [3]Or when you ask, you do not receive because the reason you ask is wrong. You want things so you can use them for your own pleasures.

[4]So, you are not loyal to God! You should know that loving the world is the same as hating God. Anyone who wants to be a friend of the world becomes God's enemy. [5]Do you think the Scripture[d] means nothing that says, "The Spirit[d] that God made to live in us wants us for himself alone." [n] [6]But God gives us even more grace, as the Scripture says,

"God is against the proud,
  but he gives grace to the humble."

Proverbs 3:34

[7]So give yourselves completely to God. Stand against the devil, and the devil will run from you. [8]Come near to God, and God will come near to you. You sinners, clean sin out of your lives. You who are trying to follow God and the world at the same time, make your thinking pure. [9]Be sad, cry, and weep! Change your laughter into crying and your joy into sadness. [10]Don't be too proud in the Lord's presence, and he will make you great.

You Are Not the Judge

[11]Brothers and sisters, do not tell evil lies about each other. If you speak against your fellow believers or judge them, you are judging and speaking against the law they follow. And when you are judging the law, you are no longer a follower of the law. You have become a judge. [12]God is the only Lawmaker

---

"The Spirit ... alone."   These words may be from Exodus 20:5.

and Judge. He is the only One who can save and destroy. So it is not right for you to judge your neighbor.

Let God Plan Your Life

13Some of you say, "Today or tomorrow we will go to some city. We will stay there a year, do business, and make money." 14But you do not know what will happen tomorrow! Your life is like a mist. You can see it for a short time, but then it goes away. 15So you should say, "If the Lord wants, we will live and do this or that." 16But now you are proud and you brag. All of this bragging is wrong. 17Anyone who knows the right thing to do, but does not do it, is sinning.

A Warning to the Rich

5 You rich people, listen! Cry and be very sad because of the troubles that are coming to you. 2Your riches have rotted, and your clothes have been eaten by moths. 3Your gold and silver have rusted, and that rust will be a proof that you were wrong. It will eat your bodies like fire. You saved your treasure for the last days. 4The pay you did not give the workers who mowed your fields cries out against you, and the cries of the workers have been heard by the Lord All-Powerful. 5Your life on earth was full of rich living and pleasing yourselves with everything you wanted. You made yourselves fat, like an animal ready to be killed. 6You have judged guilty and then murdered innocent people, who were not against you.

Be Patient

7Brothers and sisters, be patient until the Lord comes again. A farmer patiently waits for his valuable crop to grow from the earth and for it to receive the autumn and spring rains. 8You, too, must be patient. Do not give up hope, because the Lord is coming soon. 9Brothers and sisters, do not complain against each other or you will be judged guilty. And the Judge is ready to come!

10Brothers and sisters, follow the example of the prophets*d* who spoke for the Lord. They suffered many hard things, but they were patient. 11We say they are happy because they did not give up. You have heard about Job's patience, and you know the Lord's purpose for him in the end. You know the Lord is full of mercy and is kind.

Be Careful What You Say

12My brothers and sisters, above all, do not use an oath when you make a promise. Don't use the name of heaven, earth, or anything else to prove what you say. When you mean yes, say only yes, and when you mean no, say only no so you will not be judged guilty.

The Power of Prayer

13Anyone who is having troubles should pray. Anyone who is happy should sing praises. 14Anyone who is sick should call the church's elders.*d* They should pray for and pour oil on the person[n] in the name of the Lord. 15And the prayer that is said with faith will make the sick person well; the Lord will heal that person. And if the person has sinned, the sins will be forgiven. 16Confess your sins to each other and pray for each other so God can heal you. When a believing person prays, great things happen. 17Elijah was a human being just like us. He prayed that it would not rain, and it did not rain on the land for three and a half years! 18Then Elijah prayed again, and the rain came down from the sky, and the land produced crops again.

Saving a Soul

19My brothers and sisters, if one of you wanders away from the truth, and someone helps that person come back, 20remember this: Anyone who brings a sinner back from the wrong way will save that sinner's soul from death and will cause many sins to be forgiven.

---

pour oil on the person Oil was used in the name of the Lord as a sign that the person was now set apart for God's special attention and care.

1 PETER

Encouragement for Suffering Christians

1 From Peter, an apostle[d] of Jesus Christ. To God's chosen people who are away from their homes and are scattered all around the countries of Pontus, Galatia, Cappadocia, Asia, and Bithynia. ²God planned long ago to choose you by making you his holy people, which is the Spirit's[d] work. God wanted you to obey him and to be made clean by the blood of the death of Jesus Christ.

Grace and peace be yours more and more.

We Have a Living Hope

³Praise be to the God and Father of our Lord Jesus Christ. In God's great mercy he has caused us to be born again into a living hope, because Jesus Christ rose from the dead. ⁴Now we hope for the blessings God has for his children. These blessings, which cannot be destroyed or be spoiled or lose their beauty, are kept in heaven for you. ⁵God's power protects you through your faith until salvation is shown to you at the end of time. ⁶This makes you very happy, even though now for a short time different kinds of troubles may make you sad. ⁷These troubles come to prove that your faith is pure. This purity of faith is worth more than gold, which can be proved to be pure by fire but will ruin. But the purity of your faith will bring you praise and glory and honor when Jesus Christ is shown to you. ⁸You have not seen Christ, but still you love him. You cannot see him now, but you believe in him. So you are filled with a joy that cannot be explained, a joy full of glory. ⁹And you are receiving the goal of your faith — the salvation of your souls.

¹⁰The prophets[d] searched carefully and tried to learn about this salvation. They prophesied about the grace that was coming to you. ¹¹The Spirit[d] of Christ was in the prophets, telling in advance about the sufferings of Christ and about the glory that would follow those sufferings. The prophets tried to learn about what the Spirit was showing them, when those things would happen, and what the world would be like at that time. ¹²It was shown them that their service was not for themselves but for you, when they told about the truths you have now heard. Those who preached the Good News[d] to you told you those things with the help of the Holy Spirit who was sent from heaven — things into which angels desire to look.

A Call to Holy Living

¹³So prepare your minds for service and have self-control. All your hope should be for the gift of grace that will be yours when Jesus Christ is shown to you. ¹⁴Now that you are obedient children of God do not live as you did in the past. You did not understand, so you did the evil things you wanted. ¹⁵But be holy in all you do, just as God, the One who called you, is holy. ¹⁶It is written in the Scriptures:[d] "You must be holy, because I am holy."[n]

¹⁷You pray to God and call him Father, and he judges each person's work equally. So while you are here on earth, you should live with respect for God. ¹⁸You know that in the past you were living in a worthless way, a way passed down from the people who lived before you. But you were saved from that useless life. You were bought, not with something that ruins like gold or silver, ¹⁹but with the precious blood of Christ, who was like a pure and perfect lamb. ²⁰Christ was chosen before the world was made, but he was shown to the world in these last times for your sake. ²¹Through Christ you believe in God, who raised Christ from the dead and gave him glory. So your faith and your hope are in God.

²²Now that you have made your souls

pure by obeying the truth, you can have true love for your Christian brothers and sisters.[n] So love each other deeply with all your heart. [23]You have been born again, and this new life did not come from something that dies, but from something that cannot die. You were born again through God's living message that continues forever. [24]The Scripture says,

"All people are like the grass,
  and all their glory is like the flowers of
    the field.
The grass dies and the flowers fall,
[25]but the word of the Lord will live
    forever." *Isaiah 40:6-8*

And this is the word that was preached to you.

Jesus Is the Living Stone

2 So then, rid yourselves of all evil, all lying, hypocrisy,[d] jealousy, and evil speech. [2]As newborn babies want milk, you should want the pure and simple teaching. By it you can grow up and be saved, [3]because you have already examined and seen how good the Lord is.

[4]Come to the Lord Jesus, the "stone"[n] that lives. The people of the world did not want this stone, but he was the stone God chose, and he was precious. [5]You also are like living stones, so let yourselves be used to build a spiritual temple — to be holy priests who offer spiritual sacrifices to God. He will accept those sacrifices through Jesus Christ. [6]The Scripture[d] says:

"I will put a stone in the ground in
    Jerusalem.
  Everything will be built on this
    important and precious rock.
Anyone who trusts in him
  will never be disappointed." *Isaiah 28:16*

[7]This stone is worth much to you who believe. But to the people who do not believe,

"the stone that the builders rejected
  has become the cornerstone."[d]

Psalm 118:22

[8]Also, he is

"a stone that causes people to stumble,
  a rock that makes them fall." *Isaiah 8:14*

They stumble because they do not obey what God says, which is what God planned to happen to them.

[9]But you are a chosen people, royal priests, a holy nation, a people for God's own possession. You were chosen to tell about the wonderful acts of God, who called you out of darkness into his wonderful light. [10]At one time you were not a people, but now you are God's people. In the past you had never received mercy, but now you have received God's mercy.

Live for God

[11]Dear friends, you are like foreigners and strangers in this world. I beg you to avoid the evil things your bodies want to do that fight against your soul. [12]People who do not believe are living all around you and might say that you are doing wrong. Live such good lives that they will see the good things you do and will give glory to God on the day when Christ comes again.

Yield to Every Human Authority

[13]For the Lord's sake, yield to the people who have authority in this world: the king, who is the highest authority, [14]and the leaders who are sent by him to punish those who do wrong and to praise those who do right. [15]It is God's desire that by doing good you should stop foolish people from saying stupid things about you. [16]Live as free people, but do not use your freedom as an excuse to do evil. Live as servants of God. [17]Show respect for all people: Love the brothers and sisters of God's family, respect God, honor the king.

Follow Christ's Example

[18]Slaves, yield to the authority of your masters with all respect, not only those who are good and kind, but also those who are dishonest. [19]A person might have to suffer even when it is unfair, but if he thinks of God and stands the pain, God is pleased. [20]If you are beaten for doing wrong, there is no reason to praise you for being patient in your punishment. But if you suffer for doing good,

---

brothers and sisters Although the Greek text says "brothers" here and throughout this book, Peter's words were meant for the entire church, including men and women.
"stone" The most important stone in God's spiritual temple or house (his people).

and you are patient, then God is pleased. [21]This is what you were called to do, because Christ suffered for you and gave you an example to follow. So you should do as he did. [22]"He had never sinned,

and he had never lied."   *Isaiah 53:9*

[23]People insulted Christ, but he did not insult them in return. Christ suffered, but he did not threaten. He let God, the One who judges rightly, take care of him. [24]Christ carried our sins in his body on the cross so we would stop living for sin and start living for what is right. And you are healed because of his wounds. [25]You were like sheep that wandered away, but now you have come back to the Shepherd and Protector of your souls.

Wives and Husbands

3 In the same way, you wives should yield to your husbands. Then, if some husbands do not obey God's teaching, they will be persuaded to believe without anyone's saying a word to them. They will be persuaded by the way their wives live. [2]Your husbands will see the pure lives you live with your respect for God. [3]It is not fancy hair, gold jewelry, or fine clothes that should make you beautiful. [4]No, your beauty should come from within you — the beauty of a gentle and quiet spirit that will never be destroyed and is very precious to God. [5]In this same way the holy women who lived long ago and followed God made themselves beautiful, yielding to their own husbands. [6]Sarah obeyed Abraham, her husband, and called him her master. And you women are true children of Sarah if you always do what is right and are not afraid.

[7]In the same way, you husbands should live with your wives in an understanding way, since they are weaker than you. But show them respect, because God gives them the same blessing he gives you — the grace that gives true life. Do this so that nothing will stop your prayers.

Suffering for Doing Right

[8]Finally, all of you should be in agreement, understanding each other, loving each other as family, being kind and humble. [9]Do not do wrong to repay a wrong, and do not insult to repay an insult. But repay with a blessing,

because you yourselves were called to do this so that you might receive a blessing. [10]The Scripture*d* says,

"A person must do these things
to enjoy life and have many happy days.
He must not say evil things,
and he must not tell lies.
[11]He must stop doing evil and do good.
He must look for peace and work for it.
[12]The Lord sees the good people
and listens to their prayers.
But the Lord is against
those who do evil."   *Psalm 34:12-16*

[13]If you are trying hard to do good, no one can really hurt you. [14]But even if you suffer for doing right, you are blessed.

"Don't be afraid of what they fear;
do not dread those things."   *Isaiah 8:12-13*

[15]But respect Christ as the holy Lord in your hearts. Always be ready to answer everyone who asks you to explain about the hope you have, [16]but answer in a gentle way and with respect. Keep a clear conscience so that those who speak evil of your good life in Christ will be made ashamed. [17]It is better to suffer for doing good than for doing wrong if that is what God wants. [18]Christ himself suffered for sins once. He was not guilty, but he suffered for those who are guilty to bring you to God. His body was killed, but he was made alive in the spirit. [19]And in the spirit he went and preached to the spirits in prison [20]who refused to obey God long ago in the time of Noah. God was waiting patiently for them while Noah was building the boat. Only a few people — eight in all — were saved by water. [21]And that water is like baptism that now saves you — not the washing of dirt from the body, but the promise made to God from a good conscience. And this is because Jesus Christ was raised from the dead. [22]Now Jesus has gone into heaven and is at God's right side ruling over angels, authorities, and powers.

Change Your Lives

4 Since Christ suffered while he was in his body, strengthen yourselves with the same way of thinking Christ had. The person who has suffered in the body is finished with sin. [2]Strengthen yourselves so that you will live here on earth doing what God wants, not the evil things people want. [3]In the past you wasted too much time doing what nonbelievers enjoy. You were guilty of sexual sins, evil desires, drunkenness, wild and drunken parties, and hateful idol worship. [4]Nonbelievers think it is strange that you do not do the many wild and wasteful things they do, so they insult you. [5]But they will have to explain this to God, who is ready to judge the living and the dead. [6]For this reason the Good News[d] was preached to those who are now dead. Even though they were judged like all people, the Good News was preached to them so they could live in the spirit as God lives.

Use God's Gifts Wisely

[7]The time is near when all things will end. So think clearly and control yourselves so you will be able to pray. [8]Most importantly, love each other deeply, because love will cause many sins to be forgiven. [9]Open your homes to each other, without complaining. [10]Each of you has received a gift to use to serve others. Be good servants of God's various gifts of grace. [11]Anyone who speaks should speak words from God. Anyone who serves should serve with the strength God gives so that in everything God will be praised through Jesus Christ. Power and glory belong to him forever and ever. Amen.

Suffering as a Christian

[12]My friends, do not be surprised at the terrible trouble which now comes to test you. Do not think that something strange is happening to you. [13]But be happy that you are sharing in Christ's sufferings so that you will be happy and full of joy when Christ comes again in glory. [14]When people insult you because you follow Christ, you are blessed, because the glorious Spirit,[d] the Spirit of God, is with you. [15]Do not suffer for murder, theft, or any other crime, nor because you trouble other people. [16]But if you suffer because you are a Christian, do not be ashamed. Praise God because you wear that

name. [17]It is time for judgment to begin with God's family. And if that judging begins with us, what will happen to those people who do not obey the Good News[d] of God?
[18]"If it is very hard for a good person to
be saved,
the wicked person and the sinner will
surely be lost!"[n]
[19]So those who suffer as God wants should trust their souls to the faithful Creator as they continue to do what is right.

The Flock of God

5 Now I have something to say to the elders[d] in your group. I also am an elder. I have seen Christ's sufferings, and I will share in the glory that will be shown to us. I beg you to [2]shepherd God's flock, for whom you are responsible. Watch over them because you want to, not because you are forced. That is how God wants it. Do it because you are happy to serve, not because you want money. [3]Do not be like a ruler over people you are responsible for, but be good examples to them. [4]Then when Christ, the Chief Shepherd, comes, you will get a glorious crown that will never lose its beauty.

[5]In the same way, younger people should be willing to be under older people. And all of you should be very humble with each other.

"God is against the proud,
but he gives grace to the humble."

Proverbs 3:34

[6]Be humble under God's powerful hand so he will lift you up when the right time comes. [7]Give all your worries to him, because he cares about you.

[8]Control yourselves and be careful! The devil, your enemy, goes around like a roaring lion looking for someone to eat. [9]Refuse to give in to him, by standing strong in your faith. You know that your Christian family all over the world is having the same kinds of suffering.

[10]And after you suffer for a short time, God, who gives all grace, will make everything right. He will make you strong and support you and keep you from falling. He called you to share in his glory in Christ, a glory that

---

"If . . . lost!"   Quotation from Proverbs 11:31 in the Septuagint, the Greek version of the Old Testament.

will continue forever. [11]All power is his forever and ever. Amen.

Final Greetings

[12]I wrote this short letter with the help of Silas, who I know is a faithful brother in Christ. I wrote to encourage you and to tell you that this is the true grace of God. Stand strong in that grace.

[13]The church in Babylon, who was chosen like you, sends you greetings. Mark, my son in Christ, also greets you. [14]Give each other a kiss of Christian love when you meet.

Peace to all of you who are in Christ.

2 PETER

Correcting False Teachings

1 From Simon Peter, a servant and apostle*d* of Jesus Christ.

To you who have received a faith as valuable as ours, because our God and Savior Jesus Christ does what is right.

[2]Grace and peace be given to you more and more, because you truly know God and Jesus our Lord.

God Has Given Us Blessings

[3]Jesus has the power of God, by which he has given us everything we need to live and to serve God. We have these things because we know him. Jesus called us by his glory and goodness. [4]Through these he gave us the very great and precious promises. With these gifts you can share in being like God, and the world will not ruin you with its evil desires.

[5]Because you have these blessings, do your best to add these things to your lives: to your faith, add goodness; and to your goodness, add knowledge; [6]and to your knowledge, add self-control; and to your self-control, add patience; and to your patience, add service for God; [7]and to your service for God, add kindness for your brothers and sisters in Christ; and to this kindness, add love. [8]If all these things are in you and are growing, they will help you to be useful and productive in your knowledge of our Lord Jesus Christ. [9]But anyone who does not have these things cannot see clearly. He is blind and has forgotten that he was made clean from his past sins.

[10]My brothers and sisters,*n* try hard to be certain that you really are called and chosen by God. If you do all these things, you will never fall. [11]And you will be given a very great welcome into the eternal kingdom of our Lord and Savior Jesus Christ.

[12]You know these things, and you are very strong in the truth, but I will always help you remember them. [13]I think it is right for me to help you remember as long as I am in this body. [14]I know I must soon leave this body, as our Lord Jesus Christ has shown me. [15]I will try my best so that you may be able to remember these things even after I am gone.

We Saw Christ's Glory

[16]When we told you about the powerful coming of our Lord Jesus Christ, we were not telling just smart stories that someone invented. But we saw the greatness of Jesus with our own eyes. [17]Jesus heard the voice of God, the Greatest Glory, when he received honor and glory from God the Father. The voice said, "This is my Son, whom I love, and I am very pleased with him." [18]We heard that voice from heaven while we were with Jesus on the holy mountain.

[19]This makes us more sure about the message the prophets*d* gave. It is good for you to follow closely what they said as you would follow a light shining in a dark place, until the day begins and the morning star rises in your hearts. [20]Most of all, you must understand this: No prophecy in the Scriptures*d* ever comes from the prophet's own interpretation. [21]No prophecy ever came from what a person wanted to say, but people led by the Holy Spirit*d* spoke words from God.

False Teachers

2 There used to be false prophets*d* among God's people, just as you will have some false teachers in your group. They will secretly teach things that are wrong—teachings that will cause people to be lost. They will even refuse to accept the Master, Jesus, who bought their freedom. So they will bring quick ruin on themselves. [2]Many will follow their evil ways and say evil things about the way of truth. [3]Those false teachers

---

brothers and sisters Although the Greek text reads "brothers" here and throughout this book, Peter's words were meant for the entire church, including men and women.

only want your money, so they will use you by telling you lies. Their judgment spoken against them long ago is still coming, and their ruin is certain.

[4]When angels sinned, God did not let them go free without punishment. He sent them to hell and put them in caves of darkness where they are being held for judgment. [5]And God punished the world long ago when he brought a flood to the world that was full of people who were against him. But God saved Noah, who preached about being right with God, and seven other people with him. [6]And God also destroyed the evil cities of Sodom and Gomorrah[n] by burning them until they were ashes. He made those cities an example of what will happen to those who are against God. [7]But he saved Lot from those cities. Lot, a good man, was troubled because of the filthy lives of evil people. [8](Lot was a good man, but because he lived with evil people every day, his good heart was hurt by the evil things he saw and heard.) [9]So the Lord knows how to save those who serve him when troubles come. He will hold evil people and punish them, while waiting for the Judgment Day. [10]That punishment is especially for those who live by doing the evil things their sinful selves want and who hate authority.

These false teachers are bold and do anything they want. They are not afraid to speak against the angels. [11]But even the angels, who are much stronger and more powerful than false teachers, do not accuse them with insults before the Lord. [12]But these people speak against things they do not understand. They are like animals that act without thinking, animals born to be caught and killed. And, like animals, these false teachers will be destroyed. [13]They have caused many people to suffer, so they themselves will suffer. That is their pay for what they have done. They take pleasure in openly doing evil, so they are like dirty spots and stains among you. They delight in trickery while eating meals with you. [14]Every time they look at a woman they want her, and their desire for sin is never satisfied. They lead weak people into the trap

of sin, and they have taught their hearts to be greedy. God will punish them! [15]These false teachers left the right road and lost their way, following the way Balaam went. Balaam was the son of Beor, who loved being paid for doing wrong. [16]But a donkey, which cannot talk, told Balaam he was sinning. It spoke with a man's voice and stopped the prophet's crazy thinking.

[17]Those false teachers are like springs without water and clouds blown by a storm. A place in the blackest darkness has been kept for them. [18]They brag with words that mean nothing. By their evil desires they lead people into the trap of sin — people who are just beginning to escape from others who live in error. [19]They promise them freedom, but they themselves are not free. They are slaves of things that will be destroyed. For people are slaves of anything that controls them. [20]They were made free from the evil in the world by knowing our Lord and Savior Jesus Christ. But if they return to evil things and those things control them, then it is worse for them than it was before. [21]Yes, it would be better for them to have never known the right way than to know it and to turn away from the holy teaching that was given to them. [22]What they did is like this true saying: "A dog goes back to what it has thrown up,"[n] and, "After a pig is washed, it goes back and rolls in the mud."

Jesus Will Come Again

3 My friends, this is the second letter I have written you to help your honest minds remember. [2]I want you to think about the words the holy prophets[d] spoke in the past, and remember the command our Lord and Savior gave us through your apostles.[d] [3]It is most important for you to understand what will happen in the last days. People will laugh at you. They will live doing the evil things they want to do. [4]They will say, "Jesus promised to come again. Where is he? Our fathers have died, but the world continues the way it has been since it was made." [5]But they do not want to remember what happened long

---

Sodom and Gomorrah Two cities God destroyed because the people were so evil.
"A dog . . . up" Quotation from Proverbs 26:11.

ago. By the word of God heaven was made, and the earth was made from water and with water. [6]Then the world was flooded and destroyed with water. [7]And that same word of God is keeping heaven and earth that we now have in order to be destroyed by fire. They are being kept for the Judgment Day and the destruction of all who are against God.

[8]But do not forget this one thing, dear friends: To the Lord one day is as a thousand years, and a thousand years is as one day. [9]The Lord is not slow in doing what he promised — the way some people understand slowness. But God is being patient with you. He does not want anyone to be lost, but he wants all people to change their hearts and lives.

[10]But the day of the Lord will come like a thief. The skies will disappear with a loud noise. Everything in them will be destroyed by fire, and the earth and everything in it will be burned up.[n] [11]In that way everything will be destroyed. So what kind of people should you be? You should live holy lives and serve God, [12]as you wait for and look forward to the coming of the day of God. When that day comes, the skies will be destroyed with fire, and everything in them will melt with heat. [13]But God made a promise to us, and we are waiting for a new heaven and a new earth where goodness lives.

[14]Dear friends, since you are waiting for this to happen, do your best to be without sin and without fault. Try to be at peace with God. [15]Remember that we are saved because our Lord is patient. Our dear brother Paul told you the same thing when he wrote to you with the wisdom that God gave him. [16]He writes about this in all his letters. Some things in Paul's letters are hard to understand, and people who are ignorant and weak in faith explain these things falsely. They also falsely explain the other Scriptures,[d] but they are destroying themselves by doing this.

[17]Dear friends, since you already know about this, be careful. Do not let those evil people lead you away by the wrong they do. Be careful so you will not fall from your strong faith. [18]But grow in the grace and knowledge of our Lord and Savior Jesus Christ. Glory be to him now and forever! Amen.

---

will be burned up   Many Greek copies say, "will be found." One copy says, "will disappear."

1 JOHN

Love One Another

1 We write you now about what has always existed, which we have heard, we have seen with our own eyes, we have looked at, and we have touched with our hands. We write to you about the Word[n] that gives life. [2]He who gives life was shown to us. We saw him and can give proof about it. And now we announce to you that he has life that continues forever. He was with God the Father and was shown to us. [3]We announce to you what we have seen and heard, because we want you also to have fellowship with us. Our fellowship is with God the Father and with his Son, Jesus Christ. [4]We write this to you so you can be full of joy with us.

God Forgives Our Sins

[5]Here is the message we have heard from Christ and now announce to you: God is light,[n] and in him there is no darkness at all. [6]So if we say we have fellowship with God, but we continue living in darkness, we are liars and do not follow the truth. [7]But if we live in the light, as God is in the light, we can share fellowship with each other. Then the blood of Jesus, God's Son, cleanses us from every sin.

[8]If we say we have no sin, we are fooling ourselves, and the truth is not in us. [9]But if we confess our sins, he will forgive our sins, because we can trust God to do what is right. He will cleanse us from all the wrongs we have done. [10]If we say we have not sinned, we make God a liar, and we do not accept God's teaching.

Jesus Is Our Helper

2 My dear children, I write this letter to you so you will not sin. But if anyone does sin, we have a helper in the presence of the Father — Jesus Christ, the One who does what is right. [2]He is the way our sins are taken away, and not only our sins but the sins of all people.

[3]We can be sure that we know God if we obey his commands. [4]Anyone who says, "I know God," but does not obey God's commands is a liar, and the truth is not in that person. [5]But if someone obeys God's teaching, then in that person God's love has truly reached its goal. This is how we can be sure we are living in God: [6]Whoever says that he lives in God must live as Jesus lived.

The Command to Love Others

[7]My dear friends, I am not writing a new command to you but an old command you have had from the beginning. It is the teaching you have already heard. [8]But also I am writing a new command to you, and you can see its truth in Jesus and in you, because the darkness is passing away, and the true light is already shining.

[9]Anyone who says, "I am in the light,"[n] but hates a brother or sister,[n] is still in the darkness. [10]Whoever loves a brother or sister lives in the light and will not cause anyone to stumble in his faith. [11]But whoever hates a brother or sister is in darkness, lives in darkness, and does not know where to go, because the darkness has made that person blind.

[12]I write to you, dear children,
    because your sins are forgiven through Christ.
[13]I write to you, parents,
    because you know the One who existed from the beginning.
I write to you, young people,

Word The Greek word is "logos," meaning any kind of communication. Here, it means Christ, who was the way God told people about himself.
light Here, this word is used as a symbol of God's goodness or truth.
brother or sister Although the Greek text says "brother" here and throughout this book, the writer's words were meant for the entire church, including men and women.

because you have defeated the Evil
One.

[14]I write to you, children,
because you know the Father.

I write to you, parents,
because you know the One who
existed from the beginning.

I write to you, young people,
because you are strong;
the teaching of God lives in you,
and you have defeated the Evil One.

[15]Do not love the world or the things in
the world. If you love the world, the love of
the Father is not in you. [16]These are the ways
of the world: wanting to please our sinful
selves, wanting the sinful things we see, and
being too proud of what we have. None of
these come from the Father, but all of them
come from the world. [17]The world and everything that people want in it are passing
away, but the person who does what God
wants lives forever.

Reject the Enemies of Christ

[18]My dear children, these are the last days.
You have heard that the enemy of Christ*d* is
coming, and now many enemies of Christ are
already here. This is how we know that these
are the last days. [19]These enemies of Christ
were in our fellowship, but they left us. They
never really belonged to us; if they had been
a part of us, they would have stayed with us.
But they left, and this shows that none of
them really belonged to us.

[20]You have the gift*n* that the Holy One
gave you, so you all know the truth. [21]I do
not write to you because you do not know
the truth but because you do know the truth.
And you know that no lie comes from the
truth.

[22]Who is the liar? It is the person who does
not accept Jesus as the Christ. This is the enemy of Christ: the person who does not accept the Father and his Son. [23]Whoever does
not accept the Son does not have the Father.
But whoever confesses the Son has the Father, too.

[24]Be sure you continue to follow the teaching you heard from the beginning. If you continue to follow what you heard from the be-

ginning, you will stay in the Son and in the
Father. [25]And this is what the Son promised
to us — life forever.

[26]I am writing this letter about those people who are trying to lead you the wrong
way. [27]Christ gave you a special gift that is
still in you, so you do not need any other
teacher. His gift teaches you about everything, and it is true, not false. So continue to
live in Christ, as his gift taught you.

[28]Yes, my dear children, live in him so that
when Christ comes back, we can be without
fear and not be ashamed in his presence. [29]If
you know that Christ is all that is right, you
know that all who do right are God's children.

We Are God's Children

3 The Father has loved us so much that
we are called children of God. And we
really are his children. The reason the people
in the world do not know us is that they have
not known him. [2]Dear friends, now we are
children of God, and we have not yet been
shown what we will be in the future. But we
know that when Christ comes again, we will
be like him, because we will see him as he
really is. [3]Christ is pure, and all who have
this hope in Christ keep themselves pure like
Christ.

[4]The person who sins breaks God's law.
Yes, sin is living against God's law. [5]You
know that Christ came to take away sins and
that there is no sin in Christ. [6]So anyone who
lives in Christ does not go on sinning. Anyone who goes on sinning has never really understood Christ and has never known him.

[7]Dear children, do not let anyone lead you
the wrong way. Christ is all that is right. So
to be like Christ a person must do what is
right. [8]The devil has been sinning since the
beginning, so anyone who continues to sin
belongs to the devil. The Son of God came
for this purpose: to destroy the devil's work.

[9]Those who are God's children do not
continue sinning, because the new life from
God remains in them. They are not able to go
on sinning, because they have become children of God. [10]So we can see who God's children are and who the devil's children are:

gift This might mean the Holy Spirit, or it might mean teaching or truth as in verse 24.

Those who do not do what is right are not God's children, and those who do not love their brothers and sisters are not God's children.

We Must Love Each Other

[11]This is the teaching you have heard from the beginning: We must love each other. [12]Do not be like Cain who belonged to the Evil One and killed his brother. And why did he kill him? Because the things Cain did were evil, and the things his brother did were good.

[13]Brothers and sisters, do not be surprised when the people of the world hate you. [14]We know we have left death and have come into life because we love each other. Whoever does not love is still dead. [15]Everyone who hates a brother or sister is a murderer,[n] and you know that no murderers have eternal life in them. [16]This is how we know what real love is: Jesus gave his life for us. So we should give our lives for our brothers and sisters. [17]Suppose someone has enough to live and sees a brother or sister in need, but does not help. Then God's love is not living in that person. [18]My children, we should love people not only with words and talk, but by our actions and true caring.

[19-20]This is the way we know that we belong to the way of truth. When our hearts make us feel guilty, we can still have peace before God. God is greater than our hearts, and he knows everything. [21]My dear friends, if our hearts do not make us feel guilty, we can come without fear into God's presence. [22]And God gives us what we ask for because we obey God's commands and do what pleases him. [23]This is what God commands: that we believe in his Son, Jesus Christ, and that we love each other, just as he commanded. [24]The people who obey God's commands live in God, and God lives in them. We know that God lives in us because of the Spirit[d] God gave us.

Warning Against False Teachers

4 My dear friends, many false prophets[d] have gone out into the world. So do not believe every spirit, but test the spirits to see if they are from God. [2]This is how you can know God's Spirit:[d] Every spirit who confesses that Jesus Christ came to earth as a human is from God. [3]And every spirit who refuses to say this about Jesus is not from God. It is the spirit of the enemy of Christ,[d] which you have heard is coming, and now he is already in the world.

[4]My dear children, you belong to God and have defeated them; because God's Spirit, who is in you, is greater than the devil, who is in the world. [5]And they belong to the world, so what they say is from the world, and the world listens to them. [6]But we belong to God, and those who know God listen to us. But those who are not from God do not listen to us. That is how we know the Spirit that is true and the spirit that is false.

Love Comes from God

[7]Dear friends, we should love each other, because love comes from God. Everyone who loves has become God's child and knows God. [8]Whoever does not love does not know God, because God is love. [9]This is how God showed his love to us: He sent his one and only Son into the world so that we could have life through him. [10]This is what real love is: It is not our love for God; it is God's love for us in sending his Son to be the way to take away our sins.

[11]Dear friends, if God loved us that much we also should love each other. [12]No one has ever seen God, but if we love each other, God lives in us, and his love is made perfect in us.

[13]We know that we live in God and he lives in us, because he gave us his Spirit.[d] [14]We have seen and can testify that the Father sent his Son to be the Savior of the world. [15]Whoever confesses that Jesus is the Son of God has God living inside, and that person lives in God. [16]And so we know the love that God has for us, and we trust that love.

God is love. Those who live in love live in God, and God lives in them. [17]This is how love is made perfect in us: that we can be

---

Everyone … murderer If one person hates a brother or sister, then in the heart that person has killed that brother or sister. Jesus taught about this sin to his followers (Matthew 5:21-26).

without fear on the day God judges us, because in this world we are like him. [18]Where God's love is, there is no fear, because God's perfect love drives out fear. It is punishment that makes a person fear, so love is not made perfect in the person who fears.

[19]We love because God first loved us. [20]If people say, "I love God," but hate their brothers or sisters, they are liars. Those who do not love their brothers and sisters, whom they have seen, cannot love God, whom they have never seen. [21]And God gave us this command: Those who love God must also love their brothers and sisters.

Faith in the Son of God

 5 Everyone who believes that Jesus is the Christ[d] is God's child, and whoever loves the Father also loves the Father's children. [2]This is how we know we love God's children: when we love God and obey his commands. [3]Loving God means obeying his commands. And God's commands are not too hard for us, [4]because everyone who is a child of God conquers the world. And this is the victory that conquers the world — our faith. [5]So the one who wins against the world is the person who believes that Jesus is the Son of God.

[6]Jesus Christ is the One who came by water[n] and blood.[n] He did not come by water only, but by water and blood. And the Spirit[d] says that this is true, because the Spirit is the truth. [7]So there are three witnesses that tell us about Jesus: [8]the Spirit, the water, and the blood; and these three witnesses agree. [9]We believe people when they say something is true. But what God says is more important, and he has told us the truth about his own Son. [10]Anyone who believes in the Son of

God has the truth that God told us. Anyone who does not believe makes God a liar, because that person does not believe what God told us about his Son. [11]This is what God told us: God has given us eternal life, and this life is in his Son. [12]Whoever has the Son has life, but whoever does not have the Son of God does not have life.

We Have Eternal Life Now

[13]I write this letter to you who believe in the Son of God so you will know you have eternal life. [14]And this is the boldness we have in God's presence: that if we ask God for anything that agrees with what he wants, he hears us. [15]If we know he hears us every time we ask him, we know we have what we ask from him.

[16]If anyone sees a brother or sister sinning (sin that does not lead to eternal death), that person should pray, and God will give the sinner life. I am talking about people whose sin does not lead to eternal death. There is sin that leads to death. I do not mean that a person should pray about that sin. [17]Doing wrong is always sin, but there is sin that does not lead to eternal death.

[18]We know that those who are God's children do not continue to sin. The Son of God keeps them safe, and the Evil One cannot touch them. [19]We know that we belong to God, but the Evil One controls the whole world. [20]We also know that the Son of God has come and has given us understanding so that we can know the True One. And our lives are in the True One and in his Son, Jesus Christ. He is the true God and the eternal life.

[21]So, dear children, keep yourselves away from gods.

---

water   This probably means the water of Jesus' baptism.
blood   This probably means the blood of Jesus' death.

2 JOHN

Do Not Help False Teachers

[1]From the Elder.[n]

To the chosen lady[n] and her children:

I love all of you in the truth,[n] and all those who know the truth love you. [2]We love you because of the truth that lives in us and will be with us forever.

[3]Grace, mercy, and peace from God the Father and his Son, Jesus Christ, will be with us in truth and love.

[4]I was very happy to learn that some of your children are following the way of truth, as the Father commanded us. [5]And now, dear lady, this is not a new command but is the same command we have had from the beginning. I ask you that we all love each other. [6]And love means living the way God commanded us to live. As you have heard from the beginning, his command is this: Live a life of love.

[7]Many false teachers are in the world now who do not confess that Jesus Christ came to earth as a human. Anyone who does not confess this is a false teacher and an enemy of Christ.[d] [8]Be careful yourselves that you do not lose everything you have worked for, but that you receive your full reward.

[9]Anyone who goes beyond Christ's teaching and does not continue to follow only his teaching does not have God. But whoever continues to follow the teaching of Christ has both the Father and the Son. [10]If someone comes to you and does not bring this teaching, do not welcome or accept that person into your house. [11]If you welcome such a person, you share in the evil work.

[12]I have many things to write to you, but I do not want to use paper and ink. Instead, I hope to come to you and talk face to face so we can be full of joy. [13]The children of your chosen sister[n] greet you.

Elder   "Elder" means an older person. It can also mean a special leader in the church (as in Titus 1:5).
lady   This might mean a woman, or in this letter it might mean a church. If it is a church, then "her children" would be the people of the church.
truth   The truth or "Good News" about Jesus Christ that joins all believers together.
sister   Sister of the "lady" in verse 1. This might be another woman or another church.

3 JOHN

Help Christians Who Teach Truth

[1]From the Elder.[n]

To my dear friend Gaius, whom I love in the truth:[n]

[2]My dear friend, I know your soul is doing fine, and I pray that you are doing well in every way and that your health is good. [3]I was very happy when some brothers and sisters[n] came and told me about the truth in your life and how you are following the way of truth. [4]Nothing gives me greater joy than to hear that my children are following the way of truth.

[5]My dear friend, it is good that you help the brothers and sisters, even those you do not know. [6]They told the church about your love. Please help them to continue their trip in a way worthy of God. [7]They started out in service to Christ, and they have been accepting nothing from non-believers. [8]So we should help such people; when we do, we share in their work for the truth.

[9]I wrote something to the church, but Diotrephes, who loves to be their leader, will not listen to us. [10]So if I come, I will talk about what Diotrephes is doing, about how he lies and says evil things about us. But more than that, he refuses to accept the other brothers and sisters; he even stops those who do want to accept them and puts them out of the church.

[11]My dear friend, do not follow what is bad; follow what is good. The one who does good belongs to God. But the one who does evil has never known God.

[12]Everyone says good things about Demetrius, and the truth agrees with what they say. We also speak well of him, and you know what we say is true.

[13]I have many things I want to write you, but I do not want to use pen and ink. [14]I hope to see you soon and talk face to face. [15]Peace to you. The friends here greet you. Please greet each friend there by name.

Elder "Elder" means an older person. It can also mean a special leader in the church (as Titus 1:5).

truth The truth or "Good News" about Jesus Christ that joins all believers together.

brothers and sisters Although the Greek text says "brothers" here and throughout this book, the writer's words were meant for the entire church, including men and women.

JUDE

Warnings About False Teachers

[1]From Jude, a servant of Jesus Christ and a brother of James.

To all who have been called by God. God the Father loves you, and you have been kept safe in Jesus Christ:

[2]Mercy, peace, and love be yours richly.

God Will Punish Sinners

[3]Dear friends, I wanted very much to write you about the salvation we all share. But I felt the need to write you about something else: I want to encourage you to fight hard for the faith that was given the holy people of God once and for all time. [4]Some people have secretly entered your group. Long ago the prophets[d] wrote about these people who will be judged guilty. They are against God and have changed the grace of our God into a reason for sexual sin. They also refuse to accept Jesus Christ, our only Master and Lord.

[5]I want to remind you of some things you already know: Remember that the Lord saved his people by bringing them out of the land of Egypt. But later he destroyed all those who did not believe. [6]And remember the angels who did not keep their place of power but left their proper home. The Lord has kept these angels in darkness, bound with everlasting chains, to be judged on the great day. [7]Also remember the cities of Sodom and Gomorrah[n] and the other towns around them. In the same way they were full of sexual sin and people who desired sexual relations that God does not allow. They suffer the punishment of eternal fire, as an example for all to see.

[8]It is the same with these people who have entered your group. They are guided by dreams and make themselves filthy with sin. They reject God's authority and speak against the angels. [9]Not even the archangel[n]

Michael, when he argued with the devil about who would have the body of Moses, dared to judge the devil guilty. Instead, he said, "The Lord punish you." [10]But these people speak against things they do not understand. And what they do know, by feeling, as dumb animals know things, are the very things that destroy them. [11]It will be terrible for them. They have followed the way of Cain, and for money they have given themselves to doing the wrong that Balaam did. They have fought against God as Korah did, and like Korah, they surely will be destroyed. [12]They are like dirty spots in your special Christian meals you share. They eat with you and have no fear, caring only for themselves. They are clouds without rain, which the wind blows around. They are autumn trees without fruit that are pulled out of the ground. So they are twice dead. [13]They are like wild waves of the sea, tossing up their own shameful actions like foam. They are like stars that wander in the sky. A place in the blackest darkness has been kept for them forever.

[14]Enoch, the seventh descendant[d] from Adam, said about these people: "Look, the Lord is coming with many thousands of his holy angels to [15]judge every person. He is coming to punish all who are against God for all the evil they have done against him. And he will punish the sinners who are against God for all the evil they have said against him."

[16]These people complain and blame others, doing the evil things they want to do. They brag about themselves, and they flatter others to get what they want.

A Warning and Things to Do

[17]Dear friends, remember what the apostles[d] of our Lord Jesus Christ said before.

Sodom and Gomorrah Two cities God destroyed because they were so evil.
archangel The leader among God's angels or messengers.

[18]They said to you, "In the last times there will be people who laugh about God, following their own evil desires which are against God." [19]These are the people who divide you, people whose thoughts are only of this world, who do not have the Spirit.[d]

[20]But dear friends, use your most holy faith to build yourselves up, praying in the Holy Spirit. [21]Keep yourselves in God's love as you wait for the Lord Jesus Christ with his mercy to give you life forever.

[22]Show mercy to some people who have doubts. [23]Take others out of the fire, and save them. Show mercy mixed with fear to others, hating even their clothes which are dirty from sin.

Praise God

[24]God is strong and can help you not to fall. He can bring you before his glory without any wrong in you and can give you great joy. [25]He is the only God, the One who saves us. To him be glory, greatness, power, and authority through Jesus Christ our Lord for all time past, now, and forever. Amen.

REVELATION

Christ Will Win over Evil

John Tells About This Book

1 This is the revelation[n] of Jesus Christ, which God gave to him, to show his servants what must soon happen. And Jesus sent his angel to show it to his servant John, [2]who has told everything he has seen. It is the word of God; it is the message from Jesus Christ. [3]Happy is the one who reads the words of God's message, and happy are the people who hear this message and do what is written in it. The time is near when all of this will happen.

Jesus' Message to the Churches

[4]From John.

To the seven churches in the country of Asia:

Grace and peace to you from the One who is and was and is coming, and from the seven spirits before his throne, [5]and from Jesus Christ. Jesus is the faithful witness, the first among those raised from the dead. He is the ruler of the kings of the earth.

He is the One who loves us, who made us free from our sins with the blood of his death. [6]He made us to be a kingdom of priests who serve God his Father. To Jesus Christ be glory and power forever and ever! Amen.

[7]Look, Jesus is coming with the clouds, and everyone will see him, even those who stabbed him. And all peoples of the earth will cry loudly because of him. Yes, this will happen! Amen.

[8]The Lord God says, "I am the Alpha and the Omega.[n] I am the One who is and was and is coming. I am the Almighty."

[9]I, John, am your brother. All of us share with Christ in suffering, in the kingdom, and in patience to continue. I was on the island of Patmos,[n] because I had preached the word of God and the message about Jesus. [10]On the Lord's day I was in the Spirit,[d] and I heard a loud voice behind me that sounded like a trumpet. [11]The voice said, "Write what you see in a book and send it to the seven churches: to Ephesus, Smyrna, Pergamum, Thyatira, Sardis, Philadelphia, and Laodicea."

[12]I turned to see who was talking to me. When I turned, I saw seven golden lampstands [13]and someone among the lampstands who was "like a Son of Man."[n] He was dressed in a long robe and had a gold band around his chest. [14]His head and hair were white like wool, as white as snow, and his eyes were like flames of fire. [15]His feet were like bronze that glows hot in a furnace, and his voice was like the noise of flooding water. [16]He held seven stars in his right hand, and a sharp double-edged sword came out of his mouth. He looked like the sun shining at its brightest time.

[17]When I saw him, I fell down at his feet like a dead man. He put his right hand on me and said, "Do not be afraid. I am the First and the Last. [18]I am the One who lives; I was dead, but look, I am alive forever and ever! And I hold the keys to death and to the place of the dead. [19]So write the things you see, what is now and what will happen later. [20]Here is the secret of the seven stars that you saw in my right hand and the seven golden lampstands: The seven lampstands are the seven churches, and the seven stars are the angels of the seven churches.

To the Church in Ephesus

2 "Write this to the angel of the church in Ephesus:

"The One who holds the seven stars in his right hand and walks among the seven

---

revelation A making known of truth that has been hidden.
Alpha and the Omega The first and last letters of the Greek alphabet. This means "the beginning and the end."
Patmos A small island in the Aegean Sea, near the coast of Asia Minor (modern Turkey).
"like . . . Man" "Son of Man" is a name Jesus called himself. See dictionary.

golden lampstands says this: [2]I know what you do, how you work hard and never give up. I know you do not put up with the false teachings of evil people. You have tested those who say they are apostles[d] but really are not, and you found they are liars. [3]You have patience and have suffered troubles for my name and have not given up.

[4]"But I have this against you: You have left the love you had in the beginning. [5]So remember where you were before you fell. Change your hearts and do what you did at first. If you do not change, I will come to you and will take away your lampstand from its place. [6]But there is something you do that is right: You hate what the Nicolaitans[n] do, as much as I.

[7]"Every person who has ears should listen to what the Spirit[d] says to the churches. To those who win the victory I will give the right to eat the fruit from the tree of life, which is in the garden of God.

To the Church in Smyrna

[8]"Write this to the angel of the church in Smyrna:

"The One who is the First and the Last, who died and came to life again, says this: [9]I know your troubles and that you are poor, but really you are rich! I know the bad things some people say about you. They say they are Jews, but they are not true Jews. They are a synagogue[d] that belongs to Satan. [10]Do not be afraid of what you are about to suffer. I tell you, the devil will put some of you in prison to test you, and you will suffer for ten days. But be faithful, even if you have to die, and I will give you the crown of life.

[11]"Everyone who has ears should listen to what the Spirit[d] says to the churches. Those who win the victory will not be hurt by the second death.

To the Church in Pergamum

[12]"Write this to the angel of the church in Pergamum:

"The One who has the sharp, double-edged sword says this: [13]I know where you live. It is where Satan has his throne. But you are true to me. You did not refuse to tell about your faith in me even during the time of Antipas, my faithful witness who was killed in your city, where Satan lives.

[14]"But I have a few things against you: You have some there who follow the teaching of Balaam. He taught Balak how to cause the people of Israel to sin by eating food offered to idols and by taking part in sexual sins. [15]You also have some who follow the teaching of the Nicolaitans.[n] [16]So change your hearts and lives. If you do not, I will come to you quickly and fight against them with the sword that comes out of my mouth.

[17]"Everyone who has ears should listen to what the Spirit[d] says to the churches.

"I will give some of the hidden manna[d] to everyone who wins the victory. I will also give to each one who wins the victory a white stone with a new name written on it. No one knows this new name except the one who receives it.

To the Church in Thyatira

[18]"Write this to the angel of the church in Thyatira:

"The Son of God, who has eyes that blaze like fire and feet like shining bronze, says this: [19]I know what you do. I know about your love, your faith, your service, and your patience. I know that you are doing more now than you did at first.

[20]But I have this against you: You let that woman Jezebel spread false teachings. She says she is a prophetess,[d] but by her teaching she leads my people to take part in sexual sins and to eat food that is offered to idols. [21]I have given her time to change her heart and turn away from her sin, but she does not want to change. [22]So I will throw her on a bed of suffering. And all those who take part in adultery[d] with her will suffer greatly if they do not turn away from the wrongs she does. [23]I will also kill her followers. Then all the churches will know I am the One who searches hearts and minds, and I will repay each of you for what you have done.

[24]"But others of you in Thyatira have not followed her teaching and have not learned what some call Satan's deep secrets. I say to you that I will not put any other load on you.

Nicolaitans This is the name of a religious group that followed false beliefs and ideas.

25Only continue in your loyalty until I come.

26"I will give power over the nations to everyone who wins the victory and continues to be obedient to me until the end. 27'You will rule over them with an iron rod,

as when pottery is broken into pieces.'

Psalm 2:9

28This is the same power I received from my Father. I will also give him the morning star. 29Everyone who has ears should listen to what the Spirit*d* says to the churches.

To the Church in Sardis

3 "Write this to the angel of the church in Sardis:

"The One who has the seven spirits and the seven stars says this: I know what you do. People say that you are alive, but really you are dead. 2Wake up! Make yourselves stronger before what you have left dies completely. I have found that what you are doing is less than what my God wants. 3So do not forget what you have received and heard. Obey it, and change your hearts and lives. So you must wake up, or I will come like a thief, and you will not know when I will come to you. 4But you have a few there in Sardis who have kept their clothes unstained, so they will walk with me and will wear white clothes, because they are worthy. 5Those who win the victory will be dressed in white clothes like them. And I will not erase their names from the book of life, but I will say they belong to me before my Father and before his angels. 6Everyone who has ears should listen to what the Spirit*d* says to the churches.

To the Church in Philadelphia

7"Write this to the angel of the church in Philadelphia:

"This is what the One who is holy and true, who holds the key of David, says. When he opens a door, no one can close it. And when he closes it, no one can open it. 8I know what you do. I have put an open door before you, which no one can close. I know you have a little strength, but you have

obeyed my teaching and were not afraid to speak my name. 9Those in the synagogue*d* that belongs to Satan say they are Jews, but they are not true Jews; they are liars. I will make them come before you and bow at your feet, and they will know that I have loved you. 10You have obeyed my teaching about not giving up your faith. So I will keep you from the time of trouble that will come to the whole world to test those who live on earth.

11"I am coming soon. Continue strong in your faith so no one will take away your crown. 12I will make those who win the victory pillars in the temple of my God, and they will never have to leave it. I will write on them the name of my God and the name of the city of my God, the new Jerusalem,*n* that comes down out of heaven from my God. I will also write on them my new name. 13Everyone who has ears should listen to what the Spirit*d* says to the churches.

To the Church in Laodicea

14"Write this to the angel of the church in Laodicea:

"The Amen,*n* the faithful and true witness, the beginning of all God has made, says this: 15I know what you do, that you are not hot or cold. I wish that you were hot or cold! 16But because you are lukewarm—neither hot, nor cold—I am ready to spit you out of my mouth. 17You say, 'I am rich, and I have become wealthy and do not need anything.' But you do not know that you are really miserable, pitiful, poor, blind, and naked. 18I advise you to buy from me gold made pure in fire so you can be truly rich. Buy from me white clothes so you can be clothed and so you can cover your shameful nakedness. Buy from me medicine to put on your eyes so you can truly see.

19"I correct and punish those whom I love. So be eager to do right, and change your hearts and lives. 20Here I am! I stand at the door and knock. If you hear my voice and open the door, I will come in and eat with you, and you will eat with me.

21"Those who win the victory will sit with me on my throne in the same way that I won

---

Jerusalem This name is used to mean the spiritual city God built for his people. See Revelation 21-22.
Amen Used here as a name for Jesus; it means to agree fully that something is true.

the victory and sat down with my Father on his throne. [22]Everyone who has ears should listen to what the Spirit[d] says to the churches."

John Sees Heaven

4 After the vision of these things I looked, and there before me was an open door in heaven. And the same voice that spoke to me before, that sounded like a trumpet, said, "Come up here, and I will show you what must happen after this." [2]Immediately I was in the Spirit,[d] and before me was a throne in heaven, and someone was sitting on it. [3]The One who sat on the throne looked like precious stones, like jasper and carnelian. All around the throne was a rainbow the color of an emerald. [4]Around the throne there were twenty-four other thrones with twenty-four elders sitting on them. They were dressed in white and had golden crowns on their heads. [5]Lightning flashes and noises and thundering came from the throne. Before the throne seven lamps were burning, which are the seven spirits of God. [6]Also before the throne there was something that looked like a sea of glass, clear like crystal.

In the center and around the throne were four living creatures with eyes all over them, in front and in back. [7]The first living creature was like a lion. The second was like a calf. The third had a face like a man. The fourth was like a flying eagle. [8]Each of these four living creatures had six wings and was covered all over with eyes, inside and out. Day and night they never stop saying:

"Holy, holy, holy is the Lord God
    Almighty.

He was, he is, and he is coming."

[9]These living creatures give glory, honor, and thanks to the One who sits on the throne, who lives forever and ever. [10]Then the twenty-four elders bow down before the One who sits on the throne, and they worship him who lives forever and ever. They put their crowns down before the throne and say:

[11]"You are worthy, our Lord and God,

  to receive glory and honor and power,

  because you made all things.

Everything existed and was made,
  because you wanted it."

5 Then I saw a scroll in the right hand of the One sitting on the throne. The scroll had writing on both sides and was kept closed with seven seals. [2]And I saw a powerful angel calling in a loud voice, "Who is worthy to break the seals and open the scroll?" [3]But there was no one in heaven or on earth or under the earth who could open the scroll or look inside it. [4]I cried hard because there was no one who was worthy to open the scroll or look inside. [5]But one of the elders said to me, "Do not cry! The Lion[n] from the tribe[d] of Judah, David's descendant,[d] has won the victory so that he is able to open the scroll and its seven seals."

[6]Then I saw a Lamb standing in the center of the throne and in the middle of the four living creatures and the elders. The Lamb looked as if he had been killed. He had seven horns and seven eyes, which are the seven spirits of God that were sent into all the world. [7]The Lamb came and took the scroll from the right hand of the One sitting on the throne. [8]When he took the scroll, the four living creatures and the twenty-four elders bowed down before the Lamb. Each one of them had a harp and golden bowls full of incense,[d] which are the prayers of God's holy people. [9]And they all sang a new song to the Lamb:

"You are worthy to take the scroll
  and to open its seals,

because you were killed,

  and with the blood of your death you
      bought people for God

  from every tribe, language, people, and
      nation.

[10]You made them to be a kingdom of
    priests for our God,

  and they will rule on the earth."

[11]Then I looked, and I heard the voices of many angels around the throne, and the four living creatures, and the elders. There were thousands and thousands of angels, [12]saying in a loud voice:

"The Lamb who was killed is worthy
  to receive power, wealth, wisdom, and
      strength,

Lion Here refers to Christ.

honor, glory, and praise!"

13Then I heard all creatures in heaven and on earth and under the earth and in the sea saying:

"To the One who sits on the throne
and to the Lamb
be praise and honor and glory and power
forever and ever."

14The four living creatures said, "Amen," and the elders bowed down and worshiped.

6 Then I watched while the Lamb opened the first of the seven seals. I heard one of the four living creatures say with a voice like thunder, "Come!" 2I looked, and there before me was a white horse. The rider on the horse held a bow, and he was given a crown, and he rode out, determined to win the victory.

3When the Lamb opened the second seal, I heard the second living creature say, "Come!" 4Then another horse came out, a red one. Its rider was given power to take away peace from the earth and to make people kill each other, and he was given a big sword.

5When the Lamb opened the third seal, I heard the third living creature say, "Come!" I looked, and there before me was a black horse, and its rider held a pair of scales in his hand. 6Then I heard something that sounded like a voice coming from the middle of the four living creatures. The voice said, "A quart of wheat for a day's pay, and three quarts of barley for a day's pay, and do not damage the olive oil and wine!"

7When the Lamb opened the fourth seal, I heard the voice of the fourth living creature say, "Come!" 8I looked, and there before me was a pale horse. Its rider was named death, and Hades*n* was following close behind him. They were given power over a fourth of the earth to kill people by war, by starvation, by disease, and by the wild animals of the earth.

9When the Lamb opened the fifth seal, I saw under the altar the souls of those who had been killed because they were faithful to the word of God and to the message they had received. 10These souls shouted in a loud voice, "Holy and true Lord, how long until you judge the people of the earth and punish them for killing us?" 11Then each one of them was given a white robe and was told to wait a short time longer. There were still some of their fellow servants and brothers and sisters*n* in the service of Christ who must be killed as they were. They had to wait until all of this was finished.

12Then I watched while the Lamb opened the sixth seal, and there was a great earthquake. The sun became black like rough black cloth, and the whole moon became red like blood. 13And the stars in the sky fell to the earth like figs falling from a fig tree when the wind blows. 14The sky disappeared as a scroll when it is rolled up, and every mountain and island was moved from its place.

15Then the kings of the earth, the rulers, the generals, the rich people, the powerful people, the slaves, and the free people hid themselves in caves and in the rocks on the mountains. 16They called to the mountains and the rocks, "Fall on us. Hide us from the face of the One who sits on the throne and from the anger of the Lamb! 17The great day for their anger has come, and who can stand against it?"

The 144,000 People of Israel

7 After the vision of these things I saw four angels standing at the four corners of the earth. The angels were holding the four winds of the earth to keep them from blowing on the land or on the sea or on any tree. 2Then I saw another angel coming up from the east who had the seal of the living God. And he called out in a loud voice to the four angels to whom God had given power to harm the earth and the sea. 3He said to them, "Do not harm the land or the sea or the trees until we mark with a sign the foreheads of the people who serve our God." 4Then I heard how many people were marked with the sign. There were one hundred forty-four thousand from every tribe*d* of the people of Israel.

Hades   The unseen world of the dead.
brothers and sisters   Although the Greek text says "brothers" here and throughout this book, both men and women would have been included.

[5]From the tribe of Judah twelve thousand were marked with the sign,

from the tribe of Reuben twelve thousand,

from the tribe of Gad twelve thousand,

[6]from the tribe of Asher twelve thousand,

from the tribe of Naphtali twelve thousand,

from the tribe of Manasseh twelve thousand,

[7]from the tribe of Simeon twelve thousand,

from the tribe of Levi twelve thousand,

from the tribe of Issachar twelve thousand,

[8]from the tribe of Zebulun twelve thousand,

from the tribe of Joseph twelve thousand,

and from the tribe of Benjamin twelve thousand were marked with the sign.

The Great Crowd Worships God

[9]After the vision of these things I looked, and there was a great number of people, so many that no one could count them. They were from every nation, tribe,[d] people, and language of the earth. They were all standing before the throne and before the Lamb, wearing white robes and holding palm branches in their hands. [10]They were shouting in a loud voice, "Salvation belongs to our God, who sits on the throne, and to the Lamb." [11]All the angels were standing around the throne and the elders and the four living creatures. They all bowed down on their faces before the throne and worshiped God, [12]saying, "Amen! Praise, glory, wisdom, thanks, honor, power, and strength belong to our God forever and ever. Amen!"

[13]Then one of the elders asked me, "Who are these people dressed in white robes? Where did they come from?"

[14]I answered, "You know, sir."

And the elder said to me, "These are the people who have come out of the great distress. They have washed their robes[n] and made them white in the blood of the Lamb.

[15]Because of this, they are before the throne of God. They worship him day and night in his temple. And the One who sits on the throne will be present with them. [16]Those people will never be hungry again, and they will never be thirsty again. The sun will not hurt them, and no heat will burn them, [17]because the Lamb at the center of the throne will be their shepherd. He will lead them to springs of water that give life. And God will wipe away every tear from their eyes."

The Seventh Seal

8 When the Lamb opened the seventh seal, there was silence in heaven for about half an hour. [2]And I saw the seven angels who stand before God and to whom were given seven trumpets.

[3]Another angel came and stood at the altar, holding a golden pan for incense.[d] He was given much incense to offer with the prayers of all God's holy people. The angel put this offering on the golden altar before the throne. [4]The smoke from the incense went up from the angel's hand to God with the prayers of God's people. [5]Then the angel filled the incense pan with fire from the altar and threw it on the earth, and there were flashes of lightning, thunder and loud noises, and an earthquake.

The Seven Angels and Trumpets

[6]Then the seven angels who had the seven trumpets prepared to blow them.

[7]The first angel blew his trumpet, and hail and fire mixed with blood were poured down on the earth. And a third of the earth, and all the green grass, and a third of the trees were burned up.

[8]Then the second angel blew his trumpet, and something that looked like a big mountain, burning with fire, was thrown into the sea. And a third of the sea became blood, [9]a third of the living things in the sea died, and a third of the ships were destroyed.

[10]Then the third angel blew his trumpet, and a large star, burning like a torch, fell from the sky. It fell on a third of the rivers and on the springs of water. [11]The name of the star

---

washed their robes   This means they believed in Jesus so that their sins could be forgiven by Christ's blood.

is Wormwood. *n* And a third of all the water became bitter, and many people died from drinking the water that was bitter.

12Then the fourth angel blew his trumpet, and a third of the sun, and a third of the moon, and a third of the stars were struck. So a third of them became dark, and a third of the day was without light, and also the night.

13While I watched, I heard an eagle that was flying high in the air cry out in a loud voice, "Trouble! Trouble! Trouble for those who live on the earth because of the remaining sounds of the trumpets that the other three angels are about to blow!"

9 Then the fifth angel blew his trumpet, and I saw a star fall from the sky to the earth. The star was given the key to the deep hole that leads to the bottomless pit. 2Then it opened up the hole that leads to the bottomless pit, and smoke came up from the hole like smoke from a big furnace. Then the sun and sky became dark because of the smoke from the hole. 3Then locusts*d* came down to the earth out of the smoke, and they were given the power to sting like scorpions. *n* 4They were told not to harm the grass on the earth or any plant or tree. They could harm only the people who did not have the sign of God on their foreheads. 5These locusts were not given the power to kill anyone, but to cause pain to the people for five months. And the pain they felt was like the pain a scorpion gives when it stings someone. 6During those days people will look for a way to die, but they will not find it. They will want to die, but death will run away from them.

7The locusts looked like horses prepared for battle. On their heads they wore what looked like crowns of gold, and their faces looked like human faces. 8Their hair was like women's hair, and their teeth were like lions' teeth. 9Their chests looked like iron breastplates, and the sound of their wings was like the noise of many horses and chariots hurrying into battle. 10The locusts had tails with stingers like scorpions, and in their tails was their power to hurt people for five

months. 11The locusts had a king who was the angel of the bottomless pit. His name in the Hebrew language is Abaddon and in the Greek language is Apollyon. *n*

12The first trouble is past; there are still two other troubles that will come.

13Then the sixth angel blew his trumpet, and I heard a voice coming from the horns on the golden altar that is before God. 14The voice said to the sixth angel who had the trumpet, "Free the four angels who are tied at the great river Euphrates." 15And they let loose the four angels who had been kept ready for this hour and day and month and year so they could kill a third of all people on the earth. 16I heard how many troops on horses were in their army — two hundred million.

17The horses and their riders I saw in the vision looked like this: They had breastplates that were fiery red, dark blue, and yellow like sulfur. The heads of the horses looked like heads of lions, with fire, smoke, and sulfur coming out of their mouths. 18A third of all the people on earth were killed by these three terrible disasters coming out of the horses' mouths: the fire, the smoke, and the sulfur. 19The horses' power was in their mouths and in their tails; their tails were like snakes with heads, and with them they hurt people.

20The other people who were not killed by these terrible disasters still did not change their hearts and turn away from what they had made with their own hands. They did not stop worshiping demons*d* and idols made of gold, silver, bronze, stone, and wood — things that cannot see or hear or walk. 21These people did not change their hearts and turn away from murder or evil magic, from their sexual sins or stealing.

The Angel and the Small Scroll

10 Then I saw another powerful angel coming down from heaven dressed in a cloud with a rainbow over his head. His face was like the sun, and his legs were like pillars of fire. 2The angel was holding a small

Wormwood   Name of a very bitter plant; used here to give the idea of bitter sorrow.
scorpions   A scorpion is an insect that stings with a bad poison.
Abaddon, Apollyon   Both names mean "Destroyer."

scroll open in his hand. He put his right foot on the sea and his left foot on the land. ³Then he shouted loudly like the roaring of a lion. And when he shouted, the voices of seven thunders spoke. ⁴When the seven thunders spoke, I started to write. But I heard a voice from heaven say, "Keep hidden what the seven thunders said, and do not write them down."

⁵Then the angel I saw standing on the sea and on the land raised his right hand to heaven, ⁶and he made a promise by the power of the One who lives forever and ever. He is the One who made the skies and all that is in them, the earth and all that is in it, and the sea and all that is in it. The angel promised, "There will be no more waiting! ⁷In the days when the seventh angel is ready to blow his trumpet, God's secret will be finished. This secret is the Good News*d* God told to his servants, the prophets."*d*

⁸Then I heard the same voice from heaven again, saying to me: "Go and take the open scroll that is in the hand of the angel that is standing on the sea and on the land."

⁹So I went to the angel and told him to give me the small scroll. And he said to me, "Take the scroll and eat it. It will be sour in your stomach, but in your mouth it will be sweet as honey." ¹⁰So I took the small scroll from the angel's hand and ate it. In my mouth it tasted sweet as honey, but after I ate it, it was sour in my stomach. ¹¹Then I was told, "You must prophesy*d* again about many peoples, nations, languages, and kings."

The Two Witnesses

11 I was given a measuring stick like a rod, and I was told, "Go and measure the temple*d* of God and the altar, and count the people worshiping there. ²But do not measure the yard outside the temple. Leave it alone, because it has been given to those who are not God's people. And they will trample on the holy city for forty-two months. ³And I will give power to my two witnesses to prophesy*d* for one thousand two hundred sixty days, and they will be dressed in rough cloth to show their sadness."

⁴These two witnesses are the two olive trees and the two lampstands that stand before the Lord of the earth. ⁵And if anyone tries to hurt them, fire comes from their mouths and kills their enemies. And if anyone tries to hurt them in whatever way, in that same way that person will die. ⁶These witnesses have the power to stop the sky from raining during the time they are prophesying. And they have power to make the waters become blood, and they have power to send every kind of trouble to the earth as many times as they want.

⁷When the two witnesses have finished telling their message, the beast that comes up from the bottomless pit will fight a war against them. He will defeat them and kill them. ⁸The bodies of the two witnesses will lie in the street of the great city where the Lord was killed. This city is named Sodom*n* and Egypt, which has a spiritual meaning. ⁹Those from every race of people, tribe,*d* language, and nation will look at the bodies of the two witnesses for three and one-half days, and they will refuse to bury them. ¹⁰People who live on the earth will rejoice and be happy because these two are dead. They will send each other gifts, because these two prophets brought much suffering to those who live on the earth.

¹¹But after three and one-half days, God put the breath of life into the two prophets again. They stood on their feet, and everyone who saw them became very afraid. ¹²Then the two prophets heard a loud voice from heaven saying, "Come up here!" And they went up into heaven in a cloud as their enemies watched.

¹³In the same hour there was a great earthquake, and a tenth of the city was destroyed. Seven thousand people were killed in the earthquake, and those who did not die were very afraid and gave glory to the God of heaven.

¹⁴The second trouble is finished. Pay attention: The third trouble is coming soon.

The Seventh Trumpet

¹⁵Then the seventh angel blew his trum-

Sodom City that God destroyed because the people were so evil.

pet. And there were loud voices in heaven, saying:

"The power to rule the world
   now belongs to our Lord and his
      Christ,*d*

and he will rule forever and ever."

[16]Then the twenty-four elders, who sit on their thrones before God, bowed down on their faces and worshiped God. [17]They said:

"We give thanks to you, Lord God
   Almighty,

   who is and who was,

because you have used your great power
   and have begun to rule!

[18]The people of the world were angry,
   but your anger has come.

The time has come to judge the dead
and to reward your servants the
      prophets*d*

   and your holy people,

   all who respect you, great and small.

The time has come to destroy those who
      destroy the earth!"

[19]Then God's temple*d* in heaven was opened. The Ark*d* that holds the agreement God gave to his people could be seen in his temple. Then there were flashes of lightning, noises, thunder, an earthquake, and a great hailstorm.

The Woman and the Dragon

12 And then a great wonder appeared in heaven: A woman was clothed with the sun, and the moon was under her feet, and a crown of twelve stars was on her head. [2]She was pregnant and cried out with pain, because she was about to give birth. [3]Then another wonder appeared in heaven: There was a giant red dragon with seven heads and seven crowns on each head. He also had ten horns. [4]His tail swept a third of the stars out of the sky and threw them down to the earth. He stood in front of the woman who was ready to give birth so he could eat her baby as soon as it was born. [5]Then the woman gave birth to a son who will rule all the nations with an iron rod. And her child was taken up to God and to his throne. [6]The woman ran away into the desert to a place

God prepared for her where she would be taken care of for one thousand two hundred sixty days.

[7]Then there was a war in heaven. Michael[n] and his angels fought against the dragon, and the dragon and his angels fought back. [8]But the dragon was not strong enough, and he and his angels lost their place in heaven. [9]The giant dragon was thrown down out of heaven. (He is that old snake called the devil or Satan, who tricks the whole world.) The dragon with his angels was thrown down to the earth.

[10]Then I heard a loud voice in heaven saying:

"The salvation and the power and the
      kingdom of our God

   and the authority of his Christ*d* have
      now come.

The accuser of our brothers and sisters,
   who accused them day and night
      before our God,

   has been thrown down.

[11]And our brothers and sisters defeated
      him

   by the blood of the Lamb's death
   and by the message they preached.

They did not love their lives so much
   that they were afraid of death.

[12]So rejoice, you heavens
   and all who live there!

But it will be terrible for the earth and
      the sea,

   because the devil has come down to
      you!

He is filled with anger,
   because he knows he does not have
      much time."

[13]When the dragon saw he had been thrown down to the earth, he hunted for the woman who had given birth to the son. [14]But the woman was given the two wings of a great eagle so she could fly to the place prepared for her in the desert. There she would be taken care of for three and one-half years, away from the snake. [15]Then the snake poured water out of its mouth like a river toward the woman so the flood would carry her away. [16]But the earth helped the woman by opening its mouth and swallowing

Michael   The archangel—leader among God's angels or messengers (Jude 9).

the river that came from the mouth of the dragon. [17]Then the dragon was very angry at the woman, and he went off to make war against all her other children — those who obey God's commands and who have the message Jesus taught.

[18]And the dragon stood on the seashore.

The Two Beasts

13 Then I saw a beast coming up out of the sea. It had ten horns and seven heads, and there was a crown on each horn. A name against God was written on each head. [2]This beast looked like a leopard, with feet like a bear's feet and a mouth like a lion's mouth. And the dragon gave the beast all of his power and his throne and great authority. [3]One of the heads of the beast looked as if it had been killed by a wound, but this death wound was healed. Then the whole world was amazed and followed the beast. [4]People worshiped the dragon because he had given his power to the beast. And they also worshiped the beast, asking, "Who is like the beast? Who can make war against it?"

[5]The beast was allowed to say proud words and words against God, and it was allowed to use its power for forty-two months. [6]It used its mouth to speak against God, against God's name, against the place where God lives, and against all those who live in heaven. [7]It was given power to make war against God's holy people and to defeat them. It was given power over every tribe,[d] people, language, and nation. [8]And all who live on earth will worship the beast — all the people since the beginning of the world whose names are not written in the Lamb's book of life. The Lamb is the One who was killed.

[9]Anyone who has ears should listen:
[10]If you are to be a prisoner,
   then you will be a prisoner.
If you are to be killed with the sword,
   then you will be killed with the sword.
This means that God's holy people must have patience and faith.

[11]Then I saw another beast coming up out of the earth. It had two horns like a lamb, but it spoke like a dragon. [12]This beast stands be-fore the first beast and uses the same power the first beast has. By this power it makes everyone living on earth worship the first beast, who had the death wound that was healed. [13]And the second beast does great miracles[d] so that it even makes fire come down from heaven to earth while people are watching. [14]It fools those who live on earth by the miracles it has been given the power to do. It does these miracles to serve the first beast. The second beast orders people to make an idol to honor the first beast, the one that was wounded by the deadly sword but sprang to life again. [15]The second beast was given power to give life to the idol of the first one so that the idol could speak. And the second beast was given power to command all who will not worship the image of the beast to be killed. [16]The second beast also forced all people, small and great, rich and poor, free and slave, to have a mark on their right hand or on their forehead. [17]No one could buy or sell without this mark, which is the name of the beast or the number of its name. [18]This takes wisdom. Let the one who has understanding find the meaning of the number, which is the number of a person. Its number is six hundred sixty-six.

The Song of the Saved

14 Then I looked, and there before me was the Lamb standing on Mount Zion.[n] With him were one hundred forty-four thousand people who had his name and his Father's name written on their foreheads. [2]And I heard a sound from heaven like the noise of flooding water and like the sound of loud thunder. The sound I heard was like people playing harps. [3]And they sang a new song before the throne and before the four living creatures and the elders. No one could learn the new song except the one hundred forty-four thousand who had been bought from the earth. [4]These are the ones who did not do sinful things with women, because they kept themselves pure. They follow the Lamb every place he goes. These one hundred forty-four thousand were bought from among the people of the earth as people to be offered to God and the Lamb. [5]They were

Mount Zion   Another name for Jerusalem; here meaning the spiritual city of God's people.

not guilty of telling lies; they are without fault.

The Three Angels

6Then I saw another angel flying high in the air. He had the eternal Good News[d] to preach to those who live on earth — to every nation, tribe,[d] language, and people. 7He preached in a loud voice, "Fear God and give him praise, because the time has come for God to judge all people. So worship God who made the heavens, and the earth, and the sea, and the springs of water."

8Then the second angel followed the first angel and said, "Ruined, ruined is the great city of Babylon! She made all the nations drink the wine of the anger of her adultery."[d]

9Then a third angel followed the first two angels, saying in a loud voice: "If anyone worships the beast and his idol and gets the beast's mark on the forehead or on the hand, 10that one also will drink the wine of God's anger, which is prepared with all its strength in the cup of his anger. And that person will be put in pain with burning sulfur before the holy angels and the Lamb. 11And the smoke from their burning pain will rise forever and ever. There will be no rest, day or night, for those who worship the beast and his idol or who get the mark of his name." 12This means God's holy people must be patient. They must obey God's commands and keep their faith in Jesus.

13Then I heard a voice from heaven saying, "Write this: Happy are the dead who die from now on in the Lord."

The Spirit[d] says, "Yes, they will rest from their hard work, and the reward of all they have done stays with them."

The Earth Is Harvested

14Then I looked, and there before me was a white cloud, and sitting on the white cloud was One who looked like a Son of Man.[n] He had a gold crown on his head and a sharp sickle[n] in his hand. 15Then another angel came out of the temple and called out in a loud voice to the One who was sitting on the cloud, "Take your sickle and harvest from the earth, because the time to harvest has come, and the fruit of the earth is ripe." 16So the One who was sitting on the cloud swung his sickle over the earth, and the earth was harvested.

17Then another angel came out of the temple in heaven, and he also had a sharp sickle. 18And then another angel, who has power over the fire, came from the altar. This angel called to the angel with the sharp sickle, saying, "Take your sharp sickle and gather the bunches of grapes from the earth's vine, because its grapes are ripe." 19Then the angel swung his sickle over the earth. He gathered the earth's grapes and threw them into the great winepress[d] of God's anger. 20They were trampled in the winepress outside the city, and blood flowed out of the winepress as high as horses' bridles for a distance of about one hundred eighty miles.

The Last Troubles

15 Then I saw another wonder in heaven that was great and amazing. There were seven angels bringing seven disasters. These are the last disasters, because after them, God's anger is finished.

2I saw what looked like a sea of glass mixed with fire. All of those who had won the victory over the beast and his idol and over the number of his name were standing by the sea of glass. They had harps that God had given them. 3They sang the song of Moses, the servant of God, and the song of the Lamb:

"You do great and wonderful things,
                                      Psalm 111:2

  Lord God Almighty.   *Amos 3:13*
Everything the Lord does is right and
    true,   *Psalm 145:17*
  King of the nations.
4Everyone will respect you, Lord,
                                   Jeremiah 10:7
  and will honor you.
Only you are holy.
All the nations will come
  and worship you,   *Psalm 86:9-10*
because the right things you have done
  are now made known."   *Deuteronomy 32:4*

Son of Man   "Son of Man" is a name Jesus called himself. See dictionary.
sickle   A farming tool with a curved blade. It was used to harvest grain.

⁵After this I saw that the temple (the Tent*d* of the Agreement) in heaven was opened. ⁶And the seven angels bringing the seven disasters came out of the temple. They were dressed in clean, shining linen and wore golden bands tied around their chests. ⁷Then one of the four living creatures gave to the seven angels seven golden bowls filled with the anger of God, who lives forever and ever. ⁸The temple was filled with smoke from the glory and the power of God, and no one could enter the temple until the seven disasters of the seven angels were finished.

The Bowls of God's Anger

16 Then I heard a loud voice from the temple saying to the seven angels, "Go and pour out the seven bowls of God's anger on the earth."

²The first angel left and poured out his bowl on the land. Then ugly and painful sores came upon all those who had the mark of the beast and who worshiped his idol.

³The second angel poured out his bowl on the sea, and it became blood like that of a dead man, and every living thing in the sea died.

⁴The third angel poured out his bowl on the rivers and the springs of water, and they became blood. ⁵Then I heard the angel of the waters saying:

"Holy One, you are the One who is and
      who was.
    You are right to decide to punish these
      evil people.
⁶They have poured out the blood of your
      holy people and your prophets.*d*
    So now you have given them blood to
      drink as they deserve."

⁷And I heard a voice coming from the altar saying:

"Yes, Lord God Almighty,
    the way you punish evil people is right
      and fair."

⁸The fourth angel poured out his bowl on the sun, and he was given power to burn the people with fire. ⁹They were burned by the great heat, and they cursed the name of God, who had control over these disasters. But the people refused to change their hearts and lives and give glory to God.

¹⁰The fifth angel poured out his bowl on the throne of the beast, and darkness covered its kingdom. People gnawed their tongues because of the pain. ¹¹They also cursed the God of heaven because of their pain and the sores they had, but they refused to change their hearts and turn away from the evil things they did.

¹²The sixth angel poured out his bowl on the great river Euphrates so that the water in the river was dried up to prepare the way for the kings from the east to come. ¹³Then I saw three evil spirits that looked like frogs coming out of the mouth of the dragon, out of the mouth of the beast, and out of the mouth of the false prophet.*d* ¹⁴These evil spirits are the spirits of demons,*d* which have power to do miracles.*d* They go out to the kings of the whole world to gather them together for the battle on the great day of God Almighty.

¹⁵"Listen! I will come as a thief comes! Happy are those who stay awake and keep their clothes on so that they will not walk around naked and have people see their shame."

¹⁶Then the evil spirits gathered the kings together to the place that is called Armageddon in the Hebrew language.

¹⁷The seventh angel poured out his bowl into the air. Then a loud voice came out of the temple from the throne, saying, "It is finished!" ¹⁸Then there were flashes of lightning, noises, thunder, and a big earthquake — the worst earthquake that has ever happened since people have been on earth. ¹⁹The great city split into three parts, and the cities of the nations were destroyed. And God remembered the sins of Babylon the Great, so he gave that city the cup filled with the wine of his terrible anger. ²⁰Then every island ran away, and mountains disappeared. ²¹Giant hailstones, each weighing about a hundred pounds, fell from the sky upon people. People cursed God for the disaster of the hail, because this disaster was so terrible.

The Woman on the Animal

17 Then one of the seven angels who had the seven bowls came and spoke to me. He said, "Come, and I will show you the punishment that will be given to the great prostitute,*d* the one sitting over many waters. [2]The kings of the earth sinned sexually with her, and the people of the earth became drunk from the wine of her sexual sin."

[3]Then the angel carried me away by the Spirit[d] to the desert. There I saw a woman sitting on a red beast. It was covered with names against God written on it, and it had seven heads and ten horns. [4]The woman was dressed in purple and red and was shining with the gold, precious jewels, and pearls she was wearing. She had a golden cup in her hand, a cup filled with evil things and the uncleanness of her sexual sin. [5]On her forehead a title was written that was secret. This is what was written:

THE GREAT BABYLON
MOTHER OF PROSTITUTES
AND OF THE EVIL THINGS OF THE EARTH

[6]Then I saw that the woman was drunk with the blood of God's holy people and with the blood of those who were killed because of their faith in Jesus.

When I saw the woman, I was very amazed. [7]Then the angel said to me, "Why are you amazed? I will tell you the secret of this woman and the beast she rides — the one with seven heads and ten horns. [8]The beast you saw was once alive but is not alive now. But soon it will come up out of the bottomless pit and go away to be destroyed. There are people who live on earth whose names have not been written in the book of life since the beginning of the world. They will be amazed when they see the beast, because he was once alive, is not alive now, but will come again.

[9]"You need a wise mind to understand this. The seven heads on the beast are seven mountains where the woman sits. [10]And they are seven kings. Five of the kings have already been destroyed, one of the kings lives now, and another has not yet come. When he comes, he must stay a short time. [11]The beast that was once alive, but is not alive now, is also an eighth king. He belongs to the first seven kings, and he will go away to be destroyed.

[12]"The ten horns you saw are ten kings who have not yet begun to rule, but they will receive power to rule with the beast for one hour. [13]All ten of these kings have the same purpose, and they will give their power and authority to the beast. [14]They will make war against the Lamb, but the Lamb will defeat them, because he is Lord of lords and King of kings. He will defeat them with his called, chosen, and faithful followers."

[15]Then the angel said to me, "The waters that you saw, where the prostitute sits, are peoples, races, nations, and languages. [16]The ten horns and the beast you saw will hate the prostitute. They will take everything she has and leave her naked. They will eat her body and burn her with fire. [17]God made the ten horns want to carry out his purpose by agreeing to give the beast their power to rule, until what God has said comes about. [18]The woman you saw is the great city that rules over the kings of the earth."

Babylon Is Destroyed

18 After the vision of these things, I saw another angel coming down from heaven. This angel had great power, and his glory made the earth bright. [2]He shouted in a powerful voice:
"Ruined, ruined is the great city of
    Babylon!
  She has become a home for demons[d]
  and a prison for every evil spirit,
    and a prison for every unclean[d] bird
      and unclean beast.
[3]She has been ruined, because all the
    peoples of the earth
  have drunk the wine of the desire of
    her sexual sin.
  She has been ruined also because the
    kings of the earth
  have sinned sexually with her,
and the merchants of the earth
  have grown rich from the great wealth
    of her luxury."

[4]Then I heard another voice from heaven saying:
"Come out of that city, my people,
  so that you will not share in her sins,
  so that you will not receive the
    disasters that will come to her.
[5]Her sins have piled up as high as the
    sky,
  and God has not forgotten the wrongs
    she has done.

⁶Give that city the same as she gave to
  others.

  Pay her back twice as much as she
    did.

Prepare wine for her that is twice as
  strong

  as the wine she prepared for others.
⁷She gave herself much glory and rich
  living.

  Give her that much suffering and
    sadness.

She says to herself, 'I am a queen sitting
  on my throne.

  I am not a widow; I will never be
    sad.'

⁸So these disasters will come to her in
  one day:

  death, and crying, and great hunger,
and she will be destroyed by fire,

  because the Lord God who judges her
    is powerful."

⁹The kings of the earth who sinned sexually with her and shared her wealth will see
the smoke from her burning. Then they will
cry and be sad because of her death. ¹⁰They
will be afraid of her suffering and stand far
away and say:

"Terrible! How terrible for you, great
  city,

  powerful city of Babylon,

because your punishment has come in
  one hour!"

¹¹And the merchants of the earth will cry
and be sad about her, because now there is
no one to buy their cargoes— ¹²cargoes of
gold, silver, jewels, pearls, fine linen, purple
cloth, silk, red cloth; all kinds of citron wood
and all kinds of things made from ivory, expensive wood, bronze, iron, and marble;
¹³cinnamon, spice, incense,ᵈ myrrh,ᵈ frankincense,ᵈ wine, olive oil, fine flour, wheat, cattle, sheep, horses, carriages, slaves, and human lives.

¹⁴The merchants will say,

"Babylon, the good things you wanted
  are gone from you.

All your rich and fancy things have
  disappeared.

  You will never have them again."

¹⁵The merchants who became rich from selling to her will be afraid of her suffering and

will stand far away. They will cry and be sad
¹⁶and say:

"Terrible! How terrible for the great city!
  She was dressed in fine linen, purple
    and red cloth,

  and she was shining with gold,
    precious jewels, and pearls!

¹⁷All these riches have been destroyed in
  one hour!"

Every sea captain, every passenger, the
sailors, and all those who earn their living
from the sea stood far away from Babylon.
¹⁸As they saw the smoke from her burning,
they cried out loudly, "There was never a
city like this great city!" ¹⁹And they threw
dust on their heads and cried out, weeping
and being sad. They said:

"Terrible! How terrible for the great city!
  All the people who had ships on the sea
    became rich because of her wealth!

But she has been destroyed in one hour!
²⁰Be happy because of this, heaven!

  Be happy, God's holy people and
    apostlesᵈ and prophets!ᵈ

God has punished her because of what
  she did to you."

²¹Then a powerful angel picked up a large
stone, like one used for grinding grain, and
threw it into the sea. He said:

"In the same way, the great city of
    Babylon will be thrown down,
  and it will never be found again.

²²The music of people playing harps and
    other instruments, flutes, and
    trumpets,

  will never be heard in you again.
No workman doing any job

  will ever be found in you again.
The sound of grinding grain

  will never be heard in you again.
²³The light of a lamp

  will never shine in you again,
  and the voices of a bridegroom and bride
    will never be heard in you again.

Your merchants were the world's great
  people,

  and all the nations were tricked by
    your magic.

²⁴You are guilty of the death of the
    prophets and God's holy people
  and all who have been killed on
    earth."

People in Heaven Praise God

19 After this vision and announcement I heard what sounded like a great many people in heaven saying:

"Hallelujah![n]

Salvation, glory, and power belong to our God,

2 because his judgments are true and right.

He has punished the prostitute[d]
who made the earth evil with her sexual sin.

He has paid her back for the death of his servants."

[3]Again they said:

"Hallelujah!

She is burning, and her smoke will rise forever and ever."

[4]Then the twenty-four elders and the four living creatures bowed down and worshiped God, who sits on the throne. They said:

"Amen, Hallelujah!"

[5]Then a voice came from the throne, saying:

"Praise our God, all you who serve him
and all you who honor him, both small and great!"

[6]Then I heard what sounded like a great many people, like the noise of flooding water, and like the noise of loud thunder. The people were saying:

"Hallelujah!

Our Lord God, the Almighty, rules.

[7]Let us rejoice and be happy
and give God glory,

because the wedding of the Lamb has come,

and the Lamb's bride has made herself ready.

[8]Fine linen, bright and clean, was given to her to wear."

(The fine linen means the good things done by God's holy people.)

[9]And the angel said to me, "Write this: Happy are those who have been invited to the wedding meal of the Lamb!" And the angel said, "These are the true words of God."

[10]Then I bowed down at the angel's feet to worship him, but he said to me, "Do not worship me! I am a servant like you and your brothers and sisters who have the message of Jesus. Worship God, because the message about Jesus is the spirit that gives all prophecy."[d]

The Rider on the White Horse

[11]Then I saw heaven opened, and there before me was a white horse. The rider on the horse is called Faithful and True, and he is right when he judges and makes war. [12]His eyes are like burning fire, and on his head are many crowns. He has a name written on him, which no one but himself knows. [13]He is dressed in a robe dipped in blood, and his name is the Word of God. [14]The armies of heaven, dressed in fine linen, white and clean, were following him on white horses. [15]Out of the rider's mouth comes a sharp sword that he will use to defeat the nations, and he will rule them with a rod of iron. He will crush out the wine in the winepress[d] of the terrible anger of God the Almighty. [16]On his robe and on his upper leg was written this name: KING OF KINGS AND LORD OF LORDS.

[17]Then I saw an angel standing in the sun, and he called with a loud voice to all the birds flying in the sky: "Come and gather together for the great feast of God [18]so that you can eat the bodies of kings, generals, mighty people, horses and their riders, and the bodies of all people—free, slave, small, and great."

[19]Then I saw the beast and the kings of the earth. Their armies were gathered together to make war against the rider on the horse and his army. [20]But the beast was captured and with him the false prophet[d] who did the miracles[d] for the beast. The false prophet had used these miracles to trick those who had the mark of the beast and worshiped his idol. The false prophet and the beast were thrown alive into the lake of fire that burns with sulfur. [21]And their armies were killed with the sword that came out of the mouth of the rider on the horse, and all the birds ate the bodies until they were full.

The Thousand Years

20 I saw an angel coming down from heaven. He had the key to the bottomless pit and a large chain in his hand. [2]The angel grabbed the dragon, that old snake who is the devil and Satan, and tied him up for a thousand years. [3]Then he threw him into the bottomless pit, closed it, and locked it over him. The angel did this so he could not trick the people of the earth anymore until the thousand years were ended. After a thousand years he must be set free for a short time.

[4]Then I saw some thrones and people sitting on them who had been given the power to judge. And I saw the souls of those who had been killed because they were faithful to the message of Jesus and the message from God. They had not worshiped the beast or his idol, and they had not received the mark of the beast on their foreheads or on their hands. They came back to life and ruled with Christ for a thousand years. [5](The others that were dead did not live again until the thousand years were ended.) This is the first raising of the dead. [6]Happy and holy are those who share in this first raising of the dead. The second death has no power over them. They will be priests for God and for Christ and will rule with him for a thousand years.

[7]When the thousand years are over, Satan will be set free from his prison. [8]Then he will go out to trick the nations in all the earth— Gog and Magog— to gather them for battle. There are so many people they will be like sand on the seashore. [9]And Satan's army marched across the earth and gathered around the camp of God's people and the city God loves. But fire came down from heaven and burned them up. [10]And Satan, who tricked them, was thrown into the lake of burning sulfur with the beast and the false prophet.[d] There they will be punished day and night forever and ever.

People of the World Are Judged

[11]Then I saw a great white throne and the One who was sitting on it. Earth and sky ran away from him and disappeared. [12]And I saw the dead, great and small, standing before the throne. Then books were opened, and the

book of life was opened. The dead were judged by what they had done, which was written in the books. [13]The sea gave up the dead who were in it, and Death and Hades[n] gave up the dead who were in them. Each person was judged by what he had done. [14]And Death and Hades were thrown into the lake of fire. The lake of fire is the second death. [15]And anyone whose name was not found written in the book of life was thrown into the lake of fire.

The New Jerusalem

21 Then I saw a new heaven and a new earth. The first heaven and the first earth had disappeared, and there was no sea anymore. [2]And I saw the holy city, the new Jerusalem,[n] coming down out of heaven from God. It was prepared like a bride dressed for her husband. [3]And I heard a loud voice from the throne, saying, "Now God's presence is with people, and he will live with them, and they will be his people. God himself will be with them and will be their God. [4]He will wipe away every tear from their eyes, and there will be no more death, sadness, crying, or pain, because all the old ways are gone."

[5]The One who was sitting on the throne said, "Look! I am making everything new!" Then he said, "Write this, because these words are true and can be trusted."

[6]The One on the throne said to me, "It is finished. I am the Alpha and the Omega,[n] the Beginning and the End. I will give free water from the spring of the water of life to anyone who is thirsty. [7]Those who win the victory will receive this, and I will be their God, and they will be my children. [8]But cowards, those who refuse to believe, who do evil things, who kill, who sin sexually, who do evil magic, who worship idols, and who tell lies— all these will have a place in the lake of burning sulfur. This is the second death."

[9]Then one of the seven angels who had the seven bowls full of the seven last troubles came to me, saying, "Come with me, and I

Hades The place of the dead.
new Jerusalem The spiritual city where God's people live with him.
Alpha and the Omega The first and last letters of the Greek alphabet. This means "the beginning and the end."

will show you the bride, the wife of the Lamb." [10]And the angel carried me away by the Spirit[d] to a very large and high mountain. He showed me the holy city, Jerusalem, coming down out of heaven from God. [11]It was shining with the glory of God and was bright like a very expensive jewel, like a jasper, clear as crystal. [12]The city had a great high wall with twelve gates with twelve angels at the gates, and on each gate was written the name of one of the twelve tribes[d] of Israel. [13]There were three gates on the east, three on the north, three on the south, and three on the west. [14]The walls of the city were built on twelve foundation stones, and on the stones were written the names of the twelve apostles[d] of the Lamb.

[15]The angel who talked with me had a measuring rod made of gold to measure the city, its gates, and its wall. [16]The city was built in a square, and its length was equal to its width. The angel measured the city with the rod. The city was twelve thousand stadia[n] long, twelve thousand stadia wide, and twelve thousand stadia high. [17]The angel also measured the wall. It was one hundred forty-four cubits[n] high, by human measurements, which the angel was using. [18]The wall was made of jasper, and the city was made of pure gold, as pure as glass. [19]The foundation stones of the city walls were decorated with every kind of jewel. The first foundation was jasper, the second was sapphire, the third was chalcedony, the fourth was emerald, [20]the fifth was onyx, the sixth was carnelian, the seventh was chrysolite, the eighth was beryl, the ninth was topaz, the tenth was chrysoprase, the eleventh was jacinth, and the twelfth was amethyst. [21]The twelve gates were twelve pearls, each gate having been made from a single pearl. And the street of the city was made of pure gold as clear as glass.

[22]I did not see a temple in the city, because the Lord God Almighty and the Lamb are the city's temple. [23]The city does not need the sun or the moon to shine on it, because the glory of God is its light, and the Lamb is the city's lamp. [24]By its light the people of the world will walk, and the kings of the earth will bring their glory into it. [25]The city's gates will never be shut on any day, because there is no night there. [26]The glory and the honor of the nations will be brought into it. [27]Nothing unclean[d] and no one who does shameful things or tells lies will ever go into it. Only those whose names are written in the Lamb's book of life will enter the city.

22 Then the angel showed me the river of the water of life. It was shining like crystal and was flowing from the throne of God and of the Lamb [2]down the middle of the street of the city. The tree of life was on each side of the river. It produces fruit twelve times a year, once each month. The leaves of the tree are for the healing of all the nations. [3]Nothing that God judges guilty will be in that city. The throne of God and of the Lamb will be there, and God's servants will worship him. [4]They will see his face, and his name will be written on their foreheads. [5]There will never be night again. They will not need the light of a lamp or the light of the sun, because the Lord God will give them light. And they will rule as kings forever and ever.

[6]The angel said to me, "These words can be trusted and are true." The Lord, the God of the spirits of the prophets,[d] sent his angel to show his servants the things that must happen soon.

[7]"Listen! I am coming soon! Happy is the one who obeys the words of prophecy in this book."

[8]I, John, am the one who heard and saw these things. When I heard and saw them, I bowed down to worship at the feet of the angel who showed these things to me. [9]But the angel said to me, "Do not worship me! I am a servant like you, your brothers the prophets, and all those who obey the words in this book. Worship God!"

[10]Then the angel told me, "Do not keep secret the words of prophecy in this book, because the time is near for all this to happen. [11]Let whoever is doing evil continue to do evil. Let whoever is unclean continue to be unclean. Let whoever is doing right con-

---

stadia   One stadion was a distance of about two hundred yards; about one-eighth of a Roman mile.
cubits   A cubit is about half a yard, the length from the elbow to the tip of the little finger.

tinue to do right. Let whoever is holy continue to be holy."

 12"Listen! I am coming soon! I will bring my reward with me, and I will repay each one of you for what you have done. 13I am the Alpha and the Omega, *n* the First and the Last, the Beginning and the End.

14"Happy are those who wash their robes *n* so that they will receive the right to eat the fruit from the tree of life and may go through the gates into the city. 15Outside the city are the evil people, those who do evil magic, who sin sexually, who murder, who worship idols, and who love lies and tell lies.

16"I, Jesus, have sent my angel to tell you these things for the churches. I am the descendant *d* from the family of David, and I am the bright morning star."

17The Spirit *d* and the bride say, "Come!" Let the one who hears this say, "Come!" Let whoever is thirsty come; whoever wishes may have the water of life as a free gift.

18I warn everyone who hears the words of the prophecy of this book: If anyone adds anything to these words, God will add to that person the disasters written about in this book. 19And if anyone takes away from the words of this book of prophecy, God will take away that one's share of the tree of life and of the holy city, which are written about in this book.

20Jesus, the One who says these things are true, says, "Yes, I am coming soon."

Amen. Come, Lord Jesus!

21The grace of the Lord Jesus be with all. Amen.

Alpha and the Omega   The first and last letters of the Greek alphabet. This means "the beginning and the end."
wash their robes   This means they believed in Jesus so that their sins could be forgiven by Christ's blood.

DICTIONARY
with
TOPICAL CONCORDANCE

A

Aaron (AIR-ohn) *older brother of Moses.*
· before the king of Egypt, Exodus 4:14-16; 5:1-5; 7:1-2
· death of, Numbers 20:22-29

Abba (AB-uh) *word for "father" in Aramaic.*
· Jesus called God "Abba," Mark 14:36
· we can call God "Abba," Romans 8:15; Galatians 4:6

Abednego (a-BED-nee-go) *one of the three friends of Daniel whom God protected from the fiery furnace.*
· refused the king of Babylon's food, Daniel 1:3-17
· thrown into the fiery furnace, Daniel 3

Abel (AY-bul) *the second son of Adam and Eve.*
· born to Adam and Eve, Genesis 4:2
· approved by God, Genesis 4:3-4; Hebrews 11:4
· murdered by Cain, Genesis 4:8; 1 John 3:12

Abib (ah-BEEB) *first month of the Jewish calendar, about the time of year as our March or April; also called "Nisan"; means "young ears of grain."*
· the time the Israelites left Egypt, Exodus 13:3-4
· the time for the Feast of Unleavened Bread, Exodus 23:15; 34:18

Abigail, sister of David (AB-eh-gale) 1 Chronicles 2:13-17

Abigail, wife of Nabal
· brought food to David, 1 Samuel 25:14-35
· became David's wife, 1 Samuel 25:36-42

Abijah, king of Judah (a-BY-jah) 1 Kings 15:1-8; 2 Chronicles 13:1–14:1

Abijah, son of Jeroboam
· death of, 1 Kings 14:1-18

Abijah, son of Samuel, 1 Samuel 8:1-3

ability
· given by God, 2 Corinthians 3:5-6
· through Christ, Philippians 4:13
· differing abilities, 1 Corinthians 12:7-11

Abimelech, king of Gerar (a-BIM-eh-lek)
· tried to take Sarah as his wife, Genesis 20

Abimelech, king of the Philistines
· tried to take Rebekah as his wife, Genesis 26:6-11

Abimelech, son of Gideon
· birth of, Judges 8:29-31
· murdered his brothers, Judges 9:1-6
· defeated the people of Shechem, Judges 9:22-45
· burned the Tower of Shechem, Judges 9:46-49
· death of, Judges 9:50-55

Abishai (a-BISH-eye) *nephew of King David.*
· served in David's army, 2 Samuel 23:18-19; 1 Chronicles 18:12-13
· saved David's life, 2 Samuel 21:15-17

Abner (AB-nur) *commander of Saul's army.*
· at Goliath's defeat, 1 Samuel 17:55-57
· made Ish-Bosheth king of Israel, 2 Samuel 2:8-10
· later loyal to David, 2 Samuel 3:6-21
· killed by Joab, 2 Samuel 3:22-27

Abraham (AY-bra-ham) *father of the Jewish nation.*
· called from Ur by God, Genesis 12:1-4
· lied about Sarai, Genesis 12:10-20
· separated from Lot, Genesis 13
· God's agreement with, Genesis 15; 17
· name changed, Genesis 17:3-6
· father of Isaac, Genesis 21:1-7
· offered Isaac as a sacrifice, Genesis 22:1-19
· father of the faithful, Romans 4
· God's friend, James 2:23

Absalom (AB-sah-lum) *one of David's sons.*
· turned against David, 2 Samuel 15–18:8
· killed by Joab, 2 Samuel 18:9-15

abstain (ab-STAIN) *to keep from doing something.*
· from food offered to idols, Acts 15:20
· from evil, 1 Thessalonians 5:22
· from lust, 1 Peter 2:11

abyss (uh-BISS) See "bottomless pit."

accept
· a prophet not accepted, Luke 4:24
· accepted by God, Acts 10:35; 15:7-8; Romans 14:3
· each other, Romans 14:1; 15:7
· Jesus, John 12:48

accuse
· Jesus accused by the Jews, Matthew 27:12-13; Mark 15:3; Luke 6:7
· Paul accused by the Jews, Acts 23:27-29; 26:7
· the Devil, as the accuser, Revelation 12:10

Achaia (a-KA-yuh) See "Greece."

Achan (AY-can) *an Israelite who disobeyed God during the battle of Jericho,* Joshua 7

Achish (AY-kish) *king of the Philistine city of Gath.*
· David pretends to be insane, 1 Samuel 21:10-15
· David in his army, 1 Samuel 27; 29

actions
· judged by, Proverbs 20:11; Matthew 11:19; Galatians 6:4
· of love, 1 John 3:18
· of goodness, Matthew 5:16

Adam (AD-um) *the first man.*
· created by God, Genesis 1:26–2:25
· disobeyed God, Genesis 3

· compared to Christ, 1 Corinthians 15:21-22,45-49

adder, *a poisonous snake.* See "snake."

Adonijah (ad-oh-NY-jah) *David's fourth son.*
· son of Haggith, 2 Samuel 3:4
· tried to become king, 1 Kings 1
· killed by Solomon, 1 Kings 2:12-25

Adoni-Zedek (a-DOH-ny-ZEE-dek) *an Amorite king of Jerusalem.*
· defeated by Joshua, Joshua 10:1-28

Adullam (a-DOO-lum) *a city about thirteen miles from Bethlehem.*
· David hid in a cave there, 2 Samuel 23:13

adultery (ah-DUL-ter-ee) *breaking a marriage promise by having sexual relations with someone other than your husband or wife.*
· "You must not be guilty of adultery," Exodus 20:14
· Christ teaches about, Matthew 5:27-32; Luke 16:18
· woman caught in adultery, John 8:1-11

advice
· given by Ahithophel, 2 Samuel 15:30-17:23
· given to Rehoboam, 1 Kings 12:1-15
· teachings about, Proverbs 11:14; 12:5,15; 19:20

Agabus (AG-uh-bus) *a Christian prophet.*
· warned the people, Acts 11:27-30
· warned Paul about going to Jerusalem, Acts 21:10-11

Agag (AY-gag) *king of the Amalekites.*
· captured by Saul, 1 Samuel 15

agreement *a contract, promise, or covenant.*
· with Noah, Genesis 9:1-17
· with Abraham, Genesis 15; 17:1-14
· Ark of the Agreement, Exodus 25:10-22; 1 Samuel 4-5; 2 Samuel 6:1-15
· with the Israelites, Exodus 19:3-8,24; Deuteronomy 29
· new agreement, 2 Corinthians 2:12-3:18
· difference between the old and new agreements, Hebrews 8-10

Agrippa (uh-GRIP-pah) See "Herod Agrippa."

Ahab (AY-hab) *evil king of Israel who was married to Jezebel.*
· worshiped Baal, 1 Kings 16:29-33
· had Naboth killed, 1 Kings 21
· death of, 1 Kings 22:1-40

Ahasuerus (ah-HAZ-oo-EE-rus) *Hebrew word for the Greek name Xerxes.* See "Xerxes."

Ahaz, *twelfth king of Judah,* 2 Kings 16; 2 Chronicles 28

Ahaziah, king of Judah (ay-ha-ZY-uh) 2 Chronicles 22:1-9

Ahaziah, son of Ahab
· king of Israel, 1 Kings 22:40-53

Ahijah, great-grandson of Eli (a-HY-jah) 1 Samuel 14:1-23

Ahijah, the prophet
· told Jeroboam the kingdom would be divided, 1 Kings 11:29-39
· told that Jeroboam's son would die, 1 Kings 14:1-18

Ahimelech, the high priest (a-HIM-eh-lek)
· helped David, 1 Samuel 21:1-9

Ahimelech, the Hittite warrior, 1 Samuel 26:6

Ahithophel (a-HITH-oh-fel) *gave advice to King David.*
· helped Absalom rebel against David, 1 Samuel 15:31; 16:15-17:23

Ai (AY-eye) *a city completely destroyed by the Israelites,* Joshua 7-8:28

Akeldama (a-KEL-dah-mah) *field bought with the money Judas received for betraying Jesus,* Matthew 27:3-10; Acts 1:18-19

alabaster (AL-a-bass-ter) *light-colored stone with streaks or stripes through it,* Matthew 26:7; Mark 14:3; Luke 7:37

alamoth (AL-a-moth) *a musical word, which may mean "like a flute" or "high-pitched,"* Psalm 46

All-Powerful, a name for God, 1 Chronicles 11:9; Psalm 24:10; Isaiah 6:3-5; Malachi 3:1-17

Almighty, *a name for God.*
· "I am God Almighty," Genesis 17:1
· "I appeared to Abraham . . . by the name, God Almighty," Exodus 6:3
· "Holy, holy, holy is the Lord God Almighty," Revelation 4:8

almond
· design of the lampstands in Holy Tent, Exodus 25:31-36
· Aaron's stick produced, Numbers 17:8

aloes (AL-ohs) *oils from sweet-smelling sap of certain trees; used to make perfume and medicine and to prepare bodies for burial,* Psalm 45:8; Proverbs 7:17
· used to prepare Jesus' body for burial, John 19:39

Alpha and Omega (AL-fah and oh-MAY-guh) *the first and last letters of the Greek alphabet, like our A and Z.*
· used to describe Jesus, Revelation 1:8; 21:6; 22:13

altar (ALL-ter) *a place where sacrifices, gifts, or prayers were offered to a god.*
· built by Noah, Genesis 8:20
· built by Abraham, Genesis 22:9
· for burnt offerings, Exodus 27:1-8
· for incense, Exodus 30:1-10
· corners of, Exodus 27:2; 30:10; 1 Kings 1:50

· for the Temple, 2 Chronicles 4:1

Amalekites (AM-a-lah-kites) *fierce, fighting people who descended from Esau; they were enemies of Israel and were finally wiped out during the time of Hezekiah.*
· enemies of Israel, Exodus 17:8-16; 1 Samuel 15
· destroyed by King Hezekiah, 1 Chronicles 4:43

Amasa (AM-a-sa) *leader of Absalom's army when he rebelled against David,* 2 Samuel 17:25
· made leader of David's army, 2 Samuel 19:13
· killed by Joab, 2 Samuel 20:1-10

Amaziah (am-ah-ZY-uh) *the ninth king of Judah,* 2 Kings 14; 2 Chronicles 25

amen (AY-MEN or AH-MEN) *Hebrew word for "that is right,"* 1 Chronicles 16:36; Psalm 106:48; 1 Corinthians 14:16
· "Amen. Come, Lord Jesus!" Revelation 22:20

Ammonites (AM-on-ites) *descendants of Lot's son, Ben-Ammi,* Genesis 19:36-38
· enemies of Israel, Judges 10:6–11:33; 1 Samuel 11; 2 Samuel 10:1-14
· worshiped Molech, 1 Kings 11:5

Amon (AM-on) *the fifteenth king of Judah,* 2 Kings 21:18-26; 2 Chronicles 33:20-25
· an ancestor of Jesus, Matthew 1:10

Amorites (AM-or-ites) *a group of wicked people who worshiped false gods and lived in Canaan when the Israelites arrived.*
· defeated by Israel, Numbers 21:21-32; Joshua 10:1–11:14

Amos (AY-mos) *a prophet who warned Israel of God's punishment for disobedience.*
· a shepherd from Tekoa, Amos 1:1
· his visions, Amos 7–9:10

Anak/Anakites (A-nak/AN-uh-kites) *a group of large, fighting people who lived in Canaan when the Israelites arrived.*
· feared by the twelve spies, Numbers 13:22,28,33; Deuteronomy 1:26-28
· defeated by Joshua, Joshua 11:21-23

Ananias, husband of Sapphira (an-uh-NY-us)
· killed for lying to the Holy Spirit, Acts 5:1-6

Ananias, a Christian in Damascus
· helped Saul of Tarsus, Acts 9:10-19; 22:12-16

Ananias, the high priest
· at Paul's trial, Acts 23:1-5

Andrew, *a fisherman and brother of the apostle Peter.*
· chosen by Jesus to be an apostle, Mark 1:16-18; 3:13-19
· brought Peter to Jesus, John 1:40-42

· waited with the apostles in Jerusalem, Acts 1:13

angel (AIN-jel) *a heavenly being.*
· rescued Lot from Sodom, Genesis 19:1-22
· led Israel to Canaan, Exodus 23:20-23; 32:34
· announced Jesus' birth, Matthew 1:20-21; Luke 1:26-37; 2:8-15
· helped Jesus, Matthew 4:11; Luke 22:43
· helped the apostles, Acts 5:19-20; 12:6-10
· will bring judgment, Matthew 13:24-50; 24:31
· archangel, 1 Thessalonians 4:16; Jude 9
· less than Christ, Hebrews 1:4-14; 1 Peter 3:22
· rebellious angels, 2 Peter 2:4; Jude 6
· serving in heaven, Revelation 7–10

anger, *wrath.*
· of God toward people, John 3:36; Romans 1:18; 2:5-6; Colossians 3:5-6
· saved from God's anger by Christ, Romans 5:9; 1 Thessalonians 1:10; 5:9
· warnings against, Matthew 5:21-22; Ephesians 4:26,31; James 1:19-20

animal
· created by God, Genesis 1:20-25
· to be ruled by people, Genesis 1:26
· named by Adam, Genesis 2:19-20
· saved by Noah, Genesis 6:19-20
· clean, Leviticus 11:1-3,9; Deuteronomy 14:3-6
· unclean, Leviticus 11:4-8,10-12,26-44; Deuteronomy 14:7-8

Annas (AN-us) *a high priest of the Jews during Jesus' lifetime,* Luke 3:2; John 18:13
· questioned Peter and John, Acts 4:5-22

anoint (uh-NOINT) *to pour oil on.*
· to appoint a priest, Exodus 28:41; 40:13
· to appoint a king, 1 Samuel 10:1; 16:12-13; 2 Kings 9:6
· the Holy Tent, Numbers 7:1
· to heal sickness, Mark 6:13; James 5:14

Anti-Christ (AN-tee KRYST) See "enemy of Christ."

Antioch in Pisidia (AN-tee-ahk) *a small city in the country of Pisidia.*
· Paul preached there, Acts 13:14-15

Antioch in Syria, *third largest city in the Roman Empire.*
· Saul and Barnabas preached there, Acts 11:19-26
· followers first called "Christians" there, Acts 11:26
· Peter in Antioch, Galatians 2:11-12
· Paul preaches there, Acts 13:14-15

Apollos (uh-POL-us) *an educated Jew from Alexandria.*
· taught by Aquila and Priscilla, Acts 18:24-28

· preached to the Corinthians, 1 Corinthians 1:12; 3:4-6
· friend of Paul, Titus 3:13

apostle (uh-POS-'l) *someone who is sent off. Jesus chose these twelve special followers and sent them to tell the Good News about him to the whole world.*
· twelve chosen by Jesus, Mark 3:14-19
· Matthias chosen, Acts 1:12-26
· Paul chosen, 1 Corinthians 15:3-11; 2 Corinthians 12:11-12
· duties and powers of, Luke 9:1-6; Acts 5:12-16; 8:18
· leaders of the church, Acts 15; 16:4; 1 Corinthians 12:28
· false apostles, 2 Corinthians 11:13; Revelation 2:2

appearance
· not to judge by, 1 Samuel 16:7; John 7:24
· deceiving, Matthew 23:27-28
· of Jesus, Isaiah 53:2; Philippians 2:7

Aquila (AK-wi-lah) *a Jewish Christian from Rome.*
· friend of Paul, Acts 18:2-3; Romans 16:3-5
· taught Apollos, Acts 18:24-28

Arabah (AIR-uh-bah) *the Hebrew word for the Jordan Valley.* See "Jordan Valley."

Arabah, Sea of, See "Dead Sea."

Aram (AIR-um) *a country northeast of Israel,* 1 Kings 11:25; 15:18; 2 Kings 5:1; Isaiah 7:1
· known as "Syria" in the New Testament, Matthew 4:24; Acts 15:23

Aramaic (AIR-uh-MAY-ik) *the language of the people in the nation of Aram.*
· common language of the Jews, 2 Kings 18:26; John 19:13,17,20; Acts 21:40

Ararat (AIR-uh-rat) *a group of mountains located in what is now Turkey and the Soviet Union.*
· Noah's boat landed there, Genesis 8:14

Araunah (a-RAW-nah) *a Jebusite who was also called Ornan.*
· sold his threshing floor to King David, 2 Samuel 24:15-25; 1 Chronicles 21:18-28

archangel (ark-AIN-jel) *the leader of God's angels,* 1 Thessalonians 4:16; Jude 9

Areopagus (AI R-ee-OP-uh-gus) *a council or group of important leaders in Athens.*
· Paul spoke there, Acts 17:16-34

argue
· the apostles argued, Mark 9:33-37; Luke 9:46-48
· avoid arguments, Philippians 2:14; 2 Timothy 2:23-26; Titus 3:9
· Michael argued with the devil, Jude 9

Aristarchus (air-i-STAR-kus) *a man from Thessalonica who often traveled with Paul,* Acts 27:2; Colossians 4:10; Philemon 24

ark, Noah's, *the huge boat that Noah built to save his family from the flood God sent to cover the earth.* See "boat."

Ark of the Agreement, *a special box made of acacia wood and gold. Inside were the stone tablets on which the Ten Commandments were written. Later, a pot of manna and Aaron's walking stick were also put into the Ark. It was to remind the people of Israel of God's promise to be with them.*
· building of, Exodus 25:10-22; 37:1-9
· crossing the Jordan River, Joshua 3:1-17
· captured by the Philistines, 1 Samuel 4—7:1
· touched by Uzzah, 2 Samuel 6:1-8; 1 Chronicles 13
· placed in the Temple, 2 Chronicles 5:2-10
· contents of, Hebrews 9:4-5

Ark of the Covenant, See "Ark of the Agreement."

armor
· of Saul, 1 Samuel 17:38-39; 31:9-10
· of God, Ephesians 6:10-17

arrest
· John the Baptist arrested, Matthew 14:3; Mark 6:17
· Jesus arrested, Matthew 26:50-57; Mark 14:44-50; John 18:1-14
· Peter arrested, Acts 12:1-4
· Paul arrested, Acts 28:17-20

Artaxerxes (ar-tah-ZERK-sees) *the title or name of Persian kings,* Ezra 4:7; Nehemiah 2:1
· his letter to Ezra, Ezra 7:11-26

Artemis (AR-tuh-mis) *a goddess that many Greeks worshiped,* Acts 19:23-41

Asa (AY-sah) *the third king of Judah,* 1 Kings 15:9-24; 2 Chronicles 14—16

Asaph (AY-saf) *a leader of singers when David was king,* 1 Chronicles 16:5,7; 25:1-2; 2 Chronicles 5:12
· songs of, Psalms 73—83

ascension (uh-SIN-shun) *lifted up; used to describe Jesus' return to heaven,* Acts 1:2-11; 2:32-33

ashamed
· of Jesus, Mark 8:38; Luke 9:26; 2 Timothy 1:8
· for suffering as a Christian, 1 Peter 4:16

Ashdod (ASH-dahd) *one of the five strong, walled cities of the Philistines; called Azotus in the New Testament.*
· Ark of the Agreement there, 1 Samuel 5:1-8
· later called "Azotus," Acts 8:40

Asherah (ah-SHIR-ah) *a Canaanite goddess thought to be the wife of the god Baal.*
· worshiped by Israelites, 1 Kings 14:14-15,22-23; 15:13
· worship forbidden, Exodus 34:13-14; Deuteronomy 16:21-22

Ashkelon (ASH-keh-lon) *one of the five important cities of the Philistines,* Judges 1:18; Zephaniah 2:4,7
· thirty of its men killed by Samson, Judges 14:19

Ashtoreth (ASH-toh-reth) *a goddess of the people of Assyria and Canaan. At times the Israelites forgot God and built idols to worship her.* Judges 2:13; 1 Samuel 7:3-4; 12:10
· worshiped by Solomon, 1 Kings 11:5,33

Asia (AY-zhuh) *the western part of the country now called "Turkey."*
· Paul preached there, Acts 19:10,26
· seven churches of, Revelation 1:4

assembly (a-SEM-blee) *a meeting; a group of people gathered for a purpose.*
· of the church, Hebrews 10:24-25
· conduct in, James 2:1-4

assurance (uh-SHURE-ans) *with confidence; without doubts.*
· about the gospel, 1 Thessalonians 1:5
· before God, Hebrews 10:22-23; 1 John 5:14-15
· faith as, Hebrews 11:1

Assyria (uh-SEER-ee-uh) *a powerful nation north and east of Israel.*
· enemy of Israel, 2 Kings 15:19-20; 17:3-6
· enemy of Judah, 2 Kings 18:13–19:36; Isaiah 36–37:37

Astarte (ah-STAR-tay) *another name for the goddess Ashtoreth. See "Ashtoreth."*

Athaliah (ath-uh-LY-uh) *the only woman who ruled over Judah,* 2 Kings 11; 2 Chronicles 22:10–23:21

Athens (ATH-enz) *the leading city of the country of Greece.*
· Paul preached there, Acts 17:16-34

atonement (uh-TONE-ment) *to remove or forgive sins.*
· through animal sacrifices, Exodus 30:10; Leviticus 17:11; Numbers 25:13
· through faith in the blood of Jesus' death, Romans 3:25; Hebrews 2:17; 9:22; 10:11-12

Atonement, Day of, See "Cleansing, Day of."

Augustus Caesar (aw-GUS-tus SEE-zer) *or Caesar Augustus, the first Roman emperor,* Luke 2:1

authority (uh-THAR-uh-tee) *power or right to control.*

· proper use of, Matthew 20:25-26; Luke 22:24-30; Titus 2:15
· respect for, Luke 20:20-26; Romans 13:1-7; 1 Timothy 2:2; 1 Peter 2:13-17; Hebrews 13:17
· Jesus' authority, Matthew 7:29; 9:6; Mark 11:27-33; Luke 5:24; John 5:19-29

B

Baal (BAY-el) *a god of the Canaanites; "Baal" was the common word for "master, lord." He was known as the son of Dagon, or the son of El, who was known as the father of the false gods.*
· worshiped by Israelites, Judges 2:10-11; Jeremiah 11:13
· Elijah defeated prophets of Baal, 1 Kings 18:1-40
· Baal worship destroyed by Jehu, 2 Kings 10:18-28

Baal-Zebub, See "Beelzebul."

Baasha (BAY-ah-shah) *the third king of Israel,* 1 Kings 15:27–16:7; 2 Chronicles 16:1-6; Jeremiah 41:9

Babel (BAY-bel) *a tower built to reach the sky,* Genesis 11:1-9

baby
· Moses as, Exodus 2:1-10
· Solomon determined mother of, 1 Kings 3:16-28
· Elizabeth's, Luke 1:39-44
· Jesus as, Luke 2:6-21
· as a symbol of new Christians, 1 Peter 2:2

Babylon (BAB-uh-lun) *city on the Euphrates River; capital of Babylonia.*
· captives in Babylon, Psalm 137:1; Jeremiah 29:10
· destruction predicted, Jeremiah 51:36-37
· as a symbol of evil, Revelation 14:8; 17:5

Babylonians (bab-e-LONE-e-unz) *people of the country Babylonia. Also called "Chaldeans."*
· capture warned by Jeremiah, Jeremiah 21; 25
· captured the people of Judah, 2 Kings 20:12-18; 24–25; Jeremiah 39:1-10
· Daniel in Babylon, Daniel 1–4
· released Israelite captives, Ezra 2

Balaam (BAY-lum) *a prophet from Midian.*
· asked by Balak to prophesy, Numbers 22–24; 2 Peter 2:15-16; Revelation 2:14
· death of, Numbers 31:8

balm, *oil from a plant used as medicine,* Genesis 37:25; Jeremiah 8:22; 51:8; Ezekiel 27:17

Baptist, John the (BAP-tist) *someone who baptizes. John, a relative of Jesus, was called this because he baptized many people.* Matthew 3:1-6
· condemned Pharisees and Sadducees, Matthew 3:7-10

- preached about Jesus, Matthew 3:11-12
- baptized Jesus, Matthew 3:13-17
- in prison, Matthew 11:1-6; Luke 7:18-23
- described by Jesus, Matthew 11:7-12; 17:10-13; Luke 7:24-28
- death of, Matthew 14:1-12; Mark 6:14-29
- baptism of, Matthew 21:25-26; Acts 10:37; 18:25; 19:3-4
- Jesus mistaken for, Matthew 16:13-14; Mark 8:27-28; Luke 9:18-19

baptism (BAP-tiz-em) *dipping or immersing.*
- by John, Matthew 3:6; Mark 1:4; Luke 3; Acts 19:3
- of Jesus, Matthew 3:13-17
- examples of, Acts 2:38-41; 8:36-38; 16:15,33
- with fire, Matthew 3:11; Luke 3:16
- with the Holy Spirit, Mark 1:8; Acts 1:5; 11:16

Barabbas (bah-RAB-us) *a robber who had murdered someone in Jerusalem. He was freed instead of Jesus.* Matthew 27:15-26; Mark 15:6-11

Barak (BAY-rak) *a leader of Israel's army when Deborah was judge,* Judges 4–5

Bar-Jesus, See "Elymas."

barley (BAR-lee) *a type of grain.*
- harvest of, Ruth 1:22; 2:17,23; 2 Samuel 21:9
- loaves of, John 6:9-13

barn
- storing in, Matthew 6:26
- rich man's, Luke 12:16-20

Barnabas (BAR-nah-bus) *an encourager who helped the apostles,* Acts 4:36; 11:23
- worked with Paul, Acts 11:26; 13–15
- influenced by hypocrites, Galatians 2:13

Bartholomew (bar-THOL-oh-mew) *one of the twelve apostles of Jesus,* Matthew 10:3; Mark 3:18; Luke 6:14; Acts 1:13

Bartimaeus (bar-teh-MAY-us) *a blind man who was healed by Jesus,* Mark 10:46-52

Baruch (BAH-rook) *a friend of the prophet Jeremiah,* Jeremiah 36

Bathsheba (bath-SHE-buh) *the mother of Solomon and wife of David,* 2 Samuel 11–12:25; 1 Kings 1–2; 22

beatitude (bee-A-ti-tyood) *blessed or happy; often used for Jesus' teaching in Matthew 5:3-12; Luke 6:20-22.*

Beelzebul (bee-EL-ze-bull) *false god of the Philistines; in the New Testament it often refers to the devil.*
- name for Satan, Matthew 12:24; Mark 3:22; Luke 11:15

Beersheba (beer-SHE-buh) *the town farthest south in the land of Judah,* 2 Samuel 3:10; 2 Chronicles 30:5
- Abraham made an agreement there, Genesis 21:14-34

beg
- Jesus begged by demons, Matthew 8:28-34; Mark 5:1-13; Luke 8:26-33
- Jesus begged by people, Matthew 14:36; Mark 7:24-26,32; 8:22

beggar
- Bartimaeus, Mark 10:46-52
- Lazarus, Luke 16:19-31
- at Beautiful Gate, Acts 3:1-10
- man born blind, John 9:1-12

Bel, *a false god of the Babylonians,* Jeremiah 50:2; 51:44

believe
- in God, Acts 16:34; Romans 4:24
- in Jesus, Matthew 18:6; John 12:44; 14:11-12; 1 John 5:10
- in the Good News, Mark 1:15; 11:24; Acts 15:7
- rewards of believing, Matthew 21:22; John 20:31; 1 Thessalonians 2:13
- a lie, 2 Thessalonians 2:11

believers (be-LEE-vers) *the followers of Jesus,* John 3:16; Acts 4:32; 5:14; Galatians 6:10

Belshazzar (bell-SHAZ-er) *a ruler of Babylon,* Daniel 5

Belteshazzar (BELL-teh-SHAZ-er) *the Babylonian name that Nebuchadnezzar gave to Daniel,* Daniel 4:8; 5:12

Benaiah (bee-NAY-uh) *the captain of David's bodyguard,* 2 Samuel 23:20-23
- commander of Solomon's army, 1 Kings 2:34-35

Ben-Hadad (ben-HAY-dad) *two or three Syrian kings who often fought against Israel,* 1 Kings 20:1-34; 2 Kings 6:24–8:15

Benjamin (BEN-jah-min) *the youngest son of Jacob and Rachel.*
- birth of, Genesis 35:16-20
- reunited with Joseph, Genesis 42–45

Bernice (bur-NY-see) *the oldest daughter of Herod Agrippa I,* Acts 25:13–26:32

Bethany (BETH-uh-nee) *a small town about two miles from Jerusalem.*
- home of Mary, Martha, and Lazarus, John 11:1; 12:1
- home of Simon, Mark 14:3

Bethel (BETH-el) *a town about twelve miles north of Jerusalem.*
- named by Jacob, Genesis 28:10-19
- Jeroboam built idols there, 1 Kings 12:26-33

Bethesda (be-THES-da) See "Bethzatha, pool of."

Bethlehem (BETH-le-hem) *a small town five miles from Jerusalem.*
- hometown of King David, 1 Samuel 16:1,13
- birthplace of Jesus, Matthew 2:1; Luke 2:15-17

Bethsaida (beth-SAY-ih-duh) *a city in Galilee and home of Peter, Andrew, and Philip,* John 1:44; 12:21
- rejected Jesus, Matthew 11:20-21; Luke 10:13

Bethzatha, pool of (beth-ZAY-tha) *a pool in Jerusalem near the Sheep Gate.*
- Jesus healed a man there, John 5:1-18

betray (be-TRAY) *to turn against.*
- families against each other, Mark 13:12-13
- Jesus betrayed, Matthew 26:20-25; Mark 14:18-46; John 13:2-30

birds
- created by God, Genesis 1:20-21
- saved by Noah, Genesis 6:19-20; 7:1-3
- unclean, Leviticus 11:13-19
- cared for by God, Matthew 6:25-27; Luke 12:24

birth
- spiritual birth, John 1:13; 3:3-8; 1 Peter 1:23

bishop, See "elder."

bitter
- water, Exodus 15:22-25; Numbers 5:18-27; Revelation 8:11
- herbs, Exodus 12:8

bitterness (BIT-er-nes) *sorrow or pain; anger or hatred.*
- warning against, Acts 8:23; Ephesians 4:31; James 3:14

blasphemy (BLAS-feh-mee) *saying things against God or not showing respect for God.*
- examples of, 1 Timothy 1:13; Revelation 13:6
- warnings against, Matthew 12:31-32; Mark 3:28-29
- Jesus accused of, Matthew 9:3; 26:65; Mark 2:6-7; John 10:36

blessing (BLES-ing) *a gift from God; asking God's favor on.*
- promised to Abraham, Genesis 12:1-3
- Isaac blessed Jacob, Genesis 27:1-41
- from God, Acts 3:25; Romans 10:12; 15:27; Hebrews 6:7
- by Jesus, Mark 10:16; Luke 24:50; John 1:16
- by each other, Luke 6:28; 1 Corinthians 4:12; 1 Peter 3:9

blind
- the blind healed, Matthew 9:27-31; 15:30; Mark 8:22-26; John 9
- Saul struck blind, Acts 9:8-9
- spiritually blind, Matthew 23:16-26; John 9:35-41; 2 Peter 1:5-9

blood, *sometimes used to mean "death."*
- water turned into, Exodus 7:14-24
- used in the Passover, Exodus 12:13-23
- not to be eaten, Leviticus 3:17; Deuteronomy 12:16; 1 Samuel 14:31-34
- of animal sacrifices, Leviticus 1; 3; 4; Hebrews 9:12-13; 10:4
- of Christ, Matthew 26:28; Romans 5:9; Hebrews 9:14; 1 John 1:7

boasting, See "bragging."

boat, *ark.*
- built by Noah, Genesis 6:11-21
- of the apostles, Matthew 4:21-22; John 21:3-11
- used by Jesus, Matthew 8:23; 13:2; 14:13-34

body
- made of dust, Genesis 2:7; 3:19
- health of, Proverbs 3:7-8; 4:20-22; 14:30
- attitudes toward, Matthew 6:25; Romans 6:13; Ephesians 5:29
- warnings against misuse, Romans 8:13; 1 Corinthians 6:18-20; 1 Thessalonians 4:5

body of Christ, *sometimes means Jesus' human body; also a way of describing Christians.*
- Christ's physical body, John 2:19-21; 19:38; Acts 2:31; 1 Corinthians 11:24; 1 Timothy 3:16; 1 Peter 3:18
- the Church as Christ's spiritual body, Romans 12:5; 1 Corinthians 12:12-31; Ephesians 1:23; 4:4; 5:23

bone
- "whose bones came from my bones," Genesis 2:23
- Ezekiel's vision of, Ezekiel 37:1-14
- none of Jesus' bones to be broken, John 19:36

book, *parchments, scroll.*
- Book of the Teachings, Deuteronomy 30:10; Joshua 1:8; 2 Chronicles 34:14-32; Ezra 8
- book of life, Philippians 4:3; Revelation 3:5; 13:8; 20:12; 21:27
- "Jesus did many other miracles. . .not written in this book." John 20:30
- "the whole world would not be big enough for all the books," John 21:25

bottomless pit, *the place where the devil and his demons live,* Luke 8:31; Revelation 9:1-11; 11:7; 17:8; 20:1-3

box of Scriptures, *small leather boxes that some Jews tied to their foreheads and left arms; also called "phylacteries" or "frontlets."*
- held the Law of Moses, Deuteronomy 6:6-8
- Jesus criticized misuse of, Matthew 23:5

bragging, *boasting.*
- warnings against, Proverbs 27:1; 2 Corinthians 10:12-18; James 4:16; Jude 16
- about the Lord, 1 Corinthians 1:31; 2 Corinthians 10:17; Galatians 6:14

bread, *the most important food in New Testament times; usually made of barley or wheat.*
- to feed 5,000 people, Matthew 14:13-21; Mark 6:30-44; Luke 9:10-17; John 6:1-13
- to feed 4,000 people, Matthew 15:32-39; Mark 8:1-10
- Jesus, the bread of life, John 6:25-59
- "A person does not live by eating only bread," Matthew 4:4; Luke 4:4
- "Give us the food we need for each day," Luke 11:3
- in the Lord's Supper, Luke 22:19; Acts 20:7; 1 Corinthians 10:16; 11:17-34

bread that shows we are in God's presence, *twelve loaves of bread that were kept on the table in the Holy Tent and later in the Temple; also called "Bread of the Presence" or "showbread,"* Leviticus 24:5-9
- eaten by David, Matthew 12:3-4; Mark 2:25-26; Luke 6:4

bride, Song of Solomon 4:8-12
- belongs to the bridegroom, John 3:29
- of Christ, Revelation 21:2,9

bridegroom
- sun compared to, Psalm 19:5
- Jesus compared to, Matthew 9:15; Mark 2:19-20; Luke 5:34
- Jesus' story of, Matthew 25:1-13
- at Jesus' first miracle, John 2:9

brother, *a family member; people from the same country; or Christians.*
- physical brothers, Proverbs 18:24; Matthew 19:29; Mark 12:18-23
- Jesus' brothers, Matthew 13:55; Mark 3:31; John 2:12; 7:3; Acts 1:14; 1 Corinthians 9:5
- spiritual brothers, Romans 8:29; 12:10; 1 Timothy 6:2; Hebrews 2:11; 1 Peter 2:17

burn
- sacrifices, Exodus 29:10-42; Leviticus 1–4
- incense, Exodus 30:7-8; Numbers 16:40; Jeremiah 48:35; Luke 1:9
- Jericho burned by Israelites, Joshua 6:24
- idols burned by Josiah, 2 Kings 23:4-20
- jealousy like a fire, Psalm 79:5
- chaff, Matthew 3:12; Luke 3:17
- lake of burning sulfur, Revelation 21:8

burnt offerings, *a whole animal sacrificed as a gift to God.*
- rules about, Leviticus 1; 6:8-13; Numbers 28–29
- less important than obedience, 1 Samuel 15:22; Psalm 51:16-19

- less important than love, Hosea 6:6; Mark 12:32-33

bury, Matthew 8:21-22; Luke 9:59-60
- Abraham buried Sarah, Genesis 23
- Jacob not to be buried in Egypt, Genesis 47:29-30; 50:1-14
- strangers, Matthew 27:7
- in baptism, Romans 6:4

C

Caesar (SEE-zer) *a famous Roman family; used as the title of the Roman emperors.*
- Augustus, Luke 2:1
- Tiberius, Luke 3:1; 20:22; John 19:12
- Claudius, Acts 11:28; 17:7; 18:2
- Nero, Acts 25:8; 27:24; Philippians 4:22

Caesarea (SES-uh-REE-uh) *a city on the Mediterranean Sea,* Acts 10:1; 21:8; 23:32

Caesarea Philippi (SES-uh-REE-uh fih-LIP-eye) *a city at the base of Mount Hermon,* Matthew 16:13; Mark 8:27

Caiaphas (KAY-uh-fus) *the Jewish high priest from A.D. 18 to 36.*
- plotted to kill Jesus, Matthew 26:3-5; John 11:45-54
- father-in-law to Annas, John 18:13
- at Jesus' trial, Matthew 26:57-67
- questioned Peter and John, Acts 4:5-22

Cain, *the first son of Adam and Eve.*
- killed his brother Abel, Genesis 4:1-24; 1 John 3:12

Caleb (KAY-leb) *one of the twelve men Moses sent to spy out Canaan.*
- explored Canaan, Numbers 13–14
- given the city of Hebron, Joshua 14:6-15

calf
- gold idol, Exodus 32:1-20; 1 Kings 12:26-30; 2 Kings 10:28-29
- fatted, Luke 15:23,27,30

camel, Genesis 37:25; 1 Samuel 30:17; 1 Kings 10:2
- Rebekah watered Abraham's camels, Genesis 24:10-20
- "easier for a camel to go through the eye of a needle," Matthew 19:24; Mark 10:25; Luke 18:25
- "swallows a camel," Matthew 23:24

Cana (KAY-nah) *a small town near the city of Nazareth in Galilee.*
- place of Jesus' first miracle, John 2:1-11

Canaan (KAY-nun) *land God promised to the Israelites,* Leviticus 25:38; Numbers 13:2; 33:51; Psalm 105:11

Capernaum (kay-PUR-nay-um) *a city on the western shore of Lake Galilee.*
- Jesus lived there, Matthew 4:12-13
- Jesus healed there, Matthew 8:5-13; Luke 4:31-41

· rejected Jesus, Matthew 11:23-24

capital, *the top of a pillar, usually decorated with beautiful carvings.*
· in the Temple, 1 Kings 7:16-20; 2 Kings 25:17

captive
· Israelites as captives, Deuteronomy 28:41; 2 Kings 25:21; Jeremiah 30:3

cassia (CASH-ah) *a pleasant-smelling powder. Its odor is like the bark of the cinnamon plant.* Exodus 30:23-24; Psalm 45:8

census (SIN-sus) *a count of the number of people who live in an area.*
· the Israelites counted, Numbers 1:2; 26:2
· ordered by David, 1 Chronicles 21:1-2
· ordered by Augustus Caesar, Luke 2:1-3

centurion (sin-TUR-ree-un) *a Roman army officer who commanded a hundred soldiers.*
· centurion's servant healed by Jesus, Matthew 8:5-13; Luke 7:1-10
· at Jesus' death, Matthew 27:54; Mark 15:39; Luke 23:47
· Cornelius, Acts 10

Cephas (SEE-fuss) *the Aramaic word for "rock"; in Greek, "Peter." Jesus gave this name to the apostle Simon.* John 1:42

chaff (CHAF) *the husk of a head of grain. Farmers would toss the grain and chaff into the air. Since the chaff is lighter, the wind would blow it away, and the good grain would fall back to the threshing floor.*
· sinners to be destroyed like chaff, Psalms 1:4; 35:5; Matthew 3:12; Luke 3:17

Chaldeans, See "Babylonians."

change of heart and life, *repentance.*
· commanded, Matthew 3:2; Mark 1:15; Luke 13:3; Acts 3:19; 17:30
· causes of, Romans 2:4; 2 Corinthians 7:9-10
· examples of, Matthew 12:41; Luke 11:32

chariot
· Egyptians' chariots destroyed, Exodus 14:5-28
· of fire, 2 Kings 2:11; 6:17
· Ethiopian taught in a chariot, Acts 8:27-31

Chemosh (KEE-mosh) *a god of the Moabites,* Jeremiah 48:13
· worshiped by Solomon, 1 Kings 11:7

cherubim (CHAIR-uh-bim) *heavenly beings with wings and the faces of men and animals.*
· guarded the garden of Eden, Genesis 3:24
· on the Ark of the Agreement, Exodus 25:18-22; 1 Kings 6:23-28
· seen by Ezekiel, Ezekiel 10:1-20

children
· of God, John 1:12; Romans 8:14; 1 Peter 1:14; 1 John 3:1-10
· training of, Ephesians 6:4; Colossians 3:21

· obedience of, Ephesians 6:1; Colossians 3:20; 1 Timothy 3:4
· become like, Matthew 18:3-4
· "Let the little children come to me," Matthew 19:14; Mark 10:14; Luke 18:16

chosen
· Israelites chosen by God, Deuteronomy 7:7-8; 9:4-5; Isaiah 44:1
· people chosen by God, Romans 8:33; Ephesians 1:4-5; 2 Timothy 2:10; 1 Peter 1:2; 2:9
· Jesus chosen by God, Hebrews 1:2; 1 Peter 2:4

Christ (KRYST) *anointed (or chosen) one. Jesus is the Christ, chosen by God to save people from their sins.*
· active in creation, John 1:1-3; Colossians 1:15-17; Hebrews 1:2,10
· equal with God, John 5:23; 10:30; Philippians 2:6; Colossians 2:9; Hebrews 1:3
· purpose of his death, Romans 5:6; 14:9; Hebrews 9:28; 1 Peter 3:18
· gives life, John 5:21; 6:35; 10:28; 11:25; 14:6
· as Savior, Matthew 1:21; John 12:47
· as judge, Matthew 10:32-33; 25:31-46; John 5:22; Acts 17:31
· living in Christians, John 17:23; Romans 8:10; 2 Corinthians 1:21; Ephesians 3:17
· his return, Acts 1:11; 1 Thessalonians 5:1-11; Hebrews 9:28; 2 Peter 3:10
· enemy of, 1 John 2:18,22; 4:3; 2 John 7

Christians (KRIS-chuns) *Christ's followers,* Acts 11:26; 26:28; 1 Peter 4:16

church
· established by Christ, Matthew 16:18
· Christ as its head, Ephesians 1:22; 5:23; Colossians 1:18
· Christ died for, Ephesians 5:25
· activities of, Acts 12:5; 1 Corinthians 14:26-40; 1 Timothy 5:16; Hebrews 10:24-25

circumcision (SIR-kum-SIH-zhun) *the cutting off of the foreskin of the male sex organ; each Jewish boy was circumcised on the eighth day after he was born; this was done as a sign of the agreement God had made with his people, the Jews.*
· commanded by God, Genesis 17; Leviticus 12:1-3
· spiritual circumcision, Philippians 3:3; Colossians 2:11

city of refuge, See "safety, city of."

Claudius (CLAW-dee-us) *the fourth Roman emperor. He ruled from A.D. 41 to 54.* Acts 11:28; 17:7; 18:2

clean, *the state of a person, animal, or action that is pleasing to God. Under the Teachings of Moses, unclean animals could not be eaten. People who were considered clean could live and serve God normally.*

- clean and unclean animals, Deuteronomy 14:1-21; Mark 7:19; Acts 10
- clean and unclean people, Leviticus 13
- spiritually clean, Ephesians 5:26; Hebrews 9:14; 2 Peter 1:9

Cleansing, Day of, *the Day of Atonement; the most special day of the year for the Israelites when the high priest could go into the Most Holy Place. Animals were sacrificed for the sins of the people as a sign that people were cleansed of their sins for a year.*
- rules about, Leviticus 23:26-32; 25:9

cloud
- Israel led by pillar of cloud, Exodus 13:21
- cloud as small as a fist, 1 Kings 18:44
- Jesus leaves and will return in clouds, Luke 21:27; Acts 1:9; 1 Thessalonians 4:17; Revelation 1:7

Colossae (koh-LAH-see) *a city in the country of Turkey,* Colossians 1:1-2

comfort, *to help ease someone's pain, grief, or trouble.*
- bad comforters, Job 16:2
- by shepherd's rod, Psalm 23:4
- from God, Isaiah 49:13; Matthew 5:4; 2 Corinthians 1:3-4
- from the Holy Spirit, John 14:16-18

commands
- to be taught, Deuteronomy 6:1-7; Matthew 5:19
- to be obeyed, Deuteronomy 8:6; Proverbs 19:16; John 15:10
- a new command, John 13:34
- to love, Galatians 5:14; 1 Timothy 1:5; 2 John 6

communion (KUH-myu-nyun) See "Lord's Supper."

complain
- Pharisees complained, Luke 5:30
- disciples complained, John 6:61
- warnings against, Philippians 2:14

concubine (KON-kyu-bine) See "slave woman."

condemn (kun-DIM) *to judge someone guilty of doing wrong,* John 3:16-18; Romans 2:1; 8:1

coney, See "rock badger."

confess
- admitting sin, Psalm 32:5; Proverbs 28:13; James 5:16; 1 John 1:9
- admitting Christ is Lord, Romans 10:9-10; Philippians 2:11; 1 Timothy 6:12; 1 John 4:2-3

confidence (KON-fuh-dens) *a feeling of assurance; trust.*
- from the Lord, 2 Thessalonians 3:4; 2 Timothy 1:7
- in Christ, Philippians 4:13

- before God, 1 John 3:21

conscience (KON-shunts) *a person's belief about what is right and wrong.*
- Paul's good conscience, Acts 23:1
- commanded to have a good conscience, 1 Timothy 3:9; Hebrews 9:14
- a troubled conscience, Hebrews 10:22; 1 John 3:20
- a corrupt conscience, 1 Timothy 4:2; Titus 1:15

contentment, *satisfaction.*
- Paul learned, Philippians 4:11
- with possessions, Luke 3:14; 1 Timothy 6:6; Hebrews 13:5

conversion (kon-VER-zhun) *a person's turning toward God and becoming a Christian.*
- examples of, Acts 9:1-22; 11:19-21; 1 Thessalonians 1:9

coral (KOR-al) *a type of limestone that forms in the ocean,* Job 28:18; Ezekiel 27:16

Corinth (KOR-inth) *a large seaport in the country of Greece.*
- Paul preached there, Acts 18:1-11
- Paul's letters to the church there, 1 and 2 Corinthians

Cornelius (kor-NEEL-yus) *a Roman army officer in charge of a hundred soldiers,* Acts 10

cornerstone, *the most important stone at the corner of the base of a building; Jesus is called the cornerstone of the new law.*
- Christ as the cornerstone, Ephesians 2:20; 1 Peter 2:4-8

council (KOWN-s'l) *or meeting; the highest Jewish court in the days of Jesus.*
- Jesus before the council, Matthew 26:57-68; Mark 14:53-65
- apostles before the council, Acts 4:1-22; 22:30–23:10
- Stephen before the council, Acts 6:18–7

courage
- need for, Joshua 1:6-9; Psalm 27:14; 1 Corinthians 16:13; Philippians 1:20
- examples of, Acts 4:13; 5:17-32; 20:22-24

court, courtyard, *part of a building that has walls, but no roof. The Temple had four courts:*
- the Court of the Non-Jews (Gentiles), a large open area just inside the walls of Herod's Temple, Mark 11:15-17; John 10:23; Acts 3:11
- the Court of Women, the next area, where both men and women were allowed, Mark 12:41-44
- the Court of Israel, the inner area of the Temple, where only Jewish men were allowed
- the Court of the Priests, the innermost court in the Temple, where only priests were allowed, Matthew 23:35

covenant (KUV-eh-nant) See "agreement."

covet (KUV-et) *to want strongly something that belongs to someone else.*
· forbidden by God, Exodus 20:17; Romans 13:9; Hebrews 13:5

creation
· of the world, Genesis 1–2; Job 38–41; Psalm 8; Isaiah 40:21-26; John 1:1-3; Hebrews 11:3

creator, *one who makes something out of nothing.*
· God as our Maker, Deuteronomy 32:6
· "Remember your Creator," Ecclesiastes 12:1

Crete (KREET) *an island in the Mediterranean Sea.*
· Paul visited there, Acts 27:7; Titus 1:5

cross, *two rough beams of wood nailed together; criminals were killed on crosses.*
· Jesus died on a cross, Matthew 27:31-50; Mark 15:20-37; Luke 23:26-46; John 19:16-30
· importance of, 1 Corinthians 1:18; 2:2; Galatians 6:14; Ephesians 2:16; Colossians 2:13-14
· as a symbol of death to oneself, Matthew 10:38; Luke 9:23; Romans 6:6; Galatians 5:24

crown, *a special band worn around the head.*
· a king's crown, Psalm 21:2-3; Song of Solomon 3:11; Revelation 12:3
· of thorns, Matthew 27:29; Mark 15:17; John 19:2
· of victory, 1 Corinthians 9:25; 2 Timothy 4:8; 1 Peter 5:4

crucifixion (kroo-suh-FIK-shun) *to be killed on a cross.* See "cross."

cubit (KU-bit) *a measurement in Bible times; about eighteen inches,* Revelation 21:17

cud, *an animal's food that is chewed slightly, swallowed, brought up, then chewed more completely a second time,* Leviticus 11; Deuteronomy 14

cup
· of the king of Egypt, Genesis 40:11
· of Joseph, Genesis 44:1-17
· of Lord's Supper, Matthew 26:27-29; Mark 14:22-25; Luke 22:17-20; 1 Corinthians 11:25-29
· of anger, Isaiah 51:17-23
· of water, Matthew 10:42; Mark 9:41

cupbearer, *the officer who tasted and served the king his wine.*
· to the king of Egypt, Genesis 40
· Nehemiah, cupbearer to Artaxerxes, Nehemiah 1:11

curse
· from God, Deuteronomy 11:26-29; John 7:49; Galatians 3:10-13

· forbidden to people, Matthew 15:4; Romans 12:14; James 3:9-10
· response to, Luke 6:28; 1 Corinthians 4:12

curtain
· of the Holy Tent, Exodus 26:1-2; 36:9
· of the Temple, Matthew 27:51; Mark 15:38; Luke 23:45

Cush, a country in Africa, Genesis 2:13; Psalm 68:31; Isaiah 18; 20

Cush, grandson of Noah, Genesis 10

Cyprus (SY-prus) *an island in the Mediterranean Sea,* Acts 11:19-20; 13:4; 15:39

Cyrene (sy-REE-nee) *a city in North Africa,* Acts 2:10; 6:9
· Simon of, Matthew 27:32; Mark 15:21; Luke 23:26

Cyrus (SY-rus) *a king of Persia,* Daniel 1:21
· sent captives home, Ezra 1; 6
· chosen by God, Isaiah 44:28–45:13

D

Dagon (DAY-gon) *a false god of the Philistines,* Judges 16:23; 1 Samuel 5:2-7; 1 Chronicles 10:10

Damascus (duh-MAS-kus) *a city forty miles east of Lake Galilee.*
· a chief city of Syria, 1 Kings 15:18; 2 Chronicles 24:23
· condemned by Amos, Amos 1:3,5
· Paul converted there, Acts 9:1-22

Dan, a city
· Israel's most northern city, Judges 20:1; 2 Samuel 16:11

Dan, son of Jacob, Genesis 30:6; 49:16-17; Joshua 19:40-48

Daniel (DAN-yel) *a Hebrew captive taken to Babylon as a young man.*
· taken to Babylon, Daniel 1:1-6
· became king's servant, Daniel 1:7-21
· explained Nebuchadnezzar's dreams, Daniel 2; 4
· read the writing on the wall, Daniel 5
· thrown into lions' den, Daniel 6
· his visions, Daniel 7; 8; 10
· a prophet, Matthew 24:15

Darius Hystaspes (dah-RYE-us his-TAHS-peez) *a ruler of Persia who allowed the Jews to finish rebuilding the Temple,* Ezra 5–6

Darius the Mede, *the king of Persia who made Daniel an important ruler under him,* Daniel 5:31–6:28; Haggai 1:1; Zechariah 1:1

darkness, *having no light; a symbol of evil.*
· before creation, Genesis 1:2
· as a plague, Exodus 10:21-23

- at Jesus' death, Matthew 27:45; Mark 15:33; Luke 23:44-45
- spiritual, John 1:5; Romans 13:12; Colossians 1:13
- as punishment, Matthew 8:12; 2 Peter 2:17; Jude 6; 13

David (DAY-vid) *Israel's greatest king.*
- son of Jesse, 1 Samuel 16:13-23
- played harp for Saul, 1 Samuel 16:14-23
- killed Goliath, 1 Samuel 17
- friend of Jonathan, 1 Samuel 18:1-4; 19:1-7; 20
- chased by Saul, 1 Samuel 18–19; 23:7-29
- protected Saul, 1 Samuel 24; 26
- became king, 2 Samuel 2:1-7; 5:1-14
- married Bathsheba, 2 Samuel 11–12:25
- reign of, 2 Samuel 5–1 Kings 1
- not allowed to build the Temple, 2 Samuel 7:1-17
- death of, 1 Kings 2:1-11
- Jesus as son of David, Matthew 22:42-45; Luke 1:27; 20:41-44

deacon (DEE-kun) *a person chosen to serve the church in special ways,* Philippians 1:1; 1 Timothy 3:8-13

Dead Sea, *large lake at the south end of the Jordan River. Several small streams flow into it, but it has no outlet. It is so salty that nothing lives in it. It is also called the "Sea of Arabah," the "Salt Sea," and the "Eastern Sea."* Genesis 14:3; Numbers 34:3,12; Joshua 3:16

deaf, *unable or unwilling to hear.*
- healed, Matthew 11:5; Luke 7:22
- and dumb spirit, Mark 9:25

death
- a result of sin, Genesis 2:16-17; Romans 5:12; 6:23; 1 Corinthians 15:21
- Christ's victory over, 1 Corinthians 15:24-26,54-57; 2 Timothy 1:10; Hebrews 2:14; Revelation 1:18
- spiritual death, Ephesians 2:1; Colossians 2:13

Deborah (DEB-oh-rah) *the only woman judge over Israel,* Judges 4–5

Decapolis (dee-KAP-oh-lis) *ten towns in an area southeast of Lake Galilee,* Matthew 4:25; Mark 5:20; 7:31

Delilah (dee-LYE-luh) *an evil Philistine woman whom Samson loved,* Judges 16:4-20

Demas (DEE-mus) *a Christian who helped the apostle Paul when Paul was in prison.*
- worked with Paul, Colossians 4:14; Philemon 24
- left Paul, 2 Timothy 4:10

Demetrius (deh-MEE-tree-us) *a silver worker in Ephesus,* Acts 19:23-27,38

demon, *an evil spirit from the devil. Sometimes demons lived in people, but Jesus could make them come out.*
- people possessed by, Matthew 8:28-32; 9:32-33; Mark 7:24-30; 9:17-29
- Jesus accused of demon possession, Mark 3:22; John 7:20; 8:48; 10:20-21
- demons recognized Jesus, Mark 1:23-26; 3:11-12; 5:7-8; Acts 19:15; James 2:19

deny (di-NY) *refusing to believe the truth.*
- denying Christ, Matthew 10:32-33; 2 Timothy 2:12; 1 John 2:22-23
- Peter denied Christ, Matthew 26:34-35,69-75

descendants (de-SIN-dants) *family members who are born to a person or his children; grandchildren, great-grandchildren, great-great-grandchildren and so on,* Genesis 13:14-16; 15:12-16

devil (DEV-'l) *Satan; a spirit and the enemy of God and humans.*
- Jesus tempted by, Matthew 4:1-11; Luke 4:1-13
- children of, John 8:41-44; Acts 13:10; 1 John 3:7-10
- people to oppose, Ephesians 4:27; 6:11; James 4:7

Didymus (DID-ee-mus) *another name for Thomas, one of Jesus' apostles,* John 11:16; 20:24; 21:2

disciple (dih-SYE-p'l) See "follower."

disease
- a result of sin, Exodus 15:26; Deuteronomy 7:15; 28:60-61
- healed by Jesus, Matthew 4:23-24; 15:30-31; 21:14; Luke 7:21
- healed by apostles, Acts 5:12-16; 9:32-35; 14:8-10; 19:11-12; 28:8-9

disobedience
- brought sin, Romans 5:19
- to be punished, 2 Corinthians 10:6; Hebrews 4:11

divide
- heavens and earth, Genesis 1:6-8
- Red Sea, Exodus 14:16,21
- family against itself, Matthew 12:25; Mark 3:25; Luke 11:17

divorce
- teachings about, Deuteronomy 22:13-19,28-29; 24:1-4; Matthew 5:31-32; 19:1-12; 1 Corinthians 7:10-16

dog
- drinking water like a dog, Judges 7:5-6
- returns to its vomit, Proverbs 26:11; 2 Peter 2:22
- licked Ahab's blood, 1 Kings 22:38
- licked Lazarus's sores, Luke 16:20-21

door
- Jesus as the door, John 10:1

- "Knock, and the door will open," Luke 11:9-10
- "I stand at the door and knock." Revelation 3:20

donkey
- Balaam's, Numbers 22:21-30
- jawbone of, Judges 15:15-17
- ridden by Jesus, Matthew 21:1-7

Dorcas (DOR-kus) *Tabitha; a Christian woman known for helping the poor.*
- raised from the dead, Acts 9:36-43

dove, *a small bird similar to a pigeon; often a symbol for love, peace, and the Holy Spirit.*
- sent out by Noah, Genesis 8:8-12
- form taken by the Spirit of God, Matthew 3:16; Mark 1:10
- sellers of, John 2:14-16

dreams
- Joseph's, Genesis 37:1-11
- the king of Egypt's, Genesis 41:1-36
- Nebuchadnezzar's, Daniel 2; 4
- angel appeared to Joseph, Matthew 1:20-21; 2:13,19
- "your old men will dream dreams," Acts 2:17

drunkenness
- Noah became drunk, Genesis 9:20-23
- warnings against, Romans 13:13; 1 Corinthians 6:10; Ephesians 5:18; 1 Peter 4:3

E

eagle
- "to rise up as an eagle," Isaiah 40:31

earth
- creation of, Genesis 1:9-10; Jeremiah 51:15
- belongs to God, Exodus 19:5; Psalm 24:1

earthquake
- experienced by Elijah, 1 Kings 19:11-12
- at the death of Jesus, Matthew 27:51-54
- at Jesus' resurrection, Matthew 28:2
- experienced by Paul and Silas, Acts 16:25-26

Ebal (EE-buhl) *a mountain in Samaria next to Mount Gerizim.*
- place to announce curses, Deuteronomy 11:29; 27:12-13; Joshua 8:30-35

Eden, garden of (EE-den) *the home God created for Adam and Eve,* Genesis 2:8–3:24; Ezekiel 36:35; Joel 2:3

Edom (EE-dum) *Esau; the land where Esau's descendants lived.*
- the land of Esau, Genesis 36:8-9
- refused to let Israelites pass through, Numbers 20:14-21; Judges 11:17-18
- broke away from Judah, 2 Kings 8:20-22
- to be punished, Jeremiah 49:7-22; Ezekiel 25:12-14; Obadiah

education
- of Moses, Acts 7:22

- of children, Deuteronomy 6:1-7
- brings wisdom, Proverbs 8:33; 22:6

Eglon (EGG-lon) *a king of Moab,* Judges 3:12-25

Egypt (EE-jipt) *a country in the northeast part of Africa.*
- Joseph there, Genesis 39–50
- Israelites there, Genesis 46:5-34; Exodus 1; Acts 7:9-38
- Israelites left, Exodus 12:31-51
- Jesus there, Matthew 2:13-15

Ehud (EE-hud) *the second judge of Israel,* Judges 3:12-30

elder (EL-der) *older men who led God's people; appointed leaders in the church.*
- leaders of the Jews, Numbers 11:16-25; Deuteronomy 19:11-12; Matthew 21:23; Acts 4:5-7
- leaders of the church, Acts 11:30; 14:23; 15:2; 16:4
- duties and qualities, Acts 20:28; 1 Timothy 3:1-7; Titus 1:6-9; 1 Peter 5:1-3

Eleazar (el-ee-A-zar) *son of Aaron.*
- birth of, Exodus 6:23-25
- Moses became angry with, Leviticus 10:16-20
- a high priest, Numbers 3:32
- divided the promised land, Numbers 34:17

election, *process of selecting.* See "chosen."

Eli (EE-lye) *a priest and the next-to-last judge of Israel.*
- trained Samuel, 1 Samuel 1:9-28; 2:11; 3
- didn't discipline his sons, 1 Samuel 2:12-36
- death of, 1 Samuel 4:1-18

Elihu (ee-LYE-hew) *the fourth of Job's friends to try to explain Job's troubles,* Job 32–37

Elijah (ee-LIE-juh) *a prophet who spoke for God.*
- fed by ravens, 1 Kings 17:1-6
- brought boy to life, 1 Kings 17:7-24
- against prophets of Baal, 1 Kings 18:1-40
- condemned Ahab, 1 Kings 21:17-29
- taken to heaven, 2 Kings 2:1-12
- appeared with Jesus, Matthew 17:1-13; Mark 9:2-13; Luke 9:28-36

Elisha (ee-LYE-shuh) *the prophet who took Elijah's place as God's messenger.*
- received Elijah's spirit, 2 Kings 2:9-14
- helped a Shunammite woman, 2 Kings 4:1-36
- miracles of, 2 Kings 2:19-22; 4:38-44; 6:1-7
- healed Naaman, 2 Kings 5
- death of, 2 Kings 13:14-20

Elizabeth (ee-LIZ-uh-beth) *the wife of Zechariah, a priest.*
- mother of John the Baptist, Luke 1:5-25,57-66
- visited by Mary, Luke 1:39-45

Elkanah (el-KAY-nuh) *the father of Samuel,* 1 Samuel 1–2:11

Elymas (EL-ih-mus) *Bar-Jesus; a magician in the city of Paphos in Cyprus,* Acts 13:4-12

Emmaus (ee-MAY-us) *a town seven miles from Jerusalem.*
· Jesus appeared to disciples near there, Luke 24:13-39

encourage
· encouragement from God, Romans 15:4-5
· Christians to encourage each other, 1 Thessalonians 5:14; 2 Timothy 4:2; Hebrews 3:13; 10:24-25
· examples of encouragement, Acts 11:23; 13:15; 15:31-32

endurance, See "patience."

enemy
· attitude toward, Exodus 23:4-5; Matthew 5:43-48; Luke 6:27-36; Romans 12:20
· God's enemies, Romans 5:10; Philippians 3:18-19; James 4:4

enemy of Christ, *the anti-Christ,* 1 John 2:18,22; 4:3; 2 John 7

Enoch (E-nuk) *a man who walked with God,* Genesis 5:21-24; Hebrews 11:5

enrollment, See "census."

envy, See "jealousy."

Epaphras (EP-ah-fruhs) *a Christian who started the church at Colossae,* Colossians 1:7-8; 4:12-13; Philemon 23

Epaphroditus (ee-PAF-ro-DYE-tus) *a Christian in the church at Philippi,* Philippians 2:25-30; 4:18

ephah (EE-fah) *a common measurement for dry materials, about twenty quarts,* Exodus 16:36

Ephesus (EF-eh-sus) *the capital city in the Roman state of Asia.*
· Paul's work there, Acts 18:18-20; 1 Corinthians 16:8-9
· church there, Ephesians 1:1; Revelation 2:1-7

ephod (EF-ahd) See "vest, holy."

Ephraim (EE-frah-im) *Joseph's younger son,* Genesis 41:50-52; 48:8-20
· descendants of, Numbers 26:35; Joshua 16:5-10

equality (ee-KWAHL-eh-tee) *being identical in value.*
· in death, Ecclesiastes 3:19-20
· of Jewish and non-Jewish people, Romans 10:12
· in Christ, Galatians 3:26-28

Esau (EE-saw) See "Edom."

Esther (ES-ter) *a Jewish girl who became the wife of Ahasuerus, king of Persia,* Esther 1–10
· became queen, Esther 1–2:18

· learned of the plan to kill the Jews, Esther 3–4
· saved the Jews, Esther 5–8

eternal, See "forever."

eternal life, *the new kind of life promised to those who follow Jesus.*
· conditions for, Mark 10:17-31; John 3:14-15; 12:25; 17:3; Galatians 6:7-8
· source of, John 6:27-29; 10:28; Titus 1:2; 1 John 5:11-12

Ethiopia, earlier called "Cush." See "Cush."

eunuch (YOU-nuk) *a man who cannot have sexual relations. In Bible times, eunuchs were often high officers in royal palaces or armies.* 2 Kings 9:32; Esther 2:3; Isaiah 56:3-5; Acts 8:26-40

Euphrates (you-FRAY-teez) *a long, important river in Bible lands.*
· in the garden of Eden, Genesis 2:10-14
· a boundary, Genesis 15:18; 1 Kings 4:21; 2 Kings 24:7

Eutychus (YOU-ti-cus) *a young man in the city of Troas who was brought back to life,* Acts 20:7-12

evangelist (ee-VAN-juh-list) *someone who tells the Good News.*
· Philip, the evangelist, Acts 21:8
· as a gift from Christ, Ephesians 4:11

Eve (EEV) *the first woman.*
· created by God, Genesis 2:18-25
· tricked by Satan, Genesis 3; 2 Corinthians 11:3; 1 Timothy 2:13-14

everlasting, *living forever; eternal.*
· God, Genesis 21:33; Nehemiah 9:5; Isaiah 40:28
· Christ, Isaiah 9:6
· kingdom, Daniel 4:3; 2 Peter 1:11
· fire, Matthew 18:8,25,41
· gospel, Revelation 14:6

evil
· warnings against, Amos 5:15; Romans 12:9; 1 Thessalonians 5:22
· to be punished, Proverbs 24:20; Isaiah 13:11

evil spirit, See "demon."

eye
· "eye for eye," Exodus 21:23-24; Matthew 5:38
· wood in, Matthew 7:3-5; Luke 6:41-42

eyewitness, *one who sees an occurrence and reports on it.*
· of Jesus' life, Luke 1:2; 2 Peter 1:16; 1 John 1:1

Ezekiel (ee-ZEEK-yel) *a prophet during the time the Jews were captured by the Babylonians,* Ezekiel 1:3
· his vision of dry bones, Ezekiel 37:1-14

Ezra (EZ-ra) *the leader of a group of Israelites who were allowed to return to Jerusalem from Babylon,* Ezra 7–10; Nehemiah 8

F

faith (FAYTH) *belief and trust.*
· definition of, Hebrews 11:1
· sources of, Romans 1:20; 10:17
· examples of, Matthew 8:5-10; 15:21-28; Hebrews 11
· power of, Matthew 17:20-21; Ephesians 6:16
· made right with God by, Romans 4:3; 5:1; Philippians 3:9
· salvation by, Mark 16:15-16; John 5:24; 20:31; Romans 10:9; Galatians 2:16
· blessings by, Galatians 3:1-14; Ephesians 3:12; 1 Peter 1:5
· continue in, 2 Corinthians 13:5; Colossians 1:23; 1 Timothy 1:19; 2 Timothy 2:22
· lack of, Matthew 8:26; 14:31; 16:8

faithful (FAYTH-ful) *honest, loyal, true.*
· God is faithful, Deuteronomy 32:3-4; Isaiah 49:7; 2 Timothy 2:13; Hebrews 3:6; Revelation 19:11
· God's people must be faithful, Matthew 25:21; Revelation 2:10; 14:12; 17:14

fall, *sometimes used to describe the first sin.*
· Adam and Eve sinned, Genesis 3

false
· gods, Exodus 20:3; Deuteronomy 4:28; 1 Chronicles 16:26
· prophets, Deuteronomy 13:1-11; 18:22; Jeremiah 14:13-16; Matthew 7:15
· Christs, Matthew 24:24; Mark 13:22
· apostles, 2 Corinthians 11:13
· brothers, Galatians 2:4
· teachers, 2 Peter 2:1

family
· of believers, Galatians 6:10; Hebrews 2:11; 1 Peter 4:17

famine (FAM-un) *a time of hunger when there is very little food.*
· in Egypt, Genesis 41:30-31,53-57
· in Moab, Ruth 1:1
· in Israel, 1 Kings 17:1
· in Jerusalem during Claudius's rule, Acts 11:27-28

fasting (FAST-ing) *giving up food for a while.*
· to show sorrow, 1 Samuel 1:11-12; 2 Samuel 12:15-22
· of Jesus, Matthew 4:1-2
· how to fast, Matthew 6:16-18
· combined with prayer, Ezra 8:23; Luke 5:33; Acts 13:1-3

father
· to be honored, Exodus 20:12; Ephesians 6:2
· commands to, Colossians 3:21
· God as Father, Matthew 6:9; 23:9; 2 Corinthians 6:18; Galatians 4:6; Hebrews 12:4-11

fear, *a feeling of being afraid, or one of deep respect.*
· of God, Matthew 10:26-31; Luke 23:40
· overcoming, 2 Timothy 1:7; Hebrews 13:6; 1 John 4:18
· "your salvation. . .with fear and trembling," Philippians 2:12

feast (FEEST) *a special meal and celebration for a certain purpose.*
· Feast of Dedication, an eight-day celebration for the Jews that showed they were thankful that the Temple had been cleansed again, John 10:22
· Feast of Harvest, see "Feast of Weeks."
· Feast of Purim (PURE-rim) reminded the Israelites of how they were saved from death during the time of Queen Esther, Esther 9:18-32
· Feast of Shelters, "Feast of Booths" or "Feast of Tents"; reminded the Israelites of how God had taken care of them when they left Egypt and lived in tents in the wilderness, Exodus 23:16; Deuteronomy 16:13-17
· Feast of Unleavened Bread, or "Passover"; reminded the Israelites how God brought them out of Egyptian slavery, Exodus 12:1-30; Numbers 28:16-25; Deuteronomy 16:1-8
· Feast of Weeks, or "Pentecost," the "Feast of Harvest," or the "Day of Firstfruits"; a feast of thanksgiving for the summer harvest, Exodus 34:22; Leviticus 23:15-22; Numbers 28:26-31

Felix (FEE-lix) *the Roman governor of Judea from A.D. 52 to 54.*
· put Paul on trial, Acts 23:23-24; 24

fellowship (FEL-o-ship) *sharing friendship and love with others.*
· with Christ, Matthew 18:20; 1 Corinthians 1:9; 1 John 1:3
· with the Holy Spirit, 2 Corinthians 13:14; Philippians 2:1
· with believers, Acts 2:42; 1 John 1:7

Festus (FES-tus) *governor of Judea after Felix.*
· put Paul on trial, Acts 25–26

fighting
· against evil, 2 Corinthians 10:3-6; Ephesians 6:12
· "fight the good fight," 1 Timothy 1:18
· "I have fought the good fight." 2 Timothy 4:7

fire, *used by God as a sign of his presence and power.*
· the burning bush, Exodus 3:1-6
· pillar of, Exodus 13:21-22
· chariot of, 2 Kings 2:11
· wrong kind of, Numbers 26:61
· fiery furnace, Daniel 3:25
· baptism of, Matthew 3:11

- of punishment, Matthew 5:22; 13:41-42; Mark 9:43; 2 Thessalonians 1:8; Hebrews 10:27
- everything destroyed by fire, 2 Peter 3:10
- evidence of the Holy Spirit, Acts 2:3

firstborn (FIRST-born) *the oldest child in a family; the firstborn son in a Jewish family received a double share of his father's wealth and became the leader of the family when his father died.*
- Esau sold his rights, Genesis 25:27-34
- Israelites as God's firstborn, Exodus 4:22; Jeremiah 31:9
- death of, Exodus 11:1-8
- given to God, Exodus 13:1-16

firstfruits (FIRST-fruits) *the first and best crops and animals the Israelites raised and gave to God at harvest time,* Exodus 34:26; Numbers 28:26; Deuteronomy 18:3-4

fish
- clean and unclean, Deuteronomy 14:9-10
- used in miracles, Matthew 14:17; Luke 5:1-7; John 21:1-13

flax (FLAKS) *a plant used to make clothing and ropes,* Exodus 9:31; Isaiah 19:9
- used by Rahab, Joshua 2:6

flood, Genesis 6:9-8; Matthew 24:37-39; 2 Peter 3:5-6

follower (FAHL-o-wer) *a person who is learning from someone else; a "disciple."*
- of John, Matthew 9:14; 11:2; Mark 2:18
- of Christ, Matthew 11:1; 28:18-20; John 19:38; Acts 6:1-7; 11:26

fool, *someone who is not wise,* Proverbs 10:8-23; 17:7-28; 26:1-12
- examples of, Matthew 7:24-27; 25:1-13
- rejects God, Psalms 14:1; 53:1; Romans 1:20-23

footwashing, *done as an act of hospitality in Bible times because people wore sandals.*
- examples of, 1 Samuel 25:41; Luke 7:44; John 13:1-17

forever
- God's love continues forever, 1 Chronicles 16:34; Psalm 136
- praise God forever, Psalm 44:8; Romans 9:5
- be with God forever, 1 Thessalonians 4:17; 1 John 2:17
- Jesus lives forever, Hebrews 7:24
- "word of the Lord will live forever," 1 Peter 1:25

forgiveness
- of others, Matthew 6:14-15; 18:21-35; Mark 11:25; Luke 17:3-4
- by God, Luke 24:47-48; Acts 10:43; Ephesians 1:7; 1 John 1:9
- not given, Matthew 12:31-32; Mark 3:28-29; Luke 12:10; John 20:19-23
- "Father, forgive them," Luke 23:34

fornication (for-ni-KAY-shun) *having sexual relations with someone to whom you are not married.* See "adultery."

fountain, Proverbs 10:11; 13:14; 14:27; 16:22

frankincense (FRANK-in-senz) *a very expensive, sweet-smelling perfume,* Exodus 30:34; Revelation 18:13
- given to Jesus, Matthew 2:11

freedom, *having liberty; not being a slave.*
- given to Jesus, Matthew 2:11
- in Christ, 2 Corinthians 3:17; Galatians 5:1; Hebrews 2:15
- from sin, Romans 6; 8:2; Hebrews 9:15
- to be used wisely, 1 Corinthians 8:9; Galatians 5:13; 1 Peter 2:16
- "truth will make you free," John 8:32

friend
- characteristics of, Proverbs 17:17; 18:24
- of Jesus, John 15:13-15
- Abraham, as a friend of God, James 2:23

frontlet, See "box of Scriptures."

fruit, *often used to mean "result."*
- spiritual, Matthew 7:15-20; John 15:1-17; Colossians 1:10
- of the Spirit, Galatians 5:22

fulfill (full-FILL) *to give the full meaning or to cause something to come true.*
- prophecy fulfilled, Matthew 2:14-15,17-18; Luke 4:16-21; 24:44-46; John 19:24

furnace
- Shadrach, Meshach, and Abednego thrown into, Daniel 3
- hell compared to, Matthew 13:42

G

Gabriel (GAY-bree-el) *an angel of God.*
- seen in a vision, Daniel 8:16; 9:21-27
- announced Jesus' birth, Luke 1:8-20,26-38

Gad, a prophet
- David's seer, 1 Samuel 22:5; 2 Samuel 24:11-19

Gad, son of Jacob
- birth of, Genesis 30:9-11
- land of, Deuteronomy 33:20-21; Joshua 22:1-4
- tribe of, Numbers 26:15

Gadarenes (gad-uh-REENZ) *people who lived in Gadara, southeast of Lake Galilee,* Matthew 8:28-34

Galatia (guh-LAY-shuh) *a district of Asia,* Acts 16:6; 18:23; Galatians 1:2; 1 Corinthians 16:1

Galilee (GAL-i-lee) *the country between the Jordan River and the Mediterranean Sea,* 2 Kings 15:29; Matthew 4:23; 21:11; John 7:1

Galilee, Lake (GAL-i-lee) *or "Sea of Galilee," "Sea of Kinnereth," "Lake of Gennesaret," "Sea of Tiberias"; a lake thirteen miles long and eight miles wide.*
· Jesus preached there, Matthew 4:12-22; 8:23-27; John 6:1-2,16-21

Gallio (GAL-ee-oh) *a Roman governor in the country of Achaia.*
· refused to punish Paul, Acts 18:12-17

Gamaliel (guh-MAY-lee-el) *a Pharisee and Jewish teacher of the Law of Moses.*
· prevented deaths of Peter and John, Acts 5:17-40
· Paul's teacher, Acts 22:1-3

gate
· Samson removed, Judges 16:3
· narrow, Matthew 7:13-14
· of heaven, Revelation 21:21

Gath, *one of the Philistines' five strong cities,* Joshua 13:3; 1 Samuel 21:10-12
· captured Ark taken there, 1 Samuel 5:1-10
· home of Goliath, 1 Samuel 17:4

Gaza (GAY-zuh) *one of the Philistines' five strong cities,* Joshua 13:3; Acts 8:26
· Samson in prison there, Judges 16

gazelle (gah-ZEL) *an animal of the antelope family; known for its beauty and speed,* Deuteronomy 12:15; 1 Chronicles 12:8

Gedaliah (ged-uh-LYE-uh) *made governor of Judah by Nebuchadnezzar after capturing Jerusalem,* 2 Kings 25:22-26; Jeremiah 39:14–41:18

Gehazi (geh-HAY-zye) *a servant of the prophet Elisha.*
· and the Shunammite woman, 2 Kings 4:8-37
· and Naaman, 2 Kings 5:1-27

Gehenna, See "Hinnom."

genealogy (jee-nee-AHL-o-jee) *a list of the descendants in a family.*
· of Jesus, Matthew 1:1-17; Luke 3:23-38

generosity (jen-uh-RAHS-et-ee) *unselfishness.*
· shown to Ruth, Ruth 2:14-16
· to the needy, Nehemiah 8:10
· rewarded, Proverbs 11:25; Matthew 7:11

Gennesaret, Lake of, See "Galilee, Lake."

Gentiles (JEN-tiles) *anyone not Jewish.*
· received the Good News, Acts 10:44-45; 11:18; Romans 11:11-15; Ephesians 3:6-8
· conflict with the Jews, Acts 15:5-11; Galatians 2:11-14

Gerasenes (GER-un-seenz) *or "Gadarenes."* See "Gadarenes."

Gerizim (GER-i-zim) *a mountain next to Mount Ebal about thirty miles north of Jerusalem.*
· blessings announced from there, Deuteronomy 11:29; 27:12; Joshua 8:33

Gethsemane (geth-SEM-uh-nee) *a garden of olive trees just outside Jerusalem.*
· Jesus arrested there, Matthew 26:36-56; Mark 14:32-50

Gibeah (GIB-ee-uh) *a city about three miles north of Jerusalem,* Judges 19:12–20:43; 1 Samuel 10:26

Gibeon (GIB-ee-uhn) *a town about six miles northwest of Jerusalem.*
· Joshua defeated Amorites there, Joshua 9–10

Gideon (GID-ee-uhn) *the judge who led Israel to defeat the Midianites,* Judges 6:1–8:35
· angel appeared to, Judges 6:11-24
· destroyed Baal idol, Judges 6:25-32
· defeated Midianites, Judges 6:33–8:21
· the sign of the fleece, Judges 6:36-40
· built an idol, Judges 8:22-27
· death of, Judges 8:28-32
· hero of faith, Hebrews 11:32-34

gifts, *talents or abilities.*
· spiritual, Romans 12:6-8; 1 Corinthians 7:7; 12; 14:1-25; Ephesians 4:7

Gihon (GYE-hohn) *a spring outside the walls of Jerusalem,* 1 Kings 1:38-39; 2 Chronicles 32:30; 33:14

Gilead (GIL-ee-ad) *the area that Israel owned east of the Jordan River,* Numbers 32; Deuteronomy 3:10-16

Gilgal (GIL-gal) *the first place the Israelites camped after entering the promised land,* Joshua 4:19–5:12

gittith (GIT-tith) *probably a musical word and a musical instrument,* Psalms 8; 81; 84

giving
· examples of generous giving, Mark 12:43; Acts 10:2; 11:29-30; 2 Corinthians 8:3-5
· proper attitude toward, Matthew 6:3-4; Romans 12:8; 1 Corinthians 13:3; 2 Corinthians 9:7

gleaning (GLEEN-ing) *to gather grain left in the field after harvest,* Ruth 2

glory, *visible sign of God's greatness.*
· appeared in a cloud, Exodus 16:10; 24:16-17
· seen by Moses, Exodus 33:18-23
· "The heavens tell the glory of God," Psalm 19:1
· seen by Ezekiel, Ezekiel 1:26-28; 3:23; 8:4
· at Jesus' birth, Luke 2:8-14
· of Jesus, Luke 9:28-32
· seen by Stephen, Acts 7:55
· in the temple in heaven, Revelation 15:8

gluttony (GLUH-tun-ee) *eating too much.*
· warnings against, Deuteronomy 21:20; Proverbs 23:20-21
· Jesus accused of, Matthew 11:19; Luke 7:34

goat
· for a sin offering, Leviticus 9:3

- divided from sheep, Matthew 25:32-33
- blood of, Hebrews 9:12-13; 10:4

God, *the One who made the world and every-thing in it.* See also "glory."
- the creator, Genesis 1; Acts 17:24; Romans 1:25
- nearness of, Acts 17:27-28; James 4:8
- goodness of, Matthew 19:17; Acts 14:17; Romans 2:4; 1 John 4:7-11
- eternal nature of, Psalm 102:24-28; 1 Timothy 1:17; 6:16
- names of, Exodus 3:13-14; 1 Timothy 6:15; Hebrews 12:9; James 1:17; 5:4
- power of, Job 9:4-19; Isaiah 40:12-31; Matthew 19:26
- mercy of, Exodus 20:6; Numbers 14:18; Ephesians 2:4
- justice of, Psalm 67:4; Acts 17:31; Romans 2:2

golden calf, *an idol made to worship false gods.*
- made by Aaron, Exodus 32:1-24
- made by Jeroboam, 1 Kings 12:26-33

golden rule, *a name often used for Jesus' command: "Do to others what you want them to do to you,"* Matthew 7:12; Luke 6:31

Golgotha (GOL-guh-thuh) *Calvary; the hill where Jesus was crucified,* Matthew 27:33; Mark 15:22; John 19:17

Goliath (go-LYE-eth) *the giant from Gath whom David killed,* 1 Samuel 17

Gomorrah (goh-MOR-ruh) *an evil city near Sodom.*
- destroyed by God, Genesis 18:17–19:29; Matthew 10:11-15; 2 Peter 2:6

Good News, *also called the "gospel." Jesus died on the cross, was buried, and came back to life so people can be saved.* Mark 1:1; Acts 5:42; 13:26-39
- power of, Romans 1:16-17; Colossians 1:5-6; 1 Corinthians 15:2
- preached by the apostles, Luke 9:6; Acts 8:25; Philippians 1:5,12-14

Goshen (GO-shen) *an area in the Nile delta of Egypt.*
- home for Joseph's family, Genesis 45:9-10; 47:1-6,27

gospel (GOS-p'l) *"good news." The first four books of the New Testament are called the gospels because they tell the good news of what Jesus has done for us.* See "Good News."

gossip
- to be avoided, Romans 1:28-32; 2 Corinthians 12:20; 1 Timothy 5:13

government (GUV-er-ment) *group of people in charge of managing and making laws for people in a country, state, or city.*

- to be obeyed, Matthew 22:15-21; Romans 13:1-7; Titus 3:1; 1 Peter 2:13-17

governor
- Joseph, governor of Egypt, Genesis 42:6
- Nehemiah, governor of Judah, Nehemiah 5:14
- Pilate, governor of Judea, Matthew 27:2
- Felix, governor of Judea, Acts 23:26

grace, *God's kindness and love shown to us, even though we do not deserve them.*
- source of, Ephesians 3:7; Hebrews 4:14-16
- saved by, Acts 15:11; Romans 3:24; Ephesians 2:5-8; 2 Timothy 1:9
- misuse of, Romans 6; Galatians 5:4; Jude 4

grandchildren
- a blessing, Ruth 4:15; Proverbs 17:6
- inherit grandparents' wealth, Proverbs 13:22

grave, See "tomb."

Great Sea, See "Mediterranean Sea."

Greece, *once the most powerful nation in southeast Europe. Northern Greece was called "Macedonia." Southern Greece was called "Achaia."*
- Paul preached there, Acts 16:11-12; 20:1-6

greed, *selfish desire for more than one's share of something.*
- never satisfied, Proverbs 27:20
- beware of, Luke 12:15
- love of money, 1 Timothy 6:10

Greek
- the language of Greece, John 19:20; Acts 21:37; Revelation 9:11
- the people from Greece, Acts 14:1; 16:1; Colossians 3:11

grief
- of David for Absalom, 2 Samuel 18:33
- of the disciples, Matthew 17:23; John 16:6

guidance (GYD-ns) *direction.*
- by God, Exodus 13:21
- of the humble, Psalm 25:9
- of the Holy Spirit, John 16:15

guilt, *fact of having done wrong; regret, shame.*
- for improper worship, 1 Corinthians 11:27
- for breaking the Law, James 2:10
- cleansed of, Job 33:9; Isaiah 6:7; Hebrews 10:22

H

Habakkuk (ha-BAK-uk) *a prophet who wrote about the same time as Jeremiah,* Habakkuk 1–3

Hades (HAY-deez) *the world of the dead,* Revelation 6:8; 20:13-14

Hagar (HAY-gar) *Sarah's slave girl.*
- gave birth to Ishmael, Genesis 16
- sent away by Sarah, Genesis 21:8-21

Haggai (HAG-ay-eye) *a prophet in Jerusalem when the Israelites came back from Babylon,* Ezra 5:1; 6:14; Haggai 1–2

half-tribe, *one of the two parts of the tribe of Manasseh. One half-tribe settled east of the Jordan and the other settled west of the Jordan.* Joshua 1:12-15; 13:8-9; 22

Ham, *the son of Noah, Genesis 6:10; 9:18-19; 10:6*

Haman (HAY-man) *the chief officer under Ahasuerus, king of Persia.*
· planned to kill the Jews, Esther 3–6
· hanged, Esther 7

hands, laying on, *a ceremony where a person places his hands upon another.*
· for healing, Mark 5:23; 6:5; Luke 4:40
· to receive the Holy Spirit, Acts 8:17-19; 19:6
· for blessing, Mark 10:16; Acts 13:3

Hannah (HAN-uh) *the mother of Samuel,* 1 Samuel 1–2:21

happiness
· of the people of God, Psalms 144:15; 146:5; Proverbs 16:20; Matthew 5:3-12
· comes from wisdom, Proverbs 3:13

Haran (HAY-ran)
· Abraham's brother, Genesis 11:26-31
· home of Abraham, Genesis 11:31–12:5

harlot, See "prostitute."

harp, *the favorite musical instrument of the Jews.*
· first played, Genesis 4:21
· played by David, 1 Samuel 16:23; 18:10-11
· to praise God, Psalms 33:2; 71:22; 150:3

harvest
· of the poor, Ruth 2
· as a symbol, Matthew 9:37-38; 13:24-30,39; Revelation 14:14-16

hate
· seven things God hates, Proverbs 6:16-19
· a time to, Ecclesiastes 3:8
· of the world toward Jesus, John 15:18
· equal to murder, 1 John 3:15
· commands against, Galatians 5:19-21; 1 John 4:19-21

head
· a part of the body, Genesis 3:15; Psalm 23:5; Matthew 8:20; 1 Corinthians 12:21; Revelation 14:14
· a leader, Ephesians 1:22; 5:23; Colossians 1:18

heal
· a time to, Ecclesiastes 3:3
· by faith, Matthew 9:21-22; James 5:15
· "Doctor, heal yourself." Luke 4:23

heart, *the mind or feelings; not the physical heart that pumps blood,* Deuteronomy 6:5; Matthew 22:37

heaven
· the home of God, Matthew 5:34; Mark 16:19; John 3:13; Revelation 4
· angel spoke from, Genesis 21:17; 22:11
· opened, Matthew 3:16; Acts 7:56; 10:11
· fire from, 2 Kings 1:10-14; 1 Chronicles 21:26
· third heaven, 2 Corinthians 12:2
· the new heaven, Revelation 21:1-4
· kingdom of, Matthew 3:2; 5:3,19-20

Hebrews (HEE-brooz) *another name for the Jewish people,* Exodus 7:16; 2 Corinthians 11:22; Philippians 3:5

Hebron (HEE-bron) *a city about twenty miles southwest of Jerusalem,* Genesis 13:18; Numbers 13:22; 2 Samuel 2:1-11

heir (AIR) *the person who inherits what belongs to a relative. Because through Christ we can be adopted children of God, Christians are heirs to God's riches.*
· Abraham's heir, Genesis 15:3-4
· heir of God, Romans 8:17; Galatians 4:7

hell
· home of the devil and his angels, 2 Peter 2:4
· future home of sinners, Matthew 10:28; 23:33; Revelation 21:8
· descriptions of, Matthew 13:42; Mark 9:47-48; James 3:6; Revelation 14:11

helmet
· worn in battle, 1 Samuel 17:5; Ezekiel 23:24
· a symbol of salvation, Isaiah 59:17; Ephesians 6:17; 1 Thessalonians 5:8

help
· the stone of help, 1 Samuel 7:12
· the Holy Spirit as helper, Romans 8:26; Philippians 1:19
· from God, Psalms 46:1; 121:1-2; Isaiah 41:10
· commanded, 1 Thessalonians 5:14; Hebrews 6:10

Herod I (HEH-rud) *"Herod the Great"; king of Palestine from 40 to 4 B.C.,* Matthew 2:1; Luke 1:5

Herod Agrippa I (uh-GRIP-a) *king of Palestine from A.D. 41 to 44,* Acts 12:1

Herod Agrippa II, *king of Palestine from A.D. 52 to 70,* Acts 25:13–26:32

Herod Antipas (AN-ti-pus) *king of Palestine from 4 B.C. to about A.D. 39,* Matthew 14:1; Mark 6:14; Luke 23:7

Herodias (heh-ROW-dee-us) *the granddaughter of Herod I.*
· asked for John's head, Matthew 14:3-12; Mark 6:17-28; Luke 3:19

Hezekiah (hez-eh-KY-uh) *one of the good kings of Judah.*
· destroyed idols, 2 Kings 18:1-8; 2 Chronicles 29–31

higgaion

- attacked by Assyria, 2 Kings 18:9–19:37; 2 Chronicles 32:1-23; Isaiah 36–37
- life extended by God, 2 Kings 20:1-11; Isaiah 38
- death of, 2 Kings 20:12-21; 2 Chronicles 32:24-33

higgaion (hig-GI-on) *probably a time to think quietly during a song,* Psalm 9:16

high place, *a place to worship gods,* 1 Kings 14:23; 2 Chronicles 31:1; 33:3

high priest, *the most important religious leader of the Jewish people.*
- rules for, Leviticus 21:10-15
- of the Jews, Exodus 29:30; Numbers 35:25; Matthew 26:3; Acts 23:2
- Jesus as, Hebrews 2:17; 3:1; 4:14–5:10; 8:1-6

Hilkiah (hil-KY-ah) *high priest when Josiah was king,* 2 Kings 22–23; 2 Chronicles 34

Hinnom, Valley of (HIN-num) *an area where trash was burned just outside of Jerusalem; also called "Gehenna,"* Joshua 15:8; 18:16; Nehemiah 11:30

Hiram (HY-rum) *king of Tyre when David and Solomon were kings over Israel.*
- supplied trees for Solomon's Temple, 2 Samuel 5:11; 1 Kings 5:1-18; 9:11-27; 10:22

Hittites (HIT-tites) *people who lived in what is now Turkey,* Genesis 23:1-16; Exodus 3:8; Joshua 1:4; 1 Samuel 11:3

holy (HO-lee) *pure, belonging to and willing to serve God.*
- holiness of God, Leviticus 11:45; Isaiah 6:3; Hebrews 12:10; Revelation 4:8
- holy kiss, Romans 16:16
- people to be holy, Ephesians 1:4; Colossians 1:22-23; 3:2; 1 Peter 1:15-16

Holy of Holies, See "Most Holy Place."

Holy Place, *a room in the Holy Tent and the Temple,* Exodus 26:31-35; 28:29; Leviticus 6:30; 1 Kings 8:10-11

Holy Spirit (HO-lee SPIH-rit) *one of the three persons of God. The Holy Spirit helped the apostles do miracles and led men to write God's word; he lives in Christians today.*
- in creation, Genesis 1:2
- living in Christians, John 14:15-17; 1 Corinthians 6:19; Galatians 4:6
- as a helper, John 14:25-26; 16:7-15; Romans 8:1-27; Galatians 5:22-25
- filled with, Luke 1:15; Acts 2:4; 7:55; 11:23-24
- sin against, Matthew 12:31; Acts 5:3; 1 Thessalonians 5:19; Hebrews 10:29

Holy Tent, See "Meeting Tent."

honest
- heart, Luke 8:15

- people, 2 Kings 12:15
- answer, Proverbs 24:26
- commanded, Mark 10:19; Philippians 4:8

honor
- for the old, Leviticus 19:32
- from God, 1 Samuel 2:30
- comes from humility, Proverbs 15:33
- to the deserving, Romans 13:7
- shown to parents, Exodus 20:12; Matthew 15:4
- shown to God, Proverbs 3:9; John 5:23; Revelation 4:9
- not shown to a prophet in his own town, Matthew 13:57

hope, *looking forward to something you really expect to happen.*
- reason for, Romans 5:3-5; 15:4; 2 Thessalonians 2:16; 1 Peter 1:13
- nature of, Romans 8:24-25
- results of, Colossians 1:5; Hebrews 6:18

Hophni (HOF-nee) *an evil son of Eli the priest,* 1 Samuel 2:12-34; 3:11–4:18

Horeb, Mount, See "Sinai."

horses, Exodus 14:9; 1 Kings 10:26-29; Psalm 33:16-17; James 3:3

Hosanna (ho-ZAN-ah) *a shout of joy in praising God,* Matthew 21:9,15; Mark 11:9; John 12:13

Hosea (ho-SEE-uh) *a prophet who lived about seven hundred years before Christ.*
- his unfaithful wife, Hosea 1
- his warnings to Israel, Hosea 2; 4–14

hospitality
- of Abraham, Genesis 18:1-16
- teachings about, Romans 12:13; 1 Timothy 3:2; 5:9-10; 1 Peter 4:9

hosts, *armies; God is called the "Lord of hosts."* See "Lord of hosts."

Huldah (HUL-duh) *a woman prophet,* 2 Kings 22:14-20; 2 Chronicles 34:22-28

humble (HUM-bul) *not bragging or calling attention to yourself.*
- Moses as example of, Numbers 12:3
- humility commanded, Luke 14:7-11; 22:24-27; Ephesians 4:2; Philippians 2:3
- Jesus' humility, Philippians 2:5-8

hunger
- feeding the hungry, Matthew 25:34-35; Romans 12:20
- spiritual, John 6:35; 1 Peter 2:2

husband
- responsibilities of, 1 Corinthians 7:3-5; Ephesians 5:25-33; Colossians 3:19; 1 Peter 3:7

hymn (HIM) *a song that teaches us about God or praises him,* Matthew 26:30; Ephesians 5:19; Colossians 3:16

- Jesus and apostles sang, Matthew 26:30; Mark 14:26
- teachings about, Ephesians 5:19; Colossians 3:16

hypocrisy (hi-POK-ri-see) *acting as if one is good when that is not true,* Matthew 23:28; 1 Peter 2:1

hypocrite (HIP-oh-krit) *a person who acts as if he is good but isn't.*
- warnings about, Matthew 6:2,5,16; 7:3-5; Luke 13:15-17
- Pharisees as hypocrites, Matthew 15:1-9; 23:13-32

hyssop (HIS-op) *a small bushy plant; marjoram,* Exodus 12:22; Leviticus 14:4,6; John 19:29

I

Iconium (eye-KOH-nee-um) *a city in Galatia where Paul preached,* Acts 14:1-7,19-23

idol (EYE-d'l) *a statue of a false god.* See also "Baal," "Chemosh," "Molech."
- worship of, 2 Kings 17:12-17; Acts 17:16-23; 19:24; Romans 1:25
- warnings against worship of, Leviticus 19:4; Deuteronomy 6:14-15; 1 Corinthians 5:10-11; 6:9-10
- Baal, 1 Kings 18:17-40
- Chemosh, Numbers 21:29
- Molech, Jeremiah 32:35

ignorance (IG-nur-rance) *a lack of knowledge.*
- not an excuse, Leviticus 5:17

image, *likeness.*
- God's, Genesis 1:26-27
- Caesar's, Luke 20:24
- the Lord's, 2 Corinthians 3:18
- Jesus in God's image, Hebrews 1:3

immorality (IM-mor-RAL-i-tee) *evil; sinfulness.* See also "sin."
- warnings against, 1 Corinthians 5:9-11; 6:9-10; Galatians 5:19-21; Ephesians 5:5

immortality (IM-mor-TAL-i-tee) *life after death,* Job 14:1-14; Daniel 12:1-2; 1 Corinthians 15:12-58; 2 Timothy 1:10. See also "eternal life."

impossible
- people cannot do, Matthew 19:26
- for God to lie, Hebrews 6:18
- without faith to please God, Hebrews 11:6

incense (IN-sents) *a spice burned to make a sweet smell.*
- altar of, Exodus 30:1-10,34-38; Revelation 8:3-5
- used in worship, Psalm 141:2
- as a gift, Matthew 2:11

inheritance (in-HEH-ri-tence) *something valuable that is handed down within a family.*

- of land, Numbers 36:8; Deuteronomy 3:28; Psalm 25:13

iniquity, See "sin."

inn, *a place for travelers to spend the night,* Luke 2:7; 10:34

innocence (IN-uh-sens) *not guilty of sin.*
- of Adam and Eve, Genesis 2:25
- declared by Job, Job 34:5
- declared by Pilate, Matthew 27:24

inspiration (IN-spi-RAY-shun) *"God-breathed." It is used to mean that the Bible writers wrote what God wanted them to write.* 2 Timothy 3:16; 2 Peter 1:20-21

Isaac (EYE-zak) *the son of Abraham and Sarah.*
- birth of, Genesis 21:1-4
- offered as a sacrifice, Genesis 22:1-19
- married Rebekah, Genesis 24
- tricked by Jacob, Genesis 27
- hero of faith, Hebrews 11:20

Isaiah (eye-ZAY-uh) *prophet who lived about seven hundred years before Christ.*
- became a prophet, Isaiah 6:1-8
- prophesied to Hezekiah, 2 Kings 19–20
- prophecies fulfilled, Matthew 3:3; 4:14; 13:14-15

Ish-Bosheth (ish-BOW-sheth) *son of Saul,* 2 Samuel 2:8–4

Ishmael (ISH-may-el) *son of Abraham and Hagar.*
- birth of, Genesis 16:2-16
- sent away from Abraham's camp, Genesis 21:8-21

Israel, kingdom of (IZ-rah-el) *the northern kingdom which had ten tribes.*
- beginning of, 1 Kings 11:27–12
- fall of, 2 Kings 17:1-18
- rulers of, 1 Kings 15:25–16; 22:51-53; 2 Kings 13; 14:23–17:6

Israel, son of Isaac, *Hebrew for "he who wrestles with God." Jacob's name was changed to Israel when he struggled with an angel at Bethel.* Genesis 32:22-28; 35:9-10. See also "Jacob."
- name given to Jacob's descendants, Genesis 49:28; Exodus 4:22; Psalm 22:23; Romans 9:3-5

Issachar (IS-uh-car) *a son of Jacob and Leah,* Genesis 30:18
- his descendants, Numbers 1:28-29; 26:23

ivory (EYE-voh-ree) *a creamy white bone that comes from elephant tusks,* 1 Kings 10:18; 22:39; Psalm 45:8; Ezekiel 27:15

J

Jabbok River (JAB-ok) *a stream about fifty miles long that runs into the Jordan River,* Numbers 21:24; Joshua 12:2; Judges 11:13

Jabesh Gilead (JAY-besh GIL-ee-ad) *a small town on the east side of the Jordan River,* Judges 21:6-14; 2 Samuel 2:4-7

Jabin, king of Hazor (JAY-bin) *led a group of kings against the Israelites,* Joshua 11:1-11

Jabin, king of Canaan, *defeated by Israel when Deborah was judge,* Judges 4

Jacob (JAY-cub) *one of the sons of Isaac.*
· cheated Esau, Genesis 25:29-34
· tricked Isaac, Genesis 27:1-29
· his dream of a ladder to heaven, Genesis 28:10-22
· tricked by his sons, Genesis 37:10-22
· moved to Egypt, Genesis 45:25–47:12
· hero of faith, Hebrews 11:20-21

Jacob's Portion (JAY-cubs POR-shun) *a name for God, meaning he cares for Jacob's people,* Jeremiah 10:16; 51:19

jailer, *a keeper of a jail.*
· of Paul and Silas, Acts 16:23

Jairus (jay-EYE-rus) *a ruler of the synagogue.*
· Jesus brought his daughter back to life, Matthew 9:18-26; Mark 5:21-43; Luke 8:40-56

James, brother of Jesus, Matthew 13:55; Acts 12:17; 21:18
· later an apostle, Galatians 1:19

James, son of Alphaeus, *an apostle,* Matthew 10:3; Mark 3:18; Luke 6:15; Acts 1:13

James, son of Zebedee, *an apostle of Jesus and a brother of the apostle John,* Matthew 10:2; Mark 10:35; Acts 12:2

Japheth (JAY-fith) *one of Noah's three sons,* Genesis 5:32; 7:13; 9:18-27; 10:1-5

Jashar, Book of, *a book mentioned in the Bible, but not part of it,* Joshua 10:12-13; 2 Samuel 1:17-27

Jason (JAY-son) *a Christian in Thessalonica,* Acts 17:5-9

jealousy
· to describe God, Exodus 20:5; 34:14; Deuteronomy 5:9
· examples of, Genesis 37:11; 1 Samuel 18:19; Matthew 27:18; Acts 5:17
· warnings against, Romans 13:13; 1 Corinthians 13:4; 1 Timothy 6:4; 1 Peter 2:1

Jebusites (JEB-you-sites) *people who lived around Jerusalem before the time of David,* Joshua 15:63; Judges 19:10-11; 2 Samuel 4:6-8

Jehoahaz, son of Jehu (jeh-HO-uh-haz) *king of Israel who lived about eight hundred years before Christ,* 2 Kings 13:1-9

Jehoahaz, son of Josiah, *king of Judah for only three months,* 2 Kings 23:31-34; 2 Chronicles 36:1-4

Jehoash (jeh-HO-ash) *a king of Israel,* 2 Kings 13:10–14:16

Jehoiachin (jeh-HO-uh-kin) *the next-to-last king of Judah.*
· surrendered to Babylon, 2 Kings 24:8-17
· in Babylon, 2 Kings 25:27-30

Jehoiada (jeh-HO-yah-duh) *the chief priest in Jerusalem during Joash's rule,* 2 Kings 11–12; 2 Chronicles 22:11–24

Jehoiakim (jeh-HO-uh-kim) *king of Judah about 600 B.C.,* 2 Kings 23:34–24:6
· tried to kill Jeremiah, Jeremiah 26:1-23
· burned Jeremiah's scroll, Jeremiah 36:1-23

Jehoram (jeh-HOR-am) *or "Joram"; the fifth king of Judah,* 2 Kings 8:16-29; 2 Chronicles 21:4-20

Jehoshaphat (jeh-HOSH-uh-fat) *one of the good kings of Judah.*
· faithful to God, 2 Chronicles 17:1-9
· appointed judges, 2 Chronicles 19:4-11
· defeated Moab and Ammon, 2 Chronicles 20

Jehovah (jeh-HOVE-uh) *a name for God; also translated "LORD,"* Exodus 3:15; 6:3; Deuteronomy 28:58; Psalm 83:18

Jehu (JEE-hew) *an army captain who became king of Israel.*
· appointed as king, 2 Kings 9:1-13
· killed Joram and Ahaziah, 2 Kings 9:14-29
· stopped Baal worship, 2 Kings 10:18-35

Jephthah (JEF-thuh) *one of the judges of Israel.*
· fought the Ammonites, Judges 11:1-29,32-33
· his vow, Judges 11:30-31,34-39
· fought the people of Ephraim, Judges 12:2-7

Jeremiah (jer-eh-MY-ah) *a prophet who warned the people of Judah,* Jeremiah 1–52
· became a prophet, Jeremiah 1:1-10
· songs of, 2 Chronicles 35:25
· his prophecies fulfilled, 2 Chronicles 36:21-22; Matthew 2:17; 27:9
· wrote a scroll, Jeremiah 36

Jericho (JEHR-ih-ko) *probably the oldest city in the world,* Mark 10:46; Luke 10:30; 19:1
· fall of, Joshua 2–6
· rebuilt, 1 Kings 16:34

Jeroboam, son of Jehoash (jeh-ro-BO-am) *a king of Israel,* 2 Kings 14:23-29; Amos 7:7-17

Jeroboam, son of Nebat, *first ruler of the northern kingdom of Israel.*
· given ten tribes by God, 1 Kings 11:26-40
· built idols, 1 Kings 12:26-33
· warned by God, 1 Kings 13:1-34
· death of his son, 1 Kings 14:1-20

Jerusalem (jeh-ROO-suh-lem) *"Zion" or "City of David"; the greatest city of Palestine.*
· the City of David, 2 Samuel 5:6-7

- captured by Babylonians, 2 Chronicles 36:15-23
- Jews returned to, Ezra 1–2
- the new Jerusalem, Galatians 4:26; Hebrews 12:22; Revelation 3:12; 21–22

Jesse (JEH-see) *father of King David,* 1 Samuel 16–17; 1 Chronicles 2:13-15; Luke 3:32; Romans 15:12

Jesus (JEE-zus) *"Savior"; the son of God.* See also "Christ," "Son of David," "Son of Man."
- birth and childhood of, Matthew 1–2; Luke 1–2
- temptation of, Matthew 4:1-11; Mark 1:12-13; Luke 4:1-13
- miracles of, Matthew 8–9; Mark 6:30-56; Luke 17:11; 22:50-51; John 2:1; 11
- appeared with Moses and Elijah, Matthew 17:1-13; Mark 9:2-13; Luke 9:28-36
- forced men from the Temple, Matthew 21:12-13; John 2:13-17
- the Last Supper, Matthew 26:17-30; Luke 22:1-20; John 13
- trial and death of, Matthew 26:57–27:66; Mark 15; Luke 22:66–23:56; John 18–19
- appearances after resurrection, Matthew 28; Mark 16; Luke 24; John 20–21; 1 Corinthians 15:5-8
- Son of God, Matthew 3:16-17; 26:63-64; John 1:14

Jethro (JETH-row) *father of Moses' wife,* Exodus 2:16-21
- advised Moses, Exodus 18

Jews (JOOZ) *first, the tribe of Judah; later, any of the twelve tribes,* Ezra 4:12; Esther 3–10; Acts 2:5
- against Jesus, John 5:16-18; 7:1,32-36; 10:25-42
- Jesus, king of, Matthew 2:2; 27:11-14,29; John 19:17-22
- and non-Jewish people, 1 Corinthians 12:13; Galatians 3:28; Colossians 3:11

Jezebel (JEZ-eh-bell) *the evil wife of King Ahab.*
- married Ahab, 1 Kings 16:31
- killed the Lord's prophets, 1 Kings 18:4-14
- killed Naboth, 1 Kings 21:1-23
- death of, 2 Kings 9:30-37

Jezreel (JEZ-reel) *the name of a town and a valley near the Jordan River,* Judges 6:33; 1 Kings 21:1; 2 Kings 8:29

Joab (JO-ab) *the commander of King David's army,* 2 Samuel 2:12-3; 10–11; 14; 18–20; 24; 1 Kings 1–2

Joanna (jo-ANN-uh) *a woman Jesus healed,* Luke 8:2-3; 23:55–24:11

Joash, Gideon's father (JO-ash)
- protected Gideon, Judges 6:28-32

Joash, son of Ahaziah, *became king of Judah when he was seven,* 2 Kings 11–12; 2 Chronicles 22:10–24

Job (JOBE) *a wealthy man who honored God.*
- ruined by Satan, Job 1–2:10
- wealth restored, Job 42:7
- example of patience, James 5:11

Joel (JO-el) *a prophet who wrote the book of Joel,* Joel 1–3; Acts 2:16

Johanan (jo-HAY-nan) *a Jewish army captain,* Jeremiah 40:8–43

John, the apostle, *one of the sons of Zebedee.*
- called by Jesus, Mark 1:19-20
- at Jesus' transfiguration, Mark 9:2
- with Jesus in Gethsemane, Mark 14:33-42
- in the early church, Acts 3–4
- writer of Revelation, Revelation 1:1-4,9

John the Baptist, *Jesus' relative and the son of Elizabeth and Zechariah the priest.*
- birth of, Luke 1:5-25,57-80
- preached at the Jordan River, Matthew 3:1-12
- baptized Jesus, Matthew 3:13-17
- killed by Herod, Matthew 14:1-12

John Mark, See "Mark."

Jonah (JO-nah) *a prophet whom God told to preach to the city of Nineveh.*
- ran from God, Jonah 1:1-3
- swallowed by a fish, Jonah 1:4–2:10
- went to Nineveh, Jonah 3
- complained to God, Jonah 4
- the sign of, Matthew 12:38-41; 16:4; Luke 11:29-32

Jonathan (JAH-nah-thun) *the oldest son of King Saul.*
- David's friend, 1 Samuel 18:1-4
- saved David's life, 1 Samuel 19:1-7; 20
- death of, 1 Samuel 31:2

Joppa (JOP-uh) *a city on the coast of Palestine,* Jonah 1:3
- Peter preached there, Acts 9:36-42; 10:9-36

Joram (JO-ram) *son of Ahab; also a king of Israel,* 2 Kings 3:1-3; 8:29; 9:14-29

Jordan (JOR-d'n) *the only large river in Palestine.*
- Israelites crossed, Joshua 3
- Jesus baptized in, Matthew 3:13-17; Mark 1:9-11

Jordan Valley, *the valley along the Jordan River,* Deuteronomy 1:1; 3:17; Joshua 11:2

Joseph of Arimathea (JOZ-uf) *took the body of Jesus down from the cross and buried it in a tomb Joseph had dug for himself,* Matthew 27:57-60; Mark 15:42-46; Luke 23:50-54

Joseph of Nazareth, *husband of Mary, Jesus' mother.*

- angel appeared to, Matthew 1:18-24
- went to register in Bethlehem, Luke 2:4-7
- took Jesus to the Temple, Luke 2:21-52

Joseph, son of Jacob, *one of the twelve sons of Israel.*
- sold into slavery, Genesis 37
- put into prison, Genesis 39
- interpreted dreams, Genesis 40–41
- reunited with family, Genesis 42–50

Joshua (JAH-shoo-ah) *leader of the Israelites into the promised land.*
- spied out Canaan, Numbers 13
- chosen to replace Moses, Numbers 27:12-23; Deuteronomy 34:9-10
- conquered Canaan, Joshua 1; 3–12
- death of, Joshua 23–24

Josiah (jo-SY-uh) *king of Judah about 640 to 609 B.C.*
- became king, 2 Kings 22:1-2
- found the lost laws of God, 2 Kings 22:3-20
- gave the law to the people, 2 Kings 23:1-30

Jotham, youngest son of Gideon (JO-tham) Judges 9:1-21,57

Jotham, son of Uzziah, *a king of Judah,* 2 Kings 15:32-38; 2 Chronicles 27

joy, Psalm 43:4; John 15:11; 17:13; 1 Thessalonians 1:6
- a fruit of the Holy Spirit, Galatians 5:22
- God as the source, Psalms 43:4; 45:7; Romans 15:13
- joy from the Holy Spirit, Luke 10:21; Romans 14:17; Galatians 5:22; 1 Thessalonians 1:6

Jubilee (JOO-bih-lee) *a Jewish celebration that took place once every fifty years. Israelites were to let the soil rest, to free their slaves, and to return land and houses to their first owners or their descendants.* Leviticus 25; 27:17-24; Numbers 36:4

Judah, son of Jacob (JOO-duh) Genesis 29:35
- saved Joseph, Genesis 37:26-27
- deceived by Tamar, Genesis 38
- reunited with Joseph, Genesis 43–44
- tribe of, Numbers 1:26-27; 26:20-22; Joshua 15
- Jesus, a descendant of, Matthew 1:2-3; Luke 3:33-34; Revelation 5:5

Judah, kingdom of, *the southern kingdom when Israel split in two.*
- beginning of, 1 Kings 11:27–12:20
- rulers of, 1 Kings 14:21–15:24; 22:41-50; 2 Kings 8:16-29; 11–12; 14–16; 18–24
- fall of, 2 Kings 24:18–25:22

Judas Iscariot (JOO-dus is-CARE-ee-ut) *apostle who handed Jesus over to be killed.*
- chosen by Jesus, Matthew 10:4; Mark 3:19
- apostles' treasurer, John 12:4-6; 13:27-29
- betrayed Jesus, Matthew 26:14-16,47-50; Luke 22:1-6; John 6:70-71; 13:2,21-30

- death of, Matthew 27:3-5

Judas, brother of Jesus, Matthew 13:55; Mark 6:3

Judas, son of James
- an apostle, Luke 6:16; Acts 1:13

Jude (JOOD) *brother of James,* Jude 1

Judea (joo-DEE-uh) *the land of the Jews,* Matthew 2:1; 3:1; Luke 1:5; 3:1; Acts 1:8

judges (JUHG-es) *leaders of Israel prior to the kings,* Judges 2:16-19; 3:7–4; 10–12; 1 Samuel 8:1-5

judging
- warnings against, Matthew 7:1-5; 1 Corinthians 4:5; James 4:11-12
- good kinds of judging, 1 Corinthians 5:12; 6:2; 10:15
- God's judging of people, Matthew 11:22; Acts 17:31; 2 Peter 2:9; 3:7

Judgment Day (JUJ-ment) *the day Christ will judge all people,* Matthew 11:20-24; 12:33-37; 2 Peter 2:9-10; 3:7-13

Julius (JOOL-yus) *a Roman soldier in charge of Paul while Paul was taken to Rome,* Acts 27:1-3

justify (JUS-teh-fy) *to make someone right with God,* Romans 3:24; 5:1; Galatians 2:16; Titus 3:7

K

Kadesh/Kadesh Barnea (KAY-desh BAR-nee-uh) *a town in the Desert of Zin,* Numbers 20:1-21; Joshua 10:41

Kenites (KEE-nites) *a tribe of early metal workers,* Genesis 15:19; Judges 1:16; 4:11; 1 Samuel 27:10

Kerethites (KAIR-uh-thites) *King David's bodyguards,* 2 Samuel 8:18; 1 Kings 1:38

Keturah (keh-TOO-ruh) *Abraham's second wife,* Genesis 25:1-4; 1 Chronicles 1:32-33

key, *something that solves or explains.*
- to God's kingdom, Matthew 16:19
- to death, Revelation 1:18

Kidron Valley (KEH-dron) *a valley between Jerusalem and the Mount of Olives,* 2 Samuel 15:23; John 18:1
- idols burned there, 1 Kings 15:13; 2 Kings 23:4

kill
- Cain killed, Genesis 4:10-11
- laws against, Exodus 20:13
- of baby boys, Exodus 1:16; Matthew 2:16
- Jesus killed, Matthew 27:31-50; Mark 15:20-37; Luke 23:25-46; John 19:16-30

kindness
- of God, Exodus 34:6-7; Jeremiah 9:24; Romans 2:4; Ephesians 2:4-7

· commanded, 2 Corinthians 6:6; Ephesians 4:32; Colossians 3:12; 2 Peter 1:5-7

king
· King of kings, 1 Timothy 6:15; Revelation 17:14

kingdom (KING-d'm) *the kingdom of heaven is God ruling in the lives of his people.*
· the nature of, Matthew 5:19-20; 19:14; Luke 17:20-21; Romans 14:17
· parables of, Matthew 13:24-52; 18:23-35; 20:1-16; 25:1-30; Mark 4:30-33; Luke 13:18-21
· belongs to, Matthew 5:3,10; 19:14

Kiriath Jearim (KEER-yath JEE-ah-rim) *a town in the hills about twelve miles west of Jerusalem,* 1 Samuel 6:20–7:20; 1 Chronicles 13:5-6; 2 Chronicles 1:4

Kish, *father of Saul,* 1 Samuel 9:1-2

Kishon (KY-shon) *the name of a valley and a stream,* Judges 4:13; 5:21; 1 Kings 18:40

kiss, *a greeting of friendship, love, or respect.*
· of Judas, Matthew 26:48-49; Mark 14:44-45; Luke 22:47-48
· holy kiss, Romans 16:16; 1 Corinthians 16:20; 1 Peter 5:14

Kittim (KEH-tim) *the island of Cyprus,* Genesis 10:4; Numbers 24:24; 1 Chronicles 1:7; Isaiah 23:1,12

kneel
· Solomon kneeled before God, 1 Kings 8:54
· Daniel kneeled before God, Daniel 6:10
· everyone to kneel before Jesus, Philippians 2:10

knock
· "knock, and the door will open," Matthew 7:7
· at the door, Luke 13:25
· Peter knocked, Acts 12:13,16
· Jesus knocks, Revelation 3:20

knowledge
· tree of, Genesis 2:9,17
· value of, Proverbs 1:7; 8:10; 18:15; 24:5; 2 Peter 1:5-6
· lack of, Hosea 4:6; Romans 1:28
· limitations of, 1 Corinthians 8:1-2; 13:2,8-10

Kohath (KO-hath) *a son of Levi,* Exodus 6:16-20; Numbers 3:17-19

Kohathites (KO-hath-ites) *descendants of Kohath.*
· worked in the Holy Tent and Temple, Numbers 3:27-31; 4:1-20; 1 Chronicles 9:17-32

Korah (KO-ruh) *the musician,* Psalms 42; 44–49; 84

Korah, son of Izhar, *rebelled against Moses,* Numbers 16:1-40

L

Laban (LAY-ban) *father of Leah and Rachel.*
· Jacob worked for, Genesis 29:13-30
· divided his flocks with Jacob, Genesis 30:29-43
· chased Jacob, Genesis 31:19-55

Lachish (LAY-kish) *a city about thirty miles southwest of Jerusalem.*
· Joshua defeated, Joshua 10

lake
· of Galilee, Luke 5:1-2; 8:22-23,33
· of fire, Revelation 19:20
· of sulfur, Revelation 20:10; 21:8

lamb (LAM) *an animal that the Jews often offered as a gift to God.*
· as sacrifice, Genesis 4:4; Exodus 12:3-10; Leviticus 3:6-11; 4:32-35; 5:6; 14:24-25
· Jesus, the lamb of God, John 1:29,36; 1 Corinthians 5:7; 1 Peter 1:19; Revelation 5–7

Lamech, a descendant of Cain (LAY-mek) Genesis 4:18-24

Lamech, son of Methuselah, *the father of Noah,* Genesis 5:28-31

lamp, *a small bowl which held a wick and burned olive oil, thus giving light,* Matthew 25:1-13; Luke 8:16-18
· "Your word is like a lamp for my feet," Psalm 119:105

lampstand, *a holder for a lamp.*
· in the Holy Tent, Exodus 25:31-40; Numbers 8:1-4
· in the Temple, 1 Kings 7:49
· symbol of the church, Revelation 1:12-13,20

language
· world spoke only one, Genesis 11:1,6
· confused at Babel, Genesis 11:7,9
· Aramaic, 2 Kings 18:26; Ezra 4:7; John 19:20
· Latin, John 19:20
· Greek, John 19:20; Acts 21:37

Laodicea (lay-ah-deh-SEE-uh) *a town in what is now Turkey,* Colossians 4:13-16; Revelation 3:14-22

Last Supper, *the meal Jesus ate with his followers the night before his death,* Matthew 26:17-30; Mark 14:12-26; Luke 22:7-20; 1 Corinthians 11:23-26

Latin (LAT-in) *the language spoken by the Romans during New Testament times,* John 19:20

laughter
· Sarah laughed, Genesis 18:12
· mouths filled with, Psalm 126:2
· sorrow better than, Ecclesiastes 7:3
· changed into crying, James 4:9

law
- as rules, Romans 4:15; 6:14-15; Galatians 5:18
- as God's rules or teachings, Psalm 119; Romans 7:22; 8:7; James 1:25; 1 John 3:4

Law of Moses, See "Teachings of Moses."

laying on of hands, See "hands, laying on."

Lazarus of Bethany (LAZ-uh-rus) *a brother to Mary and Martha and a friend of Jesus,* John 11:1-45; 12:1-11

Lazarus, the beggar, Luke 16:19-31

laziness
- brings poverty, Proverbs 10:4
- not to be fed, 2 Thessalonians 3:10

leadership
- blind, Matthew 15:14
- of own family, 1 Timothy 3:5
- elders worthy of honor, 1 Timothy 5:17

Leah (LEE-uh) *a wife of Jacob,* Genesis 29:15-35; 30:9-21; 49:31

leather, Leviticus 13:47-59; Matthew 3:4

leaven, See "yeast."

Lebanon (LEH-beh-nun) *a country north of Israel.*
- cedars of, 1 Kings 5:1-11; Ezra 3:7
- prophecy of Lebanon's fall, Isaiah 10:34

Legion (LEE-jun) *a man who had many evil spirits in him,* Mark 5:9; Luke 8:30

lend
- money, Exodus 22:25
- borrower, a servant to lender, Proverbs 22:7
- sinners to sinners, Luke 6:34
- to enemies, Luke 6:35

leprosy (LEH-prah-see) *bad skin disease. A person with leprosy was called a leper and had to live outside the city.* Leviticus 13:45-46
- disease of Naaman, 2 Kings 5:1-27
- healed by Jesus, Matthew 8:2-3; Luke 7:11-19

Leviathan (lee-VI-ah-than) *a sea monster; possibly a crocodile,* Job 3:8; 41:1; Psalm 74:14; Isaiah 27:1

Levites (LEE-vites) *descendants of Levi, one of Jacob's sons.*
- served as priests, Numbers 1:47-53; 8:5-26; Deuteronomy 10:8-9; 18:1-8
- towns assigned to, Joshua 21

liar
- better to be poor, Proverbs 19:22
- Satan as a, John 8:44
- Cretans as, Titus 1:12
- to be punished, Revelation 21:8

lid on the Ark of the Agreement, *the mercy seat; the gold lid on the Ark of the Agreement,* Exodus 25:17-22; Hebrews 9:5

life
- breath of, Genesis 2:7
- book of, Philippians 4:3; Revelation 3:5; 21:27
- in the blood, Leviticus 17:14
- length of, Psalm 90:10
- true life, John 12:25
- "I am the. . .life." John 14:6
- eternal, John 5:24-29; 6:35-51

light
- creation of, Genesis 1:3-4
- of the world, Matthew 5:14
- God is, 1 Timothy 6:16; 1 John 1:5
- Jesus is, John 1:4-9; 3:19-20; 8:12; 12:46
- God's word is light, Psalm 119:105
- symbol of God's presence, 2 Corinthians 4:6; Ephesians 5:8-9; 1 Peter 2:9

linen (LEH-nin) *a type of cloth made from the flax plant.*
- used for priests' clothes, Exodus 28:39-42; Leviticus 6:10
- used for royal clothes, Esther 8:15
- Jesus' body wrapped in, Matthew 27:59

lion
- killed by Samson, Judges 14:5-18
- killed by David, 1 Samuel 17:34-37
- devil like a lion, 1 Peter 5:8

lips
- touched by hot coal, Isaiah 6:5-7

loaves
- used to feed five thousand, Matthew 14:17-19
- used to feed four thousand, Matthew 15:34-38

locust (LO-cust) *an insect that looks like a grasshopper. Locusts travel in large groups and can destroy crops.*
- as a plague, Exodus 10:3-19; Deuteronomy 28:38-42; Joel 1:1-4; Nahum 3:15-17
- food for John the Baptist, Matthew 3:4; Mark 1:6

Lord, *master or one who is in control; ruler of all the world and universe.*
- God as Lord, Exodus 3:15; 7:16; Psalms 31:5; 106:48
- Jesus as Lord, Acts 2:36; 1 Corinthians 8:6; Philippians 2:11; 1 Peter 3:15
- Holy Spirit as Lord, 2 Corinthians 3:18

Lord of hosts, *one of the names used for God; also called "Lord All-Powerful" and "Lord Sabaoth,"* 1 Chronicles 11:9; Psalm 24:10; Isaiah 6:3-5; Malachi 3:1-17

Lord's day
- the first day of the week, Acts 20:7; Revelation 1:10
- as the Judgment Day, 1 Corinthians 5:5; 2 Corinthians 1:14; 1 Thessalonians 5:2; 2 Peter 3:10

Lord's Prayer, *the name often given to the model prayer Jesus taught his followers,* Matthew 6:9-13; Luke 11:1-4

Lord's Supper, *the meal Jesus' followers eat to remember how he died for them; also called "communion."*
· beginning of, Matthew 26:26-29; Mark 14:22-25; Luke 22:14-20
· examples of, Acts 20:7; 1 Corinthians 10:16; 11:17-34

Lot, *Abraham's nephew,* Genesis 11:27-30
· divided land with Abram, Genesis 13
· captured, Genesis 14:1-16
· escaped destruction of Sodom, Genesis 19:1-29
· death of wife, Genesis 19:15-26

lots, *sticks, stones, or pieces of bone thrown like dice to decide something. Often God controlled the result of the lots to let people know what he wanted them to do.*
· Canaan divided by, Numbers 26:55-56
· Jonah found guilty by, Jonah 1:7
· Jesus' clothes divided by, Luke 23:34
· Matthias chosen by, Acts 1:26

love, *a strong feeling of affection, loyalty and concern for someone.*
· love of God commanded, Deuteronomy 6:5; 11:1; Matthew 22:36-38
· of God for people, Psalm 36; John 3:16; Romans 5:8; 8:39; Ephesians 1:4; 1 John 4:10-11
· of people for God, 1 Corinthians 8:3; 1 John 5:3
· of Christ for people, John 13:1; 15:9; Romans 8:35; Galatians 2:20; 1 John 3:16
· of people for Christ, Matthew 10:37; 1 Corinthians 16:22; 1 Peter 1:8
· of people for each other, Leviticus 19:18; Luke 6:27-35; John 13:34-35; 1 Corinthians 13; 1 John 4:7

Luke, *a non-Jewish doctor who often traveled with the apostle Paul,* Colossians 4:14; 2 Timothy 4:11

lust, *wanting something evil.*
· to be avoided, Proverbs 6:25; Matthew 5:28; Colossians 3:5; 1 Thessalonians 4:5
· typical of the ungodly, Romans 1:26; 1 Peter 4:3

Lydia (LID-ee-uh) *a woman from the city of Thyatira who sold purple cloth,* Acts 16:13-15,40

lying
· warnings against, Ephesians 4:25; Colossians 3:9; Revelation 21:8
· devil as a liar, John 8:44
· to the Holy Spirit, Acts 5:1-6

lyre (LIRE) *a musical instrument with strings, similar to a harp,* 1 Chronicles 15:16; Psalms 33:2; 81:2

Lystra (LIS-tra) *a city of Lycaonia.*
· Paul preached there, Acts 14:6-20; 16:1; 2 Timothy 3:11

M

Macedonia (mas-eh-DOH-nee-uh) *the northern part of Greece.*
· Paul preached there, Acts 16:6-10; 20:1-6; 1 Corinthians 16:5-9; Philippians 4:15

Machpelah (mack-PEE-luh) *the land Abraham bought from Ephron, the Hittite.*
· Sarah buried there, Genesis 23:7-19
· Abraham buried there, Genesis 25:7-10
· Jacob buried there, Genesis 49:29-33; 50:12-13

magic (MAJ-ik) *trying to use the power of evil spirits to make unnatural things happen.*
· magicians of Egypt, Genesis 41:8; Exodus 7:11-12
· condemned, Leviticus 19:26; 20:27; Deuteronomy 18:10-12
· Simon the magician, Acts 8:9-24
· Elymas the magician, Acts 13:6-11
· Ephesian magicians burn their books, Acts 19:17-19

mahalath (mah-HAY-lath) *probably a musical word; may be the name of a tune or may mean to dance and shout,* Psalms 53; 88

Malachi (MAL-uh-ky) *a prophet who lived about the time of Nehemiah. He wrote the last book of the Old Testament.* Malachi 1:1

man, *humankind; a male.*
· created by God, Genesis 1:26-27; 2:7-23
· born of woman, Job 14:1
· important to God, Psalm 8:4-8
· woman created for, 1 Corinthians 11:9

Manasseh, son of Hezekiah (mah-NASS-uh) *a king of Judah for fifty-five years,* 2 Kings 21:1-17; 2 Chronicles 33:1-20

Manasseh, son of Joseph, *older brother of Ephraim. His descendants were the tribe of Manasseh.* Genesis 41:51; 46:20; 48:1-20
· descendants of, Numbers 1:34; 26:29-34; Joshua 13:8-13; 17
· eastern half-tribe, Joshua 1:12-17; 22
· western half-tribe, Joshua 21:5,25; 22:7

manger (MAIN-jur) *a box where animals are fed,* Luke 2:6-17

manna (MAN-ah) *the white, sweet-tasting food God gave the people of Israel in the wilderness. It appeared on the ground during the night so they could gather it in the morning.*
· God sent to Israel, Exodus 16:11-36; Joshua 5:10-12
· kept in the Ark, Exodus 16:31-34; Hebrews 9:1-4

Manoah (mah-NO-uh) *the father of Samson,* Judges 13

Marduk (MAR-dook) *a god of the Babylonians. The Babylonians believed that people were evil because Marduk had created them from the blood of an evil god.* Jeremiah 50:2

Mark, *John Mark; a cousin to Barnabas; traveled with Paul and Barnabas and wrote the Gospel of Mark,* Acts 12:12,25; 13:5; Colossians 4:10; 2 Timothy 4:11
· left Paul, Acts 13:13
· traveled with Barnabas, Acts 15:36-41

marketplace, *usually a large open area inside a city where people came to buy and sell goods,* Matthew 20:3; Mark 7:4; 12:38; Luke 7:32; Acts 16:19

marriage
· teachings about, Mark 10:6-9; 1 Corinthians 7:1-16; Hebrews 13:4; 1 Timothy 5:14
· authority in, Ephesians 5:21; Colossians 3:18

Mars Hill, See "Areopagus."

Martha (MAR-thuh) *the sister of Mary and Lazarus who lived in Bethany.*
· criticized Mary, Luke 10:38-42
· at death of Lazarus, John 11:17-44

martyr (MAR-ter) *"witness"; one who knows about something. Later, martyr came to mean a person who was killed for being a witness.*
· Stephen, first Christian martyr, Acts 7:54-60
· James killed, Acts 12:2
· heroes of faith killed, Hebrews 11:32-37

Mary Magdalene (MAG-duh-lun) *a follower of Jesus from the town of Magdala; the first person to see Jesus after he came back to life.*
· at Jesus' death, Matthew 27:55-56,61
· saw Jesus after his resurrection, Matthew 28:1-10; Mark 16:1-11; John 20:10-18

Mary, mother of Jesus
· engaged to marry Joseph, Matthew 1:18-25; Luke 2:4-5
· angel appeared to, Luke 1:26-45
· birth of Jesus, Luke 2:6-21
· with Jesus in Jerusalem, Luke 2:41-52
· at wedding in Cana, John 2:1-10
· at Jesus' death, John 19:25-27
· with the apostles, Acts 1:14

Mary of Bethany, *sister of Martha and Lazarus, and a friend of Jesus.*
· sat at Jesus' feet, Luke 10:38-42
· at death of Lazarus, John 11:1-45
· poured oil on Jesus' feet, John 12:1-8

maskil (MAS-kil) *probably a description of the kind of song that some of the Psalms were,* Psalms 32, 42, 44, 45

master, *lord; ruler.*
· "No one can serve two masters." Matthew 6:24

· not to be called, Matthew 23:10
· to be obeyed, Ephesians 6:5
· how to treat slaves, Ephesians 6:9
· in heaven, Ephesians 6:9; Colossians 4:1
· Jesus as, Luke 5:5; 8:24; 17:13

Matthew (MATH-you) *also called Levi; a tax collector; wrote the Gospel of Matthew,* Matthew 9:9-10; 10:3; Acts 1:13

Matthias (muh-THY-us) *chosen to be an apostle after Judas Iscariot killed himself,* Acts 1:15-26

meat
· given by God in the wilderness, Exodus 16:1-15; Numbers 11:4-34; Psalm 78:27
· eating meat sacrificed to idols, Acts 15:20; 1 Corinthians 8; 10:25-32

Medes (MEEDS) *the people who lived in Media, which is called "Iran" today,* 2 Kings 17:6; Ezra 6:2; Esther 1:3-19; Daniel 5:28; 6:8-15

mediator (MEE-dee-a-ter) *a go-between.*
· Jesus as, 1 Timothy 2:5

medicine
· happy heart as, Proverbs 17:22

Mediterranean Sea (med-ih-teh-RANE-ih-an) *a large sea west of Canaan; also called the "Great Sea" or the "Western Sea,"* Numbers 34:6-7; Joshua 1:4

medium (MEED-ee-um) *a person who tries to help living people talk to the spirits of the dead.*
· condemned, Leviticus 19:31; Deuteronomy 18:11-13; Isaiah 8:19-20
· of Endor, 1 Samuel 28
· Josiah destroyed mediums, 2 Kings 23:24

Meeting Tent, *"Tabernacle" or "Holy Tent"; a special tent where the Israelites worshiped God. It was used from the time they left Egypt until Solomon built the Temple in Jerusalem.*
· description of, Exodus 25—27
· set up, Exodus 39:32—40:36

Megiddo (meh-GID-oh) *important town in northern Israel where many battles were fought. The book of Revelation tells about a great battle between good and evil at "Armageddon," which means "the hill of Megiddo."* Joshua 12:8-21; 2 Kings 23:29-30; Revelation 16:16

Melchizedek (mel-KIZ-ih-dek) *priest and king who worshiped God in the time of Abraham,* Genesis 14:17-24
· Christ compared to, Hebrews 5:4-10; 7

Mene, mene, tekel, parsin (MEE-nee, TEE-kul, PAR-sun) *the words written on the wall by a mysterious hand at Belshazzar's feast,* Daniel 5

319   **mob**

Mephibosheth (me-FIB-o-sheth) *crippled son of Jonathan,* 2 Samuel 4:4
· David's agreement with, 2 Samuel 9
· tricked by Ziba, 2 Samuel 16:1-4; 19:24-30

Merab (MEE-rab) *daughter of King Saul,* 1 Samuel 14:49; 18:17-19

Merarites (mee-RAY-rites) *descendants of Merari, a son of Levi; they were responsible for caring for the frame of the Holy Tent,* Numbers 3:17,33-37; 4:29-33

mercy (MUR-see) *kindness and forgiveness.*
· God's mercy to people, Exodus 34:6; Deuteronomy 4:31; Luke 1:50; Ephesians 2:4
· people's mercy to each other, Matthew 5:7; James 2:13

mercy seat, See "lid on the Ark of the Agreement."

Mesha (MEE-shuh) *an evil king of Moab,* 2 Kings 3:4-27

Meshach (MEE-shack) *friend of Daniel who was put in the fiery furnace,* Daniel 1–3

messenger, 1 Samuel 23:27; 1 Kings 19:2
· John the Baptist as, Matthew 11:10; Mark 1:2; Luke 7:27
· of Satan, 2 Corinthians 12:7

Messiah (muh-SYE-uh) *"anointed one"; the Greek word for Messiah is "Christ." Christians believe that Jesus is the Messiah or the Christ.* John 1:40-41; 4:25-26

Methuselah (meh-THOO-zeh-lah) *lived 969 years, longer than anyone else in the Bible; the son of Enoch and the grandfather of Noah,* Genesis 5:21-27

Micah (MY-cuh) *a prophet who told the people of Israel and Judah about their sins,* Micah 1–7

Micaiah (mi-KAY-uh) *a prophet of God,* 1 Kings 22:8-28; 2 Chronicles 18

Michael (MY-kul) *the archangel of God,* Jude 9; Revelation 12:7

Michal (MY-kul) *a daughter of Saul and wife of David,* 1 Samuel 18:20-29; 19:11-17; 2 Samuel 3:13-16
· criticized David, 2 Samuel 6:16-23

Michmash (MIK-mash) *a hilly area about seven miles northeast of Jerusalem,* 1 Samuel 13:23–14:23; Isaiah 10:28

Midian (MID-ee-un) *a son of Abraham; his descendants were called "Midianites,"* Genesis 25:1-6
· Joseph sold to, Genesis 37:18-36
· Jethro, a descendant of, Exodus 2:15-21
· enemy of Israel, Judges 6–7

midnight
· when the firstborn of Egypt died, Exodus 12:29
· Paul and Silas freed from jail, Acts 16:25-26
· Paul preached until, Acts 20:7

miktam (MIK-tam) *a kind of song that may describe some of the Psalms. It may mean that it is a sad song or a song about danger.* Psalms 16; 56–60

mildew (MIL-doo) *a growth that appears on things that have been damp for a long time,* Leviticus 13:47-59; 14:33-54

milk, 1 Peter 2:2

millstones, *huge stones used for grinding grain into flour or meal,* Deuteronomy 24:6; Matthew 18:6; Luke 17:1-2
· used to kill Abimelech, Judges 9:53; 2 Samuel 11:21

minister (MIN-i-ster) *servant; one who lives serving God and others,* Romans 15:15-16; Colossians 4:7

miracle (MEER-ih-k'l) *"wonderful thing"; a great event which can be done only by God's help. Miracles are special signs to show God's power.*
· purpose of, Exodus 10:1-2; Mark 2:8-12; John 2:11; Acts 3:1-10
· over nature, Exodus 14:21-22; Joshua 10:12-13; Matthew 8:23-27; 14:22-32; 21:18-22
· of healing, Matthew 8:14-17; 9:27-31; Mark 7:31-37; Acts 14:3
· of bringing people back to life, Mark 5:21-43; John 11:1-44; Acts 9:36-43

Miriam (MEER-ee-um) *the sister of Moses and Aaron.*
· watched over Moses, Exodus 2:1-8
· song of, Exodus 15:19-21
· punished, Numbers 12:1-15
· death of, Numbers 20:1

mistress (MISS-tres) *a female head of the household,* Proverbs 30:21-23
· Hagar as, Genesis 16:4-9

Mizpah (MIZ-pah) *the place where Jacob and Laban made a pile of stones to remind them of their agreement not to be angry with each other,* Genesis 31:44-49

Mizpah, the city, *a few miles north of Jerusalem,* Judges 11:29-34; 1 Samuel 7:5-16; 2 Kings 25:23

Moab (MO-ab) *the country on the east side of the Dead Sea.*
· fought with Israel, Numbers 22:1–25:9; Judges 3:12-30
· home of Ruth, Ruth 1:2,4
· rebelled against Israel, 2 Kings 3:4-27

mob
· against Paul, Acts 17:5; 21:30-36

Molech (MO-lek) *a god of the Canaanite people. Those who worshiped Molech often sacrificed their own children to him by burning them on altars.* Leviticus 18:21; 20:1-5; 2 Kings 23:10; Jeremiah 32:35

money, *Many kinds of money were used in Bible days—gold, silver, and copper.*
· proper attitudes toward, Luke 16:13; Hebrews 13:5; 1 Timothy 3:3; 6:10

moneychangers, *people who traded money from other countries for Jewish money.*
· of the Temple, Matthew 21:12-13; Mark 11:15-17; Luke 19:45-46; John 2:13-16

Mordecai (MOR-deh-kye) *a man who helped Esther to save the Jews from death.*
· discovered a plot, Esther 2:19-23
· asked Esther to help, Esther 4
· honored by the king, Esther 6

Moriah (moh-RYE-uh) *the land where Abraham went to sacrifice Isaac,* Genesis 22:2
· site of the Temple, 2 Chronicles 3:1

mortar (MORE-tar) *a stone bowl where grain is ground into flour by pounding; also, the sticky material that holds bricks together,* Genesis 11:3; Exodus 1:14

Moses (MO-zez) *the man who led God's people out of the land of Egypt; the author of the first five books of the Old Testament.*
· birth of, Exodus 2:1-10
· in Midian, Exodus 2:11–4:17
· led Israel out of Egypt, Exodus 4:18–12:51; 13:17-31
· received the law, Exodus 20–31
· struck the rock, Numbers 20:1-13
· death of, Deuteronomy 31:14–34:12

Most Holy Place, *the inner and most special room in the Holy Tent and the Temple.*
· rules about, Leviticus 16:2-20
· in the Temple, 1 Kings 6:16-35
· entered by Christ, Hebrews 9:3-25

mother-in-law
· law about, Deuteronomy 27:23
· of Ruth, Ruth 1:3-4
· Peter's, Matthew 8:14-15; Luke 4:38-39
· family against, Matthew 10:35; Luke 12:53

mothers
· treatment of, Exodus 20:12; 21:15,17; Proverbs 1:8; Matthew 15:4; 1 Timothy 5:2,4

Mount of Olives, *a hill covered with olive trees near Jerusalem; site of the garden of Gethsemane,* Matthew 21:1; 24:3; John 8:1
· David cried there, 2 Samuel 15:30
· Jesus prayed there, Luke 22:39-53
· Jesus ascended from there, Acts 1:6-12

Mount Sinai (SYE-nye) *a mountain in the Sinai Peninsula.*
· Lord spoke with Moses there, Exodus 24:16; Acts 7:30,38

· law given on, Exodus 31:18

Mount Zion (ZI-on) *one of the hills on which Jerusalem was built; later, it became another name for the whole city of Jerusalem; also a name for heaven.*
· hill of Jerusalem, 2 Kings 19:31; Psalm 48:2,11; Isaiah 24:23
· as heaven, Hebrews 12:22; Revelation 14:1

mourning (MORN-ing) *showing sadness, especially when someone has died.*
· examples of, Genesis 50:3; Deuteronomy 34:8; 1 Samuel 31:11-13

murder
· laws against, Exodus 20:13; Deuteronomy 5:17; Matthew 5:21
· committed by Barabbas, Mark 15:7
· devil as a murderer, John 8:44
· full of, Romans 1:29

music
· to the Lord, Judges 5:3; Ephesians 5:19
· in the Temple, 1 Chronicles 25:6-7

myrrh (MUR) *sweet-smelling liquid taken from certain trees and shrubs; used as a perfume and a painkiller,* Genesis 37:25; 43:11; Proverbs 7:17
· given to Jesus, Matthew 2:11; Mark 15:23
· used in Jesus' burial, John 19:39-40

mystery (MIH-ster-ee) *a secret.*
· revealed by God, Daniel 2:28
· of the message of Christ, Romans 16:25-26; Colossians 2:2; 4:3
· of Gentiles also being saved, Ephesians 3:1-6; Colossians 1:25-27
· of life after death, 1 Corinthians 15:51

N

Naaman (NAY-uh-mun) *a commander of the Aramean army; healed by Elisha of a skin disease,* 2 Kings 5; Luke 4:27

Nabal (NAY-bal) *husband of Abigail.*
· refused to help David, 1 Samuel 25:2-13
· saved by Abigail, 1 Samuel 25:14-35
· death of, 1 Samuel 25:36-38

Naboth (NAY-both) *killed by Jezebel so she could steal his vineyard,* 1 Kings 21

Nadab (NAY-dab) *son of Aaron.*
· saw God, Exodus 24:1-11
· death of, Leviticus 10:1; Numbers 3:4; 26:61

Nahum (NAY-hum) *a prophet of God; wrote the book of Nahum,* Nahum 1–3

naked
· Adam and Eve, Genesis 2:25
· realization of nakedness, Genesis 3:7-10
· born, Job 1:21

Naomi (nay-OH-me) *mother-in-law of Ruth,* Ruth 1:1-5
· returned to Bethlehem, Ruth 1:6-22

- encouraged Ruth, Ruth 2:19–3:4
- became a grandmother, Ruth 4:13-17

Naphtali (NAF-tuh-lye) *the sixth son of Jacob; his descendants were the tribe of Naphtali,* Genesis 30:7-8; Numbers 26:48-50; Joshua 19:32-39

nard, *an expensive perfume which was imported from India,* Song of Solomon 4:13; Mark 14:3; John 12:3

Nathan (NAY-thun) *a prophet during the time of David and Solomon,* 1 Kings 1
- told David not to build the Temple, 2 Samuel 7:1-17
- told David the parable of the lamb, 2 Samuel 12:1-25

Nathanael (nuh-THAN-yul) *one of Jesus' twelve apostles; probably called "Bartholomew."* John 1:43-51

nation
- formed and spread, Genesis 10:32
- against nation, Mark 13:8
- Good News preached to every one, Revelation 14:6

Nazarene (NAZ-uh-reen) *a person from the town of Nazareth. Jesus was called a Nazarene, so his followers sometimes were also called Nazarenes.* Matthew 2:21-23; Acts 24:5

Nazareth (NAZ-uh-reth) *the city in Galilee where Jesus grew up,* Matthew 2:21-23; Luke 4:16-30; John 1:45-46

Nazirite (NAZ-e-rite) *a special promise made to God, which had rules about eating certain foods and cutting the hair.*
- rules for, Numbers 6:1-21
- made by Samson, Judges 13:2-7; 16:17

Nebo, god of the Babylonians (NEE-boh) Isaiah 46:1

Nebo, the mountain
- Moses died there, Deuteronomy 34:1-5

Nebuchadnezzar (neb-you-kud-NEZ-zur) *a Babylonian king.*
- conquered Jerusalem, 2 Kings 24–25; 2 Chronicles 36
- his dreams, Daniel 2; 4
- and fiery furnace, Daniel 3

Nebuzaradan (NEB-you-ZAR-ah-dan) *the commander of Nebuchadnezzar's army.*
- captured Jerusalem, 2 Kings 25:8-12; Jeremiah 39:8-14; 40:1-6

Neco (NECK-o) *king of Egypt from 609 to 594 B.C.*
- killed King Josiah, 2 Kings 23:29-37; 2 Chronicles 35:20-27
- captured Jehoahaz, 2 Chronicles 36:1-4
- defeated by Nebuchadnezzar, Jeremiah 46:2

Nehemiah (NEE-uh-MY-uh) *led the first group of Israelites back to Jerusalem from Babylon.*
- sent to Jerusalem, Nehemiah 2
- rebuilt walls of Jerusalem, Nehemiah 3–4; 6
- as governor, Nehemiah 8:9; 10:1

neighbor
- teachings about, Exodus 20:16-17; Leviticus 19:13-18; Proverbs 3:27-29; Matthew 19:19; Luke 10:25-37

Nephilim (NEF-eh-lim) *people who were famous for being large and strong. The ten spies who were afraid to enter Canaan had seen the Nephilim who lived there.* Genesis 6:4; Numbers 13:30-33

Ner (NUR) *father of Kish,* 1 Chronicles 8:33; 9:36,39

net
- fishing with, Matthew 4:18; Luke 5:5,6; John 21:6-11
- kingdom of heaven like, Matthew 13:47

new
- a new song, Psalms 40:3; 98:1
- a new name, Isaiah 62:2; Revelation 2:17
- new mercies every morning, Lamentations 3:22-23
- a new heart, Ezekiel 18:31; 36:26
- a new life, Romans 6:4; Ephesians 4:23-24; Colossians 3:10; 1 Peter 1:3
- a new agreement, Jeremiah 31:31; 1 Corinthians 11:25; Hebrews 8:8; 9:15; 12:24
- a new heaven and earth, 2 Peter 3:13; Revelation 21:1

New Moon, *a Jewish feast held on the first day of the month. It was celebrated with animal sacrifices and the blowing of trumpets. It was to dedicate the month to the Lord.* Numbers 10:10; 2 Chronicles 2:4; 8:13; Psalm 81:3; Isaiah 1:11-17

Nicodemus (nick-uh-DEE-mus) *an important Jewish ruler and teacher. Jesus taught him about spiritual life.* John 3:1-21; 7:45-53; 19:38-42

night, *can refer to ordinary darkness or be a symbol of distress, judgment, or evil*
- created by God, Genesis 1:5; Psalm 19:1-2
- time of distress, Psalms 30:5; 42:8; 77:6
- time of judgment, John 9:4
- symbol of evil, 1 Thessalonians 5:5
- no night in heaven, Revelation 21:25

Nile River, *a river in Africa more than twenty-five hundred miles long.*
- baby Moses placed there, Exodus 2:1-10
- turned to blood, Exodus 7:14-25
- produced plague of frogs, Exodus 8:1-15

Nineveh (NIN-eh-vuh) *one of the oldest and most important cities in the world. For many years it was the capital of Assyria.* Genesis 10:8-11

- Jonah preached there, Jonah 1:1-2; 3–4; Matthew 12:41
- Nahum prophesied against, Nahum 1–3

Noah (NO-uh) *saved his family and the animals from the flood.*
- built the boat, Genesis 6:8-22
- saved from the flood, Genesis 7–8
- agreement with God, Genesis 9:1-17

Nob, *a town where priests lived during the days of King Saul,* 1 Samuel 21:1

noise
- joyful, Psalm 66:1
- of many people, Isaiah 17:12
- skies will disappear with, 2 Peter 3:10

noon
- sun to go down at, Amos 8:9
- bright light at, Acts 22:6

O

oath, *a promise or vow.*
- rules about, Matthew 5:33-37; 23:16-22; James 5:12
- God's oath, Hebrews 6:16-18
- examples of, 1 Samuel 14:24-28; 1 Kings 1:29-30; Psalm 132:1-12

Obadiah (oh-buh-DYE-uh) *a prophet of God who warned the Edomites they would be punished,* Obadiah 1-21

obedience
- to God, Leviticus 25:18; Deuteronomy 27:10; Acts 5:29
- to parents, Ephesians 6:1; Colossians 3:20
- to government, Romans 13:1-7; Titus 3:1-2; Matthew 22:17-21
- punishment for disobedience, Ephesians 5:6; 2 Thessalonians 1:8; 1 Timothy 1:9

offering (AW-fer-ing) *a gift or sacrifice.* See "sacrifice."
- brought by Cain, Genesis 4:3-5
- of non-Jewish people, Romans 15:16
- of Christ, Hebrews 10:5-18

Og (AHG) *the king of Bashan who was defeated by the Israelites,* Numbers 21:33-35; Deuteronomy 3:1-11

oil, *in Bible times usually means olive oil; used for cooking, medicine, burning in lamps, and anointing.* See "anoint."
- for lamps, Exodus 25:5-6; Matthew 25:1-10
- as medicine, Luke 10:34
- in offerings, Leviticus 2; 14:12-31
- in cooking, 1 Kings 17:10-16

ointment, See "perfume."

olive (OL-iv) *a small fruit; its oil was used in anointing ceremonies and as medicine.* See "oil."
- leaf, Genesis 8:11
- trees, Deuteronomy 6:11; 1 Samuel 8:14; Habakkuk 3:17; John 18:1

Omega, See "Alpha and Omega."

Omri (AHM-rih) *a strong, evil king of Israel,* 1 Kings 16:15-28

Onesimus (oh-NES-ih-mus) *the slave of a Christian named Philemon,* Colossians 4:9; Philemon

Onesiphorus (OH-nih-SIF-uh-russ) *a Christian friend of Paul who lived in Ephesus,* 2 Timothy 1:16-18; 4:19

onyx (AHN-ix) *a precious stone with layers of black and white running through it,* Genesis 2:12; Job 28:16
- used in the holy vest, Exodus 25:7; 28:9-14; 39:6-7,13

Orpah (OR-pah) *the sister-in-law of Ruth,* Ruth 1:3-14

Ophir (OH-fur) *a land known for its gold and beautiful trees. Its location is uncertain.* Psalm 45:9; Isaiah 13:12
- Solomon traded with Ophir, 1 Kings 9:28; 10:11; 1 Chronicles 29:4

oven, *fire was built in the bottom of a clay barrel to bake bread,* Exodus 8:3; Leviticus 2:4; Hosea 7:4

oxen
- not to be coveted, Exodus 20:17
- as offering, Numbers 7:12-83
- not to be denied food, Deuteronomy 25:4; 1 Corinthians 9:9
- Elisha plowed with, 1 Kings 19:19-21
- pulled the cart containing the Ark, 1 Chronicles 13:9

P

pain
- of a woman in childbirth, Genesis 3:16; Isaiah 13:8; Romans 8:22; Galatians 4:19,27
- not found in the new Jerusalem, Revelation 21:4

palace
- of David, 2 Samuel 5:11-12
- of Solomon, 1 Kings 7:1-12

palm tree, *a tall tree with long, fan-shaped branches growing out of the top; gives dates for food and wood for building,* Exodus 15:27; Nehemiah 8:15
- Jericho, city of, Deuteronomy 34:3; Judges 1:16; 3:13
- branches spread before Jesus, John 12:12-13

papyrus (puh-PY-rus) *a tall reed that grows in swampy places; used to make paper,* Job 8:11; 9:26

parable (PARE-uh-b'l) *a story that teaches a lesson by comparing two things.*
- of the kingdom of God, Matthew 13; 20:1-16
- of the lost sheep, coin, and son, Luke 15:1-31

· of the Judgment Day, Matthew 25

Paradise (PARE-uh-dice) *"garden"; a place where God's people go when they die,* Luke 23:43; 2 Corinthians 12:3-4

Paran (PAY-ran) *a desert area between Egypt and Canaan,* Genesis 21:20; Numbers 10:12; 12:16; 13:1-26

parchment (PARCH-ment) *a kind of writing material; made from the skin of sheep or goats,* 2 Timothy 4:13

parents
· responsibilities of, Ephesians 6:4; Colossians 3:21

Passover Feast (PASS-o-ver FEEST) *an important holy day for the Jews in the spring of each year. They ate a special meal on this day to remind them that God had freed them from being slaves in Egypt.*
· first Passover, Exodus 12:1-30
· commanded, Numbers 9:1-14
· celebrated by Jesus, Matthew 26:2,17-19

patience (PAY-shentz) *to handle pain or difficult times calmly and without complaining.*
· of God, Romans 2:4; 2 Peter 3:9
· teachings about, 1 Corinthians 13:4,7; Hebrews 6:12
· comes from the Holy Spirit, Galatians 5:22
· commanded, Romans 12:12; Ephesians 4:2; 1 Thessalonians 5:14; James 5:7-8

Patmos (PAT-mus) *a small, rocky island in the Aegean Sea between Greece and Turkey,* Revelation 1:9

Paul, *the Roman name for "Saul." Saul was a Jew, born in the city of Tarsus. He became an apostle and a great servant of God.*
· conversion of, Acts 9:1-22
· name changed from "Saul," Acts 13:9
· healings by, Acts 14:8-10; 19:11-12; 20:7-12; 28:1-11
· imprisoned, Acts 23:35–28:31
· death of, 2 Timothy 4:6-8

peace
· from God, Psalm 29:11; John 14:27; Romans 5:1
· commanded, Romans 12:18; 14:17-19; Colossians 3:15
· Prince of Peace, Isaiah 9:6
· from the Holy Spirit, Galatians 5:22

pearl (PURL), Matthew 7:6; 1 Timothy 2:9; Revelation 21:21
· parable of, Matthew 13:45-46

Pekah (PEE-kuh) *an evil king of Israel,* 2 Kings 15:25–16:9; Isaiah 7:1-10

Pekahiah (peck-uh-HI-uh) *an evil king of Israel,* 2 Kings 15:22-26

Pelethites (PELL-eh-thites) *King David's bodyguards,* 2 Samuel 15:18; 20:6-7,23

Peninnah (pe-NIN-uh) *a wife of Elkanah,* 1 Samuel 1:2-6

Pentecost (PEN-tee-cost) *a Jewish feast day celebrating the summer harvest. The apostles began telling the Good News on Pentecost after Jesus died.* Acts 2:1-41; 20:16; 1 Corinthians 16:8

perfect
· describing Jesus, Hebrews 2:10; 5:9; 7:28
· describing God, Psalm 18:30; Matthew 5:48
· God's perfect law, James 1:25
· will of God, Romans 12:2
· love, 1 John 4:18
· people made perfect, 2 Corinthians 13:11; Hebrews 10:1-14; 11:40; 12:23

perfume
· used in idol worship, Isaiah 57:9
· poured on Jesus' feet, Mark 14:3-9; Luke 7:36-39; John 12:3

Pergamum (PER-guh-mum) *a town in the Roman province of Asia in what is now Turkey,* Revelation 2:12-17

persecution (PUR-seh-CUE-shun) *trying to hurt people. Christians in the New Testament times were often persecuted by being put in jail or killed.*
· blessings with, Matthew 5:11-12; 1 Peter 3:8-17
· examples of, Acts 8:1-4; 1 Peter 3:13-15
· response to, Matthew 5:44; Romans 12:14; 1 Corinthians 4:12; 2 Corinthians 12:2
· of Christians, Matthew 13:21; 2 Timothy 3:12

Persia (PUR-zhuh) *a powerful country during the last years of the Old Testament; now called "Iran."*
· defeated Babylon, 2 Chronicles 36:20-23
· let captives return to Jerusalem, Ezra 1:1-11

Peter, *a fisherman; he and his brother, Andrew, were the first two apostles Jesus chose. First called " Simon" or "Peter," Jesus changed his name to "Cephas," which means "rock."*
· called to follow Jesus, Matthew 4:18-20
· walked on water, Matthew 14:22-33
· at the Last Supper, John 13:1-11
· defended Jesus, John 18:10-11
· denied Jesus, Mark 14:66-72; Luke 22:54-62
· preached the Good News, Acts 2:14-40
· an elder in the church, 1 Peter 5:1

pharaoh (FAY-row) *the title given to the kings of Egypt.*
· made Joseph ruler of Egypt, Genesis 40–47
· made Israelites slaves, Exodus 1–14

Pharisees (FARE-ih-seez) *"the separate people"; they followed the Jewish religious laws and customs very strictly. Jesus often spoke against them for their religious teachings and traditions.*

· practices of, Matthew 9:14; 15:1-9; Mark 7:1-13; Luke 7:30
· against Jesus, Matthew 12:14; 22:15; John 8:1-6
· criticized by Jesus, Matthew 5:20; Matthew 23

Philadelphia (fill-uh-DEL-fee-uh) *a city in the country now called "Turkey,"* Revelation 3:7-13

Philemon (fih-LEE-mun) *a Christian in the city of Colossae,* Philemon 1-25

Philip, the apostle (FIL-ip) *friend of Peter and Andrew.*
· called by Jesus, John 1:43
· brought Nathanael to Jesus, John 1:44-50
· brought Greeks to Jesus, John 12:21-22

Philip, the evangelist, *a Greek-speaking Jew chosen to serve in the church in Jerusalem.*
· preached in Samaria, Acts 8:5-13
· preached to the Ethiopian, Acts 8:26-39
· his daughters prophesied, Acts 21:8-9

Philip, the tetrarch, *son of Herod I and Cleopatra.*
· ruler of Iturea and Trachonitis, Luke 3:1

Philippi (fih-LIP-eye) *a city in northeastern Greece,* Philippians 1:1; 4:15
· Paul in jail there, Acts 16:11-40

Philistines (FIL-ih-steens) *people who were Israel's enemy for many years; worshiped false gods.*
· Samson defeated, Judges 15—16
· captured the Ark of the Agreement, 1 Samuel 4—6
· David defeated, 1 Samuel 17—18; 2 Samuel 5:17-25; 21:15-22

Phinehas, son of Eleazar (FIN-ee-us) *a priest and grandson of Aaron,* Numbers 25:1-13

Phinehas, son of Eli, *an evil priest,* 1 Samuel 1:3; 2:34; 4:4-11

Phoebe (FEE-beh) *a woman in the church in Cenchrea,* Romans 16:1

Phoenicia (foh-NEE-shuh) *an early name for the land on the east coast of the Mediterranean Sea; called "Lebanon" today,* Mark 7:26; Acts 11:19; 15:3

phylactery (fil-LAK-tur-ee) See "box of Scriptures."

pigs
· considered unclean, Leviticus 11:7
· snout of, Proverbs 11:22
· "don't throw your pearls before pigs." Matthew 7:6
· demons sent into, Matthew 8:30-33; Mark 5:11-13; Luke 8:32-33
· fed by prodigal son, Luke 15:15-16

Pilate, Pontius (PIE-lut, PON-shus) *the Roman governor of Judea from A.D. 26 to 36,* Luke 3:1; 13:1
· handed Jesus over to be killed, Matthew 27; Mark 15; Luke 23; John 18:28–19:38

pillar (PILL-ur) *a large stone that is set upright; also a tall column of stone that supports the roof of a building.*
· of Jacob, Genesis 28:18-22
· to worship false gods, 2 Kings 17:9-12
· in the Temple, 1 Kings 7:6,15-22
· of cloud and fire, Exodus 13:21-22; 14:19-24; 33:8-10

Pisgah, Mount (PIS-guh) *one of the high spots on Mount Nebo where Moses stood to see into the promised land,* Numbers 23:14; Deuteronomy 3:27; 34:1

plague (PLAYG) *a disaster. God sent ten plagues on the land of Egypt so the Egyptians would set the Israelites free.*
· on the Egyptians, Exodus 7—11
· on the Israelites, Exodus 32:35; Numbers 11:31-33; 16:41-50; 25:1-9

plumb line (PLUM LINE) *a string with a rock or other weight on one end. People used it to see if a wall was straight.*
· symbol for God's judging, 2 Kings 21:10-13; Amos 7:7-8

pomegranate (PAHM-gran-it) *a reddish fruit about the size of an apple,* Numbers 13:23; Joel 1:12
· design on priests' clothing, Exodus 28:33-34
· design of Temple decorations, 1 Kings 7:18-20

poor
· God's care for, Psalm 140:12; Proverbs 22:22-23; Matthew 11:5; James 2:5
· treatment of, Leviticus 19:9-10; Matthew 25:34-36; Luke 14:12-14

possessions
· promised land given to Israelites, Genesis 17:8; Numbers 32:22; Joshua 1:11
· proper attitudes toward, Ecclesiastes 5:10–6:6; Luke 12:13-21; Acts 2:45; 1 John 3:17
· danger of, Matthew 19:22
· sold by Christians, Acts 2:45

Potiphar (POT-ih-fur) *an officer for the king of Egypt. He put Joseph in charge of his household.* Genesis 39

pottage (POT-edge) *a thick vegetable soup or stew,* Genesis 25:29-34; 2 Kings 4:38-41

potter (POT-ur) *a person who makes pots and dishes out of clay.*
· as a symbol of God, Jeremiah 18:1-6

power
· of Jesus, Matthew 24:30; 28:18; Luke 6:19

- of the Spirit, Luke 4:14; Acts 1:8; Romans 15:19
- of Satan, Acts 26:18
- of the apostles, Luke 9:1; Acts 4:33

praetorium (pray-TORE-ee-um) *the governor's palace in New Testament times,* Matthew 27:27; Acts 23:35

praise (PRAYZ) *to say good things about someone or something. God's people can praise him by singing, praying, and by living the way he tells us to live.* 1 Chronicles 16:4-7; Psalms 103; 104; 145–150

prayer
- teachings about, Matthew 5:44-45; 21:18-22; Philippians 4:6; James 5:15-16
- Jesus' model prayer, Matthew 6:5-15

preach, *to give a talk on a religious subject; to tell the Good News.*
- Jonah preached to Nineveh, Jonah 3:2-4
- John preached, Matthew 3:1; Mark 1:4; Luke 3:3
- Jesus preached, Matthew 4:17; Mark 2:2; Luke 4:43-44
- Good News preached, Acts 8:25,40; Galatians 2:7; 1 Thessalonians 2:9
- preaching commanded, 2 Timothy 4:2

Preparation Day (prep-a-RAY-shun DAY) *the day before the Sabbath day. On that day the Jews prepared for the Sabbath.* Luke 23:54; John 19:14,31

pride
- warnings against, Romans 12:3; 1 Corinthians 13:4; Philippians 2:3; James 4:6

priest (PREEST) *in the Old Testament, a servant of God who worked in the Holy Tent or Temple. See also "high priest."*
- clothes for, Exodus 28
- appointing of, Exodus 29:1-37
- rules for, Leviticus 21–22:16

Priscilla (prih-SIL-uh) *a friend of Paul,* Acts 18:1-4,18-19; Romans 16:3-4
- taught Apollos, Acts 18:24-26

prison
- Joseph in prison, Genesis 39:20–41:40
- Peter in prison, Acts 5:17-20
- Paul in prison, Acts 16:23-34

prodigal (PRAH-dih-gul) *careless and wasteful.*
- the prodigal son, Luke 15:11-32

promise
- from God, Joshua 1:3; 1 Kings 8:20; Galatians 3:14; Ephesians 3:6
- first commandment with, Ephesians 6:2
- Lord is not slow in keeping, 2 Peter 2:9

prophecy (PRAH-feh-see) *a message; God speaking through chosen people called "prophets,"* Ezekiel 14:9; 1 Thessalonians 5:20; 2 Peter 1:20-21

prophesy (PRAH-fes-sy) *to speak a prophecy,* Acts 2:17-18. See "prophecy."
- a spiritual gift, 1 Corinthians 14:1-5

prophet (PRAH-fet) *a messenger; one who is able, with God's help, to tell God's message correctly. Sometimes prophets told what would happen in the future.* Matthew 11:13-14
- how to judge, Deuteronomy 13:1-5; 18:21-22
- examples of, Ezra 5:1; Jeremiah 1:1-9; Matthew 3:3
- false prophets, Deuteronomy 13:1-5

prophetess (PRAH-feh-tess) *a female prophet,* Exodus 15:20; Judges 4:4; 2 Kings 22:14; Luke 2:36. See "prophet."

prostitute (PRAH-sti-toot) *a person who sells his or her body for sex.*
- warnings against, 1 Corinthians 6:15
- examples of, Genesis 38:15-16; Jeremiah 3:1-3; Hosea 3:2-3; Matthew 21:32

proverbs (PRAH-verbs) *wise sayings. The book of Proverbs contains many wise sayings that tell how to live a good and happy life.* 1 Kings 4:32; Proverbs

psalm (SAHM) *a song. The book of Psalms is like a songbook.* Ephesians 5:19; Colossians 3:16

publican (PUB-leh-kun) See "tax collector."

Publius (POOB-lih-us) *an important man of the island of Malta,* Acts 28:7-8

Pul, See "Tiglath-Pileser."

punishment
- of Cain, Genesis 4:13
- everlasting, Matthew 25:46; 2 Thessalonians 1:8-9
- for rejecting Jesus, Hebrews 10:29
- by government, Romans 13:4; 1 Peter 2:14

pure
- gold, Exodus 25:11-39; 37; 1 Kings 6:20-21
- heart, Psalm 51:10; Matthew 5:8
- describing Jesus, Hebrews 7:26
- describing people, Job 4:17; 15:14; Philippians 1:10; Titus 1:15
- water, Hebrews 10:22

Purim, See "Feast of Purim."

purple, *a color that, in Bible times, was worn by kings, queens, and other rich people. Purple cloth was expensive because the purple dye came from special shellfish.* Exodus 25:1-4; Judges 8:26; Mark 15:17; Acts 16:14

Q

quail (KWALE) *a brownish-white bird.*
- given by God to Israel, Exodus 16:11-13; Numbers 11:31-34; Psalm 105:40

quarrel
· Israelites quarreled with Moses, Exodus 17:1-7

Queen Goddess, *Ishtar; a goddess of the Babylonians,* Jeremiah 7:18; 44:15-29

Queen of Heaven, See "Queen Goddess."

queen of Sheba, See "Sheba, queen of."

question
· Solomon questioned by queen of Sheba, 1 Kings 10:1-3
· Jesus questioned, Mark 8:11; Luke 23:9; John 8:6
· asked by Jesus, Matthew 21:24
· apostles questioned by Jews, Acts 4:7; 5:27

quiet
· words, Ecclesiastes 9:17
· riot quieted, Acts 19:35-36
· life, 1 Thessalonians 4:11; 1 Timothy 2:2

Quirinius (kwy-RIN-ee-us) *the Roman governor of Syria when Jesus was born,* Luke 2:1-3

quiver (KWIH-vur) *a bag to hold arrows,* Psalm 127:5; Isaiah 49:2

R

Rabbah (RAB-uh) *the capital city of the Ammonites,* 2 Samuel 11:1; 12:26-29; Ezekiel 25:5

rabbi/rabboni (RAB-eye/rah-BONE-eye) *teacher. Jesus' followers often called him "rabbi" as a sign of respect.* John 1:38; 20:16

Rachel (RAY-chel) *a wife of Jacob and the mother of Benjamin and Joseph.*
· married Jacob, Genesis 29:1-30
· gave birth to Joseph, Genesis 30:22-24
· stole Laban's idols, Genesis 31:19-35
· death of, Genesis 35:16-20

Rahab, the dragon (RAY-hab) *In a well-known story, Rahab was defeated. Egypt was sometimes called Rahab to show that it would be defeated.* Job 9:13; Isaiah 30:7

Rahab, the prostitute, *a woman in Jericho. She hid the Israelite spies and helped them escape.*
· hid the spies, Joshua 2:1-21
· rescued from Jericho, Joshua 6:16-25
· an example of faith, Hebrews 11:31; James 2:25

rainbow
· a sign of God's agreement with people, Genesis 9:8-17

raisin, 1 Samuel 25:18; 30:12; 1 Chronicles 12:40

ram, *a male sheep.*
· offered instead of Isaac, Genesis 22:13
· used for burnt offerings, Exodus 29; Leviticus 8:18-29; Numbers 28:11–29:37

· with two horns, Daniel 8:3-22

Ramah (RAY-muh) *a town about five miles north of Jerusalem,* Jeremiah 31:15; Matthew 2:18

Rameses (RAM-eh-seez) *one of the cities built by the Israelites when they were slaves in Egypt,* Exodus 1:11; 12:37; Numbers 33:3

Ramoth Gilead (RAY-moth GIL-ee-ad) *one of the cities of safety on the east side of the Jordan River,* Joshua 20:8; 1 Kings 4:13; 2 Kings 8:28–9:14

ransom, *a payment that frees a captive.*
· Jesus as a ransom for sins, Matthew 20:28; 1 Timothy 2:6; Hebrews 9:15

Rapha (RAY-fa) *a leader of a group of people in Canaan who may have been giants. The descendants of Rapha are called "Rephaites."* 2 Samuel 21:15-22; Joshua 13:12

raven, *a large black bird similar to a crow which eats dead things.*
· sent out by Noah, Genesis 8:7
· fed Elijah, 1 Kings 17:4-6

read
· the Book of the Teachings, Joshua 8:34-35; Nehemiah 8:2-9
· reading the teachings commanded, Deuteronomy 17:18-19; 31:9-13
· brings happiness, Revelation 1:3

Rebekah (ree-BEK-uh) *the wife of Isaac and the mother of Jacob and Esau.*
· married Isaac, Genesis 24
· gave birth to Jacob and Esau, Genesis 25:19-26
· helped deceive Isaac, Genesis 27
· buried at Machpelah, Genesis 49:31

redeem (ree-DEEM) *to buy something back or to buy a slave's freedom.*
· property, Leviticus 25:23-34; Ruth 4:3-6
· slave, Leviticus 25:47-49
· redeemed by God, 1 Corinthians 6:20; Galatians 4:5; Titus 2:14

Red Sea, *Sea of Reeds; a large body of water between Africa and Arabia.*
· Israelites crossed, Exodus 13:17–14:31

refuge, *a place of safety or protection.*
· God as our refuge, Deuteronomy 33:27; 2 Samuel 22:3; Psalms 18:2; 31:2; 71:3; 91:2
· city of, Numbers 35:6-34; Joshua 20

Rehoboam (ree-ho-BO-um) *son of Solomon who took his place as king.*
· became king, 1 Kings 11:41-43
· Israel rebelled against, 1 Kings 12:1-24
· strengthened Judah, 2 Chronicles 11:5-17
· disobeyed God, 2 Chronicles 12

rejoice
- commanded to, Matthew 5:11-12; Romans 12:15; Philippians 4:4; 1 Peter 4:13
- examples of, 1 Samuel 6:13; Nehemiah 12:43

remission (rih-MISH-un) See "forgiveness."

remnant (REM-nant) *a small part that is left; a name used for the Jews who were left alive after their captivity in Babylon.*
- of Israelites who returned to Jerusalem, Ezra 9:15; Nehemiah 1:2; Isaiah 10:20-22

repent (ree-PENT) *being sorry for doing something wrong and not continuing to do that wrong.* See "change of heart and life."

Rephaites, See "Rapha."

respect
- to parents, Leviticus 19:3; 1 Timothy 3:4
- between husbands and wives, Ephesians 5:33; 1 Peter 3:7
- to all people, 1 Peter 2:17; 3:16

rest
- on the seventh day, Genesis 2:2; Exodus 31:15; Hebrews 4:4
- given by the Lord, Psalm 95:11; Jeremiah 6:16; Matthew 11:28
- heaven as a place of rest, Revelation 14:13

resurrection (REZ-uh-REK-shun) *a dead person's coming back to life.*
- of Jesus, Matthew 28:1-10; Mark 16; Luke 24; John 20–21; Acts 2:24-32; Romans 1:4
- of God's people, John 6:39; Acts 24:15; 1 Corinthians 15; Philippians 3:10-11; Hebrews 11:35

Reuben (ROO-ben) *oldest of Jacob's twelve sons.*
- birth of, Genesis 29:32
- tried to save Joseph, Genesis 37:18-29
- descendants of, Exodus 6:14; Numbers 1:20; Joshua 13:15-23

revelation (rev-uh-LAY-shun) *showing plainly something that has been hidden,* 2 Corinthians 12:1; Revelation 1:1-3

revenge
- warnings against, Leviticus 19:18; Romans 12:19; 1 Thessalonians 5:15; 1 Peter 3:9

reward
- in heaven, Matthew 5:12
- for obedience, Psalm 19:11
- for what a person does, Matthew 6:1-18; 10:42; 16:27; Colossians 3:24
- children as a reward, Psalm 127:3

Rhoda (ROAD-uh) *a servant girl in the home of John Mark's mother,* Acts 12:6-17

righteousness (RY-chuss-ness) *being right with God and doing what is right.*
- explained, Romans 3:19-26; 2 Corinthians 5:21; 6:4-7; Philippians 3:8-9

- Abraham as an example of, Romans 4:3
- right living, 2 Corinthians 6:7; Ephesians 5:9; 1 Timothy 6:11; 1 Peter 2:24

robber
- Temple as a hideout for, Jeremiah 7:11; Matthew 21:13
- attacked man on road to Jericho, Luke 10:30
- killed with Jesus, Matthew 27:38-44; John 18:40

roof
- spies hid there, Joshua 2:6
- David saw Bathsheba from there, 2 Samuel 11:2
- built room for Elisha there, 2 Kings 4:8-10
- man lowered through, Mark 2:3-4
- Peter prayed there, Acts 10:9

Rock, *often used as a name for God. As a large rock is strong and provides a hiding place, so God is strong and protects us from our enemies.* Genesis 49:24; 2 Samuel 22:32-49; Psalm 19:14

rock badger (ROK BAD-jur) *a coney; a small, tailless animal like a rabbit that hides among the mountain gorges and rocky areas of Arabia,* Psalm 104:18; Proverbs 30:26

Rome, *the capital city of the Roman Empire at the time of Christ,* Acts 2:10; 18:2; Romans 1:7
- Paul sent there, Acts 23:11; 28:14-15

Ruth (ROOTH) *a widow from Moab.*
- moved to Judah, Ruth 1
- worked in Boaz's field, Ruth 2
- married Boaz, Ruth 3–4
- birth of Obed, Ruth 4:13-22

S

Sabbath (SAB-uth) *means "rest"; the seventh day of the Jewish week; the Jews' day to worship God. They were not allowed to work on this day.*
- commands about, Exodus 20:8-11; 31:12-17
- Jesus is Lord of, Matthew 12:1-13; Mark 2:23-28; Luke 6:1-11

sackcloth (SAK-cloth) *a type of clothing made from rough cloth; worn by people to show their sadness,* Genesis 37:33-35; Esther 4:1; Matthew 11:21

sacrifice (SAK-rih-fice) *to give something valuable to God.*
- burnt sacrifices, Leviticus 6:8-13
- drink sacrifices, Leviticus 23:13; Numbers 15:5; 28:7
- penalty sacrifices, Leviticus 7:1-10
- fellowship sacrifices, Leviticus 3; 7:11-27
- sin sacrifices, Leviticus 4
- limits of, Hebrews 9; 10
- living sacrifice, Romans 12:1

Sadducees (SAD-you-seez) *a Jewish religious group that didn't believe in angels or resurrection; they believed only the first five books of the Old Testament were true.*
- challenged Jesus, Matthew 22:23-33
- arrested Peter and John, Acts 4:1-3
- arrested the apostles, Acts 5:17-42
- Paul spoke to the council, Acts 23:1-9

safety, city of, *city of refuge. In Bible times, someone who had accidentally killed another person could go to a city of safety for protection. As long as he was there, the dead person's relative could not punish him.*
- rules about, Numbers 35:6-34; Joshua 20

saffron (SAF-ron) *a purple flower; parts of it are used as a spice,* Song of Solomon 4:14

saint, *holy person; another word for "Christian,"* Acts 9:41; Romans 1:7; 1 Corinthians 14:33

Salem (SAY-lem) *means "peace"; an old name for Jerusalem.*
- home of Melchizedek, Genesis 14:18; Hebrews 7:1-2

Salome, daughter of Herodias (sah-LO-mee)
- had John the Baptist killed, Matthew 14:3-12; Mark 6:17-29

Salome, wife of Zebedee, *the mother of the apostles James and John,* Mark 15:40; 16:1

salt
- used to preserve foods, Job 6:6; Mark 9:50
- Lot's wife turned into salt, Genesis 19:15-26
- "You are the salt of the earth," Matthew 5:13

Salt Sea, See "Dead Sea."

salvation (sal-VAY-shun) *being rescued from danger; being saved from sin and its punishment.*
- as God's gift, John 3:16; Ephesians 2:8; Titus 2:11
- through Christ, Acts 4:12; 1 Thessalonians 5:9; 1 Timothy 1:15; Hebrews 5:7-9
- as a helmet, Ephesians 6:17; 1 Thessalonians 5:8
- urgency of, 2 Corinthians 6:2; Hebrews 2:3
- rejoice in, Psalms 9:14; 13:5; 51:12; Isaiah 25:9

Samaritan (sah-MEHR-ih-ton) *a person from the area of Samaria in Palestine. These people were only partly Jewish, so the Jews hated them.* John 4:9
- Jesus taught a Samaritan woman, John 4:1-42
- story of the good Samaritan, Luke 10:25-37

Samson (SAM-son) *one of Israel's judges; he was famous for his great strength.*
- birth of, Judges 13
- married a Philistine, Judges 14-15

- tricked by Delilah, Judges 16:4-22
- death of, Judges 16:23-31
- hero of faith, Hebrews 11:32

Samuel (SAM-u-el) *the last judge in Israel.*
- birth of, 1 Samuel 1:1-20
- worked in the Temple, 1 Samuel 1:21–2:26
- became a prophet, 1 Samuel 3
- appointed Saul as king, 1 Samuel 10
- appointed David as king, 1 Samuel 16:1-13
- death of, 1 Samuel 25:1

Sanballat (san-BAL-lat) *governor of Samaria who tried to stop Nehemiah from rebuilding the walls of Jerusalem,* Nehemiah 4–6

sanctify (SANK-teh-fy) *to make holy or ready for service to God,* John 17:17-19; 1 Corinthians 6:11; 1 Peter 1:2

sanctuary (SANK-choo-air-ee) See "Holy Place."

sand
- Abraham's descendants as numerous as, Genesis 22:17; 32:12
- Job's days as numerous as, Job 29:18
- house built on, Matthew 7:26-27

Sanhedrin (san-HEE-drin) See "council."

Sapphira (sah-FY-ruh) *wife of Ananias.*
- lied to the Holy Spirit, Acts 5:1-11

Sarah (SAIR-uh) *wife of Abraham,* Genesis 11:29-30
- gave Hagar to Abraham, Genesis 16:1-6
- name changed from "Sarai," Genesis 17:15-16
- gave birth to Isaac, Genesis 21:1-7
- death of, Genesis 23

Satan (SAY-ton) *means "enemy"; the devil; the enemy of God and man.*
- encouraged David to sin, 1 Chronicles 21:1
- tested Job, Job 1:6-12; 2:1-7
- tempted Jesus, Luke 4:1-13
- a fallen angel, Luke 10:18-19
- to be thrown into lake of fire, Revelation 20:10

Saul, king of Israel
- appointed king, 1 Samuel 9–10
- disobeyed God, 1 Samuel 15
- tried to kill David, 1 Samuel 19; 23:7-29
- death of, 1 Samuel 31

Saul of Tarsus, Acts 13:9. See "Paul."

savior
- God as Savior, Psalm 25:5; Isaiah 45:21; Luke 1:47; 1 Timothy 1:1
- Christ as Savior, Luke 2:11; John 4:42; Ephesians 5:23; Titus 2:13

scarlet (SCAR-let) *a bright red color,* Exodus 26:1; Joshua 2:18; Isaiah 1:18; Matthew 27:28

scepter (SEP-tur) *a wand or a rod that the king holds; a sign of his power,* Esther 4:11; Psalm 60:7

scourge (SKURJ) *to beat someone with a whip or stick,* 1 Kings 12:11
· Jesus scourged, Matthew 27:26; Mark 15:15
· Paul scourged, Acts 21:32; 2 Corinthians 11:24

scribe, *to write, to count, and to put in order. In New Testament times scribes were men who wrote copies of the Scriptures.*
· Ezra as scribe, Nehemiah 8:1
· against Jesus, Matthew 15:1-9
· condemned by Jesus, Matthew 23:13-36

Scriptures (SCRIP-churs) *special writings of God's word for people. When the word Scriptures is used in the New Testament, it usually means the Old Testament. Later, it came to mean the whole Bible.*
· fulfilled, Matthew 26:52-54; John 19:24,28,36
· given by God, 2 Timothy 3:16

scroll, *a long roll of paper used for writing,* Deuteronomy 17:18; Jeremiah 36; Revelation 5:1-5

Scythians (SITH-ee-unz) *a group of wandering people who lived near the Black Sea,* Colossians 3:11

Sea of Galilee, See "Galilee, Lake."

Sea of Reeds, See "Red Sea."

seal, *a tool with a design or picture carved on it. Kings pressed this seal into wax and used it like a signature. Sometimes these seals were worn as rings.*
· examples of, 1 Kings 21:8; Esther 8:8

seed
· created by God, Genesis 1:11,12,29
· parables of, Matthew 13:1-43

seer, *another name for prophet.* See "prophet."

Selah (SEE-lah) *probably a musical direction; used in the Psalms. It may mean to pause. The word was not intended to be spoken when reading the psalm.* Psalms 3:2,4,8; 89:4,37,45,48

Sennacherib (sen-AK-ur-ib) *king of Assyria from 705 to 681 B.C.*
· attacked Jerusalem, 2 Kings 18:13-19; 2 Chronicles 32:1-23; Isaiah 36-37

Sermon on the Mount, *a sermon Jesus preached as he was sitting on the side of a mountain near Lake Galilee,* Matthew 5-7

serpent, See "snake."

servant
· of the Lord, Deuteronomy 34:5; Joshua 2:8; 1 Kings 11:32; Luke 1:38
· Jesus as a, Philippians 2:7
· parable of, Matthew 25:14-30
· Jesus' followers to be, Matthew 20:25-27

Seth, *the third son of Adam and Eve,* Genesis 4:25-26; 5:6-8; Luke 3:38

Shadrach (SHAYD-rak) *a friend of Daniel.*
· taken into captivity, Daniel 1
· became a leader, Daniel 2:49
· saved from the furnace, Daniel 3

Shallum, king of Israel (SHAL-um) *ruled for only one month in 752 B.C.,* 2 Kings 15:10-15

Shalmaneser (shal-mah-NEE-zer) *a king of Assyria,* 2 Kings 17:1-6; 18:9

Shaphan (SHAY-fan) *an assistant to King Josiah,* 2 Kings 22:3-14; 2 Chronicles 34:8-21

sharing
· commanded, Luke 3:11; Romans 12:13; 1 Timothy 6:18
· examples of, Acts 2:42-47; 4:32; 2 Corinthians 8:1-4

Sharon (SHAIR-un) *the plain in Palestine along the coast of the Mediterranean Sea,* 1 Chronicles 5:16; 27:29; Song of Solomon 2:1; Isaiah 33:9

sheaf (SHEEF) *a bundle of grain stalks that have been cut and tied together,* Genesis 37:7; Leviticus 23:10; Job 24:10

Sheba, queen of (SHE-buh) *a queen who came to visit Solomon and see his wealth,* 1 Kings 10:1-13

Shebna (SHEB-nuh) *the manager of the palace for King Hezekiah,* 2 Kings 18:17-19:4; Isaiah 36:1-37:4

sheep
· God's people compared to, Ezekiel 34; John 10:1-18; 1 Peter 2:25
· parable of, Luke 15:1-7

Shem, *Noah's oldest son,* Genesis 6:10; 7:13; 10:21-31

sheminith (SHEM-ih-nith) *a musical term in the Psalms that means an octave (eight notes); may mean to use an instrument with eight strings,* Psalms 6; 12

shepherd
· David as, 1 Samuel 17:15,34-36
· Lord as, Psalm 23
· Jesus, the good shepherd, John 10:1-18
· elders as, 1 Peter 5:1-4

Sheshbazzar (shesh-BAZ-ur) *governor of the Jews in 538 B.C.,* Ezra 1:7-11; 5:13-16

shiggaion (shi-GY-on) *probably a musical term; used in the Psalms; may mean that the psalm is a sad song,* Psalm 7

shigionoth (shi-GY-o-noth) *probably a musical term,* Habakkuk 3:1

Shiloh (SHY-lo) *a town north of Jerusalem.*
· location of the Holy Tent, Joshua 18:1,8; Judges 18:31; Jeremiah 7:12

Shimei (SHIM-ee-i) *a relative of King Saul.*
- cursed David, 2 Samuel 16:5-14
- asked forgiveness, 2 Samuel 19:16-23
- death of, 1 Kings 2:36-46

ship, 1 Kings 9:26-28; 22:48; Acts 27

Shishak (SHY-shak) *king of Egypt during the time of Solomon and Rehoboam.*
- attacked Jerusalem, 1 Kings 14:25-28; 2 Chronicles 12:1-9

showbread, See "bread that shows we are in God's presence."

Shunammite (SHOO-nah-mite) *a person from Shunem, a town in northern Israel.*
- Shunammite woman took care of Elisha, 2 Kings 4:8-17
- her son raised from the dead, 2 Kings 4:18-37
- given back her land, 2 Kings 8:1-6

sickle (SICK-ul) *a tool for cutting grain,* Revelation 14:14-19

Sidon (SY-don) *a Phoenician city on the coast of the Mediterranean Sea,* Genesis 10:19; Matthew 11:21-22; Mark 7:31; Acts 27:3-4

siege mound (SEEJ) *dirt piled against a city wall to make it easier for attackers to climb up and attack the city,* 2 Samuel 20:15; Isaiah 37:33; Jeremiah 6:6

signet ring (SIG-net RING) *a ring worn by a king or other important person. It had his seal on it.* Genesis 41:42; Esther 3:10; 8:2-10; Daniel 6:17. See "seal."

Sihon (SY-hon) *a king of the Amorites when the Israelites came out of Egypt.*
- refused to let Israelites pass, Numbers 21:21-31; Deuteronomy 2:24-37

Silas (SY-lus) *also "Silvanus"; a teacher in the church in Jerusalem who often traveled with Paul.*
- sent to the Gentiles, Acts 15:22-23; 17:16
- joined Paul in Corinth, Acts 18:5
- helped with Peter's letter, 1 Peter 5:12

Siloam, pool of (sy-LO-um) *a pool of water in Jerusalem,* John 9:1-12

Silvanus (sil-VAY-nus) See "Silas."

Simeon of Jerusalem (SIM-ee-un) *a godly man who saw baby Jesus in the Temple,* Luke 2:25-35

Simeon, son of Israel, *one of the twelve sons of Israel,* Genesis 29:33; 42:23-36
- descendants of, Numbers 1:22-23; 26:12-14

Simon, brother of Jesus (SY-mun) Matthew 13:55

Simon of Cyrene (sy-REE-ni) *carried the cross of Jesus,* Matthew 27:32; Mark 15:21; Luke 23:26

Simon Peter, See "Peter."

Simon, the magician, *tried to buy the power of the Holy Spirit,* Acts 8:9-24

Simon, the Zealot, *an apostle of Jesus,* Matthew 10:4; Mark 3:18; Luke 6:15; Acts 1:13

sin, *a word, thought, or act against the law of God.*
- offering for, Leviticus 4; 6:24-30; Hebrews 7:27; 10:4-12
- committed by everyone, Romans 3:23; 1 John 1:8-10
- Christ died for, Romans 4:25; 1 Corinthians 15:3; 1 Peter 2:24; 1 John 2:2; 3:5
- results of, Isaiah 59:2; Romans 6:23; Ephesians 2:1; Hebrews 12:1

Sinai (SY-ny) *a mountain in the desert between Egypt and Canaan.*
- Moses received the Ten Commandments there, Exodus 19-20

singing, *a way of praising God and teaching each other,* Judges 5:3; Psalm 30:4; Ephesians 5:19; Colossians 3:16

Sisera (SIS-er-uh) *captain of a Canaanite army,* Judges 4

slave
- rules about, Exodus 21:1-11,16,26-32; Ephesians 6:5-9; 1 Timothy 6:1-2

slave woman, *concubine; she bore children for her master but was not considered equal to a wife.*
- Hagar as, Genesis 16:1-3
- of Solomon, 1 Kings 11:2-3

sleep
- God never sleeps, Psalm 121:4
- danger of, Proverbs 6:10-11
- Eutychus fell asleep, Acts 20:9
- to awake from, Romans 13:11
- a gift from the Lord, Psalm 127:2

sling, *a weapon for throwing rocks,* Judges 20:16; 1 Samuel 17:39-50; 2 Kings 3:24-25

slothful (SLAWTH-ful) *lazy and undependable,* Proverbs 6:6-11; 13:4; Matthew 25:26; Hebrews 6:12

sluggard, See "slothful."

snake
- sticks became snakes, Exodus 7:8-13
- bronze snake made by Moses, Numbers 21:4-9; John 3:14
- Paul bitten by, Acts 28:1-6

Sodom (SOD-um) *a town known for its evil people.*
- destroyed, Genesis 18:17-19:29
- symbol of evil, Matthew 10:11-15; 11:20-24; Revelation 11:8

soldier
- arrested Jesus, John 18:12-13
- made fun of Jesus, Matthew 27:27-31; Luke 23:11
- at Jesus' death, Matthew 27:32-37; Luke 23:26-38,47; John 19:1-3,16-24,28-35
- lied about Jesus' resurrection, Matthew 28:11-15
- Cornelius, Acts 10:1
- guarded Peter, Acts 12:6
- Christian compared to, 2 Timothy 2:3-4

Solomon (SOL-o-mon) *a son of David; famous for his wisdom.*
- became king, 1 Kings 1:28-53
- wisdom of, 1 Kings 3:1-15; 4:29-34
- made a wise decision, 1 Kings 3:16-28
- built the Temple, 1 Kings 6; 7:13-51
- visited by the queen of Sheba, 1 Kings 10:1-13; Matthew 12:42
- married many women, 1 Kings 11:1-8
- death of, 1 Kings 11:40-41

Solomon's Porch (SOL-o-mon's PORCH) *a covered courtyard on the east side of the Temple,* 1 Kings 7:6; John 10:23; Acts 3:11; 5:12

Son of David, *a name the Jews used for the Christ because the Savior was to come from the family of King David,* Matthew 1:1; 9:27; 15:22; 21:9

Son of Man, *a name Jesus called himself. It showed that he was God's Son, but he was also a human being.* Matthew 24:30; Mark 13:26; Luke 21:27; 22:69-70

sorcery (SOR-sir-ee) *trying to put magical spells on people or harming them by magic,* Acts 8:9-25; 19:18-19
- warnings against, Leviticus 19:26; Deuteronomy 18:14-15; 2 Kings 17:17

soul (SOLE) *what makes a person alive. Sometimes the Bible writers used words like "heart" and "soul" to mean a person's whole being or the person himself.*
- "destroy the soul and the body," Matthew 10:28
- losing, Matthew 16:26
- "all your heart and all your soul," Matthew 22:37
- joined with the spirit, Hebrews 4:12

sower, *someone who plants seeds to grow into crops,* Matthew 13:1-43; 2 Corinthians 9:6

Spirit (SPIH-rit) See "Holy Spirit."

spirit, *the part of humans that was made to be like God because God is spirit. The New Testament also talks about evil spirits.* Isaiah 26:9; 1 Thessalonians 5:23; James 2:26
- evil spirit, Matthew 12:43; Mark 1:23; 5:2; Luke 4:33

spiritual gifts, *special talents or abilities that God gives his people,* Romans 12:6-8;

1 Corinthians 12:1-11; 14; Ephesians 4:7-13

spring, *a natural fountain,* Genesis 7:11; Exodus 15:27

staff, *a shepherd's walking stick,* Exodus 4:1-5; 7:8-12; Numbers 20:6-11; Psalm 23:4

steal, See also "robber."
- commands against, Exodus 20:15; Matthew 19:18; Romans 13:9; Ephesians 4:28

Stephen (STEE-ven) *one of the seven men chosen to serve the church in Jerusalem; the first martyr for Christ.*
- chosen to serve the church, Acts 6:5-6
- killed by the Jews, Acts 6:8–7:60

stoning, *a way of killing someone by throwing rocks at him.*
- commanded, Deuteronomy 17:2-7
- Naboth stoned, 1 Kings 21:13
- Stephen stoned, Acts 7:54-60
- Paul stoned, Acts 14:19

strength
- love God with all your strength, Deuteronomy 6:5; Mark 12:30
- God as the source, Psalms 18:1; 73:26; Philippians 4:13; 1 Peter 4:11

stronghold, *a fortress, a well protected place,* 1 Samuel 22:4; 2 Samuel 5:17

suffering
- proper attitude toward, 2 Corinthians 1:3-7; James 5:10
- value of, Romans 8:17-18; 1 Peter 3:8-17
- of Jesus, Isaiah 53:3-10; Luke 24:26,46; Philippians 3:10; Hebrews 2:18

swaddling clothes, *pieces of cloth that were wrapped around a newborn baby in Jesus' time,* Luke 2:7-12

sword
- of fire, Genesis 3:24
- a weapon, Joshua 5:13; 1 Samuel 17:45; Matthew 26:51-52
- the word of God, Ephesians 6:17; Hebrews 4:12

Sychar (SY-kar) *a small town in Samaria near Jacob's well,* John 4:5-6

synagogue (SIN-uh-gog) *"a meeting." By the first century, the Jews met in synagogues to read and study the Scriptures. The building was also used as the Jewish court and as a school.*
- Jesus taught in, Matthew 4:23; Mark 1:21; Luke 4:16-17
- Paul spoke there, Acts 17:1,10

Syria (SEER-ee-uh) *an area north of Galilee and east of the Mediterranean Sea; called "Aram" in Old Testament times.* See "Aram."

- enemy of Israel, 1 Kings 11:25; 20:1-34; 2 Kings 13:22-25
- learned about Jesus, Matthew 4:24

T

tabernacle (TAB-er-NAK-'l) See "Meeting Tent."

tablets of the agreement, *two flat stones on which God wrote the Ten Commandments.*
- given to Moses, Exodus 19–20; 24:12-18
- broken by Moses, Exodus 32:15-19
- the second tablets, Exodus 34:1-4
- in the Most Holy Place, Hebrews 9:4

Tabitha (TAB-eh-thuh) See "Dorcas."

Tabor, Mount (TAY-bur) *in the Valley of Jezreel about twelve miles from Lake Galilee,* Judges 4:6-16; Psalm 89:12

tambourine (tam-bah-REEN) *a musical instrument that is beaten to keep rhythm,* Exodus 15:20; 1 Samuel 18:6; Psalm 81:2

Tarshish (TAR-shish) *a city somewhere on the western side of the Mediterranean Sea,* Jonah 1:3; 4:2

Tarsus (TAR-sus) *the most important city in Cilicia, which is now the country of Turkey,* Acts 9:30; 11:25-26
- home of Paul, Acts 9:11; 21:39; 22:3

tax collector, *a Jew hired by the Romans to collect taxes,* Matthew 9:10-11
- Matthew, Matthew 10:3; Luke 5:27
- Zacchaeus, Luke 19:1-10

teacher
- Jesus called a, Matthew 8:19; Mark 10:17; John 1:38; 3:2
- in the church, Romans 12:7; Ephesians 4:11; 1 Timothy 4:13
- false, 1 Timothy 4:1-5; 2 Peter 2:1
- to be judged more strictly, James 3:1

teaching
- commanded, Deuteronomy 6:1-7; Matthew 28:20; 2 Timothy 2:2,14-15; Titus 2

Teachings of Moses, *or the "Law of Moses,"* Deuteronomy 31:24-26; Joshua 23:6; Nehemiah 8
- purpose of, Romans 3:20; 5:20; Galatians 3:21-25
- limitations of, Romans 8:3; Galatians 2:19; Hebrews 10:1

temple (TEM-p'l) *a building where people worship. God told the Jewish people to worship him at the Temple in Jerusalem.*
- Solomon's Temple, 1 Kings 6–8; 2 Chronicles 2–7
- the Temple rebuilt, Ezra 3
- the body as a temple, John 2:19-22; 1 Corinthians 3:16-17; 6:19-20; 2 Corinthians 6:16

temptation (temp-TAY-shun) *the devil's attempt to get us to do something wrong.*

- Jesus tempted, Matthew 4:1-11; Luke 4:1-13; Hebrews 4:15-16
- a way of escape from, 1 Corinthians 10:13
- source of, James 1:13-15

Ten Commandments, *the rules God gave Moses on Mount Sinai,* Exodus 20:1-20; 31:18; 34:1-28; Deuteronomy 5:1-22

tent
- Abram's tents, Genesis 13:18
- peg, Judges 4:21-22
- makers of, Acts 18:3

Tent, See "Meeting Tent."

Thaddaeus (THAD-ee-us) *one of the twelve apostles,* Matthew 10:3; Mark 3:18

thankfulness, Psalm 107:1; 1 Thessalonians 5:8; Hebrews 12:28

Theophilus (thee-AHF-ih-lus) *the person to whom the books of Luke and Acts were written,* Luke 1:1-4; Acts 1:1

Thessalonica (THES-ah-lah-NY-kah) *the capital of the country of Macedonia, which is now northern Greece,* 1 Thessalonians 1:1; 2 Thessalonians 1:1
- Paul preached there, Acts 17:1-9

Thomas (TOM-us) *Didymus; one of the twelve apostles,* Matthew 10:2-3
- questioned Jesus, John 14:5-7
- saw Jesus after resurrection, John 20:24-29; 21:2

thorn, *sharp points on a branch or stem of a plant.*
- as a curse on Adam, Genesis 3:17-18
- crown of, Matthew 27:29; Mark 15:17; John 19:2-5

threshing floor, *a place where farmers separated grain from chaff. This was done by beating the stalks on the hard ground, throwing them in the air, and letting the wind blow the chaff away.*
- angel visited Gideon there, Judges 6:11
- David bought, 2 Samuel 24:16-25

throne
- king's throne, 1 Kings 10:18-19
- God's throne, Matthew 5:34; Hebrews 4:16; Revelation 3:21; 4

Thummim (THUM-im) *the Urim and Thummim may have been gems. They were attached to the holy vest of the high priest and were used to learn God's will.* Exodus 28:29-30; Leviticus 8:8; Deuteronomy 33:8

Thyatira (THY-ah-TY-rah) *an important city in Asia famous for its purple cloth,* Acts 16:13-14; Revelation 1:11; 2:18-29

Tiberius Caesar (tie-BEER-ee-us SEE-zur) *Roman emperor during the last half of Jesus' life,* Luke 3:1

Tiglath-Pileser (TIG-lath-peh-LEE-zur) *king of Assyria who helped Ahaz; also called "Pul."*
· attacked Israel, 2 Kings 15:19-20
· rescued Ahaz, 2 Kings 16:7-10

Tigris (TY-gris) *a great river in the eastern part of the Bible lands,* Genesis 2:14; Daniel 10:4

Timothy (TIM-oh-thee) *close friend and helper of the apostle Paul.*
· helped Paul, Acts 16:1-3; 17:13-16; 1 Corinthians 4:17
· instructed by Paul, 1 and 2 Timothy

tithe (TIETH) *"tenth." The Jews were told to give one-tenth of what they earned to God.* Leviticus 27:30-32; Deuteronomy 12:1-6; Luke 11:42; 18:12

Titus (TIE-tus) *trusted friend and helper of the apostle Paul.*
· helped Corinthians, 2 Corinthians 7:6-7,13-15; 8:6,16,23
· appointed elders, Titus 1:4-5
· Paul's instructions to, Titus 1–3

Tobiah (toe-BY-uh) *tried to keep Nehemiah from rebuilding the walls of Jerusalem,* Nehemiah 2:10-20; 6:10-19; 13:4-9

tomb
· of Lazarus, John 11:38-44
· of Jesus, Matthew 27:57–28:15; Mark 15:42–16:30; Luke 23:50–24:12; John 19:38–20:9

tongue
· lying tongue hated by God, Proverbs 6:16-17
· cannot be tamed, James 3:2-12

tower of Babel, See "Babel."

transfiguration (tranz-fig-you-RAY-shun) *"to change." Jesus was transfigured in front of Peter, James, and John when his face and clothes began to shine brightly.* Matthew 17:1-9; Mark 9:2-9; Luke 9:28-36

tree
· of knowledge of good and evil, Genesis 2:9; 3:3
· of life, Genesis 2:9; Revelation 2:7; 22:2,14
· people compared to, Psalms 1:3; 92:12; Jeremiah 17:8; Matthew 3:10; 12:33
· cross described as a tree, Galatians 3:13

trespass, See "sin."

tribe, *all descendants of a certain person. The twelve tribes of Israel were descendants of the twelve sons of Jacob, who was later named "Israel."* Numbers 1–2
· Canaan divided among, Joshua 13:7-33; 15–19

triumphal entry (tri-UMF-ul) *the time Jesus entered Jerusalem just before his death,* Matthew 21:1-11; Mark 11:1-19; Luke 19:28-44; John 12:12-15

Troas (TRO-az) *one of the most important cities in northwest Asia,* Acts 16:8-10; 20:5-12; 2 Corinthians 2:12

Trophimus (TROF-eh-mus) *non-Jewish Christian who traveled with Paul,* Acts 20:3-4; 21:27-29; 2 Timothy 4:20

trumpet (TRUM-pet) *in Bible times it was made from animal horns; used to call an army together or announce something important,* Numbers 10:2-10; Joshua 6:4-20; 1 Corinthians 15:52

trust
· a duty, Luke 16:11; 1 Corinthians 4:2; Titus 2:10
· in God, Psalm 20:7; Proverbs 3:5; 16:20; Romans 4:5; 10:11; 1 Peter 2:6
· in lesser things, Psalms 49:13-14; 118:9; Proverbs 11:28; Isaiah 2:22

truth
· speaking honestly, Psalm 15:2; Proverbs 16:13
· God's message, John 17:17; Romans 1:25; Ephesians 1:13; 1 John 1:6

tunic (TOO-nik) *a kind of coat,* Exodus 28:39-40; John 19:23

Tychicus (TIK-ih-kus) *Christian from Asia who did important jobs for Paul,* Acts 20:4; Ephesians 6:21-22; Colossians 4:7-9

Tyre (TIRE) *large, important city in Phoenicia, which is now part of the country of Lebanon,* Mark 7:24-31; Acts 12:20
· Hiram, king of, 2 Samuel 5:11; 1 Kings 9:10-14; 2 Chronicles 2
· a wicked city, Matthew 11:21-22; Luke 10:13-14

U

uncircumcised, See "circumcision."

unclean, *the state of a person, animal or action that was not pleasing to God. In the Old Testament God said certain animals were unclean and were not to be eaten. If a person disobeyed the rules about being clean, he was called unclean and could not serve God until he was made clean again.* See "clean."
· unclean animals, Leviticus 11; Acts 10:9-15
· unclean people, Leviticus 12–15
· God declared everyone to be clean, Acts 10

unleavened bread (un-LEV-'nd BREAD) *bread made without yeast.*
· used in the Passover Feast, Exodus 12:20; Deuteronomy 16:1-4

Unleavened Bread, Day of, *the first day of the Feast of Unleavened Bread or Passover,* Matthew 26:17; Luke 22:7

upper room, *upstairs room in a house.*
· Jesus and his followers met there, Mark 14:14-15; Luke 22:9-12

Ur, *a great city thousands of years ago; today in the country of Iraq.*
· home of Abram, Genesis 11:28-31

Uriah (you-RY-uh) *a soldier in King David's army.*
· killed by David, 2 Samuel 11

Urim (YOUR-im) See "Thummim."

Uzzah (UZ-uh) *touched the Ark of the Agreement and died,* 2 Samuel 6:1-8; 1 Chronicles 13:1-14

Uzziah (uh-ZY-uh) *a king of Judah,* 2 Kings 15:13-15; 2 Chronicles 26; Isaiah 6:1

V

Vashti (VASH-ty) *the wife of Ahasuerus, king of Persia,* Esther 1:1-20

veil (VALE) *a head covering usually worn by women; also, a curtain in the Temple.*
· worn by women, Genesis 24:65; Song of Solomon 4:1; Isaiah 3:19
· the Temple veil, Matthew 27:51; Mark 15:38; Luke 23:45

vest, holy, *"ephod"; a special type of clothing for the priests in the Old Testament. The holy vest for the high priest had gold and gems on it.*
· description of, Exodus 25:7; 28:6-14; 39:2-7
· one made by Micah, Judges 17:1-5; 18:14-20
· worn by David, 2 Samuel 6:14

vine
· fruit of the, Matthew 26:29; Mark 14:25; Luke 22:18
· Jesus as the, John 15:1-11

vineyard
· Naboth's, 1 Kings 21
· parables of, Matthew 20:1-16; 21:28-46; Mark 12:1-12; Luke 20:9-19

virgin (VUR-jin) *person who has not had sexual relations,* Deuteronomy 22:13-29; Isaiah 7:14; Matthew 1:23; Luke 1:34

vision (VIZ-zhun) *like a dream. God often spoke to his people in visions.*
· of Abram, Genesis 15:1
· of Daniel, Daniel 2:19
· of Peter and Cornelius, Acts 10:1-16
· of Paul, Acts 16:9

vow, *a special and serious promise often made to God.*
· rules about, Numbers 30; Deuteronomy 23:21-23
· the Nazirite, Numbers 6:1-21
· of Jephthah, Judges 11:29-40
· of Paul, Acts 18:18

W

war
· rumors of, Matthew 24:6-7; Mark 13:7-8; Luke 21:9-10
· spiritual, 2 Corinthians 10:3-4
· will end, Micah 4:1-3

watchman
· examples of, 2 Samuel 18:24-27; Psalm 130:6
· prophets as watchmen, Ezekiel 3:17; Micah 7:4

water
· in creation, Genesis 1:1-2,6-10
· bitter, Exodus 15:22-27
· from a rock, Exodus 17:1-7
· for David, 2 Samuel 23:15-17
· drink of, Matthew 10:42; Mark 9:41
· Jesus walked on, Matthew 14:22-36
· turned to wine, John 2:1-11
· living water, John 4:1-15

"Way, the," *one of the earliest names given to Christians. Jesus said he was "the way" to reach God.* Acts 9:1-2; 19:9,23; 22:4; 24:14,22

wedding, Matthew 22:1-14; Luke 14:8; John 2:1-11

Western Sea, See "Mediterranean Sea."

widow
· examples of, Ruth 4:10; 1 Kings 17:8-24; Luke 21:2-4
· care for, Deuteronomy 24:17-22; 1 Timothy 5:3-16; James 1:27

wife
· man united with, Genesis 2:24
· the good wife, Proverbs 31:10-31
· teachings about, 1 Corinthians 7:1-16
· responsibility of, Ephesians 5:21-24,33; Colossians 3:18; 1 Peter 3:1

wine
· danger of, Proverbs 20:1; Ephesians 5:18
· at wedding in Cana, John 2:1-11
· for the stomach, 1 Timothy 5:23

winepress, *a pit where grapes were mashed to get the juice out. The winepress is sometimes used to describe how enemy armies will defeat people as if they were grapes crushed in a winepress.*
· examples of, Judges 6:11; Matthew 21:33
· as a symbol of punishment, Lamentations 1:15; Revelation 14:19-20; 19:15

wisdom (WIZ-d'm) *understanding what is really important in life. This wisdom comes from God.* Proverbs 1:1-2,7; 2; 4
· Solomon asked for, 1 Kings 4:29-34
· source of, James 1:5
· a parable about, Matthew 25:1-13

wise men, *"magi"; men who studied the stars,* Genesis 41:8; Exodus 7:11; Matthew 2:1-12

witchcraft, *using the power of the devil to do magic.*
· warnings against, Deuteronomy 18:10-12; Galatians 5:19-21
· examples of, 2 Kings 9:22; 2 Chronicles 33:6

witness, Acts 1:8,22; 2:32; 22:14-15

woman
· created by God, Genesis 2:22-23
· how to treat a, 1 Timothy 5:2,14

word, *in the Bible often means God's message to us in the Scriptures. Jesus is called the "Word" because he shows us what God is like.*
· like a lamp, Psalm 119:105
· like a sword, Hebrews 4:12
· living in God's people, John 15:7; Colossians 3:16; 1 John 2:14
· lasts forever, Matthew 24:35; 1 Peter 1:25
· people's words, Proverbs 12:25; 25:11; Matthew 12:36-37
· as a message, 1 Peter 1:24-25; 1 John 2:14
· Jesus as the "Word," John 1:1-5,14; 1 John 1:1-2

world, *the planet Earth; also the people on this earth who follow Satan.*
· as the Earth, 2 Samuel 22:16; Psalm 18:15
· as a symbol of wickedness, Romans 12:2; Ephesians 2:2

worship, *to praise and serve God.*
· commanded, Exodus 34:14; Luke 4:8; John 4:20-24

X-Y

Xerxes (ZERK-sees) *a king of Persia; also called "Ahasuerus,"* Esther 1–10

yeast (YEEST) *an ingredient used to make breads and cakes rise; used in the New Testament to stand for a person's influence over others. See also "unleavened bread."*
· as a symbol for influence, Mark 8:15; Luke 13:21

yoke, *a wooden frame that fits on the necks of animals to hold them together while working.*
· examples of, Deuteronomy 21:3; 1 Kings 19:19-21

youth
· "Remember your Creator," Ecclesiastes 12:1
· teachings about, 1 Timothy 4:12

Z

Zacchaeus (za-KEE-us) *Jewish tax collector in the city of Jericho,* Luke 19:1-8

Zadok (ZAY-dok) *priest who helped King David,* 2 Samuel 15:24-36; 17:15-21; 1 Kings 1:18-45

Zarephath (ZAIR-eh-fath) *a Canaanite town where Elijah helped a widow,* 1 Kings 17:8-24; Luke 4:25-26

Zealots (ZEL-ots) *a group of Jewish men also called "Enthusiasts." They hated the Romans for controlling their home country, and they planned to force the Romans out.*
· Simon, the Zealot, Luke 6:15; Acts 1:13

Zebedee (ZEB-uh-dee) *a fisherman on Lake Galilee,* Matthew 4:21-22; Mark 1:19-20

Zechariah, father of John the Baptist, (ZEK-uh-RY-uh) *a Jewish priest,* Luke 1:5-25,57-80

Zechariah, king of Israel, *ruled for only six months; killed by Shallum,* 2 Kings 14:29; 15:8-11

Zechariah, son of Berekiah, *a prophet who wrote the next-to-the-last book in the Old Testament,* Ezra 5:1; Zechariah 1–14

Zechariah, son of Jehoiada, *a priest who taught the people to serve God,* 2 Chronicles 24:20-25

Zedekiah, son of Josiah, (zed-ee-KY-uh) *the last king of Judah,* 2 Kings 24:16–25:7

Zedekiah, son of Kenaanah, *a false prophet during the time of King Ahab,* 1 Kings 22:1-24

Zedekiah, son of Maaseiah, *a false prophet in Babylon during the time of Jeremiah,* Jeremiah 29:21-23

Zephaniah (zef-uh-NY-uh) *a prophet who lived when Josiah was king of Judah; wrote the short book of Zephaniah,* Zephaniah 1:1

Zerubbabel (zeh-RUB-uh-bull) *governor of Jerusalem after the Jews had been in captivity in Babylon for seventy years.*
· returned from exile, Ezra 2:2
· built the altar of God, Ezra 3:1-6
· rebuilt the Temple, Ezra 3:7-10; 5:2

Ziba (ZY-buh) *a servant of Saul,* 2 Samuel 9:1-11; 16:1-4; 19:24-30

Zimri (ZIM-rye) *a king of Israel,* 1 Kings 16:11-20

Zion (ZY-on) *a hill inside the city of Jerusalem.* See "Mount Zion."

Ziph (ZIF) *a city about twenty-five miles south of Jerusalem,* 1 Samuel 23:14-28; 26:1-25

Zipporah (zih-PO-ruh) *the wife of Moses,* Exodus 2:15-22; 4:24-26; 18:1-3

zither (ZITH-ur) *a type of musical instrument that had about forty strings on it,* Ezekiel 3:5,7,10,15

Abraham's Journey

→ Possible route
that Abraham followed

Caspian Sea

Persian Gulf

• Susa

▲ *Mount Ararat?*

• Nineveh

Tigris River

• Nuzi

• Asshur

• Babylon

Euphrates River

• Erech

• Ur

MESOPOTAMIA

• Mari

• Haran

PADAN ARAM

HITTITES

• Kanish

• Carchemish

• Ebla

• Kadesh

• Ugarit

• Damascus

CYPRUS

• Hazor

• Sidon
• Tyre

• Dothan
• Shechem

Mediterranean Sea

• Bethel

• Jerusalem

Dead Sea

CANAAN

• Beersheba

▲ *Mount Sinai*

Red Sea

EGYPT

• On
• Memphis

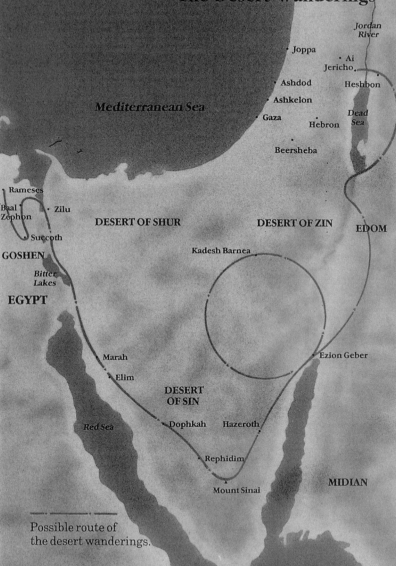

The Desert Wanderings

Jordan River

• Joppa

• Ai
Jericho •

Ashdod

Heshbon

Mediterranean Sea

Ashkelon

Gaza

Dead Sea

• Hebron

Beersheba

Rameses

Baal Zephon

• Zilu

DESERT OF SHUR

DESERT OF ZIN

EDOM

• Succoth

GOSHEN

Kadesh Barnea

Bitter Lakes

EGYPT

Marah

• Elim

DESERT OF SIN

Ezion Geber

Red Sea

• Dophkah

Hazeroth

• Rephidim

MIDIAN

Mount Sinai

Possible route of
the desert wanderings.

The Twelve Tribes During the Judges

Mediterranean Sea

• Tyre

• Dan

• Kedesh

Asher

Naphtali

ARAM

CANAAN

• Hazor

Ramah

• Kinnereth

• Ashtaroth

Lake Galilee

Zebulun

• Dor

Issachar

• Ramoth Gilead

Megiddo •

• Jezreel

Manasseh (East)

• Dothan

Manasseh (West)

• Jabesh Gilead

Jordan River

Mt. Ebal ▲

• Succoth

Mt. Gerizim ▲ • Shechem

• Joppa

• Shiloh

Ephraim

Gad

Dan

• Bethel

• Gilgal

AMMON

Ai

Gibeon •

• Jericho

Benjamin

• Heshbon

• Ashdod

• Jerusalem

▲ Mt. Nebo

• Timnah

Judah

• Bethlehem

Reuben

PHILISTIA

Adullam •

• Lachish

• Hebron

Dead Sea

• Dibon

• Aroer

• Ziklag

• Beersheba

MOAB

• Ar

Simeon

The Kingdoms of Judah and Israel

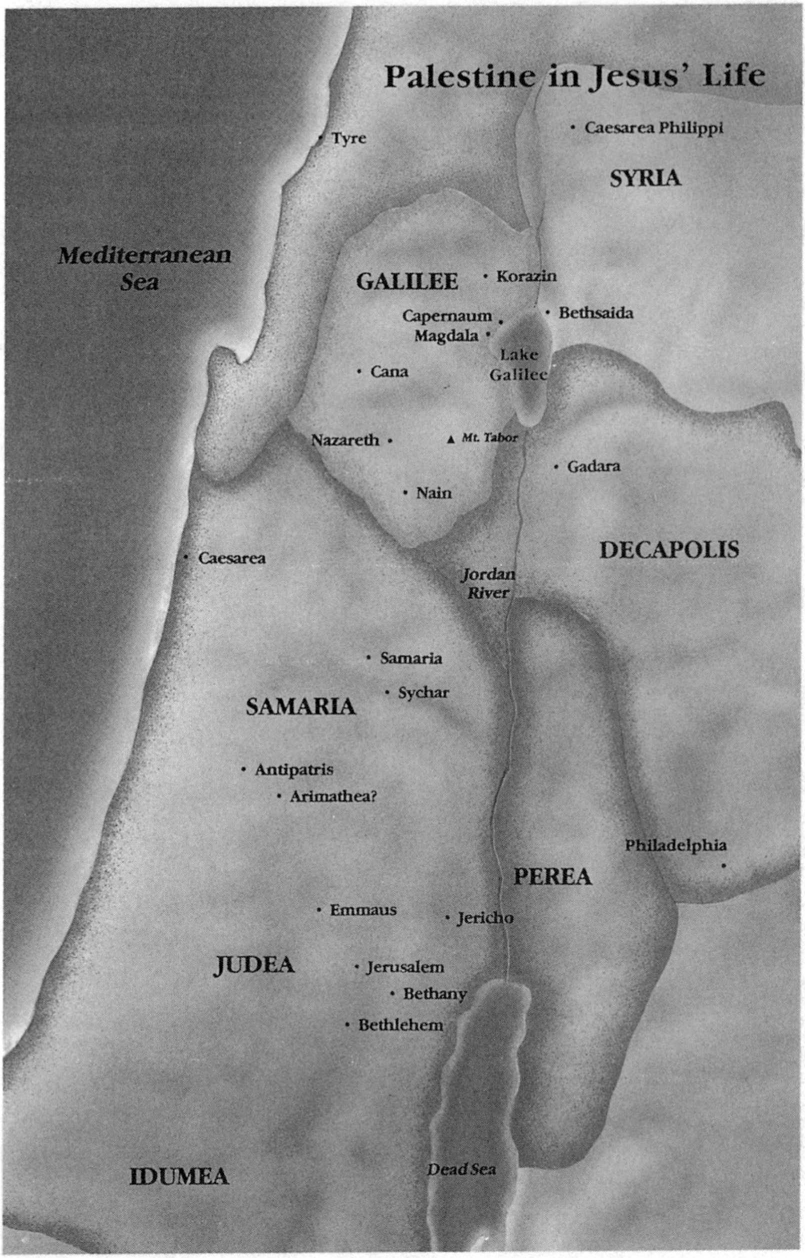

Palestine in Jesus' Life

- Tyre
- Caesarea Philippi

SYRIA

Mediterranean Sea

GALILEE
- Korazin
- Capernaum
- Magdala
- Bethsaida
- Cana

Lake Galilee

- Nazareth
▲ Mt. Tabor
- Gadara
- Nain

DECAPOLIS

- Caesarea

Jordan River

- Samaria
- Sychar

SAMARIA

- Antipatris
- Arimathea?

Philadelphia

PEREA

- Emmaus
- Jericho

JUDEA
- Jerusalem
- Bethany
- Bethlehem

IDUMEA

Dead Sea

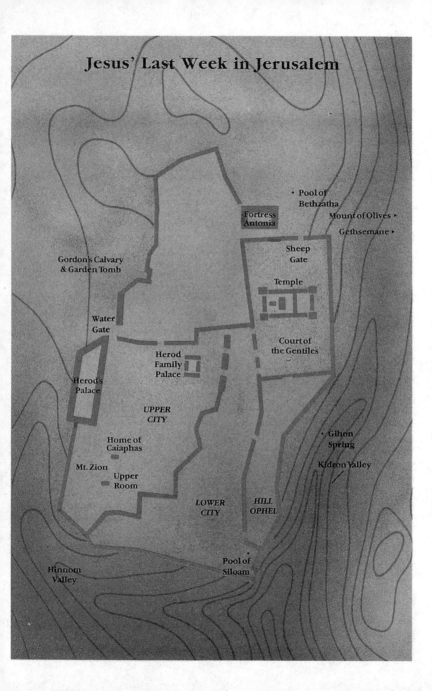

Jesus' Last Week in Jerusalem

- Pool of Bethzatha

Fortress Antonia

Mount of Olives ▸

Gethsemane ▸

Sheep Gate

Gordon's Calvary & Garden Tomb

Temple

Water Gate

Court of the Gentiles

Herod Family Palace

Herod's Palace

UPPER CITY

Gihon Spring

Home of Caiaphas

Kidron Valley

Mt. Zion

Upper Room

LOWER CITY

HILL OPHEL

Hinnom Valley

Pool of Siloam

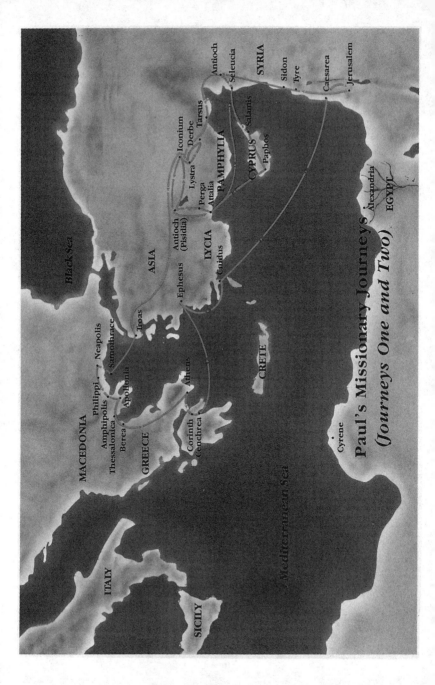

Paul's Missionary Journeys
(Journeys One and Two)

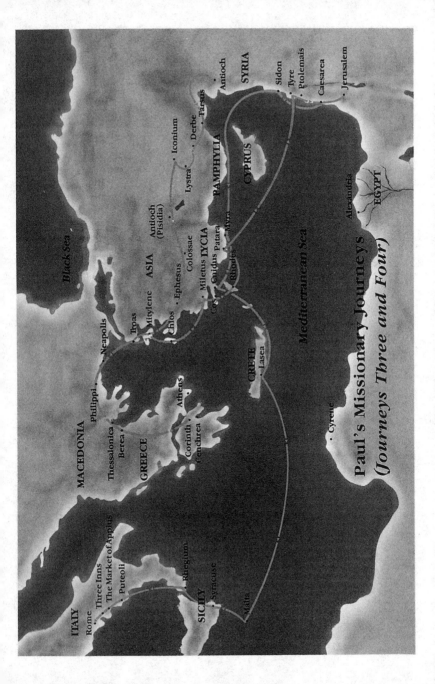

Paul's Missionary Journeys
(Journeys Three and Four)